Education Law

Education Law

Cases and Materials

THIRD EDITION

Jacqueline A. Stefkovich
PROFESSOR EMERITA
DEPARTMENT OF EDUCATION POLICY STUDIES
PENNSYLVANIA STATE UNIVERSITY

Kevin P. Brady
PROFESSOR
DEPARTMENT OF CURRICULUM AND INSTRUCTION
UNIVERSITY OF ARKANSAS

Traci N.W. Ballard
ASSOCIATE DIRECTOR
PROFESSIONAL DEVELOPMENT & LEADERSHIP ACADEMY
JEANNINE RAINBOLT COLLEGE OF EDUCATION
UNIVERSITY OF OKLAHOMA-TULSA

Lawrence F. Rossow
PROFESSOR EMERITUS
LAW AND EDUCATION
UNIVERSITY OF OKLAHOMA

CAROLINA ACADEMIC PRESS
Durham, North Carolina

Library of Congress Cataloging-in-Publication Data

Names: Rossow, Lawrence F., author. | Stefkovich, Jacqueline Anne, 1947- author. | Brady, Kevin P., author. | Ballard, Traci N.W., author.
Title: Education law : cases and materials / by Jacqueline A. Stefkovich, Kevin P. Brady, Traci N.W. Ballard, Lawrence F. Rossow.
Description: Third edition. | Durham, North Carolina : Carolina Academic Press, LLC, [2021] | Includes bibliographical references and index.
Identifiers: LCCN 2021017616 (print) | LCCN 2021017617 (ebook) | ISBN 9781531016869 (paperback) | ISBN 9781531016876 (ebook)
Subjects: LCSH: Educational law and legislation—United States—Cases. | Educational law and legislation—United States. | LCGFT: Casebooks (Law)
Classification: LCC KF4119 .R67 2021 (print) | LCC KF4119 (ebook) | DDC 344.73/07—dc23
LC record available at https://lccn.loc.gov/2021017616
LC ebook record available at https://lccn.loc.gov/2021017617

Carolina Academic Press
700 Kent Street
Durham, North Carolina 27701
(919) 489-7486
www.cap-press.com

Printed in the United States of America

To Jerome (best brother ever) and Colleen Stefkovich who generously welcomed me back as part of their family and taught me to keep it real.
Jacqueline A. Stefkovich

To my sons, Luca and Nic, who will know the impact of law on addressing equity and equality in education.
Kevin P. Brady

To my parents, educators for life; Kizer, Keaton, and Matthijs, the joys of my life; and to Matt, all my love, all my life.
Traci N.W. Ballard

To Nancy, Mara, and Marie for their continuous faith and support.
Lawrence F. Rossow

Contents

Table of Cases

Preface

After teaching education law courses both in colleges of education and in colleges of law, we have used many textbooks available for graduate-level courses. Noting the strengths and weakness of these and seeking a volume to fit our needs and those of our students, we set about to create our own. This publication serves as an attempt to capitalize on the wisdom of those who have gone before us, offering students a concise understanding of the essential concepts, key court cases, and context to inform policy and practice.

We thank those pioneering scholars and writers in our field. It is to those fine contributors that we owe gratitude for making it possible to bring education law and legal literacy for educators to the level of a teachable subject which is now included in nearly all graduate colleges of education.

The cases that shape the study of modern education law are very fact specific. These facts contain the essence of what must be known to educators in order to develop policies and practice and are essential in deciding whether a case is "on point" and useful in building clarity for any present legal challenge. While, in the interest of economy of space, concurring and dissenting opinions have been omitted, the cases included in this volume contain the unedited majority opinions, with full facts intact.

The field of law is an ever-evolving subject, and this edition seeks to provide a solid foundation of the essential historical contexts, a grounding in current jurisprudence, and a lens to understand new and emerging changes in the field. Among the most significant changes in this edition are an expanded treatment of the many issues related to the liability of schools and their personnel, the expanded use of school resource officers, and updates on the rights of transgendered students. Likewise, everything old is new again, and this edition gives modern information about topics that had for many years seemed to be somewhat settled, such as student and teacher rights in regard to First Amendment issues, drug testing, and pandemics.

Also new to this edition are contributors Kevin Brady and Traci Ballard, who bring their experiences working with both students and practitioners to the perspectives represented throughout the volume. They share the hope this book will serve the greater mission in our field to significantly improve the legal literacy of educators and others who work in schools and help them better understand the myriad of legal precedents, guidelines, and requirements regarding PK-12 education.

JACQUELINE A. STEFKOVICH

KEVIN P. BRADY

TRACI N.W. BALLARD

LAWRENCE F. ROSSOW

Acknowledgments

Drs. Stefkovich, Brady, Ballard, and Rossow wish to collectively thank all their many students over the past decades who have studied with them and provided suggestions for continuous improvement of this book. A special note of thanks to doctoral students Samantha Evans at the University of Oklahoma and Casey S. Kraichoke at the University of Arkansas for their editorial assistance in the preparation of this third edition.

Education Law

Chapter 1

Governance of Public Schools

Public schools, like other public institutions, are governed by laws from a variety of different sources. Few decisions made by school leaders throughout the school day can be made without consideration of federal or state statutes or case law. In this chapter, the pervasive role of the law in the governance of public schools will be explored. A thorough understanding of the legal framework of public education requires knowledge of how the judicial system works in consort with federal and state legislation. However, public schools are not created by the federal government. They have been established at the state level. As such, the role of the federal government in education differs widely from the state government. Nevertheless, both levels of government are closely tied to the operation of public schools. For example, while local school boards are not legislative bodies, the roles of the local education authorities are both established and limited by them.

Sources of the Law

The law comes from essentially three sources: constitutions, statutes, and case law. Public schools must comply with all these, but they do not always provide clarity about the proper course of action in a given situation. At the same time, each source provides guidance that can help schools proceed with some confidence without the fear of litigation.

Constitutions

A constitution is the highest legal source. The framers of a constitution are those who represent the people at a constitutional convention where the proposed document is drafted. Prior to having the force of law, these documents must be ratified by the public they will ultimately govern. While each individual state in the United States has a written constitution, the Constitution of the United States is the supreme law of the land and supersedes state constitutions. However, the U.S. Constitution cannot cover every conceivable topic of human life. Those topics not covered in the U.S. Constitution are left up to, or delegated to, the states to decide with their own constitutions and laws. Known as the "delegation of powers," this doctrine is derived from the Tenth Amendment to the U.S. Constitution:

> The powers not delegated to the United States by the Constitution, nor prohibited by it to the States, are reserved to the States respectively, or to the people.[1]

Education is one of many topics not specifically mentioned in the U.S. Constitution. Therefore, public education in this country is a function of the states, established by state constitutions. Further, application of the U.S. Constitution to public education is limited to those provisions applicable to the states. As a document, the U.S. Constitution has great flexibility and can be interpreted by the courts in the context of social change. Of course, the Constitution can be changed by the people. Article V of the U.S. Constitution outlines the process for amending provisions within the document, as well as future additions.

Although constitutions embody several basic principles for living in America, the following universals should be highlighted.

The separation of powers is an important principle, universal to all constitutions. The three branches of government—legislative, executive, and judicial—exist within a system of checks and balances. For example, the legislative branch of government can pass laws. The laws are binding, but not necessarily forever. The laws can be challenged and perhaps eliminated, through the judicial branch if found to be unconstitutional.

Another basic principle to be found in constitutions is the protection of fundamental rights. The Bill of Rights contains those freedoms associated with living in a democratic society. The Bill of Rights is a unique feature of the U.S. Constitution. State constitutions usually do not repeat what is contained in the Bill of Rights but mention many of the other provisions of the U.S. Constitution.

Statutes

Statutes are laws enacted by legislative bodies. Statutory law represents what the legislative branch of government produces. Every public school is compelled by the federal legislation passed by Congress and by state legislation passed in its home state. The applicability of most federal education legislation is made applicable to state created public schools by virtue of the fact that those schools receive federal funding. Therefore, penalty for failure to comply with a federal law usually involves the withholding of federal funds. Noncompliance with state statutes can result in criminal charges against school officials as well as loss of state recognition. A public school cannot operate without recognition from the state.

1. U.S. Const. Amend. X.

Regulations

Regulations lend specificity to statutes. Statutes, by design, should be narrow enough to guide those expected to follow the law, but broad enough to be able to allow for local interpretation. In the case of education-related statutes, the construction of the statutes must leave room for a federal or state agency to issue regulations which will shape how local schools might implement the will of the legislature. For most federal statutes, the regulatory agency is the U.S. Department of Education. For state statutes, the state board of education issues regulations. As with statutes, regulations carry the force of law. Failure to comply with regulations can result in the withholding of funds, removal of recognition or accreditation, and even a total take-over by the state board.

Local Board Policy

Local board policy has the force of law for those who work at or attend schools in the district. While a reference to local school board policy as law might seem a bit reaching, it is not. Board members are elected to office by strict conformity to election procedures. The board itself is a governmental body recognized by the state. If a school board were to terminate a teacher because of a failure to comply with board policy, a range of procedural and substantive due-process concerns would need to be addressed. The term "due process" is found in both the Fifth and the Fourteenth Amendments of the U.S. Constitution. The Fifth Amendment guarantees that no person shall be deprived of "life, liberty, or property, without due process of the law." The Fourteenth Amendment guarantees that no state shall "deprive any person of life, liberty, or property, without due process of law." The same is true when a board moves to expel a student. A high degree of scrutiny is required because both teachers' and students' property interests are at stake. The reality of modern-day school-board policymaking suggests an unmistakable legal function.

Case Law

Case law is court-made law. When a case is decided, it becomes binding on the litigating parties and has effect within the jurisdiction of the court. On occasion, the constitutionality of a statute is called into question. Because of the powers provided to the judicial branch in the Constitution, the court may decide that a statute is unconstitutional and is thus unenforceable. With increasing frequency, case law has begun to shape much of what happens in the public schools. In order to begin understanding the law, certain concepts must be grasped.

The law is "term intensive." For efficiency, and perhaps because of tradition, the law uses many terms not common in ordinary vocabulary. The use of Latin is common. Therefore, a legal dictionary or at least a glossary of terms should be kept nearby when reading legal material. The glossary contained in this book should be a sufficient aid throughout the beginning of your course of study in education law.

Should the reader undertake further study in the law, a legal dictionary would be invaluable.

Structure of the Law

The framework for the legal system in the United States has its roots in English Common Law. This approach commands certain minimal behaviors. If citizens fall below this behavior, a penalty is imposed. However, English Common Law is not the only approach to a system of laws. Roman law was a law of aspiration. These laws were constructed to provide goals for citizens. Penalties were imposed because of gross failures in living up to the laws.

The approach used in the United States has some elements of both English and Roman law. The more localized the law, the more likely a "goals" approach might be found. Local school board policies are examples of the aspirational aspect of law. For example, the local board policy for the Norman, Oklahoma, Public Schools on student achievement reads:

> Student achievement is an important component of the educational process, serving as a primary source of information for determining the learning progress of individual students as well as the overall effectiveness of instructional programs. Ongoing assessment of student achievement shall be conducted by the District in compliance with state law.[2]

This board's policy makes a values statement about students and the instructional program. It is more goal-oriented than compelling. However, the following example from the state statutes of Oklahoma shows the typical compelling approach usually associated with laws:

> [The] Board shall adopt a statewide system of student assessments in compliance with the Elementary and Secondary Education Act of 1965 (ESEA), as reauthorized and amended by P.L. No. 114-95, also known as the Every Student Succeeds Act (ESSA).[3]

Beyond the substantive language of statutes, regulations, or policies, the use of the terms "shall" and "may" make a difference. When the law says that the subject "shall" do such and such, there is no option. This form of law represents the compelling type which must be obeyed. However, not all laws are predicated on the "shall" verb. For example, the Illinois statute regarding the granting of sabbatical leaves for teachers says:

> Every school board may grant a sabbatical leave of absence to a teacher, principal, or superintendent performing contractual continued service, for

2. Board of Education Policies and Administrative Regulations of the Norman Public Schools, Norman, Oklahoma, No. 5001.

3. OKLA. STAT. tit. 70, §1210.508 (2018).

a period of at least four school months but not in excess of one school term, for resident study, research, travel or other purposes designed to improve the school system.[4]

Notice that the predicate for this statute is "may," not "shall." The use of the term "may" establishes a different relationship between the law and the citizen. As opposed to compelling behavior, the Illinois law provides "power" to the local board to grant a sabbatical leave under certain conditions. Hence, some laws are meant to establish a duty and compel behavior—the predicate "shall" is used in the construct. Other laws are established to provide a power to be used at the subject's discretion—the predicate "may" is used in the construct.

Stare Decisis

An important term to know when considering the importance of case law is *stare decisis*. Translated from Latin, *stare decisis* means "let the decision stand." The term itself refers to the courts' practice of following precedent. Prior to making a decision, a court will review decisions made by other courts where the facts were similar to the instant case. If the facts are similar, the rule of law announced in previous cases in the same jurisdiction will be followed. Indeed, both the plaintiff and the defendant rely on *stare decisis* when preparing their legal cases.

At the same time, the defendant argues the cases upon which the plaintiff relies as precedent can be "distinguished" from the instant case—because the facts are claimed to be different. Also, at this time, the defense presents their own line of cases in order to establish their specific legal position. As might be expected, the plaintiff then seeks to show how the defendant's line of cases can be distinguished rather than control.

If the case cited was decided by a state court outside the state deciding the present case, or in a federal court in a different circuit, the case may be deemed informative rather than dispositive—i.e., influential but not binding. For example, a state court in Colorado may consider the decision in a similar case in the state of Kansas but is not required to follow that decision. However, as both states are in the same federal circuit, a federal court in either state must follow the rulings of their shared federal appellate court.

Lower courts are particular conformists to the practice of *stare decisis*. These lower courts, which are usually federal district courts and state district courts, must adhere to the rulings of the appellate courts in their jurisdiction. Likewise, the appellate courts must adhere to the rulings of the U.S. Supreme Court.

Only at the Supreme Court level is there some abandonment of *stare decisis*. The rulings of the U.S. Supreme Court are the supreme law of the land. The Court is not

4. Ill. Rev. Stat. ch. 105, para. 24-6.1 (1979).

required to follow its own precedent. Instead, it makes precedent. State supreme courts operate in a similar way regarding *stare decisis*, except regarding matters of federal law. On federal issues, a state supreme court must follow the precedent set by the Supreme Court.

The doctrine of case or controversy is basic to the function of the courts. An early U.S. Supreme Court case noted that Article III of the U.S. Constitution limits the power of the judiciary to pronounce a judgment and carry it into effect between persons and parties who bring a case before it for decision.[5] In other words, a court does not go out and find cases. It must wait for cases to be brought to it.

Regarding the case-or-controversy doctrine, one commentator has noted that the courts do not sit to decide questions of law in a vacuum. A court decides only such questions that arise in a case or controversy.[6] In other words, parties cannot present hypothetical arguments. The problem presented must be one that is capable of legal solution. It must be a problem that will be resolved by a judgment of the court. Disputes between parties where the court serves as a vehicle for venting anger often lack case or controversy. The questions that must always be asked by those who want to file a lawsuit include: Is the court the best place to resolve the issue? Is this problem one that the law can solve? If parties are not careful to only bring a suit that meets case-or-controversy requirements, the court might penalize the parties for bringing a "frivolous" suit.

The Judicial System

The American court system is composed of both federal and state courts. While federal and state courts have similarities, there are sufficient differences to warrant a discussion about each. Education cases have been decided by both courts. The preponderance of cases is handled by state courts. However, federal litigation involving education has been rapidly increasing.

The Constitution of the United States in Article III, Section 1, gave life to the judicial branch of government when it stated: "The judicial power of the United States shall be vested in one supreme court and in such inferior courts as the Congress may from time to time ordain and establish." The court system did not take shape until 1789 when Congress passed the Judiciary Act. As Figure 1-1 shows, the federal courts are three-tiered. The first level is the U.S. District Courts. The case might then be appealed to the U.S Circuit Court of Appeals or a special federal court. Ultimately, the case could be heard by the U.S. Supreme Court.

The route of appeal through the courts is not automatic. There are certain conditions which must be met in order to proceed up the court hierarchy. The

5. Ill. Rev. Stat. ch. 105, para. 24-6.1 (1979).

6. Charles Alan Wright, Law of Federal Courts (2002).

requirements for an appeal will be discussed under the description for each court. It should be noted that in order to file a case in the federal courts, there must be a "federal question" at stake. One does not simply choose to use the federal or the state courts. The choice is often made by the facts that make it necessary to use a particular court in the first place. Either a law is broken or certain rights have been abridged. If the law or rights stem from federal laws, only then would the federal courts be used. As Figure 1-2 shows, the state courts are also three-tiered.

Figure 1-1. Federal Court System

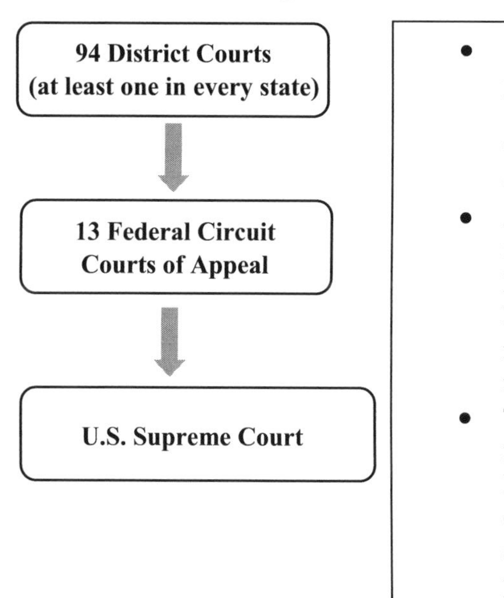

- Federal-level court cases usually progress from the district-level courts to appellate courts and then finally to the U.S. Supreme Court.
- Administrative agencies, including the U.S. Department of Education, potentially have the legal authority to make rules interpreted and enforced by federal-level courts.
- The enforcement of certain federal statutes, such as the IDEA 2004, require that the complaining party must "exhaust all administrative remedies provided within the statute."

Figure 1-2. Typical State Court System

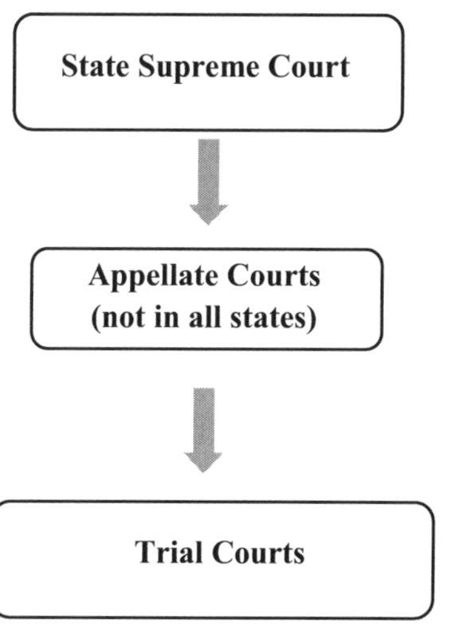

- State-level courts have the ability to resolve both state and federal claims.
- State supreme court decisions can be appealed directly to the U.S. Supreme Court on issues of federal law.

District Courts

The first, or lowest, level for the federal court system is the U.S. District Courts. The district courts are the trial courts for the system. There are 94 U.S. district courts. Ninety are in the 50 states and District of Columbia. The other four are in the United States Territories, Guam, Puerto Rico, and the Virgin Islands. Each state has at least one district court. Most states have two or more. The number and location of courts within a state depend on population density.

Because district courts are also trial courts, legal phenomena such as juries, presentation and cross-examination of witnesses, and the introduction of evidence may be present. There are 673 authorized U.S. district court judgeships distributed throughout the 94 districts. The judges are appointed by the Executive Branch of the federal government for life terms. Each court has support from service offices assigned to the district. The support group includes clerk's office, court reporters, magistrates, marshal's office, and probation officers. The court may also have bankruptcy judges assigned to it.

Courts of Appeal

The United States Courts of Appeals are in each of the 13 federal judicial circuits. There is one court for each circuit. Figure 1-3 shows that the size of the circuit is based on the population density.

Because the number of courts in each circuit is limited to one, the sparser the population, the larger the area included in the circuit. The court is usually located in the largest city within the circuit. Eleven circuits service the 50 states, Guam, Puerto Rico, and the Virgin Islands. One of the circuits services only the District of Columbia and is known as the District of Columbia Circuit. The remaining circuit is known as the Federal Circuit. It serves as a specialty appellate court, handling cases appealed from the district courts involving copyright, patents, or trademarks. Every circuit court has between six and 28 judges, depending on the average workload for the circuit. There are 179 judges in the U.S. Circuit Courts of Appeals. The judges are appointed for life by the executive branch.

Cases are brought to the circuit courts on appeal from the U.S. district courts. Without having to meet any special conditions, a disappointed suitor at the district court can have his/her case heard by the circuit court in the appropriate jurisdiction. The purpose of the appeals courts is not to retry the case, but to review the case for possible errors made by the lower court. Because the circuit courts sit in appellate review, there are no juries, witnesses, or evidence as part of the process. There is a "paper" review of the proceedings of the lower court and an opportunity for the losing party to argue for a reversal of the lower court. Of course, the successful party at the trial level will argue on appeal that the decision of the lower court should be affirmed. As noted in Figure 1-1, the courts of appeals also review actions from federal agencies and tax court. Figure 1-3 shows the distribution of states and geographical territories of the 13 federal courts of appeal.

Figure 1-3. Thirteen Federal Circuit Courts of Appeal by Geographical Boundaries

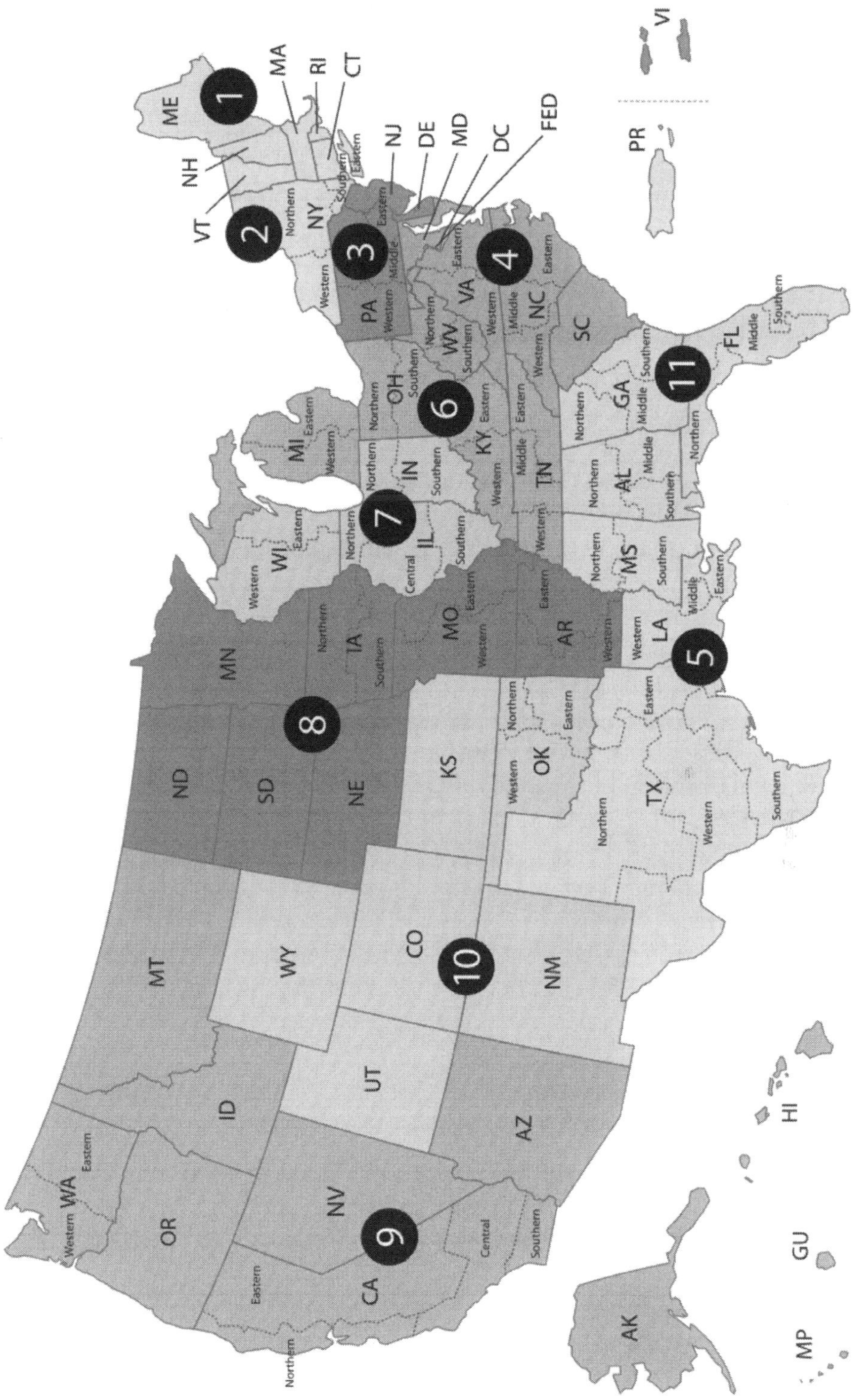

The United States Supreme Court

The highest court in the federal system is the United States Supreme Court. As noted earlier, the Supreme Court receives its authority to exist directly from Article III of the U.S. Constitution. The Supreme Court consists of nine members. There is one chief justice; the others are called associate justices.

While the appointments to the U.S. Supreme Court are for life, the justices may retire at seventy after ten years of service or at the age of sixty-five after 15 years of service. The Court has numerous supporting officers consisting of the clerk, the reporter of decisions, the librarian, and the marshal. It is required that the U.S. Supreme Court open for business on the first Monday of October. It will continue to hear cases for as long as necessary. However, tradition usually dictates that the Court hears its last case at the end of June.

Six justices must be present for a quorum. However, only four justices are required to decide to take a case by writ of certiorari. When a party petitions the Court for a writ of certiorari, it is an application for the Supreme Court to review the decision of a lower court. When a writ is issued, it represents both the Court's willingness to review the case and an authorization to send all case files to the higher court for review. If a case is presented for consideration by writ of certiorari, the Court has total discretion whether it will hear that case. Most of the cases brought before the Court are by writ of certiorari. Another route by which cases are reviewed by the Supreme Court is by appeal. A case on appeal requires that the Court consider it. However, the Court may not issue a full written opinion. In fact, only about five percent of cases presented ever are heard and given a full opinion. Some appeal cases are disposed of by issuing a summary disposition. Cases that receive only a summary disposition are either affirmed or dismissed without formal hearing or the issuance of a detailed opinion. It should be noted that a summary disposition is a decision on the merits of the case. A rejection of a case in which a party petitioned for a writ of certiorari is not a decision on the merits. Legally, nothing about the Court's interpretation or how future cases will be decided can be deduced about a case in which the Court declined to issue a writ of certiorari. However, a summary disposition that affirms the lower case establishes that the Court agrees with the conclusion of the lower case. A dismissal decision means that the Court is not in agreement with the decision of the lower court.

While the Supreme Court of the United States is primarily an appellate court, it does have original jurisdiction acting as a trial court for certain issues. These cases need not be first decided by a lower court. The Supreme Court has original jurisdiction over two areas: (1) disputes between the states, i.e., one state sues another state or (2) legal proceedings involving foreign dignitaries, i.e., an ambassador is accused of a felony.

State Courts

As with the federal courts, the state courts derive their authority from a constitution. Virtually every state constitution provides for the establishment of a court system. The system itself often resembles the three-tier system used by the federal courts. Figure 1-3 shows that the district courts handle the first-level civil or criminal cases. These courts may have names other than district court. Some of these names include superior court or county court. Often one state court is located in each county in the county seat: hence, the name county court.

Once the case is decided by a state trial court, it may then be heard by a state appellate court. The state appellate court, while often centrally located, i.e., in the state capital, is serviced by judges that come from representative areas throughout the state. This approach is designed to ensure each area of the state is represented by at least one judge on the appellate court. There are several state appellate court judges who rotate hearing cases. A decision is most often made by a three-judge bench unless the issue calls for an en banc decision, one in which all the judges on the bench of the appellate court participate. If en banc, there will be seven judges on the panel. Some states divide the responsibility between two types of appellate courts: one for criminal cases and one for civil cases.

The final appeal in a state court system is to the state supreme court. As with the state appellate courts, these are comprised of judicial representatives from each geographic area of the state. Because the number of cases reaching the state supreme court is much lower than the state appellate court, there are typically only nine state supreme court justices.

It should be noted that state court judges are elected positions. The terms of service range from two to six years. After initial election or appointment, the election of judges comes in the form of a retention ballot to the voter. The voter is asked whether the judge should remain on the bench. A positive response gives the judge another term until the question of continuing is once again placed before the voters. If the judge is removed because of negative voter response, then either a popular election is held among those wishing to run or an appointment is made by the governor. Typically, the governor selects from a group of individuals recommended for service by a state judicial nominating commission.

Figure 1-3 points out that there are specialty courts operating at a level lower than the trial courts. These specialty courts perform ministerial functions which help keep the "regular" courts from being overworked.

The Role of the Federal Government in Education

Strictly speaking, the federal government has no role in education. The framers of the Constitution of the United States left the oversight of education up to the states. The words "education" and "school" are not found in the U.S. Constitution.

Nevertheless, it is obvious that the federal government is "involved" in education. The federal government is involved for several reasons.

First, local school board members, administrators, teachers, and students, while associated with a state governmental institution, are still citizens of the United States. Therefore, issues involving fundamental freedoms, i.e., firing of teachers or suspension of students, might involve the federal courts. Federal legislation which protects individual citizens also protects those associated with the schools. In addition, the General Welfare Clause and the Commerce Clause of the U.S. Constitution stand as exceptions to the lack of a formal governmental role.

Second, education can be of national importance. The federal government offers both technical assistance and funding to schools that choose to participate in federally sponsored programs. Therefore, the federal government can "shape" education by offering attractive incentives. Therefore, you will seldom see private schools discussed in this volume. Private schools are not state actors or political subdivisions of the states in which they are located and rarely receive federal funds. However, if private educational institutions qualify for and receive federal (and sometimes state) education funding, they may subject their institutions to relevant laws.

Some amendments to the U.S. Constitution apply to the activities of individuals within the setting of the public schools. When fundamental freedoms have been allegedly violated by school authorities, the federal courts have applied the Bill of Rights to resolve the issue.

The most active parts of the Bill of Rights are the First and Fourth Amendments. The free speech clause of the First Amendment has often been an issue when teachers and students have been negatively affected by school authorities because of what they have written, worn, or said. Likewise, the religion clause of the First Amendment has been applied when teachers and students have sought to express or exercise some form of religion while in the school setting. The Fourth Amendment has been applied to issues involving student searches and seizures.

While the Fourteenth Amendment, strictly speaking, is not part of the Bill of Rights, it does provide a form of protection for students and teachers. The Fourteenth Amendment says in part:

> . . . No State shall make or enforce any law which shall abridge the privileges or immunities of citizens of the United States; nor shall any State deprive any person of life, liberty, or property, without due process of law, nor deny to any person within its jurisdiction the equal protection of the laws.[7]

The parts of the Fourteenth Amendment just quoted are known as the Due Process Clause and the Equal Protection Clause. In the school setting, the Due Process Clause is the constitutional basis for school authorities providing such procedural events as hearings before a disciplinary decision is made. The Equal Protection

---

7. U.S. Const. Amend. XIV, §1.

clause prohibits school authorities from giving different groups of teachers or students different treatment based on protected criteria such as gender, wealth, race, or religion.

Article I, Section 8, of the Constitution of the United States notes that "The Congress shall have the Power To lay and collect Taxes, Duties, Imposts and Excises, to pay the Debts and provide for the common Defense and general Welfare of the United States. . . ."[8] In essence, the General Welfare Clause allows the United States Congress to tax citizens in order to pay debts and provide for the welfare of the Union. However, the power to provide for the general welfare is not unlimited. When the general welfare involves education, Congress provides categorical aid to the states and, thus, indirectly controls educational policy. The general welfare clause does not allow Congress to directly legislate changes in education. Regulation of education in the states can only happen by the federal government offering conditional grants.

One example of Congress providing for the general welfare in education would be what was initially known as the Education for All Handicapped Children Act (EHA). Many are now familiar with the current enaction of this legislation as the Individuals with Disabilities in Education Act, or IDEA. In 1975, Congress provided large amounts of aid to states for the education of students with disabilities, then termed handicapped children. The aid was conditional upon complying with components of EHA. States were not compelled to follow EHA if they were willing to forego these federal monies. However, because providing education for those we now refer to as students with special needs has been recognized by the courts as a constitutional requirement, states must still provide for the education of its students with special needs, regardless of funding. Whether the program a state provided on its own would meet constitutional standards would be up to the courts. Therefore, Congress' version of meeting constitutional standards for the education of students with special needs, compliance with IDEA and its associated funds, becomes an attractive incentive for the states.

The Commerce Clause appears in Article I, Section 8, of the Constitution. It says that Congress shall have the power to "regulate Commerce with foreign Nations, and among the several States and with the Indian Tribes."[9] When interpreted broadly, the Commerce Clause has applied to commercial activities between and even within the states. That is, the states shall not pass laws that would restrict trade. Almost a century ago, the Supreme Court decided that "commercial activity or trade" be defined as the means for "advancement of society, labor, transportation, intelligence, care, and various mediums of exchange."[10] Congress may act not only to prevent states from impeding commerce, but may also act to improve commerce.

8. U.S. Const. Amend. XIV, §1.
9. U.S. Const. Art. I, §8, cl. 3.
10. Gibbons v. Ogden, 22 U.S. (9 Wheat.) 1 (1824).

One of the recognized purposes of education is the development of an intelligent citizenry. Therefore, the broader purposes of education fit the definition of commerce. Congress may control education within the states through the Commerce Clause depending on the issue. Thus far there have been no major cases dealing with education and the Commerce Clause. However, there have been cases dealing with other states and local government conflicts with federal authority. These cases often apply to the education setting.

The foundation for interpretation of the Commerce Clause came with the introduction of the Fair Labor Standards Act in 1938. Among other things, the Act required that there be a national minimum wage which would apply to federal government and private industry jobs. It also prohibited the shipment of goods produced by child labor. The Act was challenged as an infringement upon state sovereignty as guaranteed by the Tenth Amendment.[11] In deciding for the expansive view of the Commerce Clause, the Court noted that Congress' power over interstate commerce is not limited to activity among the states but includes those activities within the states. The broad power of the federal government to control all commerce within the nation continued for the next three decades. However, in 1976, the Supreme Court handed down a decision that temporarily reversed the broad federal power approach.

Once again, the issue focused on the Fair Labor Standards Act. This time, the 1974 Amendments to the Act extended wage standards to certain state government jobs as well as local school districts. These amendments were challenged in *National League of Cities v. Usery*.[12] As it did many years earlier, the state argued that the Tenth Amendment gave authority to states to control the wages of its workers.

This time the Court ruled for the states. Justice Rehnquist held that the state's power to set the wages of its government employees is an attribute of state sovereignty. Thus, the Tenth Amendment was violated when Congress attempted to control the wages of state government workers. A decade later the Court reversed the *Usery* decision, returning to a broad powers position in the federal government controlling state and local commerce decisions. In *Garcia v. San Antonio Metropolitan Transit Authority*,[13] the transit authority in San Antonio, Texas, challenged the Fair Labor Standards Act provision that required it to use federal minimum wage and overtime standards. It claimed that state compliance with the federal obligation would impair the states' ability to structure integral operations in areas of traditional local government functions. In ruling for San Antonio, Justice Blackmun said that assuring state sovereignty is unnecessary in our federal system. He stated that state sovereign interests are more properly protected by procedural safeguards

11. *See* United States v. Darby Lumber, 312 U.S. 100 (1941).
12. 426 U.S. 833 (1976).
13. 469 U.S. 528 (1985).

inherent in the structure of the federal system than by judicially created limitations on federal power.

No Child Left Behind

In 2002, Congress passed the No Child Left Behind Act (NCLB), the reauthorization of the 1965 Elementary and Secondary Education Act (ESEA).[14] The purpose of the Act according to Congress was to:

> ensure that all children have a fair, equal, and significant opportunity to obtain a high-quality education and reach, at a minimum, proficiency on challenging State academic achievement standards and state academic assessments.[15]

Breaking down the legislation into its basic components, 12 requirements emerge:

1. Common expectations for student academic achievement;
2. Focus on low-achieving children;
3. Close the achievement gap between minority and nonminority students and those with limited English proficiency;
4. Provide alterative school to those school that are academically failing;
5. Distribute resources to those most in need;
6. Measure achievement by an Adequate Yearly Progress;
7. Provide greater decision making authority and flexibility to schools and teachers in exchange for greater responsibility for student performance;
8. Increase enrichment programs to provide a higher quality program;
9. Lead school reform by using scientifically based instructional strategies;
10. Evaluate the quality of instruction by providing improved staff development;
11. Coordinate the requirements of NCLB to function in consort;
12. Provide increased opportunities for parent involvement in the education of their children.

It should be noted that unlike other federal government programs, NCLB provided no financial incentives. However, school districts that did not comply with the requirements were subject to having all federal funding blocked. Strictly speaking, it was an unfunded mandate.

Not associated with a civil right or other fundamental freedom, NCLB was called into question constitutionally. Because the Tenth Amendment gives authority for education to the states, some states litigated on the question of whether a state can be forced to offer programs it cannot afford. In perhaps the most-high profile of these,

14. 20 U.S.C.A. §§ 6301 *et seq.*
15. *Id.* at § 6301.

the State of Connecticut sued the Department of Education for what it claimed to be inadequate funding, seeking to force the federal government to either change its testing rules or cover the additional costs for NCLB's required testing. However, the suit was ultimately dismissed on procedural grounds.

Another issue surrounding NCLB was whether it conflicted with the Individuals with Disabilities in Education Act of 2004. It was argued that assessments of students who are in special education cannot follow the same timeframes and procedures required to comply with NCLB. The issue was addressed by the Seventh Circuit in *Board of Education of Ottawa Township High School District 140 v. Spellings*.[16] With very little rationale, the court affirmed the lower court and ruled that the two statutes did not conflict with one another.

ESSA

The Every Student Succeeds Act was signed into law in December 2015. This reauthorization of ESEA in its 50th year preempted much of NCLB and increased federal accountability for public schools in the areas of students living in poverty, minority students, limited-English-proficiency students, and those receiving special education services. State plans for compliance with ESSA must include provisions related to academic standards, annual testing, school accountability, goals for academic achievement, plans for the support and improvement of struggling schools, and methods to provide public information about schools through local and state school report cards.

The Role of State Government in Education

Both the long- and short-term history of schools in the United States establishes that education is the business of the state. All state constitutions have some provision for the establishment of a school system. A typical education provision would provide for the legislature to create statutes which help to found a system of free public education. Some state constitutions further specify that a state board of education be established to supervise the schools.[17] Other state constitutions have given recognition and certain powers to local boards.[18] However, the most common approach is for the state constitution to give plenary power to the legislature. This means that the legislature is only subject to the limitations set in the state constitution, if any. The extent of this power was aptly put by the Michigan Supreme Court:

> The legislature has entire control over the schools of the state. . . . The division of the territory of the state into districts, the conduct of the school, the

16. 517 F.3d 922 (7th Cir. 2008).
17. Okla. Const. art. XIII, § 5.
18. La. Const. art. VIII.

qualifications of teachers, the subjects to be taught therein, are all within its control. . . .[19]

Valente has summarized the authority of state legislatures by reference to case law. He finds that legislatures have the power to (1) direct or authorize the creation, modification, and abolition of school districts; (2) alter the structure and powers of school boards; (3) remove incumbent school board members and abolish their offices; (4) prescribe the school calendar and curriculum; (5) determine the sources and procedures for raising school revenues and school spending; (6) fix the appointment, term, and qualifications of teachers; (7) require local schools to admit children of non-taxpayers; and (8) revoke charters of public schools for noncompliance with state regulations.[20]

The list of legislative powers just mentioned is not exhaustive. It is illustrative. The degree of control exercised by legislatures in a particular state is a matter of tradition and, perhaps more importantly—feasibility. A state legislature is not in the best position to "run" schools. It is a law-making body that controls by creating statutes that give power to other agencies to carry out the will of the legislature. In most cases, the legislature delegates authority to a state board of education to carry out the intent of education-related statutes. Therefore, the extent to which the legislature becomes involved in controlling the schools is a matter of how specific statutes are written. The state legislatures that have a tradition of involvement will create statutes that have a higher degree of specificity than those legislatures which prefer to leave the ministerial details to an administrative agency.

In the last several decades, a popular movement in the governance of public education was to replace an elected State Superintendent of Public Education with a state board. Instead of vesting all the power in one person, a structure that was hoped to be more democratically oriented was created. All states, except the state of Wisconsin, now have state boards of education.[21]

The number of members on a state board of education varies from seven to 11. The members are usually elected or appointed from various geographic regions throughout the state, to provide maximum representation of citizens. The state board of education controls by issuing policies. The board policies are necessary to lend specificity to state statutes which are passed by the legislature. Most board policies can be traced to some state statute and are necessary to carry out the will of the legislature. In addition to creating policies, the state board of education renders certain decisions on exceptional educational matters. Some of these decisions include subjects such as school-district reorganization, school closings, and revocation of teaching and administrative credentials. The state board also sits in appellate review of certain teacher and student personnel decisions such as teacher terminations

---

19. Child Welfare Soc'y of Flint v. Kennedy Sch. Dist., 189 N.W. 1002, 1004 (Mich. 1922).

20. W. Valente & C. Valente, Law in the Schools 21 (2005).

21. Council of Chief State School Officers, *Educational Governance in the States: A Status Report on State Boards of Education, Chief State School Officers, and State Education Agencies* 23 (1983).

and student expulsions. In the last decades, state boards of education have become increasingly involved in contested decisions involving the education of students with disabilities.

The chief state school officer typically holds the title of state superintendent of public instruction. In some states the title is "commissioner of education." Regardless of title, the chief state school officer functions much like a school district superintendent would in relationship to a local board. In 27 states, the state board appoints or simply hires the chief state school officer. The State of Kansas, for example, advertises, receives applications, and conducts interviews like any executive might be hired. In 18 states, the chief school officer is found by popular election. In five states, the governor appoints the superintendent. Current trends tend toward state boards being responsible for the chief officer's hiring.[22]

State departments of public education function much like the President's cabinet. It is not possible for the state superintendent to personally carry out all policies of the state board. Therefore, a professional staff is necessary for the administration of the state board policies. Under the direction of the state superintendent, the state department issues regulations. These regulations lend specificity to the policies of the state board. In addition to issuing necessary regulations, the state department engages in a number of supervisory, enforcement, and monitoring activities. Some of these activities include: teacher certification, school accreditation, graduation requirements, financial support, and staff development.

To the dismay and even the unawareness of local school board members, local boards are not "local." Local boards are agents of the state. Local boards are legally classified as a subdivision of state government which is limited to the special purposes necessary for overseeing the operations of the school district. As units of state government, local boards of education are immune from a variety of tort liabilities (see Chapter 2 for a more detailed discussion of tort liability as it relates to educators and school districts). However, at certain times the local board acts in a proprietary manner rather than governmental. Most state statutes allow local boards to enter into contracts and sue and be sued. When local boards engage in these functions, they are acting as private corporations rather than governments. A board may not be immune from liability as a government when making corporation-like decisions.

Classifying local boards is difficult. The name of the local education authority (LEA) itself reflects regional diversity. In some states, the LEA is called a Board of School Directors. In other states, the LEA is called the Board of Education. Still, in other states, it is called simply the School Board.

Aside from labels, the organization of boards varies. The number of board members ranges from five to nine. Members serve anywhere from two- to six-year terms. In most cases, a person must live within the school district boundaries in order to be a candidate for election. Other than being a resident and registered voter in

---

22. *Id.* at 23–25.

the school district, additional qualifications for board member candidacy are rare. However, there is some movement to place a formal educational requirement for serving on a local board. For example, Oklahoma's statutes require that board members hold at least a high school diploma or equivalent.[23]

The process of electing local board members is nearly universal. At this point, it would be important to distinguish between a school board and a school district. The school district is a geopolitical entity created by the state. It represents a specific place on a state map that may or may not be contiguous with any other geopolitical border. School district lines do not have to run along city or county boundaries. In many states, a school district may lie in several counties. However, there is a movement within states toward consolidation of smaller school districts into larger ones. As consolidation becomes a goal, one solution is to create county school districts. In this case, the school district boundaries are the same as the county.

In contrast to the school district, the school board is a group of elected citizens who help decide the affairs of the school district. Officer status is different than "school employee"; a school employee has few of the characteristics of a school officer. A school officer is a person who holds office in order to carry out a delegation of sovereign power. In the case of school board members, their duties and powers are outlined in state statutes. School officers have discretionary authority to carry out their duties and are not subject to a superior power. Board members, as school officers, take an oath of office. School superintendents are often confused for school officers. However, the superintendent is a school employee as traditional case law has noted.[24]

The only time a board can act is during an officially recognized board meeting. When not sitting at a board meeting, a board member has no authority. In some states, statutes prescribe the number of meetings to be held and the form of notice of meetings which may include a time and place. State open-meeting laws typically govern such matters as public participation or attendance at the meetings. These laws pertaining to open meetings and open records are often referred to as sunshine laws. The sunshine laws cover a wide range of meeting and member behaviors.

An overview of state statutes and accompanying case law would suggest the following about how local boards must conduct business: (1) Dates and times of meetings must be published well in advance to give the board members and the public every opportunity to attend. (2) Notice of meetings must appear in a newspaper and be posted at a place where the public might get the information, i.e., bulletin board outside the school district administrative offices, and often on the district web site. (3) Meetings must be conducted in some orderly fashion, often strictly adhering to agendas included in the public notice, with minutes taken. (4) Minutes should reveal at least the decisions reached by the board. (5) All business must be discussed at an

23. 26 Okla. St. Ann. §13A-106.

24. Main v. Claremont Uniform Sch. Dist., 326 P.2d 573 (Cal. Ct. App. 1958).

open meeting where the public has an opportunity to hear. (6) There are exceptions to the business discussion requirement—when the discussion would cause harm to individual reputations or the public interest, or pertains to confidential information protected by law, the board may go into executive session. In executive session, the meeting is closed to the public. However, the board may invite individuals into the session that it feels will aid in the discussion. While some consensus might be reached in executive session, an official decision or vote must be taken at an open meeting. (7) Minutes of board meetings are considered public documents and must be open and available.[25]

The powers and duties of local boards are most often found in the state statutes. However, at least one state establishes the authority of local boards in its constitution. Duties are those areas of decision making that the board is bound by law to make. For example, if the state statute says that the local board shall hire teachers, then the board must perform that duty. The board cannot delegate that duty to the superintendent. Generally, the board cannot delegate duties that are assigned by statute. However, there are a number of duties which befall a local board which can be delegated to the administration. These are called ministerial duties.

The powers of a local board are those areas of authority that can be used in order to carry out the necessary running of the school district. When a statute is referring to a board power it often uses the predicate "may." The use of the word "may" indicates that the board has the authority to make a decision in the area being described in the statute. Whether the board can delegate a power depends on the extent to which the power is policymaking or administrative in nature. Thinking about it in practical terms, a board of education out of necessity will have to delegate most of its powers over administrative areas to the superintendent. A local board of education is not designed to make administrative decisions, while school administrators are trained and certified to make those administrative decisions. Local boards exist to exercise power over the policy-making process. While professional administrators might recommend to the board that certain policies be established, the board must decide district-wide policy.

Not all powers of local boards are specified by state statutes. It would be nearly impossible to specify all the powers which are necessary for a local board to carry out its functions. State statutes usually specify that local boards have all powers reasonably necessary for the proper and efficient management of public education. These powers are known as implied powers.

25. Valente & Valente, *supra*, 46–54. *See also* People ex rel. Gibson v. Peller, 181 N.E.2d 376 (Ill. App. Ct. 1962).

Compulsory School Attendance

The state's commitment to require that all children be educated was recognized from the initial drafting of many state constitutions. Primary articles of state constitutions often contain a section dedicated to education, evidencing the commitment states made to education from their origination. The content of these constitutional provisions often focuses not only on the establishment and maintenance of schools, but also attendance. In states where constitutions are not the source of authority for school attendance, some form of school attendance is made mandatory by statute.[26] States' constitutions are not the source of authority for school attendance; their statutes are. For example, the State of Mississippi does not require school attendance as part of its constitutional provisions but does require attendance in its education statutes.[27]

State attendance laws may be enforced by charging the parents with child neglect. Also, state prosecutors can remove a child from the parents. In some instances, the state may take action against the child directly and place the child in a custodial school.

Exemptions from Compulsory Attendance

Children of certain ages must attend a school of some kind that is recognized by the state. Some states require that any alternative to public school attendance be at a school that is accredited. Other states only require that the alternative school comply with health and safety standards. There are certain classes of children that are exempt because they are "emancipated." Young persons can gain emancipation status if the court recognizes that they are married or able to support themselves. Also, a candidate for emancipation might be an adolescent who must work to provide needed support for the family. At one time, children with special education needs could be exempt from attendance. However, since the early 1970s, public schools must provide education for a child, regardless of disability. This standard is commonly known as "zero reject."[28] Preference for the least restrictive environment ensures that the child be educated with other children to the fullest extent possible. Additional discussion on the subject of special education is presented in Chapter 5.

One of the larger bases for attendance exemption is home schooling. The next section will cover home schooling in some detail. It should be noted that home schooling has origins in certain religions in which devotees felt they needed to be exempt in order to carry out necessary elements of faith. In a famous case from 1972, *Wisconsin v. Yoder*, Amish children were kept home after the eighth grade.[29]

26. Okla. Const. art. XIII, § 4.

27. Miss. Code Ann. § 37-13-91.

28. 20 U.S.C.A. §§ 1400 *et seq.; see* Timothy W. v. Rochester, N.H., Sch. Dist., 875 F.2d 954 (1st Cir. 1989).

29. 406 U.S. 205 (1972).

The State of Wisconsin prosecuted parents for attendance-law violation. Taking the case to the U.S. Supreme Court, parents of the Amish faith were granted an exemption from the attendance law. The Court reasoned that the Amish showed the extent of coercion that would result in damage to their religion outweighed the compelling state interest in requiring all children attend school until age 16. The exemption won by the Amish was founded on the free exercise of religion.

Some courts have granted exemption from school attendance based on the presence of danger. Cases that support the danger exemption have granted this exception when parents are able to show that the child needs to be protected from grave risk of harm. However, parents must convince the court that the potential harm is sufficiently grave and that the school administration is unable to provide adequate protection.[30] Much depends on the facts and the disposition of the court. The preponderance of cases, however, support the school in its position that parents must comply with attendance law regardless of what problems their child may be having in school.

The Third Circuit affirmed a lower court decision when parents argued that the school did not sufficiently protect their child from bullying. It cited to a much earlier case wherein a parent could not withdraw a student although the child had been pushed into a wall and cut with scissors by other students.[31]

Home Schooling

Perhaps the largest number of students requesting an exemption from compulsory attendance comes from home schooling. Modern-day home school has its origins in *Wisconsin v. Yoder*, wherein the Amish won an exemption based on the Free Exercise Clause.[32] (See Chapter 6 for a detailed discussion of this decision and of home schooling as related to religion.) In the wake of *Yoder*, many states passed "Amish Acts" which provided a statutory exemption for all Amish within the state. Since that time, the emption has strayed from its foundation in a specific religious sect. States like Kansas began giving religiously orientated families an exception, even to those that were not Amish. Next, states began giving exemptions to any family that wished to teach their children at home. Families no longer had to show that religious training would be part of the home schooling.

The National Center for Education Statistics reported that in 2019, the number of home-schooled students was about 2.5 million in grades K-12 in the United States, or 3 percent to 4 percent of school-age children.[33] As the number of homeschoolers

30. *See* Kaehly v. Cty. of Pittsburgh, 687 A.2d 41 (Pa Commw. Ct. 1996).

31. *See* Commonwealth ex rel. Sch. Dist. v. Ross, 330 A.2d 290, 291 (Pa. Commw. Ct. 1975).

32. 406 U.S. 205 (1972).

33. T.D. Snyder, C. de Brey, & S.A. Dillow, *Digest of Education Statistics 2017* (NCES 2018-070) (2019).

increases, so do the home-schooling support and resource associations. The American Homeschool Association is an advocacy and support network serving homeschooling families across the nation and around the world since 1995. Some states require that home schooling be "equivalent" or "comparable" to public schools. Other states treat home schooling as they do private schools. However, a private school might also need to be accredited using the same standards as public schools. Some states have no requirements or accountability measures for home-schooled students.

In many instances, the home-schooling associations aspire to be recognized as a legitimate and even superior form of schooling in America. Many statistics concerning how home-schooled students perform compared to public school students show that homeschoolers do as well or better on standardized tests.[34] However, when data is controlled for socioeconomic status and educational attainment of adults in the home, there is little difference in performance. There is tension between states and home schools over the issue of regulation. Some states wish to fulfill a duty to provide schooling through regulation. However, homeschoolers may wish a higher degree of freedom without state oversight. Hence, the legal process has been required to settle potential disputes.

The Home School Legal Defense Association[35] (HSLDA) was founded in 1983. It provides legal advice and representation to those committed to home schooling. The litigation involving the states and home schooling has centered on "over regulation" challenges. In an early case, the State of Maine required that home-school teachers receive training and that the children be taught in a facility meeting certain health and safety standards. The court ruled that it was a reasonable requirement for the state to impose these regulations.[36] However, homeschoolers have not always lost. Homeschoolers won when a Massachusetts regulation required official home-visit inspections. The regulation was voided for not being necessary to serve a state purpose. Therefore, it was deemed unreasonable.[37]

Eligibility for special-education services under the Individuals with Disabilities Education Act, or IDEA, for homeschoolers varies from state to state. While most children residing within the boundaries of a public school district may be eligible for evaluation and identification of special needs, federal law does not specifically require states to provide services for homeschoolers. Whether a homeschooler can receive services will depend on the state's definition of "private" school. If the state recognizes home schooling as private schooling, then services must be provided. In *Hooks v. Clark County School District*,[38] the Ninth Circuit ruled that states have

---

34. M.C. Yu, P. R. Sackett, & N. R. Kuncel, *Predicting College Performance of Homeschooled Versus Traditional Students. Educational Measurement: Issues and Practice* (2016).

35. *HSLDA Letter Published in Argus Leader*, States News Service (Purcellville, VA) (May 24, 2012).

36. State v. McDonough, 468 A.2d 977 (Me. 1983).

37. Blount v. Dept. of Educ. & Cultural Servs., 551 A.2d 1377 (Me. 1988).

38. 228 F.3d 1036 (9th Cir. 2000).

discretion to determine whether home education constitutes an IDEA-qualifying educational environment. Strictly speaking, the term "private" does not include a "home in which instruction is provided" for those who are excused from compulsory attendance.[39] Whether a homeschooler can participate in extracurricular activities is also state dependent. Attempts at litigation to provide participation rights have generally failed in bringing claims of rights under the federal Constitution, i.e., Due Process and Equal Protection.

Vouchers

In his work *Capitalism and Freedom*,[40] Milton Friedman first proposed school vouchers to denationalize education. He theorized that the imposition of a minimum required level of schooling and the financing of this schooling by the state can be justified by the "neighborhood effects" of schooling. The actual administration of educational institutions, or "nationalization" by the government, is much more difficult to justify. Governments could require a minimum level of schooling financed by giving parents vouchers redeemable for a specified maximum sum per child per year if spent on "approved" educational services. Parents would then be free to spend this sum and any additional amount they themselves provided on purchasing educational services from an "approved" institution of their own choice. The educational services could be rendered by private enterprises operated for profit or by non-profit institutions. The role of government would be limited to ensuring that the schools met certain minimum standards, such as the inclusion of minimum common content in their programs.

In the last 50 years, school vouchers have had mixed results in their use by the states. The basic principle in a voucher program is to return property tax money to families so they can use it to pay for the cost of instruction in their preferred school format. The school-choice approach does not return real dollars to taxpayers. Instead, a "voucher" worth the equivalent amount paid in property taxes is given to the local school district. Of course, parents have to bear the cost of instruction that might exceed their voucher amount. In some states, scholarships are offered in order to augment cost overages.

Initial challenges to vouchers emerged when taxpayers attempted to use the vouchers at sectarian schools. This issue came to a head in the 2002 Supreme Court case of *Zelman v. Simmons Harris*.[41] This case involved the Cleveland Public Schools, which included religiously affiliated schools as part of its voucher program. As expected, parochial schools being included in the program were challenged. However, the Cleveland program had practical aspects that had not been used by previous

39. Nev. Rev. Stat. § 394.103 (2013).

40. Milton Friedman, Capitalism and Freedom 89 (1962).

41. 536 U.S. 639 (2002).

states. Parents would receive a cash amount, not a voucher that was made out to them as payee. The taxpayer or parent, however, could not use the check unless it was signed over as a third party to the school. Therefore, no state money would ever be paid *directly* to the church-related school. While state money reimbursement was eventually paid to the school, it was from the parents, not the state treasurer. The High Court considered the practical aspects of the program to provide only *indirect* aid. Indirect aid to religious institutions had been recognized as no violation of the Establishment Clause and thus, this voucher program was legal. (See Chapter 6 for a more detailed discussion of this issue as it relates to separation of church and state under the Constitution's First Amendment.)

Charter Schools

The National Education Association (NEA) reported that charter schools came into existence with two charter schools in Minnesota in 1991. There were almost 7,000 charter schools by 2019, operating in 44 states plus the District of Columbia and Puerto Rico and enrolling approximately 3.2 million students. While no one definition of a charter school can be found, several organizations and commentators have provided good descriptions. Valente says:

> Charter schools are nonsectarian schools that are created under a state law by a "charter," this establishes their structure and mode of operation. They are not subject to many regulations that govern traditional public schools, but they are accountable to the public authorities in greater degree than traditional private schools.[42]

The make-up of a charter school varies considerably from state to state and within the state. Charter schools may exist as a function of a public school, a public/private partnership, private non-profits, or as private "for profit" entities. These schools may deliver the curriculum in a traditional setting, online or "virtual" formats, or various hybrid approaches. They may differ widely as to curriculum, admission, and teacher qualifications, among other aspects. The curriculum of the charter school tends to be unique in that experimentation is supported. The school may be devoted to at-risk or gifted students, students with special needs, or even elite athletes. Others specialize in a unique field of study such as the fine arts or science. Teacher qualifications for charter schools vary from state to state. Some states require charters to adhere to the same teaching-credential requirements as those of traditional public school teachers. However, many states allow a waiver of the regular teaching credential for charter schools. Funding of charter schools may come from public and/or private sources. Like most aspects of charter schools, the balance between state and private funds varies from state to state.

---

42. Valente & Valente, *supra*, 444–45 (2005).

Now that we have explored the pervasive role of the law in the governance of public schools and provided a thorough overview of the legal framework of public education, later chapters will cover in more depth specific topics in education law and how they are shaped by this framework.

The Impact of the National Pandemic on K-12 Education

It is, perhaps, too soon to realize the full impact of the international COVID-19, pandemic that began affecting public schools in 2020. It would not be unreasonable to expect future challenges related to the adequacy and equity of funding and educational access, the rights of students with disabilities, school conditions for both teachers and students, and compulsory attendance, as well as other impacts on existing educational laws and policies at the national, state, and local levels. To date, the COVID-19 pandemic has created the largest disruption of the international education system in history, impacting approximately 1.6 billion students in more than 190 countries across all continents.[43] The closures of schools and other learning centers have impacted 94 percent of the world's student population, and up to 99 percent in low- and lower-middle income countries.[44] The crisis has unquestionably magnified pre-existing educational disparities and inequities among students by reducing the opportunities for many of the most vulnerable student populations, including but not limited to those living in poor or rural areas, refugees, students with disabilities, and forcibly displaced persons, as these students attempt to continue their learning. The pandemic is revealing deep socioeconomic and racial/ethnic inequities that have long characterized American K-12 public education. Initial research studies predict significant COVID-19-related learning deficits among students that will significantly increase already dramatic student achievement gaps, and students who are the most vulnerable will most likely bear the brunt of the learning losses, namely students with disabilities, low-income students, and students of color.[45] Historically, unexpected interruptions to schooling have been found to undermine student achievement and subsequent success in higher education. While only time will reveal the full impact of COVID-19 on education, its initial impacts have been dramatic and impactful.

---

43. United Nations, Policy Brief, *Education During COVID-19 and Beyond* (Aug. 2020), https://www.un.org/development/desa/dspd/wp-content/uploads/sites/22/2020/08/sg_policy_brief_covid-19_and_education_august_2020.pdf.

44. *Id.*

45. *Coronavirus Impacts on Education and Learning*, Walton Family Found. (Aug. 21, 2020), https://www.waltonfamilyfoundation.org/learning/coronavirus-impacts-on-education-and-learning.

Chapter 2

Liability of Educators and School Districts

This chapter focuses on tort liability and types of situations that school authorities must face in dealing with liability issues. The authors recognize that entire texts and law school courses are devoted exclusively to the area of tort liability as a distinct study of law. Understanding this, this chapter concentrates primarily on how tort liability affects educators and K-12 school districts. An overview of the law is given to refresh students who may have previous study in law and to acquaint new students with basic concepts. It is not meant, however, to provide a comprehensive explanation of this field. For more detailed information, we refer students to the many textbooks available on this topic.

Introduction

The word "tort" comes from the Latin meaning "to twist" or "twisted."[1] Prosser broadly defines tort as "a civil wrong, other than breach of contract, for which the court will provide a remedy in the form of an action for damages."[2] Different from both criminal and contract law, tort law seeks compensation for a variety of civil wrongs.

As part of the system of common law, state-level courts hear tort cases. The variance of tort law from state to state makes detailed generalizations problematic. However, there are some common characteristics of tort law across states. Torts generally fall into four categories. They include intentional torts, strict liability, non-intentional torts based on negligence, and constitutional torts. Each of these is described below and presented in terms of how they apply to educators and education law. Because the first two types of tort claims are less common in educational settings, they are only briefly discussed. Non-intentional torts based on negligence and constitutional torts are presented in much more detail as they represent far more significant litigation in the school context.

1. *Tort*, Merriam-Webster Dictionary, https://www.merriam-webster.com/dictionary/tort.
2. William L. Prosser, Law of Torts 2 (4th ed. 1971).

Intentional Torts

Intentional torts are the result of voluntary and intended behavior that brings about either desired or reasonably foreseeable outcomes, even in the absence of a desire to do harm.[3] In other words, even if an injury is not intended, if a person "invades the interests of another in a way that the law will not sanction," an intentional tort may result.[4] Intentional torts commonly associated with educational settings might include assault, battery, false imprisonment, infliction of emotional distress, defamation, libel, and slander.

Defamation, Libel, and Slander

Defamation is defined as "Malicious or groundless harm to the reputation or good name of another by the making of a false statement to a third person. . . . A false written or oral statement that damages another's reputation."[5] A defamatory statement or communication is one which is defined as "tending to harm a person's reputation, usu. [*sic*] by subjecting the person to public contempt, disgrace, or ridicule, or by adversely affecting the person's business."[6]

Libel is "a method of defamation expressed by print, writing, pictures, or signs . . . any publication that is injurious to the reputation of another."[7] Slander is "the speaking of base and defamatory words tending to prejudice another in his reputation, office, trade, business, or means of livelihood."[8] Slander has four essential elements: a false and defamatory statement about another person; unprivileged communication; "fault amounting at least to negligence on the part of the publisher"; and "either actionability of the statement irrespective of harm or the existence of special harm."[9]

Most education-related cases on defamation address school employees and either employment references or public statements. In general, court cases adhere to the standards set forth on defamation, libel, and slander mentioned above. In educational settings, tort claims of this nature may often come to loggerheads with academic freedom and free speech rights. Other types of defamation cases may arise in the context of school newspapers. In such instances, the principal has the authority to regulate what is printed.[10] See Chapter 4 for a discussion of students and the school newspaper context.

---

3. Prosser at 31.
4. *Id.*
5. *Defamation*, Black's Law Dictionary (11th ed. 2019).
6. *Defamatory*, Black's Law Dictionary (11th ed. 2019).
7. *Libel*, Black's Law Dictionary (11th ed. 2019).
8. *Slander*, Black's Law Dictionary (11th ed. 2019).
9. Restatement (Second) of Torts § 558.
10. See *Hazelwood School District v. Kuhlmeier*, 484 U.S. 260 (1988), for a discussion of school newspapers and school officials' authority to regulate content; see also *Draudt v. Wooster City*

Strict Liability

While fault is at issue in both intentional and unintentional (negligence) claims, strict liability is often referred to as "liability without fault."[11] For purposes of education law, these cases generally involve product liability, whereby the seller is responsible for ensuring that products are not defective. The strict liability doctrine means that strict liability is imposed on "the commercial distribution of defective products."[12]

Here, there is a presumption that if a seller puts goods into the stream of commerce, then these goods are suitable for their intended use. Thus, if a student or teacher falls and is hurt because he or she stands on a chair that is designed only for sitting, the doctrine of strict liability would not apply. In this case, the chair was not used for the purpose for which it was designed (unless of course there was faulty design which caused the problem and not misuse). This same rule would apply to machines improperly used in shop classes or chemicals misused in a science class. On the other hand, if a student sits on the chair properly and the chair falls apart, injuring the student, then strict liability would apply. Similarly, if the shop equipment and chemicals are used according to directions, including observing safety precautions, and damages result, then the seller is strictly liable. The vast amount of tort cases in schools do not involve strict liability; however, it is important to know the law in this area when school districts purchase or possibly produce and/or sell products.

School districts have also been plaintiffs in actions for strict liability in situations where their leadership believe that the school or students have suffered harm because of a particular product. For example, several school districts joined in mass tort claims against the maker of vaping devices and products labeled JUUL, alleging it "marketed its JUUL nicotine delivery products in a manner designed to attract minors, that JLI's marketing misrepresents or omits that JUUL products are more potent and addictive than cigarettes, that JUUL products are defective and unreasonably dangerous due to their attractiveness to minors, and that JLI promotes nicotine addiction."[13]

Unintentional Torts

Unintentional torts are those caused by negligence. Negligence is defined as "the failure to use such care as a reasonably prudent and careful person would use under similar circumstances."[14] This area of tort liability is broad and may cover anything

---

School District Board of Education, 246 F. Supp. 2d 820 (N.D. Ohio 2003), for a discussion directly bearing on defamation.

11. *Liability, strict liability*, Black's Law Dictionary (11th ed. 2019).

12. *Id.*

13. In re Juul Labs, Inc., 396 F. Supp. 3d 1366,1367 (J.P.M.L. 2019).

14. *Negligence*, Black's Law Dictionary (11th ed. 2019).

from automobile accidents to medical malpractice. Most tort cases in public schools fall under this category of unintentional torts. Here, tort liability may cover accidents caused by negligence in science laboratories or classes with heavy equipment such as vocational shops, injuries in physical education classes, and/or slip and fall cases due to wet floors or icy sidewalks.

In contrast to intentional torts, claims of negligence involve no conscious desire to harm. In an action for negligence, plaintiffs argue that some type of injury resulted from action or inaction that the defendant should have known would cause harm.[15] In order to prevail in a claim of negligence, plaintiffs must prove four elements:

1. A duty, or obligation recognized by the law, to conform to a standard of conduct, for the protection of others against unreasonable risks.
2. A breach of that duty, i.e., failure to conform to the standard of care required.
3. A legal or proximate cause between the conduct and the resulting injury.
4. Actual loss or damage.[16]

Duty

In a New Jersey case, the school violated its duty to supervise when a nine-year-old student was permanently injured after being hit by an automobile while crossing a busy street. This incident occurred when students were given an early dismissal toward the end of the school year. The district had clear policies regarding supervision as applied to dismissals at the regular time but no policies specific to early dismissals such as this one where students were not adequately supervised.[17]

In most education-related negligence cases that reach the courts, school districts have not been held responsible because they had no duty to protect. Such cases often deal with incidents outside of school hours or away from the school setting. For example, a Nebraska court found that a school district had no duty to supervise two summer school students who were assaulted at a restaurant near the school on their lunch break. One student suffered an asthma attack and died, the other sustained injuries. The court ruled that the school had no duty to protect students who are off campus, and the assault was not foreseeable.[18]

Even in cases as serious as suicide, courts have generally steered away from establishing a duty of care. In a suicide attempt at school that left the student seriously disabled, the First Circuit Court of Appeals[19] concluded that the school district owed no duty to protect this child under tort law or constitutional law:

15. *Id.*
16. *Id.*
17. Jerkins v. Anderson, 922 A.2d 1279 (N.J. 2007).
18. Wright v. Omaha Pub. Sch. Dist., 791 N.W.2d 760 (Neb. 2010).
19. Hasenfus v. LaJeunesse, 175 F.3d 68 (1st Cir. 1999).

> The federal courts have no general authority to decide when school administrators should introduce suicide prevention programs, or whether an unruly or upset school child should be sent out of class, or what should be said to other parents about a tragic incident at school. Substantive due process is not a license for judges to supersede the decisions of local officials and elected legislators on such matters.[20]

In *Rogers*,[21] the Delaware Supreme Court found no duty of care when a student committed suicide at home after having talked with the school's intervention specialist about his intentions. The specialist spent four hours with the student, decided he was no longer entertaining suicidal thoughts, and notified all appropriate school personnel in an e-mail. The court, however, recognized that the parents sufficiently presented facts to support a claim of negligence *per se* because school officials violated mandatory state and district requirements to notify a parent or guardian of the student's crisis.

One possible exception is *Eisel*,[22] where the school counselor was held liable for the death of a student who was involved in a suicide pact with a friend; however, this duty hinged largely on school policy and on Maryland state law's somewhat singular interpretation of *in loco parentis*. Fossey and Zirkel,[23] two prominent education law scholars, studied suicide cases following *Eisel* and concluded that:

> . . . [It] is inescapable that the courts—both state and federal—are inhospitable to plaintiffs seeking to hold educators legally responsible for a student's suicide death. This conclusion does not mean that educators should ignore suicidal behavior by students. Rather, school policies and programs to reduce the tragedy of student suicide are more a matter of professional discretion and ethical imperative than a necessary precaution.[24]

It is critical, therefore, that school leaders know the law in this area, including state as well as federal law, and that they use their own conscience and ethical sense of duty when the law does not hold them financially responsible.

Standard of Care

School officials clearly have a duty to protect students and employees. The question here is: How far does that duty extend? While the law does expect administrators and teachers to keep schools safe, it does not expect them to be omniscient. The standard of care for tort liability, as stated above, is that of a reasonable person. In other words, would a reasonable school official (i.e., teacher, administrator)

---

20. *Id.* at 74.

21. Rogers v. Christina Sch. Dist., 73 A.3d 1 (Del. 2013).

22. Eisel v. Bd. of Educ., 597 A.2d 447 (Md. 1991).

23. Richard Fossey & Perry A. Zirkel, *Liability for Student Suicide in the Wake of* Eisel, 10 Tex. Wesleyan L. Rev. 403 (2004).

24. *Id.* at 439.

have acted in such a manner? While the standard of care may differ based on a student's age, the scope of the duty may also be impacted by the extent of a student's disability.[25]

An important line of cases that focuses on the standard of care addresses issues of supervision and whether negligence applies. Consider *Stevens v. Chesteen.*[26] In this case, Timothy Stevens, a student who had knee surgery as the result of a motorcycle accident, was not to participate in any physical or strenuous activities that might cause further damage. As part of their physical education activities, students engaged in a game of touch football. Stevens stood on the sidelines. As he was distracted by some commotion in the stands, one of the players ran into him, re-injuring his knee. Stevens sued for negligent supervision, noting that Chesteen, the coach, was not on the field at the time of the accident but was in a storage shed on the visitor's side of the field. An Alabama Supreme Court ruled in favor of the school district stating that ". . . the reality of school life is such that a teacher cannot possibly be expected to personally supervise each student in his charge at every moment of the school day."[27]

On the other hand, teachers have been found negligent when students were hurt in unruly classrooms and on dangerous playgrounds.[28] In a Massachusetts case,[29] a principal was denied immunity when a student was seriously injured during a mandated recess period. The school had no playground, so the principal decided to hold recess in a concrete courtyard with benches that had sharp edges and corners. The court ruled that the principal had a duty to conduct recess in a safe place and it was foreseeable that first graders would run, fall, and push each other at recess, and that one might get hurt on the sharp-edged benches. There were also other safer places, such as the gymnasium, where the recess could have been held.

Causation

Causation takes two forms. The incident that occurred must be the direct cause of the damages. In other words, if a school official breached a duty but the damages occurred not because of the breach but because of some intervening event, then there would not be a direct cause and the school district would not be held responsible. Another critical factor in determining causation is foreseeability. Oftentimes, school officials are not held liable in negligence cases because the events that caused the incident were not foreseeable.

---

25. S.H. v. K & H Transp., Inc., 242 A.3d 278 (N.J. Super. Ct. App. Div. 2020).

26. 561 So.2d 1100 (Ala. 1990).

27. *Id.* at 1103.

28. *See, e.g.,* Johnson v. Sch. Dist. of Millard, 573 N.W.2d. 116 (Neb. 1998) (a student fell into a bookcase during an unsupervised game of "London Bridge" and required 50 stitches); Maynard v. Bd. of Educ. of Massena Central Sch. Dist., 663 N.Y.S.2d 717 (App. Div. 3rd Dept. 1997) (a student's eye was injured when another student used a ruler to shoot a pencil at him).

29. Gennari v. Reading Pub. Sch., 933 N.E.2d 1027 (Mass. App. Ct. 2010).

For example, in *McMahon v. St. Croix Falls,*[30] a school district was not held liable for a truant student's suicide in that the suicide was too remote an event for the school district to have known. Similarly, in *Stoddart v. Pocatello School District #25,*[31] the school district was not held responsible for the murder of a student in her friend's home even though school authorities had uncovered threats of violence from the alleged perpetrator some two-and-a-half years earlier. The court held that the school did not have an ongoing duty to monitor this person.

Damages

With schools as with tort liability cases in general, damages must be real and capable of being compensated. They need not, however, be physical. Physical damages may be easier for a jury to assess and thus easier to fashion a remedy for, but they are not the only types of damages that may apply to students in schools. Of relevance to educational settings are claims for intentional infliction of emotional distress. These claims have been used in a variety of school cases but are mostly found in situations where a child may be traumatized such as by bullying, corporal punishment, or strip searching. Irwin Hyman, a former professor of school psychology and well-known scholar who researched these last two issues for decades, contended that in such cases, students are often so affected by these incidents that they could well be diagnosed as having psychological disorders such as post-traumatic stress syndrome.[32] Professor Hyman's work makes very compelling social science arguments, including some that have been acknowledged by the Supreme Court;[33] however, legal claims based on emotional distress have not persuaded the judiciary.[34] Plaintiffs in school-related cases are increasingly asserting these state-law tort claims even though they generally fail.[35]

---

30. 596 N.W. 2d 875 (Wis. Ct. App. 1999). *See also* Mikell v. Sch. Admin. Unit # 33, 972 A.2d 1050 (N.H. 2009) (finding that it was too speculative that the guidance counselor could have prevented the suicide had she instructed the student to seek professional help).

31. 239 P.3d 784 (Idaho 2010).

32. Irwin A. Hyman & Pamela A Snook, Dangerous Schools: What We Can Do About the Physical and Emotional Abuse of our Children 87, 89 (1999); Irwin A. Hyman, Reading, Writing, and the Hickory Stick: The Appalling Story of Physical and Psychological Abuse in American Schools (1990).

33. Safford v. Redding, 557 U.S. 364, 375 (citing *The Other Side of School Violence: Educator Policies and Practices that May Contribute to Student Misbehavior,* 36 J. Sch. Psychol. 7, 13 (1998) (strip search can "result in serious emotional damage").

34. *See, e.g.,* Pendleton v. Fassett, No. 08-227-C, 2009 WL 2849542 (W.D. Ky. Sep. 1, 2009) (strip search not so outrageous as to support emotional distress claim).

35. *See, e.g.,* Kelly A. Albin, *Bullies in a Wired World: The Impact of Cyberspace Victimization on Adolescent Mental Health and the Need for Cyberbullying Legislation in Ohio,* 25 J.L. & Health 155 (2012) (noting that claims based on intentional infliction of emotional distress are very difficult to win).

Defenses to Negligence

In response to negligence claims, educators have used several defenses including contributory negligence, comparative negligence, and assumption of the risk. Contributory negligence is "a plaintiff's own negligence that played a part in causing the plaintiff's injury and that is significant enough (in a few jurisdictions) to bar the plaintiff from recovering damages."[36] This doctrine stands in contrast to the more commonly used modified comparative negligence, where negligence is assessed in terms of percentages. Here, the plaintiff would receive proportionately fewer damages based on his or her degree of negligence.[37] Pure comparative negligence allows the plaintiffs to receive the total amount minus the percentage to which they were responsible for the injury. Modified comparative negligence has a cut-off point (generally around 51 percent). In other words, if the plaintiff was 49 percent liable, they receive that percentage of damages. If they were responsible for 50 percent or more of the damages, they receive no restitution. In determining damages, therefore, it is critical to know whether your state is bound by contributory, comparative, or modified comparative negligence statutes.

Assumption of risk involves the chance of injury being understood by the plaintiff as a possibility of engaging in a known risk.[38] Classic examples of assumption of risk include riding a roller coaster and being a spectator at a baseball game, a situation where it is common for balls to fly into the audience. In the school context, assumption of risk is often associated with athletics. For example, in *Edelson*,[39] a student sued because of an injury inflicted to his jaw while he was engaged in a wrestling match. A New York appeals court maintained that the student had assumed the risk and that such an injury was foreseeable during the match. Assumption of risk, however, did not bar recovery in *Stoughtenger v. Hannibal Central School District*,[40] where a student was required to wrestle a much heavier opponent as part of a mandated activity in gym class.

Ciccone v. Bedford Central School District,[41] another New York case, involved Antonio Ciccone, a high school senior lacrosse player who was injured when he collided with another player after executing a "body check." This maneuver involved Ciccone using his head to block the opponent. The court noted that "Antonio was a highly skilled and trained athlete who had been playing lacrosse since the sixth grade" and "executed body check blocks approximately 20–30 times each game."[42]

---

36. *Negligence, contributory negligence*, Black's Law Dictionary (11th ed. 2019).

37. *Negligence, comparative negligence*, Black's Law Dictionary (11th ed. 2019).

38. *Assumption of the risk, negligence, contributory negligence*, Black's Law Dictionary (11th ed. 2019).

39. Edelson v. Uniondale Union Free Sch. Dist., 219 A.D.2d 614 (N.Y. App. Div. 2d Dept. 1995).

40. 90 A.D.3d 1696 (N.Y. App. Div. 4th Dept. 2011).

41. 21 A.D.3d 437 (N.Y. App. Div. 4th Dept. 2005).

42. *Id.* at 438.

Granting summary judgment for the school district, the court concluded that this student was aware of, and voluntarily assumed, the risks inherent in playing lacrosse.

In a California case,[43] a cheerleader injured her knee while practicing a gymnastic stunt. Here, the state appeals court granted the school summary judgment in that the cheerleader had assumed risks associated with this activity. The coach had done nothing to increase the possibility of injury, and the parents had signed a release form. An Illinois case[44] involved a father who sued the school district when his son was injured after being hit in the eye with a tennis ball. The two were watching a school tennis match and, because the bleachers were filled, were standing inside the fence surrounding tennis court. The father claimed the school had allowed them to watch the game in an unsafe area. An Illinois state appeals court ruled that the man and his son had voluntarily placed themselves in danger and that plaintiffs may not recover damages when the danger is obvious.

Liability for Third-Party Actions

There are times when school districts may be liable, at least in part, for third-party actions. For example, if a student presents a danger to another student, and school authorities are aware of this situation, then they have a duty to take reasonable measures. What these reasonable measures consist of may vary depending on state tort laws as well as other state legislation such as anti-bullying laws or cyberbullying laws. This is not to say that the school district is solely responsible. In such cases, the plaintiff student may bring claims against the school as well as personal claims against the perpetrator. This situation is most common in cases related to school safety, as discussed in Chapter 4 on students' rights, and in cases related to bullying and racial and sexual harassment, elaborated upon later in this chapter.

Limitations on Recovery

Another variable when it comes to damages in legal actions in state courts is the implementation of limitations by state legislatures on recovery against a state or its political subdivisions. Commonly referred to as governmental tort claims acts or sovereign immunity acts, these measures may limit the amount an individual claimant may recover or the total amount recoverable in a single incident where there are multiple claimants. For example, consider the 2018 mass shooting at Marjory Stoneman Douglas High School. In the tragedy, 17 victims were killed, 17 more were injured by gunfire, and numerous others experienced varying levels of trauma. However, state statute limits the recovery for each individual to $200,000 and the total recovery for a single incident to $300,000.[45] Therefore, when the Florida

---

43. Aaris v. Las Virgenes Unified Sch. Dist., 75 Cal. Rptr. 2d 801 (Ct. App. 1998).

44. Chareas v. Township High Sch. Dist., 553 N.E.2d 23 (Ill. App. Ct. 1990).

45. Fla. Stat. § 768.28 (5) (2019).

Supreme Court ruled that the mass shooting was a single event (rather than a series of incidents), the greatest cumulative monetary amount recoverable by all claimants against the school district (should they be successful) was limited to $300,000.[46] Many legal strategists prefer to bring suit in federal court, or both state *and* federal court, to ensure that their clients can recover the greatest financial verdict.

The Paul D. Coverdell Teacher Protection Act

A provision of No Child Left Behind, the Paul D. Coverdell Teacher Protection Act of 2001[47] protects teachers from liability as long as "the harm was not caused by willful or criminal misconduct, gross negligence, reckless misconduct, or a conscious, flagrant indifference to the rights or safety of the individual harmed by the teacher."[48] The underlying premise of the Act at passage was that it would allow teachers "the tools they need to undertake reasonable actions to maintain order, discipline, and an appropriate educational environment."[49]

On the other hand, teachers are not covered if their actions constitute gross negligence. *Black's Law Dictionary* defines gross negligence as: "A lack of even slight diligence or care."[50] Synonyms include "reckless negligence, wanton negligence, willful negligence."[51] It is important to note, however, that precise definitions of this term are articulated by individual states in their tort liability statutes. Some legal commentators have criticized the Act, believing that this law combined with state tort statutes serves to protect school personnel when they should be held more accountable.[52]

Civil Rights Torts and Qualified Immunity

Section 1983 of Title 42 in the U.S. Code (aka the Civil Rights Act) provides qualified immunity, which "protects government officials performing discretionary functions from civil trials . . . and from liability if their conduct violates no 'clearly

---

46. Guttenberg v. Sch. Bd., 303 So. 3d 518 (Fla. 2020).

47. Initially a part of the No Child Left Behind Act of 2001, P.L. 107–110, 20 U.S.C. § 6319 (2002), this statute was moved to § 7946. Limitation on liability for teachers, 20 U.S.C.S. § 7946 (Current through Public Law 116–193, approved October 30, 2020.).

48. *Id.* at § 7946 (a)(4).

49. No Child Left Behind Act of 2001, P.L. 107–110, 20 U.S.C. § 2362 (2002).

50. *Negligence, gross negligence*, Black's Law Dictionary (11th ed. 2019).

51. *Id.*

52. *See, e.g.*, Joshua Flynt, *Saved by the Bell: An Overview of Liability Rules for Professional Employees of Texas School Districts*, 57 Baylor L. Rev. 833 (Fall 2005) (noting that in Texas, damages for gross negligence are capped at $100,000); Brian J. Gorman, Catherine J. Wynne, Christopher J. Morse & James T. Todd, *Psychology and Law in the Classroom: How the Use of Clinical Fads in the Classroom May Awaken the Educational Malpractice Claim*, 2011 BYU Educ. & L.J. 29, 31 (2011) (contending that federal law (Coverdell) does not open a wide berth for educational malpractice suits).

established statutory or constitutional rights of which a reasonable person would have known.'"[53] For decades, students or teachers seeking to hold schools accountable in cases where there is an allegation of violations of constitutional rights have used § 1983 of the Civil Rights Act of 1871 to supplement their claims. Originally intended to suppress Ku Klux Klan violence and mandate the Fourteenth Amendment, § 1983 offers a remedy to plaintiffs for the violation of both civil and constitutional rights by state actors. Although § 1983 does not create any rights, this law allows plaintiffs to seek monetary damages in cases where constitutional rights have been violated. Section 1983 states:

> Every person who, under color of any statute, ordinance, regulation, custom or usage of any State or Territory or the District of Columbia, subjects or causes to be subjected, any citizen of the United States or other person within the jurisdiction thereof to the deprivation of any rights, privileges, or immunities secured by the Constitution and laws, shall be liable to the party injured in any action at law, suit in equity, or other proper proceeding for redress.[54]

Section 1983 offers complex case law that spans over a century. Largely disregarded for its first 70 years, the 1939 case of *Hague v. CIO*[55] offered the first modern opinion for § 1983 claims. It was not until *Monroe v. Pape*[56] in 1961 and *Monell v. Department of Social Services*[57] in 1978 that the real impact of § 1983 began to be felt. In *Monroe*,[58] a husband and wife filed claims against Chicago police for breaking into their home, searching it, and detaining the husband—all without a warrant. Here, the U.S. Supreme Court reversed two lower court findings by maintaining that the plaintiffs had a cause of action against the police and were thus permitted to file claims under 42 U.S.C. § 1983. The plaintiffs did not have a cause of action against the City of Chicago because municipalities are not persons under the law and therefore cannot be held liable. In *Monell*,[59] a case dealing with the New York City Department of Social Services, which required pregnant employees to take leaves of absences earlier than medically required, the U.S. Supreme Court reversed two lower court findings and overruled *Monroe* by maintaining, among other things, that local governments, municipal corporations, and school boards were "persons" under the law. Thus, such entities were not wholly immune from liability under § 1983.

To set forth a § 1983 claim, a plaintiff must identify the person or entity to be sued and prove that they were operating under the "color of the law" when the violation

53. Civil Rights Act of 1871, 42 U.S.C. § 1983.
54. *Id.*
55. 307 U.S. 496 (1939).
56. 365 U.S. 167 (1961).
57. 436 U.S. 658 (1978).
58. 365 U.S. 167 (1961).
59. 436 U.S. 658 (1978).

occurred. Furthermore, the plaintiff must show that the person or entity being sued directly caused the violation that resulted in the deprivation of rights. Once this criterion is met, the use of § 1983 creates a civil action, which offers several distinct advantages to the plaintiff. Specifically, § 1983 offers recovery of attorney fees, a wider range of rights that may be litigated, an increased number of defendants, generous federal law for assessing damages, and circumvention of state-law immunity.[60]

While there has been a history of ambiguity surrounding the application of § 1983 to individuals, several points have been made clear by the courts. Since § 1983 is meant to apply to any person who acts under the "color of state law," it cannot be used to seek monetary damages from private actors.[61] Therefore, in education-related contexts, § 1983 would apply to employees (e.g., teachers, principals) completing job-related activities who have directly caused a deprivation of rights. Section 1983 claims have also been brought against supervisors of employees who have committed a violation.

Therefore, if a teacher violates a student's civil rights, then there is a possibility that both the teacher and the supervisor (principal) may be held liable. In addition to applying to employees of the school, the Supreme Court has ruled that school board members and the school district in its entirety may also be sued under § 1983.[62] However, in such cases, the courts have determined that there must be some evidence that the supervisor also committed the wrong. More specifically, some circuits require the supervisor's deliberate indifference to the wrongdoing; others require that the supervisor demonstrate gross negligence or direct encouragement of the denial of rights.[63] Consider *Oliver v. McClung.*[64] Here, all students in a physical education class in Indiana were strip searched after two students reported a missing $4.50. The search was deemed illegal, but the court ruled that the school board and superintendent were not liable under § 1983 because there was no custom or practice of such searches in the school. On the other hand, the principal, food-service worker, and teacher who conducted the searches were liable because such searches were a clear constitutional violation.

Section 1983 claims cannot stand alone. They must be accompanied by a claim that one's civil rights have been violated under either the U.S. Constitution (e.g., the Fourth Amendment) or federal code (e.g., Title IX). Section 1983 claims must be set forth at the same time as the initial claim. In addition, the plaintiff cannot succeed at a § 1983 claim unless he or she first succeeds in the original claim. Finally, the standard for winning a § 1983 case is much higher than for the original claim.

60. DeShaney v. Winnebago Cnty. Dept. of Soc. Servs., 489 U.S. 189 (1989).

61. Robert L. Phillips, *Peer Abuse in Public Schools: Should Schools Be Liable for Student to Student Injuries Under Section 1983?*, BYU L. Rev. 237 (1995).

62. Wood v. Strickland, 420 U.S. 308 (1975); Monell v. Dept. of Soc. Servs., 436 U.S. 658 (1978).

63. Gail P. Sorenson, *School District Liability for Federal Civil Rights Violations Under § 1983*, 76 Educ. Law Rep. 313 (1992).

64. Oliver *ex rel* Hines v. McClung, 919 F. Supp. 1206 (N.D. Ind. 1995).

Therefore, a plaintiff may well be successful in the civil rights claim but may still not meet the standard for the §1983 claim. For qualified immunity to apply, the court must believe officials have acted without malice and that they could not have reasonably known that the act in question would have violated the rights of the plaintiff.[65]

As mentioned previously, qualified-immunity claims may be combined with a variety of federal civil-rights claims. For the most part, plaintiffs have not been successful in these claims, particularly as they relate to the U.S. Constitution. This is due partly to the fact that students' rights are so limited in schools. Also, courts are hesitant to interfere with the everyday workings of school districts or to question the judgment of school officials. Thus, even when students do succeed in their constitutional claims, the actions on the part of school officials are often not so egregious as to merit financial remuneration. Section 1983 claims combined with violations of the Fourth Amendment's prohibition on illegal searches and seizures and allegations of sexual harassment under Title IX are among the most likely to gain success in the school setting.

Corporal Punishment

The use of corporal punishment in the schools began with the first day of school in America. Likewise, litigation for schools using corporal punishment goes back as far as 1853, when parents sued an Indiana teacher. It seems their son spelled a word incorrectly and then refused to try to correct his mistake. The teacher hit the student in the head with his fist, kicked him in the face, and wore out two whips on him.[66]

What is corporal punishment? *Black's Law Dictionary* defines it simply as "physical punishment; punishment that is inflicted on the body (including imprisonment)."[67] Therefore, it seems to rule out the mere "touching" of a student. The problem is that the teacher can never know the extent of the student's personal condition. For example, patting the student on the back may have an entirely innocent and unaffecting result. However, if the student suffers from hemophilia or a related physical problem, a pat on the head could result in pain and punishment for the student. The cases show that corporal punishment may involve any number of physically related events between student and teacher.

Corporal punishment, if severe enough, could evolve into intentional torts of assault, battery, aggravated assault, and/or other offenses enunciated in the individual state's tort law. Some plaintiffs have linked corporal punishment with deprivation of liberty under the Fourteenth Amendment (substantive due process) and thus were able to attach a §1983 claim seeking monetary damages for deprivation of

65. *Id.*

66. 36 Educ. Law Rep. 267 (citing Gardner v. State, 4 Ind. 632 (1853)).

67. *Punishment, corporal Punishment*, Black's Law Dictionary (11th ed. 2019).

a Constitutional right. Less frequently, but still important to mention, some plaintiffs have claimed that corporal punishment constitutes an illegal seizure under the Fourth Amendment and have attached a § 1983 claim.

In most instances, corporal punishment cases are brought against the school as a tort action. In other words, parents use civil law to claim negligence, allowing them to recover damages for injury to the child. In the mid-1970s, however, in *Baker v. Owen*,[68] parents brought claims under the Eighth Amendment of the U.S. Constitution for cruel and unusual punishment and under the Fourteenth Amendment for procedural due process violations when their child was paddled despite their objections. A North Carolina district court ruled that the paddling did not constitute cruel and unusual punishment and that the state had a right to discipline students in schools to maintain order.[69] Two years later, Florida parents argued that corporal punishment, as to their child's paddling, was unconstitutional as a violation of the Eighth Amendment and due process rights under the Fourteenth Amendment. Their arguments became part of the first U.S. Supreme Court opinion to determine whether the Eighth Amendment applies to corporal punishment of children in public schools—*Ingraham v. Wright*.[70] **[*See* Case No. 2-1.]**

The facts grew out of a situation where a junior high school student was given 20 licks with a paddle while being held over a table in the principal's office. The paddling was so severe that he suffered a hematoma requiring medical attention. In their lawsuit, the parents argued that corporal punishment is such a deprivation that students must be given due process before inflicting this type of discipline. In addition, it was argued that the use of corporal punishment is cruel and unusual punishment, which is forbidden by the Eighth Amendment.

In ruling for the school district, the Court noted that the Eighth Amendment was intended to protect criminals. It has no place in the public schools. The justices also rejected the due process argument. While the Court recognized that students may have a liberty interest (good name, honor, and reputation) in corporal punishment, it is not the same as a suspension. Suspensions deprive students of their property rights and therefore require procedural due process. However, with corporal punishment, the student remains in school. In addition, the purpose of corporal punishment would be diluted if elaborate procedures had to be followed prior to its use. The *Ingraham* Court did not leave parents and students without hope. It informed the public that state laws could always provide protection where the U.S. Constitution does not. Also, the common law of battery could be used by parents whenever corporal punishment became excessive.

68. 395 F. Supp. 294 (M.D.N.C. 1975), *aff'd*, 423 U.S. 907 (1975).

69. *Id.*

70. 430 U.S. 651 (1977).

State Laws and Local Policies

As of November 2020, 31 states and the District of Columbia had banned corporal punishment either by state statute or state board-of-education regulation.[71] However, when the legislature or the state board of education is silent on the use of corporal punishment, local boards of education may decide to ban this practice or allow it. Many large cities eliminated the use of corporal punishment decades ago, primarily due to increased insurance premiums. A school system allowing corporal punishment will face more legal liability than one that does not—hence higher insurance costs.

Banning corporal punishment or allowing it is not the only choice. Statutes, state board regulations, or even local board policies may allow corporal punishment, but only under certain conditions, which might include that (1) students are informed in advance which misbehavior could lead to corporal punishment; (2) students are given options in lieu of being corporally punished (e.g., two licks or write an essay); (3) a witness is present; (4) written information about the incident leading to the corporal punishment is provided to parents upon request; (5) only a paddle may be used to administer the corporal punishment to an area of the body restricted to the buttocks; and (6) school officials consider the age, sex, and condition of the student in deciding the extent of the corporal punishment.

Constitutional Claims

While students may not have an Eighth Amendment or procedural due process claim under the Fourteenth Amendment, the *Ingraham* ruling did not foreclose the possibility of a Fourteenth Amendment *substantive due process* claim, which can also be combined with §1983. As we discuss these claims based on a variety of fact patterns, it is important to know that so much has been written on this area of the law, and with more cases emerging, we could not possibly provide a comprehensive view of this topic in one chapter. As with other aspects of the law, it is critical that school officials check with their school attorneys or professional associations to locate any new rulings in their state or federal jurisdiction. With these caveats in mind, the remainder this discussion will provide a broad overview as to the status of the law on this topic.

Substantive due process violations related to corporal punishment would be implicated whenever "the force applied caused injury so severe, was so disproportionate to the need presented, and was so inspired by malice or sadism rather than a merely careless or unwise excess of zeal that it amounted to a brutal and inhumane

71. *Country Report for the USA: Summary of Necessary Legal Reform to Achieve Full Prohibition*, Global Partnership to End Violence Against Children, http://endcorporalpunishment.org/reports-on-every-state-and-territory/usa/ (visited Nov. 19, 2020).

abuse of official power literally shocking to the conscience."[72] Scott Bloom, a legal scholar, has asserted that "[t]eachers and school administrators have consistently gone beyond the pale of authority and administered corporal punishment in a manner that shocks the conscience."[73] The courts, however, have not generally agreed with Professor Bloom.

When is the injury to the child sufficiently "shocking" to amount to a substantive due process violation? Examples of punishment found to be *inadequate* to "shock the conscience" include piercing a student's arm with a pin,[74] restraining a disruptive student until his eyes swelled and his lips turned blue,[75] grabbing a student's neck and squeezing it,[76] slapping a seventh-grade boy with an open hand at full force causing physical pain and emotional pain resulting in the need for psychotherapy,[77] pushing a student backwards resulting in a condition of chronic back pain,[78] and paddling a student five times on the buttocks causing swelling and bruising.[79]

Moreover, the Fifth Circuit Court of Appeals has maintained that students do not have a substantive due process right when it comes to corporal punishment if there are state remedies, civil or criminal. Courts in other circuits have been more forthright in asserting that students have substantive due process rights in this regard but have set the bar very high when it comes to determining exactly what shocks the conscience.

Starting with the Fifth Circuit, the decisions in *Cunningham v. Beavers*,[80] *Fee v. Herndon*,[81] and *Moore v. Willis Independent School District*[82] all concluded that students have no right to §1983 claims. *Cunningham* involved female kindergarten students who were bruised from being paddled. *Herndon* centered on a student classified as emotionally disturbed who, after a particularly harsh beating by the

72. Brooks v. Sch. Bd. of Richmond, 569 F. Supp. 1534 (E.D. Va. 1983); Brown v. Johnson, 710 F. Supp. 183 (E.D. Ky. 1989).

73. Scott Bloom, *Spare the Rod, Spoil the Child? A Legal Framework for Recent Corporal Punishment Proposals,* 25 Golden Gate U. L. Rev. 361, 384 (1995). *See also* Courtney Mitchell, *Corporal Punishment in the Public Schools: An Analysis of Federal Constitutional Claims*, 73 Law & Contemp. Probs. 321 (Spring 2010) (documenting corporal punishment substantive due process claims and offering support for Fourth Amendment claims); Nicole Mortorano, *Protecting Children's Rights Inside of the Schoolhouse Gates: Ending Corporal Punishment in Schools*, 102 Geo. L.J. 481 (Jan. 2014) (advocating both constitutional and legislative approaches to eliminate corporal punishment); and Lewis M. Wasserman, *Corporal Punishment in K-12 Public School Settings: Reconsideration of Its Constitutional Dimensions Thirty Years After* Ingraham v. Wright, 26 Touro L. Rev. 1029 (2011) (providing in-depth analysis of the history of corporal punishment in the courts).

74. Brooks v. Sch. Bd. of Richmond, 569 F. Supp. 1534 (E.D. Va. 1983).

75. T.W. v. Sch. Bd. of Seminole Cnty., Fla., 610 F.3d 588 (11th Cir. 2010).

76. Peterson v. Baker, 504 F.3d 1331 (11th Cir, 2007).

77. Smith *ex rel* Smith v. Half Hollow Hills Central Sch. Dist., 298 F.3d 168 (2d Cir. 2002).

78. Gottlieb ex rel Calabria v. Laurel Highlands Sch. Dist., 272 F.3d 168 (3d Cir. 2001).

79. Saylor v. Bd. of Educ. of Harlan County, Kentucky, 118 F.3d 507 (6th Cir. 1997).

80. 858 F.2d 269 (5th Cir. 1988), *cert. denied,* 489 U.S. 1067 (1989).

81. 900 F.2d 804 (5th Cir. 1990).

82. 233 F.3d 871 (5th Cir. 2000).

school principal, was forced to remain in psychiatric rehabilitation for months. In *Moore*,[83] the Fifth Circuit did not find a substantive due process violation when a track coach made a student do 100 squat thrusts in a row. A male middle school student was talking during roll call on the day of try out for the boys' track team. As punishment, the coach made the boy do squat thrusts. After the incident, the coach told the boy's mother, "With junior high kids, you have to inflict pain, or they don't remember."[84]

The student was hospitalized and missed three weeks of school. He continued to experience fatigue and was unable to participate in school sports or physical education class. The court ruled that the parents had not met their burden for a substantive due process violation. It cited to its previous ruling in *Fee v. Herndon* when it stated, "Corporal punishment in public schools is a deprivation of substantive due process when it is arbitrary, capricious, or wholly unrelated to the legitimate state goal of maintaining an atmosphere conducive to learning."[85] The court concluded that educators in states which proscribe student mistreatment and provide a remedy do not by definition act arbitrarily, a necessary predicate for substantive due process relief. Parents in *Moore* had available relief under the Texas state statutes. Section 22.051 (a) of the Texas Education Code states, "A professional employee of a school district is not liable . . . except in circumstances in which a professional employee uses excessive force in the discipline of students or negligence resulting in bodily injury to students."

In *Hall v. Tawney*,[86] a Fourth Circuit Court of Appeals maintained that there could be a separate federal cause of action to plaintiffs under §1983. In this case, a West Virginia student had been beaten so severely with a thick rubber paddle that he required emergency treatment and was hospitalized for 10 days. In ruling for the student, the *Hall* court crafted a three-part test that considers (1) the severity of the injury caused by the punishment, (2) the proportionality of the force applied to the need presented, and (3) whether the force was inspired by malice or sadism so that it amounted to an abuse of power so brutal and inhumane as to be shocking to the conscience.

Using the *Hall* test but rejecting the element of malice, a Tenth Circuit court[87] found in favor of a nine-year-old student whose teacher held her upside down and beat her on the front of her legs with a split paddle which grabbed her, causing her to bleed. *Webb v. McCullough*,[88] a Sixth Circuit case, involved a student who was knocked to the ground, grabbed from the floor, thrown against the wall,

83. *Id.*
84. *Id.* at 873.
85. *Id.* at 875 (5th Cir. 1990) (citing 900 F.2d 804), *cert. denied,* 498 U.S. 908 (1990).
86. 621 F.2d 607 (4th Cir. 1980).
87. Garcia v. Miera, 817 F.2d 650 (10th Cir. 1987).
88. 828 F.2d 1151, 1158 (6th Cir. 1987).

and slapped by her principal on a field trip.[89] Recognizing that the actions were off school property and did not appear to fall within the disciplinary context of schooling, the court remanded this case for further proceedings, acknowledging that the principal's actions could be characterized as brutal, inhumane, and shocking to the conscience.[90] Accordingly, in *Metzger v. Osbeck*,[91] a Third Circuit court found that treatment of a student was arbitrary, capricious, and egregious enough to warrant a substantive due process claim when a swimming coach put a student in a chokehold, which caused the student to lose consciousness. The student fell on the school's swimming pool deck, breaking his nose and teeth.[92]

The Eleventh Circuit found a substantive due process violation in *Neal v. Fulton County Board of Education*,[93] a case involving a high school member of the varsity football team who had a fight after practice with one of his teammates. While the fight ensued, the football coach and the principal were in the immediate area. Neither of them stopped the fight, but the coach came over and began dumping the contents of the plaintiff's bag on the ground, shouting repeatedly "what did you hit him with; if you hit him with it, I am going to hit you with it." The facts showed that the plaintiff had a weight lock from the weight room in his duffle bag. The coach, in the presence of the principal, proceeded to pick up the weight lock and struck the student in the left eye. As a result of the blow, the student's eye was knocked completely out of its socket leaving it destroyed and dismembered, causing permanent blindness in that eye. The court characterized Coach Ector as "using an obviously excessive amount of force that presented a reasonably foreseeable risk of serious bodily injury."[94] The court decided that the plaintiff clearly had a claim under the Fourteenth Amendment and remanded the case for further proceedings.[95]

In *Johnson v. Newburgh Enlarged School District*,[96] a Second Circuit case, parents of an eighth-grade student succeeded in their claims when their son was battered by his gym teacher during class. The facts showed that teacher had asked for the students to hand in the balls after a game of dodge ball. The student in question threw one of the balls as requested. The ball landed near, but did not hit, the teacher. In response, the teacher threw two balls back at the student and yelled, "You think that's funny." The teacher then grabbed the student by the throat and shouted, "I'll kick the shit out of you!" He lifted him off the ground by his neck and dragged him across the gym floor to the bleachers. The teacher then choked the student and slammed the back of the student's head against the bleachers four times. The teacher

89. *Id.* at 1154.
90. *Id.* at 1159.
91. 841 F.2d 518, 520 (3d Cir. 1988).
92. *Id.*
93. 229 F.3d 1069 (11th Cir. 2000).
94. *Id.* at 1076.
95. *Id.* at 1076–77.
96. 239 F.3d 246 (2d Cir. 2001).

also rammed the student's forehead into a metal fuse box located on the gym wall and punched him in the face.

In *Wise v. Pea Ridge School District*,[97] an Eighth Circuit court adopted a modified version of the *Hall* test. In this case, one girl received an in-school suspension and the other was spanked twice in physical education class with a paddle. Deciding for the school district, the court considered (a) the need for the use of corporal punishment, (b) the relationship between the need and the amount of punishment, (c) the extent of injury, and (d) whether the punishment was administered in good faith to maintain discipline or maliciously to cause harm. Two other Eighth Circuit opinions followed *Wise*. In *London v. DeWitt*,[98] a 1999 decision, the court considered the four *Wise* factors and ruled for the school district. The court maintained that that the school officials' actions, which involved grabbing the student and dragging him, were not so egregious as to shock the conscience.[99] In 2002, this same circuit determined that a principal's treatment of a sixth grader, which caused the child to have a sprained neck, also did not constitute excessive force so as to shock the conscience.[100] In this case, *Golden v. Anders*,[101] the principal grabbed the student by the neck and "threw" him on a bench after the student had an altercation with a teacher for kicking a vending machine.[102]

Garcia v. Miera,[103] decided by the Tenth Circuit Court of Appeals, recognized a violation of a nine-year-old female student's substantive due process rights when she was hung upside down by a teacher while the principal struck so hard that it split the paddle. The student suffered severe bruises and cuts and was left permanently physically scarred. In a later decision, *Harris v. Robinson*,[104] this same court drew a comparison with *Miera*. In *Harris*, a mother sued on behalf of her son against his teacher and the school district, claiming that the teacher violated the boy's substantive due process rights by making him clean out a toilet with his bare hands. The court held that the boy's injuries were not as severe as those in *Miera*, and the teacher's actions were not so brutal to shock the conscience. The court conceded that the teacher exercised poor judgment, but her actions were not "inspired by malice or sadism,"[105] and were not enough to violate the boy's civil rights.

The Eleventh Circuit Court of Appeals denied immunity to an Alabama school principal who hit a 13-year-old student in the head, ribs, and back with a metal cane. In this case, *Kirkland v. Greene County Board of Education*,[106] the administrator

---

97. 855 F. 2d 560 (8th Cir. 1988).
98. 194 F.3d 873 (8th Cir. 1999).
99. *Id.* at 877.
100. 324 F.3d 650, 655 (8th Cir. 2003).
101. *Id.* at 652.
102. *Id.*
103. 817 F.2d 650 (10th Cir. 1987), *cert. denied*, 485 U.S. 959 (1988).
104. 273 F.3d 927 (10th Cir. 2001).
105. *Id.* at 931.
106. 347 F.3d 903 (11th Cir. 2003).

based his actions on the fact that the student had previously brought a weapon to school. The court maintained that the student's previous weapons possession did not justify this type of beating.

In another line of cases, federal appeals courts, notably those in the Seventh and Ninth Circuits, have begun to interpret excessive force under the Fourth Amendment as opposed to a violation of substantive due process under the Fourteenth Amendment. This rationale comes from the U.S. Supreme Court's 1989 decision in *Graham v. Connor*.[107] The facts in *Graham* were not school-related, and this decision has not been applied universally to corporal punishment cases involving excessive force. When it is applied, however, the legal test is one of "objective reasonableness under the circumstances"[108] as opposed to the substantive due process standard of force applied "maliciously and sadistically to cause harm."[109] For more detailed information on the *Graham* test and how it applies to student seizures under the Fourth Amendment, see our discussion of school resource officers later in this chapter.

Wallace v. Batavia School District,[110] a Seventh Circuit decision, was the first to apply the Fourth Amendment excessive-force analysis to corporal punishment in schools.[111] This case involved two teenage girls who were shouting obscenities. A fight was about to break out when the teacher separated the girls and ordered one out of the classroom — briefly seizing her arm in the process. Entering a summary judgment for the school district, the court declared, "This emphatically is not a matter rising to the level of constitutional violation. This type of § 1983 litigation denigrates the Constitution and is a disservice to school systems, the federal courts, and the public they serve."[112]

Several years later, the Ninth Circuit ruled in favor of the plaintiffs in two separate cases that involved corporal punishment as excessive force. In *Doe v. Hawaii*,[113] a second-grade student continued to misbehave even after the vice principal threatened to tape him to a tree if he did not stop. The principal carried through with his threat until a fifth-grade student questioned his actions. The court ruled that this punishment constituted a seizure as well as excessive force under the Fourth Amendment. The court refused to grant the principal immunity. *Preschooler II v. Clark County Board of Trustees*,[114] another Ninth Circuit case, involved a special

107. 490 U.S. 386 (1989).

108. *Id.* at 399.

109. *Id.* at 397.

110. 68 F.3d 1010 (7th Cir. 1995).

111. *See also* P.B. v. Koch, 96 F.3d 1298 (9th Cir. 1996) (upholding substantive due process claims on an excessive force case on students in a high school).

112. 68 F.3d at 1016.

113. Doe *ex rel* Doe v. State of Hawaii Dept. of Educ., 334 F.3d 906 (9th Cir. 2003).

114. 479 F.3d 1175 (9th Cir. 2007); Roe v. Nevada, 621 F. Supp. 2d 1039 (D. Nev. 2007) (further court actions regarding preschooler's expert witnesses). *See also* Payne v. Peninsula Sch. Dist. 653 F.3d 863 (9th Cir. 2011), *cert denied*, 132 S. Ct. 1540 (2012).

education teacher who slammed an autistic four-year-old into a chair after having forced him to repeatedly slap himself. This child was diagnosed with tuberous sclerosis, a condition that causes tumors in the eyes and brain. The court concluded that:

> In light of the clear constitutional prohibition of excessive physical abuse of schoolchildren, and the heightened protections for disabled pupils, no reasonable special education teacher would believe that it is lawful to force a seriously disabled four-year old child to beat himself or to violently throw or slam him.[115]

In sum, whether and what constitutional claims apply to corporal punishment are dependent on the law in the federal circuit where your school is located. The Fifth Circuit stands alone as basically rejecting constitutional claims in favor of claims based on civil and/or criminal state law.[116] The First, Second, Third, Fourth, Sixth, Eighth, Tenth, and Eleventh Circuits have supported substantive due process claims with varying outcomes. The *Hall* and *Wise* courts have provided relatively clear standards as to when substantive due process is violated. The threshold of "shocking the conscience," however, is high and has made it difficult for plaintiffs to succeed even if the court recognizes their claims. It has also been an exceedingly controversial standard questioned by numerous educational and legal commentators.[117]

Corporal Punishment versus Battery

The fact that a state statute, regulation, or local policy permits corporal punishment is not a viable defense in the commission of a battery. As the Court pointed out in *Ingraham*, parents have the recourse of invoking the common law of battery as a

115. 479 F.3d at 1182.

116. *See* Kristina Rico, Note, *Excessive Exercise as Corporal Punishment in* Moore v. Willis Independent School District *—Has the Fifth Circuit Totally Isolated Itself in Its Position?* 9 VILL. SPORTS & ENT. L. FORUM 351, 353 (2002) (demonstrating that Fifth Circuit stands alone in its rejection of substantive due process in corporal punishment cases).

117. *See, e.g.*, Irwin A. Hyman, Jacqueline A. Stefkovich, & Shannon Taich, *Paddling and Pro-Paddling Polemics: Refuting Nineteenth Century Pedagogy*, 31 J.L. & EDUC. 74, 78 (2002) (pointing out that over half the states and numerous school districts in other states prohibit corporal punishment); Jerry R. Parkinson, *Federal Court Treatment of Corporal Punishment in Public Schools: Jurisprudence that Is Literally Shocking to the Conscience*, 39 S.D. L. REV. 276, 302 (urging the Supreme Court to take a stand on the corporal punishment issue); Lekha Menon, *Spare the Rod, Save a Child: Why the Supreme Court Should Revisit* Ingraham v. Wright *and Protect the Substantive Due Process Rights of Students Subjected to Corporal Punishment*, 39 CARDOZO L. REV. 313 (2017), (suggesting that the U.S. Supreme Court reconsider the use of corporal punishment in substantive due process claims); Steven J. Dick, Kerri D. Prejean, & Richard Fossey, *School-Based Corporal Punishment of Students with Disabilities: A Law and Policy Analysis*, 358 EDUC. LAW REP. 733 (2018) (stating that in some states, students with disabilities receive corporal punishment at a much higher level than other students).

protection against the use of excessive force by school officials. Battery can violate both criminal and civil law.

There can be a fine line between using the authorized law to administer corporal punishment and battery. In fact, what might constitute acceptable behavior under a corporal punishment law could otherwise violate the law of battery. Battery has been defined as "an unlawful touching, beating, wounding, laying hold, however trifling, of another's person or clothes without his consent."[118] The question is, when does a school official commit a battery? The simple answer is whenever sufficient evidence of the event can be recorded. Anytime the corporal punishment results in some "marks" that can be witnessed, photographed, or otherwise recorded, the potential is there for proving battery. Therefore, it is up to those administering the punishment to know if they have gone too far and committed battery. The problem for the teacher is to know the condition of the child and what specific instruments of pain are going to leave marks. How can a teacher know this? The result is a great legal gamble each time a teacher uses corporal punishment.

The Ninth Circuit Court's decision in *P.B. v. Koch*[119] provides a good example of how corporal punishment can lead to battery. The court used the *Hall* test to rule in favor of three Idaho high school students who were subjected to excessive force. The court maintained that no force had been necessary in these instances and that school officials had been put on notice that excessive force was illegal. The punishment in one instance was so severe that the principal pleaded guilty to criminal assault and battery charges. That incident involved the principal walking by a student and hearing the words "Heil Hitler." He assumed they were directed at him. Without giving the student a chance to explain, the principal hit the student with his back hand and then front hand across the mouth. He grabbed the student's neck and squeezed, causing bruises which turned purple and lasted for a couple of days. The student went to the emergency room and was given Advil and an ice pack. He was hoarse for several days. The student reported the incident to the police. The principal was charged and convicted of criminal battery. The case before the Ninth Circuit was for the civil side of the incident in which the student was also successful.

Corporal Punishment versus Child Abuse

A permissive corporal punishment law can fool the educator into committing a battery and can also lead to a charge of child abuse. For example, the Florida state law on child abuse includes "excessive corporal punishment" in the definition of child abuse. In addition, Florida has a statute that establishes a registry of convicted child abusers. Initially, educators in the state welcomed the registry and found it useful when hiring. However, the number of principals showing up on the registry for having used corporal punishment caused schools to rethink. In 1989, after hearings, the

118. Cochran's Law Lexicon (5th ed.).

119. 96 F.3d 1298 (9th Cir. 1996).

Florida Department of Health and Rehabilitative Services (HRS) placed the names of 71 educators on the list. The total number of people listed was 208.[120] As for the educators on the list, many used corporal punishment in accordance with state and local policies.

Two of the affected educators decided to challenge the application of the child abuse laws to the corporal punishment that was meted out in their cases. The educators were both administrators in Florida schools but in different locations. One was a dean of students who paddled a student in accordance with the state statute and local board policy. The paddling left bruises that lasted for about a week. The other incident involved a female school principal who paddled a student, also leaving bruises that lasted a week. When these cases came before HRS for a hearing, it was concluded that punishment inflicting bruises on a child that last six to seven days constitutes excessive force. On appeal, the Florida District Court of Appeals affirmed the decision of HRS. It agreed on the use of a strict "bruising rule" as constituting child abuse in corporal punishment cases.[121]

While this decision was technically not overruled, subsequent sister courts in Florida questioned length of time, stating that: "there is no rational connection between the length of time a bruise remains visible and the ultimate fact of excessive corporal punishment."[122] After these holdings, HRS formally amended its position to include bruising as only one of several factors to be considered in determining excessive corporal punishment. Others may include the nature and severity of the injury, location of the injury, whether the action resulted in additional injuries, the child's age, the manner of infliction, and the appropriateness of the discipline as related to the offense's seriousness.[123]

Clearly, this is an area that becomes complicated when the student in question has identified special needs. However, there may, in a court's view, be a line between abuse and a constitutional violation. The teacher in question in *Domingo v. Kowalski*[124] employed practices in the classroom ranging from gagging a student with a bandana to stop him from spitting, to strapping a student to a toilet to keep her from falling from the toilet, to forcing yet another to sit with her pants down on a training toilet in full view of her classmates to assist her with toilet-training. Their parents sued, alleging violations of substantive due process, but did not allege any serious physical or psychological injury.

---

120. Lisa Jennings, *Educators Balk as Paddlers Put on Child-Abuse List*, EDUC. WEEK (Oct. 11, 1989), https://www.edweek.org/education/educators-balk-as-paddlers-put-on-child-abuse-list/1989/10.

121. B.L. v. Dept. of Health and Rehab. Servs., 545 So. 2d 289 (Fla. Dist. Ct. App. 1989). Motion to strike judicial brief and appendix denied, 553 So. 2d 1164 (Fla. 1989).

122. B.R. & W.C. v. Dept. of Health and Rehab. Servs., 558 So. 2d 1027, 1029 (Fla. Dist. Ct. App. 1989); D. J. v. Dept. of Health and Rehab. Servs., 565 So. 2d 863 (Fla. Dist. Ct. App. 1990).

123. Department of HRS v. S. K. H, 9 Fla. Admin. L. Rep. 6509, 6511 (1987).

124. 810 F.3d 403 (6th Cir. 2016).

On appeal, the Sixth Circuit analyzed the case as if it were a corporal punishment case, inquiring "whether the force applied caused injury so severe, was so disproportionate to the need presented, and was so inspired by malice or sadism rather than a merely careless or unwise excess of zeal that it amounted to a brutal and inhumane abuse of official power literally shocking the conscience,"[125] while balancing the relationship of the allegedly unconstitutional conduct to any legitimate pedagogical purpose. Ultimately, the court affirmed the district court's determination that the actions, "while inappropriate and even 'abusive,' did not rise to the conscience-shocking level required of a substantive due process claim" because the teacher's supervisors had insufficient notice of her actions to be found deliberately indifferent and because the district's policies and practices were not constitutionally inadequate.[126]

Teachers' use of corporal punishment has led to termination in some cases. Whether court challenges have been brought on constitutional or damage claims, teachers lost only about 40 percent of the time.[127] However, it must be noted that teachers and other school employees can be terminated for failure to comply with a no-corporal-punishment ban. The termination could also be based on a teacher's misapplication of the conditions associated with the use of corporal punishment in situations where it is legal. Several courts have upheld terminations based upon insubordination for failure to comply with local board requirements in administering corporal punishment.[128]

Bullying and Constitutional Claims

As mentioned earlier, most liability claims related to bullying fall under state tort liability and anti-bullying statutes; however, constitutional claims are also available. Like corporal punishment, plaintiffs may file a § 1983 claim in conjunction with a Fourteenth Amendment substantive due process claim. For the most part, courts are inclined to side with the school district in these instances. As mentioned previously, the bar for § 1983/substantive due process claims is difficult to reach. For example, consider the Third Circuit Court of Appeals' decision in *Morrow v. Balaski*.[129]

Here, Brittany and Emily Morrow were subjected to bullying, a series of threats, and physical assaults by Shaquana Anderson, a student who was later charged by the police with simple assault, terroristic threats, and harassment. Among other things, Shaquana tried to push Brittany down a set of steps and allegedly called her "a 'cracker,' told her she was 'retarded,' and that she 'had better learn to fight

125. *Id.* at 411.

126. *Id.* at 406.

127. 36 Educ. L. Rep. 267, 270. *See* Daniels v. Gordon, 503 S.E.2d 72 (Ga. App. 1998).

128. Burton v. Kirby, 775 S.W.2d 834 (Tex. App. 1989).

129. 719 F.3d 160 (3d Cir. 2013).

back.'"[130] Despite the fact that the juvenile court put Anderson on probation for these actions and prohibited her from having contact with Brittany, Shaquana continued to threaten the girl, and Shaquana's friend assaulted Brittany on the school bus. Claiming that school officials failed to resolve this situation, the Morrows withdrew their daughters from the school, and sued for violation of substantive due process and money damages under § 1983.[131]

While the court conveyed sympathy for the Morrows, it ruled that school authorities did not have an affirmative duty to protect students against private actions. This reasoning was based on the Supreme Court's *DeShaney*[132] decision, where it found no affirmative obligation on the part of a social service agency that returned an abused child to his home only to have the child suffer brain damage as the result his father's subsequently beating him.

Strip Searching

As mentioned above, the Fourth Amendment to the U.S. Constitution guarantees freedom from unreasonable searches and seizures by government officials. (This topic is discussed in more detail in the chapters on teachers' rights and students' rights.) While § 1983 claims frequently accompany Fourth Amendment violations, courts have generally granted immunity to school personnel. A possible exception is strip searching, but even here the standard for denying immunity is high. For example, in the Eleventh Circuit, it took some ten years of litigation to finally establish that school authorities should have known that highly intrusive strip searches for small amounts of money clearly violated the students' constitutional rights.

This series of cases began with *Jenkins v. Talladega*,[133] where a teacher and guidance counselor at the Graham Elementary School in Talladega, Alabama, strip searched two eight-year-old second graders for a missing $7. While the Eleventh Circuit court did not speak to the legality of the search as such, it did hold that those persons conducting the search would not be liable under § 1983. The court maintained it was not necessarily so that school officials would have known such a search was illegal because there was no precedent in the state or circuit. Two years later in a Georgia case, *Thomas v. Roberts*,[134] this same circuit court denied a similar § 1983 claim when a class of elementary school students was strip searched for $26. In its opinion, the Eleventh Circuit pointed out that the incident had occurred before its decision in *Talladega* and, therefore, there was no precedent that school personnel

---

130. *Id.* at 164.

131. *Id.* at 164–65.

132. *Id.* at 166 (citing DeShaney v. Winnebago Cnty. Dep't of Social Servs., 489 U.S. 189, 197 (1989)).

133. 95 F.3d 1036 (11th Cir. 1996), *reh'g en banc*, 115 F.2d 821 (11th Cir.), *cert. denied*, 118 S. Ct. 412 (1997).

134. 323 F.3d 950 (11th Cir. 2003).

could have followed. All those persons involved in the search, including the teacher, a resource officer, and the vice principal who approved the search were not given fair warning that the search would violate students' rights. Thus, these persons were entitled to qualified immunity.

It was not until ten years after *Talladega* that a court in this circuit finally found a school district liable for money damages in a student strip search for a minor offense ($12). In a 2007 opinion, *H.Y. v. Russell County Board of Education*,[135] a federal district court in Alabama found the strip searching of 15 students for $12 to be excessively intrusive given the interest at stake. The school district was required to pay damages for violation of the students' rights (based on *Talladega* and *Thomas*); however, they were relieved of civil liability claims for battery, invasion of privacy, and outrage. Two years later, a district court in Georgia refused to grant summary judgment on immunity issues for an assistant principal and disciplinary secretary who conducted an illegal strip search.[136] Thus, for all intents and purposes, school officials in the Eleventh Circuit are clearly on notice that they will not be immune from money damages if they conduct illegal strip searches on students. As noted above, strip searching a student or groups of students for small amounts of money constitutes an illegal strip search.

This same line of reasoning also applies to educators in the Sixth Circuit, which handed down similar decisions on a like series of cases, starting with *Beard v. Whitmore Lake School District*.[137] The federal appeals court in *Beard* constructed a three-part test to determine the viability of a qualified immunity claim.[138] First, the court must decide "based on applicable law" whether a constitutional violation has occurred. Facts must be considered "in the light most favorable to the plaintiff." Second, the court must apply a reasonable person standard to determine whether a clearly established right had been violated. In other words, would a reasonable person have known? Third, the plaintiff must provide sufficient evidence to show "what the official allegedly did was objectively unreasonable in light of the clearly established constitutional rights."[139] Applying this test, the court determined that even though the strip search of some 25 students in a gym class for missing prom money was illegal, the law was not clearly established within the Sixth Circuit.[140] Thus school officials were immune from § 1983 claims.

Five years later, in *Knisley v. Pike County Joint Vocational School District*,[141] the Sixth Circuit cited *Beard* in denying immunity to officials who had illegally strip

135. 490 F. Supp. 2d 1174 (M.D. Ala. 2007).

136. Foster v. Raspberry, 652 F. Supp. 2d 1342 (M.D. Ga. 2009).

137. 402 F.3d 598 (6th Cir. 2005).

138. *Id. See also*, Sanchez v. Stockstill, No. SA-04-CA-110-XR, 2005 WL 552139 (W.D. Tex. Mar. 9, 2005) (describing a similar two-part test for qualified immunity provided by the Fifth Circuit).

139. 402 F.3d at 603 (citing Champion v. Outlook Nashville, Inc. 380 F.3d 893, 900-01 (6th Cir. 2004)).

140. *Id.* at 608.

141. 604 F.3d 977 (6th Cir. 2010).

searched some 15–16 students in a nursing class for missing money, gift cards, and a credit card. The school had appealed an earlier decision to the U.S. Supreme Court which remanded the case to the Sixth Circuit ordering that it be reevaluated based on *Safford v. Redding*, a U.S. Supreme Court decision addressing §1983 immunity in student strip-search cases. In this second *Knisley* opinion, the court directly, and emphatically, stated that qualified immunity would not apply to those who conduct illegal strip searches of students and officially put school officials on notice that they would not be immune from money damages under §1983. The court stated the following:

> The United States Supreme Court has asked us to reconsider this case in light of *Redding* [italics added throughout], in which the Court invalidated a strip search of a female student when looking for ibuprofen tablets.... Essentially, the *Redding* defendants were entitled to qualified immunity because neither the Supreme Court nor the Ninth Circuit had clearly established case law on point and there was no national consensus on this issue among the Circuits at the time of the *Redding* search.... However, this Circuit's law on student strip searches was clearly established as early as 2005, when we published our opinion in *Beard*. We read *Redding* to affirm our constitutional holding in *Beard*. Thus, because *Beard* remains good constitutional law and because that law was clearly established at the time of the strip search in this case, *Redding* does not require a result contrary to that reached in *Knisley I*. Our Circuit's clearly established case law on this issue put the school and its employees on notice that this search was unconstitutional, so defendants are not entitled to qualified immunity protection. [Footnotes and citations omitted].[142]

Safford v. Redding,[143] decided in 2009, is the U.S. Supreme Court's landmark decision on immunity and school strip searches. In this case, school personnel strip searched a 14-year-old female middle-school student for prescription-strength ibuprofen. While the Court found the search to be unconstitutional, the justices granted school authorities immunity under §1983. Upon reviewing several lower court opinions with differing outcomes and noting that there were no court decisions in the state of Arizona prohibiting such actions, the Court reasoned that the law on strip searching students in schools was not sufficiently clear to deny immunity.

Thus, the question of qualified immunity rests on whether there is established law. As mentioned above, the law is now clearly established in the Sixth and Eleventh Circuits. In addition, there are seven states with statutes prohibiting strip searching students in public schools. These states are California, Iowa, New Jersey, North Carolina, Oklahoma, Washington, and Wisconsin. Even though the *Safford* Court granted school officials immunity, some legal commentators believe that this

142. *Id.* at 982–84.

143. 557 U.S. 364 (2009).

decision puts school districts on notice so that in the future they may well be liable for money damages if they conduct an unreasonable strip search for minor offenses.[144] Others assert that the *Safford* Court, in granting immunity, lost an opportunity to set a precedent if schools did not take action to prohibit strip searching.[145] (See Chapter 4 on students' rights for more information about students' Fourth Amendment rights and when and how school officials may, or may not, search students.)

As is typical of court decisions, outcomes are fact dependent. In the years following *Redding*, the details of student strip search cases have varied widely. For example, a relatively new line of cases has arisen that involves school nurses inspecting the genital areas of young children for possible infection or injury. While several courts have declared that these inspections are searches under the Fourth Amendment, the question of liability is still unclear. For example, in the *Hearring*,[146] a federal district court found that School Nurse Sliwowski conducted an unreasonable search of a young child's genital area after suspecting a urinary tract infection, but the Sixth Circuit Court of Appeals reversed this opinion based on *Beard* and *Safford*. This court maintained that the law was not clear on this issue either in the State of Tennessee or in the Sixth Circuit.

In another case, *Herrera v. Santa Fe Public Schools*,[147] a federal district court in New Mexico recognized that suspicion-less pat-down searches of students attending an off-campus prom were unreasonable but that school authorities were immune under § 1983 because the law was not clearly established that pat downs of all students entering a prom were illegal. In this case, the search, conducted by a private security firm hired by the school district, involved employees touching a student's arms and stomach and cupping and shaking her breasts.

In *Littell v. Houston Independent School District*,[148] the Fifth Circuit went one step further than previous strip-search renderings by addressing the issue of whether the school district should have trained its personnel regarding the legality of certain searches. In this case, parents of female middle-school students who were subjected to strip searches at school brought a § 1983 claim against the school district, alleging that the strip searches were illegal and seeking an injunction requiring the school district to clarify its search policy and provide at least some Fourth Amendment training.

During a sixth-grade choir class, an assistant principal ordered a mass, suspicionless strip search of the underwear of 22 preteen girls. All agree the search violated the girls' constitutional rights under Texas and federal law. Even so, the district court

---

144. Joseph O. Oluwole, *Danger or Resort to Underwear, The* Safford United School District No. 1 v. Redding *Standard for Strip Searching Public School Students*, 41 St. Mary's L.J. 479 (2010).

145. Alexis Karteron, *Arrested Development: Rethinking Fourth Amendment Standards for Seizures and Use of Force in Schools*,18 Nev. L.J. 863 (2018).

146. Hearring v. Sliwowski, 712 F.3d 275 (6th Cir. 2013).

147. 41 F. Supp. 3d 1027 (D.N.M. 2014).

148. 894 F.3d 616 (5th Cir. 2018).

dismissed the girls' lawsuit against the school district for failure to state a claim. The Fifth Circuit reversed, holding that the school officials' strip search of students violated the students' Fourth Amendment rights and the parents sufficiently alleged that deliberate indifference caused the Fourth Amendment violation.

The issues of deliberate indifference and a need to train personnel are new to school strip-search decisions but have been required for years in sexual harassment cases. It is possible that requests for training may become more common regarding searches. Even if training is not enacted for preventative purposes, it would nonetheless be a good idea for school districts either to pass a policy allowing strip searches only in dire circumstances (i.e., when safety is at stake) or, better yet, prohibit all strip searches. Either way, training on searching students could be made available.

To summarize, school officials can be held personally liable *if* a student can prove that the official acted with malice in denying constitutional rights. Personal liability can also occur when a school official acts with ignorance or disregard for the law. Absent these conditions, a school official has immunity. For the most part, with some notable exceptions, courts are unwilling to support immunity in strip-searching cases if the search is clearly not reasonable. This especially applies to searches for small amounts of money. As illustrated by the decisions above, even though a school official may be protected from personal liability under certain circumstances, a student may still be successful in a suit against the school for civil damages under 42 U.S.C. § 1983.

School Resource Officers

Since the mid-1980s, the presence of school resource officers (SROs) and/or police in schools has increased exponentially. With these increases has come more litigation. Most of these cases include allegations of Fourth Amendment violations accompanied by claims for monetary damages under § 1983 and state statutes. We caution readers that involvement of police and SROs is a very broad topic that relies heavily on state and federal laws and, as with other aspects of the law that we have discussed, court decisions are very fact specific. Therefore, it is difficult to make conclusive recommendations. We can, however, provide a broad overview of the types of litigation that have emerged, especially in the past few years, and any trends that we see.

Legal scholars and commentators[149] have been consistent in identifying the rise in cases involving SROs, the tendency for school authorities to prevail despite some disturbing disciplinary choices, and a disconnect between best pedagogical

149. *See* Kevin P. Brady, *School Resource Officers and the Unsettled Legal Standard for Establishing Student Excessive Physical Force Claims*, 359 Educ. Law Rep. 689 (2018); Alexis Karteron, *Arrested Development: Rethinking Fourth Amendment Standards for Seizures and Use of Force in Schools*,18 Nev. L.J. 863 (2018); Kerrin C. Wolf, *Assessing Students' Civil Rights Claims Against*

practices and what is legally permissible.[150] Some of these concerns are based on the judiciary's long-standing view that courts should not micromanage schools and that even when school personnel violate students' constitutional rights, there must be a blatant disregard of these rights to be awarded money damages. Others mention the rise of school disturbance laws that criminalize student behavior formerly handled through suspensions and other disciplinary actions.[151] The fluidity of the SRO's role only complicates matters further. This official has been described as, among others, a counselor, a confident, an instructor, a police officer, a role model, and a disciplinarian.[152] Each of these functions requires training, experience, and sometimes conflicting legal/ethical expectations.[153] Besides illegal searches (often done at the behest of school personnel), a burgeoning area of Fourth Amendment litigation involves claims that SROs have violated students' rights through illegal seizures and/or excessive force. The following cases illustrate a wide array of situations brought before federal circuit courts of appeal.

A Sixth Circuit case, *Machan v. Olney*,[154] involved a police officer (Olney) assigned to the middle school who took a student to the hospital for a blood draw and mental evaluation. The student, T.R., a seventh grader, told Principal Gill Williams that she had been thinking about suicide and she had been seeing guns at home and knives to hurt herself. Williams told Olney, who called T.R.'s father, Machan, and told him that T.R. was suicidal and he planned to take her to the hospital. Olney took T.R. to the hospital. The attending physician drew T.R.'s blood and talked to T.R. about suicidal thoughts. Then T.R.'s father arrived at the hospital.

The hospital staff told Mechan to take T.R. to a nearby mental health center, which he did. After being at the mental health center for 45 minutes, Mechan took T.R. home. These facts provided Olney with ample grounds to think that T.R. posed a danger to herself and thus provided probable cause for Olney to take T.R. into protective custody for a mental evaluation. When a person is suicidal, a mental evaluation can reasonably include a determination whether the person has already acted upon her suicidal thoughts, which means the officer can authorize a blood draw as part of that evaluation.

Machan, T.R.'s father, claimed Olney violated T.R's constitutional right to be free from illegal seizures. The district court ruled that Olney did not have qualified immunity; the Sixth Circuit Court of Appeals reversed, maintaining that Olney

---

School Resource Officers, 38 Pace L. Rev. 215 (2018); Perry A. Zirkel, *An Empirical Analysis of Recent Case Law Arising from the Use of School Resource Officers*, 48 J.L. & Educ. 305 (2019).

150. *See* Maryam Ahranjani, *The Prisonization of America's Public Schools*, 45 Hofstra L. Rev. 1097 (2017).

151. Noelia Rivera-Calderón, *Arrested at the Schoolhouse Gate: Criminal School Disturbance Laws and Children's Rights in Schools*, 76 Nat'l L. Guild Rev. 1 (2019).

152. *See supra* note 149.

153. *See* Jacqueline A. Stefkovich & William C. Frick, Best Interests of the Student: Applying Ethical Constructs to Legal Cases (3d ed.) (2021).

154. 958 F. 3d 1212 (6th Cir. 2020).

had probable cause to believe T.R. was a danger to herself. Therefore, her Fourth Amendment rights against illegal seizures were not violated and immunity was not required. Mechan also argued that, rather than take T.R. to the hospital for a mental evaluation without his consent, Olney should have simply detained T.R. at the school for 90 minutes until Mechan could arrive to take her home. But Olney had reason to fear that T.R. might hurt herself at home, given that T.R. herself had just said that "she sees things" there (i.e., guns and knives) that made "her want to hurt herself." Moreover, seizures, by definition, are not consensual; and the existence of probable cause meant that Olney did not need Machan's consent to take T.R. to the hospital for a mental evaluation. Olney therefore did not violate the Fourth Amendment when he took T.R. to the hospital and authorized the blood draw.

In *J.W. v. Birmingham Board of Education*,[155] SROs employed by the Birmingham Police Department and stationed at schools had the authority to use Freeze +P, an incapacitating chemical spray, i.e., pepper spray, on students under certain circumstances. Six Birmingham High School students who were sprayed with or exposed to Freeze +P in 2009, 2010, and 2011 filed a civil rights lawsuit under § 1983 against the Birmingham Board of Education, the Chief of the BPD, and the SROs who used the spray against them or in their vicinity. These students alleged that the SROs used excessive force in violation of the Fourth Amendment by spraying them and by failing to adequately decontaminate them. The court awarded $5,000 each to the six students. They also claimed that the constitutional violations were the result of a policy or custom of the Birmingham Police Department. The Eleventh Circuit held that the SROs who were initially held individually liable on the students' Fourth Amendment decontamination claims are entitled to qualified immunity.

The district court requested that both parties meet and arrive at a mutually agreed upon training and procedure plan. This lower court offered some guidelines based on general practice:

> (1) unless doing so would endanger the student, officer, or bystanders, after an [SRO] sprays a student with Freeze +P and has secured the student, the officer must provide the student with an opportunity to decontaminate with water, either in the form of a shower, washing at a sink, or using an eye wash station; (2) because of the lingering exposure from contaminated clothing, at all times, Chief Roper must maintain at each school where the B.P.D. allows [SROs] to spray students with Freeze +P a sufficient number (as agreed by the parties) of sweat suits in varying sizes, and must allow the student to change out of his or her contaminated clothes; (3) the [SRO] must then place the student in front of a fan; (4) Chief Roper must ensure that [SROs] have available sealable plastic and/or garbage bags that an affected student can use to store her contaminated clothing; and (5) Chief Roper must replace each sweat suit a student uses so that the total number

155. 904 F.3d 1248 (11th Cir. 2018).

> available at the start of each week is always the same as the initial number agreed on by the parties.[156]

This lower court also suggested that a one-page pamphlet describing the need for and methods of decontamination be posted and distributed for others to see in case they were in the vicinity of the pepper spray and could possibly be contaminated. The Eleventh Circuit panel accepted this district court order and maintained that, for practical reasons, it would be accepted as precedent. The circuit court noted, however, that it did not generally endorse prescriptive solutions.

As to the merits of the case, there was no appeal based on the damages that the students were awarded; therefore, the circuit court did not address this issue. Neither did the court address whether the Fourth Amendment had been violated; that issue could be appealed but was not part of this case which dealt exclusively with the remaining claim, i.e., whether the SROs were liable for damages based their failure to decontaminate the students who were sprayed. Assuming this incident resulted in a constitutional violation based on excessive force, the circuit court ruled that the SROs could not have known that what they did in 2009, 2010, and 2011 violated the students' civil rights under § 1983 as there was no relevant case law in either the Eleventh Circuit or at the state supreme court level. Therefore, the SROs were immune from liability.

The following year, this same circuit court granted qualified immunity to another SRO in *Hines v. Jefferson*.[157] In this case, a female student had been involved in a fight in a school hallway that was ultimately handled by the SRO and resulted in the student being charged with obstructing an officer and disorderly conduct. (These charges were later dismissed.) The student alleged that the officer told her she was under arrest and put her in a choke hold as she was escorted to the SRO's office and that the SRO held her by her neck while she fought to get away. She further asserted that she told the officer she could not breathe. According to the SRO, the student refused to comply with directives to stand up and go to the office, scratched the officer's arm, and tried to grab the officer by the neck of her shirt. The SRO maintained that she stood behind the student and secured the student's upper body as the student continued to fight while being escorted to the SRO office. After complaining of neck pain, bruising, and swelling, the student was taken by her mother to a physician. The physician reported no external bruises or abnormal breathing, and an x-ray of the student's neck was normal.

The student's parent filed a § 1983 claim against the SRO alleging malicious prosecution and excessive force in violation of the Fourteenth and Fourth Amendments and claims of excessive corporal punishment against the SRO and the school system. The district court granted summary judgment in favor of the SRO and the school district. It concluded that the SRO's actions were objectively reasonable, that

---

156. *Id.* at 1254.

157. 795 Fed. Appx. 707 (11th Cir. 2019).

the SRO was entitled to qualified immunity, and that the parent's claims failed as a matter of law. The Eleventh Circuit Court of Appeals determined the SRO's use of force was not grossly disproportionate to the situation and that any reasonable officer in her position would inevitably conclude the use of force was lawful, nor was her conduct so far beyond the hazy border between excessive and acceptable force that the officer had to know she was violating the Constitution. The SRO had arguable probable cause to charge a student that had recently been fighting and was combative with the officer, and the SRO's use of force did not constitute corporal punishment.

E.W. v. Dolgos[158] involved the parents of an elementary school student who brought a §1983 action against a school resource officer, Dolgos claiming that the officer's decision to handcuff a calm, compliant elementary school student for fighting with another student three days prior violated the student's Fourth Amendment rights and Maryland law. A ten-year-old student, E.W., rode a school bus. E.W. sat in an aisle seat on one side of the bus while another student, A.W., sat diagonally across from her in an aisle seat one row behind E.W. on the opposite side of the bus. E.W. stood over A.W. and began hitting her, swinging her arms downward because of their height difference. Although the seat in front of A.W. obscured the camera's view of the scuffle, the way A.W. was sitting suggests that E.W.'s swings likely landed on A.W.'s left arm, shoulder, and possibly her head. This exchange drew the attention of the bus driver, who called both E.W. and A.W. to the front of the bus and eventually suspended both girls from the bus for three days.

Three days later, after school authorities had time to review the bus tapes of this incident, E.W. was removed from class and placed in a closed office with an SRO and two school administrators. The SRO, Dolgos, placed E.W. in handcuffs from behind and reseated her. Immediately after being handcuffed, E.W. began to cry. She explained that she did not want to go to jail and that she would not hit A.W. again. The SRO kept her handcuffed for about two minutes as she cried and apologized. Officer Dolgos indicated that E.W. never complained that the handcuffs were too tight or displayed bruises to her. Rather, responding to E.W.'s show of remorse, the SRO decided not to arrest E.W. and removed the handcuffs. The school contacted E.W.'s mother, T.W., and Dolgos informed T.W. that she would refer the matter to the department of juvenile services.

The Fourth Circuit held that based on the totality of the circumstances, the SRO's decision to handcuff the minor student was objectively unreasonable under the Fourth Amendment. The court arrived at this decision after applying three factors suggested by the U.S. Supreme Court in *Graham v. Connor.*[159] This analysis includes "the severity of the crime at issue, whether the suspect poses an immediate threat to the safety of the officers or others, and whether he is actively resisting

158. 884 F.3d 172 (4th Cir. 2018).

159. *Id.* at 179 (citing Graham v. Connor, 490 U.S. 386 (1989)).

arrest or attempting to evade arrest by flight."[160] Based on a related U.S. Supreme Court decision,[161] the *E.W.* court considered other circumstances relevant to the use of excessive force, in this case, the suspect's age and the school setting.

The *E.W.* court determined that the crime in this case was not that serious (an assault, but a misdemeanor), there was no immediate threat (especially considering the small size of the student compared to that of the security guard), and the student was passive (not actively resisting). Also, the student was only ten years old and in elementary school, a place where children should be given supervision and protection. Considering all these factors, the court determined that this seizure was unreasonable. On the other hand, the judges granted federal qualified immunity to Officer Dolgos and found her immune under the Maryland Tort Claims Act ("MTCA"). The court reasoned that Dolgos did not have sufficient notice because it was not apparent that her conduct was unlawful. There had been decisions in the Fourth Circuit stating that "the use of handcuffs would 'rarely' be considered excessive force when the officer has probable cause for the underlying arrest."[162] This decision, however, puts school personnel (in the Fourth Circuit) on notice for future cases of excessive force applied to students. Noting the preponderance of police in schools, the court concluded that:

> While the officers' presence surely keeps the nation's children safe, officers should not handcuff young students who may have committed minor offenses but do not pose an immediate threat to safety and will not evade arrest. Unnecessarily handcuffing and criminally punishing young schoolchildren is undoubtedly humiliating, scarring, and emotionally damaging. We must be mindful of the long-lasting impact such actions have on these children and their ability to flourish and lead prosperous lives — an impact that should be a matter of grave concern for us all.[163]

Educators should not see this decision as a blanket restriction on SROs handcuffing students if an incident is more serious and jeopardizes the safety of others.[164] Not all circuits have employed the *Graham* standard; therefore, it is important to know what your particular jurisdiction has ruled as well as your school's policy (if they have one) on the matter. Probably the best advice that we can offer if there is no precedent in your circuit or state is to refrain from using handcuffs on students, especially those at the elementary school level, and never use handcuffs as a punishment or scare tactic. The following case is a good example of an SRO not having immunity from liability.

160. *Id.* at 179 (citing *Graham* at 396).

161. Kingsley v. Hendrickson, 576 U.S. 389 (2015).

162. 884 F.3d 186 (citing Brown v. Gilmore, 278 F.3d 362, 369 (4th Cir. 2002)).

163. *Id.* at 176.

164. K.W.P. v. Kansas City Pub. Schs., 931 F.3d 813 (8th Cir. 2019).

In *Scott v. County of San Bernadino*,[165] a middle school assistant principal asked the sheriff's deputy, a school resource officer, to counsel a group of seven girls who had been involved in ongoing incidents of bullying and fighting. Some of these students were the bullies; others were victims. After concluding that the girls were unresponsive and disrespectful, the deputy arrested them "to prove a point"[166] and "make [them] mature a lot faster."[167] He also called in another deputy as backup. The United States Court of Appeals for the Ninth Circuit found that the arrest of this group of students was unreasonable under the Fourth Amendment of the U.S. Constitution because the seizure was not justified at its inception in that the officers only had generalized allegations that some of the students had been bickering and fighting. Even if the warrantless arrests of the students were justified at their inception, they were not reasonably related to any circumstances justifying interference. The summary arrest, handcuffing, and police transport to the station of middle school girls was a disproportionate response to the school's need. Thus, the court concluded that "[n]o reasonable officer could have reasonably believed that the law authorizes the arrest of a group of middle schoolers in order to prove a point."[168] This court affirmed the district court's denial of qualified immunity to the SRO because the students were arrested without any consideration of fault.

Sexual Harassment: Title IX and § 1983 Claims

Figure 2-1. Title IX Sex Discrimination

UNITED STATES CODE ANNOTATED

TITLE 20. EDUCATION

CHAPTER 38—DISCRIMINATION BASED ON SEX OR BLINDNESS

Sec. 1681. Sex

(a) Prohibition against discrimination; exceptions

No person in the United States shall, on the basis of sex, be excluded from participation in, be denied the benefits of, or be subjected to discrimination under any education program or activity receiving Federal financial assistance, except that:

(1) Classes of educational institutions subject to prohibition

in regard to admissions to educational institutions, this section shall apply only to institutions of vocational education, professional education, and graduate higher education, and to public institutions of undergraduate higher education;

165. 903 F.3d 943 (9th Cir. 2018).
166. *Id.* at 946.
167. *Id.*
168. *Id.* at 951.

(2) Educational institutions commencing planned change in admissions

in regard to admissions to educational institutions, this section shall not apply

(A) for one year from June 23, 1972, nor for six years after June 23, 1972, in the case of an educational institution which has begun the process of changing from being an institution which admits only students of one sex to being an institution which admits students of both sexes, but only if it is carrying out a plan for such a change which is approved by the Secretary of Education or

(B) for seven years from the date an educational institution begins the process of changing from being an institution which admits only students of only one sex to being an institution which admits students of both sexes, but only if it is carrying out a plan for such a change which is approved by the Secretary of Education, whichever is the later;

(3) Educational institutions of religious organizations with contrary religious tenets

this section shall not apply to an educational institution which is controlled by a religious organization if the application of this subsection would not be consistent with the religious tenets of such organization;

(4) Educational institutions training individuals for military services or merchant marine

this section shall not apply to an educational institution whose primary purpose is the training of individuals for the military services of the United States, or the merchant marine;

(5) Public educational institutions with traditional and continuing admissions policy

in regard to admissions this section shall not apply to any public institution of undergraduate higher education which is an institution that traditionally and continually from its establishment has had a policy of admitting only students of one sex;

(6) Social fraternities or sororities; voluntary youth service organizations

this section shall not apply to membership practices—

(A) of a social fraternity or social sorority which is exempt from taxation under section 501(a) of title 26, the active membership of which consists primarily of students in attendance at an institution of higher education, or

(B) of the Young Men's Christian Association, Young Women's Christian Association, Girl Scouts, Boy Scouts, Camp Fire Girls, and voluntary youth service organizations which are so exempt, the membership of which has traditionally been limited to persons of one sex and principally to persons of less than nineteen years of age;

(7) Boy or Girl conferences

this section shall not apply to—

(A) any program or activity of the American Legion undertaken in connection with the organization or operation of any Boys State conference, Boys Nation conference, Girls State conference, or Girls Nation conference; or

(B) any program or activity of any secondary school or educational institution specifically for—

(i) the promotion of any Boys State conference, Boys Nation conference, Girls State conference, or Girls Nation conference; or

(ii) the selection of students to attend any such conference;

(8) Father-son or mother-daughter activities at educational institutions

this section shall not preclude father-son or mother-daughter activities at an educational institution, but if such activities are provided for students of one sex, opportunities for reasonably comparable activities shall be provided for students of the other sex; and

(9) Institution of higher education scholarship awards in "beauty" pageants

this section shall not apply with respect to any scholarship or other financial assistance awarded by an institution of higher education to any individual because such individual has received such award in any pageant in which the attainment of such award is based upon a combination of factors related to the personal appearance, poise, and talent of such individual and in which participation is limited to individuals of one sex only, so long as such pageant is in compliance with other nondiscrimination provisions of Federal law.

(b) Preferential or disparate treatment because of imbalance in participation or receipt of Federal benefits; statistical evidence of imbalance

Nothing contained in subsection (a) of this section shall be interpreted to require any educational institution to grant preferential or disparate treatment to the members of one sex on account of an imbalance which may exist with respect to the total number or percentage of persons of that sex participating in or receiving the benefits of any federally supported program or activity, in comparison with the total number or percentage of persons of that sex in any community, State, section, or other area: *Provided*, That this subsection shall not be construed to prevent the consideration in any hearing or proceeding under this chapter of statistical evidence tending to show that such an imbalance exists with respect to the participation in, or receipt of the benefits of, any such program or activity by the members of one sex.

(c) "Educational institution" defined

For purposes of this chapter an educational institution means any public or private preschool, elementary, or secondary school, or any institution of vocational, professional, or higher education, except that in the case of an educational institution composed of more than one school, college, or department which are administratively separate units, such term means each such school, college, or department.[169]

Sexual Harassment

One of the areas of school law where plaintiffs have been most successful in their § 1983 claims is in matters of sexual harassment. Here, the plaintiff typically couples the § 1983 claim for monetary damages with a Title IX claim. Title IX prohibits gender discrimination on the part of agencies receiving federal monies [*see* **Figure 2-1**]. Failure to comply with this law could result in the loss of federal funding.[170] There are several important court opinions addressing sexual harassment as it relates to employers/employees, teachers/students, and peers (i.e., student-to-student incidents).

Sexual harassment includes instances of *quid pro quo* which involve one person, usually the person in power, asking another person for sex in exchange for some favor, i.e., a better job, a promotion, or the ability to stay in one's current position. To come into conflict with the law, this offer needs to be made only once. In other words, no pattern needs to be shown. A second type of sexual harassment involves a hostile environment. Here, harassment must be sexual and unwanted and there usually needs to be a pattern of such behavior. Because this topic is elaborated on in Chapter 3 on teachers' rights, the following discussion will focus primarily on cases dealing with students.

Franklin v. Gwinnett County Public Schools[171] involved a female high-school student who was sexually harassed by a male teacher. In this 1992 decision, the U.S. Supreme Court ruled that monetary damages were available as a remedy under Title IX. Six years later, in *Gebser v. Lago Vista Independent School District*,[172] a case involving a Title IX claim by a student who had a sexual relationship with her teacher, the Court applied a deliberate-indifference standard. Ruling in favor of the school district, the Court maintained that there was insufficient evidence to support the notion that school authorities should have known about the relationship. In this case, plaintiffs needed both actual notice and deliberate indifference to gain monetary damages under § 1983.

The following year, in 1999, the U.S. Supreme Court ruled in favor of a female student who had a Title IX claim for peer-on-peer sexual harassment. In this case,

---

169. (Pub. L. 92-318, title IX, Sec. 901, June 23, 1972, 86 Stat. 373; Pub. L. 93-568, Sec. 3(a), Dec. 31, 1974, 88 Stat. 1862; Pub. L. 94-482, title IV, Sec. 412(a), Oct. 12, 1976, 90 Stat. 2234; Pub. L. 96-88, title III, Sec. 301(a)(1), title V, Sec. 507, Oct. 17, 1979, 93 Stat. 677, 692; Pub. L. 99-514, Sec. 2, Oct. 22, 1986, 100 Stat. 2095.)

170. Title IX, 20 U.S.C. § 1681 provides that, "No person in the United States shall, on the basis of sex, be excluded from participation in, be denied the benefits of or be subjected to discrimination under any educational program or activity receiving federal financial assistance."

171. 503 U.S. 60 (1992).

172. 524 U.S. 274 (1998).

Davis v. Monroe County Board of Education,[173] [*see* **Case No. 2-2**] a female fifth-grade student complained of sexual harassment from a classmate. In determining liability, the Court applied *Gebser*'s actual notice and deliberate-indifference standard and added a requirement that the behavior must be so "severe, pervasive, and objectively offensive" that it systematically deprives the student of access to educational opportunities at the school.[174] A fourth case, *Fitzgerald v. Barnstable School Committee*[175] reached the Supreme Court in 2009. This case involved repeated sexual harassment of a kindergartener by a third-grade boy on the school bus and later in the school itself. Here, the issue was whether § 1983 claims could be used as a remedy for violation of Fourteenth Amendment equal protection in gender discrimination cases. Overturning a First Circuit court's ruling, the Court asserted that § 1983 could be applied and that Title IX was not the exclusive remedy for these types of violations.

There have been many lawsuits involving students and sexual harassment in the years since *Gebser*, *Davis*, and *Fitzgerald*. For the most part, these claims have been filed under Title IX and § 1983, and their legality has generally rested on the actual notice and deliberate indifference doctrine. Consider *Matthis v. Wayne County Board of Education*,[176] where eighth-grade basketball players sexually harassed seventh graders in the locker room by, among other things, anal penetration with a magic marker and sticking naked buttocks in a student's face. The coach ignored these initial incidents, and the school board was slow to act, resulting in a lawsuit and a jury's award of $100,000 each to the students who were violated. On appeal, the Sixth Circuit affirmed the district court's determination.[177]

In a 2010 unpublished opinion,[178] the Tenth Circuit Court of Appeals affirmed a lower court decision whereby J.M., a 14-year-old Oklahoma student, was awarded well over half a million dollars in federal and state tort claims due to sexual harassment by the school's band director, Brian Giacomo, who reportedly took her out of other classes regularly to have sex with him in the band room. They engaged in "vaginal intercourse, anal sex, oral sex, kissing, hugging, and touching"[179] and had sex at his home, her home, and in the band room. They also had oral sex in Giacomo's automobile. In his deposition, Giacomo admitted he recognized that J.M. had low self-esteem and that "he could take advantage of her through his position of authority."[180] Giacomo further testified that "he cultivated an inappropriate sexual relationship with J.M. by telling her she was beautiful, helping her with her musical skills, showing her special favoritism, including giving her awards, and

173. 526 U.S. 629 (1999).

174. *Id.* at 650.

175. 555 U.S. 246 (1st Cir. 2009).

176. 782 F. Supp. 2d 542 (M.D. Tenn. 2011).

177. Matthis v. Wayne Cnty. Bd. of Educ., 496 Fed. Appx. 513 (6th Cir. 2012).

178. J.M. v. Hilldale Ind. Sch. Dist., 397 Fed. Appx. 445 (10th Cir. 2010).

179. J.M. v. Hilldale Ind. Sch. Dist., No. CIV 07-367-JHP, 2008 U.S. Dist. LEXIS 57098 at *5 (E.D. Okla. July 25, 2008) (*summary judgment denied*).

180. *Id.*

making her a section leader in the band."[181] He also testified that the sex was consensual—something that is not possible given the age of this student.

According to the record, most of the students in the band knew of the relationship between Giacomo and J.M. In addition, when one student, Mikel Pembrook, reported information to the assistant principal, the AP yelled at him and warned him not to say anything as he might ruin Giacomo's career. At a subsequent meeting, the AP "threatened Pembrook's parents that if the 'pedophile rumors' did not stop, Pembrook would be suspended or expelled."[182] It was not until the mother of another student discovered that Giacomo was having sex with her daughter that these incidents were reported at a higher level and action was taken. J.M.'s parents brought forth claims under Title IX, § 1983, and state tort law. While disturbing, this case presents a good example of what can happen regarding both the welfare of the student and the legal costs incurred when school officials are deliberately indifferent to reports of sexual harassment.

Conversely, courts in the Fifth, Seventh, and Eighth Circuits have ruled that students' claims did not meet the test set forth in *Davis v. Monroe*.[183] In the Fifth Circuit, a female student claimed that a cheerleader sexually harassed her by calling her a "ho," starting a rumor about a hickey, wiping tears from her eyes, and slapping her boyfriend's buttocks.[184] Ruling in favor of the school district, the court determined that the alleged harassment was not based on sex nor was it adequately severe or pervasive, and the school administrators were not deliberately indifferent to these incidents. Similarly, an Eighth Circuit panel ruled that teasing, name-calling, and falsely accusing a student of being a homosexual was not sufficiently severe or pervasive to win a Title IX claim.[185]

In the Seventh Circuit,[186] Rita Trentadue, a student in the high school's Junior ROTC program, was sexually assaulted by Sgt. Mark Cole, an instructor in the program. The abuse, which continued for several months, occurred in the JROTC staff office at the high school and also while out on drills. On several occasions, Cole moved his hand across the student's chest or down the back of her pants while giving her a hug. He also put his hand between her legs while she was a passenger in his car returning from drill practice and put his hand inside her pants and touched her genital area while she was asleep under a tree. When Trentadue finally told her mother about this abuse, they reported these incidents to the school guidance counselor and to the principal who immediately informed the superintendent and assistant superintendent. Cole was questioned, admitted to the abuse, and upon request

181. *Id.*

182. J.M. v. Hilldale Ind. Sch. Dist., 397 Fed. Appx. 445, 447 (10th Cir. 2010).

183. 526 U.S. 629 (1999).

184. Sanches v. Carrollton-Farmers Branch Ind. Sch. Dist., 647 F.3d 156 (5th Cir. 2010).

185. 648 F.3d 860 (8th Cir. 2011).

186. Trentadue v. Redmon, 619 F.3d 648 (7th Cir. 2010).

turned in his resignation. While the court found Cole's behavior to be appalling, the judges found nothing to suggest either a Title IX or a § 1983 claim against the school.

Another Seventh Circuit[187] case involved a 26-year-old female teacher who exchanged a series of sexually suggestive text messages with a 14-year-old male student. They also met at her apartment once and kissed for some 15–20 minutes, an incident that allegedly involved some petting, which she denied. Upon discovering evidence of this affair via her son's e-mails, the student's mother notified the school district and subsequently placed her son in a private school. The teacher was fired and pled guilty to sexual assault charges. The mother brought Title IX claims but was unsuccessful because even though school personnel had suspicions and had investigated, the teacher lied when questioned. Thus, there was no real evidence of involvement. When the parent notified the school with some tangible proof, authorities reacted immediately.

Similarly, in the Eleventh Circuit case *J.F.K. v. Troup County School District*,[188] parents were unable to show that the principal had actual notice when a 45-year-old female homeroom teacher sexually molested O.K.K., their 12-year-old son. The principal had been made aware of several lesser incidents that he discussed with the teacher. He characterized her behavior as "inappropriate, devoid of professionalism, and reek[ing] of immaturity."[189] This conduct included interfering in students' personal business, frequently e-mailing students, and acting overly possessive with O.K.K., but nothing indicated the ongoing sexual harassment that was happening, including numerous occurrences of oral sex.

To summarize, if school officials are put on actual notice as to incidents of sexual harassment, they are obliged to investigate immediately and take any necessary action. Deliberate indifference to these reports could result in loss of federal funding for the school district under Title IX and money damages under § 1983 in addition to state tort law remedies.

Transgender Students

This section addresses the rights of transgender students and the laws that protect these individuals. Title IX, a civil rights act passed as part of the Education Amendments of 1972, provides in part that "[n]o person in the United States shall, on the basis of sex, be excluded from participation in, be denied the benefits of or be subjected to discrimination under any educational program or activity receiving federal financial assistance. . . ."[190] Title IX is usually thought of as a law protecting

187. Doe. v. St. Francis Sch. Dist., 694 F.3d 869 (7th Cir. 2012). (This is a public school; St. Francis is the name of the town where the school is located — Eds.).

188. 678 F.3d 1254 (11th Cir. 2012).

189. *Id.* at 1261.

190. 20 U.S.C. § 1681 (emphasis added).

the rights of students in relation to athletics, admission to single-gender educational institutions, and/or sexual harassment. While most Title IX legal claims involve the rights of female students, this law also includes males who are discriminated against based on their gender. More recently, this law has been applied to protect the rights of transgender students. We are discussing transgender-related cases in this liability chapter because, like sexual harassment (discussed above), violation of Title IX can result in an institution's (school district's) loss of federal funding. Also, claims for monetary damages under § 1983 can be made if an individual's civil rights under the U.S. Constitution or a federal law (such as Title IX) are violated.

Since the last edition of this book, there has been an upsurge in legal cases addressing the needs of transgender students in K-12 public schools. Between 2017 and 2020, five different U.S. circuit courts of appeals were the first to rule on these students' rights to access appropriate bathrooms and/or locker rooms. In each situation, the transgender student won. These opinions include *Doe v. Boyertown*[191] (Third Circuit), *Grimm v. Gloucester*[192] (Fourth Circuit), *Whitaker*[193] (Seventh Circuit), *Parents for Privacy*[194] (Ninth Circuit), and *Adams*[195] (Eleventh Circuit). Of these five cases, two (*Whitaker* and *Grimm*) were based on the transgender student's Fourteenth Amendment Due Process rights under the U.S. Constitution as well as Title IX claims. Three others (*Parents for Privacy, Boyertown*, and *Adams*) originated from the Title IX claims of cisgender (those who can easily identify with the sex assigned to them at birth) students and/or parents on their cisgender children's behalf. In all five cases, the circuit courts ruled in favor of the transgender students and their rights under both Title IX and the Equal Protection Clause of the Fourteenth Amendment.

We will discuss two of these cases—*Grimm* and *Boyertown*—in greater detail, as we believe they can offer some clarity and guidance on this issue for school personnel. Before proceeding with our analysis, we offer four caveats: (1) This is an incredibly fast-moving area of law, and it is imperative that you consult with your professional association or school attorney to see if there are relevant court decisions in your particular jurisdiction, especially if your school is not in one of the five circuits that have already rendered an opinion. (2) If you work in the Third, Fourth, Seventh, Ninth, or Eleventh Circuits, you are bound to the decisions in *Boyer, Grimm, Whitaker, Parents for Privacy*, and *Adams*, respectively. (3) These decisions all involve transgender students who were born female but who identify with the male gender. (4) These cases and subsequent decisions are restricted to transgender students' use of bathrooms and/or locker room facilities.

191. Doe *ex. rel.* Doe v. Boyertown Area Sch. Dist., 897 F.3d 518 (3d. Cir. 2018).

192. Grimm v. Gloucester Cnty. Sch. Bd., 972 F.3d 586 (4th Cir. 2020).

193. Whitaker by Whitaker v. Kenosha Unified Sch. Dist. No. 1 Bd. of Educ., 858 F.3d 1034 (7th Cir. 2017).

194. Parents for Privacy v. Barr, 949 F.3d 1210 (9th Cir. 2020).

195. Adams by and through Kasper v. Sch. Bd. of St. John's Cnty., 968 F.3d 1286 (11th Cir. 2020).

With these restrictions in mind, let us first consider *Grimm v. Gloucester County School Board*. In this case, Gavin Grimm, a transgender student who identifies as a male, was denied use of the boys' restrooms. For seven weeks, school officials allowed Gavin to use the male facilities with no complaints. It was only when the community and school board members got involved that these rights were taken away. This case's journey through the courts was a long and tedious one and did not get resolved until Gavin was out of high school and in community college. The *Grimm* court began by explaining the concept of transgender, pointing out that most people are cisgender and, therefore, never give any thought to which bathroom they use. Transgender individuals comprise approximately 0.6 percent of the U.S. adult population. Like cisgender, this is natural and not a choice.[196] Persons who are transgender are up to three times more likely than the general population to be diagnosed with mental health problems including gender dysphoria, a clinical condition arising from debilitating anxiety and distress associated with reconciling the differences between the gender they identify with and the one they were assigned at birth. Depression, self-harm (e.g., mutilation), substance abuse, and suicide are among the problems associated with untreated gender dysphoria.

Listed in the fifth edition of the American Psychiatric Association's *Diagnostic and Statistical Manual of Mental Disorders*,[197] incongruence between gender identity and assigned sex is a clinical diagnosis. Specific markers include a marked incongruence between one's experienced/expressed gender and primary and/or secondary sex characteristics; a strong conviction that one has the typical feelings and reactions of the other gender; and a strong desire to have the primary and/or secondary sex characteristics of the other gender, to be of the other gender, to be treated as the other gender, or to be rid of one's primary and/or secondary sex characteristics. To be gender dysphoric, one must have symptoms for at least six months and be clinically diagnosed. Medical and mental health professionals have agreed-upon standards of care and treatment protocols for gender dysphoria.[198]

In the spring of his freshman year, Grimm disclosed to his mother that he was transgender. He immediately began therapy at his own request with a psychologist who counsels transgender youth. The therapist diagnosed Grimm with gender dysphoria, referred him for hormone treatment, and stated in a treatment letter that he should be treated as a male and be allowed to use the boys' restrooms at school. Late that summer, as Gavin was preparing to enter his sophomore year, he and his mother met with the school guidance counselor to discuss transition plans. Gavin was initially permitted to use the nurse's bathroom, but this resulted in anxiety, shame, and stigmatization and caused him to be late to class because it was so far from the classrooms. After consultation with the district's superintendent and the school principal, Gavin was allowed to use the boys' restrooms. The school board was not informed of

196. 972 F.3d at 613.
197. APA, DSM-5 (2013).
198. 972 F.3d at 595 (citing APA, DSM-5 (2013) at 452).

this decision, and for seven weeks, Gavin used the male restrooms with no incident. Locker rooms posed no problem as Gavin's physical education classes were online.

However, the superintendent, principal, and some of the school board members began receiving complaints from adults in the community, neighboring communities, and even other states. Only one student complained, and that was prior to improvements in the restrooms, which included panels between urinals, privacy strips on stall doors, and three separate unisex bathrooms available to all students. In response to these complaints, one board member proposed a policy that male and female restroom and locker room facilities in its schools be limited to their corresponding biological genders, and "students with gender identity issues"[199] be provided an alternative, appropriate private facility.

After the school-board policy passed, Gavin avoided restrooms and suffered from frequent urinary tract infections, which are common with transgender students denied access to appropriate restrooms. In his junior year, Gavin was hospitalized for suicidal ideation resulting from being in an environment that made him feel "unsafe, anxious, and disrespected." During this time, Grimm continued with his transition by having chest reconstruction surgery (a double mastectomy), obtaining state identification from the Department of Motor Vehicles that reflected his gender as male, successfully getting his birth certificate changed to male, and requesting that the school change his records to reflect his gender as male. More than two months later, in January 2017, Grimm received a letter from the Board, through its attorney, declining Gavin's request without providing a reason. The Board denied this request even though Gavin was in compliance with the Family Educational Rights and Privacy Act[200] regulations.

Agreeing with its previous decision and that of the lower court, the Fourth Circuit maintained that Gavin, as a transgender student, had an equal protection right to use the boys' restrooms. Following the equal protection standards set forth by the U.S. Supreme Court in *Bowen v. Gilliard*[201] and *City of Cleburne v. Cleburne Living Center*,[202] the court applied a four-factor analysis to determine whether transgender persons (Gavin) constitute a quasi-suspect class. Such a classification would mean that the state (school) needed an "exceedingly persuasive justification"[203] to deny Gavin his rights.

First, the class must be historically subject to discrimination.[204] Second, there must be "a defining characteristic that bears a relation to its ability to perform or contribute to society."[205] Third, "the class may be defined as a discrete group by

199. 972 F.3d at 599.

200. FERPA, 20 U.S.C. §1232g; 34 C.F.R. Part 99 (1974).

201. 483 U.S. 587, 602 (1987).

202. 473 U.S. 432 (1985).

203. 972 F.3d at 608 (citing United States v. Virginia (VMI), 518 U.S. 515, 534 (1996)).

204. *Id.* at 611 (citing *Bowen*, 483 U.S. 587 at 602).

205. *Id.* (citing *Cleburne*, 473 U.S.at 440–41).

obvious, immutable, or distinguishing characteristics."[206] Fourth, the class must be "a minority lacking political power"[207] (only 0.6 percent of the population is transgender). Using the background information provided earlier in this case, the court ruled that Gavin, as a transgender male, easily passed all four prongs of the test for a quasi-suspect class and that the school did not have "an exceedingly persuasive justification"[208] to deny him his rights.

Gavin also succeeded in his Title IX claims, which required him to prove that he was excluded from participation in an education program "on the basis of sex," the educational institution was receiving federal financial assistance at the time, and improper discrimination caused him harm.[209] The court concluded there was no question that bathroom use was part of the educational program, the school received federal funding, and the school board's actions, relying "on the basis of sex," caused Gavin harm.[210] The U.S. Supreme Court's 2020 *Bostock*[211] decision made it clear that "on the basis of sex" applies to people who are transgender.[212] (For more information about this court opinion, see Chapter 3 on teachers' rights.) These actions caused harm such as the inconvenience of finding appropriate restrooms and the stigma attached to requiring the use of separate bathrooms—the latter constituting segregation. Similarly, the court ruled that the school's refusal to change Gavin's records was made "on the basis of sex" and caused damage to Gavin, constituting yet another Title IX violation.[213]

Noting that the adults, not the students, were the school's greatest obstacle, the court concluded that "the Board acted to protect cisgender boys from Gavin's mere presence—a special kind of discrimination against a child that he will no doubt carry with him for life." Gloucester's Board of Education ignored medical research, the results of a large national survey putting numbers to the extent of discrimination against transgender persons, and lawful practices in schools across the state of Virginia. The Board also gave support to the predator myth that boys would pretend to be transgender to gain access to girls' bathrooms and locker rooms, something that has been debunked. Ending on a somewhat optimistic note, the court stated:

> The proudest moments of the federal judiciary have been when we affirm the burgeoning values of our bright youth, rather than preserve the prejudices of the past. How shallow a promise of equal protection that would not protect Grimm from the fantastical fears and unfounded prejudices of his adult community.... One administrator noted: As to the students, I am most

---

206. *Id.* (citing *Bowen*, 483 U.S. 587 at 602).
207. *Id.*
208. *Id.* at 608 (citing United States v. Virginia (VMI), 518 U.S. at 534).
209. *Id.* at 616 (citing Preston v. Va. *ex rel.* New River Cmty. Coll., 31 F.3d 203, 206 (4th Cir. 1994)).
210. *Id.* at 617–18.
211. Bostock v. Clayton Cnty., 590 U.S. __, 140 S. Ct. 1731 (2020).
212. 972 F.3d at 616 (citing Bostock, 140 S. Ct. at 1741).
213. 972 F.3d at 619.

> impressed. They are very understanding and accepting of their classmates. It feels like the adult community is struggling with it more. As another explained, "Young people are pretty savvy and comfortable, and can understand and empathize with someone who just wants to use the bathroom."[214]

Along with *Parents for Privacy* and *Adams, Doe v. Boyertown*[215] presents the transgender issue from the perspective of some cisgender students who claim that school policies supporting transgender students violate their (cisgender) constitutional right to privacy, Title IX, and Pennsylvania tort law. A federal district court in Pennsylvania denied these students a preliminary injunction to stop this policy. Praising the thorough record set by this lower court, the Third Circuit Court of Appeals agreed that there was no basis for granting the injunction. To be granted an injunction, the cisgender students would have to show a likelihood of success on the merits, irreparable harm on their part if the injunction is denied, that granting the relief will not result in greater harm for the transgender students, and that public interest favors the relief. Based on established law as well as the facts of this case, the appeals court agreed with the district court that the cisgender students' arguments were not persuasive, and their claims were unlikely to succeed.

In addition to describing possible complaints from cisgender students and how the court responded to them, we included this case to provide an example of a well-thought-out policy to grant transgender students their rights. We do not advocate one certain way of proceeding, as all schools have their own needs and physical facilities. Originally, the Boyertown Area Senior High School (BASH) required students to use bathrooms and locker rooms aligned with their sex determined at birth, but the district changed this policy in 2016 to allow transgender students to use those facilities aligned with their gender identity. BASH developed this new policy after a careful process based on their analysis of student needs.

Before students were granted permission to use facilities that matched their gender identity, they were required to meet with a licensed counselor trained to address these issues who would consult with other school personnel. Once approved, the student could not return to using facilities associated with their gender at birth. Like other appeals court opinions, the court described the characteristics of transgender individuals and the negative effects of gender dysphoria. To ensure privacy, BASH has several multi-user bathrooms with individual toilet stalls. There are four single-user restrooms always available to all students and four more available depending on the time of day. The locker rooms consist of common areas, private team rooms (by which one would not have to walk through the locker rooms), and shower facilities. Students must change into gym clothes but do not have to change in the locker room. They can instead change privately in one of the single-user facilities, the private shower stalls, or team rooms.[216]

---

214. 972 F.3d at 620.
215. 897 F.3d 518 (3d. Cir. 2018).
216. *Id.* at 524–25.

Rendering their decision, the Third Circuit Court of Appeals saw no violation of Title IX as there was no discrimination based on sex. As to the plaintiffs' other claims, the judges concluded that "under the circumstances here, the presence of transgender students in the locker and restrooms is no more offensive to constitutional or Pennsylvania-law privacy interests than the presence of the other students who are not transgender."[217]

Racial Harassment & Title VI Claims

While it is always important to consider school policies and state laws regarding discrimination and harassment, there has been a trend of students gaining large settlements for racial harassment under Title VI.[218] An illustrative decision from the Second Circuit Court of Appeals, *Zeno v. Pine Plains Central School District*,[219] involved Anthony Zeno, a biracial (half-white, half-Latino), 16-year-old freshman who moved from Long Island to Pine Plains, New York. Anthony's new school was homogenous, with only 5 percent of the students coming from minority groups. After about three weeks at the school, students began accosting Anthony with racial slurs and harassing him. When Anthony's mother approached the principal with her concerns, he told her that the town is small and she should not start "burning . . . bridges."[220] As the incidents continued, Mrs. Zeno wrote to the school board and the district superintendent, neither of which followed up with her, nor the school principal.

The incidents escalated with physical as well as verbal attacks and death threats. During Anthony's sophomore year, the family's attorney advised the school to provide Anthony with a "shadow" to accompany him at school and to implement a zero-tolerance based racial sensitivity program.[221] The district responded by implementing a one-day program that focused on bullying and sexual harassment with little attention to race. During all this time and into his junior year, Anthony suffered continued abuse, including threats of lynching and of raping his sister. While the district suspended the perpetrators, others rose to take their place. Finally, in the beginning of his fourth year and with no let-up, Anthony elected to receive an IEP diploma that would allow him to attend community college but was not recognized by most four-year or trade schools. Anthony was ultimately awarded $1 million for violations of his civil rights under Title VI, an award that was upheld by the

217. *Id.* at 521.

218. Title VI, 42 U.S.C. § 2000d provides that, "No person in the United States shall, on the ground of race, color, or national origin, be excluded from participation in, be denied the benefits of, or be subjected to discrimination under any educational program or activity receiving Federal financial assistance."

219. 702 F.3d 655 (2d Cir. 2012).

220. *Id.* at 659.

221. *Id.* at 660.

Second Circuit Court of Appeals. The court applied a standard of "deliberate indifference," which was introduced in *Davis v. Monroe County Board of Education*,[222] a sexual harassment case decided by the U.S. Supreme Court and discussed later in this chapter. The appeals court also cited several racial harassment cases that had applied this standard as well as other claims in the second circuit and elsewhere.[223]

Educational Malpractice

Over the years, various incarnations of school reform have brought forth calls for accountability on many different levels. Reaching their peak in the mid- to late-1970s through the 1980s and then tapering off in the 1990s, this desire to hold schools accountable for educating youth has manifested itself in legal cases challenging school districts' responsibility to educate students.[224] More specifically, plaintiffs in these cases have attempted to identify a failure on behalf of a given school district to adequately educate an individual student. Such cases, generally referred to as educational malpractice or educational liability cases, focus on the quality of education. In the attempt to demonstrate either the failure or inappropriateness of education, plaintiffs and legal scholars have relied on four general theories to forward their claims: tort theory, statutory theory, state and federal constitutional theories, and contract theory.[225]

---

222. 526 U.S. 629 (1999).

223. *Zeno*, 702 F.3d at 665 n.10 (citing DiStiso, 691 F.3d at 226 (violation of §1983)); Hayut v. State Univ. of N.Y., 352 F.3d 733 (2d Cir. 2003) (violation of Fourteenth Amendment Equal Protection Clause); Gant *ex rel.* Gant v. Wallingford Bd. of Educ., 195 F.3d 134 (2d Cir. 1999) (violation of §1981); Bryant v. Indep. Sch. Dist. No. I-38 of Garvin Cnty., 334 F.3d 928, 934 (10th Cir. 2003) (applying *Davis* to a Title VI student-on-student harassment claim); Saxe v. State Coll. Area Sch. Dist., 240 F.3d 200, 206 n.5 (3d Cir. 2001) (acknowledging that *Davis* "applies equally" to harassment under Title VI or other federal anti-discrimination statutes).

224. *See, e.g.*, Peter W. v. San Francisco Unified Sch. Dist., 60 Cal. App. 3d 814 (1976); Donohue v. Copiague Union Free Sch. Dist., 391 N.E.2d 1352 (N.Y. 1979); Hoffman v. Bd. of Educ., 400 N.E.2d 317 (N.Y. 1979); Loughran v. Flanders, 470 F. Supp. 110 (D. Conn. 1979); Smith v. Almeda Cnty. Soc. Serv., 90 Cal. App. 3d 929 (1979); D.S.W. v. Fairbanks N. Star Borough Sch. Dist., 628 P.2d 554 (Alaska 1981); B.M. v. State, 649 P.2d 425 (Mont. 1982); Hunter v. Bd. of Educ., 439 A.2d 582 (Md. 1982); Doe v. Bd. of Educ. of Montgomery Cnty., 295 Md. 67 (1982); Tubell v. Dade County Pub. Sch., 419 So. 2d 388 (Fla. Dist. Ct. App. 1982); Snow v. State, 475 N.E.2d 454 (N.Y. 1984); Torres v. Little Flower Children's Serv., 474 N.E.2d 223 (N.Y. 1984); Wickstrom v. North Idaho College, 725 P.2d 155, 157 (Idaho 1986); Agostine v. Sch. Dist. of Phila., 527 A.2d 193 (Pa. Commw. Ct. 1987); Silano v. Tirozzi, 651 F. Supp. 1021 (D.C. Conn. 1987); Poe v. Hamilton, 565 N.E. 2d. 887 (Ohio 1990); Rich v. Kentucky Country Day, Inc., 793 S.W.2d 832 (Ky. Ct. App. 1990); Brantley v. District of Columbia, 640 A.2d 181, 184 (D.C. Cir. 1994); Doe v. Town of Framingham, 965 F.Supp. 226 (D. Mass. 1997); Sellers v. Sch. Bd. of Manassas, Virginia, 960 F. Supp. 1006 (E.D. Va. 1997); Bell v. Bd. of Educ. of West Haven, 739 A.2d 321 (Conn. App. Ct. 1999).

225. *See* Julie F. Mead & Preston C. Green III, *Keeping Promises: An Examination of Charter Schools' Vulnerability to Claims of Educational Liability*, 2001 B.Y.U. EDUC. & L.J. 35 (2001); Geoffrey Rapp, *Reconsidering Educational Liability: Property—Owners as Litigants, Constructive Trust as Remedy*, 18 YALE L. & POL'Y REV. 463 (2001).

Despite these varied strategies, plaintiffs have had very limited success in the courts with claims of educational malpractice.[226] In the earliest cases, often borrowing from medical legal models, plaintiffs relied on tort theory to forward their malpractice claims. Tort cases have claimed either negligence or misrepresentation on the part of the school district. The failure to educate is often based on an assumption of a duty to educate on the part of the school. These cases attempt to demonstrate a breach of this duty due to "improper or inadequate instruction, testing, placement, or counseling of a child."[227] But negligence claims are problematic for several reasons. To be successful, educational malpractice claims based on negligence require plaintiffs to demonstrate a duty recognized by law, prove the person or entity being sued has breached this duty, prove that this breach was the proximate cause of the individual's injury, and demonstrate that an actual injury or loss has occurred.[228]

Peter W. v. San Francisco Unified School District[229] [*see* **Case No. 2-3**] is perhaps the most frequently cited education malpractice decision. If ever there was a test case for educational malpractice, this is it. Peter W. graduated from high school with good grades yet was functionally illiterate, not knowing even the most rudimentary math and reading skills. Yet, the court ruled for the school district, maintaining that there is no agreed-upon standard to determine whether the school had been negligent. Additionally, there was no way in this case for the court to determine proximate cause. Finally, the court found that accountability on the part of the school district places too much of a burden on the school. In other words, the court refused on public policy grounds to consider the claim of educational malpractice.

Plaintiffs have filed tort claims based on misrepresentation. Generally, there are two types of misrepresentation claims: negligent misrepresentation and intentional misrepresentation.[230] Kevin McJessy observed that courts have rejected these arguments[231] based upon the same public policy issues identified in *Peter W.* In all these cases, academic abstention has been a major legal argument. Elaborating on the significance of the *Peter W.* decision, McJessy makes the following observation:

> Peter W. has had a profound impact on the theory of "educational liability." It gave substance to the theoretical murmuring of the legal profession, spawned a great deal of new scholarship on the subject of educational liability, and inspired other attorneys to attempt similar actions in other states.

---

226. *See* Sharan E. Brown & Kim Cannon, *Educational Malpractice Actions: A Remedy for What Ails Our Schools?* 78 Educ. Law. Rep. 643 (1993); Albert C. Jurenas, *Will Educational Malpractice Be Revived?* 74 Educ. Law. Rep. 449 (1992); Alice Klein, Note, *Educational Malpractice: A Lesson in Professional Accountability*, 32 B.C. L. Rev. 899 (1991).

227. Deborah D. Dye, Note, *Educational Malpractice: A Cause of Action that Failed to Pass the Test*, 90 W. Va. L. Rev. 499 (1987/1988).

228. W. Page Keeton, et al., Prosser & Keeton on the Law of Torts 30 (5th ed. 1984).

229. 60 Cal. App. 3d 814 (1976).

230. Mead & Green at 38.

231. Kevin P. McJessy, Comment, *Contract Law: The Proper Framework for Litigating Educational Liability Claims*, 89 NW. U. L. Rev. 1768 (1995).

> Paradoxically, the greatest legacy of *Peter W.* is that nearly every court to consider the propriety of an educational liability claim since that decision has relied on *Peter W.* as support for invoking the doctrine of academic abstention and dismissing the claim. Despite virtually uniform endorsement of educational liability actions by the legal community, the bench has almost uniformly opposed such actions.[232]

Finally, as this commentator points out, there is a history of legal commentary supporting educational malpractice claims based on the belief that success in this area would improve public education.[233]

It was speculated[234] at the inception of the accountability requirements set forth in the No Child Left Behind Act[235] and expanded through the federal Race to the Top[236] stimulus, particularly as they related to teacher effectiveness, that school districts would become more vulnerable to educational malpractice lawsuits. That transformation did not occur to any great extent. The failure of tort theory to be successful in education malpractice cases has led to additional legal strategies, with mixed results. Statutory theory poses the argument that states have established a standard of care through statutes. By their failure to educate, school districts have fallen short of this standard.[237] The courts have been reluctant to find for plaintiffs when statutory theory has been set forth, often relying on the same public-policy grounds considered in tort cases.[238]

While tort and statutory claims have offered little success to plaintiffs, claims based on constitutional theory have achieved some success. Such claims argue that both federal and individual state constitutions set forth a duty to educate. The Supreme Court effectively eliminated a federal constitutional argument when it ruled in *San Antonio v. Rodriguez*[239] that education is not a fundamental right. While constitutional theory has had some success at the state level, the wording of state constitutions varies considerably and thus interpretation of the law in one state is likely not applicable to other states.[240] In addition, many states have been

---

232. *Id.* at 1770.

233. *See, e.g.*, Sharan E. Brown & Kim Cannon, *Educational Malpractice Actions: A Remedy for What Ails Our Schools?* 78 Educ. L. Rep. 643 (1993), and Melanie Natasha Henry, *No Child Left Behind? Educational Malpractice Litigation for the 21st Century*, 92 Calif. L. Rev. 1117 (July 2004).

234. *See* Todd DeMitchell, Terri DeMitchell & Douglas Gagnon, *Teacher Effectiveness and Value-Added Modeling: Building a Pathway to Educational Malpractice?* 2012 B.Y.U. Educ. & L.J. 257 (2012), and Ethan Hutt & Aaron Tang, *The New Education Malpractice Litigation*, 99 Va L. Rev. 419 (May 2013).

235. NCLB Act of 2001, Pub. L. No. 107-110, § 115, Stat. 1425 (2002).

236. H.R. 1532–112th Congress: Race to the Top Act of 2011, http://www.govtrack.us/congress/bills/112/hr1532.

237. Mead & Green at 40.

238. *Id.*

239. 411 U.S. 1 (1973).

240. McJessy at 1770.

reluctant to declare education a fundamental right, often because this would open a floodgate of public entities insisting that their services are fundamental.[241]

In the over 40 years following *Peter W.*, some 80 court cases alleged educational malpractice. Of those, only one plaintiff was successful, and that ruling was based not on a federal educational right but on specific language in a state constitution.[242] However, in 2020, pursuant to litigation in the Sixth Circuit Court of Appeals in *Gary B. v. Whitmer*,[243] plaintiffs argued that students have a fundamental right to a basic minimum education and that conditions in the Detroit public schools denied that right, in violation of both the Due Process and Equal Protection clauses. Essentially, the plaintiffs sought recognition that they had been denied a basic minimum education and thus have been deprived of access to literacy.

In its deliberation, the *Gary B.* court conducted a review of the Supreme Court's education cases, finding an application of their principles to the substantive due process framework that demonstrated the court should recognize a basic minimum education to be a fundamental right.[244] The court stated, "[A]ccess to a foundational level of literacy—provided through public education—has an extensive historical legacy and is so central to our political and social system as to be 'implicit in the concept of ordered liberty,'" and, "In short, without the literacy provided by a basic minimum education, it is impossible to participate in our democracy."[245] The parties reached a settlement before the courts could assess damages. A California case resulted in a similar, if less significant, settlement which resulted in millions of dollars being distributed among low-performing elementary schools.[246] Many more are likely to follow.

Contract law provides another strategy to persuade the courts to recognize educational malpractice claims. Contract theory offers that there is breach of a contract between the school and the pupil when a failure to educate exists. Meade and Green observe that plaintiffs in such cases may assert that "schools promised to provide a minimal level of education"[247] and failed to make good on that claim. McJessy,[248] who also advocates for this strategy, provides several reasons for its use, such as the ineffectiveness of other claims to the emerging contractual relationship between schools and students. He points out that educational malpractice claims fit well with

241. Kelly Thompson Cochran, *Beyond School Financing: Defining the Constitutional Right to an Adequate Education,* 78 N.C. L. Rev. 399, 409 (Jan. 2000).

242. Mark Dynarski, *Can Schools Commit Malpractice*, Brookings Inst. (July 26, 2018), https://www.brookings.edu/research/can-schools-commit-malpractice-it-depends/.

243. 957 F.3d 616 (6th Cir. 2020).

244. *Id.* at 621. *See also* Derek W. Black, *The Fundamental Right to Education*, 94 Notre Dame L. Rev. 1059 (2019).

245. 957 F.3d at 642.

246. Dana Goldstein, *Detroit Students Have a Constitutional Right to Literacy, Court Rules*, N.Y Times (Mar. 27, 2020), https://www.nytimes.com/by/dana-goldstein.

247. Mead & Green at 41.

248. McJessy at 1784.

the goal of contract law, which is to protect reasonable expectations of parties; that contract law, unlike tort liability, does not encourage courts to abstain; and because there has been some limited success in this area, albeit at the post-secondary level, courts will not see it as making new law, something that has discouraged the judiciary in the past.[249]

All in all, contract law is another way to counteract educational malpractice; however, it is more likely to be successful in charter schools and private schools where the promises made are much more explicit than in traditional public schools. For example, in a Denver case[250] where 3,400 parents sued the public schools claiming a contract violation in that their children were not adequately educated, the Colorado state appeals court ruled that there is no contract in this situation and concluded that:

> Plaintiffs cannot hold a public school district to the implementation of its educational objectives in a judicial setting. This matter is of a political nature, in as much as the school district is a political entity and, therefore, such policy issues should be addressed at the ballot box, not presented as a judicially enforceable contract claim.[251]

Still in its early stages, this approach to litigation bears watching.

Conclusions

In sum, it should be recognized that courts, in general, are reluctant to hold schools liable for monetary damages. Clearly, schools do not have "deep pockets." And, just as important, courts recognize that for school officials to be able to do their jobs effectively, they, as with other government agents, must be free from constant governmental interference. As indicated in this chapter, court decisions as well as state statutes have provided considerable guidance to schools in determining the legality and liability of their actions.

Selected Case Law

[2-1] *Ingraham v. Wright*

[2-2] *Davis v. Monroe County Board of Education*

[2-3] *Peter W. v. San Francisco Unified School District*

---

249. *Id.*

250. Denver Parents Ass'n v. Denver Bd. of Educ., 10 P.3d 662 (Colo. Ct. App. 2000).

251. *Id.* at 665.

[Case No. 2-1]

School corporal punishment is not cruel and unusual in violation of the Eighth Amendment.

Ingraham v. Wright

Supreme Court of the United States
430 U.S. 651 (1977)

Mr. Justice POWELL delivered the opinion of the Court.

This case presents questions concerning the use of corporal punishment in public schools: First, whether the paddling of students as a means of maintaining school discipline constitutes cruel and unusual punishment in violation of the Eighth Amendment; and, second, to the extent that paddling is constitutionally permissible, whether the Due Process Clause of the Fourteenth Amendment requires prior notice and an opportunity to be heard.

I

Petitioners James Ingraham and Roosevelt Andrews filed the complaint in this case on January 7, 1971, in the United States District Court for the Southern District of Florida.[252] At the time both were enrolled in the Charles R. Drew Junior High School in Dade County, Fla., Ingraham in the eighth grade and Andrews in the ninth. The complaint contained three counts, each alleging a separate cause of action for deprivation of constitutional rights, under 42 U.S.C. ss 1981–1988. Counts one and two were individual actions for damages by Ingraham and Andrews based on paddling incidents that allegedly occurred in October 1970 at Drew Junior High School. Count three was a class action for declaratory and injunctive relief filed on behalf of all students in the Dade County schools.[253] Named as defendants in all counts were respondents Willie J. Wright (principal at Drew Junior High School), Lemmie Deliford (an assistant principal), Solomon Barnes (an assistant to the principal), and Edward L. Whigham (superintendent of the Dade County School System).[254]

Petitioners presented their evidence at a week-long trial before the District Court. At the close of petitioners' case, respondents moved for dismissal of count three "on the ground that upon the facts and the law the plaintiff has shown no right to relief,"

---

252. As Ingraham and Andrews were minors, the complaint was filed in the names of Eloise Ingraham, James' mother, and Willie Everett, Roosevelt's father.

253. The District Court certified the class, under Fed. Rules Civ. Proc. 23(b)(2) and (c)(1), as follows: "'All students of the Dade County School system who are subject to the corporal punishment policies issued by the Defendant, Dade County School Board. . . .'" App. 17. One student was specifically excepted from the class by request.

254. The complaint also named the Dade County School Board as a defendant, but the Court of Appeals held that the Board was not amenable to suit under 42 U.S.C. ss 1981–1988 and dismissed the suit against the Board for want of jurisdiction. 525 F.2d 909, 912 (CA5 1976). This aspect of the Court of Appeals' judgment is not before us.

Fed. Rule Civ. Proc. 41(b), and for a ruling that the evidence would be insufficient to go to a jury on counts one and two.[255] The District Court granted the motion as to all three counts, and dismissed the complaint without hearing evidence on behalf of the school authorities. App. 142–150.

Petitioners' evidence may be summarized briefly. In the 1970–1971 school year many of the 237 schools in Dade County used corporal punishment as a means of maintaining discipline pursuant to Florida legislation and a local School Board regulation.[256] The statute then in effect authorized limited corporal punishment by negative inference, proscribing punishment which was "degrading or unduly severe" or which was inflicted without prior consultation with the principal or the teacher in charge of the school. Fla. Stat. Ann. s 232.27 (1961).[257] The regulation,

255. Petitioners had waived their right to jury trial on the claims for damages in counts one and two, but respondents had not. The District Court proceeded initially to hear evidence only on count three, the claim for injunctive relief. At the close of petitioners' case, however, the parties agreed that the evidence offered on count three (together with certain stipulated testimony) would be considered, for purposes of a motion for directed verdict, as if it had also been offered on counts one and two. It was understood that respondents could reassert a right to jury trial if the motion were denied. App. 142.

256. The evidence does not show how many of the schools actually employed corporal punishment as a means of maintaining discipline. The authorization of the practice by the School Board extended to 231 of the schools in the 1970–1971 school year, but at least 10 of those schools did not administer corporal punishment as a matter of school policy. Id., at 137–139.

257. In the 1970–1971 school year, s 232.27 provided:

"Each teacher or other member of the staff of any school shall assume such authority for the control of pupils as may be assigned to him by the principal and shall keep good order in the classroom and in other places in which he is assigned to be in charge of pupils, but he shall not inflict corporal punishment before consulting the principal or teacher in charge of the school, and in no case shall such punishment be degrading or unduly severe in its nature. . . ."

Effective July 1, 1976, the Florida Legislature amended the law governing corporal punishment. Section 232.27 now reads: "Subject to law and to the rules of the district school board, each teacher or other member of the staff of any school shall have such authority for the control and discipline of students as may be assigned to him by the principal or his designated representative and shall keep good order in the classroom and in other places in which he is assigned to be in charge of students. If a teacher feels that corporal punishment is necessary, at least the following procedures shall be followed:

"(1) The use of corporal punishment shall be approved in principle by the principal before it is used, but approval is not necessary for each specific instance in which it is used.

"(2) A teacher or principal may administer corporal punishment only in the presence of another adult who is informed beforehand, and in the student's presence, of the reason for the punishment.

"(3) A teacher or principal who has administered punishment shall, upon request, provide the pupil's parent or guardian with a written explanation of the reason for the punishment and the name of the other (adult) who was present." Fla. Stat. Ann. s 232.27 (1977) (codifier's notation omitted).

Corporal punishment is now defined as "the moderate use of physical force or physical contact by a teacher or principal as may be necessary to maintain discipline or to enforce school rules." s 228.041(28). The local school boards are expressly authorized to adopt rules governing student conduct and discipline and are directed to make available codes of student conduct. s 230.23(6). Teachers and principals are given immunity from civil and criminal liability for enforcing disciplinary rules, "(e)xcept in the case of excessive force or cruel and unusual punishment. . . ." s 232.275.

Dade County School Board Policy 5144, contained explicit directions and limitations.[258] The authorized punishment consisted of paddling the recalcitrant student on the buttocks with a flat wooden paddle measuring less than two feet long, three to four inches wide, and about one-half inch thick. The normal punishment was limited to one to five "licks" or blows with the paddle and resulted in no apparent physical injury to the student. School authorities viewed corporal punishment as a less drastic means of discipline than suspension or expulsion. Contrary to the procedural requirements of the statute and regulation, teachers often paddled students on their own authority without first consulting the principal.[259]

Petitioners focused on Drew Junior High School, the school in which both Ingraham and Andrews were enrolled in the fall of 1970. In an apparent reference to Drew, the District Court found that "(t)he instances of punishment which could be characterized as severe, accepting the students' testimony as credible, took place in one junior high school." App. 147. The evidence, consisting mainly of the testimony of 16 students, suggests that the regime at Drew was exceptionally harsh. The testimony of Ingraham and Andrews, in support of their individual claims for damages, is illustrative. Because he was slow to respond to his teacher's instructions, Ingraham was subjected to more than 20 licks with a paddle while being held over a table in the principal's office. The paddling was so severe that he suffered a hematoma[260] requiring medical attention and keeping him out of school for several days.[261] Andrews was paddled several times for minor infractions. On two occasions he was struck on his arms, once depriving him of the full use of his arm for a week.[262]

---

258. In the 1970–1971 school year, Policy 5144 authorized corporal punishment where the failure of other means of seeking cooperation from the student made its use necessary. The regulation specified that the principal should determine the necessity for corporal punishment, that the student should understand the seriousness of the offense and the reason for the punishment, and that the punishment should be administered in the presence of another adult in circumstances not calculated to hold the student up to shame or ridicule. The regulation cautioned against using corporal punishment against a student under psychological or medical treatment, and warned that the person administering the punishment "must realize his own personal liabilities" in any case of physical injury. App. 15.

While this litigation was pending in the District Court, the Dade County School Board amended Policy 5144 to standardize the size of the paddles used in accordance with the description in the text, to proscribe striking a child with a paddle elsewhere than on the buttocks, to limit the permissible number of "licks" (five for elementary and intermediate grades and seven for junior and senior grades), and to require a contemporaneous explanation of the need for the punishment to the student and a subsequent notification to the parents. App. 126–128.

259. 498 F.2d 248, 255, and n. 7 (1974) (original panel opinion), vacated on rehearing, 525 F.2d 909 (1976); App. 48, 138, 146; Exhibits 14, 15.

260. Stedman's Medical Dictionary (23d ed. 1976) defines "hematoma" as "(a) localized mass of extravasated blood that is relatively or completely confined within an organ or tissue . . . ; the blood is usually clotted (or partly clotted), and, depending on how long it has been there, may manifest various degrees of organization and decolorization."

261. App. 3–4, 18–20, 68–85, 129–136.

262. *Id.*, at 4–5, 104–113. The similar experiences of several other students at Drew, to which they individually testified in the District Court, are summarized in the original panel opinion in

The District Court made no findings on the credibility of the students' testimony. Rather, assuming their testimony to be credible, the court found no constitutional basis for relief. With respect to count three, the class action, the court concluded that the punishment authorized and practiced generally in the county schools violated no constitutional right. Id., at 143, 149. With respect to counts one and two, the individual damages actions, the court concluded that while corporal punishment could in some cases violate the Eighth Amendment, in this case a jury could not lawfully find "the elements of severity, arbitrary infliction, unacceptability in terms of contemporary standards, or gross disproportion which are necessary to bring 'punishment' to the constitutional level of 'cruel and unusual punishment.'" Id., at 143.

A panel of the Court of Appeals voted to reverse. 498 F.2d 248 (CA5 1974). The panel concluded that the punishment was so severe and oppressive as to violate the Eighth and Fourteenth Amendments, and that the procedures outlined in Policy 5144 failed to satisfy the requirements of the Due Process Clause. Upon rehearing, the en banc court rejected these conclusions and affirmed the judgment of the District Court. 525 F.2d 909 (1976). The full court held that the Due Process Clause did not require notice or an opportunity to be heard:

> In essence, we refuse to set forth, as constitutionally mandated, procedural standards for an activity which is not substantial enough, on a constitutional level, to justify the time and effort which would have to be expended by the school in adhering to those procedures or to justify further interference by federal courts into the internal affairs of public schools.

Id., at 919.

The court also rejected the petitioners' substantive contentions. The Eighth Amendment, in the court's view, was simply inapplicable to corporal punishment in public schools. Stressing the likelihood of civil and criminal liability in state law, if petitioners' evidence were believed, the court held that "(t)he administration of corporal punishment in public schools, whether or not excessively administered, does not come within the scope of Eighth Amendment protection." Id., at 915. Nor was there any substantive violation of the Due Process Clause. The court noted that "(p)addling of recalcitrant children has long been an accepted method of promoting good behavior and instilling notions of responsibility and decorum into the mischievous heads of school children." Id., at 917. The court refused to examine instances of punishment individually:

> We think it a misuse of our judicial power to determine, for example, whether a teacher has acted arbitrarily in paddling a particular child for certain behavior or whether in a particular instance of misconduct five licks would have been a more appropriate punishment than ten licks....

Ibid.

---

the Court of Appeals, 498 F.2d, at 257–259.

We granted certiorari, limited to the questions of cruel and unusual punishment and procedural due process. 425 U.S. 990, 96 S. Ct. 2200, 48 L. Ed. 2d 815.[263]

II

In addressing the scope of the Eighth Amendment's prohibition on cruel and unusual punishment this Court has found it useful to refer to "(t)raditional common-law concepts," Powell v. Texas, 392 U.S. 514, 535, 88 S. Ct. 2145, 2155, 20 L. Ed. 2d 1254 (1968) (plurality opinion), and to the "attitude(s) which our society has traditionally taken." Id., at 531, 88 S. Ct., at 2153. So, too, in defining the requirements of procedural due process under the Fifth and Fourteenth Amendments, the Court has been attuned to what "has always been the law of the land," United States v. Barnett, 376 U.S. 681, 692, 84 S. Ct. 984, 990, 12 L.Ed.2d 23 (1964), and to "traditional ideas of fair procedure." Greene v. McElroy, 360 U.S. 474, 508, 79 S. Ct. 1400, 1419, 3 L. Ed. 2d 1377 (1959). We therefore begin by examining the way in which our traditions and our laws have responded to the use of corporal punishment in public schools.

The use of corporal punishment in this country as a means of disciplining school children dates back to the colonial period.[264] It has survived the transformation of primary and secondary education from the colonials' reliance on optional private arrangements to our present system of compulsory education and dependence on public schools.[265] Despite the general abandonment of corporal punishment as a means of punishing criminal offenders,[266] the practice continues to play a role in the public education of school children in most parts of the country.[267] Professional and

263. We denied review of a third question presented in the petition for certiorari: "Is the infliction of severe corporal punishment upon public school students arbitrary, capricious and unrelated to achieving any legitimate educational purpose and therefore violative of the Due Process Clause of the Fourteenth Amendment?" Pet. for Cert. 2.

264. See H. Falk, Corporal Punishment 11–48 (1941); N. Edwards & H. Richey, The School in the American Social Order 115–116 (1947).

265. Public and compulsory education existed in New England before the Revolution, see id., at 50–68, 78–81, 97–113, but the demand for free public schools as we now know them did not gain momentum in the country as a whole until the mid-1800's, and it was not until 1918 that compulsory school attendance laws were in force in all the States. See Brown v. Board of Education, 347 U.S. 483, 489 n. 4, 74 S. Ct. 686, 689, 98 L. Ed. 873 (1954), citing Cubberley, Public Education in the United States 408–423, 563–565 (1934 ed.); cf. Wisconsin v. Yoder, 406 U.S. 205, 226, and n. 15, 92 S. Ct. 1526, 1538, 32 L. Ed. 2d 15 (1972).

266. See Jackson v. Bishop, 404 F.2d 571, 580 (CA8 1968); Falk, supra, at 85–88.

267. See K. Larson & M. Karpas, Effective Secondary School Discipline 146 (1963); A. Reitman, J. Follman, & E. Ladd, Corporal Punishment in the Public Schools 2–5 (ACLU Report 1972).

public opinion is sharply divided on the practice,[268] and has been for more than a century.[269] Yet we can discern no trend toward its elimination.

At common law a single principle has governed the use of corporal punishment since before the American Revolution: Teachers may impose reasonable but not excessive force to discipline a child.[270] Blackstone catalogued among the "absolute rights of individuals" the right "to security from the corporal insults of menaces, assaults, beating, and wounding," 1 W. Blackstone, Commentaries * 134, but he did not regard it a "corporal insult" for a teacher to inflict "moderate correction" on a child in his care. To the extent that force was "necessary to answer the purposes for which (the teacher) is employed," Blackstone viewed it as "justifiable or lawful." Id., at * 453; 3 id., at * 120. The basic doctrine has not changed. The prevalent rule in this country today privileges such force as a teacher or administrator "reasonably believes to be necessary for (the child's) proper control, training, or education." Restatement (Second) of Torts s 147(2) (1965); see id., s 153(2). To the extent that the force is excessive or unreasonable, the educator in virtually all States is subject to possible civil and criminal liability.[271]

Although the early cases viewed the authority of the teacher as deriving from the parents,[272] the concept of parental delegation has been replaced by the view more consonant with compulsory education laws that the State itself may impose such corporal punishment as is reasonably necessary "for the proper education of the child and for the maintenance of group discipline." 1 F. Harper & F. James, Law of Torts s 3.20, p. 292 (1956).[273] All of the circumstances are to be taken into account in determining whether the punishment is reasonable in a particular case. Among the

268. For samplings of scholarly opinion on the use of corporal punishment in the schools, see F. Reardon & R. Reynolds, Corporal Punishment in Pennsylvania 1–2, 34 (1975); National Education Association, Report of the Task Force on Corporal Punishment (1972); K. James, Corporal Punishment in the Public Schools 8–16 (1963). Opinion surveys taken since 1970 have consistently shown a majority of teachers and of the general public favoring moderate use of corporal punishment in the lower grades. See Reardon & Reynolds, supra, at 2, 23–26; Delaware Department of Public Instruction, Report on the Corporal Punishment Survey 48 (1974); Reitman, Follman, & Ladd, supra, at 34–35; National Education Association, supra, at 7.

269. See Falk, supra, 66–69; cf. Cooper v. McJunkin, 4 Ind. 290 (1853).

270. See 1 F. Harper & F. James, The Law of Torts s 3.20, pp. 288–292 (1956); Proehl, Tort Liability of Teachers, 12 Vand. L. Rev. 723, 734–738 (1959); W. Prosser, The Law of Torts 136–137 (4th ed. 1971).

271. See cases cited n. 28, supra. The criminal codes of many States include provisions explicitly recognizing the teacher's common-law privilege to inflict reasonable corporal punishment. E.g., Ariz. Rev. Stat. Ann. s 13-246(A)(1) (1956); Conn. Gen. Stat. s 53a-18 (1977); Neb. Rev. Stat. s 28-840(2) (1975); N.Y. Penal Law s 35.10 (McKinney 1975 and Supp. 1976); Ore. Rev. Stat. s 161.205(1) (1975).

272. See Proehl, supra, at 726, and n. 13.

273. Today, corporal punishment in school is conditioned on parental approval only in California. Cal. Educ. Code s 49001 (West Supp. 1977). Cf. Morrow v. Wood, 35 Wis. 59 (1874). This Court has held in a summary affirmance that parental approval of corporal punishment is not constitutionally required. Baker v. Owen, 423 U.S. 907, 96 S. Ct. 210, 46 L. Ed. 2d 137 (1975), aff'g 395 F. Supp. 294 (M.D.N.C.).

most important considerations are the seriousness of the offense, the attitude and past behavior of the child, the nature and severity of the punishment, the age and strength of the child, and the availability of less severe but equally effective means of discipline. Id., at 290–291; Restatement (Second) of Torts s 150, Comments c–e, p. 268 (1965).

Of the 23 States that have addressed the problem through legislation, 21 have authorized the moderate use of corporal punishment in public schools.[274] Of these States only a few have elaborated on the common-law test of reasonableness, typically providing for approval or notification of the child's parents,[275] or for infliction of punishment only by the principal[276] or in the presence of an adult witness.[277] Only two States, Massachusetts and New Jersey, have prohibited all corporal punishment in their public schools.[278] Where the legislatures have not acted, the state courts have uniformly preserved the common-law rule permitting teachers to use reasonable force in disciplining children in their charge.[279]

Against this background of historical and contemporary approval of reasonable corporal punishment, we turn to the constitutional questions before us.

III

The Eighth Amendment provides: "Excessive bail shall not be required, nor excessive fines imposed, nor cruel and unusual punishments inflicted." Bail, fines, and punishment traditionally have been associated with the criminal process, and by subjecting the three to parallel limitations the text of the Amendment suggests an intention to limit the power of those entrusted with the criminal-law function of

---

274. Cal. Educ. Code ss 49000–49001 (West Supp. 1977); Del. Code Ann., Tit. 14, s 701 (Supp. 1976); Fla. Stat. Ann. s 232.27 (1977); Ga. Code Ann. ss 32-835, 32-836 (1976); Haw. Rev. Stat. ss 298-16 (1975 Supp.), 703-309(2) (Spec. Pamphlet 1975); Ill. Ann. Stat., c. 122, ss 24-24, 34-84a (1977 Supp.); Ind. Code Ann. s 20-8.1-5-2 (1975); Md. Ann. Code, Art. 77, s 98B (1975) (in specified counties); Mich. Comp. Laws Ann., s 340.756 (1970); Mont. Rev. Codes Ann. s 75-6109 (1971); Nev. Rev. Stat. s 392.465 (1973); N.C. Gen. Stat. s 115-146 (1975); Ohio Rev. Code Ann. s 3319.41 (1972); Okla. Stat. Ann., Tit. 70, s 6-114 (1972); Pa. Stat. Ann., Tit. 24, s 13-1317 (Supp. 1976); S.C. Code s 59-63-260 (1977); S.D. Compiled Laws Ann. s 13-32-2 (1975); Vt. Stat. Ann., Tit. 16, s 1161 (Supp. 1976); Va. Code Ann. s 22-231.1 (1973); W.Va. Code, s 18A-5-1 (1977); Wyo. Stat. s 21.1-64 (Supp. 1975).

275. Cal. Educ. Code s 49001 (West Supp. 1977) (requiring prior parental approval in writing); Fla. Stat. Ann. s 232.27(3) (1977) (requiring a written explanation on request); Mont. Rev. Codes Ann. s 75-6109 (1971) (requiring prior parental notification).

276. Md. Ann. Code, Art. 77, s 98B (1975).

277. Fla. Stat. Ann. s 232.27 (1977); Haw. Rev. Stats. s 298-16 (1975 Supp.); Mont. Rev. Codes Ann. s 75-6109 (1971).

278. Mass. Gen. Laws Ann., c. 71, s 37G (Supp. 1976); N.J. Stat. Ann. s 18A:6-1 (1968).

279. E.g., Suits v. Glover, 260 Ala. 449, 71 So.2d 49 (1954); La Frentz v. Gallagher, 105 Ariz. 255, 462 P.2d 804 (1969); Berry v. Arnold School Dist., 199 Ark. 1118, 137 S.W.2d 256 (1940); Andreozzi v. Rubano, 145 Conn. 280, 141 A.2d 639 (1958); Tinkham v. Kole, 252 Iowa 1303, 110 N.W.2d 258 (1961); Carr v. Wright, 423 S.W.2d 521 (Ky. 1968); Christman v. Hickman, 225 Mo. App. 828, 37 S.W.2d 672 (1931); Simms v. School Dist. No. 1, 13 Or. App. 119, 508 P.2d 236 (1973); Marlar v. Bill, 181 Tenn. 100, 178 S.W.2d 634 (1944); Prendergast v. Masterson, 196 S.W. 246 (Tex. Civ. App.1917). See generally sources cited n. 19, supra.

government. An examination of the history of the Amendment and the decisions of this Court construing the proscription against cruel and unusual punishment confirms that it was designed to protect those convicted of crimes. We adhere to this longstanding limitation and hold that the Eighth Amendment does not apply to the paddling of children as a means of maintaining discipline in public schools.

A

The history of the Eighth Amendment is well known.[280] The text was taken, almost verbatim, from a provision of the Virginia Declaration of Rights of 1776, which in turn derived from the English Bill of Rights of 1689. The English version, adopted after the accession of William and Mary, was intended to curb the excesses of English judges under the reign of James II. Historians have viewed the English provision as a reaction either to the "Bloody Assize," the treason trials conducted by Chief Justice Jeffreys in 1685 after the abortive rebellion of the Duke of Monmouth,[281] or to the perjury prosecution of Titus Oates in the same year.[282] In either case, the exclusive concern of the English version was the conduct of judges in enforcing the criminal law. The original draft introduced in the House of Commons provided: "The requiring excessive bail of persons committed in criminal cases and imposing excessive fines, and illegal punishments, to be prevented."[283]

Although the reference to "criminal cases" was eliminated from the final draft, the preservation of a similar reference in the preamble[284] indicates that the deletion was without substantive significance. Thus, Blackstone treated each of the provision's three prohibitions as bearing only on criminal proceedings and judgments.[285]

The Americans who adopted the language of this part of the English Bill of Rights in framing their own State and Federal Constitutions 100 years later feared the imposition of torture and other cruel punishments not only by judges acting beyond their lawful authority, but also by legislatures engaged in making the laws by which judicial authority would be measured. Weems v. United States, 217 U.S. 349,

---

280. See Gregg v. Georgia, 428 U.S. 153, 168–173, 96 S. Ct. 2909, 2920–2925, 49 L. Ed. 2d 859 (1976) (joint opinion of Stewart, Powell, and Stevens, JJ.) (hereinafter joint opinion); Furman v. Georgia, 408 U.S. 238, 316–328, 92 S. Ct. 2726, 2765–2772, 33 L. Ed. 2d 346 (1972) (Marshall, J., concurring); Granucci, "Nor Cruel and Unusual Punishments Inflicted:" The Original Meaning, 57 Calif. L. Rev. 839 (1969).

281. See I. Brant, The Bill of Rights 155 (1965).

282. See Granucci, supra, at 852–860.

283. Id., at 855.

284. The preamble reads in part:

"WHEREAS the late King James the Second, by the assistance of divers evil counsellors, judges, and ministers employed by him, did endeavor to subvert and extirpate . . . the laws and liberties of this kingdom.

"10. And excessive bail hath been required of persons committed in criminal cases, to elude the benefit of the laws made for the liberty of the subjects.

"11. And excessive fines have been imposed; and illegal and cruel punishments inflicted. . . ." R. Perry & J. Cooper, Sources of Our Liberties 245–246 (1959).

285. 4 W. Blackstone, Commentaries * 297 (bail), * 379 (fines and other punishments).

371–373, 30 S. Ct. 544, 550–551, 54 L. Ed. 793 (1910). Indeed, the principal concern of the American Framers appears to have been with the legislative definition of crimes and punishments. In re Kemmler, 136 U.S. 436, 446–447, 10 S. Ct. 930, 933–934, 34 L. Ed. 519 (1890); Furman v. Georgia, 408 U.S. 238, 263, 92 S. Ct. 2726, 2739, 33 L.Ed.2d 346 (1972) (Brennan, J., concurring). But if the American provision was intended to restrain government more broadly than its English model, the subject to which it was intended to apply the criminal process was the same.

At the time of its ratification, the original Constitution was criticized in the Massachusetts and Virginia Conventions for its failure to provide any protection for persons convicted of crimes.[286] This criticism provided the impetus for inclusion of the Eighth Amendment in the Bill of Rights. When the Eighth Amendment was debated in the First Congress, it was met by the objection that the Cruel and Unusual Punishments Clause might have the effect of outlawing what were then the common criminal punishments of hanging, whipping, and earcropping. 1 Annals of Cong. 754 (1789). The objection was not heeded, "precisely because the legislature would otherwise have had the unfettered power to prescribe punishments for crimes." Furman v. Georgia, supra, at 263, 92 S. Ct., at 2739.

B

In light of this history, it is not surprising to find that every decision of this Court considering whether a punishment is "cruel and unusual" within the meaning of the Eighth and Fourteenth Amendments has dealt with a criminal punishment. See Estelle v. Gamble, 429 U.S. 97, 97 S. Ct. 285, 50 L. Ed. 2d 251 (1976) (incarceration without medical care); Gregg v. Georgia, 428 U.S. 153, 96 S. Ct. 2909, 49 L. Ed. 2d 859 (1976) (execution for murder); Furman v. Georgia, supra (execution for murder); Powell v. Texas, 392 U.S. 514, 88 S. Ct. 2145, 20 L. Ed. 2d 1254 (1968) (plurality opinion) ($20 fine for public drunkenness); Robinson v. California, 370 U.S. 660, 82 S. Ct. 1417, 8 L. Ed. 2d 758 (1962) (incarceration as a criminal for addiction to narcotics); Trop v. Dulles, 356 U.S. 86, 78 S. Ct. 590, 2 L. Ed. 2d 630 (1958) (plurality opinion) (expatriation for desertion); Louisiana ex rel Francis v. Resweber, 329 U.S. 459, 67 S. Ct. 374, 91 L. Ed. 422 (1947) (execution by electrocution after a failed first attempt); Weems v. United States, supra (15 years' imprisonment and other penalties for falsifying an official document); Howard v. Fleming, 191 U.S. 126, 24 S. Ct. 49, 48 L. Ed. 121 (1903) (10 years' imprisonment for conspiracy to defraud); In re Kemmler, supra (execution by electrocution); Wilkerson v. Utah, 99 U.S. 130, 25 L. Ed. 345 (1879)

---

286. Abraham Holmes of Massachusetts complained specifically of the absence of a provision restraining Congress in its power to determine "what kind of punishments shall be inflicted on persons convicted of crimes." 2 J. Elliot, Debates on the Federal Constitution 111 (1876). Patrick Henry was of the same mind:

"What says our (Virginia) bill of rights? 'that excessive bail ought not to be required, nor excessive fines imposed, nor cruel and unusual punishments inflicted.' Are you not, therefore, now calling on those gentlemen who are to compose Congress, to prescribe trials and define punishments without this control? Will they find sentiments there similar to this bill of rights? You let them loose; you do more you depart from the genius of your country. . . ." 3 id., at 447.

(execution by firing squad); Pervear v. Commonwealth, 5 Wall. 475, 18 L. Ed. 608 (1867) (fine and imprisonment at hard labor for bootlegging).

These decisions recognize that the Cruel and Unusual Punishments Clause circumscribes the criminal process in three ways: First, it limits the kinds of punishment that can be imposed on those convicted of crimes, e.g., Estelle v. Gamble, supra; Trop v. Dulles, supra; second, it proscribes punishment grossly disproportionate to the severity of the crime, e.g., Weems v. United States, supra; and third, it imposes substantive limits on what can be made criminal and punished as such, e.g., Robinson v. California, supra. We have recognized the last limitation as one to be applied sparingly. "The primary purpose of (the Cruel and Unusual Punishments Clause) has always been considered, and properly so, to be directed at the method or kind of punishment imposed for the violation of criminal statutes. . . ." Powell v. Texas, supra, at 531–532, 88 S. Ct., at 2154 (plurality opinion).

In the few cases where the Court has had occasion to confront claims that impositions outside the criminal process constituted cruel and unusual punishment, it has had no difficulty finding the Eighth Amendment inapplicable. Thus, in Fong Yue Ting v. United States, 149 U.S. 698, 13 S. Ct. 1016, 37 L. Ed. 905 (1893), the Court held the Eighth Amendment inapplicable to the deportation of aliens on the ground that "deportation is not a punishment for crime." Id., at 730, 13 S. Ct., at 1028; see Mahler v. Eby, 264 U.S. 32, 44 S. Ct. 283, 68 L. Ed. 549 (1924); Bugajewitz v. Adams, 228 U.S. 585, 33 S. Ct. 607, 57 L. Ed. 978 (1913). And in Uphaus v. Wyman, 360 U.S. 72, 79 S. Ct. 1040, 3 L. Ed. 2d 1090 (1959), the Court sustained a judgment of civil contempt, resulting in incarceration pending compliance with a subpoena, against a claim that the judgment imposed cruel and unusual punishment. It was emphasized that the case involved "'essentially a civil remedy designed for the benefit of other parties . . . exercised for centuries to secure compliance with judicial decrees.'" Id., at 81, 79 S. Ct., at 1047, quoting Green v. United States, 356 U.S. 165, 197, 78 S. Ct. 632, 650, 2 L. Ed. 2d 672 (1958) (dissenting opinion).[287]

C

Petitioners acknowledge that the original design of the Cruel and Unusual Punishments Clause was to limit criminal punishments, but urge nonetheless that the prohibition should be extended to ban the paddling of schoolchildren. Observing that the Framers of the Eighth Amendment could not have envisioned our present

287. In urging us to extend the Eighth Amendment to ban school paddlings, petitioners rely on the many decisions in which this Court has held that the prohibition against "cruel and unusual" punishments is not "'fastened to the obsolete but may acquire meaning as public opinion becomes enlightened by a humane justice.'" Gregg v. Georgia, 428 U.S., at 171, 96 S. Ct., at 2924 (joint opinion); see, e.g., Trop v. Dulles, 356 U.S. 86, 100–101, 78 S. Ct. 590, 597–598, 2 L. Ed. 2d 630 (1958) (plurality opinion); Weems v. United States, 217 U.S. 349, 373, 378, 30 S. Ct. 544, 551–553, 54 L. Ed. 793 (1910). This reliance is misplaced. Our Eighth Amendment decisions have referred to "evolving standards of decency," Trop v. Dulles, supra, 356 U.S., at 101, 78 S. Ct., at 598, only in determining whether criminal punishments are "cruel and unusual" under the Amendment.

system of public and compulsory education, with its opportunities for noncriminal punishments, petitioners contend that extension of the prohibition against cruel punishments is necessary lest we afford greater protection to criminals than to schoolchildren. It would be anomalous, they say, if schoolchildren could be beaten without constitutional redress, while hardened criminals suffering the same beatings at the hands of their jailers might have a valid claim under the Eighth Amendment. See Jackson v. Bishop, 404 F.2d 571 (CA8 1968); cf. Estelle v. Gamble, supra. Whatever force this logic may have in other settings,[288] we find it an inadequate basis for wrenching the Eighth Amendment from its historical context and extending it to traditional disciplinary practices in the public schools.

The prisoner and the schoolchild stand in wholly different circumstances, separated by the harsh facts of criminal conviction and incarceration. The prisoner's conviction entitles the State to classify him as a "criminal," and his incarceration deprives him of the freedom "to be with family and friends and to form the other enduring attachments of normal life." Morrissey v. Brewer, 408 U.S. 471, 482, 92 S. Ct. 2593, 2600, 33 L. Ed. 2d 484 (1972); see Meachum v. Fano, 427 U.S. 215, 224–225, 96 S. Ct. 2532, 2538, 49 L. Ed. 2d 451 (1976). Prison brutality, as the Court of Appeals observed in this case, is "part of the total punishment to which the individual is being subjected for his crime and, as such, is a proper subject for Eighth Amendment scrutiny." 525 F.2d, at 915.[289] Even so, the protection afforded by the Eighth Amendment is limited. After incarceration, only the "'unnecessary and wanton infliction of pain,'" Estelle v. Gamble, 429 U.S., at 103, 97 S. Ct., at 291, quoting Gregg v. Georgia, 428 U.S. at 173, 96 S. Ct., at 2925, constitutes cruel and unusual punishment forbidden by the Eighth Amendment.

The schoolchild has little need for the protection of the Eighth Amendment. Though attendance may not always be voluntary, the public school remains an open institution. Except perhaps when very young, the child is not physically restrained from leaving school during school hours; and at the end of the school day, the child is invariably free to return home. Even while at school, the child brings with him the support of family and friends and is rarely apart from teachers and other pupils who may witness and protest any instances of mistreatment.

---

288. Some punishments, though not labeled "criminal" by the State, may be sufficiently analogous to criminal punishments in the circumstances in which they are administered to justify application of the Eighth Amendment. Cf. In re Gault, 387 U.S. 1, 87 S. Ct. 1428, 18 L. Ed. 2d 527 (1967). We have no occasion in this case, for example, to consider whether or under what circumstances persons involuntarily confined in mental or juvenile institutions can claim the protection of the Eighth Amendment.

289. Judge Friendly similarly has observed that the Cruel and Unusual Punishments Clause "can fairly be deemed to be applicable to the manner in which an otherwise constitutional sentence . . . is carried out by an executioner, see Louisiana ex rel. Francis v. Resweber, 329 U.S. 459, 67 S. Ct. 374, 91 L. Ed. 422 (1947), or to cover conditions of confinement which may make intolerable an otherwise constitutional term of imprisonment." Johnson v. Glick, 481 F.2d 1028, 1032 (CA2), cert. denied, 414 U.S. 1033, 94 S. Ct. 462, 38 L. Ed. 2d 32 (1973) (citation omitted).

The openness of the public school and its supervision by the community afford significant safeguards against the kinds of abuses from which the Eighth Amendment protects the prisoner. In virtually every community where corporal punishment is permitted in the schools, these safeguards are reinforced by the legal constraints of the common law. Public school teachers and administrators are privileged at common law to inflict only such corporal punishment as is reasonably necessary for the proper education and discipline of the child; any punishment going beyond the privilege may result in both civil and criminal liability. See Part II, supra. As long as the schools are open to public scrutiny, there is no reason to believe that the common-law constraints will not effectively remedy and deter excesses such as those alleged in this case.[290]

We conclude that when public school teachers or administrators impose disciplinary corporal punishment, the Eighth Amendment is inapplicable. The pertinent constitutional question is whether the imposition is consonant with the requirements of due process.[291]

---

290. Putting history aside as irrelevant, the dissenting opinion of Mr. Justice WHITE argues that a "purposive analysis" should control the reach of the Eighth Amendment. Post, at 1420–1421. There is no support whatever for this approach in the decisions of this Court. Although an imposition must be "punishment" for the Cruel and Unusual Punishments Clause to apply, the Court has never held that all punishments are subject to Eighth Amendment scrutiny. See n. 40, infra. The applicability of the Eighth Amendment always has turned on its original meaning, as demonstrated by its historical derivation. See Gregg v. Georgia, 428 U.S., at 169–173, 96 S. Ct., at 2923–2925 (joint opinion); Furman v. Georgia, 408 U.S., at 315–328, 92 S. Ct., at 2765–2772 (Marshall J., concurring).

The dissenting opinion warns that as a consequence of our decision today, teachers may "cut off a child's ear for being late to class." Post, at 1419. This rhetoric bears no relation to reality or to the issues presented in this case. The laws of virtually every State forbid the excessive physical punishment of schoolchildren. Yet the logic of the dissent would make the judgment of which disciplinary punishments are reasonable and which are excessive a matter of constitutional principle in every case, to be decided ultimately by this Court. The hazards of such a broad reading of the Eighth Amendment are clear. "It is always time to say that this Nation is too large, too complex and composed of too great a diversity of peoples for any one of us to have the wisdom to establish the rules by which local Americans must govern their local affairs. The constitutional rule we are urged to adopt is not merely revolutionary it departs from the ancient faith based on the premise that experience in making local laws by local people themselves is by far the safest guide for a nation like ours to follow." Powell v. Texas, 392 U.S. 514, 547–548, 88 S. Ct. 2145, 2161, 20 L. Ed. 2d 1254 (1968) (opinion of Black, J.).

291. Eighth Amendment scrutiny is appropriate only after the State has complied with the constitutional guarantees traditionally associated with criminal prosecutions. See United States v. Lovett, 328 U.S. 303, 317–318, 66 S. Ct. 1073, 1079–1080, 90 L. Ed. 1252 (1946). Thus, in Trop v. Dulles, 356 U.S. 86, 78 S. Ct. 590, 2 L. Ed. 2d 630 (1958), the plurality appropriately took the view that denationalization was an impermissible punishment for wartime desertion under the Eighth Amendment, because desertion already had been established at a criminal trial. But in Kennedy v. Mendoza-Martinez, 372 U.S. 144, 83 S. Ct. 554, 9 L. Ed. 2d 644 (1963), where the Court considered denationalization as a punishment for evading the draft, the Court refused to reach the Eighth Amendment issue, holding instead that the punishment could be imposed only through the criminal process. Id., at 162–167, 186, 83 S. Ct., at 564–567, 576 and n. 43. As these cases demonstrate, the State does not acquire the power to punish with which the Eighth Amendment is concerned until after it has secured a formal adjudication of guilt in accordance with due process of law. Where the

IV

The Fourteenth Amendment prohibits any state deprivation of life, liberty, or property without due process of law. Application of this prohibition requires the familiar two-stage analysis: We must first ask whether the asserted individual interests are encompassed within the Fourteenth Amendment's protection of "life, liberty or property"; if protected interests are implicated, we then must decide what procedures constitute "due process of law." Morrissey v. Brewer, 408 U.S. at 481, 92 S. Ct., at 2600; Board of Regents v. Roth, 408 U.S. 564, 569–572, 92 S. Ct. 2701, 2705–2707, 33 L. Ed. 2d 548 (1972). See Friendly, Some Kind of Hearing, 123 U. Pa. L. Rev. 1267 (1975). Following that analysis here, we find that corporal punishment in public schools implicates a constitutionally protected liberty interest, but we hold that the traditional common-law remedies are fully adequate to afford due process.

A

"(T)he range of interests protected by procedural due process is not infinite." Board of Regents v. Roth, supra, at 570, 92 S. Ct., at 2705. We have repeatedly rejected "the notion that any grievous loss visited upon a person by the State is sufficient to invoke the procedural protections of the Due Process Clause." Meachum v. Fano, 427 U.S. at 224, 96 S. Ct., at 2538. Due process is required only when a decision of the State implicates an interest within the protection of the Fourteenth Amendment. And "to determine whether due process requirements apply in the first place, we must look not to the 'weight' but to the nature of the interest at stake." Roth, supra, 408 U.S., at 570–571, 92 S. Ct., at 2705.

The Due Process Clause of the Fifth Amendment, later incorporated into the Fourteenth, was intended to give Americans at least the protection against governmental power that they had enjoyed as Englishmen against the power of the Crown. The liberty preserved from deprivation without due process included the right "generally to enjoy those privileges long recognized at common law as essential to the orderly pursuit of happiness by free men." Meyer v. Nebraska, 262 U.S. 390, 399, 43 S. Ct. 625, 626, 67 L. Ed. 1042 (1923); see Dent v. West Virginia, 129 U.S. 114, 123–124, 9 S. Ct. 231, 233–234, 32 L. Ed. 623 (1889). Among the historic liberties so protected was a right to be free from and to obtain judicial relief, for unjustified intrusions on personal security.[292]

State seeks to impose punishment without such an adjudication, the pertinent constitutional guarantee is the Due Process Clause of the Fourteenth Amendment.

292. See 1 W. Blackstone, Commentaries * 134. Under the 39th Article of the Magna Carta, an individual could not be deprived of this right of personal security "except by the legal judgment of his peers or by the law of the land." Perry & Cooper, supra, n. 33, at 17. By subsequent enactments of Parliament during the time of Edward III, the right was protected from deprivation except "by due process of law." See Shattuck, The True Meaning of the Term "Liberty," 4 Harv. L. Rev. 365, 372–373 (1891).

While the contours of this historic liberty interest in the context of our federal system of government have not been defined precisely,[293] they always have been thought to encompass freedom from bodily restraint and punishment. See Rochin v. California, 342 U.S. 165, 72 S. Ct. 205, 96 L. Ed. 183 (1952). It is fundamental that the state cannot hold and physically punish an individual except in accordance with due process of law.

This constitutionally protected liberty interest is at stake in this case. There is, of course a de minimis level of imposition with which the Constitution is not concerned. But at least where school authorities, acting under color of state law, deliberately decide to punish a child for misconduct by restraining the child and inflicting appreciable physical pain, we hold that Fourteenth Amendment liberty interests are implicated.[294]

B

"(T)he question remains what process is due." Morrissey v. Brewer, supra, at 481, 92 S. Ct., at 2600. Were it not for the common-law privilege permitting teachers, to inflict reasonable corporal punishment on children in their care, and the availability of the traditional remedies for abuse, the case for requiring advance procedural safeguards would be strong indeed.[295] But here we deal with a punishment paddling

---

293. See, e.g., Skinner v. Oklahoma, 316 U.S. 535, 541, 62 S. Ct. 1110, 1113, 86 L. Ed. 1655 (1942) (sterilization); Jacobson v. Massachusetts, 197 U.S. 11, 25 S. Ct. 358, 49 L. Ed. 643 (1905) (vaccination); Union Pacific R. Co. v. Botsford, 141 U.S. 250, 251–252, 11 S. Ct. 1000, 1001, 35 L. Ed. 734 (1891) (physical examinations); cf. ICC v. Brimson, 154 U.S. 447, 479, 14 S. Ct. 1125, 1134, 38 L. Ed. 1047 (1894).

The right of personal security is also protected by the Fourth Amendment, which was made applicable to the States through the Fourteenth because its protection was viewed as "implicit in 'the concept of ordered liberty' . . . enshrined in the history and the basic constitutional documents of English-speaking peoples." Wolf v. Colorado, 338 U.S. 25, 27–28, 69 S. Ct. 1359, 1361, 93 L. Ed. 1782 (1949). It has been said of the Fourth Amendment that its "overriding function . . . is to protect personal privacy and dignity against unwarranted intrusion by the State." Schmerber v. California, 384 U.S. 757, 767, 86 S. Ct. 1826, 1834, 16 L. Ed. 2d 908 (1966). But the principal concern of that Amendment's prohibition against unreasonable searches and seizures is with intrusions on privacy in the course of criminal investigations. See Whalen v. Roe, 429 U.S. 589, 604 n. 32, 97 S. Ct. 869, 879, 51 L. Ed. 2d 64 (1977). Petitioners do not contend that the Fourth Amendment applies, according to its terms, to corporal punishment in public school.

294. Unlike Goss v. Lopez, 419 U.S. 565, 95 S. Ct. 729, 42 L. Ed. 2d 725 (1975), this case does not involve the state-created property interest in public education. The purpose of corporal punishment is to correct a child's behavior without interrupting his education. That corporal punishment may, in a rare case, have the unintended effect of temporarily removing a child from school affords no basis for concluding that the practice itself deprives students of property protected by the Fourteenth Amendment.

Nor does this case involve any state-created interest in liberty going beyond the Fourteenth Amendment's protection of freedom from bodily restraint and corporal punishment. Cf. Meachum v. Fano, 427 U.S. 215, 225–227, 96 S. Ct. 2532, 2538–2539, 49 L. Ed. 2d 451 (1976).

295. If the common-law privilege to inflict reasonable corporal punishment in school were inapplicable, it is doubtful whether any procedure short of a trial in a criminal or juvenile court could satisfy the requirements of procedural due process for the imposition of such punishment.

within that tradition, and the question is whether the common-law remedies are adequate to afford due process.

"'(D)ue process,' unlike some legal rules, is not a technical conception with a fixed content unrelated to time, place and circumstances.... Representing a profound attitude of fairness... 'due process' is compounded of history, reason, the past course of decisions, and stout confidence in the strength of the democratic faith which we profess...." Anti-Fascist Comm. v. McGrath, 341 U.S. 123, 162–163, 71 S. Ct. 624, 643, 95 L. Ed. 817 (1951) (Frankfurter, J., concurring).

Whether in this case the common-law remedies for excessive corporal punishment constitute due process of law must turn on an analysis of the competing interests at stake, viewed against the background of "history, reason, (and) the past course of decisions." The analysis requires consideration of three distinct factors: "First, the private interest that will be affected...; second, the risk of an erroneous deprivation of such interest... and the probable value, if any, of additional or substitute procedural safeguards; and, finally, the (state) interest, including the function involved and the fiscal and administrative burdens that the additional or substitute procedural requirement would entail." Mathews v. Eldridge, 424 U.S. 319, 335, 96 S. Ct. 893, 903, 47 L. Ed. 2d 18 (1976). Cf. Arnett v. Kennedy, 416 U.S. 134, 167–168, 94 S. Ct. 1633, 1650–1651, 40 L. Ed. 2d 15 (1974) (Powell, J., concurring).

1

Because it is rooted in history, the child's liberty interest in avoiding corporal punishment while in the care of public school authorities is subject to historical limitations. Under the common law, an invasion of personal security gave rise to a right to recover damages in a subsequent judicial proceeding. 3 W. Blackstone, Commentaries * 120–121. But the right of recovery was qualified by the concept of justification. Thus, there could be no recovery against a teacher who gave only "moderate correction" to a child. Id., at * 120. To the extent that the force used was reasonable in light of its purpose, it was not wrongful, but rather "justifiable or lawful." Ibid.

The concept that reasonable corporal punishment in school is justifiable continues to be recognized in the laws of most States. See Part II, supra. It represents "the balance struck by this country," Poe v. Ullman, 367 U.S. 497, 542, 81 S. Ct. 1752, 1776, 6 L. Ed. 2d 989 (1961) (Harlan, J., dissenting), between the child's interest in personal security and the traditional view that some limited corporal punishment may be necessary in the course of a child's education. Under that longstanding accommodation of interests, there can be no deprivation of substantive rights as long as disciplinary corporal punishment is within the limits of the common-law privilege.

This is not to say that the child's interest in procedural safeguards is insubstantial. The school disciplinary process is not "a totally accurate, unerring process, never mistaken and never unfair...." Goss v. Lopez, 419 U.S. 565, 579–580, 95 S. Ct.

See United States v. Lovett, 328 U.S., at 317–318, 66 S. Ct. 1073, 1079–1080, 90 L. Ed. 1252; cf. Breed v. Jones, 421 U.S. 519, 528–529, 95 S. Ct. 1779, 1785–1786, 44 L. Ed. 2d 346 (1975).

729, 739, 42 L. Ed. 2d 725 (1975). In any deliberate infliction of corporal punishment on a child who is restrained for that purpose, there is some risk that the intrusion on the child's liberty will be unjustified and therefore unlawful. In these circumstances the child has a strong interest in procedural safeguards that minimize the risk of wrongful punishment and provide for the resolution of disputed questions of justification.

We turn now to a consideration of the safeguards that are available under applicable Florida law.

2

Florida has continued to recognize, and indeed has strengthened by statute, the common-law right of a child not to be subjected to excessive corporal punishment in school. Under Florida law the teacher and principal of the school decide in the first instance whether corporal punishment is reasonably necessary under the circumstances in order to discipline a child who has misbehaved. But they must exercise prudence and restraint. For Florida has preserved the traditional judicial proceedings for determining whether the punishment was justified. If the punishment inflicted is later found to have been excessive not reasonably believed at the time to be necessary for the child's discipline or training the school authorities inflicting it may be held liable in damages to the child and, if malice is shown, they may be subject to criminal penalties.[296]

Although students have testified in this case to specific instances of abuse, there is every reason to believe that such mistreatment is an aberration. The uncontradicted evidence suggests that corporal punishment in the Dade County schools was, "(w)ith the exception of a few cases, . . . unremarkable in physical severity." App. 147. Moreover, because paddlings are usually inflicted in response to conduct directly observed by teachers in their presence, the risk that a child will be paddled without cause is typically insignificant. In the ordinary case, a disciplinary paddling neither threatens seriously to violate any substantive rights nor condemns the child "to

296. See supra, at 1404–1405, 1407. The statutory prohibition against "degrading" or unnecessarily "severe" corporal punishment in former s 232.27 has been construed as a statement of the common law principle. See 1937 Op. Fla. Atty. Gen., Biennial Report of the Atty. Gen. 169 (1937–1938); cf. 1957 Op. Fla. Atty. Gen., Biennial Report of the Atty. Gen. 7, 8 (1957–1958). Florida Stat. Ann. s 827.03(3) (1976) makes malicious punishment of a child a felony. Both the District Court, App. 144, and the Court of Appeals, 525 F.2d, at 915, expressed the view that the common-law tort remedy was available to the petitioners in this case. And petitioners conceded in this Court that a teacher who inflicts excessive punishment on a child may be held both civilly and criminally liable under Florida law. Brief for Petitioners 33 n. 11, 34; Tr. of Oral Arg. 17, 52–53. In view of the statutory adoption of the common-law rule, and the unanimity of the parties and the courts below, the doubts expressed in Mr. Justice White's dissenting opinion as to the availability of tort remedies in Florida can only be viewed as chimerical. The dissent makes much of the fact that no Florida court has ever "recognized" a damages remedy for unreasonable corporal punishment. Post, at 1424 n. 11, 1427. But the absence of reported Florida decisions hardly suggests that no remedy is available. Rather, it merely confirms the common-sense judgment that excessive corporal punishment is exceedingly rare in the public schools.

suffer grievous loss of any kind." Anti-Fascist Comm. v. McGrath, 341 U.S., at 168, 71 S. Ct., at 647 (Frankfurter, J., concurring).

In those cases where severe punishment is contemplated, the available civil and criminal sanctions for abuse considered in light of the openness of the school environment afford significant protection against unjustified corporal punishment. See, supra, at 1412. Teachers and school authorities are unlikely to inflict corporal punishment unnecessarily or excessively when a possible consequence of doing so is the institution of civil or criminal proceedings against them.[297]

It still may be argued, of course, that the child's liberty interest would be better protected if the common-law remedies were supplemented by the administrative safeguards of prior notice and a hearing. We have found frequently that some kind of prior hearing is necessary to guard against arbitrary impositions on interests protected by the Fourteenth Amendment. See, e.g., Board of Regents v. Roth, 408 U.S., at 569–570, 92 S. Ct., at 2705; Wolff v. McDonnell, 418 U.S. 539, 557–558, 94 S. Ct. 2963, 2975–2976, 41 L. Ed. 2d 935 (1974); cf. Friendly, 123 U. Pa. L. Rev., at 1275–1277. But where the State has preserved what "has always been the law of the land," United States v. Barnett, 376 U.S. 681, 84 S. Ct. 984, 12 L. Ed. 2d 23 (1964), the case for administrative safeguards is significantly less compelling.[298]

There is a relevant analogy in the criminal law. Although the Fourth Amendment specifically proscribes "seizure" of a person without probable cause, the risk that police will act unreasonably in arresting a suspect is not thought to require an advance determination of the facts. In United States v. Watson, 423 U.S. 411, 96 S. Ct. 820, 46 L. Ed. 2d 598 (1976), we reaffirmed the traditional common-law rule that

297. The low incidence of abuse, and the availability of established judicial remedies in the event of abuse, distinguish this case from Goss v. Lopez, 419 U.S. 565, 95 S. Ct. 729, 42 L. Ed. 2d 725 (1975). The Ohio law struck down in Goss provided for suspensions from public school of up to 10 days without "any written procedure applicable to suspensions." Id., at 567, 95 S. Ct., at 733. Although Ohio law provided generally for administrative review, Ohio Rev. Code Ann. s 2506.01 (Supp. 1973), the Court assumed that the short suspensions would not be stayed pending review, with the result that the review proceeding could serve neither a deterrent nor a remedial function. 419 U.S., at 581 n. 10, 95 S. Ct., at 740. In these circumstances, the Court held the law authorizing suspensions unconstitutional for failure to require "that there be at least an informal give-and-take between student and disciplinarian, preferably prior to the suspension. . . ." Id., at 584, 95 S. Ct., at 741. The subsequent civil and criminal proceedings available in this case may be viewed as affording substantially greater protection to the child than the informal conference mandated by Goss.

298. "(P)rior hearings might well be dispensed with in many circumstances in which the state's conduct, if not adequately justified, would constitute a common-law tort. This would leave the injured plaintiff in precisely the same posture as a common-law plaintiff, and this procedural consequence would be quite harmonious with the substantive view that the fourteenth amendment encompasses the same liberties as those protected by the common law." Monaghan, Of "Liberty" and "Property," 62 Cornell L. Rev. 405, 431 (1977) (footnote omitted). See Bonner v. Coughlin, 517 F.2d 1311, 1319 (CA7 1975), modified en banc, 545 F.2d 565 (1976), cert. pending, No. 76-6204.

We have no occasion in this case, see supra, at 1406, and n. 12, to decide whether or under what circumstances corporal punishment of a public school child may give rise to an independent federal cause of action to vindicate substantive rights under the Due Process Clause.

police officers may make warrantless public arrests on probable cause. Although we observed that an advance determination of probable cause by a magistrate would be desirable, we declined "to transform this judicial preference into a constitutional rule when the judgment of the Nation and Congress has for so long been to authorize warrantless public arrests on probable cause. . . ." Id., at 423, 96 S. Ct., at 828; see id., at 429, 96 S. Ct., at 830 (Powell, J., concurring). Despite the distinct possibility that a police officer may improperly assess the facts and thus unconstitutionally deprive an individual of liberty, we declined to depart from the traditional rule by which the officer's perception is subjected to judicial scrutiny only after the fact.[299] There is no more reason to depart from tradition and require advance procedural safeguards for intrusions on personal security to which the Fourth Amendment does not apply.

3

But even if the need for advance procedural safeguards were clear, the question would remain whether the incremental benefit could justify the cost. Acceptance of petitioners' claims would work a transformation in the law governing corporal punishment in Florida and most other States. Given the impracticability of formulating a rule of procedural due process that varies with the severity of the particular imposition,[300] the prior hearing petitioners seek would have to precede any paddling, however moderate or trivial.

Such a universal constitutional requirement would significantly burden the use of corporal punishment as a disciplinary measure. Hearings even informal hearings require time, personnel, and a diversion of attention from normal school pursuits. School authorities may well choose to abandon corporal punishment rather than incur the burdens of complying with the procedural requirements. Teachers, properly concerned with maintaining authority in the classroom, may well prefer to rely on other disciplinary measures which they may view as less effective rather than confront the possible disruption that prior notice and a hearing may entail.[301] Paradoxically, such an alteration of disciplinary policy is most likely to occur in the ordinary case where the contemplated punishment is well within the common-law privilege.[302]

---

299. See also Terry v. Ohio, 392 U.S. 1, 88 S. Ct. 1868, 20 L. Ed. 2d 889 (1968). The reasonableness of a warrantless public arrest may be subjected to subsequent judicial scrutiny in a civil action against the law enforcement officer or in a suppression hearing to determine whether any evidence seized in the arrest may be used in a criminal trial.

300. "(P)rocedural due process rules are shaped by the risk of error inherent in the truth-finding process as applied to the generality of cases, not the rare exceptions. . . ." Mathews v. Eldridge, 424 U.S. 319, 344, 96 S. Ct. 893, 907, 47 L. Ed. 2d 18 (1976).

301. If a prior hearing, with the inevitable attendant publicity within the school, resulted in rejection of the teacher's recommendation, the consequent impairment of the teacher's ability to maintain discipline in the classroom would not be insubstantial.

302. The effect of interposing prior procedural safeguards may well be to make the punishment more severe by increasing the anxiety of the child. For this reason, the school authorities in Dade

Elimination or curtailment of corporal punishment would be welcomed by many as a societal advance. But when such a policy choice may result from this Court's determination of an asserted right to due process, rather than from the normal processes of community debate and legislative action, the societal costs cannot be dismissed as insubstantial.[303] We are reviewing here a legislative judgment, rooted in history and reaffirmed in the laws of many States, that corporal punishment serves important educational interests. This judgment must be viewed in light of the disciplinary problems common-place in the schools. As noted in Goss v. Lopez, 419 U.S., at 580, 95 S. Ct., at 739: "Events calling for discipline are frequent occurrences and sometimes require immediate, effective action."[304] Assessment of the need for, and the appropriate means of maintaining, school discipline is committed generally to the discretion of school authorities subject to state law. "(T)he Court has repeatedly emphasized the need for affirming the comprehensive authority of the States and of school officials, consistent with fundamental constitutional safeguards, to prescribe and control conduct in the schools." Tinker v. Des Moines School Dist., 393 U.S. 503, 507, 89 S. Ct. 733, 737, 21 L. Ed. 2d 731 (1969).[305]

"At some point the benefit of an additional safeguard to the individual affected ... and to society in terms of increased assurance that the action is just, may be outweighed by the cost." Mathews v. Eldridge, 424 U.S., at 348, 96 S. Ct., at 909. We think that point has been reached in this case. In view of the low incidence of abuse, the openness of our schools, and the common-law safeguards that already exist, the risk of error that may result in violation of a schoolchild's substantive rights can only be regarded as minimal. Imposing additional administrative safeguards as a constitutional requirement might reduce that risk marginally, but would also entail a significant intrusion into an area of primary educational responsibility. We

---

County found it desirable that the punishment be inflicted as soon as possible after the infraction. App. 48–49.

303. "It may be true that procedural regularity in disciplinary proceedings promotes a sense of institutional rapport and open communication, a perception of fair treatment, and provides the offender and his fellow students a showcase of democracy at work. But ... (r)espect for democratic institutions will equally dissipate if they are thought too ineffectual to provide their students an environment of order in which the educational process may go forward. ..." Wilkinson, Goss v. Lopez: The Supreme Court as School Superintendent, 1975 Sup. Ct. Rev. 25, 71–72.

304. The seriousness of the disciplinary problems in the Nation's public schools has been documented in a recent congressional report, Senate Committee on the Judiciary, Subcommittee to Investigate Juvenile Delinquency, Challenge for the Third Century: Education in a Safe Environment Final Report on the Nature and Prevention of School Violence and Vandalism, 95th Cong., 1st Sess. (Comm. Print 1977).

305. The need to maintain order in a trial courtroom raises similar problems. In that context, this Court has recognized the power of the trial judge "to punish summarily and without notice or hearing contemptuous conduct committed in his presence and observed by him." Taylor v. Hayes, 418 U.S. 488, 497, 94 S. Ct. 2697, 2702, 41 L. Ed. 2d 897 (1974), citing Ex parte Terry, 128 U.S. 289, 9 S. Ct. 77, 32 L. Ed. 405 (1888). The punishment so imposed may be as severe as six months in prison. See Codispoti v. Pennsylvania, 418 U.S. 506, 513–515, 94 S. Ct. 2687, 2691–2693, 41 L. Ed. 2d 912 (1974); cf. Muniz v. Hoffman, 422 U.S. 454, 475–476, 95 S. Ct. 2178, 2190, 45 L. Ed. 2d 319 (1975).

conclude that the Due Process Clause does not require notice and a hearing prior to the imposition of corporal punishment in the public schools, as that practice is authorized and limited by the common law.[306]

V

Petitioners cannot prevail on either of the theories before us in this case. The Eighth Amendment's prohibition against cruel and unusual punishment is inapplicable to school paddlings, and the Fourteenth Amendment's requirement of procedural due process is satisfied by Florida's preservation of common-law constraints and remedies. We therefore agree with the Court of Appeals that petitioners' evidence affords no basis for injunctive relief, and that petitioners cannot recover damages on the basis of any Eighth Amendment or procedural due process violation.

Affirmed.

[Case No. 2-2]

School may be liable for monetary damages in cases of student-on-student sexual harassment.

Davis v. Monroe County Board of Education

Supreme Court of the United States
526 U.S. 629 (1999)

Justice O'CONNOR delivered the opinion of the Court.

Petitioner brought suit against the Monroe County Board of Education and other defendants, alleging that her fifth-grade daughter had been the victim of sexual harassment by another student in her class. Among petitioner's claims was a claim for monetary and injunctive relief under Title IX of the Education Amendments of 1972 (Title IX), 86 Stat. 373, as amended, 20 U.S.C. § 1681 et seq. The District Court dismissed petitioner's Title IX claim on the ground that "student-on-student," or peer, harassment provides no ground for a private cause of action under the statute.

---

306. Mr. Justice WHITE's dissenting opinion offers no manageable standards for determining what process is due in any particular case. The dissent apparently would require, as a general rule, only "an informal give-and-take between student and disciplinarian." Post, at 1423. But the dissent would depart from these "minimal procedures" requiring even witnesses, counsel, and cross-examination in cases where the punishment reaches some undefined level of severity. Post, at 1427 n. 18. School authorities are left to guess at the degree of punishment that will require more than an "informal give-and-take" and at the additional process that may be constitutionally required. The impracticability of such an approach is self-evident, and illustrates the hazards of ignoring the traditional solution of the common law.

We agree with the dissent that the Goss procedures will often be, "if anything, less than a fair-minded school principal would impose upon himself." Post, at 1427, quoting Goss, 419 U.S., at 583, 95 S. Ct., at 740. But before this Court invokes the Constitution to impose a procedural requirement, it should be reasonably certain that the effect will be to afford protection appropriate to the constitutional interests at stake. The dissenting opinion's reading of the Constitution suggests no such beneficial result and, indeed, invites a lowering of existing constitutional standards.

The Court of Appeals for the Eleventh Circuit, sitting en banc, affirmed. We consider here whether a private damages action may lie against the school board in cases of student-on-student harassment. We conclude that it may, but only where the funding recipient acts with deliberate indifference to known acts of harassment in its programs or activities. Moreover, we conclude that such an action will lie only for harassment that is so severe, pervasive, and objectively offensive that it effectively bars the victim's access to an educational opportunity or benefit.

I

Petitioner's Title IX claim was dismissed under Federal Rule of Civil Procedure 12(b)(6) for failure to state a claim upon which relief could be granted. Accordingly, in reviewing the legal sufficiency of petitioner's cause of action, "we must assume the truth of the material facts as alleged in the complaint." Summit Health, Ltd. v. Pinhas, 500 U.S. 322, 325, 111 S. Ct. 1842, 114 L. Ed. 2d 366 (1991).

A

Petitioner's minor daughter, LaShonda, was allegedly the victim of a prolonged pattern of sexual harassment by one of her fifth-grade classmates at Hubbard Elementary School, a public school in Monroe County, Georgia. According to petitioner's complaint, the harassment began in December 1992, when the classmate, G.F., attempted to touch LaShonda's breasts and genital area and made vulgar statements such as "'I want to get in bed with you'" and "'I want to feel your boobs.'" Complaint 7. Similar conduct allegedly occurred on or about January 4 and January 20, 1993. Ibid. LaShonda reported each of these incidents to her mother and to her classroom teacher, Diane Fort. Ibid. Petitioner, in turn, also contacted Fort, who allegedly assured petitioner that the school principal, Bill Querry, had been informed of the incidents. Ibid. Petitioner contends that, notwithstanding these reports, no disciplinary action was taken against G.F. Id., ¶ 16.

G.F.'s conduct allegedly continued for many months. In early February, G.F. purportedly placed a door stop in his pants and proceeded to act in a sexually suggestive manner toward LaShonda during physical education class. Id., 8. LaShonda reported G.F.'s behavior to her physical education teacher, Whit Maples. Ibid. Approximately one week later, G.F. again allegedly engaged in harassing behavior, this time while under the supervision of another classroom teacher, Joyce Pippin. Id., 9. Again, LaShonda allegedly reported the incident to the teacher, and again petitioner contacted the teacher to follow up. Ibid.

Petitioner alleges that G.F. once more directed sexually harassing conduct toward LaShonda in physical education class in early March, and that LaShonda reported the incident to both Maples and Pippen. Id., 10. In mid-April 1993, G.F. allegedly rubbed his body against LaShonda in the school hallway in what LaShonda considered a sexually suggestive manner, and LaShonda again reported the matter to Fort. Id., 11.

The string of incidents finally ended in mid-May, when G.F. was charged with, and pleaded guilty to, sexual battery for his misconduct. Id., 14. The complaint alleges that LaShonda had suffered during the months of harassment, however; specifically, her previously high grades allegedly dropped as she became unable to concentrate on her studies, id., 15, and, in April 1993, her father discovered that she had written a suicide note, ibid. The complaint further alleges that, at one point, LaShonda told petitioner that she "'didn't know how much longer she could keep [G.F.] off her.'" Id., 12.

Nor was LaShonda G.F.'s only victim; it is alleged that other girls in the class fell prey to G.F.'s conduct. Id., 16. At one point, in fact, a group composed of LaShonda and other female students tried to speak with Principal Querry about G.F.'s behavior. Id., 10. According to the complaint, however, a teacher denied the students' request with the statement, "'If [Querry] wants you, he'll call you.'" Ibid.

Petitioner alleges that no disciplinary action was taken in response to G.F.'s behavior toward LaShonda. Id., 16. In addition to her conversations with Fort and Pippen, petitioner alleges that she spoke with Principal Querry in mid-May 1993. When petitioner inquired as to what action the school intended to take against G.F., Querry simply stated, "'I guess I'll have to threaten him a little bit harder.'" Id., 12. Yet, petitioner alleges, at no point during the many months of his reported misconduct was G.F. disciplined for harassment. Id., 16 Indeed, Querry allegedly asked petitioner why LaShonda "'was the only one complaining.'" Id., 12.

Nor, according to the complaint, was any effort made to separate G.F. and LaShonda. Id., 16. On the contrary, notwithstanding LaShonda's frequent complaints, only after more than three months of reported harassment was she even permitted to change her classroom seat so that she was no longer seated next to G.F. Id., 13. Moreover, petitioner alleges that, at the time of the events in question, the Monroe County Board of Education (Board) had not instructed its personnel on how to respond to peer sexual harassment and had not established a policy on the issue. Id., 17.

B

On May 4, 1994, petitioner filed suit in the United States District Court for the Middle District of Georgia against the Board, Charles Dumas, the school district's superintendent, and Principal Querry. The complaint alleged that the Board is a recipient of federal funding for purposes of Title IX, that "[t]he persistent sexual advances and harassment by the student G.F. upon [LaShonda] interfered with her ability to attend school and perform her studies and activities," and that "[t]he deliberate indifference by Defendants to the unwelcome sexual advances of a student upon LaShonda created an intimidating, hostile, offensive and abus[ive] school environment in violation of Title IX." Id., 27, 28. The complaint sought compensatory and punitive damages, attorney's fees, and injunctive relief. Id., 32.

The defendants (all respondents here) moved to dismiss petitioner's complaint under Federal Rule of Civil Procedure 12(b)(6) for failure to state a claim upon which relief could be granted, and the District Court granted respondents' motion. See D. v. Monroe Cty. Bd. of Educ., 862 F. Supp. 363, 368 (M.D.Ga. 1994). With regard to petitioner's claims under Title IX, the court dismissed the claims against individual defendants on the ground that only federally funded educational institutions are subject to liability in private causes of action under Title IX. Id., at 367. As for the Board, the court concluded that Title IX provided no basis for liability absent an allegation "that the Board or an employee of the Board had any role in the harassment." Ibid.

Petitioner appealed the District Court's decision dismissing her Title IX claim against the Board, and a panel of the Court of Appeals for the Eleventh Circuit reversed. Davis v. Monroe Cty. Bd. of Educ., 74 F.3d 1186, 1195 (1996). Borrowing from Title VII law, a majority of the panel determined that student-on-student harassment stated a cause of action against the Board under Title IX: "[W]e conclude that as Title VII encompasses a claim for damages due to a sexually hostile working environment created by co-workers and tolerated by the employer, Title IX encompasses a claim for damages due to a sexually hostile educational environment created by a fellow student or students when the supervising authorities knowingly fail to act to eliminate the harassment." Id., at 1193. The Eleventh Circuit panel recognized that petitioner sought to state a claim based on school "officials' failure to take action to stop the offensive acts of those over whom the officials exercised control," ibid., and the court concluded that petitioner had alleged facts sufficient to support a claim for hostile environment sexual harassment on this theory, id., at 1195.

The Eleventh Circuit granted the Board's motion for rehearing en banc, Davis v. Monroe Cty. Bd. of Educ., 91 F.3d 1418 (1996), and affirmed the District Court's decision to dismiss petitioner's Title IX claim against the Board, 120 F.3d 1390 (1997). The en banc court relied, primarily, on the theory that Title IX was passed pursuant to Congress' legislative authority under the Constitution's Spending Clause, U.S. Const., Art. I, § 8, cl. 1, and that the statute therefore must provide potential recipients of federal education funding with "unambiguous notice of the conditions they are assuming when they accept" it. 120 F.3d, at 1399. Title IX, the court reasoned, provides recipients with notice that they must stop their employees from engaging in discriminatory conduct, but the statute fails to provide a recipient with sufficient notice of a duty to prevent student-on-student harassment. Id., at 1401.

Writing in dissent, four judges urged that the statute, by declining to identify the perpetrator of discrimination, encompasses misconduct by third parties: "The identity of the perpetrator is simply irrelevant under the language" of the statute. Id., at 1412 (Barkett, J., dissenting). The plain language, the dissenters reasoned, also provides recipients with sufficient notice that a failure to respond to student-on-student harassment could trigger liability for the district. Id., at 1414.

We granted certiorari, 524 U.S. 980, 119 S. Ct. 29, 141 L. Ed. 2d 789 (1998), in order to resolve a conflict in the Circuits over whether, and under what circumstances, a recipient of federal educational funds can be liable in a private damages action arising from student-on-student sexual harassment, compare 120 F.3d 1390 (C.A.11 1997) (case below), and Rowinsky v. Bryan Independent School Dist., 80 F.3d 1006,

1008 (C.A.5) (holding that private damages action for student-on-student harassment is available under Title IX only where funding recipient responds to these claims differently based on gender of victim), cert. denied, 519 U.S. 861, 117 S. Ct. 165, 136 L. Ed. 2d 108 (1996), with Doe v. University of Illinois, 138 F.3d 653, 668 (C.A.7 1998) (upholding private damages action under Title IX for funding recipient's inadequate response to known student-on-student harassment), vacated and remanded, 526 U.S. 1142, 119 S. Ct. 2016, 143 L. Ed. 2d 1028 (1999), Brzonkala v. Virginia Polytechnic Institute and State University, 132 F.3d 949, 960–961 (C.A.4 1997) (same), vacated and District Court decision affirmed en banc, 169 F.3d 820 (C.A.4 1999) (not addressing merits of Title IX hostile environment sexual harassment claim and directing District Court to hold this claim in abeyance pending this Court's decision in the instant case), and Oona R.S. v. McCaffrey, 143 F.3d 473, 478 (C.A.9 1998) (rejecting qualified immunity claim and concluding that Title IX duty to respond to student-on-student harassment was clearly established by 1992–1993), cert. denied, 526 U.S. 1154, 119 S. Ct. 2039, 143 L. Ed. 2d 1047 (1999). We now reverse.

II

Title IX provides, with certain exceptions not at issue here, that

> "[n]o person in the United States shall, on the basis of sex, be excluded from participation in, be denied the benefits of, or be subjected to discrimination under any education program or activity receiving Federal financial assistance." 20 U.S.C. § 1681(a).

Congress authorized an administrative enforcement scheme for Title IX. Federal departments or agencies with the authority to provide financial assistance are entrusted to promulgate rules, regulations, and orders to enforce the objectives of § 1681, see § 1682, and these departments or agencies may rely on "any . . . means authorized by law," including the termination of funding, ibid., to give effect to the statute's restrictions.

There is no dispute here that the Board is a recipient of federal education funding for Title IX purposes. 74 F.3d, at 1189. Nor do respondents support an argument that student-on-student harassment cannot rise to the level of "discrimination" for purposes of Title IX. Rather, at issue here is the question whether a recipient of federal education funding may be liable for damages under Title IX under any circumstances for discrimination in the form of student-on-student sexual harassment.

A

Petitioner urges that Title IX's plain language compels the conclusion that the statute is intended to bar recipients of federal funding from permitting this form of discrimination in their programs or activities. She emphasizes that the statute prohibits a student from being "subjected to discrimination under any education program or activity receiving Federal financial assistance." 20 U.S.C. § 1681(a) (emphasis added). It is Title IX's "unmistakable focus on the benefited class," Cannon v. University of Chicago, 441 U.S. 677, 691, 99 S. Ct. 1946, 60 L. Ed. 2d 560 (1979), rather than the perpetrator, that, in petitioner's view, compels the conclusion that the statute works to protect students from the discriminatory misconduct of their peers.

Here, however, we are asked to do more than define the scope of the behavior that Title IX proscribes. We must determine whether a district's failure to respond to student-on-student harassment in its schools can support a private suit for money damages. See Gebser v. Lago Vista Independent School Dist., 524 U.S. 274, 283, 118 S. Ct. 1989, 141 L. Ed. 2d 277 (1998) ("In this case, . . . petitioners seek not just to establish a Title IX violation but to recover damages . . ."). This Court has indeed recognized an implied private right of action under Title IX, see Cannon v. University of Chicago, supra, and we have held that money damages are available in such suits, Franklin v. Gwinnett County Public Schools, 503 U.S. 60, 112 S. Ct. 1028, 117 L. Ed. 2d 208 (1992). Because we have repeatedly treated Title IX as legislation enacted pursuant to Congress' authority under the Spending Clause, however, see, e.g., Gebser v. Lago Vista Independent School Dist., supra, at 287, 118 S. Ct. 1989 (Title IX); Franklin v. Gwinnett County Public Schools, supra, at 74–75, and n. 8, 112 S. Ct. 1028 (Title IX); see also Guardians Assn. v. Civil Serv. Comm'n of New York City, 463 U.S. 582, 598–599, 103 S. Ct. 3221, 77 L. Ed. 2d 866 (1983) (opinion of White, J.) (Title VI), private damages actions are available only where recipients of federal funding had adequate notice that they could be liable for the conduct at issue. When Congress acts pursuant to its spending power, it generates legislation "much in the nature of a contract: in return for federal funds, the States agree to comply with federally imposed conditions." Pennhurst State School and Hospital v. Halderman, 451 U.S. 1, 17, 101 S. Ct. 1531, 67 L. Ed. 2d 694 (1981). In interpreting language in spending legislation, we thus "insis[t] that Congress speak with a clear voice," recognizing that "[t]here can, of course, be no knowing acceptance [of the terms of the putative contract] if a State is unaware of the conditions [imposed by the legislation] or is unable to ascertain what is expected of it." Ibid.; see also id., at 24–25, 101 S. Ct. 1531.

Invoking Pennhurst, respondents urge that Title IX provides no notice that recipients of federal educational funds could be liable in damages for harm arising from student-on-student harassment. Respondents contend, specifically, that the statute only proscribes misconduct by grant recipients, not third parties. Respondents argue, moreover, that it would be contrary to the very purpose of Spending Clause legislation to impose liability on a funding recipient for the misconduct of third parties, over whom recipients exercise little control. See also Rowinsky v. Bryan Independent School Dist., 80 F.3d, at 1013.

We agree with respondents that a recipient of federal funds may be liable in damages under Title IX only for its own misconduct. The recipient itself must "exclud[e] [persons] from participation in, . . . den[y] [persons] the benefits of, or . . . subjec[t] [persons] to discrimination under" its "program[s] or activit[ies]" in order to be liable under Title IX. The Government's enforcement power may only be exercised against the funding recipient, see § 1682, and we have not extended damages liability under Title IX to parties outside the scope of this power. See National Collegiate Athletic Assn. v. Smith, 525 U.S. 459, 467, n. 5, 119 S. Ct. 924, 929, n. 5, 142 L. Ed. 2d

929 (1999) (rejecting suggestion "that the private right of action available under . . . § 1681(a) is potentially broader than the Government's enforcement authority"); cf. Gebser v. Lago Vista Independent School Dist., supra, at 289, 118 S. Ct. 1989 ("It would be unsound, we think, for a statute's express system of enforcement to require notice to the recipient and an opportunity to come into voluntary compliance while a judicially implied system of enforcement permits substantial liability without regard to the recipient's knowledge or its corrective actions upon receiving notice").

We disagree with respondents' assertion, however, that petitioner seeks to hold the Board liable for G. F.'s actions instead of its own. Here, petitioner attempts to hold the Board liable for its own decision to remain idle in the face of known student-on-student harassment in its schools. In Gebser, we concluded that a recipient of federal education funds may be liable in damages under Title IX where it is deliberately indifferent to known acts of sexual harassment by a teacher. In that case, a teacher had entered into a sexual relationship with an eighth-grade student, and the student sought damages under Title IX for the teacher's misconduct. We recognized that the scope of liability in private damages actions under Title IX is circumscribed by Pennhurst's requirement that funding recipients have notice of their potential liability. 524 U.S., at 287–288, 118 S. Ct. 1989. Invoking Pennhurst, Guardians Assn., and Franklin, in Gebser we once again required "that 'the receiving entity of federal funds [have] notice that it will be liable for a monetary award'" before subjecting it to damages liability. 524 U.S., at 287, 118 S. Ct. 1989 (quoting Franklin v. Gwinnett County Public Schools, 503 U.S., at 74, 112 S. Ct. 1028). We also recognized, however, that this limitation on private damages actions is not a bar to liability where a funding recipient intentionally violates the statute. Id., at 74–75, 112 S. Ct. 1028; see also Guardians Assn. v. Civil Serv. Comm'n of New York City, supra, at 597–598, 103 S. Ct. 3221 (opinion of White, J.) (same with respect to Title VI). In particular, we concluded that Pennhurst does not bar a private damages action under Title IX where the funding recipient engages in intentional conduct that violates the clear terms of the statute.

Accordingly, we rejected the use of agency principles to impute liability to the district for the misconduct of its teachers. 524 U.S., at 283, 118 S. Ct. 1989. Likewise, we declined the invitation to impose liability under what amounted to a negligence standard — holding the district liable for its failure to react to teacher-student harassment of which it knew or should have known. Ibid. Rather, we concluded that the district could be liable for damages only where the district itself intentionally acted in clear violation of Title IX by remaining deliberately indifferent to acts of teacher-student harassment of which it had actual knowledge. Id., at 290, 118 S. Ct. 1989. Contrary to the dissent's suggestion, the misconduct of the teacher in Gebser was not "treated as the grant recipient's actions." Post, at 1680 (opinion of KENNEDY, J.). Liability arose, rather, from "an official decision by the recipient not to remedy the violation." Gebser v. Lago Vista Independent School Dist., supra, at 290, 118 S. Ct. 1989. By employing the "deliberate indifference" theory already used to establish municipal liability under Rev. Stat. §1979, 42 U.S.C. §1983, see Gebser v. Lago Vista Independent School Dist., supra, at 290–291, 118 S. Ct. 1989 (citing Board of Comm'rs of Bryan Cty. v. Brown, 520 U.S. 397, 117 S. Ct. 1382, 137 L. Ed. 2d 626 (1997), and City of Canton v. Harris, 489 U.S. 378, 109 S. Ct. 1197, 103 L. Ed. 2d 412 (1989)), we concluded in Gebser that recipients could be liable in damages only where their own deliberate indifference effectively "cause[d]" the discrimination, 524 U.S., at 291, 118 S. Ct. 1989; see also Canton v. Harris, supra, at 385, 109 S. Ct. 1197 (recognizing that a municipality will be liable under §1983 only if "the municipality itself causes the constitutional violation at issue" (emphasis in original)). The high standard imposed in Gebser sought to eliminate any "risk that the recipient would be liable in damages not for its own official decision but instead for its employees' independent actions." 524 U.S., at 290–291, 118 S. Ct. 1989.

Gebser thus established that a recipient intentionally violates Title IX, and is subject to a private damages action, where the recipient is deliberately indifferent to known acts of teacher-student discrimination. Indeed, whether viewed as "discrimination" or "subject[ing]" students to discrimination, Title IX "[u]nquestionably . . . placed on [the Board] the duty not" to permit teacher-student harassment in its schools, Franklin v. Gwinnett County Public Schools, supra, at 75, 112 S. Ct. 1028, and recipients violate Title IX's plain terms when they remain deliberately indifferent to this form of misconduct.

We consider here whether the misconduct identified in Gebser—deliberate indifference to known acts of harassment—amounts to an intentional violation of Title IX, capable of supporting a private damages action, when the harasser is a student rather than a teacher. We conclude that, in certain limited circumstances, it does. As an initial matter, in Gebser we expressly rejected the use of agency principles in the Title IX context, noting the textual differences between Title IX and Title VII. 524 U.S., at 283, 118 S. Ct. 1989; cf. Faragher v. City of Boca Raton, 524 U.S. 775, 791–792, 118 S. Ct. 2275, 141 L. Ed. 2d 662 (1998) (invoking agency principles on ground that definition of "employer" in Title VII includes agents of employer); Meritor Savings Bank, FSB v. Vinson, 477 U.S. 57, 72, 106 S. Ct. 2399, 91 L. Ed. 2d 49 (1986) (same). Additionally, the regulatory scheme surrounding Title IX has long provided funding recipients with notice that they may be liable for their failure to respond to the discriminatory acts of certain nonagents. The Department of Education requires recipients to monitor third parties for discrimination in specified circumstances and to refrain from particular forms of interaction with outside entities that are known to discriminate. See, e.g., 34 CFR §§106.31(b)(6), 106.31(d), 106.37(a)(2), 106.38(a), 106.51(a)(3) (1998).

The common law, too, has put schools on notice that they may be held responsible under state law for their failure to protect students from the tortious acts of third parties. See Restatement (Second) of Torts §320, and Comment a (1965). In fact, state courts routinely uphold claims alleging that schools have been negligent in failing to protect their students from the torts of their peers. See, e.g., Rupp v. Bryant, 417 So.2d 658, 666–667 (Fla. 1982); Brahatcek v. Millard School Dist., 202

Neb. 86, 99–100, 273 N.W.2d 680, 688 (1979); McLeod v. Grant County School Dist. No. 128, 42 Wash.2d 316, 320, 255 P.2d 360, 362–363 (1953).

This is not to say that the identity of the harasser is irrelevant. On the contrary, both the "deliberate indifference" standard and the language of Title IX narrowly circumscribe the set of parties whose known acts of sexual harassment can trigger some duty to respond on the part of funding recipients. Deliberate indifference makes sense as a theory of direct liability under Title IX only where the funding recipient has some control over the alleged harassment. A recipient cannot be directly liable for its indifference where it lacks the authority to take remedial action.

The language of Title IX itself—particularly when viewed in conjunction with the requirement that the recipient have notice of Title IX's prohibitions to be liable for damages—also cabins the range of misconduct that the statute proscribes. The statute's plain language confines the scope of prohibited conduct based on the recipient's degree of control over the harasser and the environment in which the harassment occurs. If a funding recipient does not engage in harassment directly, it may not be liable for damages unless its deliberate indifference "subject[s]" its students to harassment. That is, the deliberate indifference must, at a minimum, "cause [students] to undergo" harassment or "make them liable or vulnerable" to it. Random House Dictionary of the English Language 1415 (1966) (defining "subject" as "to cause to undergo the action of something specified; expose" or "to make liable or vulnerable; lay open; expose"); Webster's Third New International Dictionary 2275 (1961) (defining "subject" as "to cause to undergo or submit to: make submit to a particular action or effect: EXPOSE"). Moreover, because the harassment must occur "under" "the operations of" a funding recipient, see 20 U.S.C. § 1681(a); § 1687 (defining "program or activity"), the harassment must take place in a context subject to the school district's control, Webster's Third New International Dictionary, supra, at 2487 (defining "under" as "in or into a condition of subjection, regulation, or subordination"; "subject to the guidance and instruction of"); Random House Dictionary of the English Language, supra, at 1543 (defining "under" as "subject to the authority, direction, or supervision of").

These factors combine to limit a recipient's damages liability to circumstances wherein the recipient exercises substantial control over both the harasser and the context in which the known harassment occurs. Only then can the recipient be said to "expose" its students to harassment or "cause" them to undergo it "under" the recipient's programs. We agree with the dissent that these conditions are satisfied most easily and most obviously when the offender is an agent of the recipient. Post, at 1680. We rejected the use of agency analysis in Gebser, however, and we disagree that the term "under" somehow imports an agency requirement into Title IX. See post, at 1679–1680. As noted above, the theory in Gebser was that the recipient was directly liable for its deliberate indifference to discrimination. See supra, at 1671. Liability in that case did not arise because the "teacher's actions [were] treated" as those of the funding recipient, post, at 1680; the district was directly liable for its own failure to act. The terms "subjec[t]" and "under" impose limits, but nothing about these terms requires the use of agency principles.

Where, as here, the misconduct occurs during school hours and on school grounds — the bulk of G.F.'s misconduct, in fact, took place in the classroom — the misconduct is taking place "under" an "operation" of the funding recipient. See Doe v. University of Illinois, 138 F.3d, at 661 (finding liability where school fails to respond properly to "student-on-student sexual harassment that takes place while the students are involved in school activities or otherwise under the supervision of school employees"). In these circumstances, the recipient retains substantial control over the context in which the harassment occurs. More importantly, however, in this setting the Board exercises significant control over the harasser. We have observed, for example, "that the nature of [the State's] power [over public schoolchildren] is custodial and tutelary, permitting a degree of supervision and control that could not be exercised over free adults." Vernonia School Dist. 47J v. Acton, 515 U.S. 646, 655, 115 S. Ct. 2386, 132 L. Ed. 2d 564 (1995). On more than one occasion, this Court has recognized the importance of school officials' "comprehensive authority . . . , consistent with fundamental constitutional safeguards, to prescribe and control conduct in the schools." Tinker v. Des Moines Independent Community School Dist., 393 U.S. 503, 507, 89 S. Ct. 733, 21 L. Ed. 2d 731 (1969); see also New Jersey v. T.L.O., 469 U.S. 325, 342, n. 9, 105 S. Ct. 733, 83 L. Ed. 2d 720 (1985) ("The maintenance of discipline in the schools requires not only that students be restrained from assaulting one another, abusing drugs and alcohol, and committing other crimes, but also that students conform themselves to the standards of conduct prescribed by school authorities"); 74 F.3d, at 1193 ("The ability to control and influence behavior exists to an even greater extent in the classroom than in the workplace . . ."). The common law, too, recognizes the school's disciplinary authority. See Restatement (Second) of Torts § 152 (1965). We thus conclude that recipients of federal funding may be liable for "subject[ing]" their students to discrimination where the recipient is deliberately indifferent to known acts of student-on-student sexual harassment and the harasser is under the school's disciplinary authority.

At the time of the events in question here, in fact, school attorneys and administrators were being told that student-on-student harassment could trigger liability under Title IX. In March 1993, even as the events alleged in petitioner's complaint were unfolding, the National School Boards Association issued a publication, for use by "school attorneys and administrators in understanding the law regarding sexual harassment of employees and students," which observed that districts could be liable under Title IX for their failure to respond to student-on-student harassment. See National School Boards Association Council of School Attorneys, Sexual Harassment in the Schools: Preventing and Defending Against Claims v, 45 (rev. ed.). Drawing on Equal Employment Opportunity Commission guidelines interpreting Title VII, the publication informed districts that, "if [a] school district has constructive notice of severe and repeated acts of sexual harassment by fellow students, that may form the basis of a [T]itle IX claim." Ibid. The publication even correctly anticipated a form of Gebser's actual notice requirement: "It is unlikely that courts will hold a school district liable for sexual harassment by students against students in the absence of actual knowledge or notice to district employees." Sexual Harassment in the Schools, supra, at 45. Although we do not rely on this publication as an "indicium of congressional notice," see post, at 1685, we do find support for our reading of Title IX in the fact that school attorneys have rendered an analogous interpretation.

Likewise, although they were promulgated too late to contribute to the Board's notice of proscribed misconduct, the Department of Education's Office for Civil Rights (OCR) has recently adopted policy guidelines providing that student-on-student harassment falls within the scope of Title IX's proscriptions. See Department of Education, Office of Civil Rights, Sexual Harassment Guidance: Harassment of Students by School Employees, Other Students, or Third Parties, 62 Fed. Reg. 12034, 12039–12040 (1997) (OCR Title IX Guidelines); see also Department of Education, Racial Incidents and Harassment Against Students at Educational Institutions, 59 Fed. Reg. 11448, 11449 (1994).

We stress that our conclusion here — that recipients may be liable for their deliberate indifference to known acts of peer sexual harassment — does not mean that recipients can avoid liability only by purging their schools of actionable peer harassment or that administrators must engage in particular disciplinary action. We thus disagree with respondents' contention that, if Title IX provides a cause of action for student-on-student harassment, "nothing short of expulsion of every student accused of misconduct involving sexual overtones would protect school systems from liability or damages." See Brief for Respondents 16; see also 120 F.3d, at 1402 (Tjoflat, J.) ("[A] school must immediately suspend or expel a student accused of sexual harassment"). Likewise, the dissent erroneously imagines that victims of peer harassment now have a Title IX right to make particular remedial demands. See post, at 1691 (contemplating that victim could demand new desk assignment). In fact, as we have previously noted, courts should refrain from second-guessing the disciplinary decisions made by school administrators. New Jersey v. T.L.O., supra, at 342–343, n. 9, 105 S. Ct. 733.

School administrators will continue to enjoy the flexibility they require so long as funding recipients are deemed "deliberately indifferent" to acts of student-on-student harassment only where the recipient's response to the harassment or lack thereof is clearly unreasonable in light of the known circumstances. The dissent consistently mischaracterizes this standard to require funding recipients to "remedy" peer harassment, post at 1678, 1680, 1683, 1690, and to "ensur[e] that . . . students conform their conduct to" certain rules, post at 1682. Title IX imposes no such requirements. On the contrary, the recipient must merely respond to known peer harassment in a manner that is not clearly unreasonable. This is not a mere "reasonableness" standard, as the dissent assumes. See post, at 1688. In an appropriate case, there is no reason why courts, on a motion to dismiss, for summary judgment, or for a directed verdict, could not identify a response as not "clearly unreasonable" as a matter of law.

Like the dissent, see post, at 1681–1683, we acknowledge that school administrators shoulder substantial burdens as a result of legal constraints on their disciplinary authority. To the extent that these restrictions arise from federal statutes, Congress can review these burdens with attention to the difficult position in which such legislation may place our Nation's schools. We believe, however, that the standard set out here is sufficiently flexible to account both for the level of disciplinary authority available to the school and for the potential liability arising from certain forms of disciplinary action. A university might not, for example, be expected to exercise the same degree of control over its students that a grade school would enjoy, see post, at 1682–1683, and it would be entirely reasonable for a school to refrain from a form of disciplinary action that would expose it to constitutional or statutory claims.

While it remains to be seen whether petitioner can show that the Board's response to reports of G.F.'s misconduct was clearly unreasonable in light of the known circumstances, petitioner may be able to show that the Board "subject[ed]" LaShonda to discrimination by failing to respond in any way over a period of five months to complaints of G.F.'s in-school misconduct from LaShonda and other female students.

B

The requirement that recipients receive adequate notice of Title IX's proscriptions also bears on the proper definition of "discrimination" in the context of a private damages action. We have elsewhere concluded that sexual harassment is a form of discrimination for Title IX purposes and that Title IX proscribes harassment with sufficient clarity to satisfy Pennhurst's notice requirement and serve as a basis for a damages action. See Gebser v. Lago Vista Independent School Dist., 524 U.S., at 281, 118 S. Ct. 1989; Franklin v. Gwinnett County Public Schools, 503 U.S., at 74–75, 112 S. Ct. 1028. Having previously determined that "sexual harassment" is "discrimination" in the school context under Title IX, we are constrained to conclude that student-on-student sexual harassment, if sufficiently severe, can likewise rise to the level of discrimination actionable under the statute. See Bennett v. Kentucky Dept. of Ed., 470 U.S. 656, 665–666, 105 S. Ct. 1544, 84 L. Ed. 2d 590 (1985) (rejecting claim of insufficient notice under Pennhurst where statute made clear that there were some conditions placed on receipt of federal funds, and noting that Congress need not "specifically identif[y] and proscrib[e]" each condition in the legislation). The statute's other prohibitions, moreover, help give content to the term "discrimination" in this context. Students are not only protected from discrimination, but also specifically shielded from being "excluded from participation in" or "denied the benefits of" any "education program or activity receiving Federal financial assistance." § 1681(a). The statute makes clear that, whatever else it prohibits, students must not be denied access to educational benefits and opportunities on the basis of gender. We thus conclude that funding recipients are properly held liable in damages only where they are deliberately indifferent to sexual harassment, of which they have actual knowledge, that is so severe, pervasive, and objectively offensive that it can be said to deprive the victims of access to the educational opportunities or benefits provided by the school.

The most obvious example of student-on-student sexual harassment capable of triggering a damages claim would thus involve the overt, physical deprivation of access to school resources. Consider, for example, a case in which male students physically threaten their female peers every day, successfully preventing the female students from using a particular school resource—an athletic field or a computer lab, for instance. District administrators are well aware of the daily ritual, yet they deliberately ignore requests for aid from the female students wishing to use the resource. The district's knowing refusal to take any action in response to such behavior would fly in the face of Title IX's core principles, and such deliberate indifference may appropriately be subject to claims for monetary damages. It is not necessary, however, to show physical exclusion to demonstrate that students have been deprived by the actions of another student or students of an educational opportunity on the basis of sex. Rather, a plaintiff must establish sexual harassment of students that is so severe, pervasive, and objectively offensive, and that so undermines and detracts from the victims' educational experience, that the victim-students are effectively denied equal access to an institution's resources and opportunities. Cf. Meritor Savings Bank, FSB v. Vinson, 477 U.S., at 67, 106 S. Ct. 2399.

Whether gender-oriented conduct rises to the level of actionable "harassment" thus "depends on a constellation of surrounding circumstances, expectations, and relationships," Oncale v. Sundowner Offshore Services, Inc., 523 U.S. 75, 82, 118 S. Ct. 998, 140 L. Ed. 2d 201 (1998), including, but not limited to, the ages of the harasser and the victim and the number of individuals involved, see OCR Title IX Guidelines 12041–12042. Courts, moreover, must bear in mind that schools are unlike the adult workplace and that children may regularly interact in a manner that would be unacceptable among adults. See, e.g., Brief for National School Boards Association et al. as Amici Curiae 11 (describing "dizzying array of immature . . . behaviors by students"). Indeed, at least early on, students are still learning how to interact appropriately with their peers. It is thus understandable that, in the school setting, students often engage in insults, banter, teasing, shoving, pushing, and gender-specific conduct that is upsetting to the students subjected to it. Damages are not available for simple acts of teasing and name-calling among school children, however, even where these comments target differences in gender. Rather, in the context of student-on-student harassment, damages are available only where the behavior is so severe, pervasive, and objectively offensive that it denies its victims the equal access to education that Title IX is designed to protect.

The dissent fails to appreciate these very real limitations on a funding recipient's liability under Title IX. It is not enough to show, as the dissent would read this opinion to provide, that a student has been "teased," post, at 1688, or "called . . . offensive names," post, at 1689. Comparisons to an "overweight child who skips gym class because the other children tease her about her size," the student who "refuses to wear glasses to avoid the taunts of 'four-eyes,'" and "the child who refuses to go to school because the school bully calls him a 'scaredy-cat' at recess," post, at 1688, are inapposite and misleading. Nor do we contemplate, much less hold, that a mere "decline in grades is enough to survive" a motion to dismiss. Ibid. The dropoff in LaShonda's grades provides necessary evidence of a potential link between her education and G.F.'s misconduct, but petitioner's ability to state a cognizable claim here depends equally on the alleged persistence and severity of G.F.'s actions, not to mention the Board's alleged knowledge and deliberate indifference. We trust that the dissent's characterization of our opinion will not mislead courts to impose more sweeping liability than we read Title IX to require.

Moreover, the provision that the discrimination occur "under any education program or activity" suggests that the behavior be serious enough to have the systemic effect of denying the victim equal access to an educational program or activity. Although, in theory, a single instance of sufficiently severe one-on-one peer harassment could be said to have such an effect, we think it unlikely that Congress would have thought such behavior sufficient to rise to this level in light of the inevitability of student misconduct and the amount of litigation that would be invited by entertaining claims of official indifference to a single instance of one-on-one peer harassment. By limiting private damages actions to cases having a systemic effect on educational programs or activities, we reconcile the general principle that Title IX prohibits official indifference to known peer sexual harassment with the practical realities of responding to student behavior, realities that Congress could not have meant to be ignored. Even the dissent suggests that Title IX liability may arise when a funding recipient remains indifferent to severe, gender-based mistreatment played out on a "widespread level" among students. Post, at 1690.

The fact that it was a teacher who engaged in harassment in Franklin and Gebser is relevant. The relationship between the harasser and the victim necessarily affects the extent to which the misconduct can be said to breach Title IX's guarantee of equal access to educational benefits and to have a systemic effect on a program or activity. Peer harassment, in particular, is less likely to satisfy these requirements than is teacher-student harassment.

C

Applying this standard to the facts at issue here, we conclude that the Eleventh Circuit erred in dismissing petitioner's complaint. Petitioner alleges that her daughter was the victim of repeated acts of sexual harassment by G.F. over a 5-month period, and there are allegations in support of the conclusion that G.F.'s misconduct was severe, pervasive, and objectively offensive. The harassment was not only verbal; it included numerous acts of objectively offensive touching, and, indeed, G.F. ultimately pleaded guilty to criminal sexual misconduct. Moreover, the complaint alleges that there were multiple victims who were sufficiently disturbed by G.F.'s misconduct to seek an audience with the school principal. Further, petitioner contends that the harassment had a concrete, negative effect on her daughter's ability to receive an education. The complaint also suggests that petitioner may be able to show both actual knowledge and deliberate indifference on the part of the

Board, which made no effort whatsoever either to investigate or to put an end to the harassment.

On this complaint, we cannot say "beyond doubt that [petitioner] can prove no set of facts in support of [her] claim which would entitle [her] to relief." Conley v. Gibson, 355 U.S. 41, 45–46, 78 S. Ct. 99, 2 L. Ed. 2d 80 (1957). See also Scheuer v. Rhodes, 416 U.S. 232, 236, 94 S. Ct. 1683, 40 L. Ed. 2d 90 (1974) ("The issue is not whether a plaintiff will ultimately prevail but whether the claimant is entitled to offer evidence to support the claims"). Accordingly, the judgment of the United States Court of Appeals for the Eleventh Circuit is reversed, and the case is remanded for further proceedings consistent with this opinion.

It is so ordered.

[Case No. 2-3]

Students inadequately educated may not bring tort claims against the school district.

Peter W. v. San Francisco Unified Sch. Dist.[307]

Court of Appeal of California, First Appellate District, Division 4
60 Cal. App. 3d 814 (1976)

RATTIGAN, J.

The novel — and troublesome — question on this appeal is whether a person who claims to have been inadequately educated, while a student in a public school system, may state a cause of action in tort against the public authorities who operate and administer the system. We hold that he may not.

The appeal reaches us upon plaintiff's first amended complaint (hereinafter the "complaint"), which purports to state seven causes of action. Respondents (San Francisco Unified School District, its superintendent of schools, its governing board, and the individual board members) appeared to it by filing general demurrers to all seven counts; we hereinafter refer to them as "defendants." The trial court sustained their demurrers with 20 days' leave to amend. When plaintiff failed to amend within that period, the court entered a judgment dismissing his action.

On plaintiff's appeal, which is from the judgment, the question is whether a cause of action is stated against defendants in any of the complaint's seven counts. (Glaire v. La Lanne-Paris Health Spa, Inc. (1974) 12 Cal. 3d 915, 918 [117 Cal. Rptr. 541, 528 P.2d 357].) (*1*) We must treat the demurrers as having provisionally admitted all material facts properly pleaded in it (ibid.), but not such allegations — which appear throughout it — as amount to "'contentions, deductions, or conclusions of fact or law.'" (Venuto v. Owens-Corning Fiberglas Corp. (1971) 22 Cal. App. 3d 116, 122 [99 Cal. Rptr. 350].) We limit our summary of its contents accordingly.

---

307. This case was previously titled *Doe v. San Francisco Unified School District.*

The First Cause of Action

The first count, which is the prototype of the others (each of which incorporates all of its allegations by reference), sounds in negligence. Its opening allegations may be summarized, and quoted in part, as follows:

Defendant district is "a unified school district . . . existing under the laws of the State of California" and functioning under the direction of its governing board and superintendent of schools. Plaintiff is an 18-year-old male who was recently graduated from a high school operated by the district. He had theretofore been enrolled in its schools, and had attended them, for a period of 12 years. Allegations explicitly charging negligence next appear, as follows:

"XI. Defendant school district, its agents and employees, negligently and carelessly failed to provide plaintiff with adequate instruction, guidance, counseling and/or supervision in basic academic skills such as reading and writing, although said school district had the authority, responsibility and ability . . . [to do so]. . . . Defendant school district, its agents and employees, negligently failed to use reasonable care in the discharge of its duties to provide plaintiff with adequate instruction . . . in basic academic skills[,] and failed to exercise that degree of professional skill required of an ordinary prudent educator under the same circumstances[,] as exemplified, but not limited to[,] the following acts:"

In five enumerated subsections which follow in the same paragraph ("XI."), plaintiff alleges that the school district and its agents and employees, "negligently and carelessly" in each instance, (1) failed to apprehend his reading disabilities, (2) assigned him to classes in which he could not read "the books and other materials," (3) allowed him "to pass and advance from a course or grade level" with knowledge that he had not achieved either its completion or the skills "necessary for him to succeed or benefit from subsequent courses," (4) assigned him to classes in which the instructors were unqualified or which were not "geared" to his reading level, and (5) permitted him to graduate from high school although he was "unable to read above the eighth grade level, as required by Education Code section 8573, . . . thereby depriving him of additional instruction in reading and other academic skills."

The first count continues with allegations of proximate cause and injury: "XII. . . . [A]s a direct and proximate result of the negligent acts and omissions by the defendant school district, its agents and employees, plaintiff graduated from high school with a reading ability of only the fifth grade [sic]. As a further proximate result . . . [thereof] . . . , plaintiff has suffered a loss of earning capacity by his limited ability to read and write and is unqualified for any employment other than . . . labor which requires little or no ability to read or write. . . ."

In the closing paragraphs of the first count, plaintiff alleges general damages based upon his "permanent disability and inability to gain meaningful employment"; special damages incurred as the cost of compensatory tutoring allegedly required by reason of the "negligence, acts and omissions of defendants"; that he had presented to the school district an appropriate and timely claim for such damages; and that the claim had been rejected in its entirety.

We proceed to assess the first count for the cause of action in negligence which it purports to plead; the others are separately treated below. In his own assessment of the count, plaintiff initially points out that the doctrine of governmental immunity from tort liability was abolished in Muskopf v. Corning Hospital Dist. (1961) 55 Cal. 2d 211 [11 Cal. Rptr. 89, 359 P.2d 457]; that Muskopf further established that governmental liability for negligence is the rule, and immunity the exception; that, as to the conduct pleaded in his first count, immunity from liability is not expressly granted by any provision of the 1963 Tort Claims Act which succeeded Muskopf (Gov. Code, § 810 et seq.); and that, in fact, one provision thereof makes defendant district vicariously liable for any tortious conduct of its employees which would give rise to a cause of action against them personally. (Gov. Code, § 815.2, subd. (a).)[308]

The thrust of these observations is that defendants do not have statutory immunity from the negligence liability with which the first count would charge them. However, Muskopf holds that liability is the rule, and immunity the exception, only "*when there is negligence*." (Muskopf v. Corning Hospital Dist., supra, 55 Cal. 2d 211 at p. 219 [italics added].) The 1963 Tort Claims Act did not change this "basic teaching." (Johnson v. State of California (1968) 69 Cal. 2d 782, 798 [73 Cal. Rptr. 240, 447 P.2d 352].) Since its enactment, all governmental liability in California has been dependent upon its provisions. (Gov. Code, § 815; Susman v. City of Los Angeles (1969) 269 Cal. App. 2d 803, 808 [75 Cal. Rptr. 240].) (2) This means that, to state a cause of action against a public entity, every fact material to the existence of its statutory liability must be pleaded with particularity. (Susman v. City of Los Angeles, supra, at p. 809.)

A public entity may be held vicariously liable for the conduct of its employee, under Government Code section 815.2, subdivision (a) (see fn. 1, ante), only if it is established that the employee would be personally liable for the conduct upon some "acceptable theory of liability." (Van Alstyne, Cal. Government Tort Liability (Cont. Ed. Bar 1964) § 5.33, p. 144.) Plaintiff's immunity points thus mean that he may state a cause of action for negligence. They do not mean that he has stated one, nor do they relieve him of the pleading requirements he must meet for this purpose.

According to the familiar California formula, the allegations requisite to a cause of action for negligence are (1) facts showing a duty of care in the defendant, (2) negligence constituting a breach of the duty, and (3) injury to the plaintiff as a proximate

308. "815.2. (a) A public entity is liable for injury proximately caused by an act or omission of an employee of the public entity within the scope of his employment if the act or omission would, apart from this section, have given rise to a cause of action against the employee or his personal representative."

result. (3 Witkin, Cal. Procedure (2d ed. 1971) Pleading, § 450, p. 2103.) The present parties do not debate the adequacy of plaintiff's first count with respect to the elements of negligence, proximate cause, and injury; they focus exclusively upon the issue (which we find dispositive, as will appear) of whether it alleges facts sufficient to show that defendants owed him a "duty of care."

The facts which it shows in this respect — or not — appear in its allegations that he had been a student undergoing academic instruction in the public school system operated and administered by defendants. He argues that these facts alone show the requisite "duty of care" upon three judicially recognized theories, for which he cites authorities, pertaining to the public schools.

According to the first theory, "[a]ssumption of the function of instruction of students imposes the duty to exercise reasonable care in its discharge." (Summarizing this and the other two theories advanced by plaintiff, we quote the pertinent captions of his opening brief.) The decisions he cites for his first theory have no application here; in each, the question was whether a public employee's discharge of a function, the performance of which he had "assumed" in the exercise of his discretion, was reached by statutes which granted him immunity from tort liability for the results of his discretionary actions. (Morgan v. County of Yuba (1964) 230 Cal. App. 2d 938, 940–943 [41 Cal. Rptr. 508]; Sava v. Fuller (1967) 249 Cal. App. 2d 281, 283–285 [57 Cal. Rptr. 312]. See also McCorkle v. City of Los Angeles (1969) 70 Cal. 2d 252, 258–262 [74 Cal. Rptr. 389, 449 P.2d 453].)

Plaintiff's second theory is that "[t]here is a special relationship between students and teachers which supports [the teachers'] duty to exercise reasonable care." He cites for this theory a wide-ranged array of decisions which enforced or addressed various "rights," "opportunities," or privileges of public school students (particularly in equal protection contexts), but none of which involved the question whether the school authorities owed them a "duty of care" in the process of their academic education. (See, e.g., Lau v. Nichols (1973) 414 U.S. 563, 564–568 [39 L. Ed. 2d 1, 3–6, 94 S. Ct. 786]; Ward v. Flood (1874) 48 Cal. 36, 50–51; Serrano v. Priest (1971) 5 Cal. 3d 584, 606–607 [96 Cal. Rptr. 601, 487 P.2d 1241]; Governing Board v. Metcalf (1974) 36 Cal. App. 3d 546, 550 [111 Cal. Rptr. 724].) The third theory is that the "[d]uty of teachers to exercise reasonable care in instruction and supervision of students is recognized in California." The decisions cited here are inapplicable because they establish only that public school authorities have a duty to exercise reasonable care for the physical safety of students under their supervision. (See, e.g., Dailey v. Los Angeles Unified Sch. Dist. (1970) 2 Cal. 3d 741, 745–747 [87 Cal. Rptr. 376, 470 P.2d 360].)

For want of relevant authority in each instance, plaintiff's allegations of his enrollment and attendance at defendants' schools do not plead the requisite "duty of care," relative to his academic instruction, upon any of the three theories he invokes. Of course, no reasonable observer would be heard to say that these facts did not impose upon defendants a "duty of care" within any common meaning of the term;

given the commanding importance of public education in society, we state a truism in remarking that the public authorities who are dutybound to educate are also bound to do it with "care." But the truism does not answer the present inquiry, in which "duty of care" is not a term of common parlance; it is instead a legalistic concept of "duty" which will sustain liability for negligence in its breach, and it must be analyzed in that light.

The concept reflects the longstanding language of decisions in which the existence of a "duty of care," in a defendant, has been repeatedly defined as a requisite element of his liability for negligence. (See, e.g., Means v. Southern California Ry. Co. (1904) 144 Cal. 473, 478 [77 P. 1001]; Dahms v. General Elevator Co. (1932) 214 Cal. 733, 737 [7 P.2d 1013]; Richards v. Stanley (1954) 43 Cal. 2d 60, 63 [271 P.2d 23]; Raymond v. Paradise Unified School Dist. (1963) 218 Cal. App. 2d 1, 6 [31 Cal. Rptr. 847]; 4 Witkin, Summary of Cal. Law (8th ed. 1974) Torts, § 488, p. 2749.) The concept has not been treated as immutable; with respect to physical injury resulting from emotional "spectator" shock, for example, it now incorporates a test—the foreseeability of the injury—which it had previously excluded. (Dillon v. Legg (1968) 68 Cal. 2d 728, 730, 733–735 [69 Cal. Rptr. 72, 441 P. 912, 29 A.L.R.3d 1316] [overruling Amaya v. Home Ice, Fuel & Supply Co. (1963) 59 Cal. 2d 295, 310 et seq. (29 Cal. Rptr. 33, 379 P.2d 513)]. See Mobaldi v. Board of Regents (1976) 55 Cal. App. 3d 573, 576, 579–581 [127 Cal. Rptr. 720]; 4 Witkin, op. cit. supra, Torts, § 494, p. 2759.)

Despite such changes in the concept, several constants are apparent from its evolution. One is that the concept itself is still an essential factor in any assessment of liability for negligence. (See, e.g., United States Liab. Ins. Co. v. Haidinger-Hayes, Inc. (1970) 1 Cal. 3d 586, 594 [83 Cal. Rptr. 418, 463 P.2d 770]; Valdez v. J. D. Diffenbaugh Co. (1975) 51 Cal. App. 3d 494, 504 [124 Cal. Rptr. 467].) Another is that whether a defendant owes the requisite "duty of care," in a given factual situation, presents a question of law which is to be determined by the courts alone. (Raymond v. Paradise Unified School Dist., supra, 218 Cal. App. 2d 1 at p. 8; 4 Witkin, op. cit. supra, Torts, § 493, p. 2756.) A third, and the one most important in the present case, is that judicial recognition of such duty in the defendant, with the consequence of his liability in negligence for its breach, is initially to be dictated or precluded by considerations of public policy. From among an array of judicial statements to this effect, the following language by the Raymond court is particularly pertinent here: "An affirmative declaration of duty [of care] simply amounts to a statement that two parties stand in such relationship that the law will impose on one a responsibility for the exercise of care toward the other. Inherent in this simple description are various and sometimes delicate *policy judgments*. The social utility of the activity out of which the injury arises, compared with the risks involved in its conduct; the kind of person with whom the actor is dealing; the workability of a rule of care, especially in terms of the parties' relative ability to adopt practical means of preventing injury; the relative ability of the parties to bear the financial burden of injury and the availability of means by which the loss may be shifted or spread; the body of statutes and judicial precedents which color the parties' relationship; the prophylactic effect of a rule of liability; in the case of a public agency defendant, the extent of its powers, the role imposed upon it by law and the limitations imposed upon it by budget; and finally, the moral imperatives which judges share with their fellow citizens — such are the factors which play a role in the determination of duty. [Citations.] Occasions for judicial determination of a duty of care are infrequent, because in 'run of the mill' accident cases the existence of a duty may be — and usually is — safely assumed. Here the problem is squarely presented." (Raymond v. Paradise Unified School Dist., supra, 218 Cal. App. 2d 1 at pp. 8–9 [italics added].)

In Rowland v. Christian (1968) 69 Cal. 2d 108 [70 Cal. Rptr. 97, 443 P.2d 561, 32 A.L.R.3d 496], the Supreme Court used similar terminology in defining various public policy considerations as exceptional factors which might alone warrant nonliability for negligence. The court declared that the foundation of all negligence liability in this state was Civil Code section 1714,[309] paraphrased the section in terms of duty of care (as expressing the principle that "[a]ll persons are required to use ordinary care to prevent others being injured as the result of their conduct"), and stated that liability was to flow from this "fundamental principle" in all cases except where a departure from it was "clearly supported by public policy." The court then described the pertinent factors of public policy, and their role, as follows:

"A departure from this fundamental principle involves the balancing of a number of considerations; the major ones are the foreseeability of harm to the plaintiff, the degree of certainty that the plaintiff suffered injury, the closeness of the connection between the defendant's conduct and the injury suffered, the moral blame attached to the defendant's conduct, the policy of preventing future harm, the extent of the burden to the defendant and the consequences to the community of imposing a duty to exercise care with resulting liability for breach, and the availability, cost, and prevalence of insurance for the risk involved. [Citations.]" (Rowland v. Christian, supra, 69 Cal. 2d 108 at pp. 112–113. See 4 Witkin, op. cit. supra, Torts, § 487, pp. 2748–2749.)

Such policy factors, and their controlling role in the determination whether a defendant owes a "duty of care" which will underlie his liability for negligence in its breach, have been similarly defined in other decisions. (See, e.g., Connor v. Great Western Sav. & Loan Assn. (1968) 69 Cal. 2d 850, 865 [73 Cal. Rptr. 369, 447 P.2d 609, 39 A.L.R.3d 224] and cases cited; Valdez v. J. D. Diffenbaugh Co., supra, 51 Cal. App. 3d 494 at p. 507. See also Prosser, Law of Torts (4th ed. 1971) pp. 21–23.) Some have been classified as "administrative factors" which involve such considerations as the possibility of "feigned claims," and the difficulty of proof, of a particular injury; others, as "socio-economic and moral factors" involving the prospect of limitless

309. Section 1714 provides in pertinent part: "Everyone is responsible, not only for the result of his willful acts, but also for an injury occasioned to another by his want of ordinary care or skill in the management of his property or person. . . ." Id., at p. 112.)

liability for the same injury. (See Amaya v. Home Ice, Fuel & Supply Co., supra, 59 Cal. 2d 295 at pp. 310–315 [applying the factors to negate "duty"]; compare Dillon v. Legg, supra, 68 Cal. 2d 728 at pp. 735–746 [acknowledging the factors but disregarding them as limitations upon liability].)

It has also been pointed out that the concept of "duty" may actually focus upon the rights of the injured plaintiff rather than upon the obligations of the defendant, but that the same public policy considerations will control whether the one may state a cause of action for negligence, against the other, in a given factual situation. In these respects, the Supreme Court has stated:

"The assertion that liability must nevertheless be denied because defendant bears no 'duty' to plaintiff 'begs the essential question—whether the plaintiff's interests are entitled to legal protection against the defendant's conduct.... It [duty] is a shorthand statement of a conclusion, rather than an aid to analysis in itself.... But it should be recognized that "duty" is not sacrosanct in itself, but only an expression of *the sum total of those considerations of policy which lead the law to say that the particular plaintiff is entitled to protection.*'"[310] Dillon v. Legg, supra, 68 Cal.2d 728 at p. 734, quoting from Prosser, Law of Torts (3d ed. 1964) pp. 332–333 [italics added here]. See also Prosser, op. cit. (4th ed. 1971) pp. 325–326.)

On occasions when the Supreme Court has opened or sanctioned new areas of tort liability, it has noted that the wrongs and injuries involved were both comprehensible and assessable within the existing judicial framework. (See, e.g., State Rubbish etc. Assn. v. Siliznoff (1952) 38 Cal. 2d 330, 338 [240 P.2d 282]; Dillon v. Legg, supra, 68 Cal. 2d 728 at pp. 735–747.) This is simply not true of wrongful conduct and injuries allegedly involved in educational malfeasance. Unlike the activity of the highway or the marketplace, classroom methodology affords no readily acceptable standards of care, or cause, or injury. The science of pedagogy itself is fraught with different and conflicting theories of how or what a child should be taught, and any layman might—and commonly does—have his own emphatic views on the subject. The "injury" claimed here is plaintiff's inability to read and write. Substantial professional authority attests that the achievement of literacy in the schools, or its failure, are influenced by a host of factors which affect the pupil subjectively, from outside the formal teaching process, and beyond the control of its ministers. They may be physical, neurological, emotional, cultural, environmental; they may be present but not perceived, recognized but not identified.[311]

---

310. "Protection" of the plaintiff is the initial element in the Restatement formula defining the requisites of a cause of action for negligence. The formula's essentials include negligence, causation, and injury (the "invasion of an interest" of the plaintiff) but, unlike the California formula, the first element is not a "duty of care" in the defendant: it is the condition that the "*interest invaded is protected.*" (Rest. 2d Torts, § 281 [italics added].)

311. From among innumerable authorities to these effects, defendants cite Gagne, Conditions of Learning (1965); Schubert & Torgerson, Improving the Reading Program (1968); Flesch, Why Johnny Can't Read (1965).

We find in this situation no conceivable "workability of a rule of care" against which defendants' alleged conduct may be measured (Raymond v. Paradise Unified School Dist., supra, 218 Cal. App. 2d 1 at p. 8), no reasonable "degree of certainty that . . . plaintiff suffered injury" within the meaning of the law of negligence (see fn. 3, ante, referring to Rest. 2d Torts, § 281), and no such perceptible "connection between the defendant's conduct and the injury suffered," as alleged, which would establish a causal link between them within the same meaning. (Rowland v. Christian, supra, 69 Cal. 2d 108 at p. 113.)

These recognized policy considerations alone negate an actionable "duty of care" in persons and agencies who administer the academic phases of the public educational process. Others, which are even more important in practical terms, command the same result. Few of our institutions, if any, have aroused the controversies, or incurred the public dissatisfaction, which have attended the operation of the public schools during the last few decades. Rightly or wrongly, but widely, they are charged with outright failure in the achievement of their educational objectives; according to some critics, they bear responsibility for many of the social and moral problems of our society at large. Their public plight in these respects is attested in the daily media, in bitter governing board elections, in wholesale rejections of school bond proposals, and in survey upon survey. To hold them to an actionable "duty of care," in the discharge of their academic functions, would expose them to the tort claims — real or imagined — of disaffected students and parents in countless numbers. They are already beset by social and financial problems which have gone to major litigation, but for which no permanent solution has yet appeared. (See, e.g., Crawford v. Board of Education (1976) 17 Cal. 3d 280 [130 Cal. Rptr. 724, 551 P.2d 28]; Serrano v. Priest, supra, 5 Cal. 3d 584.) The ultimate consequences, in terms of public time and money, would burden them — and society — beyond calculation.

Upon consideration of the role imposed upon the public schools by law and the limitations imposed upon them by their publicly supported budgets (Raymond v. Paradise Unified School Dist., supra, 218 Cal. App. 2d 1 at p. 8), and of the just-cited "consequences to the community of imposing [upon them] a duty to exercise care with resulting liability for breach" (Rowland v. Christian, supra, 69 Cal. 2d 108 at p. 118), we find no such "duty" in the first count of plaintiff's complaint. As this conclusion is dispositive, other problems presented by the pleading need not be discussed: it states no cause of action.

The Last Five Causes of Action

In each of his last five counts (the third through the seventh, inclusive), plaintiff repleads all the allegations of the first one. He further alleges, in each, that he had incurred "the damages alleged herein" "as a direct and proximate result" of a specified violation, by one or more of the defendants and as to him, of a respectively described "duty" (or "mandatory duty") allegedly imposed upon them by an express provision of law.[312] The theory of each count is that it states a cause of action for breach of a "mandatory duty" under Government Code section 815.6.[313]

If it be assumed that each of these counts effectively pleads the district's failure to have exercised "reasonable diligence to discharge the duty" respectively alleged, as mentioned in the statute (see fn. 6, ante), none states a cause of action. This is because the statute imposes liability for failure to discharge only such "mandatory duty" as is "imposed by an enactment that is designed to protect against the risk of a particular kind of injury." (See ibid.) The various "enactments" cited in these counts (see fn. 5, ante) are not so "designed." We have already seen that the failure of educational achievement may not be characterized as an "injury" within the meaning of tort law. It further appears that the several "enactments" have been conceived as provisions directed to the attainment of optimum educational results, but not as safeguards against "injury" of any kind: i.e., as administrative but not protective. Their violation accordingly imposes no liability under Government Code section 815.6.

The Second Cause of Action

Plaintiff's second count requires separate treatment because the theory of liability invoked in it is materially different from those reflected in the others. After incorporating into it all the allegations of the first count, he further alleges as follows:

"Defendant school district, its agents and employees, falsely and fraudulently represented to plaintiff's mother and natural guardian that plaintiff was performing at or near grade level in basic academic skills such as reading and writing. . . ." The representations were false. The charged defendants knew that they were false, or had no basis for believing them to be true. "As a direct and proximate result of the intentional or negligent misrepresentation made, plaintiff suffered the damages set forth herein."

---

312. The third count thus refers to the district's and the governing board's having violated their "mandatory duty," allegedly imposed upon them by Education Code section 10759 and title 5 of the California Administrative Code, "of keeping the parents and natural guardians of minor school children advised as to their accurate educational progress and achievements." The fourth count alleges a violation, by the district, of its "duty of instructing plaintiff, and other students, in the basic skills of reading and writing" as imposed "under the Constitution and laws of the State of California." The fifth count refers to the district's having graduated plaintiff from high school as a violation of a "mandatory duty not to graduate students from high school without demonstration of proficiency in basic skills" as allegedly imposed by Education Code section 8573 et seq. The sixth count speaks to a violation, by the governing board, of its "mandatory duty" to inspect and evaluate the district's educational program pursuant to Education Code sections 1053 and 8002; the seventh, to the district's violation of its "mandatory duty," allegedly imposed by Education Code section 8505, "to design the course of instruction offered in the public schools to meet the needs of the pupils for which the course of study is prescribed."

313. "815.6. Where a public entity is under a mandatory duty imposed by an enactment that is designed to protect against the risk of a particular kind of injury, the public entity is liable for an injury of that kind proximately caused by its failure to discharge the duty unless the public entity establishes that it exercised reasonable diligence to discharge the duty."

For the public policy reasons heretofore stated with respect to plaintiff's first count, we hold that this one states no cause of action for negligence in the form of the "misrepresentation" alleged. The possibility of its stating a cause of action for intentional misrepresentation, to which it expressly refers in the alternative, is assisted by judicial limitations placed upon the scope of the governmental immunity which is granted, as to liability for "misrepresentation," by Government Code section 818.8. (See Johnson v. State of California, supra, 69 Cal. 2d 782 at pp. 799–800; Connelly v. State of California (1970) 3 Cal. App. 3d 744, 752 [84 Cal. Rptr. 257]. See also Gov. Code, § 822.2.)

The second count nevertheless does not state a cause of action, for intentional misrepresentation, because it alleges no facts showing the requisite element of reliance upon the "misrepresentation" it asserts. (See 3 Witkin, Cal. Procedure, op. cit. supra, Pleading, §§ 573–574, pp. 2210–2212.) Plaintiff elected to stand upon it without exercising his leave to amend. The trial court's action, in sustaining defendant's general demurrer to it, is therefore to be regarded as conclusive for our purposes. (O'Hara v. L.A. County Flood etc. Dist. (1941) 19 Cal. 2d 61, 64 [119 P.2d 23]; Susman v. City of Los Angeles, supra, 269 Cal. App. 2d 803 at p. 822.)

The judgment of dismissal is affirmed.

Chapter 3

Teachers' Rights and Responsibilities

The subject of teachers' rights can be looked upon as a balancing of competing interests. On the one side exists the teachers' freedom to exercise personal rights. On the other side exists governmental authority to restrict these rights for the welfare of the schools. The tension between these two interests has produced a multitude of case law flanked by a substantial volume of state and federal legislation. Understanding teachers' rights involves three areas: (1) the rights of teachers protected by the U.S. Constitution, (2) teachers' protection against employer discrimination, and (3) teachers' rights when being dismissed.

Constitutional Rights of Teachers

Teachers' Free Speech Rights

Many teachers' constitutional rights have come to be legally recognized as a result of some deprivation of the exercise of free speech and expression. Generally, a teacher may not be dismissed, demoted, or transferred because of their exercise of free speech and expression. The leading case on this matter is *Pickering v. Board of Education*.[1] [**See Case No. 3-1.**] Prior to *Pickering*, the courts viewed teacher employment as a privilege. This *privilege doctrine* was used by the courts to sustain the dismissal of teachers for whatever reason a board of education may have articulated. In 1968, when the U.S. Supreme Court decided *Pickering*, a new judicial view was forwarded concerning the constitutional rights of teachers. The Court believed that the interest of the government to impose restrictions on teachers must be weighed against the interests of the teachers. Neither the government's interest nor the teachers' is absolute.

In the case itself, Marvin Pickering, a public-school teacher in Will County, Illinois, was terminated after he wrote a letter to the local newspaper criticizing the board of education. Specifically, Mr. Pickering disagreed with the board's disparate expenditure of funds between the educational and athletic programs. The board claimed that the letter contained false statements damaging the reputations

1. 391 U.S. 563 (1968).

of the board members and school administrators. In using a balancing-of-interests approach in analyzing the case, the Court asked: (1) Was the substance of the letter a matter of public concern? and (2) Did the letter produce disruption in the school system?[2] The Court concluded that the letter was a matter of public concern. Also, the record revealed that the letter did not precipitate any disruption in the system. In determining the lack of disruption, the Court noted that the letter was not directed at anyone with whom Pickering would have daily contact in the work environment.[3] Given its analysis, the Court concluded that absent proof of false statements, knowingly or recklessly made, a teacher's views on public issues cannot form the basis for dismissal.[4]

An additional dimension was added to the *Pickering* criteria in 1977 when the U.S. Supreme Court decided *Mt. Healthy City School District v. Doyle.*[5] [***See* Case No. 3-2.**] In *Mt. Healthy*, a non-tenured teacher telephoned a radio station to criticize the dress code for teachers. The teacher, Doyle, had previously been involved in altercations of a reprimanding nature. However, Doyle challenged his dismissal as an impermissible curtailment of his right to free speech. In addition to 1968 precedents, the Court asked whether the teacher could show that his free speech was a substantial factor in the board's decision to terminate. A positive answer would trigger the need for the authorities to show by a preponderance of the evidence that the board would have reached the same decision to terminate absent the free-speech exercise. Finding for Doyle, the Court concluded that the exercise of protected speech should place an employee in a position that is no better or worse regarding continued employment.[6] The Court found that the board would not have reached the same conclusion if it were not for Doyle's phone call to the radio station.

While not a case concerning a teacher, *Connick v. Myers*,[7] [***see* Case No. 3-3**] further shaped the analysis of speech for all employees of government or quasi-governmental entities including schools. Sheila Myers, an assistant district attorney, objected to being transferred to another section of the office. Consequently, she developed a questionnaire to be completed by her co-workers. The questionnaire asked questions which in part challenged the authority of the district attorney. She passed out the questionnaire at the office. Upon learning of its distribution, the district attorney dismissed Ms. Myers for insubordination. In analyzing the issue of whether Ms. Myers was protected by the speech clause for her activities, the Court for the first time applied a means of "evaluating" the quality of the speech against the employer's need to operate an efficient workplace. The Court noted that Myers' speech must be viewed in relation to *content, form, and context*. Unlike the approach

2. *Id.* at 570.
3. *Id.* at 572–73.
4. *Id.* at 574.
5. 429 U.S. 274 (1977).
6. *Id.* at 285–86.
7. 461 U.S. 138 (1983).

used in *Pickering*, where the teacher's speech was taken "as is" as long as it was of public concern, here the Court considered the nature of the employee's speech. For *content*, the Court noted that 13 of the 14 questions on the questionnaire had to do with the employee's own personal issues. This would rank value of the speech low from a constitutional perspective. The more the issues related to broad social policy considerations, the higher the Court would have valued the content.

As to *form*, the method of the questionnaire was not as highly valued as it might have been had she spoken out at a meeting or with each co-worker face to face. The questionnaire was a somewhat pre-textual approach to dealing with the subject. In other words, it was not the most honest way to express the speech. Therefore, her marks were also low in terms of the form of the speech. Lastly, the *context* of the speech was low. This is so because the speech was given during the workday and at the workplace. If the speech activity had occurred before or after work, during the lunch hour, or better yet, if the questionnaire had been mailed to her coworkers' homes, the context criterion would have been higher. For many years, the three cases taken together, *Pickering*, *Mt. Healthy*, and *Connick*, provided the essence of what principals must know when making a negative employment decision about a teacher when the issue involves speech. Taken together, it seemed reasonable to conclude that teachers could enjoy some level of protection when expressing their opinions. That was about to change.

In 1994, 11 years after *Connick*, a U.S. Supreme Court decision regarding public employees' rights made it much easier for a school board to dismiss teachers for speech-related activities. *Waters v. Churchill*,[8] [*see* **Case No. 3-4**] involved a public hospital nurse who was dismissed for insubordination when it was learned that she spoke negatively about the hospital's internal transfer policy. Cheryl Waters was fired from her nursing job at a public hospital, allegedly because of statements she made to a co-worker during a work break. What Waters said during the conversation is in dispute. The employer's version was based on interviews with the co-worker and one other employee who overheard part of the conversation. The witnesses indicated that Waters made disruptive statements critical of her department and of the administration. Waters' version, which was corroborated by others who also overheard part of the conversation, indicated that her speech was largely limited to non-disruptive statements critical of the hospital's cross-training policy which she believed threatened patient care.

The United States District Court for the Central District of Illinois granted summary judgment in favor of the hospital, holding that management could fire Waters with impunity because neither version of the conversation was protected under *Connick*. The Court of Appeals for the Seventh Circuit reversed, concluding that Waters' speech, viewed in the light most favorable to her, was on a matter of public concern and was not disruptive. The appellate court ruled that the inquiry must

---

8. 511 U.S. 661 (1994).

turn on what her speech was as determined by a jury, not on what the employer believed it to be.

In vacating the decision of the Seventh Circuit, the U.S. Supreme Court held that the *Connick* test should be applied to what the government employer reasonably thought was said, not to what the trier of fact ultimately determines to have been said.[9] The Seventh Circuit's approach would require that the government employer come to its factual conclusions through procedures identical to the rules of evidence used by the courts but, in reality, employment decisions are often made on hearsay, past conduct, personal knowledge, and other factors that the courts ignore.

The High Court maintained that the *Connick* test can be applied to the facts as the employer thought them to be but *must* also consider the *reasonableness* of the employer's conclusions. It is necessary that the employer reach conclusions about what was said in *good faith* rather than as a pretext. The Court indicated that it may be unreasonable for an employer to arrive at a conclusion with no evidence at all. Likewise, it would be unreasonable for the employer to act based on extremely weak evidence when strong evidence is clearly available. For example, if an employee is accused of writing an improper letter to an editor, the employer should be expected to read the letter rather than deciding based on hearsay. In applying the procedural standard set above, the Court concluded that Waters' speech discouraged people from coming to work in the obstetrics department. This qualifies as disruption. Waters argued that much of what she said was not disruptive. Those parts were ignored by the employer. The Court noted that if the *Connick* test was applied to the speech for which Churchill was fired, it is irrelevant that the employer did not take into consideration other forms of speech at the event.

The Supreme Court's most recent decision addressing public employees' free-speech rights is *Garcetti v. Ceballos*,[10] [*see* **Case No. 3-5**] an opinion handed down in 2006. In many ways, this decision changed everything by restricting free-speech rights further than any previous ruling. In this case, Ceballos, a California deputy district attorney, found that a search warrant affidavit contained serious misrepresentations and recommended dismissing the case. He was reassigned and transferred. Ruling against Ceballos, the Court determined that statements made pursuant to a position as a public employee, rather than a private citizen, result in no First Amendment protections. When public employees are speaking on matters concerning official duties, they are not speaking as citizens but as employees; therefore, the speech of public employees made pursuant to official duties is not protected speech under the First Amendment.

Applying the *Garcetti* standard to education cases, most courts, including several federal courts of appeals, have ruled in favor of the school district. For example, David Weintraub, a fifth-grade teacher in Brooklyn, New York, filed a grievance

9. *Id.* at 667–68.
10. 547 U.S. 410 (2006).

because school administrators would not discipline a student who hit him with a book on two separate occasions in two consecutive days. Weintraub told other teachers about his grievance and was later discharged for allegedly bad performance, assault charges, and sexually abusing a student. The criminal charges were ultimately dropped. Weintraub claimed retaliation and violation of his free-speech rights.[11] Basing its decision on *Garcetti*, the Second Circuit Court of Appeals ruled in favor of the school district. The court recognized disciplinary issues as official duties of the teacher and hence as unprotected speech. Agreeing with other circuit decisions, the appeals court noted that these duties do not have to be "specifically designated"[12] in an employee's job description.

Applying *Garcetti*, numerous courts have not protected public school teachers' questioning administrative decisions. These teacher complaints address a wide range of issues related to budgetary expenditures, operations and management, policy implementation, and programs serving students with disabilities. Courts have rendered decisions with these outcomes in the Fifth,[13] Sixth,[14] Seventh,[15] Eighth,[16] Ninth,[17] and Tenth[18] Circuit Courts of Appeals. Administrators should also be aware that courts have arrived at similar outcomes when principals and superintendents have been involved in reporting on matters related to their jobs.[19] Further, while

---

11. Weintraub v. Bd. of Educ. of the Dist. of City of N.Y., 593 F.3d 196 (2d Cir. 2010).

12. *Id.* at 201–02.

13. *See, e.g.*, Williams v. Dallas Indep. Sch. Dist., 480 F.3d 689 (5th Cir. 2007) (upheld firing of coach after he repeatedly requested information regarding funds needed to operate his department).

14. *See, e.g.*, Fox v. Traverse City Area Pub. Schs. Bd. of Educ., 605 F.3d 345 (6th Cir.), *cert. denied*, 131 S. Ct. 643 (2010) (upholding school board's non-renewal of a probationary special education teacher's contract for reporting that her caseload exceeded legal mandates).

15. *See, e.g.*, Mayer v. Monroe Cnty. Cmty. Sch. Corp., 474 F.3d 477 (7th Cir. 2007) (not protecting teacher's political speech infused into the curriculum); Craig v. Rich Twp. High Sch. Dist. 227, 736 F.3d 1110 (7th Cir. 2013) (not protecting guidance counselor's sexually related, self-published advice book in that this speech may interfere with job performance and personnel relationships); Brown v. Chicago Bd. of Educ., 824 F.3d 713 (7th Cir. 2016) (upholding suspension of teacher for repeating racial slurs to illustrate inappropriate language in sixth grade class).

16. *See, e.g.*, Anderson v. Douglas Cnty. Sch. Dist., 342 Fed. Appx. 223 (8th Cir. 2009) (upholding the firing of a technical support coordinator who told staff about pay irregularities, invalid contracts, and funding discrepancies).

17. *See, e.g.*, Richerson v. Beckon, 337 Fed. Appx. 637 (9th Cir. 2009) (finding that a curriculum specialist's blog criticizing other employees undermined her ability to perform her job); Coomes v. Edmonds Sch. Dist. No. 15, 816 F.3d 1255 (9th Cir. 2016) (not protecting teacher's opposition to special education placements communicated through the chain of command).

18. *See, e.g.*, Brammer-Holter v. Twin Peaks Charter Acad., 492 F.3d 1192 (10th Cir. 2007) (protecting charter-school teachers' political speech but not their criticisms of the school's operation and management even though administration encouraged open comment); Duvall v. Putnam City Sch. Dist., 530 Fed. Appx. 804 (10th Cir. 2013) (not protecting special education teacher's voiced concerns and dissenting letters against her school's full inclusion model).

19. *See, e.g.*, McArdle v. Peoria Sch. Dist. No. 150, 705 F.3d 751, 754 (7th Cir. 2013) (questioning another administrator's misuse of funds was not protected speech); Casey v. West Las Vegas Indep. Sch. Dist., 473 F.3d 1323 (10th Cir. 2007) (upholding superintendent's demotion for reporting Head Start violations against school board advice); D'Angelo v. Sch. Bd. of Polk County, Florida, 497 F.3d

many states have laws protecting whistleblowers, these laws vary across states in their ability to protect the informer from retaliation.[20]

Another application of *Garcetti*'s balance between employer control and individual freedom played out in the 2020 case of *Kennedy v. Bremerton School District.*[21] Kennedy, a high-school assistant football-coach, had a ritual of offering a roughly 30-second prayer on one knee at the 50-yard line immediately after the players and coaches shook hands after the game. The majority of the team eventually began to take part and the practice evolved to include inspirational religious post-game talks. The school district's administration was not aware of the practice until an opposing team's coach commented on Kennedy's invitation to the opposing team's coaches and players to join him. After inquiry, the administration directed Kennedy to abstain from the practice to comply with district policy by which school staff were to neither encourage nor discourage students from engaging in religious activity. Undeterred, Kennedy continued this behavior, and a media circus resulted. Kennedy was eventually placed on administrative leave and ultimately declined to reapply for his position.

Kennedy sued the school district in federal court, alleging violation of his First Amendment rights of free speech and free exercise as well as claims under Title VII of the Civil Rights Act.

In ruling on behalf of the district, the Ninth Circuit Court of Appeals determined that Kennedy's "speech" did not amount to speaking on a matter of public concern, such speech was made in his capacity as a public employee, and the coercive effect of Kennedy's actions violated the Establishment Clause, all of which justified the district's decision to place him on leave (giving them a legitimate, nondiscriminatory reason for the negative employment action). "While public schools do not have unfettered discretion to restrict an employee's religious speech, they do have the ability to prevent a coach from praying at the center of the football field immediately after games."[22]

1203 (11th Cir. 2007) (upholding contract non-renewal when principal spoke out to convert low-performing school to a charter school).

20. *See, e.g.*, Richard Moberly, *Sarbanes-Oxley's Whistleblower Provisions: Ten Years Later*, 64 S.C. L. Rev. 1 (2012) (arguing that the act has failed to protect whistleblowers from retaliation and has not resolved the underlying problems); Diane Norcross, *Comment: Separating the Employee from the Citizen: The Social Science Implications of Garcetti v. Ceballos*, 40 U. Balt. L. Rev. 543 (Spring 2011) (advocating for a return to the *Connick-Pickering* balancing test in light of federal and state laws' inability to prevent retaliation); Susan L. Wynne & Michael S. Vaughn, Ph.D., *Silencing Matters of Public Concern: An Analysis of State Legislative Protection of Whistleblowers in Light of the Supreme Court's Ruling in* Garcetti v. Ceballos, 8 Ala. C.R. & C.L. L. Rev. 239 (2017) (suggesting that states strengthen their whistle-blower protections).

21. 443 F. Supp. 3d 1223 (W.D. Wash. 2020), *affirmed*, No. 20-35222, 2021 U.S. App. LEXIS 7911 (9th Cir. Wash., Mar. 18, 2021).

22. 443 F. Supp. 3d at 1245.

Other controversies have arisen with teachers' expression in their clothing choices, apart from the religious garb discussed elsewhere in this chapter. Examples include wearing "thin blue line" clothing in support of law enforcement or slogans for or against the Black Lives Matter, MeToo, and other social movements. For practitioners, this is a perfect example demonstrating that not all controversies seen in the media make it to the courtroom.

Finally, school principals should note that whether teachers choose to exercise their free speech in public or private will not change the protection provided teachers by the First Amendment. This standard was announced by the Supreme Court in *Givhan v. Western Line Consolidated School District.*[23] Bessie Givhan, a junior-high English teacher, met privately with her principal to criticize school policies on racial discrimination. The principal alleged that Givhan was insulting, loud, hostile, and arrogant in manner during their meeting, and she was therefore terminated for insubordination. In holding for the teacher, the Court refused to recognize a lesser degree of protection for free speech because the communication was made in a private setting.

To summarize the discussion of free-speech rights for teachers, a school leader should remember the following points: (1) A teacher may not be punished (dismissed, transferred, or demoted) for engaging in free speech as a citizen, that is, on a matter of public concern on their own time. (2) The principal can assume that the teacher is protected unless there are conditions that cancel the teacher's protection. (3) A teacher may not be protected if the speech is purely personal in nature and interferes with the smooth running of the school. (4) A teacher is not protected if the speech is related to the duties of the job; these duties do not have to be a part of the teacher's written job description. (5) Unlike their counterparts in higher education, elementary and secondary school teachers have very little freedom when it comes to speech in the classroom or in carrying out their duties.

Teachers' Fourth Amendment Rights

As with students' privacy rights (discussed in Chapter 4), cases regarding teachers' Fourth Amendment rights generally fall into one of two categories. First are those cases where there is individualized suspicion, and second are those situations involving mass or random testing of teachers for drug use. Unlike student-search decisions, which number in the hundreds, there are few decisions regarding the searching of teachers, and most focus on suspected drug use.

---

23. 439 U.S. 410 (1979).

Searches with Individualized Suspicion

A typical case involving individualized suspicion would center on a specific teacher who shows symptoms that would lead school officials to believe that the teacher is under the influence of drugs or alcohol. While government officials generally need probable cause to search individuals, this standard changes in the school context; a standard of reasonable suspicion, rather than probable cause, usually applies to teachers in schools. Individual states may grant additional protections based on their own privacy laws and could raise the standard to probable cause. Negotiated agreements and other union-type agreements may also establish certain rights for school employees. Therefore, it is important to check state laws and local policies.

In most of these cases, there is a local or state policy that school officials must follow. *Hearn v. Board of Public Education*,[24] an Eleventh Circuit case, is an important and controversial decision that vividly demonstrates the limits of teachers' rights. Sherry Hearn, the plaintiff in the case, was a high-school social-studies and constitutional-law teacher. During a random drug search of the school parking lot, police allowed a canine to enter the teacher's unlocked car through an open window, which alerted the officer to a fragment of marijuana in her ashtray. Both the search of the automobile and seizure of the content were conducted without the teacher's consent or presence.[25]

The school's "Safe School Plan," however, called for "zero-tolerance" of drugs, alcohol, and weapons.[26] Consequently, the Board had in place a "Drug-Free Workplace Policy." This policy mandated that when a supervisor observes, or when known circumstances indicate suspicion, that the employee is using drugs, that employee must submit to drug testing within two hours of the incident. Refusal would give cause for that person's position to be terminated. If a person tests positive, they would also be terminated.[27] In accordance with this school policy, Hearn was ordered to undergo a urinalysis drug test within two hours of notification that the substance had been discovered. She refused to undergo the test because she felt her car had been illegally searched (based on her teacher contract). Also, she did not want to act until she had sought the advice of her attorney who could not be reached until the next day.[28] She did, however, take the test after consulting with her attorney and was found to be drug free. The police closed their investigation; nevertheless, the school board terminated Ms. Hearn for insubordination and the Eleventh Circuit Court of Appeals upheld this action.[29] (See this chapter's section on insubordination for more information on this topic.)

24. 191 F.3d 1329 (11th Cir. 1999).
25. *Id.* at 1331.
26. *Id.* at 1330.
27. *Id.* at 1334.
28. *Id.* at 1331.
29. *Id.* at 1334.

In a later case decided by Mississippi's Supreme Court, *Smith County School District. v. Barnes*,[30] first-grade students found their teacher lying on the classroom floor with her eyes closed. The teacher refused a drug test but later admitted to using opiates and taking Xanax and Ambien. The teacher was dismissed from her job because of her refusal to take the drug test, coupled with her erratic behavior, absenteeism, tardiness, and deteriorating work performance. The court deferred to the board's discretion in firing the teacher. In *Donegan v. Livingston*,[31] a federal district court in Pennsylvania denied summary judgment to an instructional aide who claimed her Fourth Amendment rights were violated when she was subjected to a breathalyzer test after smelling of alcohol. Applying the Fourth Amendment's special needs exemption enunciated in *Chandler v. Miller*[32] (described below) to the school context, the court determined that Donegan's limited search and detention were reasonable.

Even though suspicion-based testing may be justified, the search must align in scope with the suspicion. In one instance, a teaching assistant who was reported by a parent for smelling strongly of alcohol and consequently was subjected to both a breathalyzer and a drug test was determined by a federal court to have been the victim of a Fourth Amendment violation.[33] While the district may have had reasonable, individualized suspicion that the employee was in violation of policies against certain alcohol use, that suspicion was not sufficient basis for drug testing for all mind-altering substances and was not reasonably related in scope to the circumstances that justified the search at its inception. Further, under the circumstances, urinalysis was deemed unreasonably intrusive in light of the suspicion of alcohol use (where a breathalyzer would have been sufficient).

Mass Drug Testing of Teachers

There has been neither federal legislation nor any U.S. Supreme Court decision relative to mass or random drug- or alcohol testing of teachers. Thus, most of the law on this topic comes from lower court decisions. As of early 2020, two federal courts of appeals (in the Sixth and Eleventh Circuits), a few lower federal courts, and two state supreme courts have rendered decisions on this issue. Their findings, however, have been inclusive and fact specific. These decisions will be addressed after a brief overview of U.S. Supreme Court decisions on random drug testing of public employees in general.

Case law regulating drug testing of school employees applies U.S. Supreme Court precedent stemming from decisions addressing drug testing of adults in places other than schools. In two of these decisions, handed down on the same day in 1989, the Court established a test which has generally been applied to adult workers in school

30. 90 So. 3d 63 (Miss. 2012).

31. 877 F. Supp. 2d 212 (M.D. Pa. 2012).

32. 520 U.S. 305 (1997).

33. Robertson v. Sch. Bd., No. 3:18-cv-371-JAG, 2019 WL 5691946 (E.D. Va. Nov. 4, 2019).

settings. The first decision, *Skinner v. Railway Labor Executives' Association*,[34] involved drug testing of railroad employees. After balancing the government's need to search against the privacy rights of these individuals, the Court determined that drug testing without individualized suspicion was reasonable in cases involving accidents or issues of safety. Also, because of physical fitness requirements, employees had diminished expectations of privacy. In a companion decision, *National Treasury Employees Union v. Von Raab*,[35] the Court maintained as reasonable drug testing of customs agents. Agents had a diminished expectation of privacy because of the government's interest in preventing bribery and misuse of firearms and because these individuals were subject to fitness and character examinations.

A third U.S. Supreme Court decision, *Chandler v. Miller*,[36] handed down in 1997, involved the constitutionality of a Georgia statute which required candidates for certain high offices in that state to submit to and pass a drug test 30 days prior to nomination. Here, the Court balanced the privacy rights of the candidates against the government's interest in preventing drug use and found the drug-testing program unconstitutional. Citing *Skinner* and *Von Raab*, the Court based its reasoning on the "special needs" exception to the Fourth Amendment. This exception requires demonstration of a "special need" to overcome the Amendment's requirement for individualized suspicion. Because there was no demonstrated drug problem among officeholders in Georgia, the Court was unable to uphold the suspicionless drug-testing program.

As mentioned above, there are only a few published cases involving mass drug testing of teachers. *Patchogue* is the earliest recorded decision on this topic.[37] This case involved a school district which required certain probationary teachers to undergo urinalyses to detect the use of controlled substances. This policy was enacted despite no indication that any of these teachers had a drug problem.[38] In deciding for the teachers, a New York appellate court determined that the testing was clearly not part of a "medical examination" as required by the teachers' contract.[39]

---

34. 489 U.S. 602 (1989).

35. 489 U.S. 656 (1989).

36. 520 U.S. 305 (1997).

37. Patchogue-Medford Congress of Teachers v. Bd. of Educ. of the Patchogue-Medford Union Free Sch. Dist., 119 A.D.2d 35 (N.Y. App. Div. 2d Dept. 1986).

38. *Id.* at 36. *See also* Richard Fossey & Robert C. Cloud, *The Eleventh Circuit's* Friedenberg v. School Board of Palm Beach County *and Drug Testing District Employees: An Analysis of Federal Case Law*, 363 Educ. Law Rep. 909 (2019) (concluding that bus drivers, custodians, and possibly substitute teaching applicants may be randomly drug tested but not fulltime teachers); Charles J. Russo, Commentary, *Drug Testing of Teachers and the Fourth Amendment*, 35 Educ. Law Rep. 899, 903 (1987) (characterizing this decision as a cornerstone in the law relative to the drug testing of teachers); Charles J. Russo, *Drug Testing of Teachers:* Patchogue-Medford Congress of Teachers *Revisited*, 40 Educ. Law Rep. 607, 614 (1987) (expressing concern that this decision did not resolve the question of whether individualized suspicion is needed).

39. 119 A.D.2d at 37.

Preceding *Skinner* and *Von Raab* by two years, *Patchogue* foreshadows important points made later by the Supreme Court. Considering teachers' rights under the Fourth Amendment, the Court balanced the invasion of privacy against the need for such testing and the benefits that would result, i.e., identifying individuals unfit to teach.[40] In assessing privacy rights, the court looked to other decisions which addressed privacy rights of persons working in industries that are highly regulated due to the possibility of criminal behavior. Such businesses included those involved with liquor, firearms, casino gambling, and horseracing but not teaching.[41] Moreover, the *Patchogue* court pointed out that controlling drug use in the teaching profession is not nearly so important as it is in other governmental positions such as police officer, bus driver, firefighter, and train engineer.[42] In these positions, "the use of controlled substances would ordinarily pose situations fraught with imminent and grave consequences to public safety."[43]

Other lower courts, in rendering decisions after *Skinner* and *Von Raab*, were equally as reluctant to characterize teachers' work as rising to the level of danger equivalent to that imposed on railway workers or customs officials. A Washington, D.C., circuit court overruled a random drug testing program for employees of the Department of the Interior, which included teachers employed by the Bureau of Indian Affairs.[44] In *Georgia Association of Educators v. Harris*,[45] a federal district court applied the *Skinner* and *Von Raab* tests and held that Georgia's Applicant Drug Screening Test, which required drug screening of all public employees, including teachers, was unconstitutional. Here, the court observed that defendants seemed to ignore *Von Raab*'s requirement that the interest in drug testing must have a connection to the plaintiff's job duties. The court noted, "Instead, defendants attempt to justify their comprehensive drug testing program based on a generalized governmental interest in maintaining a drug-free workplace."[46]

This logic continued in a post-*Chandler* Louisiana case[47] in which the Fifth Circuit Court of Appeals examined the special-needs requirement in *Chandler* to determine if pre-employment drug-testing programs in two Louisiana school districts was constitutional. Here, drug testing was instituted because insurance companies would not cover drug-related accidents.[48] In this case, a male monitor was present as male teachers were observed urinating with their back to the monitor.

---

40. *Id.* at 38.

41. *Id.* at 38–39 (citing Colonnade Corp. v. United States, 397 U.S. 72, 77 (1970)) (liquor); United States v. Biswell 406 U.S. 311, 316 (firearms); Matter of Martin, 447 A.2d 1290 (N.J. Sup. Ct. 1982) (casino gambling); and Shoemaker v. Handel, 608 F. Supp. 1151 (D.N.J. 1985) (horseracing).

42. 119 A.D.2d at 39.

43. *Id.*

44. Bangert v. Hodel, 705 F. Supp. 643, 649 (D.D.C. 1989).

45. 749 F. Supp. 1110 (N.D. Ga. 1990).

46. *Id.* at 1114.

47. United Teachers of New Orleans v. Orleans Par. Sch. Bd., 142 F.3d 853 (5th Cir. 1998).

48. *Id.* at 855–56.

Female teachers urinated in a stall with the door closed as a female monitor stood outside listening for signs of tampering.[49] The court emphasized the importance of individualized suspicion and noted that no incidents had occurred which would indicate a problem in the district or among the teachers. Neither was the pervasive drug problem in our society a justification for drug testing teachers. As the court pointed out:

> Special needs are just that, an exception to the command of the Fourth Amendment. It cannot be the case that a state's preference for means of detection is enough to waive off the protections of privacy insisting upon individualized suspicion. It is true that the principles we apply are not absolute in their restraint of government, but it equally true that they do not kneel to the convenience of government or allow their teaching to be so lightly slipped past. Surely then it is self-evident that we cannot rest upon the rhetoric of the drug wars. As destructive as drugs are and as precious are the charges of our teachers, special needs must rest on demonstrated realities.[50]

This logic, however, was neither followed by the Sixth Circuit Court in *Knox County Education Association v. Knox County Board of Education*[51] nor the Eleventh Circuit in *Friedenberg v. School Board of Palm Beach County*.[52]

In *Knox County*, the Sixth Circuit Court of Appeals upheld a program that required mandatory drug testing of all persons *applying* for teaching positions in the Knox County, Tennessee, school system. It did not extend to teachers already employed in the district. *Knox County* is a very narrow decision in that "it is a one-time test, with advance notice and with no random testing component, and because the school system in which the employees work is heavily regulated, particularly as to drug usage."[53] In addition, there was a documented drug problem in the school. While the court fell short of classifying teaching positions as "safety sensitive,"[54] the majority opinion noted that younger children can be active and unpredictable and need close attention and supervision, especially in emergency situations. Of special note is the *Knox* plaintiff's petition for a rehearing of the case *en banc*. There were not enough votes to rehear the case; however, four judges felt so strongly about the decision that they wrote a dissenting opinion. In their dissent, they echoed assertions of earlier courts, stating that this drug-testing program does not meet the standards articulated in *Vernonia*, *Chandler*, *Skinner*, and *Von Raab*.[55]

---

49. *Id.* at 855.

50. *Id.* at 857.

51. 158 F.3d 361 (6th Cir. 1998), *rehearing en banc denied* (Feb. 4, 1999), *cert. denied*, 528 U.S. 812 (1999).

52. 911 F.3d 1084 (11th Cir. 2018).

53. 158 F.3d at 384.

54. *Id.* at 386.

55. *Id.*

The *Friedenberg*[56] case involved a Palm Beach County school policy requiring *applicants* for *substitute* teaching positions to be drug tested after they were conditionally accepted for the job. Unlike most previous decisions, this court categorized teachers as holding safety-sensitive positions. Nonetheless, the judges rendered a narrow decision focusing only applicability to the drug testing of substitute teacher applicants who had been conditionally hired. The *Friedenberg* ruling opposes several other state and federal court decisions regarding random drug testing of teachers which do not characterize these positions as highly safety sensitive. For example, a federal district court in West Virginia[57] declared unconstitutional a random drug-testing program of public employees including teachers, stating specifically that teachers are not in high-security positions.

In *Association of Independent Schools of Greater Washington v. District of Columbia*, a D.C. district court struck down a city law requiring random drug testing of teachers working in private child-development facilities, noting teachers' "robust interest in their personal privacy."[58] Furthermore, the court noted that the defendants "offered no evidence of any drug use by any nursery-school teachers" and "[no] indication of any pervasive 'drug culture' among those individuals,"[59] two identifiers associated with safety-sensitive positions. Moreover, the court characterized the defendant's concerns as speculative rather than evidence based. Finally, as late as 2018, a state appellate court in North Carolina rejected the random drug testing of all school-board employees in Graham County. In this decision, *Jones v. Graham City Board of Education*,[60] the state court determined that there was no reduced expectation of privacy for these individuals and that there was no evidence that these plaintiffs' drug or alcohol use had harmed anyone.

In sum, it is reasonable to conclude that, with the possible exception of the Eleventh Circuit, mass or random drug testing of teachers is likely illegal or at least certainly will be challenged in the courts. Requiring drug testing of *applicants* for teaching positions is more likely to succeed but is also questionable. Moreover, case law has not explored what other positions might be safety sensitive, so questions remain about whether it could be argued that such positions include course content involving laser use or other educational technology equipment, performing chemistry experiments and the like, or supervising interactions with large animals in husbandry courses.

56. 911 F.3d 1084 (11th Cir. 2018).

57. *See, e.g.*, American Fed'n of Teachers–West Virginia, AFL-CIO v. Kanawha Cnty. Bd. of Educ., 592 F. Supp. 2d 883 (S.D. W.Va. 2009).

58. 311 F.Supp.3d 262, 274 (2018). Order amended by Association of Independent Schools of Greater Washington v. District of Columbia, 311 F.Supp.3d 355 (2018).

59. *Id.* at 279.

60. 677 S.E.2d 171 (N.C. Ct. App. 2009).

Drug Testing of Other School Employees

While it is arguable whether teachers are engaged in a dangerous profession, this stand may be more compelling for other seemingly higher-risk positions such as school custodians and bus drivers. Again, there are few cases on point, but one opinion, *Aubrey v. School Board of Lafayette Parish*,[61] emanating from the Fifth Circuit, poses compelling arguments. Here, the court had to decide whether a school custodian on drugs might pose a substantial risk to students. The school considered the custodial position to be "safety sensitive" in that the custodian handled potentially dangerous machinery and hazardous substances in a school with a large number of young children.[62] Holding for the school district, the court agreed that Aubrey did hold a safety-sensitive position, while also noting that Aubrey had notice and that the intrusiveness of the search was minimal.[63] The court concluded, "It is clear that unlike *Chandler*, the special need in this case is substantially more than symbolic or a desire to project a public image."[64]

Finally, random drug testing of school bus drivers is usually considered to be legal because of the imminent danger that would occur if drivers were on drugs. This drug testing generally falls under U.S. Department of Transportation rules and regulations or may be governed by state statutes.[65] There is little case law as to other workers, but *Aubrey* probably provides the best guidance thus far in the arena as well as any laws that may exist in individual states. As more and more states enact laws legalizing previously controlled intoxicating substances, especially those that may be permitted under state law but prohibited by federal law, it is possible that a new generation of cases will give new life to the debate on the legality of drug testing for teachers and other employees.

Employment Discrimination in Teaching

Social and political movements of the 1970s and 1980s produced several federal acts which resulted in an increase in teacher protections, not only by degree but in kind. The Civil Rights Act of 1964, the Age Discrimination in Employment Act, the Pregnancy Protection Act, and the Americans with Disabilities Act all stand to safeguard against discrimination based on race, sex, age, religion, or disability, respectively. In addition to these federal acts, most states have enacted companion legislation that gives protection equal to, or in some cases greater than, that provided by federal law. The school principal must be aware that local board policies and collective-bargaining contracts may also be a source of legal protection for

61. 148 F.3d 559 (5th Cir. 1998).
62. *Id.* at 561.
63. *Id.* at 564.
64. *Id.*
65. 49 C.F.R. Part 382, 66 F.R. 43097 (Aug. 17, 2001).

teachers. The principal will benefit from an understanding of the federal discrimination laws discussed below. Through the federal laws, the principal can become acquainted with those areas that are likely to be sensitive when dealing with teacher employment issues. Protections against discrimination in employment cover race, sex, religion, age, and disability.

Race Discrimination

The primary source of protection for race discrimination comes from Title VII of the Civil Rights Act of 1964. Title VII prohibits employers with 15 or more employees from discriminating on the basis of race and covers hiring, promotion, compensation packages, and most conditions of employment.[66] When attempting to show racial discrimination, teachers or other school employees have two possible avenues. They may try to evidence that the employment practice has an *adverse impact* on the minority group with which they identify so that they should receive the protection of Title VII. Another approach is to allege that the employment practice resulted in their experiencing *disparate treatment* because of their race. *Adverse impact* has been defined as "employment practices that are facially neutral in their treatment of different groups but that in fact fall more harshly on one group than another. Proof of discriminatory motive . . . is not required."[67]

To establish a case of *adverse impact*, the employee must show a causal connection between the facially neutral employment practice and the disproportionate exclusion of the protected group from that portion of the workforce under scrutiny. The disproportionate exclusion is shown by using statistics. If the school employee is successful in showing disparate statistics, the burden of proof shifts to the employer, who must prove that the policy or practice is justified by a valid job necessity. For example, in 1981, a school district successfully defended a race discrimination challenge based on their use of teachers' test scores. In *Newman v. Crews*,[68] the school district determined teachers' salaries on scores from the National Teachers Examination. This practice resulted in the denial of pay raises to a much larger proportion of black teachers than white teachers. However, the court found no fault with the practice since it was justified by the need to attract well-qualified teachers and to encourage self-improvement.

To establish a case of *disparate treatment*, a much greater burden of proof rests with the employee. The employee must show that the school district *intended* to treat individuals differently because of their race. Three specific methods are available to the school district employee for proving disparate treatment. First, the teacher may present evidence that the employer has made statements that point to a discriminatory motive. Second, the teacher can try to establish that they were treated

66. 42 U.S.C. § 2000 *et seq.*

67. Int'l Bhd. of Teamsters v. United States, 431 U.S. 324, 335 (1977).

68. 651 F.2d 222 (4th Cir. 1981).

differently than persons with whom they were similarly situated. In other words, the rejected teacher could attempt to prove that the employer kept the position open after they were rejected and continued to seek applicants with their qualifications. For cases of alleged discrimination involving conditions of employment, such as vacation or termination, the application of the similarly-situated standard becomes important. The school district is not expected to apply the terms of employment evenly to all employees. For example, teachers who are classified as head teachers or master teachers may conceivably be treated differently than regular classroom teachers. If the district were to decide that it must eliminate a teaching position because of financial needs, it could eliminate the only minority teacher in the district provided that previously established objective criteria, such as teacher evaluation scores and seniority, were used. If the choice became one of terminating a black teacher or a white teacher, the black teacher might be terminated legitimately if that teacher's evaluation scores were lower than the white teacher's, even if both had the same seniority and teacher status. In one such case, two teachers were not similarly situated (different evaluation scores) and therefore could not provide the basis for proof by comparative evidence.[69]

Third, the teacher could utilize statistics. The validity of the use of statistics as evidence lies in the assumption that an employer who does not discriminate will have a workforce that mirrors the racial and ethnic composition of the area from which the workforce is drawn.[70] An inference of disparate treatment through the use of statistics might be drawn if, for example, minority teachers have been confined primarily to a few schools with predominantly minority pupils. Once the teacher claiming discrimination establishes the case, the school district can attempt to rebut the charge by articulating a nondiscriminatory reason for the action. Then the burden of proof remains with the teacher to show by a preponderance of the evidence that the legitimate reasons offered are really a pretext for racial discrimination. In one such case in the Third Circuit, a teacher of Egyptian descent identifying as a non-practicing Muslim alleged wrongful termination based on his race, ethnicity, and religion.[71] However, the supervisor claimed the teacher was terminated for legitimate cause related to disseminating links to anti-Semitic online articles through the school's official channels, expressing no remorse for this conduct, and having a history of teaching Holocaust denial theories to their students. Regardless of the supervisor's disparaging remarks regarding his race, the teacher was not able show that his teaching anti-Semitic views to his students was a pretext for discrimination that led to his termination.

School districts seem to have won their cases when the courts found that the reasons for differential treatment were based on quality of performance or other

69. EEOC Compliance Manual, Vol. 2, Sec. 604, Office of Compliance, Decisions Division, Bureau of National Affairs.

70. Brandt v. Shop 'N Save Warehouse, 108 F.3d 935 (8th Cir. 1997).

71. Ali v. Woodbridge Twp. Sch. Dist., 957 F.3d 174 (3d Cir. 2020).

considerations unrelated to race. Employers are not required to accord preference to minorities if nonminority applicants are considered better or even merely equally qualified for available positions. The principal should not confuse this standard with those employer actions taken for the sake of affirmative action. A school district may elect to participate in improving the racial balance in the teaching force and therefore give preference to a minority teacher.

If the school district is under a court order to remedy past practices of discrimination, then it is possible that the differential treatment of minority teachers would preclude the employers' allowed discretion under Title VII. A teacher who is successful in a Title VII discrimination suit may be awarded back pay accruing from two years prior to the filing of the charge. In addition, the court may order that the victim be hired, promoted, or reinstated in the next available position. The court may also grant retroactive seniority. However, seniority systems that are not maintained with the intent to discriminate may not be eliminated by the court even though the system perpetuates the effects of past discrimination.[72]

Gender Discrimination

As is the case with racial discrimination claims, a major source of protection in sex-discrimination claims is Title VII of the Civil Rights Act of 1964 [*see* **Figure 3-1**]. Protection from sex discrimination is covered under Title VII by the sexual harassment provision which was added later. Unfortunately, Congress did not choose the best word when it sought to offer protection under this entitlement — ex-discrimination protection under the original legislation is meant to protect *gender* discrimination. In other words, the discussion here is about gender discrimination even through the term used in the legislation is sex.

This clarification was solidified by the Supreme Court in *Bostock v. Clayton County*.[73] The opinion consolidated three *separate* cases related to the termination of employees: one case involved an employee who was fired for conduct "unbecoming" a county employee shortly after he began participating in a gay recreational softball league, another involved an employee who was fired mere days after he mentioned being gay, and a third involved an employee who presented as a male when she was hired but who was terminated after informing her employer that she planned to "live and work full-time as a woman."[74]

In its landmark decision, the Supreme Court determined that it is impossible to discriminate against a person for being homosexual or transgender without discriminating against that individual based on sex, and therefore all three terminations violated Title VII of the Civil Rights Act which prohibits all forms of sex discrimination.

---

72. Daniels v. Pipe Fitters Ass'n, Local Union 597, 113 F.3d 685 (7th Cir. 1997).
73. 140 S. Ct. 1731 (2020).
74. *Id.* at 1734.

> An employer violates Title VII when it intentionally fires an individual employee based in part on sex. It makes no difference if other factors besides the plaintiff's sex contributed to the decision or that the employer treated women as a group the same when compared to men as a group. A statutory violation occurs if an employer intentionally relies in part on an individual employee's sex when deciding to discharge the employee. Because discrimination on the basis of homosexuality or transgender status requires an employer to intentionally treat individual employees differently because of their sex, an employer who intentionally penalizes an employee for being homosexual or transgender also violates Title VII. There is no escaping the role intent plays: Just as sex is necessarily a but-for cause when an employer discriminates against homosexual or transgender employees, an employer who discriminates on these grounds inescapably intends to rely on sex in its decisionmaking.[75]

The conditions necessary for the teacher to successfully receive a judgment as well as those conditions necessary for a school employer to defend are essentially the same when filing for sex discrimination under Title VII. Since 1982, however, sex-discrimination claims have also been brought under Title IX of the Education Amendments of 1972.

While school employees, as individuals, have a right to sue under Title IX, the act does not allow for personal remedies, such as a reinstatement or back pay, as are provided by Title VII. The sanction for a Title IX violation is the cutoff of federal funds to the program in the school district where the violation is found. The threat of the interruption of federal funds is a powerful incentive for a school district to amend its program and thus provides the employee with an opportunity previously barred.

Title IX applies to any public or private educational institution, whether a preschool or an elementary, secondary, vocational, professional, or postsecondary school. However, an institution is excluded from the Act if it is controlled by a religious organization to the extent that the enforcement of Title IX would conflict with a religious precept of that organization.[76] Title IX violations are proven and defended in the same way that they are under Title VII. As discussed earlier, the decision of whether to use Title VII or Title IX is based upon what the alleged victim wishes to accomplish. Most cases that are filed with the hope of a change in institutional policy are brought under Title IX. If individual employee damages are sought, Title VII is the more common vehicle.

Sex-discrimination claims often arise in the context of pregnancy-related policies or sexual harassment. Since only women can get pregnant, any employment disadvantage befalling women because of pregnancy can result in a claim of sex

---

75. *Id.* at 1735.

76. 20 U.S.C. § 1681(a)(3), (4).

discrimination. An employer is prohibited from excluding pregnancy benefits in comprehensive medical insurance plans.[77] Maternity-leave provisions are also prescribed under Title VII. Pregnancy must be treated as an illness would be. Just as employees are permitted to decide when they are too sick to work, the school district cannot decide for the pregnant employee when she must terminate work. The courts have also decided that Title VII requires school district policies to allow teachers to use accumulated sick leave for pregnancy-related illness.

In addition to sick leave, employees often take unpaid leave if additional time off is needed to recover from giving birth. The Supreme Court has held that Title VII requires school districts to recognize accumulated seniority upon the return from maternity leave. The courts have also required that districts not exclude maternity leave while including other leaves in computing a teacher's probationary period toward tenure.[78] Teachers who are unwed parents are also protected by Title VII. School districts' claims that unwed parenthood constitutes immorality or that the employment of unwed parents in schools contributes to the problem of pregnancies among high school girls have repeatedly been rejected by the courts.[79]

Figure 3-1. Title VII of the Civil Rights Act of 1964

42 U.S.C.A. § 2000e-2 Unlawful employment practices

(a) Employer practices

It shall be an unlawful employment practice for an employer—

(1) to fail or refuse to hire or to discharge any individual, or otherwise to discriminate against any individual with respect to his compensation, terms, conditions, or privileges of employment, because of such individual's race, color, religion, sex, or national origin; or

(2) to limit, segregate, or classify his employees or applicants for employment in any way which would deprive or tend to deprive any individual of employment opportunities or otherwise adversely affect his status as an employee, because of such individual's race, color, religion, sex, or national origin.

(b) Employment agency practices

It shall be an unlawful employment practice for an employment agency to fail or refuse to refer for employment, or otherwise to discriminate against, any individual because of his race, color, religion, sex, or national origin, or to classify or refer for employment any individual on the basis of his race, color, religion, sex, or national origin.

(c) Labor organization practices

It shall be an unlawful employment practice for a labor organization—

77. 42 U.S.C.A. § 2000(e), (k) (1978).

78. Hilow v. Rome City Sch. Dist., No. 91-CV-567, 1994 WL 328625 (N.D.N.Y. June 29, 1994).

79. *See, e.g.*, Andrews v. Drew Mun. Separate Sch. Dist., 507 F.2d 611 (5th Cir. 1975).

(1) to exclude or to expel from its membership, or otherwise to discriminate against, any individual because of his race, color, religion, sex, or national origin;

(2) to limit, segregate, or classify its membership or applicants for membership, or to classify or fail or refuse to refer for employment any individual, in any way which would deprive or tend to deprive any individual of employment opportunities, or would limit such employment opportunities or otherwise adversely affect his status as an employee or as an applicant for employment, because of such individual's race, color, religion, sex, or national origin; or

(3) to cause or attempt to cause an employer to discriminate against an individual in violation of this section.

(d) Training programs

It shall be an unlawful employment practice for any employer, labor organization, or joint labor-management committee controlling apprenticeship or other training or retraining, including on-the-job training programs to discriminate against any individual because of his race, color, religion, sex, or national origin in admission to, or employment in, any program established to provide apprenticeship or other training.

(e) Businesses or enterprises with personnel qualified on basis of religion, sex, or national origin; educational institutions with personnel of particular religion

Notwithstanding any other provision of this subchapter, (1) it shall not be an unlawful employment practice for an employer to hire and employ employees, for an employment agency to classify, or refer for employment any individual, for a labor organization to classify its membership or to classify or refer for employment any individual, or for an employer, labor organization, or joint labor management committee controlling apprenticeship or other training or retraining programs to admit or employ any individual in any such program, on the basis of his religion, sex, or national origin in those certain instances where religion, sex, or national origin is a bona fide occupational qualification reasonably necessary to the normal operation of that particular business or enterprise, and (2) it shall not be an unlawful employment practice for a school, college, university, or other educational institution or institution of learning to hire and employ employees of a particular religion if such school, college, university, or other educational institution or institution of learning is, in whole or in substantial part, owned, supported, controlled, or managed by a particular religion or by a particular religious corporation, association, or society, or if the curriculum of such school, college, university, or other educational institution or institution of learning is directed toward the propagation of a particular religion.

(f) Members of Communist Party or Communist-action or Communist-front organizations

As used in this subchapter, the phrase "unlawful employment practice" shall not be deemed to include any action or measure taken by an employer, labor organization, joint labor management committee, or employment agency with respect to an individual who is a member of the Communist Party of the United States or of any other organization required to register as a Communist-action or Communist-front organization by final order of the Subversive Activities Control Board pursuant to the Subversive Activities Control Act of 1950 *[50 U.S.C. 781 et seq.]*.

(g) National security

Notwithstanding any other provision of this subchapter, it shall not be an unlawful employment practice for an employer to fail or refuse to hire and employ any individual for any position, for an employer to discharge any individual from any position, or for an employment agency to fail or refuse to refer any individual for employment in any position, or for a labor organization to fail or refuse to refer any individual for employment in any position, if-

(1) the occupancy of such position, or access to the premises in or upon which any part of the duties of such position is performed or is to be performed, is subject to any requirement imposed in the interest of the national security of the United States under any security program in effect pursuant to or administered under any statute of the United States or any Executive order of the President; and

(2) such individual has not fulfilled or has ceased to fulfill that requirement.

(h) Seniority or merit system; quantity or quality of production; ability tests; compensation based on sex and authorized by minimum wage provisions

Notwithstanding any other provision of this subchapter, it shall not be an unlawful employment practice for an employer to apply different standards of compensation, or different terms, conditions, or privileges of employment pursuant to a bona fide seniority or merit system, or a system which measures earnings by quantity or quality of production or to employees who work in different locations, provided that such differences are not the result of an intention to discriminate because of race, color, religion, sex, or national origin, nor shall it be an unlawful employment practice for an employer to give and to act upon the results of any professionally developed ability test provided that such test, its administration or action upon the results is not designed, intended or used to discriminate because of race, color, religion, sex or national origin. It shall not be an unlawful employment practice under this subchapter for any employer to differentiate upon the basis of sex in determining the amount of the wages or compensation paid or to be paid to employees of such employer if such differentiation is authorized by the provisions of section 206(d) of Title 29 *[section 6(d) of the Labor Standards Act of 1938, as amended]*.

(i) Businesses or enterprises extending preferential treatment to Indians

Nothing contained in this subchapter shall apply to any business or enterprise on or near an Indian reservation with respect to any publicly announced employment practice of such business or enterprise under which a preferential treatment is given to any individual because he is an Indian living on or near a reservation.

(j) Preferential treatment not to be granted on account of existing number or percentage imbalance

Nothing contained in this subchapter shall be interpreted to require any employer, employment agency, labor organization, or joint labor-management committee subject to this subchapter to grant preferential treatment to any individual or to any group because of the race, color, religion, sex, or national origin of such individual or group on account of an imbalance which may exist with respect to the total number or percentage of persons of any race, color, religion, sex, or national origin employed by any employer, referred or classified for employment by any employment agency or labor organization, admitted to membership or classified by any labor organization, or admitted to, or employed in, any apprenticeship or other training program, in comparison with the total number or percentage of persons of such race, color, religion, sex, or national origin in any community, State, section, or other area, or in the available work force in any community, State, section, or other area.

(k) Burden of proof in disparate impact cases

(1) (A) An unlawful employment practice based on disparate impact is established under this subchapter only if—

(i) a complaining party demonstrates that a respondent uses a particular employment practice that causes a disparate impact on the basis of race, color, religion, sex, or national origin and the respondent fails to demonstrate that the challenged practice is job related for the position in question and consistent with business necessity; or

(ii) the complaining party makes the demonstration described in subparagraph (C) with respect to an alternative employment practice and the respondent refuses to adopt such alternative employment practice.

(B) (i) With respect to demonstrating that a particular employment practice causes a disparate impact as described in subparagraph (A)(i), the complaining party shall demonstrate that each particular challenged employment practice causes a disparate impact, except that if the complaining party can demonstrate to the court that the elements of a respondent's decisionmaking process are not capable of separation for analysis, the decisionmaking process may be analyzed as one employment practice.

(ii) If the respondent demonstrates that a specific employment practice does not cause the disparate impact, the respondent shall not be required to demonstrate that such practice is required by business necessity.

(C) The demonstration referred to by subparagraph (A)(ii) shall be in accordance with the law as it existed on June 4, 1989, with respect to the concept of "alternative employment practice".

(2) A demonstration that an employment practice is required by business necessity may not be used as a defense against a claim of intentional discrimination under this subchapter.

(3) Notwithstanding any other provision of this subchapter, a rule barring the employment of an individual who currently and knowingly uses or possesses a

controlled substance, as defined in schedules I and II of section 102(6) of the Controlled Substances Act (21 U.S.C. 802(6)), other than the use or possession of a drug taken under the supervision of a licensed health care professional, or any other use or possession authorized by the Controlled Substances Act *[21 U.S.C. 801 et seq.]* or any other provision of Federal law, shall be considered an unlawful employment practice under this subchapter only if such rule is adopted or applied with an intent to discriminate because of race, color, religion, sex, or national origin.

(l) Prohibition of discriminatory use of test scores

It shall be an unlawful employment practice for a respondent, in connection with the selection or referral of applicants or candidates for employment or promotion, to adjust the scores of, use different cutoff scores for, or otherwise alter the results of, employment related tests on the basis of race, color, religion, sex, or national origin.

(m) Impermissible consideration of race, color, religion, sex, or national origin in employment practices

Except as otherwise provided in this subchapter, an unlawful employment practice is established when the complaining party demonstrates that race, color, religion, sex, or national origin was a motivating factor for any employment practice, even though other factors also motivated the practice.

(n) Resolution of challenges to employment practices implementing litigated or consent judgments or orders

(1) (A) Notwithstanding any other provision of law, and except as provided in paragraph (2), an employment practice that implements and is within the scope of a litigated or consent judgment or order that resolves a claim of employment discrimination under the Constitution or Federal civil rights laws may not be challenged under the circumstances described in subparagraph (B).

(B) A practice described in subparagraph (A) may not be challenged in a claim under the Constitution or Federal civil rights laws—

(i) by a person who, prior to the entry of the judgment or order described in subparagraph (A), had—

(I) actual notice of the proposed judgment or order sufficient to apprise such person that such judgment or order might adversely affect the interests and legal rights of such person and that an opportunity was available to present objections to such judgment or order by a future date certain; and

(II) a reasonable opportunity to present objections to such judgment or order; or

(ii) by a person whose interests were adequately represented by another person who had previously challenged the judgment or order on the same legal grounds and with a similar factual situation, unless there has been an intervening change in law or fact.

(2) Nothing in this subsection shall be construed to—

(A) alter the standards for intervention under rule 24 of the Federal Rules of Civil Procedure or apply to the rights of parties who have successfully intervened pursuant to such rule in the proceeding in which the parties intervened;

(B) apply to the rights of parties to the action in which a litigated or consent judgment or order was entered, or of members of a class represented or sought to be represented in such action, or of members of a group on whose behalf relief was sought in such action by the Federal Government;

(C) prevent challenges to a litigated or consent judgment or order on the ground that such judgment or order was obtained through collusion or fraud, or is transparently invalid or was entered by a court lacking subject matter jurisdiction; or

(D) authorize or permit the denial to any person of the due process of law required by the Constitution.

(3) Any action not precluded under this subsection that challenges an employment consent judgment or order described in paragraph (1) shall be brought in the court, and if possible before the judge, that entered such judgment or order. Nothing in this subsection shall preclude a transfer of such action pursuant to section 1404 of Title 28.

Sexual Harassment

Title VII is the primary source of protection against sexual harassment. Sexual harassment has been defined as repeated and unwelcome advances, derogatory statements based on sex, or sexually demeaning gestures or acts.[80] Claims are filed when the victim has experienced adverse employment consequences, such as termination, demotion, or a bar to benefits, in connection with the sexual harassment. The school district has an affirmative obligation under Title VII to investigate teachers' complaints of sexual harassment by supervisors. Failure to investigate complaints can lead to a judgment against the school district.

In order for victims to find success in the charge, they need not prove that the harassment actually resulted in the loss of tangible job benefits. The Equal Employment Opportunity Commission (EEOC) has issued guidelines [*see* **Figure 3-2**] concerning sexual harassment in the workplace. The EEOC would inquire if sexual harassment is:

1. an explicit or implicit term on condition of employment
2. used as a basis for employment decisions
3. has the effect of unreasonably interfering with individuals' work performance
4. creates an intimidating, hostile, or offensive working environment.[81]

---

80. 29 C.F.R. § 1604.11(a) (1985).
81. 29 C.F.R. § 1604.11(a) (1980).

Initially, the federal government sought to prevent *quid pro quo* sexual harassment, which in Latin means "this for that." *Black's Law Dictionary* defines this type of sexual harassment as that "in which an employment decision is based on the satisfaction of a sexual demand."[82] A supervisor (employer) for *quid pro quo* sexual-harassment purposes is anyone who has the authority to hire, fire, promote, demote, or in any way affect the employment status of an individual or a person who participates in the decision-making process of the employee. In the case of a teacher, the principal would of course qualify as a supervisor but so would the assistant superintendent for personnel or the superintendent. However, the director of transportation might not qualify as a supervisor.

As of 1986, the Supreme Court recognized another form of sexual harassment known as *hostile environment* sexual harassment. Hostile environment sexual harassment results when the employee experiences sexually stereotypical insults, demeaning propositions, or unwanted touching that poison the psychological and work environment.[83] Exposure to vulgar language in itself has not constituted hostile environment sexual harassment nor has the occasional display of nude posters.[84] Situations which involve women harassing men or individuals of the same sex are also covered.[85]

School districts are directly responsible only for sexual harassment of employees by supervisors. Harassment occurring among workers at the same level is beyond the purview of the EEOC guidelines. An exception takes place when the employer knew of or should have known of harassment among employees and failed to take corrective measures.

Figure 3-2. EEOC Guidelines on Sexual Harassment

CODE OF FEDERAL REGULATIONS
TITLE 29 — LABOR
SUBTITLE B — REGULATIONS RELATING TO LABOR
CHAPTER XIV — EQUAL EMPLOYMENT OPPORTUNITY COMMISSION
PART 1604 — GUIDELINES ON DISCRIMINATION BECAUSE OF SEX
29 C.F.R. § 1604.11
§ 1604.11 Sexual harassment.

(a) Harassment on the basis of sex is a violation of section 703 of title VII.[1] Unwelcome sexual advances, requests for sexual favors, and other verbal or physical conduct of a sexual nature constitute sexual harassment when (1) submission to such conduct is made either explicitly or implicitly a term or condition of an individual's employment, (2) submission to or rejection of such conduct by an individual is used

82. *Sexual harassment, quid pro quo sexual harassment*, Black's Law Dictionary (11th ed. 2019).

83. Meritor Savings Bank v. Vinson, 477 U.S. 57 (1986).

84. Robinson v. Jacksonville, 760 F. Supp. 1486 (M.D. Fla. 1991).

85. Wright v. Methodist Youth Servs., 511 F. Supp. 307 (N.D. Ill. 1981).

as the basis for employment decisions affecting such individual, or (3) such conduct has the purpose or effect of unreasonably interfering with an individual's work performance or creating an intimidating, hostile, or offensive working environment.

Footnote(s):[1] The principles involved here continue to apply to race, color, religion, or national origin.

(b) In determining whether alleged conduct constitutes sexual harassment, the Commission will look at the record as a whole and at the totality of the circumstances, such as the nature of the sexual advances and the context in which the alleged incidents occurred. The determination of the legality of a particular action will be made from the facts, on a case by case basis.

(c) [Reserved]

(d) With respect to conduct between fellow employees, an employer is responsible for acts of sexual harassment in the workplace where the employer (or its agents or supervisory employees) knows or should have known of the conduct, unless it can show that it took immediate and appropriate corrective action.

(e) An employer may also be responsible for the acts of non-employees, with respect to sexual harassment of employees in the workplace, where the employer (or its agents or supervisory employees) knows or should have known of the conduct and fails to take immediate and appropriate corrective action. In reviewing these cases the Commission will consider the extent of the employer's control and any other legal responsibility which the employer may have with respect to the conduct of such non-employees.

(f) Prevention is the best tool for the elimination of sexual harassment. An employer should take all steps necessary to prevent sexual harassment from occurring, such as affirmatively raising the subject, expressing strong disapproval, developing appropriate sanctions, informing employees of their right to raise and how to raise the issue of harassment under Title VII, and developing methods to sensitize all concerned.

(g) Other related practices: Where employment opportunities or benefits are granted because of an individual's submission to the employer's sexual advances or requests for sexual favors, the employer may be held liable for unlawful sex discrimination against other persons who were qualified for but denied that employment opportunity or benefit.

Religious Discrimination

As is the case with racial and sex discrimination, Title VII of the Civil Rights Act of 1964 also protects employees from religious discrimination. The Free Exercise Clause of the First Amendment requires that employers not force teachers to relinquish their religious beliefs as a condition of employment. Teachers also have the right to abstain from certain school activities that they claim would conflict with their religious beliefs.

At the same time, there is a limit to teachers' free-exercise rights. For example, teachers abstaining from school activities can be disallowed if the absence would disrupt the operation of the school or impede the instructional program in some way. While there is no prohibition against teachers praying or otherwise engaging in religious practice during non-instructional time outside the view of students, that exercise can in no way interfere with the orderly operation of the school program or advance a particular religious belief in any way. In addition, teachers cannot use the free-exercise protection to refuse to teach a portion of a state-required curriculum because it is claimed to conflict with their religious views.

Many religious discrimination claims surround the school districts' failure to accommodate teachers with certain religious beliefs. Section 701(j) of Title VII places an affirmative duty upon the employer to accommodate employees' religious beliefs so long as that can be done without undue hardship on the conduct of the employer's business. What is undue hardship? The leading Supreme Court case on this issue is *Ansonia Board of Education v. Philbrook.*[86] In this case, Mr. Philbrook missed six school days for religious observations consistent with his Worldwide Church of God faith. He was docked two days' pay because only four of the six days could be covered as leave or personal business. Mr. Philbrook claimed that his being docked pay for the two days was religious discrimination. Ultimately, the Supreme Court ruled that when the school district provided Mr. Philbrook with some days off, it was "reasonably accommodating" him. It might have been different if the school district did not provide Mr. Philbrook with any days. The Court noted that for an employer to comply with Title VII, it need not grant every aspect of the employee's religiously based request(s). Reasonable accommodation for the Ansonia school district occurred when it gave him four of the six days.

At least one state (Pennsylvania) has a religious garb statute that prohibits public school teachers from wearing religious clothing and/or headdresses while on duty.[87] These issues tread a line between religious exercise and speech and have been the subject of litigation.[88] However, there is some indication that small symbols of religion, such as small cross or Star of David that does not include a message, would likely be permitted, lacking demonstration of a resulting disruption, controversy, or disturbance, or evidence of perceived government endorsement of the teacher's religion.[89]

---

86. 479 U.S. 60 (1986).

87. Pa. Public School Code of 1949, Act 14 § 1112.

88. *See, e.g.*, United States v. Bd. of Educ. for the Sch. Dist. of Philadelphia, 911 F.2d 882 (3d Cir. 1990) (garb statute prohibits teacher from wearing Muslim headdress in the school).

89. Nichol v. ARIN Intermediate Unit 28, 268 F. Supp. 2d 536 (W.D. Pa. 2003).

In sum, a school district must try to accommodate the religious beliefs of its employees to the extent that work activities do not force the employees to do something contrary to their religion. The employer may be expected to use a variety of methods to accommodate, such as accepting voluntary substitutes, permitting work-shift exchanges, using flexible scheduling, and changing job assignments. However, the employer is not required to place undue hardship on the school district in total deference to the need to accommodate. For example, a teacher may use their classroom or other areas to pray when students are not present; however, a school is not required to provide a dedicated area for that teacher to engage in mandatory prayer. Indeed, school districts cannot confer specific benefits on employees for religious reasons, such as paid leave available only for sectarian observances. In addition, a certain amount of impairment of the teachers' religious beliefs may be required to protect vulnerable public school children from religious inculcation.

Age Discrimination

Persons who have reached the age of 40 are protected against age discrimination by the Age Discrimination in Employment Act (ADEA) [*see* **Figure 3-3**]. There is no upper age limit for this protection. While some states have laws that protect younger workers from age discrimination, there is nothing in federal law that prohibits an employer from favoring older workers over younger ones. Initially passed by Congress in 1967, the ADEA and its amendments prohibit all forms of adverse employment conditions resulting from employer discrimination because of an employee's age.

Figure 3-3. § 623. Prohibition of Age Discrimination

(a) Employer practices

It shall be unlawful for an employer—

(1) to fail or refuse to hire or to discharge any individual or otherwise discriminate against any individual with respect to his compensation, terms, conditions, or privileges of employment, because of such individual's age;

(2) to limit, segregate, or classify his employees in any way which would deprive or tend to deprive any individual of employment opportunities or otherwise adversely affect his status as an employee, because of such individual's age; or

(3) to reduce the wage rate of any employee in order to comply with this chapter.

(b) Employment agency practices

It shall be unlawful for an employment agency to fail or refuse to refer for employment, or otherwise to discriminate against, any individual because of such individual's age, or to classify or refer for employment any individual on the basis of such individual's age.

(c) Labor organization practices

It shall be unlawful for a labor organization—

(1) to exclude or to expel from its membership, or otherwise to discriminate against, any individual because of his age;

(2) to limit, segregate, or classify its membership, or to classify or fail or refuse to refer for employment any individual, in any way which would deprive or tend to deprive any individual of employment opportunities, or would limit such employment opportunities or otherwise adversely affect his status as an employee or as an applicant for employment, because of such individual's age;

(3) to cause or attempt to cause an employer to discriminate against an individual in violation of this section.

(d) Opposition to unlawful practices; participation in investigations, proceedings, or litigation

It shall be unlawful for an employer to discriminate against any of his employees or applicants for employment, for an employment agency to discriminate against any individual, or for a labor organization to discriminate against any member thereof or applicant for membership, because such individual, member or applicant for membership has opposed any practice made unlawful by this section, or because such individual, member or applicant for membership has made a charge, testified, assisted, or participated in any manner in an investigation, proceeding, or litigation under this chapter.

(e) Printing or publication of notice or advertisement indicating preference, limitation, etc.

It shall be unlawful for an employer, labor organization, or employment agency to print or publish, or cause to be printed or published, any notice or advertisement relating to employment by such an employer or membership in or any classification or referral for employment by such a labor organization, or relating to any classification or referral for employment by such an employment agency, indicating any preference, limitation, specification, or discrimination, based on age.

(f) Lawful practices; age an occupational qualification; other reasonable factors; laws of foreign workplace; seniority system; employee benefit plans; discharge or discipline for good cause

It shall not be unlawful for an employer, employment agency, or labor organization—

(1) to take any action otherwise prohibited under subsections (a), (b), (c), or (e) of this section where age is a bona fide occupational qualification reasonably necessary to the normal operation of the particular business, or where the differentiation is based on reasonable factors other than age, or where such practices involve an employee in a workplace in a foreign country, and compliance with such subsections

would cause such employer, or a corporation controlled by such employer, to violate the laws of the country in which such workplace is located;

(2) to take any action otherwise prohibited under subsection (a), (b), (c), or (e) of this section—

(A) to observe the terms of a bona fide seniority system that is not intended to evade the purposes of this chapter, except that no such seniority system shall require or permit the involuntary retirement of any individual specified by section 631(a) of this title because of the age of such individual; or

(B) to observe the terms of a bona fide employee benefit plan—

(i) where, for each benefit or benefit package, the actual amount of payment made or cost incurred on behalf of an older worker is no less than that made or incurred on behalf of a younger worker, as permissible under *section 1625.10, title 29, Code of Federal Regulations* (as in effect on June 22, 1989); or

(ii) that is a voluntary early retirement incentive plan consistent with the relevant purpose or purposes of this chapter.

Notwithstanding clause (i) or (ii) of subparagraph (B), no such employee benefit plan or voluntary early retirement incentive plan shall excuse the failure to hire any individual, and no such employee benefit plan shall require or permit the involuntary retirement of any individual specified by section 631(a) of this title, because of the age of such individual. An employer, employment agency, or labor organization acting under subparagraph (A), or under clause (i) or (ii) of subparagraph (B), shall have the burden of proving that such actions are lawful in any civil enforcement proceeding brought under this chapter; or

(3) to discharge or otherwise discipline an individual for good cause.

(g) Repealed. *Pub.L. 101-239, Title VI, § 6202(b)(3)(C)(i),* Dec. 19, 1989, 103 Stat. 2233

(h) Practices of foreign corporations controlled by American employers; foreign employers not controlled by American employers; factors determining control

(1) If an employer controls a corporation whose place of incorporation is in a foreign country, any practice by such corporation prohibited under this section shall be presumed to be such practice by such employer.

(2) The prohibitions of this section shall not apply where the employer is a foreign person not controlled by an American employer.

(3) For the purpose of this subsection the determination of whether an employer controls a corporation shall be based upon the—

(A) interrelation of operations,

(B) common management,

(C) centralized control of labor relations, and

(D) common ownership or financial control, of the employer and the corporation.

(i) Employee pension benefit plans; cessation or reduction of benefit accrual or of allocation to employee account; distribution of benefits after attainment of normal retirement age; compliance; highly compensated employees

(1) Except as otherwise provided in this subsection, it shall be unlawful for an employer, an employment agency, a labor organization, or any combination thereof to establish or maintain an employee pension benefit plan which requires or permits—

(A) in the case of a defined benefit plan, the cessation of an employee's benefit accrual, or the reduction of the rate of an employee's benefit accrual, because of age, or

(B) in the case of a defined contribution plan, the cessation of allocations to an employee's account, or the reduction of the rate at which amounts are allocated to an employee's account, because of age.

(2) Nothing in this section shall be construed to prohibit an employer, employment agency, or labor organization from observing any provision of an employee pension benefit plan to the extent that such provision imposes (without regard to age) a limitation on the amount of benefits that the plan provides or a limitation on the number of years of service or years of participation which are taken into account for purposes of determining benefit accrual under the plan.

(3) In the case of any employee who, as of the end of any plan year under a defined benefit plan, has attained normal retirement age under such plan—

(A) if distribution of benefits under such plan with respect to such employee has commenced as of the end of such plan year, then any requirement of this subsection for continued accrual of benefits under such plan with respect to such employee during such plan year shall be treated as satisfied to the extent of the actuarial equivalent of in-service distribution of benefits, and

(B) if distribution of benefits under such plan with respect to such employee has not commenced as of the end of such year in accordance with section 1056(a)(3) of this title and section 401(a)(14)(C) of Title 26, and the payment of benefits under such plan with respect to such employee is not suspended during such plan year pursuant to section 1053(a)(3)(B) of this title or section 411(a)(3)(B) of Title 26, then any requirement of this subsection for continued accrual of benefits under such plan with respect to such employee during such plan year shall be treated as satisfied to the extent of any adjustment in the benefit payable under the plan during such plan year attributable to the delay in the distribution of benefits after the attainment of normal retirement age.

The provisions of this paragraph shall apply in accordance with regulations of the Secretary of the Treasury. Such regulations shall provide for the application of the preceding provisions of this paragraph to all employee pension benefit plans subject to this subsection and may provide for the application of such provisions, in the case of any such employee, with respect to any period of time within a plan year.

(4) Compliance with the requirements of this subsection with respect to an employee pension benefit plan shall constitute compliance with the requirements of this section relating to benefit accrual under such plan.

(5) Paragraph (1) shall not apply with respect to any employee who is a highly compensated employee (within the meaning of section 414(q) of Title 26) to the extent provided in regulations prescribed by the Secretary of the Treasury for purposes of precluding discrimination in favor of highly compensated employees within the meaning of subchapter D of chapter 1 of Title 26.

(6) A plan shall not be treated as failing to meet the requirements of paragraph (1) solely because the subsidized portion of any early retirement benefit is disregarded in determining benefit accruals or it is a plan permitted by subsection (m) of this section.

(7) Any regulations prescribed by the Secretary of the Treasury pursuant to clause (v) of section 411(b)(1)(H) of Title 26 and subparagraphs (C) and (D) of section 411(b)(2) of Title 26 shall apply with respect to the requirements of this subsection in the same manner and to the same extent as such regulations apply with respect to the requirements of such sections 411(b)(1)(H) and 411(b)(2).

(8) A plan shall not be treated as failing to meet the requirements of this section solely because such plan provides a normal retirement age described in section 1002(24)(B) of this title and section 411(a)(8)(B) of Title 26.

(9) For purposes of this subsection—

(A) The terms "employee pension benefit plan", "defined benefit plan", "defined contribution plan", and "normal retirement age" have the meanings provided such terms in section 1002 of this title.

(B) The term "compensation" has the meaning provided by section 414(s) of Title 26.

(j) Employment as firefighter or law enforcement officer

It shall not be unlawful for an employer which is a State, a political subdivision of a State, an agency or instrumentality of a State or a political subdivision of a State, or an interstate agency to fail or refuse to hire or to discharge any individual because of such individual's age if such action is taken—

(1) with respect to the employment of an individual as a firefighter or as a law enforcement officer, the employer has complied with section 3(d)(2) of the Age Discrimination in Employment Amendments of 1996 if the individual was discharged after the date described in such section, and the individual has attained—

(A) the age of hiring or retirement, respectively, in effect under applicable State or local law on March 3, 1983; or

(B)(i) if the individual was not hired, the age of hiring in effect on the date of such failure or refusal to hire under applicable State or local law enacted after September 30, 1996; or

(ii) if applicable State or local law was enacted after September 30, 1996, and the individual was discharged, the higher of—

(I) the age of retirement in effect on the date of such discharge under such law; and

(II) age 55; and

(2) pursuant to a bona fide hiring or retirement plan that is not a subterfuge to evade the purposes of this chapter.

(k) Seniority system or employee benefit plan; compliance

A seniority system or employee benefit plan shall comply with this chapter regardless of the date of adoption of such system or plan.

(l) Lawful practices; minimum age as condition of eligibility for retirement benefits; deductions from severance pay; reduction of long-term disability benefits

Notwithstanding clause (i) or (ii) of subsection (f)(2)(B) of this section—

(1) It shall not be a violation of subsection (a), (b), (c), or (e) of this section solely because—

(A) an employee pension benefit plan (as defined in section 1002(2) of this title) provides for the attainment of a minimum age as a condition of eligibility for normal or early retirement benefits; or

(B) a defined benefit plan (as defined in section 1002(35) of this title) provides for—

(i) payments that constitute the subsidized portion of an early retirement benefit; or

(ii) social security supplements for plan participants that commence before the age and terminate at the age (specified by the plan) when participants are eligible to receive reduced or unreduced old-age insurance benefits under title II of the Social Security Act (*42 U.S.C. 401* et seq.), and that do not exceed such old-age insurance benefits.

(2)(A) It shall not be a violation of subsection (a), (b), (c), or (e) of this section solely because following a contingent event unrelated to age—

(i) the value of any retiree health benefits received by an individual eligible for an immediate pension;

(ii) the value of any additional pension benefits that are made available solely as a result of the contingent event unrelated to age and following which the individual is eligible for not less than an immediate and unreduced pension; or

(iii) the values described in both clauses (i) and (ii); are deducted from severance pay made available as a result of the contingent event unrelated to age.

(B) For an individual who receives immediate pension benefits that are actuarially reduced under subparagraph (A)(i), the amount of the deduction available pursuant to subparagraph (A)(i) shall be reduced by the same percentage as the reduction in the pension benefits.

(C) For purposes of this paragraph, severance pay shall include that portion of supplemental unemployment compensation benefits (as described in section 501(c)(17) of Title 26) that—

(i) constitutes additional benefits of up to 52 weeks;

(ii) has the primary purpose and effect of continuing benefits until an individual becomes eligible for an immediate and unreduced pension; and

(iii) is discontinued once the individual becomes eligible for an immediate and unreduced pension.

(D) For purposes of this paragraph and solely in order to make the deduction authorized under this paragraph, the term "retiree health benefits" means benefits provided pursuant to a group health plan covering retirees, for which (determined as of the contingent event unrelated to age)—

(i) the package of benefits provided by the employer for the retirees who are below age 65 is at least comparable to benefits provided under title XVIII of the Social Security Act (*42 U.S.C. 1395* et seq.);

(ii) the package of benefits provided by the employer for the retirees who are age 65 and above is at least comparable to that offered under a plan that provides a benefit package with one-fourth the value of benefits provided under title XVIII of such Act; or

(iii) the package of benefits provided by the employer is as described in clauses (i) and (ii).

(E)(i) If the obligation of the employer to provide retiree health benefits is of limited duration, the value for each individual shall be calculated at a rate of $3,000 per year for benefit years before age 65, and $750 per year for benefit years beginning at age 65 and above.

(ii) If the obligation of the employer to provide retiree health benefits is of unlimited duration, the value for each individual shall be calculated at a rate of $48,000 for individuals below age 65, and $24,000 for individuals age 65 and above.

(iii) The values described in clauses (i) and (ii) shall be calculated based on the age of the individual as of the date of the contingent event unrelated to age. The values are effective on October 16, 1990, and shall be adjusted on an annual basis, with respect to a contingent event that occurs subsequent to the first year after October 16, 1990, based on the medical component of the Consumer Price Index for all-urban consumers published by the Department of Labor.

(iv) If an individual is required to pay a premium for retiree health benefits, the value calculated pursuant to this subparagraph shall be reduced by whatever percentage of the overall premium the individual is required to pay.

(F) If an employer that has implemented a deduction pursuant to subparagraph (A) fails to fulfill the obligation described in subparagraph (E), any aggrieved individual may bring an action for specific performance of the obligation described in subparagraph (E). The relief shall be in addition to any other remedies provided under Federal or State law.

(3) It shall not be a violation of subsection (a), (b), (c), or (e) of this section solely because an employer provides a bona fide employee benefit plan or plans under which long-term disability benefits received by an individual are reduced by any pension benefits (other than those attributable to employee contributions)—

(A) paid to the individual that the individual voluntarily elects to receive; or

(B) for which an individual who has attained the later of age 62 or normal retirement age is eligible.

(m) Voluntary retirement incentive plans

Notwithstanding subsection (f)(2)(b) of this section, it shall not be a violation of subsection (a), (b), (c), or (e) of this section solely because a plan of an institution of higher education (as defined in section 1001 of Title 20) offers employees who are serving under a contract of unlimited tenure (or similar arrangement providing for unlimited tenure) supplemental benefits upon voluntary retirement that are reduced or eliminated on the basis of age, if—

(1) such institution does not implement with respect to such employees any age-based reduction or cessation of benefits that are not such supplemental benefits, except as permitted by other provisions of this chapter;

(2) such supplemental benefits are in addition to any retirement or severance benefits which have been offered generally to employees serving under a contract of unlimited tenure (or similar arrangement providing for unlimited tenure), independent of any early retirement or exit-incentive plan, within the preceding 365 days; and

(3) any employee who attains the minimum age and satisfies all non-age-based conditions for receiving a benefit under the plan has an opportunity lasting not less than 180 days to elect to retire and to receive the maximum benefit that could then be elected by a younger but otherwise similarly situated employee, and the plan does not require retirement to occur sooner than 180 days after such election.

An age-discrimination claim results when an employee younger than those within the protected age group is in some way preferred over the older employee and that preference is based solely on age. The United States Department of Labor and certain federal courts have interpreted ADEA to also include a prohibition on age discrimination among employees *within* the protected age group. Therefore, a school district could not give preferential treatment to someone who is 42 over someone who is 61.

Within the definition of employer, the ADEA indicates a qualification of at least 20 employees. Therefore, school districts with under 20 employees each working a day in each of 20 or more calendar weeks in the current or preceding calendar year would be outside the protection of the Act.[90]

For an employee to prove an ADEA violation, most courts require that the disparate-treatment standard of review be used. (We mentioned this theory earlier when we discussed racial discrimination.) Thus, the teacher would need to show that the school district *intentionally* discriminated based upon age. The burden of proof rests with the teacher, and the requirement to show intentional disparate treatment on account of age is particularly difficult.

Aging is an unavoidable condition that all persons will experience, regardless of their race, creed, or sex. The aging process and its concomitant effect on certain physical abilities and mental faculties gives rise to a natural turnover in the workforce. Older people leave and younger people enter. Therefore, the replacement of an older employee by a younger one does not give rise to the same inference of discrimination as the replacement of a black employee by a white employee.

The school district has several avenues of defense in an ADEA case. The first is an affirmative defense based on the ADEA's permitting age discrimination if age is a bona fide occupational qualification (BFOQ) necessary for the operation of the business. In order to succeed with this defense, the school district must establish that there is a factual basis for believing that nearly all persons of a certain age group are incapable of performing the work safely and efficiently and that the foundation of the operation of the school district would be in peril if persons of that age were employed.

The school district might also attempt to establish that the age-discriminatory action was taken based on reasonable factors other than age or for good cause.[91] This defense attempts to defend by rebuttal, that is, to establish that the action was taken for a legitimate, nondiscriminatory reason. An action for a good cause is viewed as being motivated by the teacher's failure to perform the job at a minimally acceptable level of competence or by the failure to comply with reasonable school-district regulations. The reasonable-factors-other-than-age defense will pertain to a situation

---

90. 29 U.S.C. § 630 (b).

91. 29 U.S.C.A. § 623(f)(1), (3).

not arising from the teacher's work performance. For example, when an individual applied for an assistant principal position after their previous role as dean was eliminated under a reorganization and ultimately lost out to a younger applicant, they filed suit in federal court. The Eleventh Circuit sided with the school district, finding that the competing, and ultimately successful, applicant's additional certification provided a plainly nondiscriminatory basis for the hiring decision.[92]

Finally, the school district can successfully defend itself by establishing that it was taking actions that complied with a bona fide seniority system or bona fide employment benefits plan, except that the system or plan can neither require nor permit compulsory retirement based upon age. Generally, a bona fide seniority system or benefits plan is one established for reasons unrelated to age. Some states have laws that require mandatory retirement at a stated age if the licensing or other aspects of the job state age as a bona fide occupational qualification, as is the case for some state judges and elected officials who are not considered traditional employees under the federal law and those in high policymaking positions. While these may affect some administrators, such as those who spend 80 percent or more of their time on supervisory or management duties, rarely will any of these apply to most public-school employees.

In matters related to the rights of citizens, states can always provide protections where none exist at the federal level. More often, states will extend those rights that are only minimums by federal law, and several states have enacted companion statutes that protect against age discrimination in employment at the state level. Since the state can provide even more protection than is afforded at the federal level, principals should check the status of any age-discrimination statutes in their state.

Teacher Dismissal

The term *dismissal* must be distinguished from terms that may seem similar but are quite different. *Dismissal* is the termination of a tenured teacher at any point, or the termination of a probationary teacher's employment at any time prior to the end of the contract period. A *nonrenewal* is the termination of a probationary teacher's employment at the end of the contract period by board option not to renew. Therefore, the word *termination* is general and simply means the separation of teachers from their jobs. It is not sufficiently specific to be used in a legal framework. Certainly, the term *fired* is not used in the school setting, as this term suggests activities more typical in private industry.

The distinctions between dismissal and nonrenewal are important, since one or the other calls for a different level of due process that must be afforded the teacher

92. Bruno v. Greene Cty. Sch., 801 Fed. Appx. 681 (11th Cir. 2020).

prior to the action taken. What is *due process*? The concept of due process stems from the Fourteenth Amendment to the U.S. Constitution:

> No state shall make or enforce any law which shall abridge the privileges or immunities of citizens of the United States nor shall any State deprive any person of life, liberty, or property without due process of law, nor deny to any person within its jurisdiction the equal protection of the laws.

While very difficult to define precisely, due process can be discussed broadly as meaning that an individual has both liberty and property interests in their employment. These rights cannot be taken without notice and an opportunity for a hearing. Beyond these minimums, the level of due process that must be given depends generally on the status of the teacher (tenured or probationary) and on whether a liberty interest is involved in the termination.

A teacher's property interest is simply their right to do a job. This right is created by the employment contract in the case of probationary teachers and usually by the states' tenure laws for those teachers on tenure. A *liberty interest* is an interest in one's good name. A liberty interest may be implicated if the reason for dismissal involved damage to the teacher's potential for future employment. The leading U.S. Supreme Court case which provides the doctrines of liberty and property interests for teachers is *Board of Regents v. Roth.*[93] The determination of potential damage to future employment should be anticipated by school authorities, especially if the dismissal might create a stigma or might damage an individual's reputation. Failure to provide due process to a teacher whose liberty interest is involved can result in the nullification of the school authorities' action. If eligible, full procedural due-process rights would include the following:

1. notice of charges
2. impartial hearing
3. representation by counsel
4. presentation of witnesses on the teacher's behalf
5. cross-examination of adverse witnesses and challenge of incriminating evidence
6. opportunity to appeal to higher legal authority, including access to courts.

Dismissal of Non-Tenured Teachers

The level of due process required for the nonrenewal of a probationary teacher's contract is determined by state law. Generally, however, untenured teachers' contracts may be non-renewed at the end of any probationary year. This may be done without providing a hearing. Depending on whether the nonrenewal comes

93. 408 U.S. 564 (1972).

at the end of the first, second, or third year of probation, the board may not even be required to provide reasons for the nonrenewal. The number of years that a teacher must remain on probation varies from state to state, although the principal would not find much variation in the one-to-three-year standard. In most states, only the minimal procedural guarantee of a timely notice is required for the dismissal of a non-tenured teacher. Thus, states recognize some property rights for non-tenured teachers, but these rights are far less than those offered the tenured teacher.

A dismissal that might involve a teacher's liberty interest is an exception to the minimum procedural due process. If a liberty interest is involved, the teacher would be eligible for full procedural due-process rights. It should be noted that a teacher must do more than simply claim a liberty interest. The possibility of damage to the teacher's good name must be proved. Once more, the mere fact that the teacher was dismissed is not in itself sufficient proof that damage to good name took place. The court in *Roth* said that "it stretches the concept too far to suggest that a person is deprived of 'liberty' when he simply is not rehired in one job but remains as free as before to seek another."[94]

An additional exception to minimum procedural due process occurs when the non-tenured teacher is dismissed prior to the expiration of the contract year. The contract itself establishes a property right. Therefore, full due-process procedures must be given to those who are dismissed during the term of the contract.

Even though a teacher may not be tenured, some due process must be provided. In *Cleveland Board of Education v. Loudermill*,[95] the U.S. Supreme Court considered the due-process challenge of a school security guard who was terminated for dishonesty in filling out his employment application. The guard was given no opportunity to respond to the charge, nor was he granted any kind of hearing prior to his dismissal. In addressing the "property interest" issue, the Court concluded that the relevant Ohio statute "plainly create[d] such an interest" in the plaintiff because it specifically set forth the grounds for a dismissal: such an employee could be dismissed for "incompetency, inefficiency, dishonesty, drunkenness, immoral conduct, insubordination, discourteous treatment of the public, neglect of duty, violation of such section or the rules of the director of administrative services or the commission, or any other failure of good behavior, or any other acts of misfeasance, malfeasance, or nonfeasance in office."[96]

Connecticut Education Association, Inc. v. Tirozzi[97] also provides a good example of a state-created property interest in a teaching certificate. In that case, the Supreme Court of Connecticut held that the rights of public-school teachers in their teaching certificates constitute protected property interests because a Connecticut statute declares that a teacher's certificate can be revoked only "for cause." Even though the

94. 408 U.S. 564, 575 (1972).
95. 470 U.S. 532 (1985).
96. *Id.* at 538–39.
97. 554 A.2d 1065 (Conn. 1989).

types of "cause" justifying a dismissal were not set forth in detail as they were in *Loudermill*, the statutory language was enough to invoke the Due Process Clause: "A teacher who is given by statute the right to continued employment except upon a showing of cause . . . acquires a property right that is entitled to protection under the due process clause."[98]

Dismissal of Tenured Teachers

Before tenured teachers can be dismissed, the full procedural due-process rights outlined by state law must be provided. Once more, school authorities cannot dismiss the tenured teacher unless they have cause. As is the case with tenure laws generally, the definition of the word *cause* will vary from state to state.

The most common causes listed by statute for the dismissal of tenured teachers are incompetency, insubordination, and immorality. Regardless of which cause is used, the board of education must have evidence that the teacher did in fact perform, or fail to perform, in certain ways that must result in dismissal. The board may not simply allege that the teacher is incompetent, insubordinate, or immoral without evidence. It is at this point that the board must rely heavily on the administration to supply the evidence. It is typically the building principal who has gathered the necessary documentation which provides the support for the dismissal.

The principal should be aware of the basic legal standards that have emerged pertaining to the nature of evidence for dismissal of tenured teachers. Six ideas should be kept in mind before the principal contemplates a dismissal:

1. The evidence must be substantial.
2. It must be relevant to establish the alleged facts.
3. It must be developed in a constitutionally approved way (no illegal wire taps, for example).
4. It must be documented, which, in its simplest form, means recording the time, date, and place, with witnesses listed, if any.
5. Evidence presented at the hearing should be limited to charges made.
6. The rules of evidence applicable in court proceedings do not apply in a strict sense to dismissal hearings.

The written evaluation is often used in connection with dismissal for incompetency. *Incompetency* has been broadly defined by the courts. However, the term can be used to connote a lack of some requisite ability. Among the three most widely asserted grounds for dismissal, incompetency is the most difficult to prove and requires the most documentation. In addition, some states, such as Illinois,[99] require that a distinction be made between those causes that are remediable and those that

98. *Id.* at 1070.

99. 105 Ill. Comp. Stat. 5/24A-5 (effective July 1, 2014).

are not. If the teacher has been found to be incompetent and is consequently dismissed, the court will look to see whether the incompetency was remediable. If it is found to be remediable, the school must show that attempts were made to remediate the teacher's incompetency.

School authorities' use of immorality as a cause for dismissal has come under closer scrutiny by the courts in recent years. Generally, the courts will require that there be proof of a relationship between the immoral conduct and unfitness to teach. The exception seems to be sexual conduct between the teacher and student; courts have consistently held that such behavior is sufficient cause for dismissal. In other words, there is a presumption of unfitness to teach when teacher-student sexual conduct is found.

Insubordination, the willful disregard for or refusal to obey school regulations and official orders, is the easiest to prove among the three most common causes for dismissal. Since conduct is measured against the existence of a rule or policy, insubordination is more readily documented by school authorities and is thus more supportable than other causes. A dismissal based upon insubordination is likely to be upheld by the court if the teacher acted willfully, deliberately, fraudulently, evasively, defiantly, or contemptuously with respect to a policy, rule, or order from a superior. However, a dismissal may be held unjustifiable if the order that the teacher disobeyed was unreasonable. Teachers dismissed improperly on insubordination grounds have been reinstated by courts for various reasons, including insufficient evidence to prove the misconduct had occurred, insufficient showing of the existence of the alleged rule violated, lack of authority for issuance of the rule or order by the board, bias or discrimination against the teacher in the enforcement of the rule, or a violation of the teacher's First Amendment academic freedom or freedom of speech.

Documentation for Dismissal: Sufficiency of Evidence

It is important for school authorities to have developed a record of the lack of teacher performance to dismiss. State statutes frequently require that a teacher's performance be evaluated before the district terminates the contract.[100] The number of annual evaluations conducted varies but usually are more frequent for probationary teachers than for tenured teachers. When not renewing or terminating teachers' contracts, statutes typically require that only certain grounds serve as bases for termination. Often the statutes identify "grounds" to be used when terminating tenured teachers but refer to "reasons" for dismissing probationary teachers.[101] The difference between grounds and reasons is largely one of specificity. Grounds are statutorily stipulated and usually consist of three of four areas of deficiency. Reasons

100. For a thorough treatment of this topic, see LAWRENCE F. ROSSOW & LAUREL A. LOGAN, THE LAW OF TEACHER EVALUATION (3d ed. 2013).

101. *See, e.g.*, TEX. EDUC. CODE ANN. § 21.211 (2012).

could be anything the local board of education feels accurately describes the basis for the termination. However, the reasons should be rationally related to a legitimate objective of the board in retaining qualified teachers. It should be noted that local boards may also use statutory grounds as reasons for terminating non-tenured teachers. The most typical statutory grounds are incompetence, immorality, insubordination, and other just causes.

To show that a teacher has violated one of these grounds, school authorities must have proof. Therefore, the question becomes, what kind or level of evidence is sufficient? While proving each of the grounds is different, there are some general principles that can be followed. Local boards of education have considerable discretionary power in assembling evidence. The board's assessment of the facts to determine whether there are grounds or reasons for terminating teachers' contracts in most cases will be accepted by a reviewing court. For example, in a teacher dismissal case, a South Carolina court concluded that "if any of the charges against a teacher are supported by substantial evidence, the school board's decision to dismiss must be sustained. We defined 'substantial evidence' as 'evidence which, considering the record as a whole, would allow reasonable minds to reach the conclusion that *the administrative agency* reached or must have reached in order to justify its action.'"[102]

Incompetence

Perhaps more than any other charge used for dismissal, removing a teacher for incompetence requires that repeated evaluations clearly show un-remediated deficiencies. The establishment of incompetence rarely rests on a single incident. *American Law Reports* concludes that the courts' view of teacher incompetence is driving the multiple deficiencies requirement:

> [T]he incompetent teacher is rarely deficient in one respect alone; rather, incompetence seems to manifest itself in a pervasive pattern encompassing a multitude of sins and bringing in its wake disorganization, disharmony, and an atmosphere unproductive for the acquisition of knowledge or any other ancillary benefit.[103]

Compared to other grounds that are used to terminate teachers, incompetence is the most time-consuming and demanding of documentation. Nevertheless, it remains one of the most often-used grounds for removing teachers. Incompetence is the deficiency most related to the teaching process. When a board of education attempts to carry out its goal of retaining "good teachers," removing those that are incompetent seems to follow. While incompetence can consist of several different deficiencies, the areas most litigated include student control problems and instructional failures.

---

102. Brown v. James, 697 S.E.2d 604, 609 (S.C. Ct. App. 2010).
103. 4 A.L.R. 3d 1090, 1102.

Regardless of the difficulty in dismissing on grounds of incompetence, an increase in the knowledge of the laws of teacher evaluation can help the administrator ward off feelings of discouragement. For school boards, caution should be exercised in the use of the incompetence ground when the evidence points not to the teacher's inadequacy but to some other misbehavior. In *M.T. v. Department of Education*,[104] a Pennsylvania teacher successfully defended his dismissal when he was able to show that he was a competent music teacher. The school district's reason for the dismissal was based on the teacher's alleged sexual misconduct with a student. However, the dismissal proceeding used incompetence as the grounds.

While lack of classroom control is one of the major problems leading to nonrenewal of probationary teachers' contracts, the dismissals that have most often produced litigation are those of tenured teachers. In many court decisions, school districts have been successful against challenges from teachers. In *Alexander v. Reeves*,[105] an elementary school principal recommended that a middle-school health teacher be terminated from his position. The basis for the termination was "neglect of duty," specifically his failure to supervise his classroom adequately and the failure to report an incident to the administrator regarding an assault on a student by other students. The teacher argued that the decision to dismiss was arbitrary and capricious and that there were other teachers who had classroom-management problems who were not dismissed.

For a school board's decision to be arbitrary and capricious, it must be shown to have been made without substantial evidence. In *Alexander*, there was no testimony that other similarly situated teachers were treated differently. Additionally, the principal testified that Alexander's classroom management was far "more troubling" than that of other teachers, stating that "[n]othing comes close" to it. She added, "His were safety issues, kids pushing, running, pulling desks, that kind of thing. It's a really an out-of-control classroom."[106] The court held that the record showed that there was a rational and factual basis for Alexander's termination and no indication that the decision was based on improper criteria. Therefore, the court found that there was sufficient evidence to support the decision to terminate Alexander.[107]

In some states, neglect of duty is seen as a form of incompetence. The use of neglect-of-duty grounds potentially could require less documentation. A single event, depending on severity, might be sufficient for dismissal. Nevertheless, the use of incompetence as grounds for dismissal or nonrenewal will require some level of longitudinal documentation. For example, in *Salerno v. Seaford Union Free School District*,[108] a special education teacher was found to have had classroom-management problems across a period of two years. These problems were documented

104. 56 A.3d 1 (Pa. Commw. Ct. 2012).

105. 90 So. 3d 1273 (Miss. Ct. App. 2012).

106. *Id.* at 1282.

107. *Id.*

108. 958 N.Y.S.2d 648 (Sup. Ct. 2011).

in written observations such as "[her] students had a great deal of difficulty following directions," "[she should] consider methods and techniques to handle students' misbehavior," and "she must be more sensitive to her students' needs and the manner and need of resolving disciplinary problems." In *Salerno*, it was noted in the teacher's evaluation that several students were acting out throughout the observed lesson and that she was advised to continue to assist students who do not model appropriate behavior and explore the advice of colleagues and the administration to resolve the problem. The result was that in eight out of eight observation reports, the teacher was found to be unsuccessful in handling classroom incidents or emergencies efficiently.[109]

Immorality

Immorality continues to be an often-used ground for teacher termination. The following section provides examples of case law concerning teacher immorality. A sample of cases is used because the number of cases decided is too large for individual treatment. Determining that a teacher has not met the standard for moral fitness is a subject for the evaluation process. While immorality would be difficult to connect to actual in-class performance, its detection is no less significant. Typically, moral unfitness is a judgment call by the school board. The need to decide a teacher's moral fitness is thrust upon the board by events "reported" by the administration, students, or the public. While the moral fitness components of an evaluation are not subject to precise measurement, it becomes part of the overall summative evaluation. The U.S. Supreme Court has recognized the importance of local authorities considering the moral fitness of teachers.[110] The more difficult questions are: How is immorality defined? What teacher behaviors have courts considered to be within this definition?

The California Court of Appeals in *San Diego Unified School District v. Commission on Professional Competence*[111] provided a good definition of teacher immorality in stating that:

> The term "immoral" has been defined generally as that which is hostile to the welfare of the general public and contrary to good morals. Immorality has not been confined to sexual matters, but includes conduct inconsistent with rectitude, or indicative of corruption, indecency, depravity, dissoluteness; or as willful, flagrant, or shameless conduct showing moral indifference to the opinions of respectable members of the community, and as an inconsiderate attitude toward good order and the public welfare.[112] Moreover, the definition of immoral or unprofessional conduct must be

109. *Id.*

110. *See* Bd. of Educ. v. Pico, 457 U.S. 853 (1982).

111. 124 Cal. Rptr. 3d 320 (2011).

112. *Id.* at 329 (citing Bd. of Educ. v. Weiland, 179 Cal. App. 2d 808, 811, 4 Cal. Rptr. 286 (1960)).

> considered in conjunction with the unique position of public-school teachers, upon whom are imposed "responsibilities and limitations on freedom of action which do not exist in regard to other callings."[113]

The preponderance of cases in the last decade involving termination on grounds of immorality has been won by the school districts. Immorality is a broad category which is manifested in several forms including sexual misconduct (also commonly referred to as *moral turpitude*). State statutes tend to include *dishonesty* as a manifestation of immorality. Later in this section, the specific misbehaviors of teachers who were terminated for dishonesty will be recalled from an earlier decade. Most recently, the courts have considered potential immoral behavior such as sexually explicit internet solicitation, drug possession, acts of violence, lewd speech, and traffic violations.

In *San Diego Unified School District,* a tenured middle school teacher posted information on Craigslist that he was interested in meeting for sex. The ad also contained four pictures of the teacher Frank Lampedusa: the first of his face, torso, and abdomen; the second of his anus; the third of his genitalia; and the fourth of his face and upper torso. An anonymous tip to the local police was brought to the attention of the school district's area superintendent. The teacher in question was called by the administration which suggested that he remove the listing. The teacher agreed and immediately left the school to go home and remove the listing. The listing was up for approximately two days. Later that evening, the teacher searched the internet further and took steps to ensure there was no other link to the listing or any other information on the internet that would tie him to it.[114]

The teacher was dismissed for unfitness to teach. However, upon appeal, the California Commission on Professional Competence found that the school district did not have substantial evidence of Lampedusa's unfitness to teach. It found no nexus between the ads and any adverse effect on his ability to be an effective teacher. The decision was challenged in the Superior Court of California, which upheld the commission's opinion. On appeal, the school district argued that Lampedusa's actions clearly established that he was unfit. In making their decision, the state appeals court used criteria announced decades earlier by the California Supreme Court in *Morrison v. State Board of Education.*[115] The *Morrison* court articulated the following factors in determining a teacher's unfitness to teach. They are:

> [1] the likelihood that the conduct may have adversely affected students or fellow teachers, [2] the degree of such adversity anticipated, [3] the proximity or remoteness in time of the conduct, [4] the type of teaching certificate held by the party involved, [5] the extenuating or aggravating circumstances, if any, surrounding the conduct, [6] the praiseworthiness or

113. *Id.* (citing Bd. of Trs. v. Stubblefield, 16 Cal. App. 3d 820, 826, 94 Cal. Rptr. 318 (1971)).
114. *Id.* at 323.
115. 1 Cal. 3d 214 (1969).

> blameworthiness of the motives resulting in the conduct, [7] the likelihood of the recurrence of the questioned conduct, and [8] the extent to which disciplinary action may inflict an adverse impact or chilling effect upon the constitutional rights of the teacher involved or other teachers.[116]

These factors have been developed to aid the school board in determining a teacher's fitness to teach and "in determining whether the teacher's *future* classroom performance and overall impact on his students are likely to meet the [school district's] standards" (emphasis added).[117]

Reversing the trial court, the court of appeals noted that the commission and therefore the superior court ignored the evidence that a parent and an educator *did* view the ad. Thus, the evidence established that Lampedusa's conduct interfered with his ability to serve as a role model at school. It appears that the lower court and commission relied too heavily on the notion that the teacher's misconduct was not job related. In addition, they seemed to believe that actual damages or adverse effects need to be present for the teacher to be dismissed, whereas the Court of Appeals' analysis placed the bar much lower. It concluded that a reasonable forecast of adverse effect is dispositive of unfitness.

Professional Misconduct as Immorality

Unprofessional conduct by a school employee is conduct that does not rise to the level of immoral conduct, which the courts have held to be a higher form of misconduct. In *McFerren v. Farrell Area School District*,[118] a Pennsylvania court considered an appeal from an African American school administrator who was dismissed for telling an African American student that "the white man is going to kick your ass." The board's dismissal was based on immorality as determined by local community morals. However, on appeal, the court found that the district did not make its case. It said:

> The Secretary erred in holding that McFerren's use of the phrase "the white man" was *per se* immoral. It was the District's burden to present evidence of the morals of the community and evidence that McFerren's comment offended those morals, and it did not do so. Accordingly, we reverse the Secretary's conclusion that McFerren committed an act of immorality.[119]

Political correctness should not be confused with morality. McFerren's choice of words was unfortunate, as much for the unnecessary anatomical reference as for the reference to race. It is human nature to say things thoughtlessly, particularly in stressful situations that are later regretted. Context is also important in evaluating whether speech is offensive.

---

116. *Id.* at 229.

117. *Id.* at 229–30.

118. 993 A.2d 344 (Pa. Commw. Ct. 2010).

119. *Id.* at 356.

In *Alston v. Unemployment Compensation Board of Review*,[120] an African American employee was dismissed, in part, for using "the 'N' word during a conversation with another employee";[121] the matter was remanded on procedural grounds. McFerren argued that by pointing out the race of the speaker and the addressee, the *Alston* court acknowledged that the context in which racial remarks are made should be considered. Irrespective of *Alston*, McFerren's point on context is a good one. The use of the "N" word conveys a different message when spoken by African Americans than when spoken by white people. Likewise, McFerren's comment, if made to a white student, might have touched upon morality in the way it did not in Savage's case. Furthermore, an immoral act generally requires premeditation, as in the commission of a *crimen falsi* or the distribution of racist materials.[122]

Unethical Behavior and Dishonesty as Immorality

The Missouri Court of Appeals upheld a tenured teacher's dismissal for engaging in immoral conduct. The teacher was in charge of the Parents as Teachers (PAT) program, a support program for increasing parent and teacher cooperation. One of the parents and program participants was jailed for an immigration violation. During the incarceration, the program director authorized a visit for the purpose of persuading the inmate to give up an 11-month-old infant for adoption.[123] The teacher covered up the purpose of the visit while requesting mileage reimbursement. The school district considered the teacher's cover-up to be a violation of the *Supervisor's Manual and Program Administration Guide, Born to Learn™ Components: Ethical Considerations for Parent Educators*[124] and concluded that the teacher's behavior was unethical, dishonest, and therefore immoral.

Some courts require further evidence to support a justification for dismissal on grounds of immorality. For example, the court in *Broney v. California Commission on Teacher Credentialing*[125] concluded that a school district could not dismiss a teacher whose behavior it did not like absent a showing that it directly affected teaching performance. In other words, the immorality must render the teacher *unfit*. Citing to the *Morrison* decision, it said:

> Terms such as "immoral or unprofessional conduct" or "moral turpitude" stretch over so wide a range that they embrace an unlimited area of conduct. In using them the Legislature surely did not mean to endow the employing agency with the power to dismiss any employee whose personal, private conduct incurred its disapproval. Hence the courts have consistently

120. 967 A.2d 432 (Pa. Commw. Ct. 2009).
121. *Id.* at 433.
122. 993 A.2d at 356.
123. Homa v. Carthage R-IX Sch. Dist., 345 S.W.3d 266 (Mo. Ct. App. 2011).
124. *Id.* at 270.
125. 108 Cal. Rptr. 3d 832 (2010).

> related the terms to the issue of whether, when applied to the performance of the employee on the job, the employee has disqualified himself. . . .[126]

In other words, does the conduct at issue render the petitioner "unfit to teach"?[127]

Unbecoming Conduct as Immorality

Conduct unbecoming a teacher is a legal term emanating from state laws that have been used both to suspend and dismiss teachers. For example, in *Board of Education of Fayette County v. Hurley-Richards*,[128] Kentucky state law defined "conduct unbecoming a teacher" as "conduct that is unsuitable, indecorous, or improper for a teacher." In this case, a teacher was initially suspended with pay for allegedly coercing a student to go to the office after he had been pulling his sister's hair in the school's hallway. There had also been a claim, later disproved, that the male child was choking. A hearing tribunal found this conduct to fall within the "conduct unbecoming" statute but the Kentucky Supreme Court ruled otherwise, viewing the teacher's conduct as an appropriate method of discipline.

Another case, *Robinson v. Ohio Department of Education*,[129] dealing with charges of unbecoming conduct involved Craig Robinson, a middle school teacher who during his planning period received and viewed an email containing four pictures of a woman posing. In three of the pictures, the woman was wearing a bikini; the fourth picture showed her bare breasts and pubic area. (The images were attached to a message from a fraternity brother of Robinson regarding the nursing care of another fraternity brother who had undergone surgery.) Later that day, Robinson accessed the email on the classroom computer of another teacher, Billy Brooks, to show the pictures to Brooks.

There were students in Brooks' classroom at the time, but there was no evidence that the students saw or were intended to see the pictures. Brooks believed that the fourth image was pornographic, and he reported what occurred to the principal. After an investigation, Robinson was placed on administrative leave. After a hearing, he was suspended without pay for a period of five days. The Dayton Public Schools filed an educator misconduct reporting form with the Ohio Department of Education. Following another investigation, the Ohio Department of Education notified Robinson that the State Board of Education intended to determine whether to limit, suspend, or revoke his teaching license. Robinson requested a hearing on the matter at which he testified that the email's images were inappropriate for students to view but that his conduct was not "conduct unbecoming an educator."[130]

126. Morrison v. State Bd. of Educ., 1 Cal. 3d at 224–25 (1969).
127. *Id.* at 230.
128. 396 S.W.3d 879 (Ky. 2013).
129. 971 N.E.2d 977 (Ohio Ct. App. 2012).
130. *Id.* at 980.

> The hearing officer considered Ohio law,' R.C. 3319.31(B), Ohio Adm. Code 3301-73-21 and the Licensure Code of Professional Conduct for Ohio Educators and concluded that "Mr. Robinson violated this standard, along with the aforementioned applicable law, through his use of school e-mail, school computers, and the school network to view lewd photos, one including nudity, during the school day and with students in the classroom." The hearing officer considered Robinson's "conduct and work activity before the misconduct, his lack of previous misconduct or discipline, and the five-day suspension already imposed by the Dayton Public Schools" to be mitigating factors. The officer considered Robinson's belief that his conduct was not inappropriate for an educator to be an aggravating factor.
>
> The hearing officer concluded that Robinson's conduct constituted conduct unbecoming a teacher, in violation of R.C. 3319.31(B)(1). The officer further concluded that there was a nexus between Robinson's conduct and his performance as a teacher. The officer recommended that Robinson's license be suspended for one year, with all but 60 days suspended, to be served in the summer months.[131]

In a North Dakota Supreme Court case,[132] a teacher's "unbecoming conduct" included telling a student to lose weight, calling another student "stupid," and making comments about "skinny Ethiopian women."[133] These events occurred in such a manner that other students could hear the remarks. Moreover, the school principal had worked with this teacher for some seven years to help improve his relations with students.

Sexual Activities with Students as Immorality

In *M.T. v. Department of Education*,[134] a high-school band director was dismissed for immorality when he was found to have had a sexual relationship with one of the student band members. At the hearing level, the Pennsylvania Professional Standards and Practices Commission citing Pennsylvania Code[135] agreed that the teacher engaged in immoral conduct. It noted that:

> the Commission has promulgated regulations to define terms in the Act that describe the conduct for which the Commission may impose discipline.... Those regulations define "immorality" as "conduct which offends the morals of the Commonwealth and is a bad example to the youth whose ideals a professional educator ... has a duty to foster and elevate".... Based upon the factual findings regarding the nature of the physical contact M.T.

---

131. *Id.*
132. Kilber v. Grand Forks Pub. Sch. Dist., 820 N.W.2d 96 (N.D. 2012).
133. *Id.* at 98.
134. 56 A.3d 1 (Pa. Commw. Ct. 2010).
135. 22 Pa. Code § 237.3 (2002).

> initiated with Student, we conclude that the Commission did not err in concluding as a matter of law that M.T.'s conduct was immoral.[136]

While not exactly "sexual relations," in *City School District of the City of New York v. McGraham*,[137] a 36-year-old tenured high school teacher was the subject of disciplinary charges pursuant to her improper conduct with respect to a 15-year-old male student. The teacher corresponded with the student electronically outside of school hours—sometimes late at night—about a variety of personal matters and tried to discuss with him the nature of their relationship, which, in her view, was potentially romantic. There was, however, no physical contact between the two and none of her communications was of a sexual nature. The teacher agreed to disciplinary arbitration in which the arbitrator found the teacher guilty of serious misconduct unbecoming a person in her position and imposed a 90-day suspension without pay and reassignment, rather than termination.

Cruelty as Immorality

In *M.T.*,[138] the Pennsylvania State Department of Education made a unique argument regarding cruelty. It concluded that the band director's sexual misbehavior constituted cruelty.

> [T]he Department refers us to the definition of "malicious," which Black's Law Dictionary describes as meaning "substantially certain to cause injury without just cause or excuse." Black's Law Dictionary 969 (7th ed. 1999). The Department argues that cruelty can involve both physical and psychological harm to a person and that, as a result of M.T.'s persistent sexual conduct with Student, Student became withdrawn from friends and family. The Commission, adopting the Hearing Officer's analysis, reasoned that M.T.'s conduct was cruel because it "was certain to cause psychological injury and was without just cause or excuse."[139]

The state court went on to affirm the decision of the commission. All of M.T.'s teaching licenses were revoked.

Douglas v. New York City Board /Department of Education[140] involved a New York City high school chemistry teacher who was terminated for immorality when he engaged in inappropriate, sexually explicit communication with a student. The teacher "asked Student A whether she liked anyone or had a boyfriend; told her that she was dressing sexy lately; asked her to touch her breast and demonstrated how he wanted her to do that; and touched his genitals in front of her . . . [He] simulated a

136. 56 A.3d at 11.
137. 958 N.E.2d 897 (N.Y. 2011).
138. 56 A.3d 1.
139. *Id.* at 9.
140. 87 A.D.3d 856 (N.Y. App. Div. 1st Dept. 2011).

woman's breast with a balloon, which he squeezed while stating words to the effect that 'we got some chemistry going on.'"[141] The teacher argued that the punishment of termination was so disproportionate to the offense, in light of all the circumstances, as to be "shocking to one's sense of fairness" and thus a violation of substantive due process. The court disagreed and concluded that the teacher's behavior was unbecoming of the profession. It upheld the dismissal.

Criminal Activity as Immorality

In *Hutchison v. Kentucky Unemployment Insurance Commission*,[142] teacher Carolyn Hutchison was arrested for third-degree terroristic threatening and two counts of fourth-degree assault (all misdemeanors) in addition to first-degree burglary (a felony). These charges arose from Hutchison's behavior following the breakup of a 16-year romantic relationship. She pleaded guilty. The employer informed Hutchison that her employment was terminated because she had engaged in conduct which rendered her unable to be a role model for her students. Hutchison filed for unemployment benefits, and her request was denied. She appealed the initial determination to a referee. The teacher argued that she should be eligible for unemployment compensation because her termination was based on conduct that was not connected to her job.

While the court recognized that under ordinary circumstances, some nexus between conduct and job performance would be required, there are exceptions. The teaching profession is one of those exceptions. The court noted that there is a heightened standard of conduct for teachers. "The purpose of teacher tenure laws is to promote good order in the school system by preventing the arbitrary removal of capable and experienced teachers by political or personal whim. It is not to protect those who violate the criminal law."[143]

In *Watkins v. McDowell County Board of Education*,[144] a West Virginia sixth-grade science teacher was convicted of a misdemeanor battery charge following an altercation with a parent during a school meeting. The teacher was subsequently terminated for immorality. The appeal of her termination was upheld by an administrative law judge, state district court, and court of appeals.

Fraud is another form of immorality as grounds for termination. In *Cipollaro v. New York City Department of Education*,[145] the court affirmed a hearing officer's determination that a teacher knowingly defrauded the New York City Department of Education out of $98,000 over a two-year period by enrolling two of her children in New York City public schools. She and her family lived in Westchester County

141. *Id.* at 858.

142. 329 S.W.3d 353 (Ky. Ct. App. 2010).

143. *Id.* at 356–57.

144. 729 S.E.2d 822 (W. Va. 2012).

145. 83 A.D.3d 543 (N.Y. App. Div. 1st Dept. 2011).

and thus would have had to bear the full cost of instruction. The teacher termination was upheld.

In *Powell v. Paine*,[146] a West Virginia science teacher and head football coach disciplined his then nine-year-old son to a point where the Department of Health and Human Resources and law enforcement began investigations. While the teacher was initially charged with felony child abuse for the injuries inflicted upon his son, the case was ultimately resolved with a plea to one count of misdemeanor domestic battery. The teacher/coach was sentenced to 30 days of incarceration to be served on weekends and a fine, but he was subsequently dismissed from his job for immorality.

In *Timpani v. Lakeside School District*,[147] an Arkansas teacher who took funds from a student book-purchasing program was terminated even though criminal charges were never brought. The teacher had accumulated "bonus points" as a result of her students' purchasing books from an outside vendor. With these bonus points, the teacher ordered personal items such as refrigerators and toasters. Once it was discovered that the teacher was taking such items for use in her home, the school superintendent proceeded to recommend the teacher for dismissal. Accepting the recommendation of the superintendent, the board moved to dismiss the teacher for immorality. On appeal to the state court, the teacher argued to no avail that it was standard practice for teachers to take the proceeds of bonus points for personal use. Finding insufficient evidence for the teacher's argument, the court upheld the dismissal.

Other issues which have led to teacher dismissal include carrying on a long-term immoral adulterous relationship with the parent of a child in class;[148] refusing to take a drug test in violation of the school district's drug and alcohol policy;[149] masturbating while standing in a school parking lot while looking at a group of girls;[150] falsifying college transcripts;[151] and possession of cocaine, possession of marijuana, possession of a firearm, monetary instrument abuse (possession of counterfeit money), and possession of drug paraphernalia.[152]

In sum, among the primary grounds for teacher dismissal, the greatest increase has occurred in the area of immorality.

146. 697 S.E.2d 161 (W. Va. 2010).

147. 386 S.W.3d 588, 2011 (Ark. Ct. App. 2011).

148. Posner v. Lewis, 80 A.D.3d 308 (N.Y. App. Div. 1st Dept. 2010).

149. Smith Cnty. Sch. Dist. v. Barnes, 90 So. 3d 63 (Miss. 201,2).

150. Elsass v. St. Mary's City Sch. Dist. Bd. of Educ., No. 2-10-30, 2011 WL 1458154 (Ohio Ct. App. Dec. 16, 2011).

151. Haynam v. Ohio State Bd. of Educ., No. L-11-1100, 2011 WL 6365144 (Ohio Ct. App. Apr. 18, 2011).

152. Sias v. Iberia Par. Sch. Bd., 74 So. 3d 800 (La. Ct. App. 2011).

Insubordination

Insubordination among teachers has been defined as the willful disregard for or refusal to obey school regulations and official orders.[153] Among the various reasons used by boards to evaluate or dismiss teachers, insubordination is the easiest to show. Unlike incompetence or immorality, which often rest on the sufficiency of evidence, a teacher either disobeyed a rule/order or did not. Perhaps the reason these violations are not more often the focus of terminations is because insubordination is less closely related to the teaching process. Philosophically, it would seem more appropriate to remove a teacher for being an unfit teacher than for "not being a good soldier." Nevertheless, there are school systems that expressly require a high degree of compliance by teachers.

In *Griffith v. Seattle School District No. 1*,[154] two special education teachers refused to administer the state's required achievement test, the Washington Assessment of Student Learning (WASL), to their students who had Individualized Education Programs (IEPs). The teachers argued that "[w]e have a legal obligation to serve our students and fulfill their IEP minutes. Participation in the WAAS [Washington Alternative Assessment of Student] process detracts from the implementation of their IEP goals and objectives . . . that [a]dministering the WAAS to our students in order to maintain the appearance of adequate yearly progress is not in the best interest of our students and their families."[155] The teachers were sent a letter warning them that refusal constituted insubordination and would lead to disciplinary action. Even after repeated follow-up emails from the administration warning them of disciplinary action, they refused to administer the test, stating that their refusal was based *on principle*. After a hearing, the district imposed a ten-day suspension without pay, pending other disciplinary actions. On appeal, the Washington appellate court affirmed the decision of the hearing officer, noting that there was sufficient cause for the disciplinary action. The ruling in effect eliminates standing *on principle* as a teacher's defense when there exists a willful refusal to obey a reasonable regulation governing conduct.

In *Crosby v. Holt*,[156] a Tennessee school district directed a male teacher to stop communication with a female high school student when it was suspected that there was a sexually inappropriate relationship between the two. Rather than proceeding to discipline on the grounds of immorality, it decided to issue a warning. When the teacher and student ignored the warning, the district dismissed the teacher for insubordination.

---

153. Jeffrey F. Ghent, Annot., *What Constitutes "Insubordination" as Ground for Dismissal of a Public School Teacher*, 78 A.L.R.3d 83 (1977).

154. 266 P.3d 932 (Wash. Ct. App. 2011), *cert. denied*, 278 P.3d 1111 (Wash. 2012) (Table).

155. 266 P.3d 935.

156. 320 S.W.3d 805 (Tenn. Ct. App. 2009).

Although insubordination as grounds for dismissal can assume a wide variety of fact patterns, one common thread runs throughout: in each of these cases, the teacher was given a warning and put on a plan of improvement or reprimanded before formal steps were taken to dismiss. Regardless of the category of alleged misconduct, failure to comply with the remedy prescribed can result in dismissal.

Controversial Nature of Teacher Protections

Laws that protect unionized employees often cause controversy, and laws that apply to unionized teachers are no exception. Some argue that the protections in many states are outdated and do not reflect the needs of the modern workforce. In some areas, the laws are vague and used in ways that are to the detriment of teachers, while others are so specific that they require schools to maintain the employment of individuals who may no longer effectively perform their job duties. Some argue that tenure laws have the potential to force decisionmakers to retain individuals who may be less effective than non-tenured peers.

For example, the Sixth Circuit found that a reduction in force achieved through using factors such as a teacher's effectiveness and qualifications to determine teacher reemployment — a process that did not require principals to give preference to tenured teachers over non-tenured teachers — violated the Tennessee Teacher Tenure Act.[157] However, a Third Circuit court found that a Pennsylvania school district did not violate the contract's clause in suspending tenured teachers because the action was a necessary and reasonable measure to advance the school district's significant and legitimate public purpose of combatting the budget shortage that it faced.[158] Some plaintiffs, as well as legal commentators, have argued that tenure laws create inequitable conditions for minority and socioeconomically disadvantaged students. In *Vergara v. State of California*,[159] public school students claimed that the protections in the California Education Code governing tenure, dismissal, and seniority-based layoffs of K-12 public school teachers created an oversupply of grossly ineffective teachers in violation of the Equal Protection Clause by providing poor and minority students an education that was inadequate and disproportionate to that of their white and privileged peers. The California state appeals court ruled against these students, concluding that (1) students assigned to grossly ineffective teachers were not a sufficiently identifiable group for purposes of equal protection, and (2) statutes did not inevitably cause low-income and minority students to be disproportionately assigned to grossly ineffective teachers in violation of equal protection.

157. Kelley v. Shelby Cty. Bd. of Educ., 751 Fed. Appx. 650, (6th Cir. 2018).

158. Watters v. Bd. of Sch. Dirs. of Scranton, 975 F.3d 406 (3d Cir. 2020).

159. 209 Cal. Rptr. 3d 532 (Ct. App.), *cert. denied*, No. S234741, 2016 Cal. LEXIS 8387 (Aug. 22, 2016).

In a situation that may have had more to do with how the case was presented to the court than with the intent of the action, the plaintiff's claims failed. Not only did they complain about the statutes themselves rather than the *effects* of their implementation, but they failed to show data proving that the statutes resulted in poor or minority students being any more likely to be assigned ineffective teachers. Furthermore, the plaintiffs did not adequately provide facts to overcome evidence of the role administrators played in the assignment of teachers within each district.[160]

Constitutional Restrictions on Teacher Dismissals

As a general proposition, teachers do not relinquish their First Amendment rights by choosing to teach in the public schools.[161] Therefore, school authorities may not dismiss a teacher for the exercise of a First Amendment right. The rights of the teacher in the context of the First Amendment include the freedom to speak out on matters of public concern, the freedom to speak symbolically on political matters, academic freedom, and the freedom to express oneself through association.

If teachers believe that they have been dismissed because of conduct that is constitutionally protected, they have the burden to prove that their exercise of these rights was a substantial or motivating factor in the board's decision. If they meet that burden, the board must then respond by a preponderance of the evidence to show that it would have arrived at the same decision without having considered the protected conduct. The teachers must be placed in no worse a position than they would be in if they had not engaged in the protected conduct.

Assuming the dismissal was ordered as a punishment for the exercise of First Amendment rights, the analysis moves to another level. The First Amendment does not give the teacher absolute protection. Rather, the court will consider the school's need to promote an efficient public service in balance with the teacher's rights. Since community standards and state interests vary, a case-by-case approach to the balancing test is used.

---

160. *See* Todd A. DeMitchell & Joseph J. Onosko, Vergara v. State of California: *The End of Teacher Tenure or a Flawed Ruling?* 25 S. Cal. Interdisc. L.J. 589 (2016); Michael Lynch, Note, *Saving Students from Ineffective Teachers: The* Vergara *Decision and Its Potential Constitutional Implications*, 30 J. Civ. Rts. & Econ. Dev 31 (2017); Lyanne Prieto, *"Shocking the Conscience" or Suffering as Scapegoats?: Why the* Vergara *Opinion Misinterpreted the Role That Teachers and Tenure Play in Disadvantaging Poor and Minority Students*, 17 Rutgers Race & L. Rev. 85 (2016).

161. Tinker v. Des Moines Ind. Sch. Dist., 393 U.S. 503, 506 (1969).

Applying the Teacher Speech Doctrines: Criticism of Authority

Given the constitutional doctrines applying to teachers' speech discussed in the previous section, it is helpful to look at how the lower courts have applied these doctrines in deciding more recent issues. It is not uncommon for teachers to criticize their principals or other supervisors from time to time. Criticism of legitimate authority can be risky for the teacher. At what point does *criticism* spill over into *insubordination*? The next section will explore the contours of insubordination. For now, it is important to look at those occasions when teachers have been protected and when they have not. The speech clause seems to offer no protection if the employer has conducted a good-faith, (no pretext) reasonable investigation prior to the termination. Of course, the employer must conclude that there is no protected speech being used as the basis of the termination. The employer will be held harmless for a "wrong" conclusion.

The Ninth Circuit decided that a public junior college teacher's dismissal based on the discovery of anonymous letters should be upheld. In *Wasson v. Sonoma County Junior College*,[162] a series of letters were disseminated throughout the district. The letters accused the administration of various types of misconduct. The board hired a private investigator to determine the origin of the letters.

An instructor, Wasson, was identified as the author of the letters. She was dismissed for having authored the letters which, according to the board, contained statements about the superintendent that were "false and defamatory and which had the purpose or effect of undermining his leadership of the district."[163] The teacher's argument was that the dismissal amounted to "free speech retaliation" that was imputed wrongfully to her authorship. The court ruled that:

> ... [A] First Amendment retaliation claim seeks to vindicate a public employee's exercise of free speech rights when she has suffered an adverse employment action in response to having spoken out publicly. It cannot be used to remedy a cause of mistaken identity. In fact, the Supreme Court has never held that it is a violation of the Constitution for a government employer to discharge an employee based on substantively incorrect information.[164]

In *Wales v. Board of Education of Community Unit School District 300*,[165] the Seventh Circuit decided that a memo sent to the principal of the school where the teacher worked was not protected speech; therefore, her subsequent dismissal which was in part based on the memo was valid. The teacher, Colleen Wales, objected to the principal's management approach. Wales felt that insufficient support was being

162. 203 F.3d 659 (9th Cir. 2000).

163. *Id.* at 662.

164. *Id.* at 663.

165. 120 F.3d 82 (7th Cir. 1997).

provided for disciplining students and submitted a memo to the principal protesting her management. The memo caused their relationship to deteriorate. Wales' annual evaluation, which was conducted some months after the memo incident, reflected a concern that the principal had for continued positive relationships with the teacher. The court said, "an employee's decision to deliver a message in private supports an inference that the real concern is the employment relation—and a school district as employer may react to speech about the workplace in ways a government as regulator may not."[166]

Apparently, a public employee may not even be protected by *not* speaking. In *Coover v. Saucon Valley School District*,[167] the Pennsylvania district court ruled that a school district could dismiss a superintendent for unprofessional conduct when she remained silent during a presentation by a politically controversial speaker. The school district had a policy which prohibited "using school time or property for political purposes."[168] The superintendent invited the political speaker to address the district's administrators. During the presentation, the superintendent remained silent. The board concluded that the superintendent's silence sent a message to district employees that a degree of agreement may exist between the superintendent and the speaker. At trial, the superintendent's primary argument was that her silence was protected speech. In rejecting the superintendent's argument, the court noted that for her speech to be protected, she would have needed to meet the threshold requirement of *Pickering*. That is, she would have needed to be speaking (or in this case not speaking) as a citizen on a matter of public concern. However, she was present for the speech event as an employee, not a citizen.[169] Given the post-*Waters* line of cases, it is difficult not to conclude that the pendulum of teachers' speech rights versus employer authority to dismiss has shifted in favor of school authorities. Even if the teacher engages in protected speech, if the administration does not think so after it conducts a good faith, reasonable investigation, then the teacher is not protected.

Nevertheless, there is one example of a school employee successfully defending herself from a dismissal based on speech. In *Kirchmann v. Lake Elsinore Unified School District*, plaintiff Norma Kirchmann was a secretary at a school district facilities department. Noticing that there were some irregularities in the bidding process for architectural services, she investigated. Kirchmann discovered that the architect selected by the administration had a conflict of interest with officials in the district. She faxed an anonymous letter to those firms that were not selected, informing them of the conflict of interest and suggesting there was bias in the selection process. Upon discovering Kirchmann's faxing activity, the district notified her that she was suspended, without pay, for 30 days. The notice charged her with "failure to follow

166. *Id.* at 84. *See also* Cliff v. Indianapolis Bd. of Sch. Comm'rs, 42 F.3d 403 (7th Cir. 1994).
167. 955 F. Supp. 392 (E.D. Pa. 1997).
168. *Id.* at 395.
169. *Id.* at 400.

directions of a superior, dishonesty, and misuse or misappropriation of district property."[170] The charge of failing to follow directions was based on Kirchmann's transmission of the fax after having been told by the assistant superintendent that any communication with outside vendors had to be approved by the administration. The charges of dishonesty and misuse of district property were based on her unauthorized use of the list of bidders.

The lower court denied relief, concluding that the district's interest in promoting efficiency of its operations outweighed Kirchmann's free-speech interest. The court of appeals reversed. The secretary argued that the district used the faxing event as an excuse to dismiss her and that there was no objective job-related reason for the dismissal. The district argued that she did not engage in protected speech. It averred that the purpose of the fax was to seek revenge against the administration and that she had no interest in facilitating public discussion. It is interesting that the appellate court relied on a Seventh Circuit decision when it opined:

> It is often the case that those who speak out are also involved in personal disputes with employers and other employees. Consequently, a plaintiff's speech could be characterized as a matter of public concern even if the speaker stands to gain a personal benefit in addition to bringing the wrongdoing to light. [However] [a]n employee's personal motive may vitiate the public concern element if the speech concerns a subject of public interest, but the *expression* addresses only the personal effect upon the employee.[171]

The court's ruling was based on the conclusion that the seriousness of the subject of the secretary's fax (conflict of interest and bias in the bidding process) was not outweighed by the district's need for efficiency. There was no evidence of any of the *Pickering* or *Connick* employer concerns. Perhaps most important, the administration did not show that it conducted a "good faith, reasonable investigation" before it concluded that there was no protected speech.

Conditions of Employment

Most states provide for a "continuing contract" for tenured teachers. Once the teacher has been employed for a certain number of years in the same school district (from one to three years), the move from a probationary to a continuing contract is automatic, i.e., there need not be any special resolution of the board for the teacher to move from probationary to tenured status. If the teacher is not dismissed before the requisite years of continuous service are met, tenure is typically a statutory inevitability.

170. 67 Cal. Rptr. 2d 268, 272 (Ct. App. 1997).

171. *Id.* at 274 (quoting Marshall v. Porter Cnty. Planning Comm'n, 32 F.3d 1215, 1219 (7th Cir. 1994).

What is also provided with some regularity among the states is the written contract. The purpose of the written contract is to bind obligations of both parties to certain conditions of employment such as salary, regular and/or extra-duty assignments, and other compensation considerations. The written contract is not "the employment" contract; it is the "conditions of employment" contract. The employment contract is conditioned by statute. As long as the teacher can find her name in the minutes of the board meeting where she was hired, the legal obligation for the teacher's employment is extended. For example, failure of a teacher to sign the annual written contract does not mean the teacher is not employed. It may mean, however, that the teacher's salary and other job benefits are frozen at the previous year's level of compensation.

In addition to the contract, state statutes often describe responsibilities or "duties" for teachers. In Illinois, for example, the state statute requires that teachers be responsible for the "discipline of students."[172] It is also common for states to require teachers to report suspicions of child abuse, bullying among students, and the observation of peer sexual harassment.

There are often disputes regarding the relative position of the teachers' primary teaching contract and the extra-duty contract. Many teachers perform extra duties as part of their job but not as part of their teaching career. In other words, teachers gain tenure and job security in their primary teaching activities as guaranteed in their state statutes; meanwhile, some teaching positions come with significant extra duties, sometimes even coaching assignments. The question then becomes, Can a teacher gain tenure in an extra-duty assignment? The answer seems to be "no." Because extra-duty assignments are arranged by annual contracts not shaped by any state statutes, only contract law would control the relationship between teacher and school district regarding extra-duty assignments. The extra-duty assignments are typically subject to annual individual contracts. In effect, one duty is not dependent on the other. There are cases in which the teacher's extra-duty contract may not be renewed, but this has no effect on the primary employment relationship the teacher has with the school district "as a teacher." These issues often surface with coaching activities. For example, if the coach has a losing season which causes the school district to dismiss the coach, she may continue to stay on as a teacher.[173]

Teachers' Rights Considerations in Pandemics and Other Crises

One of the many novelties to arise in 21st-century school law has been the reemergence of pandemics, the likes of which have not been seen in decades. In 2019, measles cases in the United States topped 1,200 in 31 states, whereas only 55 cases were

172. 105 Ill. Comp. Stat. 5/24-24.

173. *See* Farner v. Idaho Falls Sch. Dist. No. 91, 17 P.3d 281 (Idaho 2000).

reported the previous year.[174] In January 2020, the Centers for Disease Control and Prevention announced the first confirmed U.S. case of COVID-19, and by November of that year, over 11 million had been confirmed as infected.[175] Not since the flu and polio pandemics of the 20th century had schools faced shutdowns and disease-control challenges of such magnitude.[176] School closures and online learning were widely implemented. For schools that continued to operate in person, even partially, measures such as temperature checks and virus testing for teachers and others were implemented.

These, and other measures, have the capacity to impact teachers' rights on a variety of levels. Chief among these considerations is the ADA (*see* above, this chapter). Particularly, public school employers must consider the ADA's limitations on disability-related inquiries and medical examinations, its measures prohibiting the exclusion of individuals with disabilities from the workplace for health or safety concerns absent a "direct threat," and its requirements that reasonable accommodations for those with disabilities be made absent undue hardship, despite pandemic conditions.[177]

While the ADA may prohibit both requiring employees to submit to a medical examination and questioning the nature and severity of an employee's disability, some level of examination or inquiry may be permissible if it is shown to be job related and consistent with business necessity.[178] In short, if the employer reasonably believes (based on objective evidence) the employee's ability to perform the essential functions of the job may be impaired by a medical condition or that the employee will pose a direct threat due to a medical condition, then a disability-related inquiry or medical examination of an employee is considered "job-related and consistent with business necessity."[179]

Equal employment laws including the ADA and Rehabilitation Act, while still applicable, do not interfere with or prevent employers from following the guidelines

174. *See Measles: Cases and Outbreaks*, Centers for Disease Control, https://www.cdc.gov/measles/cases-outbreaks.html (viewed November 20, 2020).

175. First Travel-related Case of 2019 Novel Coronavirus Detected in United States, Centers for Disease Control, https://www.cdc.gov/media/releases/2020/p0121-novel-coronavirus-travel-case.html (viewed November 20, 2020); *Covid Data Tracker, Centers for Disease Control*, https://covid.cdc.gov/covid-data-tracker/#cases_totalcases (viewed November 20, 2020).

176. *See* K. Meyers & M. A. Thomasson, *Can pandemics affect educational attainment? Evidence from the polio epidemic of 1916*, Cliometrica 1–35 (2020)..

177. 42 U.S.C. § 12112(d)(4)(A); 42 U.S.C. §§ 12111(3), (8); 29 C.F.R. §§ 1630.2(r), 1630.15(b)(2); 42 U.S.C. § 12112(b)(5); *see also* § 12111(3); 29 C.F.R. § 1630.2(r); *see also Pandemic Preparedness in the Workplace and the Americans with Disabilities Act*, EEOC (reissued Mar. 19, 2020), https://www.eeoc.gov/laws/guidance/pandemic-preparedness-workplace-and-americans-disabilities-act.

178. 42 U.S.C. § 12112(d)(4)(A).

179. *Enforcement Guidance on Disability-Related Inquiries and Medical Examinations of Employees under the ADA*, EEOC (July 27, 2000), , https://www.eeoc.gov/laws/guidance/enforcement-guidance-disability-related-inquiries-and-medical-examinations-employees#4.

and suggestions made by the CDC or state and local public health authorities about steps employers should take regarding COVID-19.

Notably, the EEOC's guidance for the COVID-19 epidemic includes the following:

1. During a pandemic, ADA-covered employers may ask such employees if they are experiencing symptoms of the pandemic virus. For COVID-19, these include symptoms such as fever, chills, cough, shortness of breath, sore throat, or any other symptom identified by the CDC or other public health authorities. Employers must maintain all information about employee illness as a confidential medical record in compliance with the ADA.

2. While generally measuring an employee's body temperature is considered a medical examination, for the purposes of preventing the spread of COVID-19, employers may measure employees' body temperature.

3. The ADA does not interfere with employers requiring employees who become ill with symptoms of COVID-19 to leave the workplace.

4. Requiring doctors' notes, certifications of fitness for duty, and other related inquires before a COVID-19 diagnosed employee returns to work are permitted under the ADA because they would not be disability related.

5. Employers may take screening steps to determine if employees entering the workplace have COVID-19 because an individual with the virus will pose a direct threat to the health of others. Therefore, an employer may choose to administer COVID-19 testing to employees before initially permitting them to enter the workplace and/or periodically to determine if their presence in the workplace poses a direct threat to others. The ADA does not interfere with employers following recommendations by the CDC or other public health authorities regarding whether, when, and for whom testing or other screening is appropriate. Testing administered by employers consistent with current CDC guidance will meet the ADA's "business necessity" standard.

6. The ADA allows an employer to bar an employee from physical presence in the workplace if he refuses to have his temperature taken or refuses to answer questions about whether he has COVID-19, has symptoms associated with COVID-19, or has been tested for COVID-19.[180]

180. *What You Should Know About COVID-19 and the ADA, the Rehabilitation Act, and Other EEO Laws*, EEOC (updated Sept. 8, 2020), https://www.eeoc.gov/wysk/what-you-should-know-about-covid-19-and-ada-rehabilitation-act-and-other-eeo-laws.

Selected Case Law

[3-1] *Pickering v. Board of Education of Township High School District 205, Will County, Ill.*

[3-2] *Mt. Healthy City School District Board of Education v. Doyle*

[3-3] *Connick v. Myers*

[3-4] *Waters v. Churchill*

[3-5] *Garcetti v. Ceballos*

[Case No. 3-1]

Comments by teachers on matters of public concern that are substantially correct may not furnish grounds for dismissal even though they are critical in tone.

Pickering v. Board of Education of Township High School District 205, Will County, Illinois

Supreme Court of the United States
391 U.S. 563 (1968)

Mr. Justice MARSHALL delivered the opinion of the Court.

Appellant Marvin L. Pickering, a teacher in Township High School District 205, Will County, Illinois, was dismissed from his position by the appellee Board of Education for sending a letter to a local newspaper in connection with a recently proposed tax increase that was critical of the way in which the Board and the district superintendent of schools had handled past proposals to raise new revenue for the schools. Appellant's dismissal resulted from a determination by the Board, after a full hearing, that the publication of the letter was 'detrimental to the efficient operation and administration of the schools of the district' and hence, under the relevant Illinois statute, Ill. Rev. Stat., c. 122, s 10-22.4 (1963), that 'interests of the schools require(d) (his dismissal).'

Appellant's claim that his writing of the letter was protected by the First and Fourteenth Amendments was rejected. Appellant then sought review of the Board's action in the Circuit Court of Will County, which affirmed his dismissal on the ground that the determination that appellant's letter was detrimental to the interests of the school system was supported by substantial evidence and that the interests of the schools overruled appellant's First Amendment rights. On appeal, the Supreme Court of Illinois, two Justices dissenting, affirmed the judgment of the Circuit Court. 36 Ill.2d 568, 225 N.E.2d 1 (1967). We noted probable jurisdiction of appellant's claim that the Illinois statute permitting his dismissal on the facts of this case was unconstitutional as applied under the First and Fourteenth Amendments.[181] 389

181. Appellant also challenged that statutory standard on which the Board based his dismissal as vague and overbroad. See Keyishian v. Bd. of Regents, 385 U.S. 589, 87 S. Ct. 675, 17 L. Ed. 2d 629

U.S. 925 88 S. Ct. 291, 19 L. Ed. 2d 276 (1967). For the reasons detailed below we agree that appellant's rights to freedom of speech were violated and we reverse.

I.

In February of 1961 the appellee Board of Education asked the voters of the school district to approve a bond issue to raise $4,875,000 to erect two new schools. The proposal was defeated. Then, in December of 1961, the Board submitted another bond proposal to the voters which called for the raising of $5,500,000 to build two new schools. This second proposal passed and the schools were built with the money raised by the bond sales. In May of 1964 a proposed increase in the tax rate to be used for educational purposes was submitted to the voters by the Board and was defeated. Finally, on September 19, 1964, a second proposal to increase the tax rate was submitted by the Board and was likewise defeated. It was in connection with this last proposal of the School Board that appellant wrote the letter to the editor (which we reproduce in an Appendix to this opinion) that resulted in his dismissal.

Prior to the vote on the second tax increase proposal a variety of articles attributed to the District 205 Teachers' Organization appeared in the local paper. These articles urged passage of the tax increase and stated that failure to pass the increase would result in a decline in the quality of education afforded children in the district's schools. A letter from the superintendent of schools making the same point was published in the paper two days before the election and submitted to the voters in mimeographed form the following day. It was in response to the foregoing material, together with the failure of the tax increase to pass, that appellant submitted the letter in question to the editor of the local paper.

The letter constituted, basically, an attack on the School Board's handling of the 1961 bond issue proposals and its subsequent allocation of financial resources between the schools' educational and athletic programs. It also charged the superintendent of schools with attempting to prevent teachers in the district from opposing or criticizing the proposed bond issue.

The Board dismissed Pickering for writing and publishing the letter. Pursuant to Illinois law, the Board was then required to hold a hearing on the dismissal. At the hearing the Board charged that numerous statements in the letter were false and that the publication of the statements unjustifiably impugned the 'motives, honesty, integrity, truthfulness, responsibility and competence' of both the Board and the school administration. The Board also charged that the false statements damaged the professional reputations of its members and of the school administrators, would be disruptive of faculty discipline, and would tend to foment 'controversy, conflict and dissension' among teachers, administrators, the Board of Education, and the residents of the district. Testimony was introduced from a variety of witnesses on

(1967); NAACP v. Button, 371 U.S. 415, 83 S. Ct. 328, 9 L. Ed. 2d 405 (1963); Shelton v. Tucker, 364 U.S. 479, 81 S. Ct. 247, 5 L. Ed. 2d 231 (1960). Because of our disposition of this case we do not reach appellant's challenge to the statute on its face.

the truth or falsity of the particular statements in the letter with which the Board took issue. The Board found the statements to be false as charged. No evidence was introduced at any point in the proceedings as to the effect of the publication of the letter on the community as a whole or on the administration of the school system in particular, and no specific findings along these lines were made.

The Illinois courts reviewed the proceedings solely to determine whether the Board's findings were supported by substantial evidence and whether, on the facts as found, the Board could reasonably conclude that appellant's publication of the letter was 'detrimental to the best interests of the schools.' Pickering's claim that his letter was protected by the First Amendment was rejected on the ground that his acceptance of a teaching position in the public schools obliged him to refrain from making statements about the operation of the schools 'which in the absence of such position he would have an undoubted right to engage in.' It is not altogether clear whether the Illinois Supreme Court held that the First Amendment had no applicability to appellant's dismissal for writing the letter in question or whether it determined that the particular statements made in the letter were not entitled to First Amendment protection.

In any event, it clearly rejected Pickering's claim that, on the facts of this case, he could not constitutionally be dismissed from his teaching position.

II.

To the extent that the Illinois Supreme Court's opinion may be read to suggest that teachers may constitutionally be compelled to relinquish the First Amendment rights they would otherwise enjoy as citizens to comment on matters of public interest in connection with the operation of the public schools in which they work, it proceeds on a premise that has been unequivocally rejected in numerous prior decisions of this Court. E.g., Wieman v. Updegraff, 344 U.S. 183, 73 S. Ct. 215, 97 L.Ed. 216 (1952); Shelton v. Tucker, 364 U.S. 479, 81 S. Ct. 247 (1960); Keyishian v. Board of Regents, 385 U.S. 589, 87 S. Ct. 675 (1967). '(T)he theory that public employment which may be denied altogether may be subjected to any conditions, regardless of how unreasonable, has been uniformly rejected.' Keyishian v. Board of Regents, supra, 385 U.S. at 605–606, 87 S. Ct. at 685. At the same time it cannot be gainsaid that the State has interests as an employer in regulating the speech of its employees that differ significantly from those it possesses in connection with regulation of the speech of the citizenry in general. The problem in any case is to arrive at a balance between the interests of the teacher, as a citizen, in commenting upon matters of public concern and the interest of the State, as an employer, in promoting the efficiency of the public services it performs through its employees.

III.

The Board contends that 'the teacher by virtue of his public employment has a duty of loyalty to support his superiors in attaining the generally accepted goals of education and that, if he must speak out publicly, he should do so factually and accurately, commensurate with his education and experience.' Appellant, on the other hand, argues that the test applicable to defamatory statements directed against public officials by persons having no occupational relationship with them, namely, that statements to be legally actionable must be made 'with knowledge that (they were) * * * false or with reckless disregard of whether (they were) * * * false or not,' New York Times Co. v. Sullivan, 376 U.S. 254, 280, 84 S. Ct. 710, 726, 11 L. Ed. 2d 686 (1964), should also be applied to public statements made by teachers. Because of the enormous variety of fact situations in which critical statements by teachers and other public employees may be thought by their superiors, against whom the statements are directed to furnish grounds for dismissal, we do not deem it either appropriate or feasible to attempt to lay down a general standard against which all such statements may be judged. However, in the course of evaluating the conflicting claims of First Amendment protection and the need for orderly school administration in the context of this case, we shall indicate some of the general lines along which an analysis of the controlling interests should run.

An examination of the statements in appellant's letter objected to by the Board[182] reveals that they, like the letter as a whole, consist essentially of criticism of the Board's allocation of school funds between educational and athletic programs, and of both the Board's and the superintendent's methods of informing, or preventing the informing of, the district's taxpayers of the real reasons why additional tax revenues were being sought for the schools. The statements are in no way directed towards any person with whom appellant would normally be in contact in the course of his daily work as a teacher. Thus no question of maintaining either discipline by immediate superiors or harmony among coworkers is presented here. Appellant's employment relationships with the Board and, to a somewhat lesser extent, with the superintendent are not the kind of close working relationships for which it can persuasively be claimed that personal loyalty and confidence are necessary to their proper functioning. Accordingly, to the extent that the Board's position here can be taken to suggest that even comments on matters of public concern that are substantially correct, such as statements (1)–(4) of appellant's letter, see Appendix, infra, may furnish grounds for dismissal if they are sufficiently critical in tone, we unequivocally reject it.[183]

---

182. We have set out in the Appendix our detailed analysis of the specific statements in appellant's letter which the Board found to be false, together with our reasons for concluding that several of the statements were, contrary to the findings of the Board, substantially correct.

183. It is possible to conceive of some positions in public employment in which the need for confidentiality is so great that even completely correct public statements might furnish a permissible ground for dismissal. Likewise, positions in public employment in which the relationship between superior and subordinate is of such a personal and intimate nature that certain forms of public criticism of the superior by the subordinate would seriously undermine the effectiveness of the working relationship between them can also be imagined. We intimate no views as to how we would resolve any specific instances of such situations, but merely note that significantly different considerations would be involved in such cases.

We next consider the statements in appellant's letter which we agree to be false. The Board's original charges included allegations that the publication of the letter damaged the professional reputations of the Board and the superintendent and would foment controversy and conflict among the Board, teachers, administrators, and the residents of the district. However, no evidence to support these allegations was introduced at the hearing. So far as the record reveals, Pickering's letter was greeted by everyone but its main target, the Board, with massive apathy and total disbelief. The Board must, therefore, have decided, perhaps by analogy with the law of libel, that the statements were per se harmful to the operation of the schools.

However, the only way in which the Board could conclude, absent any evidence of the actual effect of the letter, that the statements contained therein were per se detrimental to the interest of the schools was to equate the Board members' own interests with that of the schools. Certainly an accusation that too much money is being spent on athletics by the administrators of the school system (which is precisely the import of that portion of appellant's letter containing the statements that we have found to be false, see Appendix, infra) cannot reasonably be regarded as per se detrimental to the district's schools. Such an accusation reflects rather a difference of opinion between Pickering and the Board as to the preferable manner of operating the school system, a difference of opinion that clearly concerns an issue of general public interest.

In addition, the fact that particular illustrations of the Board's claimed undesirable emphasis on athletic programs are false would not normally have any necessary impact on the actual operation of the schools, beyond its tendency to anger the Board. For example, Pickering's letter was written after the defeat at the polls of the second proposed tax increase. It could, therefore, have had no effect on the ability of the school district to raise necessary revenue, since there was no showing that there was any proposal to increase taxes pending when the letter was written.

More importantly, the question whether a school system requires additional funds is a matter of legitimate public concern on which the judgment of the school administration, including the School Board, cannot, in a society that leaves such questions to popular vote, be taken as conclusive. On such a question free and open debate is vital to informed decision-making by the electorate. Teachers are, as a class, the members of a community most likely to have informed and definite opinions as to how funds allotted to the operations of the schools should be spent. Accordingly, it is essential that they be able to speak out freely on such questions without fear of retaliatory dismissal.

In addition, the amounts expended on athletics which Pickering reported erroneously were matters of public record on which his position as a teacher in the district did not qualify him to speak with any greater authority than any other taxpayer. The Board could easily have rebutted appellant's errors by publishing the accurate figures itself, either via a letter to the same newspaper or otherwise. We are thus not presented with a situation in which a teacher has carelessly made false statements about matters so closely related to the day-to-day operations of the schools that any harmful impact on the public would be difficult to counter because of the teacher's presumed greater access to the real facts. Accordingly, we have no occasion to consider at this time whether under such circumstances a school board could reasonably require that a teacher make substantial efforts to verify the accuracy of his charges before publishing them.[184]

What we do have before us is a case in which a teacher has made erroneous public statements upon issues then currently the subject of public attention, which are critical of his ultimate employer but which are neither shown nor can be presumed to have in any way either impeded the teacher's proper performance of his daily duties in the classroom[185] or to have interfered with the regular operation of the schools generally. In these circumstances we conclude that the interest of the school administration in limiting teachers' opportunities to contribute to public debate is not significantly greater than its interest in limiting a similar contribution by any member of the general public.

IV.

The public interest in having free and unhindered debate on matters of public importance—the core value of the Free Speech Clause of the First Amendment—is so great that it has been held that a State cannot authorize the recovery of damages by a public official for defamatory statements directed at him except when such statements are shown to have been made either with knowledge of their falsity or with reckless disregard for their truth or falsity. New York Times Co. v. Sullivan, 376 U.S. 254, 84 S. Ct. 710 (1964); St. Amant v. Thompson, 390 U.S. 727, 88 S. Ct. 1323, 20 L. Ed. 2d 262 (1968). Compare Linn v. United Plant Guard Workers, 383 U.S. 53, 86 S. Ct. 657, 15 L. Ed. 2d 582 (1966). The same test has been applied to suits for invasion of privacy based on false statements where a 'matter of public interest' is involved. Time, Inc. v. Hill, 385 U.S. 374, 87 S. Ct. 534, 17 L. Ed. 2d 456 (1967). It is therefore perfectly clear that, were appellant a member of the general public, the State's power to afford the appellee Board of Education or its members any legal right to sue him for writing the letter at issue here would be limited by the requirement that the letter be judged by the standard laid down in New York Times.

This Court has also indicated, in more general terms, that statements by public officials on matters of public concern must be accorded First Amendment protection despite the fact that the statements are directed at their nominal superiors. Garrison v. State of Louisiana, 379 U.S. 64, 85 S. Ct. 209, 13 L. Ed. 2d 125 (1964); Wood

---

184. There is likewise no occasion furnished by this case for consideration of the extent to which teachers can be required by narrowly drawn grievance procedures to submit complaints about the operation of the schools to their superiors for action thereon prior to bringing the complaints before the public.

185. We also note that this case does not present a situation in which a teacher's public statements are so without foundation as to call into question his fitness to perform his duties in the classroom. In such a case, of course, the statements would merely be evidence of the teacher's general competence, or lack thereof, and not an independent basis for dismissal.

v. Georgia, 370 U.S. 375, 82 S. Ct. 1364, 8 L. Ed. 2d 569 (1962). In Garrison, the New York Times test was specifically applied to a case involving a criminal defamation conviction stemming from statements made by a district attorney about the judges before whom he regularly appeared.

While criminal sanctions and damage awards have a somewhat different impact on the exercise of the right to freedom of speech from dismissal from employment, it is apparent that the threat of dismissal from public employment is nonetheless a potent means of inhibiting speech. We have already noted our disinclination to make an across-the-board equation of dismissal from public employment for remarks critical of superiors with awarding damages in a libel suit by a public official for similar criticism. However, in a case such as the present one, in which the fact of employment is only tangentially and insubstantially involved in the subject matter of the public communication made by a teacher, we conclude that it is necessary to regard the teacher as the member of the general public he seeks to be.

In sum, we hold that, in a case such as this, absent proof of false statements knowingly or recklessly made by him,[186] a teacher's exercise of his right to speak on issues of public importance may not furnish the basis for his dismissal from public employment. Since no such showing has been made in this case regarding appellant's letter, see Appendix, infra, his dismissal for writing it cannot be upheld and the judgment of the Illinois Supreme Court must, accordingly, be reversed and the case remanded for further proceedings not inconsistent with this opinion. It is so ordered.

Judgment reversed and case remanded with directions.

APPENDIX TO OPINION OF THE COURT

A. Appellant's letter.

LETTERS TO THE EDITOR

* * * **Graphic Newspapers, Inc. Thursday, September 24, 1964, Page 4**

Dear Editor:

I enjoyed reading the back issues of your paper which you loaned to me. Perhaps others would enjoy reading them in order to see just how far the two new high schools have deviated from the original promises by the Board of Education. First, let me state that I am referring to the February thru November, 1961 issues of your paper, so that it can be checked.

One statement in your paper declared that swimming pools, athletic fields, and auditoriums had been left out of the program. They may have been left out but they

186. Because we conclude that appellant's statements were not knowingly or recklessly false, we have no occasion to pass upon the additional question whether a statement that was knowingly or recklessly false would, if it were neither shown nor could reasonably be presumed to have had any harmful effects, still be protected by the First Amendment.

got put back in very quickly because Lockport West has both an auditorium and athletic field. In fact, Lockport West has a better athletic field than Lockport Central. It has a track that isn't quite regulation distance even though the board spent a few thousand dollars on it. Whose fault is that? Oh, I forgot, it wasn't supposed to be there in the first place. It must have fallen out of the sky. Such responsibility has been touched on in other letters but it seems one just can't help noticing it. I am not saying the school shouldn't have these facilities, because I think they should, but promises are promises, or are they?

Since there seems to be a problem getting all the facts to the voter on the twice defeated bond issue, many letters have been written to this paper and probably more will follow, I feel I must say something about the letters and their writers. Many of these letters did not give the whole story. Letters by your Board and Administration have stated that teachers' salaries total $1,297,746 for one year. Now that must have been the total payroll, otherwise the teachers would be getting $10,000 a year. I teach at the high school and I know this just isn't the case. However, this shows their 'stop at nothing' attitude. To illustrate further, do you know that the superintendent told the teachers, and I quote, 'Any teacher that opposes the referendum should be prepared for the consequences.' I think this gets at the reason we have problems passing bond issues. Threats take something away; these are insults to voters in a free society. We should try to sell a program on its merits, if it has any.

Remember those letters entitled 'District 205 Teachers Speak,' I think the voters should know that those letters have been written and agreed to by only five or six teachers, not 98% of the teachers in the high school. In fact, many teachers didn't even know who was writing them. Did you know that those letters had to have the approval of the superintendent before they could be put in the paper? That's the kind of totalitarianism teachers live in at the high school, and your children go to school in.

In last week's paper, the letter written by a few uninformed teachers threatened to close the school cafeteria and fire its personnel. This is ridiculous and insults the intelligence of the voter because properly managed school cafeterias do not cost the school district any money. If the cafeteria is losing money, then the board should not be packing free lunches for athletes on days of athletic contests. Whatever the case, the taxpayer's child should only have to pay about 30 cents for his lunch instead of 35 cents to pay for free lunches for the athletes.

In a reply to this letter your Board of Administration will probably state that these lunches are paid for from receipts from the games. But $20,000 in receipts doesn't pay for the $200,000 a year they have been spending on varsity sports while neglecting the wants of teachers.

You see we don't need an increase in the transportation tax unless the voters want to keep paying $50,000 or more a year to transport athletes home after practice and to away games, etc. Rest of the $200,000 is made up in coaches' salaries, athletic directors' salaries, baseball pitching machines, sodded football fields, and thousands of dollars for other sports equipment.

These things are all right, provided we have enough money for them. To sod football fields on borrowed money and then not be able to pay teachers' salaries is getting the cart before the horse.

If these things aren't enough for you, look at East High. No doors on many of the classrooms, a plant room without any sunlight, no water in a first aid treatment room, are just a few of many things. The taxpayers were really taken to the cleaners. A part of the sidewalk in front of the building has already collapsed. Maybe Mr. Hess would be interested to know that we need blinds on the windows in that building also.

Once again, the board must have forgotten they were going to spend $3,200,000 on the West building and $2,300,000 on the East building.

As I see it, the bond issue is a fight between the Board of Education that is trying to push tax-supported athletics down our throats with education, and a public that has mixed emotions about both of these items because they feel they are already paying enough taxes, and simply don't know whom to trust with any more tax money.

I must sign this letter as a citizen, taxpayer and voter, not as a teacher, since that freedom has been taken from the teachers by the administration. Do you really know what goes on behind those stone walls at the high school?

Respectfully,

Marvin L. Pickering.

[Case No. 3-2]

Discharged teacher's claims that the board of education violated his First and Fourteenth Amendment rights were not defeated by the fact that he did not have tenure.

Mt. Healthy City School District Board of Education v. Doyle

Supreme Court of the United States
429 U.S. 274 (1977)

Mr. Justice REHNQUIST delivered the opinion of the Court.

Respondent Doyle sued petitioner Mt. Healthy Board of Education in the United States District Court for the Southern District of Ohio. Doyle claimed that the Board's refusal to renew his contract in 1971 violated his rights under the First and Fourteenth Amendments to the United States Constitution. After a bench trial the District Court held that Doyle was entitled to reinstatement with backpay. The Court of Appeals for the Sixth Circuit affirmed the judgment, 529 F.2d 524, and we granted the Board's petition for certiorari, 425 U.S. 933, 96 S. Ct. 1662, 48 L. Ed. 2d 174, to consider an admixture of jurisdictional and constitutional claims.

I

Although the respondent's complaint asserted jurisdiction under both 28 U.S.C. s 1343 and 28 U.S.C. s 1331, the District Court rested its jurisdiction only on s 1331. Petitioner's first jurisdictional contention, which we have little difficulty disposing of, asserts that the $10,000 amount in controversy required by that section is not satisfied in this case.

The leading case on this point is St. Paul Indemnity Co. v. Red Cab Co., 303 U.S. 283, 58 S. Ct. 586, 82 L. Ed. 845 (1938), which stated this test:

> "(T)he sum claimed by the plaintiff controls if the claim is apparently made in good faith. It must appear to a legal certainty that the claim is really for less than the jurisdictional amount to justify dismissal. The inability of plaintiff to recover an amount adequate to give the court jurisdiction does not show his bad faith or oust the jurisdiction."

Id., at 288–289, 58 S. Ct., at 590 (footnotes omitted).

We have cited this rule with approval as recently as Weinberger v. Wiesenfeld, 420 U.S. 636, 642 n. 10, 95 S. Ct. 1225, 1230, 43 L. Ed. 2d 514 (1975), and think it requires disposition of the jurisdictional question tendered by the petition in favor of the respondent. At the time Doyle brought this action for reinstatement and $50,000 damages, he had already accepted a job in a different school system paying approximately $2,000 per year less than he would have earned with the Mt. Healthy Board had he been rehired. The District Court in fact awarded Doyle compensatory damages in the amount of $5,158 by reason of income already lost at the time it ordered his reinstatement. Even if the District Court had chosen to award only compensatory damages and not reinstatement, it was far from a "legal certainty" at the time of suit that Doyle would not have been entitled to more than $10,000.

II

The Board has filed a document entitled "Supplemental Authorities" in which it raises quite a different "jurisdictional" issue from that presented in its petition for certiorari and disposed of in the preceding section of this opinion. Relying on the District Court opinion in Weathers v. West Yuma County School Dist., 387 F. Supp. 552, 556 (Colo.1974), the Board contends that even though Doyle may have met the jurisdictional amount requirement of s 1331 it may not be subjected to liability in this case because Doyle's only substantive constitutional claim arises under 42 U.S.C. s 1983. Because it is not a "person" for purposes of s 1983, the Board reasons, liability may no more be imposed on it where federal jurisdiction is grounded on 28 U.S.C. s 1331 than where such jurisdiction is grounded on 28 U.S.C. s 1343.

The District Court avoided this issue by reciting that it had not "stated any conclusion on the possible Monroe-Kenosha problem in this case since it seems that the case is properly here as a s 1331 case, as well as a s 1983 one." Pet. for Cert. 14a–15a. This reference to our decisions in Monroe v. Pape, 365 U.S. 167, 81 S. Ct. 473, 5 L. Ed. 2d 492 (1961), and City of Kenosha v. Bruno, 412 U.S. 507, 93 S. Ct. 2222, 37 L. Ed. 2d 109 (1973), where it was held that a municipal corporation is not a suable "person" under s 1983, raises the question whether petitioner Board in this case is sufficiently like the municipal corporations in those cases so that it, too, is excluded from s 1983 liability.

The quoted statement of the District Court makes clear its view that if the jurisdictional basis for the action is s 1331, the limitations contained in 42 U.S.C. s 1983 do not apply. The Board argues, on the contrary, that since Congress in s 1983 has expressly created a remedy relating to violations of constitutional rights under color of state law, one who seeks to recover for such violations is bound by the limitations contained in s 1983 whatever jurisdictional section he invokes.

The question of whether the Board's arguments should prevail, or whether as respondent urged in oral argument, we should, by analogy to our decision in Bivens v. Six Unknown Fed. Narcotics Agents, 403 U.S. 388, 91 S. Ct. 1999, 29 L. Ed. 2d 619 (1971), imply a cause of action directly from the Fourteenth Amendment which would not be subject to the limitations contained in s 1983, is one which has never been decided by this Court. Counsel for respondent at oral argument suggested that it is an extremely important question and one which should not be decided on this record. We agree with respondent.

The Board has raised this question for the first time in a document filed after its reply brief in this Court. Were it in truth a contention that the District Court lacked jurisdiction, we would be obliged to consider it, even as we are obliged to inquire sua sponte whenever a doubt arises as to the existence of federal jurisdiction. Liberty Mutual Ins. Co. v. Wetzel, 424 U.S. 737, 740, 96 S. Ct. 1202, 1204, 47 L. Ed. 2d 435 (1976); Louisville & Nashville R. Co. v. Mottley, 211 U.S. 149, 152, 29 S. Ct. 42, 43, 53 L. Ed. 126 (1908). And if this were a s 1983 action, brought under the special jurisdictional provision of 28 U.S.C. s 1343 which requires no amount in controversy, it would be appropriate for this Court to inquire, for jurisdictional purposes whether a statutory action had in fact been alleged. City of Kenosha v. Bruno, supra. However, where an action is brought under s 1331, the catchall federal-question provision requiring in excess of $10,000 in controversy, jurisdiction is sufficiently established by allegation of a claim under the Constitution or federal statutes, unless it "clearly appears to be immaterial and made solely for the purpose of obtaining jurisdiction. . . ." Bell v. Hood, 327 U.S. 678, 682, 66 S. Ct. 773, 776, 90 L. Ed. 939 (1946); Montana-Dakota Utilities Co. v. Northwestern Pub. Serv. Co., 341 U.S. 246, 249, 71 S. Ct. 692, 694, 95 L. Ed. 912 (1951).

Here respondent alleged that the Board had violated his rights under the First and Fourteenth Amendments and claimed the jurisdictionally necessary amount of damages. The claim that the Board is a "person" under s 1983, even assuming the correctness of the Board's argument that the s 1331 action is limited by the restrictions of s 1983, is not so patently without merit as to fail the test of Bell v. Hood, supra. Therefore, the question as to whether the respondent stated a claim for relief under s 1331 is not of the jurisdictional sort which the Court raises on its own motion. The related question of whether a school district is a person for purposes of s 1983 is likewise not before us. We leave those questions for another day, and assume, without deciding, that the respondent could sue under s 1331 without regard to the limitations imposed by 42 U.S.C. s 1983.

III

The District Court found it unnecessary to decide whether the Board was entitled to immunity from suit in the federal courts under the Eleventh Amendment, because it decided that any such immunity had been waived by Ohio statute and decisional law. In view of the treatment of waiver by a State of its Eleventh Amendment immunity from suit in Ford Motor Co. v. Dept. of Treasury, 323 U.S. 459, 464–466, 65 S. Ct. 347, 350–351, 89 L. Ed. 389 (1945), we are less sure than was the District Court that Ohio had consented to suit against entities such as the Board in the federal courts. We prefer to address instead the question of whether such an entity had any Eleventh Amendment immunity in the first place, since if we conclude that it had none it will be unnecessary to reach the question of waiver.

The bar of the Eleventh Amendment to suit in federal courts extends to States and state officials in appropriate circumstances, Edelman v. Jordan, 415 U.S. 651, 94 S. Ct. 1347, 39 L. Ed. 2d 662 (1974); Ford Motor Co. v. Dept. of Treasury, supra, but does not extend to counties and similar municipal corporations. See Lincoln County v. Luning, 133 U.S. 529, 530, 10 S. Ct. 363, 33 L. Ed. 766 (1890); Moor v. County of Alameda, 411 U.S. 693, 717–721, 93 S. Ct. 1785, 1799–1801, 36 L. Ed. 2d 596 (1973). The issue here thus turns on whether the Mt. Healthy Board of Education is to be treated as an arm of the State partaking of the State's Eleventh Amendment immunity, or is instead to be treated as a municipal corporation or other political subdivision to which the Eleventh Amendment does not extend. The answer depends, at least in part, upon the nature of the entity created by state law. Under Ohio law the "State" does not include "political subdivisions," and "political subdivisions" do include local school districts. Ohio Rev. Code Ann. s 2743.01 (Page Supp.1975). Petitioner is but one of many local school boards within the State of Ohio. It is subject to some guidance from the State Board of Education, Ohio Rev. Code Ann. s 3301.07 (Page 1972 and Supp.1975), and receives a significant amount of money from the State. Ohio Rev. Code Ann. s 3317 (Page 1972 and Supp.1975). But local school boards have extensive powers to issue bonds, Ohio Rev. Code Ann. s 133.27 (Page 1969), and to levy taxes within certain restrictions of state law. Ohio Rev. Code Ann. ss 5705.02, 5705.03, 5705.192, 5705.194 (Page 1973 and Supp.1975). On balance, the record before us indicates that a local school board such as petitioner is more like a county or city than it is like an arm of the State. We therefore hold that it was not entitled to assert any Eleventh Amendment immunity from suit in the federal courts.

IV

Having concluded that respondent's complaint sufficiently pleaded jurisdiction under 28 U.S.C. s 1331, that the Board has failed to preserve the issue whether that complaint stated a claim upon which relief could be granted against the Board, and that the Board is not immune from suit under the Eleventh Amendment, we now proceed to consider the merits of respondent's claim under the First and Fourteenth Amendments.

Doyle was first employed by the Board in 1966. He worked under one-year contracts for the first three years, and under a two-year contract from 1969 to 1971. In 1969 he was elected president of the Teachers' Association, in which position he worked to expand the subjects of direct negotiation between the Association and the Board of Education. During Doyle's one-year term as president of the Association, and during the succeeding year when he served on its executive committee, there was apparently some tension in relations between the Board and the Association.

Beginning early in 1970, Doyle was involved in several incidents not directly connected with his role in the Teachers' Association. In one instance, he engaged in an argument with another teacher which culminated in the other teacher's slapping him. Doyle subsequently refused to accept an apology and insisted upon some punishment for the other teacher. His persistence in the matter resulted in the suspension of both teachers for one day, which was followed by a walkout by a number of other teachers, which in turn resulted in the lifting of the suspensions.

On other occasions, Doyle got into an argument with employees of the school cafeteria over the amount of spaghetti which had been served him; referred to students, in connection with a disciplinary complaint, as "sons of bitches"; and made an obscene gesture to two girls in connection with their failure to obey commands made in his capacity as cafeteria supervisor. Chronologically the last in the series of incidents which respondent was involved in during his employment by the Board was a telephone call by him to a local radio station. It was the Board's consideration of this incident which the court below found to be a violation of the First and Fourteenth Amendments.

In February 1971, the principal circulated to various teachers a memorandum relating to teacher dress and appearance, which was apparently prompted by the view of some in the administration that there was a relationship between teacher appearance and public support for bond issues. Doyle's response to the receipt of the memorandum on a subject which he apparently understood was to be settled by joint teacher-administration action was to convey the substance of the memorandum to a disc jockey at WSAI, a Cincinnati radio station, who promptly announced the adoption of the dress code as a news item. Doyle subsequently apologized to the principal, conceding that he should have made some prior communication of his criticism to the school administration.

Approximately one month later the superintendent made his customary annual recommendations to the Board as to the rehiring of non-tenured teachers. He recommended that Doyle not be rehired. The same recommendation was made with respect to nine other teachers in the district, and in all instances, including Doyle's, the recommendation was adopted by the Board. Shortly after being notified of this decision, respondent requested a statement of reasons for the Board's actions. He received a statement citing "a notable lack of tact in handling professional matters which leaves much doubt as to your sincerity in establishing good school relationships." That general statement was followed by references to the radio station incident and to the obscene-gesture incident.[187]

The District Court found that all of these incidents had in fact occurred. It concluded that respondent Doyle's telephone call to the radio station was "clearly protected by the First Amendment," and that because it had played a "substantial part" in the decision of the Board not to renew Doyle's employment, he was entitled to reinstatement with backpay. App. to Pet. for Cert. 12a–13a. The District Court did not expressly state what test it was applying in determining that the incident in question involved conduct protected by the First Amendment, but simply held that the communication to the radio station was such conduct. The Court of Appeals affirmed in a brief per curiam opinion. 529 F.2d 524.

Doyle's claims under the First and Fourteenth Amendments are not defeated by the fact that he did not have tenure. Even though he could have been discharged for no reason whatever, and had no constitutional right to a hearing prior to the decision not to rehire him, Board of Regents v. Roth, 408 U.S. 564, 92 S. Ct. 2701, 33 L. Ed. 2d 548 (1972), he may nonetheless establish a claim to reinstatement if the decision not to rehire him was made by reason of his exercise of constitutionally protected First Amendment freedoms. Perry v. Sindermann, 408 U.S. 593, 92 S. Ct. 2694, 33 L. Ed. 2d 570 (1972).

That question of whether speech of a government employee is constitutionally protected expression necessarily entails striking "a balance between the interests of the teacher, as a citizen, in commenting upon matters of public concern and the interest of the State, as an employer, in promoting the efficiency of the public services it performs through its employees." Pickering v. Board of Education, 391 U.S. 563, 568, 88 S. Ct. 1731, 1734, 20 L. Ed. 2d 811 (1968). There is no suggestion by the Board that Doyle violated any established policy, or that its reaction to his communication to the radio station was anything more than an ad hoc response to Doyle's action in making the memorandum public. We therefore accept the District Court's finding that the communication was protected by the First and Fourteenth

187. "I. You have shown a notable lack of tact in handling professional matters which leaves much doubt as to your sincerity in establishing good school relationships.

"A. You assumed the responsibility to notify W.S.A.I. Radio Station in regards to the suggestion of the Board of Education that teachers establish an appropriate dress code for professional people. This raised much concern not only within this community, but also in neighboring communities.

"B. You used obscene gestures to correct students in a situation in the cafeteria causing considerable concern among those students present.

"Sincerely yours,
"Rex Ralph
"Superintendent"

Amendments. We are not, however, entirely in agreement with that court's manner of reasoning from this finding to the conclusion that Doyle is entitled to reinstatement with backpay.

The District Court made the following "conclusions" on this aspect of the case:

> "1) If a non-permissible reason, e.g., exercise of First Amendment rights, played a substantial part in the decision not to renew even in the face of other permissible grounds the decision may not stand (citations omitted).
>
> "2) A non-permissible reason did play a substantial part. That is clear from the letter of the Superintendent immediately following the Board's decision, which stated two reasons the one, the conversation with the radio station clearly protected by the First Amendment. A court may not engage in any limitation of First Amendment rights based on 'tact' that is not to say that the 'tactfulness' is irrelevant to other issues in this case."

App. to Pet. for Cert. 12a–13a.

At the same time, though, it stated that

> "(i)n fact, as this Court sees it and finds, both the Board and the Superintendent were faced with a situation in which there did exist in fact reason . . . independent of any First Amendment rights or exercise thereof, to not extend tenure." Id., at 12a.

Since respondent Doyle had no tenure, and there was therefore not even a state-law requirement of "cause" or "reason" before a decision could be made not to renew his employment, it is not clear what the District Court meant by this latter statement. Clearly the Board legally could have dismissed respondent had the radio station incident never come to its attention. One plausible meaning of the court's statement is that the Board and the Superintendent not only could, but in fact would have reached that decision had not the constitutionally protected incident of the telephone call to the radio station occurred. We are thus brought to the issue whether, even if that were the case, the fact that the protected conduct played a "substantial part" in the actual decision not to renew would necessarily amount to a constitutional violation justifying remedial action. We think that it would not.

A rule of causation which focuses solely on whether protected conduct played a part, "substantial" or otherwise, in a decision not to rehire, could place an employee in a better position as a result of the exercise of constitutionally protected conduct than he would have occupied had he done nothing. The difficulty with the rule enunciated by the District Court is that it would require reinstatement in cases where a dramatic and perhaps abrasive incident is inevitably on the minds of those responsible for the decision to rehire, and does indeed play a part in that decision even if the same decision would have been reached had the incident not occurred. The constitutional principle at stake is sufficiently vindicated if such an employee is placed in no worse a position than if he had not engaged in the conduct. A borderline or marginal candidate should not have the employment question resolved against him because of constitutionally protected conduct. But that same candidate ought not to be able, by engaging in such conduct, to prevent his employer from assessing his performance record and reaching a decision not to rehire on the basis of that record, simply because the protected conduct makes the employer more certain of the correctness of its decision.

This is especially true where, as the District Court observed was the case here, the current decision to rehire will accord "tenure." The long-term consequences of an award of tenure are of great moment both to the employee and to the employer. They are too significant for us to hold that the Board in this case would be precluded, because it considered constitutionally protected conduct in deciding not to rehire Doyle, from attempting to prove to a trier of fact that quite apart from such conduct Doyle's record was such that he would not have been rehired in any event.

In other areas of constitutional law, this Court has found it necessary to formulate a test of causation which distinguishes between a result caused by a constitutional violation and one not so caused. We think those are instructive in formulating the test to be applied here.

In *Lyons v. Oklahoma*, 322 U.S. 596, 64 S. Ct. 1208, 88 L. Ed. 1481 (1944), the Court held that even though the first confession given by a defendant had been involuntary, the Fourteenth Amendment did not prevent the State from using a second confession obtained 12 hours later if the coercion surrounding the first confession had been sufficiently dissipated as to make the second confession voluntary. In Wong Sun v. United States, 371 U.S. 471, 491, 83 S. Ct. 407, 419, 9 L. Ed. 2d 441 (1963), the Court was willing to assume that a defendant's arrest had been unlawful but held that "the connection between the arrest and the statement (given several days later) had 'become so attenuated as to dissipate the taint.' Nardone v. United States, 308 U.S. 338, 341, 60 S. Ct. 266, 84 L. Ed. 307." Parker v. North Carolina, 397 U.S. 790, 796, 90 S. Ct. 1458, 25 L. Ed. 2d 785 (1970), held that even though a confession be assumed to have been involuntary in the constitutional sense of the word, a guilty plea entered over a month later met the test for the voluntariness of such a plea. The Court in Parker relied on the same quoted language from Nardone, supra, as did the Court in Wong Sun, supra. While the type of causation on which the taint cases turn may differ somewhat from that which we apply here, those cases do suggest that the proper test to apply in the present context is one which likewise protects against the invasion of constitutional rights without commanding undesirable consequences not necessary to the assurance of those rights.

Initially, in this case, the burden was properly placed upon respondent to show that his conduct was constitutionally protected, and that this conduct was a "substantial factor" or to put it in other words, that it was a "motivating factor"[188] in

188. See Village of Arlington Heights v. Metropolitan Housing Development Corp., 429 U.S., at 270–271, n. 21, 97 S. Ct., at 566.

the Board's decision not to rehire him. Respondent having carried that burden, however, the District Court should have gone on to determine whether the Board had shown by a preponderance of the evidence that it would have reached the same decision as to respondent's reemployment even in the absence of the protected conduct.

We cannot tell from the District Court opinion and conclusions, nor from the opinion of the Court of Appeals affirming the judgment of the District Court, what conclusion those courts would have reached had they applied this test. The judgment of the Court of Appeals is therefore vacated, and the case remanded for further proceedings consistent with this opinion.

So ordered.

[Case No. 3-3]

Whether a public employee's speech addresses a matter of public concern so as to shield the employee from discharge for expressing those views must be determined by the content, form, and context of the given statement, as revealed by the whole record.

Connick v. Myers

Supreme Court of the United States
461 U.S. 138 (1983)

Justice WHITE delivered the opinion of the Court.

In *Pickering v. Board of Education,* 391 U.S. 563, 88 S. Ct. 1731, 20 L. Ed. 2d 811 (1968), we stated that a public employee does not relinquish First Amendment rights to comment on matters of public interest by virtue of government employment. We also recognized that the State's interests as an employer in regulating the speech of its employees "differ significantly from those it possesses in connection with regulation of the speech of the citizenry in general." *Id.,* at 568, 88 S. Ct., at 1734. The problem, we thought, was arriving "at a balance between the interests of the [employee], as a citizen, in commenting upon matters of public concern and the interest of the State, as an employer, in promoting the efficiency of the public services it performs through its employees." *Ibid.* We return to this problem today and consider whether the First and Fourteenth Amendments prevent the discharge of a state employee for circulating a questionnaire concerning internal office affairs.

I

The respondent, Sheila Myers, was employed as an Assistant District Attorney in New Orleans for five and a half years. She served at the pleasure of petitioner Harry Connick, the District Attorney for Orleans Parish. During this period Myers competently performed her responsibilities of trying criminal cases.

In the early part of October, 1980, Myers was informed that she would be transferred to prosecute cases in a different section of the criminal court. Myers was strongly opposed to the proposed transfer[189] and expressed her view to several of her supervisors, including Connick. Despite her objections, on October 6 Myers was notified that she was being transferred. Myers again spoke with Dennis Waldron, one of the first assistant district attorneys, expressing her reluctance to accept the transfer. A number of other office matters were discussed and Myers later testified that, in response to Waldron's suggestion that her concerns were not shared by others in the office, she informed him that she would do some research on the matter.

That night Myers prepared a questionnaire soliciting the views of her fellow staff members concerning office transfer policy, office morale, the need for a grievance committee, the level of confidence in supervisors, and whether employees felt pressured to work in political campaigns.[190] Early the following morning, Myers typed and copied the questionnaire. She also met with Connick who urged her to accept the transfer. She said she would "consider" it. Connick then left the office. Myers then distributed the questionnaire to 15 assistant district attorneys. Shortly after noon, Dennis Waldron learned that Myers was distributing the survey. He immediately phoned Connick and informed him that Myers was creating a "mini-insurrection" within the office. Connick returned to the office and told Myers that she was being terminated because of her refusal to accept the transfer. She was also told that her distribution of the questionnaire was considered an act of insubordination. Connick particularly objected to the question which inquired whether employees "had confidence in and would rely on the word" of various superiors in the office, and to a question concerning pressure to work in political campaigns which he felt would be damaging if discovered by the press.

Myers filed suit under 42 U.S.C. §1983, contending that her employment was wrongfully terminated because she had exercised her constitutionally-protected right of free speech. The District Court agreed, ordered Myers reinstated, and awarded backpay, damages, and attorney's fees. 507 F. Supp. 752 (E.D. La. 1981).[191] The District Court found that although Connick informed Myers that she was being fired because of her refusal to accept a transfer, the facts showed that the questionnaire was the real reason for her termination. The court then proceeded to hold that Myers' questionnaire involved matters of public concern and that the state had not "clearly demonstrated" that the survey "substantially interfered" with the operations of the District Attorney's office.

---

189. Myers' opposition was at least partially attributable to her concern that a conflict of interest would have been created by the transfer because of her participation in a counseling program for convicted defendants released on probation in the section of the criminal court to which she was to be assigned.

190. The questionnaire is reproduced as Appendix A.

191. Petitioner has also objected to the assessment of damages as being in violation of the Eleventh Amendment and to the award of attorney's fees. Because of our disposition of the case, we do not reach these questions.

Connick appealed to the United States Court of Appeals for the Fifth Circuit, which affirmed on the basis of the District Court's opinion. 654 F.2d 719 (1981). Connick then sought review in this Court by way of certiorari, which we granted. 455 U.S. 999, 102 S. Ct. 1629, 71 L. Ed. 2d 865 (1982).

II

For at least 15 years, it has been settled that a state cannot condition public employment on a basis that infringes the employee's constitutionally protected interest in freedom of expression. *Keyishian v. Board of Regents,* 385 U.S. 589, 605–606, 87 S. Ct. 675, 684–685, 17 L. Ed. 2d 629 (1967); *Pickering v. Board of Education,* 391 U.S. 563, 88 S. Ct. 1731, 20 L. Ed. 2d 811 (1968); *Perry v. Sindermann,* 408 U.S. 593, 597, 92 S. Ct. 2694, 2697, 33 L. Ed. 2d 570 (1972); *Branti v. Finkel,* 445 U.S. 507, 515–516, 100 S. Ct. 1287, 1293, 63 L. Ed. 2d 574 (1980). Our task, as we defined it in *Pickering,* is to seek "a balance between the interests of the [employee], as a citizen, in commenting upon matters of public concern and the interest of the State, as an employer, in promoting the efficiency of the public services it performs through its employees." 391 U.S., at 568, 88 S. Ct., at 1734. The District Court, and thus the Court of Appeals as well, misapplied our decision in *Pickering* and consequently, in our view, erred in striking the balance for respondent.

A

The District Court got off on the wrong foot in this case by initially finding that, "[t]aken as a whole, the issues presented in the questionnaire relate to the effective functioning of the District Attorney's Office and are matters of public importance and concern." 507 F. Supp., at 758. Connick contends at the outset that no balancing of interests is required in this case because Myers' questionnaire concerned only internal office matters and that such speech is not upon a matter of "public concern," as the term was used in *Pickering.* Although we do not agree that Myers' communication in this case was wholly without First Amendment protection, there is much force to Connick's submission. The repeated emphasis in *Pickering* on the right of a public employee "as a citizen, in commenting upon matters of public concern," was not accidental. This language, reiterated in all of *Pickering's* progeny,[192] reflects both the historical evolvement of the rights of public employees, and the common sense realization that government offices could not function if every employment decision became a constitutional matter.[193]

---

192. See *Perry v. Sindermann,* 408 U.S. 593, 598, 92 S. Ct. 2694, 2698, 33 L. Ed. 2d 570 (1972); *Mt. Healthy City School Dist. Board of Ed. v. Doyle,* 429 U.S. 274, 284, 97 S. Ct. 568, 574, 50 L. Ed. 2d 471 (1977); *Givhan v. Western Line Consolidated School District,* 439 U.S. 410, 414, 99 S. Ct. 693, 695, 58 L. Ed. 2d 619 (1979).

193. The question of whether expression is of a kind that is of legitimate concern to the public is also the standard in determining whether a common-law action for invasion of privacy is present. See Restatement (Second) of Torts, § 652D. See also *Cox Broadcasting Co. v. Cohn,* 420 U.S. 469, 95 S. Ct. 1029, 43 L. Ed. 2d 328 (1975) (action for invasion of privacy cannot be maintained when the subject-matter of the publicity is matter of public record); *Time, Inc. v. Hill,* 385 U.S. 374, 387–388, 87 S. Ct. 534, 541–542, 17 L. Ed. 2d 456 (1967).

For most of this century, the unchallenged dogma was that a public employee had no right to object to conditions placed upon the terms of employment—including those which restricted the exercise of constitutional rights. The classic formulation of this position was Justice Holmes', who, when sitting on the Supreme Judicial Court of Massachusetts, observed: "A policeman may have a constitutional right to talk politics, but he has no constitutional right to be a policeman." *McAuliffe v. Mayor of New Bedford,* 155 Mass. 216, 220, 29 N.E. 517, 517 (1892). For many years, Holmes' epigram expressed this Court's law. *Adler v. Board of Education,* 342 U.S. 485, 72 S. Ct. 380, 96 L. Ed. 517 (1952); *Garner v. Board of Public Works,* 341 U.S. 716, 71 S. Ct. 909, 95 L. Ed. 1317 (1951); *United Public Workers v. Mitchell,* 330 U.S. 75, 67 S. Ct. 556, 91 L. Ed. 754 (1947); *United States v. Wurzbach,* 280 U.S. 396, 50 S. Ct. 167, 74 L. Ed. 508 (1930); *Ex parte Curtis,* 106 U.S. 371, 1 S. Ct. 381, 27 L. Ed. 232 (1882).

The Court cast new light on the matter in a series of cases arising from the widespread efforts in the 1950s and early 1960s to require public employees, particularly teachers, to swear oaths of loyalty to the state and reveal the groups with which they associated. In *Wiemann v. Updegraff,* 344 U.S. 183, 73 S. Ct. 215, 97 L. Ed. 216 (1952), the Court held that a State could not require its employees to establish their loyalty by extracting an oath denying past affiliation with Communists. In *Cafeteria Workers v. McElroy,* 367 U.S. 886, 81 S. Ct. 1743, 6 L. Ed. 2d 1230 (1961), the Court recognized that the government could not deny employment because of previous membership in a particular party. See also *Shelton v. Tucker,* 364 U.S. 479, 490, 81 S. Ct. 247, 253, 5 L. Ed. 2d 231 (1960); *Torcaso v. Watkins,* 367 U.S. 488, 81 S. Ct. 1680, 6 L. Ed. 2d 982 (1961); *Cramp v. Board of Public Instruction,* 368 U.S. 278, 82 S. Ct. 275, 7 L. Ed. 2d 285 (1961). By the time *Sherbert v. Verner,* 374 U.S. 398, 83 S. Ct. 1790, 10 L. Ed. 2d 965 (1963), was decided, it was already "too late in the day to doubt that the liberties of religion and expression may be infringed by the denial of or placing of conditions upon a benefit or privilege." *Id.,* at 404, 83 S. Ct., at 1794. It was therefore no surprise when in *Keyishian v. Board of Regents,* 385 U.S. 589, 87 S. Ct. 675, 17 L. Ed. 2d 629 (1967), the Court invalidated New York statutes barring employment on the basis of membership in "subversive" organizations, observing that the theory that public employment which may be denied altogether may be subjected to any conditions, regardless of how unreasonable, had been uniformly rejected. *Id.,* at 605–606, 87 S. Ct., at 684–685.

In all of these cases, the precedents in which *Pickering* is rooted, the invalidated statutes and actions sought to suppress the rights of public employees to participate in public affairs. The issue was whether government employees could be prevented or "chilled" by the fear of discharge from joining political parties and other associations that certain public officials might find "subversive." The explanation for the Constitution's special concern with threats to the right of citizens to participate in political affairs is no mystery. The First Amendment "was fashioned to assure unfettered interchange of ideas for the bringing about of political and social changes desired by the people." *Roth v. United States,* 354 U.S. 476, 484, 77 S. Ct. 1304, 1308, 1 L. Ed. 2d 1498; *New York Times Co. v. Sullivan,* 376 U.S. 254, 269, 84 S.

Ct. 710, 720, 11 L. Ed. 2d 686 (1964). "[S]peech concerning public affairs is more than self-expression; it is the essence of self-government." *Garrison v. Louisiana,* 379 U.S. 64, 74–75, 85 S. Ct. 209, 215–216, 13 L. Ed. 2d 125 (1964). Accordingly, the Court has frequently reaffirmed that speech on public issues occupies the "highest rung of the hierarchy of First Amendment values," and is entitled to special protection. *NAACP v. Claiborne Hardware Co.,* 458 U.S. 886, 913, 102 S. Ct. 3409, 3426, 73 L. Ed. 2d 1215 (1982); *Carey v. Brown,* 447 U.S. 455, 467, 100 S. Ct. 2286, 2293, 65 L. Ed. 2d 263 (1980).

Pickering v. Board of Education, supra, followed from this understanding of the First Amendment. In *Pickering,* the Court held impermissible under the First Amendment the dismissal of a high school teacher for openly criticizing the Board of Education on its allocation of school funds between athletics and education and its methods of informing taxpayers about the need for additional revenue. Pickering's subject was "a matter of legitimate public concern" upon which "free and open debate is vital to informed decision-making by the electorate." 391 U.S., at 571–572, 88 S. Ct., at 1736.

Our cases following *Pickering* also involved safeguarding speech on matters of public concern. The controversy in *Perry v. Sindermann,* 408 U.S. 593, 92 S. Ct. 2694, 33 L. Ed. 2d 570 (1972), arose from the failure to rehire a teacher in the state college system who had testified before committees of the Texas legislature and had become involved in public disagreement over whether the college should be elevated to four-year status—a change opposed by the Regents. In *Mt. Healthy City Board of Ed. v. Doyle,* 429 U.S. 274, 97 S. Ct. 568, 50 L. Ed. 2d 471 (1977), a public school teacher was not rehired because, allegedly, he had relayed to a radio station the substance of a memorandum relating to teacher dress and appearance that the school principal had circulated to various teachers. The memorandum was apparently prompted by the view of some in the administration that there was a relationship between teacher appearance and public support for bond issues, and indeed, the radio station promptly announced the adoption of the dress code as a news item. Most recently, in *Givhan v. Western Line Consolidated School District,* 439 U.S. 410, 99 S. Ct. 693, 58 L. Ed. 2d 619 (1979), we held that First Amendment protection applies when a public employee arranges to communicate privately with his employer rather than to express his views publicly. Although the subject-matter of Mrs. Givhan's statements were not the issue before the Court, it is clear that her statements concerning the school district's allegedly racially discriminatory policies involved a matter of public concern.

Pickering, its antecedents and progeny, lead us to conclude that if Myers' questionnaire cannot be fairly characterized as constituting speech on a matter of public concern, it is unnecessary for us to scrutinize the reasons for her discharge.[194] When

194. See *Clark v. Holmes,* 474 F.2d 928 (CA7 1972) cert. denied, 411 U.S. 972, 93 S. Ct. 2148, 36 L. Ed. 2d 695 (1973); *Schmidt v. Fremont County School Dist.,* 558 F.2d 982, 984 (CA10 1977).

employee expression cannot be fairly considered as relating to any matter of political, social, or other concern to the community, government officials should enjoy wide latitude in managing their offices, without intrusive oversight by the judiciary in the name of the First Amendment. Perhaps the government employer's dismissal of the worker may not be fair, but ordinary dismissals from government service which violate no fixed tenure or applicable statute or regulation are not subject to judicial review even if the reasons for the dismissal are alleged to be mistaken or unreasonable. *Board of Regents v. Roth,* 408 U.S. 564, 92 S. Ct. 2701, 33 L. Ed. 2d 548 (1972); *Perry v. Sindermann,* 408 U.S. 593, 92 S. Ct. 2694, 33 L. Ed. 2d 570 (1972); *Bishop v. Wood,* 426 U.S. 341, 349–350, 96 S. Ct. 2074, 2079–2080, 48 L. Ed. 2d 684 (1976).

We do not suggest, however, that Myers' speech, even if not touching upon a matter of public concern, is totally beyond the protection of the First Amendment. "The First Amendment does not protect speech and assembly only to the extent that it can be characterized as political. 'Great secular causes, with smaller ones, are guarded.'" *United Mine Workers v. Illinois State Bar Association,* 389 U.S. 217, 223, 88 S. Ct. 353, 356, 19 L. Ed. 2d 426 (1967), *quoting Thomas v. Collins,* 323 U.S. 516, 531, 65 S. Ct. 315, 323, 89 L. Ed. 430 (1945). We in no sense suggest that speech on private matters falls into one of the narrow and well-defined classes of expression which carries so little social value, such as obscenity, that the state can prohibit and punish such expression by all persons in its jurisdiction. See *Chaplinsky v. New Hampshire,* 315 U.S. 568, 62 S. Ct. 766, 86 L. Ed. 1031 (1942); *Roth v. United States,* 354 U.S. 476, 77 S. Ct. 1304, 1 L. Ed. 2d 1498 (1957); *New York v. Ferber,* 458 U.S. 747, 102 S. Ct. 3348, 73 L. Ed. 2d 1113 (1982). For example, an employee's false criticism of his employer on grounds not of public concern may be cause for his discharge but would be entitled to the same protection in a libel action accorded an identical statement made by a man on the street. We hold only that when a public employee speaks not as a citizen upon matters of public concern, but instead as an employee upon matters only of personal interest, absent the most unusual circumstances, a federal court is not the appropriate forum in which to review the wisdom of a personnel decision taken by a public agency allegedly in reaction to the employee's behavior. *Cf. Bishop v. Wood,* 426 U.S. 341, 349–350, 96 S. Ct. 2074, 2079–2080, 48 L. Ed. 2d 684 (1976). Our responsibility is to ensure that citizens are not deprived of fundamental rights by virtue of working for the government; this does not require a grant of immunity for employee grievances not afforded by the First Amendment to those who do not work for the state.

Whether an employee's speech addresses a matter of public concern must be determined by the content, form, and context of a given statement, as revealed by the whole record.[195] In this case, with but one exception, the questions posed by Myers to her coworkers do not fall under the rubric of matters of "public concern." We view the questions pertaining to the confidence and trust that Myers' coworkers

195. The inquiry into the protected status of speech is one of law, not fact.

possess in various supervisors, the level of office morale, and the need for a grievance committee as mere extensions of Myers' dispute over her transfer to another section of the criminal court. Unlike the dissent, *post,* at 1698, we do not believe these questions are of public import in evaluating the performance of the District Attorney as an elected official. Myers did not seek to inform the public that the District Attorney's office was not discharging its governmental responsibilities in the investigation and prosecution of criminal cases. Nor did Myers seek to bring to light actual or potential wrongdoing or breach of public trust on the part of Connick and others. Indeed, the questionnaire, if released to the public, would convey no information at all other than the fact that a single employee is upset with the status quo. While discipline and morale in the workplace are related to an agency's efficient performance of its duties, the focus of Myers' questions is not to evaluate the performance of the office but rather to gather ammunition for another round of controversy with her superiors. These questions reflect one employee's dissatisfaction with a transfer and an attempt to turn that displeasure into a cause celebre.[196]

To presume that all matters which transpire within a government office are of public concern would mean that virtually every remark—and certainly every criticism directed at a public official—would plant the seed of a constitutional case. While as a matter of good judgment, public officials should be receptive to constructive criticism offered by their employees, the First Amendment does not require a public office to be run as a roundtable for employee complaints over internal office affairs.

One question in Myers' questionnaire, however, does touch upon a matter of public concern. Question 11 inquires if assistant district attorneys "ever feel pressured to work in political campaigns on behalf of office supported candidates." We have recently noted that official pressure upon employees to work for political candidates not of the worker's own choice constitutes a coercion of belief in violation of fundamental constitutional rights. *Branti v. Finkel,* 445 U.S. 507, 515–516, 100 S. Ct. 1287, 1293, 63 L. Ed. 2d 574 (1980); *Elrod v. Burns,* 427 U.S. 347, 96 S. Ct. 2673, 49 L. Ed. 2d 547 (1976). In addition, there is a demonstrated interest in this country that government service should depend upon meritorious performance rather than political service. *CSC v. Letter Carriers,* 413 U.S. 548, 93 S. Ct. 2880, 37 L. Ed. 2d 796 (1973); *United Public Workers v. Mitchell,* 330 U.S. 75, 67 S. Ct. 556, 91 L. Ed. 754 (1947). Given this history, we believe it apparent that the issue of whether assistant

---

196. This is not a case like *Givhan,* where an employee speaks out as a citizen on a matter of general concern, not tied to a personal employment dispute, but arranges to do so privately. Mrs. Givhan's right to protest racial discrimination—a matter inherently of public concern—is not forfeited by her choice of a private forum. 439 U.S., at 415–416, 99 S. Ct., at 696–697. Here, however, a questionnaire not otherwise of public concern does not attain that status because its subject matter could, in different circumstances, have been the topic of a communication to the public that might be of general interest. The dissent's analysis of whether discussions of office morale and discipline could be matters of public concern is beside the point—it does not answer whether *this* questionnaire is such speech.

district attorneys are pressured to work in political campaigns is a matter of interest to the community upon which it is essential that public employees be able to speak out freely without fear of retaliatory dismissal.

B

Because one of the questions in Myers' survey touched upon a matter of public concern, and contributed to her discharge we must determine whether Connick was justified in discharging Myers. Here the District Court again erred in imposing an unduly onerous burden on the state to justify Myers' discharge. The District Court viewed the issue of whether Myers' speech was upon a matter of "public concern" as a threshold inquiry, after which it became the government's burden to "clearly demonstrate" that the speech involved "substantially interfered" with official responsibilities. Yet *Pickering* unmistakably states, and respondent agrees,[197] that the state's burden in justifying a particular discharge varies depending upon the nature of the employee's expression. Although such particularized balancing is difficult, the courts must reach the most appropriate possible balance of the competing interests.[198]

C

The *Pickering* balance requires full consideration of the government's interest in the effective and efficient fulfillment of its responsibilities to the public. One hundred years ago, the Court noted the government's legitimate purpose in "promot[ing] efficiency and integrity in the discharge of official duties, and to maintain proper discipline in the public service." *Ex parte Curtis,* 106 U.S. 371, 373, 1 S. Ct. 381, 384, 27 L. Ed. 232 (1882). As Justice POWELL explained in his separate opinion in *Arnett v. Kennedy,* 416 U.S. 134, 168, 94 S. Ct. 1633, 1651, 40 L. Ed. 2d 15 (1974):

> "To this end, the Government, as an employer, must have wide discretion and control over the management of its personnel and internal affairs. This

---

197. See Brief for Respondent 9 ("These factors, including the degree of the 'importance' of plaintiff's speech, were proper considerations to be weighed in the *Pickering* balance."); Tr. of Oral Arg. 30 (Counsel for Respondent) ("I certainly would not disagree that the content of the questionnaire, whether it affects a matter of great public concern or only a very narrow internal matter, is a relevant circumstance to be weighed in the *Pickering* analysis.").

198. "The Constitution has imposed upon this Court final authority to determine the meaning and application of those words of that instrument which require interpretation to resolve judicial issues. With that responsibility, we are compelled to examine for ourselves the statements in issue and the circumstances under which they are made to see whether or not they ... are of a character which the principles of the First Amendment, as adopted by the Due Process Clause of the Fourteenth Amendment, protect." *Pennekamp v. Florida,* 328 U.S. 331, 335, 66 S. Ct. 1029, 1031, 90 L. Ed. 1295 (1946) (footnote omitted).

Because of this obligation, we cannot "avoid making an independent constitutional judgment on the facts of the case." *Jacobellis v. Ohio,* 378 U.S. 184, 190, 84 S. Ct. 1676, 1679, 12 L. Ed. 2d 793 (1964) (Opinion of BRENNAN, J.). See *Edwards v. South Carolina,* 372 U.S. 229, 235, 83 S. Ct. 680, 683, 9 L. Ed. 2d 697 (1963); *New York Times v. Sullivan,* 376 U.S. 254, 285, 84 S. Ct. 710, 728, 11 L. Ed. 2d 686 (1964); *NAACP v. Claiborne Hardware Co.,* 458 U.S. 886, 915–916, n. 50, 102 S. Ct. 3409, 3427, n. 50, 73 L. Ed. 2d 1215 (1982).

> includes the prerogative to remove employees whose conduct hinders efficient operation and to do so with dispatch. Prolonged retention of a disruptive or otherwise unsatisfactory employee can adversely affect discipline and morale in the work place, foster disharmony, and ultimately impair the efficiency of an office or agency."

We agree with the District Court that there is no demonstration here that the questionnaire impeded Myers' ability to perform her responsibilities. The District Court was also correct to recognize that "it is important to the efficient and successful operation of the District Attorney's office for Assistants to maintain close working relationships with their superiors." 507 F. Supp., at 759. Connick's judgment, and apparently also that of his first assistant Dennis Waldron, who characterized Myers' actions as causing a "mini-insurrection", was that Myers' questionnaire was an act of insubordination which interfered with working relationships.[199] When close working relationships are essential to fulfilling public responsibilities, a wide degree of deference to the employer's judgment is appropriate. Furthermore, we do not see the necessity for an employer to allow events to unfold to the extent that the disruption of the office and the destruction of working relationships is manifest before taking action.[200] We caution that a stronger showing may be necessary if the employee's speech more substantially involved matters of public concern.

The District Court rejected Connick's position because "unlike a statement of fact which might be deemed critical of one's superiors, [Myers'] questionnaire was not a statement of fact, but the presentation and solicitation of ideas and opinions," which are entitled to greater constitutional protection because "under the First Amendment there is no such thing as a false idea." 507 F. Supp., at 759. This approach, while perhaps relevant in weighing the value of Myers' speech, bears no logical relationship to the issue of whether the questionnaire undermined office relationships. Questions, no less than forcefully stated opinions and facts, carry messages and it requires no unusual insight to conclude that the purpose, if not the likely result, of the questionnaire is to seek to precipitate a vote of no confidence in Connick and his supervisors. Thus, Question 10, which asked whether or not the Assistants had confidence in and relied on the word of five named supervisors, is a statement that carries the clear potential for undermining office relations.

---

199. Waldron testified that from what he had learned of the events on October 7, Myers "was trying to stir up other people not to accept the changes [transfers] that had been made on the memorandum and that were to be implemented." App. 167. In his view, the questionnaire was a "final act of defiance" and that, as a result of Myers' action, "there were going to be some severe problems about the changes." *Ibid.* Connick testified that he reached a similar conclusion after conducting his own investigation. "After I satisfied myself that not only wasn't she accepting the transfer but that she was affirmatively opposing it and disrupting the routine of the office by this questionnaire, I called her in . . . [and dismissed her]." App. 130.

200. Cf. *Perry Ed. Assn. v. Perry Local Ed. Assn.,* 460 U.S. 37, 52, n. 12, 103 S. Ct. 948, 957, 74 L. Ed. 2d 794 (1983) (proof of future disruption not necessary to justify denial of access to non-public forum on grounds that the proposed use may disrupt the property's intended function.); *Greer v. Spock,* 424 U.S. 828, 96 S. Ct. 1211, 47 L. Ed. 2d 505 (1976) (same).

Also relevant is the manner, time, and place in which the questionnaire was distributed. As noted in *Givhan v. Western Line Consolidated School Dist., supra* at 415, n. 4, 99 S. Ct., at 696, n. 4, "Private expression . . . may in some situations bring additional factors to the *Pickering* calculus. When a government employee personally confronts his immediate superior, the employing agency's institutional efficiency may be threatened not only by the content of the employee's message but also by the manner, time, and place in which it is delivered." Here the questionnaire was prepared, and distributed at the office; the manner of distribution required not only Myers to leave her work but for others to do the same in order that the questionnaire be completed.[201] Although some latitude in when official work is performed is to be allowed when professional employees are involved, and Myers did not violate announced office policy,[202] the fact that Myers, unlike Pickering, exercised her rights to speech at the office supports Connick's fears that the functioning of his office was endangered.

Finally, the context in which the dispute arose is also significant. This is not a case where an employee, out of purely academic interest, circulated a questionnaire so as to obtain useful research. Myers acknowledges that it is no coincidence that the questionnaire followed upon the heels of the transfer notice. When employee speech concerning office policy arises from an employment dispute concerning the very application of that policy to the speaker, additional weight must be given to the supervisor's view that the employee has threatened the authority of the employer to run the office. Although we accept the District Court's factual finding that Myers' reluctance to accede to the transfer order was not a sufficient cause in itself for her dismissal, and thus does not constitute a sufficient defense under *Mt. Healthy City Board of Ed. v. Doyle,* 429 U.S. 274, 97 S. Ct. 568, 50 L. Ed. 2d 471 (1977), this does not render irrelevant the fact that the questionnaire emerged after a persistent dispute between Myers and Connick and his deputies over office transfer policy.

III

Myers' questionnaire touched upon matters of public concern in only a most limited sense; her survey, in our view, is most accurately characterized as an employee grievance concerning internal office policy. The limited First Amendment interest involved here does not require that Connick tolerate action which he reasonably believed would disrupt the office, undermine his authority, and destroy close working relationships. Myers' discharge therefore did not offend the First Amendment. We reiterate, however, the caveat we expressed in *Pickering, supra,* at 569, 88 S. Ct., at 1735: "Because of the enormous variety of fact situations in which

201. The record indicates that some, though not all, of the questionnaires were distributed during lunch. Employee speech which transpires entirely on the employee's own time, and in non-work areas of the office, bring different factors into the *Pickering* calculus, and might lead to a different conclusion. Cf. *NLRB v. Magnavox Co.,* 415 U.S. 322, 94 S. Ct. 1099, 39 L. Ed. 2d 358 (1974).

202. The violation of such a rule would strengthen Connick's position. See *Mt. Healthy City Board of Ed. v. Doyle,* 429 U.S. at 284, 97 S. Ct. at 574.

critical statements by . . . public employees may be thought by their superiors . . . to furnish grounds for dismissal, we do not deem it either appropriate or feasible to lay down a general standard against which all such statements may be judged."

Our holding today is grounded in our long-standing recognition that the First Amendment's primary aim is the full protection of speech upon issues of public concern, as well as the practical realities involved in the administration of a government office. Although today the balance is struck for the government, this is no defeat for the First Amendment. For it would indeed be a Pyrrhic victory for the great principles of free expression if the Amendment's safeguarding of a public employee's right, as a citizen, to participate in discussions concerning public affairs were confused with the attempt to constitutionalize the employee grievance that we see presented here. The judgment of the Court of Appeals is

Reversed.

APPENDIX A

Questionnaire distributed by respondent on October 7, 1980

PLAINTIFF'S EXHIBIT 2, App. 191

Please take the few minutes it will require to fill this out. You can freely express your opinion *WITH ANONYMITY GUARANTEED.*

* * *

1. How long have you been in the Office? ____________

2. Were you moved as a result of the recent transfers? ____________

3. Were the transfers as they effected [sic] you discussed with you by any superior prior to the notice of them being posted? ____________

4. Do you think as a matter of policy, they should have been? ____________

5. From your experience, do you feel office procedure regarding transfers has been fair? ____________

6. Do you believe there is a rumor mill active in the office? ____________

7. If so, how do you think it effects [sic] overall working performance of A.D.A. personnel? ____________

8. If so, how do you think it effects [sic] office morale? ____________

9. Do you generally first learn of office changes and developments through rumor? ____________

10. Do you have confidence in and would you rely on the word of:

    Bridget Bane ____________

    Fred Harper ____________

    Lindsay Larson ____________

    Joe Meyer ____________

    Dennis Waldron ____________

11. Do you ever feel pressured to work in political campaigns on behalf of office supported candidates? ______

12. Do you feel a grievance committee would be a worthwhile addition to the office structure? ______

13. How would you rate office morale? ______

14. Please feel free to express any comments or feelings you have. ______

THANK YOU FOR YOUR COOPERATION IN THIS SURVEY.

[Case No. 3-4]

For a government employee's speech to be protected, it must be a matter of public concern and the employee's interest must not be outweighed by any injury to that of the state employer in promoting efficiency of public services.

Waters v. Churchill

Supreme Court of the United States
511 U.S. 661 (1994)

Justice O'CONNOR announced the judgment of the Court.

In *Connick v. Myers,* 461 U.S. 138, 103 S. Ct. 1684, 75 L. Ed. 2d 708 (1983), we set forth a test for determining whether speech by a government employee may, consistently with the First Amendment, serve as a basis for disciplining or discharging that employee. In this case, we decide whether the *Connick* test should be applied to what the government employer thought was said, or to what the trier of fact ultimately determines to have been said.

I

This case arises out of a conversation that respondent Cheryl Churchill had on January 16, 1987, with Melanie Perkins-Graham. Both Churchill and Perkins-Graham were nurses working at McDonough District Hospital; Churchill was in the obstetrics department, and Perkins-Graham was considering transferring to that department. The conversation took place at work during a dinner break. Petitioners heard about it, and fired Churchill allegedly because of it. There is, however, a dispute about what Churchill actually said, and therefore about whether petitioners were constitutionally permitted to fire Churchill for her statements.

The conversation was overheard in part by two other nurses, Mary Lou Ballew and Jean Welty, and by Dr. Thomas Koch, the clinical head of obstetrics. A few days later, Ballew told Cynthia Waters, Churchill's supervisor, about the incident. According to Ballew, Churchill took "'the cross trainee into the kitchen for ... at least 20 minutes to talk about [Waters] and how bad things are in [obstetrics] in general.'" 977 F.2d 1114, 1118 (CA7 1992). Ballew said that Churchill's statements led Perkins-Graham to no longer be interested in switching to the department. Supplemental App. of Defendants-Appellees in No. 91-2288 (CA7), p. 60.

Shortly after this, Waters met with Ballew a second time for confirmation of Ballew's initial report. Ballew said that Churchill "was knocking the department" and that "in general [Churchill] was saying what a bad place [obstetrics] is to work." Ballew said she heard Churchill say Waters "was trying to find reasons to fire her." Ballew also said Churchill described a patient complaint for which Waters had supposedly wrongly blamed Churchill. *Id.*, at 67–68.

Waters, together with petitioner Kathleen Davis, the hospital's vice president of nursing, also met with Perkins-Graham, who told them that Churchill "had indeed said unkind and inappropriate negative things about [Waters]." *Id.*, at 228. Also, according to Perkins-Graham, Churchill mentioned a negative evaluation that Waters had given Churchill, which arose out of an incident in which Waters had cited Churchill for an insubordinate remark. *Ibid.* The evaluation stated that Churchill "'promotes an unpleasant atmosphere and hinders constructive communication and cooperation,'" 977 F.2d, at 1118, and "'exhibits negative behavior towards [Waters] and [Waters'] leadership through her actions and body language'"; the evaluation said Churchill's work was otherwise satisfactory, *id.*, at 1116. Churchill allegedly told Perkins-Graham that she and Waters had discussed the evaluation, and that Waters "wanted to wipe the slate clean . . . but [Churchill thought] this wasn't possible." Supplemental App. of Defendants-Appellees in No. 91-2288, at 228. Churchill also allegedly told Perkins-Graham "that just in general things were not good in OB and hospital administration was responsible." *Id.*, at 229. Churchill specifically mentioned Davis, saying Davis "was ruining MDH." *Ibid.* Perkins-Graham told Waters that she knew Davis and Waters "could not tolerate that kind of negativism." *Ibid.*

Churchill's version of the conversation is different. For several months, Churchill had been concerned about the hospital's "cross-training" policy, under which nurses from one department could work in another when their usual location was overstaffed. Churchill believed this policy threatened patient care because it was designed not to train nurses but to cover staff shortages, and she had complained about this to Davis and Waters. According to Churchill, the conversation with Perkins-Graham primarily concerned the cross-training policy. 977 F.2d, at 1118. Churchill denies that she said some of what Ballew and Perkins-Graham allege she said. She does admit she criticized Davis, saying her staffing policies threatened to "ruin" the hospital because they "'seemed to be impeding nursing care.'" *Ibid.* She claims she actually defended Waters and encouraged Perkins-Graham to transfer to obstetrics. *Ibid.*

Koch's and Welty's recollections of the conversation match Churchill's. *Id.*, at 1122. Davis and Waters, however, never talked to Koch or Welty about this, and they did not talk to Churchill until the time they told her she was fired. Moreover, Churchill claims, Ballew was biased against Churchill because of an incident in which Ballew apparently made an error and Churchill had to cover for her. Brief for Respondents 9, n. 12.

After she was discharged, Churchill filed an internal grievance. The president of the hospital, petitioner Stephen Hopper, met with Churchill in regard to this and heard her side of the story. App. to Pet. for Cert. 75–77. He then reviewed Waters' and Davis' written reports of their conversations with Ballew and Perkins-Graham, and had Bernice Magin, the hospital's vice president of human resources, interview Ballew one more time. Supplemental App. of Defendants-Appellees in No. 91-2288, at 108, 139–142. After considering all this, Hopper rejected Churchill's grievance.

Churchill then sued under Rev.Stat. §1979, 42 U.S.C. §1983, claiming that the firing violated her First Amendment rights because her speech was protected under *Connick v. Myers,* 461 U.S. 138, 103 S. Ct. 1684, 75 L. Ed. 2d 708 (1983). In May 1991, the United States District Court for the Central District of Illinois granted summary judgment to petitioners. The court held that neither version of the conversation was protected under *Connick:* Regardless of whose story was accepted, the speech was not on a matter of public concern, and even if it was on a matter of public concern, its potential for disruption nonetheless stripped it of First Amendment protection. Therefore, the court held, management could fire Churchill for the conversation with impunity. App. to Pet. for Cert. 45–49.

The United States Court of Appeals for the Seventh Circuit reversed. 977 F.2d 1114 (1992). The court held that Churchill's speech, viewed in the light most favorable to her, was protected speech under the *Connick* test: It was on a matter of public concern—"the hospital's [alleged] violation of state nursing regulations as well as the quality and level of nursing care it provides its patients," *id.,* at 1122—and it was not disruptive, *id.,* at 1124.

The court also concluded that the inquiry must turn on what the speech actually was, not on what the employer thought it was. "If the employer chooses to discharge the employee without sufficient knowledge of her protected speech as a result of an inadequate investigation into the employee's conduct," the court held, "the employer runs the risk of eventually being required to remedy any wrongdoing whether it was deliberate or accidental." *Id.,* at 1127 (footnote omitted).

We granted certiorari, 509 U.S. 903, 113 S. Ct. 2991, 125 L. Ed. 2d 686 (1993), to resolve a conflict among the Circuits on this issue. Compare the decision below with *Atcherson v. Siebenmann,* 605 F.2d 1058 (CA8 1979); *Wulf v. Wichita,* 883 F.2d 842 (CA10 1989); *Sims v. Metropolitan Dade County,* 972 F.2d 1230 (CA11 1992).

II

A

There is no dispute in this case about when speech by a government employee is protected by the First Amendment: To be protected, the speech must be on a matter of public concern, and the employee's interest in expressing herself on this matter must not be outweighed by any injury the speech could cause to "'the interest of the State, as an employer, in promoting the efficiency of the public services it performs through its employees.'" *Connick, supra,* 461 U.S., at 142, 103 S. Ct., at 1687 (quoting

Pickering v. Board of Ed. of Township High School Dist. 205, Will Cty., 391 U.S. 563, 568, 88 S. Ct. 1731, 1735, 20 L. Ed. 2d 811 (1968)). It is also agreed that it is the court's task to apply the *Connick* test to the facts. 461 U.S., at 148, n. 7, and 150, n. 10, 103 S. Ct., at 1690, n. 7, and 1692, n. 10.

The dispute is over how the factual basis for applying the test—what the speech was, in what tone it was delivered, what the listener's reactions were, see *id.*, at 151–153, 103 S. Ct., at 1692–1693—is to be determined. Should the court apply the *Connick* test to the speech as the government employer found it to be, or should it ask the jury to determine the facts for itself? The Court of Appeals held that the employer's factual conclusions were irrelevant, and that the jury should engage in its own fact-finding. Petitioners argue that the employer's factual conclusions should be dispositive. Respondents take a middle course: They suggest that the court should accept the employer's factual conclusions, but only if those conclusions were arrived at reasonably, see Brief for Respondents 39, something they say did not happen here.

We agree that it is important to ensure not only that the substantive First Amendment standards are sound, but also that they are applied through reliable procedures. This is why we have often held some procedures—a particular allocation of the burden of proof, a particular quantum of proof, a particular type of appellate review, and so on—to be constitutionally required in proceedings that may penalize protected speech. See *Freedman v. Maryland,* 380 U.S. 51, 58–60, 85 S. Ct. 734, 738–740, 13 L. Ed. 2d 649 (1965) (government must bear burden of proving that speech is unprotected); *Speiser v. Randall,* 357 U.S. 513, 526, 78 S. Ct. 1332, 1342, 2 L. Ed. 2d 1460 (1958) (same); *Philadelphia Newspapers, Inc. v. Hepps,* 475 U.S. 767, 775–778, 106 S. Ct. 1558, 1563–1565, 89 L. Ed. 2d 783 (1986) (libel plaintiff must bear burden of proving that speech is false); *Masson v. New Yorker Magazine, Inc.,* 501 U.S. 496, 510, 111 S. Ct. 2419, 2429, 115 L. Ed. 2d 447 (1991) (actual malice must be proved by clear and convincing evidence); *Bose Corp. v. Consumers Union of United States, Inc.,* 466 U.S. 485, 503–511, 104 S. Ct. 1949, 1960–1965, 80 L. Ed. 2d 502 (1984) (appellate court must make independent judgment about presence of actual malice).

These cases establish a basic First Amendment principle: Government action based on protected speech may under some circumstances violate the First Amendment even if the government actor honestly believes the speech is unprotected. And though Justice SCALIA suggests that this principle be limited to licensing schemes and to "deprivation[s] of the freedom of speech specifically *through the judicial process,*" *post,* at 1894 (emphasis in original), we do not think the logic of the cases supports such a limitation. Speech can be chilled and punished by administrative action as much as by judicial processes; in no case have we asserted or even implied the contrary. In fact, in *Speiser v. Randall,* we struck down procedures, on the grounds that they were insufficiently protective of free speech, which involved both administrative and judicial components. *Speiser,* like this case, dealt with a government decision to deny a speaker certain benefits—in *Speiser* a tax exemption, in this case a government job—based on what the speaker said. Our holding there did not depend on the deprivation taking place "specifically through the judicial process," and we cannot see how the result could have been any different had the process been entirely administrative, with no judicial review. We cannot sweep aside *Speiser* and the other cases cited above as easily as Justice SCALIA proposes.

Nonetheless, not every procedure that may safeguard protected speech is constitutionally mandated. True, the procedure adopted by the Court of Appeals may lower the chance of protected speech being erroneously punished. A speaker is more protected if she has two opportunities to be vindicated—first by the employer's investigation and then by the jury—than just one. But each procedure involves a different mix of administrative burden, risk of erroneous punishment of protected speech, and risk of erroneous exculpation of unprotected speech. Though the First Amendment creates a strong presumption against punishing protected speech even inadvertently, the balance need not always be struck in that direction. We have never, for instance, required proof beyond a reasonable doubt in civil cases where First Amendment interests are at stake, though such a requirement would protect speech more than the alternative standards would. *Compare, e.g., California ex rel. Cooper v. Mitchell Brothers' Santa Ana Theater,* 454 U.S. 90, 93, 102 S. Ct. 172, 173, 70 L. Ed. 2d 262 (1981) (*per curiam*), with *McKinney v. Alabama,* 424 U.S. 669, 686, 96 S. Ct. 1189, 1198, 47 L. Ed. 2d 387 (1976) (Brennan, J., concurring in judgment in part). Likewise, the possibility that defamation liability would chill even true speech has not led us to require an actual malice standard in all libel cases. *Dun & Bradstreet, Inc. v. Greenmoss Builders, Inc.,* 472 U.S. 749, 761, 105 S. Ct. 2939, 2946, 86 L. Ed. 2d 593 (1985) (plurality opinion); *Gertz v. Robert Welch, Inc.,* 418 U.S. 323, 94 S. Ct. 2997, 41 L. Ed. 2d 789 (1974). Nor has the possibility that overbroad regulations may chill commercial speech convinced us to extend the overbreadth doctrine into the commercial speech area. *Bates v. State Bar of Ariz.,* 433 U.S. 350, 380–381, 97 S. Ct. 2691, 2707–2708, 53 L. Ed. 2d 810 (1977).

We have never set forth a general test to determine when a procedural safeguard is required by the First Amendment—just as we have never set forth a general test to determine what constitutes a compelling state interest, *see Boos v. Barry,* 485 U.S. 312, 324, 108 S. Ct. 1157, 1165, 99 L. Ed. 2d 333 (1988), or what categories of speech are so lacking in value that they fall outside the protection of the First Amendment, *New York v. Ferber,* 458 U.S. 747, 763–764, 102 S. Ct. 3348, 3357–3358, 73 L. Ed. 2d 1113 (1982), or many other matters—and we do not purport to do so now. But though we agree with Justice SCALIA that the lack of such a test is inconvenient, see *post,* at 1894, this does not relieve us of our responsibility to decide the case that is before us today. Both Justice SCALIA and we agree that some procedural requirements are mandated by the First Amendment and some are not. See *post,* at 1893. None of us have discovered a general principle to determine where the line is to be drawn. See *post,* at 1893–1894. We must therefore reconcile ourselves to answering the question on a case-by-case basis, at least until some workable general rule emerges.

Accordingly, all we say today is that the propriety of a proposed procedure must turn on the particular context in which the question arises—on the cost of the procedure and the relative magnitude and constitutional significance of the risks it would decrease and increase. And to evaluate these factors here we have to return to the issue we dealt with in *Connick* and in the cases that came before it: What is it about the government's role as employer that gives it a freer hand in regulating the speech of its employees than it has in regulating the speech of the public at large?

B

We have never explicitly answered this question, though we have always assumed that its premise is correct—that the government as employer indeed has far broader powers than does the government as sovereign. *See, e.g., Pickering,* 391 U.S., at 568, 88 S. Ct., at 1735; *Civil Service Comm'n v. Letter Carriers,* 413 U.S. 548, 564, 93 S. Ct. 2880, 2890, 37 L. Ed. 2d 796 (1973); *Connick,* 461 U.S., at 147, 103 S. Ct., at 1689. This assumption is amply borne out by considering the practical realities of government employment, and the many situations in which, we believe, most observers would agree that the government must be able to restrict its employees' speech.

To begin with, even many of the most fundamental maxims of our First Amendment jurisprudence cannot reasonably be applied to speech by government employees. The First Amendment demands a tolerance of "verbal tumult, discord, and even offensive utterance," as "necessary side effects of... the process of open debate," *Cohen v. California,* 403 U.S. 15, 24–25, 91 S. Ct. 1780, 1788, 29 L. Ed. 2d 284 (1971). But we have never expressed doubt that a government employer may bar its employees from using Mr. Cohen's offensive utterance to members of the public or to the people with whom they work. "Under the First Amendment there is no such thing as a false idea," *Gertz, supra,* at 339, 94 S. Ct., at 3006, the "fitting remedy for evil counsels is good ones," *Whitney v. California,* 274 U.S. 357, 375, 47 S. Ct. 641, 648, 71 L. Ed. 1095 (1927) (Brandeis, J., concurring). But when an employee counsels her co-workers to do their job in a way with which the public employer disagrees, her managers may tell her to stop, rather than relying on counterspeech. The First Amendment reflects the "profound national commitment to the principle that debate on public issues should be uninhibited, robust, and wide-open." *New York Times Co. v. Sullivan,* 376 U.S. 254, 270, 84 S. Ct. 710, 721, 11 L. Ed. 2d 686 (1964). But though a private person is perfectly free to uninhibitedly and robustly criticize a state governor's legislative program, we have never suggested that the Constitution bars the governor from firing a high-ranking deputy for doing the same thing. *Cf. Branti v. Finkel,* 445 U.S. 507, 518, 100 S. Ct. 1287, 1294, 63 L. Ed. 2d 574 (1980). Even something as close to the core of the First Amendment as participation in political campaigns may be prohibited to government employees. *Broadrick v. Oklahoma,* 413 U.S. 601, 93 S. Ct. 2908, 37 L. Ed. 2d 830 (1973); *Letter Carriers, supra; Public Workers v. Mitchell,* 330 U.S. 75, 67 S. Ct. 556, 91 L. Ed. 754 (1947).

Government employee speech must be treated differently with regard to procedural requirements as well. For example, speech restrictions must generally precisely define the speech they target. *Baggett v. Bullitt,* 377 U.S. 360, 367–368, 84 S. Ct. 1316, 1320–1321, 12 L. Ed. 2d 377 (1964); *Hustler Magazine, Inc. v. Falwell,* 485 U.S. 46, 55, 108 S. Ct. 876, 881, 99 L. Ed. 2d 41 (1988). Yet surely a public employer may, consistently with the First Amendment, prohibit its employees from being "rude to customers," a standard almost certainly too vague when applied to the public at large. *Cf. Arnett v. Kennedy,* 416 U.S. 134, 158–162, 94 S. Ct. 1633, 1646–1648, 40 L. Ed. 2d 15 (1974) (plurality opinion) (upholding a regulation that allowed discharges for speech that hindered the "efficiency of the service"); *id.,* at 164, 94 S. Ct., at 1649 (Powell, J., concurring in part and concurring in result in part) (agreeing on this point).

Likewise, we have consistently given greater deference to government predictions of harm used to justify restriction of employee speech than to predictions of harm used to justify restrictions on the speech of the public at large. Few of the examples we have discussed involve tangible, present interference with the agency's operation. The danger in them is mostly speculative. One could make a respectable argument that political activity by government employees is generally not harmful, see *Public Workers v. Mitchell, supra,* 330 U.S. at 99, 67 S. Ct., at 569, or that high officials should allow more public dissent by their subordinates, *see Connick, supra,* 461 U.S., at 168–169, 103 S. Ct., at 1701–1702 (Brennan, J., dissenting); Whistleblower Protection Act of 1989, 103 Stat. 16, or that even in a government workplace the free market of ideas is superior to a command economy. But we have given substantial weight to government employers' reasonable predictions of disruption, even when the speech involved is on a matter of public concern, and even though when the government is acting as sovereign our review of legislative predictions of harm is considerably less deferential. *Compare, e.g., Connick, supra,* at 151–152, 103 S. Ct., at 1692–1693; *Letter Carriers, supra,* 413 U.S., at 566–567, 93 S. Ct., at 2890–2891, with *Sable Communications of Cal., Inc. v. FCC,* 492 U.S. 115, 129, 109 S. Ct. 2829, 2838, 106 L. Ed. 2d 93 (1989); *Texas v. Johnson,* 491 U.S. 397, 409, 109 S. Ct. 2533, 2542, 105 L. Ed. 2d 342 (1989). Similarly, we have refrained from intervening in government employer decisions that are based on speech that is of entirely private concern. Doubtless some such speech is sometimes nondisruptive; doubtless it is sometimes of value to the speakers and the listeners. But we have declined to question government employers' decisions on such matters. *Connick, supra,* 461 U.S., at 146–149, 103 S. Ct., at 1689–1691.

This does not, of course, show that the First Amendment should play no role in government employment decisions. Government employees are often in the best position to know what ails the agencies for which they work; public debate may gain much from their informed opinions, *Pickering, supra,* 391 U.S., at 572, 88 S. Ct., at 1736. And a government employee, like any citizen, may have a strong, legitimate interest in speaking out on public matters. In many such situations the government may have to make a substantial showing that the speech is, in fact, likely to be disruptive before it may be punished. *See, e.g., Rankin v. McPherson,* 483 U.S. 378, 388, 107 S. Ct. 2891, 2899, 97 L. Ed. 2d 315 (1987); *Connick, supra,* 461 U.S., at 152, 103 S. Ct., at 1692; *Pickering, supra,* 391 U.S., at 569–571, 88 S. Ct., at 1735–1736. Moreover, the government may certainly choose to give additional protections to its employees beyond what is mandated by the First Amendment, out of respect for the values underlying the First Amendment, values central to our social order as well as our legal system. *See, e.g.,* Whistleblower Protection Act of 1989, *supra.*

But the above examples do show that constitutional review of government employment decisions must rest on different principles than review of speech restraints imposed by the government as sovereign. The restrictions discussed above are allowed not just because the speech interferes with the government's operation. Speech by private people can do the same, but this does not allow the government to suppress it.

Rather, the extra power the government has in this area comes from the nature of the government's mission as employer. Government agencies are charged by law with doing particular tasks. Agencies hire employees to help do those tasks as effectively and efficiently as possible. When someone who is paid a salary so that she will contribute to an agency's effective operation begins to do or say things that detract from the agency's effective operation, the government employer must have some power to restrain her. The reason the governor may, in the example given above, fire the deputy is not that this dismissal would somehow be narrowly tailored to a compelling government interest. It is that the governor and the governor's staff have a job to do, and the governor justifiably feels that a quieter subordinate would allow them to do this job more effectively.

The key to First Amendment analysis of government employment decisions, then, is this: The government's interest in achieving its goals as effectively and efficiently as possible is elevated from a relatively subordinate interest when it acts as sovereign to a significant one when it acts as employer. The government cannot restrict the speech of the public at large just in the name of efficiency. But where the government is employing someone for the very purpose of effectively achieving its goals, such restrictions may well be appropriate.

C

1

The Court of Appeals' decision, we believe, gives insufficient weight to the government's interest in efficient employment decisionmaking. In other First Amendment contexts the need to safeguard possibly protected speech may indeed outweigh the government's efficiency interests. *See, e.g., Freedman v. Maryland,* 380 U.S. 51, 85 S. Ct. 734, 13 L. Ed. 2d 649 (1965); *Speiser v. Randall,* 357 U.S., at 526, 78 S. Ct., at 1342. But where the government is acting as employer, its efficiency concerns should, as we discussed above, be assigned a greater value.

The problem with the Court of Appeals' approach — under which the facts to which the *Connick* test is applied are determined by the judicial factfinder — is that it would force the government employer to come to its factual conclusions through procedures that substantially mirror the evidentiary rules used in court. The government manager would have to ask not what conclusions she, as an experienced professional, can draw from the circumstances, but rather what conclusions a jury would later draw. If she relies on hearsay, or on what she knows about the accused employee's character, she must be aware that this evidence might not be usable in court. If she knows one party is, in her personal experience, more credible than another, she must realize that the jury will not share that personal experience. If she thinks the alleged offense is so egregious that it is proper to discipline the accused employee even though the evidence is ambiguous, she must consider that a jury might decide the other way.

But employers, public and private, often do rely on hearsay, on past similar conduct, on their personal knowledge of people's credibility, and on other factors that the judicial process ignores. Such reliance may sometimes be the most effective way for the employer to avoid future recurrences of improper and disruptive conduct. What works best in a judicial proceeding may not be appropriate in the employment context. If one employee accuses another of misconduct, it is reasonable for a government manager to credit the allegation more if it is consistent with what the manager knows of the character of the accused. Likewise, a manager may legitimately want to discipline an employee based on complaints by patrons that the employee has been rude, even though these complaints are hearsay.

It is true that these practices involve some risk of erroneously punishing protected speech. The government may certainly choose to adopt other practices, by law or by contract. But we do not believe that the First Amendment requires it to do so. Government employers should be allowed to use personnel procedures that differ from the evidentiary rules used by courts, without fear that these differences will lead to liability.

2

On the other hand, we do not believe that the court must apply the *Connick* test only to the facts as the employer thought them to be, without considering the reasonableness of the employer's conclusions. Even in situations where courts have recognized the special expertise and special needs of certain decisionmakers, the deference to their conclusions has never been complete. Cf. *New Jersey v. T.L.O.,* 469 U.S. 325, 342–343, 105 S. Ct. 733, 743–744, 83 L. Ed. 2d 720 (1985); *United States v. Leon,* 468 U.S. 897, 914, 104 S. Ct. 3405, 3416, 82 L. Ed. 2d 677 (1984); *Universal Camera Corp. v. NLRB,* 340 U.S. 474, 490–491, 71 S. Ct. 456, 465–466, 95 L. Ed. 456 (1951). It is necessary that the decisionmaker reach its conclusion about what was said in good faith, rather than as a pretext; but it does not follow that good faith is sufficient. Justice SCALIA is right in saying that we have often held various laws to require only an inquiry into the decisionmaker's intent, see *post,* at 1895–1896, but, as discussed *supra* in Part II-A, this has not been our view of the First Amendment.

We think employer decisionmaking will not be unduly burdened by having courts look to the facts as the employer *reasonably* found them to be. It may be unreasonable, for example, for the employer to come to a conclusion based on no evidence at all. Likewise, it may be unreasonable for an employer to act based on extremely weak evidence when strong evidence is clearly available — if, for instance, an employee is accused of writing an improper letter to the editor, and instead of just reading the letter, the employer decides what it said based on unreliable hearsay.

If an employment action is based on what an employee supposedly said, and a reasonable supervisor would recognize that there is a substantial likelihood that what was actually said was protected, the manager must tread with a certain amount of care. This need not be the care with which trials, with their rules of evidence and procedure, are conducted. It should, however, be the care that a reasonable manager would use before making an employment decision — discharge, suspension, reprimand, or whatever else — of the sort involved in the particular case. Justice SCALIA correctly points out that such care is normally not constitutionally required unless the employee has a protected property interest in her job, *post,* at 1894; *see also Board of Regents of State Colleges v. Roth,* 408 U.S. 564, 576–578, 92 S. Ct. 2701, 2708–2710, 33 L. Ed. 2d 548 (1972); but we believe that the possibility of inadvertently punishing someone for exercising her First Amendment rights makes such care necessary.

Of course, there will often be situations in which reasonable employers would disagree about who is to be believed, or how much investigation needs to be done, or how much evidence is needed to come to a particular conclusion. In those situations, many different courses of action will necessarily be reasonable. Only procedures outside the range of what a reasonable manager would use may be condemned as unreasonable.

Petitioners argue that *Mt. Healthy City Bd. of Ed. v. Doyle,* 429 U.S. 274, 97 S. Ct. 568, 50 L. Ed. 2d 471 (1977), forecloses a reasonableness test, and holds instead that the First Amendment was not violated unless "'the defendant [s'] *intent* [was] to violate the plaintiff['s] constitutional rights.'" Brief for Petitioners 25; *see also post,* at 1895–1896 (SCALIA, J., dissenting). Justice SCALIA makes a similar argument based on *Pickering, Connick,* and *Perry,* which alluded to the impropriety of management "retaliation" for protected speech. *Post,* at 1895. But in all those cases the employer assertedly knew the true content of the employee's protected speech, and fired the employee in part because of it. In none of them did we have occasion to decide what should happen if the defendants hold an erroneous and unreasonable belief about what plaintiff said. These cases cannot be read as foreclosing an argument that they never dealt with. *United States v. L.A. Tucker Truck Lines, Inc.,* 344 U.S. 33, 38, 73 S. Ct. 67, 69, 97 L. Ed. 54 (1952).

3

We disagree with Justice STEVENS' contention that the test we adopt "provides less protection for a fundamental constitutional right than the law ordinarily provides for less exalted rights." *Post,* at 1898. We have never held that it is a violation of the Constitution for a government employer to discharge an employee based on substantively incorrect information. Where an employee has a property interest in her job, the only protection we have found the Constitution gives her is a right to adequate procedure. And an at-will government employee — such as Churchill apparently was, App. to Pet. for Cert. 70 — generally has no claim based on the Constitution at all.

Of course, an employee may be able to challenge the substantive accuracy of the employer's factual conclusions under state contract law, or under some state statute or common-law cause of action. In some situations, the employee may even have a federal statutory claim. *See NLRB v. Burnup & Sims, Inc.*, 379 U.S. 21, 85 S. Ct. 171, 13 L. Ed. 2d 1 (1964). Likewise, the State or Federal Governments may, if they choose, provide similar protection to people fired because of their speech. But this protection is not mandated by the Constitution.

The one pattern from which our approach does diverge is the broader protection normally given to people in their relationship with the government as sovereign. *See, e.g., New York Times Co., v. Sullivan*, 376 U.S., at 279–280, 84 S. Ct., at 725–726, cited *post*, at 1898–1899, 1900 (STEVENS, J., dissenting). But the reasons for this are those discussed *supra* in Part II-B: "[O]ur 'profound national commitment' to the freedom of speech," *post*, at 1900 (STEVENS, J., dissenting), must of necessity operate differently when the government acts as employer rather than sovereign.

III

Applying the foregoing to this case, it is clear that if petitioners really did believe Perkins-Graham's and Ballew's story, and fired Churchill because of it, they must win. Their belief, based on the investigation they conducted, would have been entirely reasonable. After getting the initial report from Ballew, who overheard the conversation, Waters and Davis approached and interviewed Perkins-Graham, and then interviewed Ballew again for confirmation. In response to Churchill's grievance, Hopper met directly with Churchill to hear her side of the story, and instructed Magin to interview Ballew one more time. Management can spend only so much of their time on any one employment decision. By the end of the termination process, Hopper, who made the final decision, had the word of two trusted employees, the endorsement of those employees' reliability by three hospital managers, and the benefit of a face-to-face meeting with the employee he fired. With that in hand, a reasonable manager could have concluded that no further time needed to be taken. As respondents themselves point out, "if the belief an employer forms supporting its adverse personnel action is 'reasonable,' an employer has no need to investigate further." Brief for Respondents 39.

And under the *Connick* test, Churchill's speech as reported by Perkins-Graham and Ballew was unprotected. Even if Churchill's criticism of cross-training reported by Perkins-Graham and Ballew was speech on a matter of public concern — something we need not decide — the potential disruptiveness of the speech as reported was enough to outweigh whatever First Amendment value it might have had. According to Ballew, Churchill's speech may have substantially dampened Perkins-Graham's interest in working in obstetrics. Discouraging people from coming to work for a department certainly qualifies as disruption. Moreover, Perkins-Graham perceived Churchill's statements about Waters to be "unkind and inappropriate," and told management that she knew they could not continue to "tolerate that kind of negativism" from Churchill. This is strong evidence that Churchill's complaining, if not dealt with, threatened to undermine management's authority in Perkins-Graham's eyes. And finally, Churchill's statement, as reported by Perkins-Graham, that it "wasn't possible" to "wipe the slate clean" between her and Waters could certainly make management doubt Churchill's future effectiveness. As a matter of law, this potential disruptiveness was enough to outweigh whatever First Amendment value the speech might have had.

This is so even if, as Churchill suggests, Davis and Waters were "[d]eliberately [i]ndifferent," Brief for Respondents 31, to the possibility that much of the rest of the conversation was solely about cross-training. So long as Davis and Waters discharged Churchill only for the part of the speech that was either not on a matter of public concern, or on a matter of public concern but disruptive, it is irrelevant whether the rest of the speech was, unbeknownst to them, both on a matter of public concern and nondisruptive. The *Connick* test is to be applied to the speech for which Churchill was fired. Cf. *Connick,* 461 U.S., at 149, 103 S. Ct., at 1691 (evaluating the disruptiveness of part of plaintiff's speech because that part was "upon a matter of public concern *and contributed to [plaintiff's] discharge*" (emphasis added)); *Mt. Healthy, supra,* 429 U.S., at 286–287, 97 S. Ct., at 575–576. An employee who makes an unprotected statement is not immunized from discipline by the fact that this statement is surrounded by protected statements.

Nonetheless, we agree with the Court of Appeals that the District Court erred in granting summary judgment in petitioners' favor. Though Davis and Waters would have been justified in firing Churchill for the statements outlined above, there remains the question whether Churchill was actually fired because of those statements, or because of something else. *See Mt. Healthy,* 429 U.S., at 286–287, 97 S. Ct., at 575–576.

Churchill has produced enough evidence to create a material issue of disputed fact about petitioners' actual motivation. Churchill had criticized the cross-training policy in the past; management had exhibited some sensitivity about the criticisms; Churchill pointed to some other conduct by hospital management that, if viewed in the light most favorable to her, would show that they were hostile to her because of her criticisms. 977 F.2d, at 1125–1126. A reasonable factfinder might therefore, on this record, conclude that petitioners actually fired Churchill not because of the disruptive things she said to Perkins-Graham, but because of nondisruptive statements about cross-training that they thought she may have made in the same conversation, or because of other statements she may have made earlier. If this is so, then the court will have to determine whether those statements were protected speech, a different matter than the one before us now.

Because of our conclusion, we need not determine whether the defendants were entitled to qualified immunity. We also need not decide whether the defendants were acting pursuant to hospital policy or custom, because that question, though argued by petitioners in their merits brief, was not presented in the petition for certiorari. *See Izumi Seimitsu Kogyo Kabushiki Kaisha v. U.S. Philips Corp.,* 510 U.S. 27, 114 S. Ct. 425, 126 L. Ed. 2d 396 (1993) (*per curiam*). Rather, we vacate the judgment of the Court of Appeals and remand the case for further proceedings consistent with this opinion.

So ordered.

[Case No. 3-5]

The U.S. Constitution's First Amendment held not to prohibit managerial discipline of public employees for making statements pursuant to employees' official duties.

Garcetti v. Ceballos

Supreme Court of the United States
547 U.S. 410 (2006)

Justice KENNEDY delivered the opinion of the Court.

It is well settled that "a State cannot condition public employment on a basis that infringes the employee's constitutionally protected interest in freedom of expression." Connick v. Myers, 461 U.S. 138, 142, 103 S. Ct. 1684, 75 L. Ed. 2d 708 (1983). The question presented by the instant case is whether the First Amendment protects a government employee from discipline based on speech made pursuant to the employee's official duties.

I

Respondent Richard Ceballos has been employed since 1989 as a deputy district attorney for the Los Angeles County District Attorney's Office. During the period relevant to this case, Ceballos was a calendar deputy in the office's Pomona branch, and in this capacity he exercised certain supervisory responsibilities over other lawyers. In February 2000, a defense attorney contacted Ceballos about a pending criminal case. The defense attorney said there were inaccuracies in an affidavit used to obtain a critical search warrant. The attorney informed Ceballos that he had filed a motion to traverse, or challenge, the warrant, but he also wanted Ceballos to review the case. According to Ceballos, it was not unusual for defense attorneys to ask calendar deputies to investigate aspects of pending cases.

After examining the affidavit and visiting the location it described, Ceballos determined the affidavit contained serious misrepresentations. The affidavit called a long driveway what Ceballos thought should have been referred to as a separate roadway. Ceballos also questioned the affidavit's statement that tire tracks led from a stripped-down truck to the premises covered by the warrant. His doubts arose from his conclusion that the roadway's composition in some places made it difficult or impossible to leave visible tire tracks.

Ceballos spoke on the telephone to the warrant affiant, a deputy sheriff from the Los Angeles County Sheriff's Department, but he did not receive a satisfactory explanation for the perceived inaccuracies. He relayed his findings to his supervisors, petitioners Carol Najera and Frank Sundstedt, and followed up by preparing a disposition memorandum. The memo explained Ceballos' concerns and recommended dismissal of the case. On March 2, 2000, Ceballos submitted the memo to Sundstedt for his review. A few days later, Ceballos presented Sundstedt with another memo, this one describing a second telephone conversation between Ceballos and the warrant affiant.

Based on Ceballos' statements, a meeting was held to discuss the affidavit. Attendees included Ceballos, Sundstedt, and Najera, as well as the warrant affiant and other employees from the sheriff's department. The meeting allegedly became heated, with one lieutenant sharply criticizing Ceballos for his handling of the case.

Despite Ceballos' concerns, Sundstedt decided to proceed with the prosecution, pending disposition of the defense motion to traverse. The trial court held a hearing on the motion. Ceballos was called by the defense and recounted his observations about the affidavit, but the trial court rejected the challenge to the warrant.

Ceballos claims that in the aftermath of these events he was subjected to a series of retaliatory employment actions. The actions included reassignment from his calendar deputy position to a trial deputy position, transfer to another courthouse, and denial of a promotion. Ceballos initiated an employment grievance, but the grievance was denied based on a finding that he had not suffered any retaliation. Unsatisfied, Ceballos sued in the United States District Court for the Central District of California, asserting, as relevant here, a claim under Rev. Stat. §1979, 42 U.S.C. §1983. He alleged petitioners violated the First and Fourteenth Amendments by retaliating against him based on his memo of March 2.

Petitioners responded that no retaliatory actions were taken against Ceballos and that all the actions of which he complained were explained by legitimate reasons such as staffing needs. They further contended that, in any event, Ceballos' memo was not protected speech under the First Amendment. Petitioners moved for summary judgment, and the District Court granted their motion. Noting that Ceballos wrote his memo pursuant to his employment duties, the court concluded he was not entitled to First Amendment protection for the memo's contents. It held in the alternative that even if Ceballos' speech was constitutionally protected, petitioners had qualified immunity because the rights Ceballos asserted were not clearly established.

The Court of Appeals for the Ninth Circuit reversed, holding that "Ceballos's allegations of wrongdoing in the memorandum constitute protected speech under the First Amendment." 361 F.3d 1168, 1173 (2004). In reaching its conclusion the court looked to the First Amendment analysis set forth in Pickering v. Board of Educ., 391 U.S. 563, 88 S. Ct. 1731, 20 L. Ed. 2d 811 (1968), and Connick, supra. Connick instructs courts to begin by considering whether the expressions in question were made by the speaker "as a citizen upon matters of public concern." See id., at 146–147, 103 S. Ct. 1684, 75 L. Ed. 2d 708. The Court of Appeals determined that Ceballos' memo, which recited what he thought to be governmental misconduct, was "inherently a matter of public concern." 361 F.3d, at 1174. The court did not, however, consider whether the speech was made in Ceballos' capacity as a citizen. Rather, it relied on Circuit precedent rejecting the idea that "a public employee's speech is deprived of First Amendment protection whenever those views are expressed, to government workers or others, pursuant to an employment responsibility." Id., at 1174–1175 (citing cases including Roth v. Veteran's Admin. of Govt. of United States, 856 F.2d 1401 (CA9 1988)). Having concluded that Ceballos' memo satisfied the public-concern requirement, the Court of Appeals proceeded to balance Ceballos' interest in his speech against his supervisors' interest in responding to it. See Pickering, supra, at 568, 88 S. Ct. 1731, 20 L. Ed. 2d 811. The court struck the balance in Ceballos' favor, noting that petitioners "failed even to suggest disruption or inefficiency in the workings of the District Attorney's Office" as a result of the memo. See 361 F.3d, at 1180. The court further concluded that Ceballos' First Amendment rights were clearly established and that petitioners' actions were not objectively reasonable. See id., at 1181–1182.

Judge O'Scannlain specially concurred. Agreeing that the panel's decision was compelled by Circuit precedent, he nevertheless concluded Circuit law should be revisited and overruled. See id., at 1185. Judge O'Scannlain emphasized the distinction "between speech offered by a public employee acting as an employee carrying out his or her ordinary job duties and that spoken by an employee acting as a citizen expressing his or her personal views on disputed matters of public import." Id., at 1187. In his view, "when public employees speak in the course of carrying out their routine, required employment obligations, they have no personal interest in the content of that speech that gives rise to a First Amendment right." Id., at 1189.

We granted certiorari, 543 U.S. 1186, 125 S. Ct. 1395, 161 L. Ed. 2d 188 (2005), and we now reverse.

II

As the Court's decisions have noted, for many years "the unchallenged dogma was that a public employee had no right to object to conditions placed upon the terms of employment — including those which restricted the exercise of constitutional rights." Connick, 461 U.S., at 143, 103 S. Ct. 1684, 75 L. Ed. 2d 708. That dogma has been qualified in important respects. See id., at 144–145, 103 S. Ct. 1684, 75 L. Ed. 2d 708. The Court has made clear that public employees do not surrender all their First Amendment rights by reason of their employment. Rather, the First Amendment protects a public employee's right, in certain circumstances, to speak as a citizen addressing matters of public concern. See, e.g., Pickering, supra, at 568, 88 S. Ct. 1731, 20 L. Ed. 2d 811; Connick, supra, at 147, 103 S. Ct. 1684, 75 L. Ed. 2d 708; Rankin v. McPherson, 483 U.S. 378, 384, 107 S. Ct. 2891, 97 L. Ed. 2d 315 (1987); United States v. National Treasury Emples. Union, 513 U.S. 454, 466, 115 S. Ct. 1003, 130 L. Ed. 2d 964 (1995).

Pickering provides a useful starting point in explaining the Court's doctrine. There the relevant speech was a teacher's letter to a local newspaper addressing issues including the funding policies of his school board. 391 U.S., at 566, 88 S. Ct. 1731, 20 L. Ed. 2d 811. "The problem in any case," the Court stated, "is to arrive at a balance between the interests of the teacher, as a citizen, in commenting upon matters of public concern and the interest of the State, as an employer, in promoting the efficiency of the public services it performs through its employees." Id., at 568, 88 S. Ct. 1731 20 L. Ed. 2d 811. The Court found the teacher's speech "neither [was] shown nor can be presumed to have in any way either impeded the teacher's proper performance of his daily duties in the classroom or to have interfered with the regular operation of the schools generally." Id., at 572–573, 88 S. Ct. 1731, 20 L. Ed. 2d 811 (footnote omitted). Thus, the Court concluded that "the interest of the school administration in limiting teachers' opportunities to contribute to public debate is not significantly greater than its interest in limiting a similar contribution by any member of the general public." Id., at 573, 88 S. Ct. 1731, 20 L. Ed. 2d 811.

Pickering and the cases decided in its wake identify two inquiries to guide interpretation of the constitutional protections accorded to public employee speech. The first requires determining whether the employee spoke as a citizen on a matter of public concern. See id., at 568, 88 S. Ct. 1731, 20 L. Ed. 2d 811. If the answer is no, the employee has no First Amendment cause of action based on his or her employer's reaction to the speech. See Connick, supra, at 147, 103 S. Ct. 1684, 75 L. Ed. 2d 708. If the answer is yes, then the possibility of a First Amendment claim arises. The question becomes whether the relevant government entity had an adequate justification for treating the employee differently from any other member of the general public. See Pickering, 391 U.S., at 568, 88 S. Ct. 1731, 20 L. Ed. 2d 811. This consideration reflects the importance of the relationship between the speaker's expressions and employment. A government entity has broader discretion to restrict speech when it acts in its role as employer, but the restrictions it imposes must be directed at speech that has some potential to affect the entity's operations.

To be sure, conducting these inquiries sometimes has proved difficult. This is the necessary product of "the enormous variety of fact situations in which critical statements by teachers and other public employees may be thought by their superiors ... to furnish grounds for dismissal." Id., at 569, 88 S. Ct. 1731, 20 L. Ed. 2d 811. The Court's overarching objectives, though, are evident.

When a citizen enters government service, the citizen by necessity must accept certain limitations on his or her freedom. See, e.g., Waters v. Churchill, 511 U.S. 661, 671, 114 S. Ct. 1878, 128 L. Ed. 2d 686 (1994) (plurality opinion) ("[T]he government as employer indeed has far broader powers than does the government as sovereign"). Government employers, like private employers, need a significant degree of control over their employees' words and actions; without it, there would be little chance for the efficient provision of public services. Cf. Connick, supra, at 143, 103 S. Ct. 1684, 75 L. Ed. 2d 708 ("[G]overnment offices could not function if every employment decision became a constitutional matter"). Public employees, moreover, often occupy trusted positions in society. When they speak out, they can express views that contravene governmental policies or impair the proper performance of governmental functions.

At the same time, the Court has recognized that a citizen who works for the government is nonetheless a citizen. The First Amendment limits the ability of a public employer to leverage the employment relationship to restrict, incidentally or intentionally, the liberties employees enjoy in their capacities as private citizens. See Perry v. Sindermann, 408 U.S. 593, 597, 92 S. Ct. 2694, 33 L. Ed. 2d 570 (1972). So long as employees are speaking as citizens about matters of public concern, they must face only those speech restrictions that are necessary for their employers to operate efficiently and effectively. See, e.g., Connick, supra, at 147, 103 S. Ct. 1684, 75 L. Ed. 2d 708 ("Our responsibility is to ensure that citizens are not deprived of fundamental rights by virtue of working for the government").

The Court's employee-speech jurisprudence protects, of course, the constitutional rights of public employees. Yet the First Amendment interests at stake extend beyond the individual speaker. The Court has acknowledged the importance of promoting the public's interest in receiving the well-informed views of government employees engaging in civic discussion. Pickering again provides an instructive example. The Court characterized its holding as rejecting the attempt of school administrators to "limi[t] teachers' opportunities to contribute to public debate." 391 U.S., at 573, 88 S. Ct. 1731, 20 L. Ed. 2d 811. It also noted that teachers are "the members of a community most likely to have informed and definite opinions" about school expenditures. Id., at 572, 88 S. Ct. 1731, 20 L. Ed. 2d 811. The Court's approach acknowledged the necessity for informed, vibrant dialogue in a democratic society. It suggested, in addition, that widespread costs may arise when dialogue is repressed. The Court's more recent cases have expressed similar concerns. See, e.g., San Diego v. Roe, 543 U.S. 77, 82, 125 S. Ct. 521, 160 L. Ed. 2d 410 (2004) (per curiam) ("Were [public employees] not able to speak on [the operation of their employers], the community would be deprived of informed opinions on important public issues. The interest at stake is as much the public's interest in receiving informed opinion as it is the employee's own right to disseminate it" (citation omitted)); cf. Treasury Emples., 513 U.S., at 470, 115 S. Ct. 1003, 130 L. Ed. 2d 964 ("The large-scale disincentive to Government employees' expression also imposes a significant burden on the public's right to read and hear what the employees would otherwise have written and said").

The Court's decisions, then, have sought both to promote the individual and societal interests that are served when employees speak as citizens on matters of public concern and to respect the needs of government employers attempting to perform their important public functions. See, e.g., Rankin, 483 U.S., at 384, 107 S. Ct. 2891, 97 L. Ed. 2d 315 (recognizing "the dual role of the public employer as a provider of public services and as a government entity operating under the constraints of the First Amendment"). Underlying our cases has been the premise that while the First Amendment invests public employees with certain rights, it does not empower them to "constitutionalize the employee grievance." Connick, 461 U.S., at 154, 103 S. Ct. 1864, 75 L. Ed. 2d 708.

III

With these principles in mind we turn to the instant case. Respondent Ceballos believed the affidavit used to obtain a search warrant contained serious misrepresentations. He conveyed his opinion and recommendation in a memo to his supervisor. That Ceballos expressed his views inside his office, rather than publicly, is not dispositive. Employees in some cases may receive First Amendment protection for expressions made at work. See, e.g., Givhan v. Western Line Consol. School Dist., 439 U.S. 410, 414, 99 S. Ct. 693, 58 L. Ed. 2d 619 (1979). Many citizens do much of their talking inside their respective workplaces, and it would not serve the goal of treating public employees like "any member of the general public," Pickering, 391 U.S., at 573, 88 S. Ct. 1731, 20 L. Ed. 2d 811, to hold that all speech within the office is automatically exposed to restriction.

The memo concerned the subject matter of Ceballos' employment, but this, too, is nondispositive. The First Amendment protects some expressions related to the speaker's job. See, e.g., ibid.; Givhan, supra, at 414, 99 S. Ct. 693, 58 L. Ed. 2d 619. As the Court noted in Pickering: "Teachers are, as a class, the members of a community most likely to have informed and definite opinions as to how funds allotted to the operation of the schools should be spent. Accordingly, it is essential that they be able to speak out freely on such questions without fear of retaliatory dismissal." 391 U.S., at 572, 88 S. Ct. 1731, 20 L. Ed. 2d 811. The same is true of many other categories of public employees.

The controlling factor in Ceballos' case is that his expressions were made pursuant to his duties as a calendar deputy. See Brief for Respondent 4 ("Ceballos does not dispute that he prepared the memorandum 'pursuant to his duties as a prosecutor'"). That consideration—the fact that Ceballos spoke as a prosecutor fulfilling a responsibility to advise his supervisor about how best to proceed with a pending case—distinguishes Ceballos' case from those in which the First Amendment provides protection against discipline. We hold that when public employees make statements pursuant to their official duties, the employees are not speaking as citizens for First Amendment purposes, and the Constitution does not insulate their communications from employer discipline.

Ceballos wrote his disposition memo because that is part of what he, as a calendar deputy, was employed to do. It is immaterial whether he experienced some personal gratification from writing the memo; his First Amendment rights do not depend on his job satisfaction. The significant point is that the memo was written pursuant to Ceballos' official duties. Restricting speech that owes its existence to a public employee's professional responsibilities does not infringe any liberties the employee might have enjoyed as a private citizen. It simply reflects the exercise of employer control over what the employer itself has commissioned or created. Cf. Rosenberger v. Rector and Visitors of Univ. of Va., 515 U.S. 819, 833, 115 S. Ct. 2510, 132 L. Ed. 2d 700 (1995) ("[W]hen the government appropriates public funds to promote a particular policy of its own it is entitled to say what it wishes"). Contrast, for example, the expressions made by the speaker in Pickering, whose letter to the newspaper had no official significance and bore similarities to letters submitted by numerous citizens every day.

Ceballos did not act as a citizen when he went about conducting his daily professional activities, such as supervising attorneys, investigating charges, and preparing filings. In the same way he did not speak as a citizen by writing a memo that addressed the proper disposition of a pending criminal case. When he went to work and performed the tasks he was paid to perform, Ceballos acted as a government employee. The fact that his duties sometimes required him to speak or write does not mean his supervisors were prohibited from evaluating his performance.

This result is consistent with our precedents' attention to the potential societal value of employee speech. See supra, at ___–___, 164 L. Ed. 2d, at 699–700, 126 S. Ct. 1951. Refusing to recognize First Amendment claims based on government employees' work product does not prevent them from participating in public debate. The employees retain the prospect of constitutional protection for their contributions to the civic discourse. This prospect of protection, however, does not invest them with a right to perform their jobs however they see fit.

Our holding likewise is supported by the emphasis of our precedents on affording government employers sufficient discretion to manage their operations. Employers have heightened interests in controlling speech made by an employee in his or her professional capacity. Official communications have official consequences, creating a need for substantive consistency and clarity. Supervisors must ensure that their employees' official communications are accurate, demonstrate sound judgment, and promote the employer's mission. Ceballos' memo is illustrative. It demanded the attention of his supervisors and led to a heated meeting with employees from the sheriff's department. If Ceballos' superiors thought his memo was inflammatory or misguided, they had the authority to take proper corrective action.

Ceballos' proposed contrary rule, adopted by the Court of Appeals, would commit state and federal courts to a new, permanent, and intrusive role, mandating judicial oversight of communications between and among government employees and their superiors in the course of official business. This displacement of managerial discretion by judicial supervision finds no support in our precedents. When an employee speaks as a citizen addressing a matter of public concern, the First Amendment requires a delicate balancing of the competing interests surrounding the speech and its consequences. When, however, the employee is simply performing his or her job duties, there is no warrant for a similar degree of scrutiny. To hold otherwise would be to demand permanent judicial intervention in the conduct of governmental operations to a degree inconsistent with sound principles of federalism and the separation of powers.

The Court of Appeals based its holding in part on what it perceived as a doctrinal anomaly. The court suggested it would be inconsistent to compel public employers to tolerate certain employee speech made publicly but not speech made pursuant to an employee's assigned duties. See 361 F.3d, at 1176. This objection misconceives the theoretical underpinnings of our decisions. Employees who make public statements outside the course of performing their official duties retain some possibility of First Amendment protection because that is the kind of activity engaged in by citizens who do not work for the government. The same goes for writing a letter to a local newspaper, see Pickering, supra, or discussing politics with a co-worker, see Rankin, 483 U.S. 378, 107 S. Ct. 2891, 97 L. Ed. 2d 315. When a public employee speaks pursuant to employment responsibilities, however, there is no relevant analogue to speech by citizens who are not government employees.

The Court of Appeals' concern also is unfounded as a practical matter. The perceived anomaly, it should be noted, is limited in scope: It relates only to the expressions an employee makes pursuant to his or her official responsibilities, not to statements or complaints (such as those at issue in cases like Pickering and Connick) that are made outside the duties of employment. If, moreover, a government employer is troubled by the perceived anomaly, it has the means at hand to avoid it. A public employer that wishes to encourage its employees to voice concerns privately retains the option of instituting internal policies and procedures that are receptive to employee criticism. Giving employees an internal forum for their speech will discourage them from concluding that the safest avenue of expression is to state their views in public.

Proper application of our precedents thus leads to the conclusion that the First Amendment does not prohibit managerial discipline based on an employee's expressions made pursuant to official responsibilities. Because Ceballos' memo falls into this category, his allegation of unconstitutional retaliation must fail.

Two final points warrant mentioning. First, as indicated above, the parties in this case do not dispute that Ceballos wrote his disposition memo pursuant to his employment duties. We thus have no occasion to articulate a comprehensive framework for defining the scope of an employee's duties in cases where there is room for serious debate. We reject, however, the suggestion that employers can restrict employees' rights by creating excessively broad job descriptions. See post, at ___, n 2, 164 L. Ed. 2d, at 707 (Souter, J., dissenting). The proper inquiry is a practical one. Formal job descriptions often bear little resemblance to the duties an employee actually is expected to perform, and the listing of a given task in an employee's written job description is neither necessary nor sufficient to demonstrate that conducting the task is within the scope of the employee's professional duties for First Amendment purposes.

Second, Justice Souter suggests today's decision may have important ramifications for academic freedom, at least as a constitutional value. See post, at ______, 164 L. Ed. 2d, at 712. There is some argument that expression related to academic scholarship or classroom instruction implicates additional constitutional interests that are not fully accounted for by this Court's customary employee-speech jurisprudence. We need not, and for that reason do not, decide whether the analysis we conduct today would apply in the same manner to a case involving speech related to scholarship or teaching.

IV

Exposing governmental inefficiency and misconduct is a matter of considerable significance. As the Court noted in Connick, public employers should, "as a matter of good judgment," be "receptive to constructive criticism offered by their employees." 461 U.S., at 149, 103 S. Ct. 1684, 75 L. Ed. 2d 708. The dictates of sound judgment are reinforced by the powerful network of legislative enactments — such as whistle--blower protection laws and labor codes — available to those who seek to expose wrongdoing. See, e.g., 5 U.S.C. § 2302(b)(8); Cal. Govt. Code Ann. § 8547.8 (West 2005); Cal. Lab. Code Ann. § 1102.5 (West Supp. 2006). Cases involving government attorneys implicate additional safeguards in the form of, for example, rules of conduct and constitutional obligations apart from the First Amendment. See, e.g., Cal. Rule Prof. Conduct 5-110 (2005) ("A member in government service shall not institute or cause to be instituted criminal charges when the member knows or should know that the charges are not supported by probable cause"); Brady v. Maryland, 373 U.S. 83, 83 S. Ct. 1194, 10 L. Ed. 2d 215 (1963). These imperatives, as well as obligations arising from any other applicable constitutional provisions and mandates of the criminal and civil laws, protect employees and provide checks on supervisors who would order unlawful or otherwise inappropriate actions.

We reject, however, the notion that the First Amendment shields from discipline the expressions employees make pursuant to their professional duties. Our precedents do not support the existence of a constitutional cause of action behind every statement a public employee makes in the course of doing his or her job.

The judgment of the Court of Appeals is reversed, and the case is remanded for proceedings consistent with this opinion. *It is so ordered.*

Chapter 4

Students' Rights and Discipline

The law applicable to students' rights has changed dramatically over the years. The pendulum had swung from the right to the left and, in the 1990s, was on its way back to the right. Before the 1969 United States Supreme Court decision in *Tinker v. Des Moines Independent Community School District*,[1] students were not thought to have legal rights which might limit the authority of the school. Teachers stood *in loco parentis* (in place of parents). A teacher could do anything a parent could do. When *Tinker* was decided, the Supreme Court recognized the rights of students in the educational setting under the U.S. Constitution.

In the 1970s, student civil rights were at their height. Many court decisions during those years were decided in favor of students. Students' rights were expanded to areas of speech, dress, assembly, and due process. Schools were required to provide both procedural and substantive protections when dealing with issues of student rights.

By the 1980s, however, these rights began to be circumscribed. In the landmark U.S. Supreme Court decision *New Jersey v. T.L.O.*,[2] the State of New Jersey used *in loco parentis* as a defense, in part, in attempting to show that students did not have any right to privacy in school. Although the Court ruled that students do have privacy rights, it gave schools more authority to control those rights. *T.L.O.* marked the re-entry into a period of greater control in the hands of school authorities to deal with the perceived increase in danger in the school environment.

Legal Basis for Disciplining Students

In this section, we will discuss two U.S. Supreme Court decisions regarding school disciplinary procedures. The first, decided in 1975, is *Goss v. Lopez*,[3] which addressed short-term (less than 10 days) suspensions, ruling that students must have due process (notice and a right to be heard) before being suspended. [*See* **Case No. 4-1.**] As to longer-term suspensions and expulsions, the Court noted that, with this greater loss of property, students should be given procedural safeguards in addition to those required by *Goss*. In response, states as well as school districts

1. 393 U.S. 503 (1969).
2. 469 U.S. 325 (1985).
3. 419 U.S. 565 (1975).

have carefully outlined such procedures. Most school administrators are familiar with their district policies and state laws in this regard, but it is always important to review these procedures periodically as they may change and vary from state to state; procedural violations are common grounds for a lawsuit. The second decision, *J.D.B. v. North Carolina*,[4] focused on whether and when school officials must read students their *Miranda*[5] rights. [**See Case No. 4-2.**] Before we discuss these legal decisions, let us consider the scope of school leaders' authority in matters of student discipline.

Scope of School Leaders' Authority

Both state statutes and case law have supported the notion that not only do school officials have the authority to discipline students but the *duty* to discipline. While the doctrine of *in loco parentis* is no longer viable as an absolute standard, there have been examples where either a state legislature or a court has used the doctrine to support increased school authority. In Oklahoma, a state statute entitled "Control and Discipline of Child" essentially empowers teachers with the same rights as parents:

> ... The teacher of a child attending a public school shall have the same right as a parent or guardian to control and discipline such child according to local policies during the time the child is in attendance or in transit to or from the school or any other school function authorized by the school district or classroom presided over by the teacher.[6]

At least three other states have statutes similar to Oklahoma's regarding teachers' *in loco parentis* authority in maintaining discipline.[7] As to specific disciplinary methods, school personnel have wide discretion; punishments might range from corporal punishment to withholding of privileges. However, the trend in the use of corporal punishment has been to ban or severely limit its use. Over half of the states do not allow corporal punishment by state statute. Withholding privileges seems only limited by school authorities ensuring that personnel are withholding privileges and not infringing on a right or a property interest.

All students have some constitutional rights. Before any of those rights can be withheld, several special conditions have to exist. These conditions will be explored later in this chapter. As to property interests, all students have a property interest in attending school. All state constitutions contain a "right to free public education" section which establishes the students' property interest. Due process must be provided before the school can withhold these privileges (by suspending the student).

---

4. 564 U.S. 261 (2011).
5. Miranda v. Arizona, 384 U.S. 436 (1966).
6. 70 O.S. 2002, § 24-100.4.
7. Alabama (Ala. Stat. § 16-28-12); Georgia (Ga. Stat. §§ 20-2-215, 738) and Illinois (Ill. St. Ch. 105 § 5/24-24).

Grade Reductions as Punishment

When courts have addressed the issue of grade reductions, most often it has been in connection with suspension from school. In other words, the suspended student's grades were either reduced as a result of missing something like an examination or as the result of an additional penalty imposed on top of the suspension. Some courts have held for suspended students when automatic grade reductions were imposed. It is reasonable to conclude that if the misconduct in question does not rise to the level of an offense meriting suspension, it is doubtful whether grade reductions for lesser offenses would be upheld (e.g., classroom misbehaviors such as lack of attention, tardiness, or homework problems). The basic theory advanced by the courts is that grade reductions for misbehavior are improper because they result in misrepresentation of a student's academic achievement. Early on, a Pennsylvania court stated, "Misrepresentation of achievement is equally improper and, we think, illegal whether the achievement is misrepresented by upgrading or by downgrading, if either is done for reasons that are irrelevant to the achievement being graded."[8]

A federal district court in Indiana agreed with the Pennsylvania court sometime later. In *Smith et al. v. School City of Hobart*,[9] students had been caught drinking beer during school hours and were given an out-of-school suspension for five days.

> Smith argued that the school violated her substantive due process rights when it reduced her grades by twenty percent (20%) for the nine-week grading period. Her position was that the use of academic sanctions for nonacademic misconduct constituted arbitrary and capricious action, as the penalty was not rationally related to the misconduct and not rationally related to the disciplinary purpose. Moreover, Smith averred that the school's imposition of both a suspension and grade reduction amounted to excessive double punishment. Although it was not patently clear, it appeared that Smith's grades were reduced by four percent (4%) for each class missed during the time of her suspension, a total of five days, because she was punished with out-of-school suspension as opposed to in-school suspension.

The Indiana federal court agreed with the plaintiff, ruling that the school's policy was both unreasonable and arbitrary on its face. Both parties stipulated that the disciplinary action was for the student's behavior (drinking alcohol) and not for lack of academic effort even though the school asserted, without any evidence related to the facts in this case, that alcohol adversely affects academics. Finally, the court found no relationship between the 4% grade reduction and the amount of effort exerted by students who remained in class and concluded that academic sanctions must be related directly to academic performance.

However, a student's class grade can be affected by the mere fact that the student is absent due to an out-of-school suspension. The school is not under any constitutional

8. Katzman v. Cumberland Valley Sch. Dist., 479 A.2d 671, 675 (1984).
9. 811 F. Supp. 391 (N.D. Ind. 1993).

obligation to "preserve" a student's grade in such a situation. In *John S. v. Ozark R-VI School District*,[10] a student received a ten-day out-of-school suspension in addition to a 50 percent reduction in her grade for any work submitted during the time of the suspension. The court stated that "the suspension and grade reduction were two separate punishments" and ruled that the 50 percent grade reduction was unlawful.

Expulsion and Suspension[11]

The terms *expulsion* and *suspension* are really adjectives rather than nouns. In a practical sense, they refer generally to the length of time the student is removed from school. The term *expulsion* was originally used for the school's decision to permanently remove a student from attendance. Currently, most state statutes limit the length of removal from school. Usually, school authorities are limited to removal from the current semester and one semester beyond. These "maximum" removals are more accurately called "long-term suspensions." However, a long-term suspension for due-process purposes is any suspension over ten days. Thus, the term expulsion is more nostalgic than accurate but is sometimes used as a synonym for a long-term suspension. A "short-term" suspension is a removal for ten days or less. Regardless of the length of the removal, severing the student's education is the ultimate punishment in the law. The Supreme Court considered school suspensions severe enough to apply the Fourteenth Amendment to issues surrounding their use.

The Fourteenth Amendment

The constitutional basis for due process for students can be traced to the Fourteenth Amendment. It states in part that ". . . shall any State deprive any person of life, liberty, or property, without due process of law. . . ." Because the public schools are considered "the State," life, liberty, or property cannot be deprived without providing due process. *Goss v. Lopez*[12] established that a student's education is a *property* interest. The *Goss* Court also held that when a student is suspended, a student's liberty interest is implicated. The recording of the suspension in the student's file could have serious ramifications for future education. Any activity of the state (school) that results in the possible damage to a citizen's (student's) good name, honor, or reputation implicates a liberty interest. The presence of a liberty interest requires that due process be provided.

The Due Process Clause, while eloquent in context, is conceptually abstruse. Defining due process of law can be extremely difficult, and it is not a new problem. The Supreme Court commented several decades ago:

---

10. No. 11-3031-CV-S-RED, 2012 WL 176226 (W.D. Mo. Jan. 18, 2012).

11. For a thorough treatment on the topic of student suspensions, see LAWRENCE F. ROSSOW & KATHRINE J. GUTIERREZ, THE LAW OF STUDENT EXPULSIONS AND SUSPENSIONS, (3d ed. 2012).

12. 419 U.S. 565 (1975).

> Due process is an elusive concept. Its exact boundaries are indefinable, and its content varies according to specific factual contexts . . . whether the Constitution requires that a particular right obtained in a specific proceeding depends upon a complexity of factors.[13]

Short-Term Suspensions

Defining Minimum Due Process — *Goss v. Lopez*

The Goss decision (see case No. 4.1) contributed to the general notion of "when" and "how much" due process must be given students should be noted. Prior to the 1975 *Goss* decision, the courts did not recognize the need to provide due process of any kind for students being suspended for short periods of time. However, the definition of "short-term" and "long-term" was not universal. A specified number of days of suspension in one state (15 days, for example) might have been viewed as a short-term suspension. The same number of days in another state could be viewed as a long-term suspension. In addition to the lack of quantitative indices for short-term/long-term suspensions, what constituted due process for even long-term suspensions was not always clear. Perhaps it was fortunate for the Court that the *Goss* case involved the suspension of students without due process for ten days. The amount of time for which the students were suspended plus the absence of any due process gave the Court the opportunity to provide quantitative guidelines to answer the questions *when* and *how much* due process.

For students involved in a suspension of ten days or less, the Court said, "At the very minimum . . . students facing suspension and the consequent interference with a protected property interest must be given some kind of notice and afforded some kind of hearing," and that "[l]onger suspensions or expulsions for the remainder of the school term, or permanently, may require more formal procedures."[14]

The holding sent a message to all states that suspensions of 10 days or less are of the short-term variety and require a minimum due-process procedure of notice and informal hearing. Suspensions of more than ten days require more than notice and informal hearing. While the *Goss* decision focused on short-term suspensions, it helped shape the guidelines for all suspensions. As a result, school authorities can distinguish between short-term and long-term suspensions, and, more precisely, how much due process may be due a student facing sanction. Establishing that due process for suspensions is not a question of "if" but rather "how much," the Court outlined the minimum requirements for due process for a suspension of 10 days or less. Before being suspended, the student must be afforded (1) oral or written notice

13. Lawrence F. Rossow, *Administrative Discretion and Student Suspension: A Lion in Waiting*, 13 J.L. & Educ. 418, 419 (1984).

14. 419 U.S. at 579.

of the charges, (2) an explanation of the evidence if the student denies the charges, and (3) some kind of hearing where the student has an opportunity to present his/her side of the story.

The Court also provided for an "emergency" exception to the notice and hearing requirement. It felt that there might be an occasion when "[s]tudents whose presence poses a continuing danger to persons or property or an ongoing threat of disrupting the academic process may be immediately removed from the school." In these cases, the notice and hearing requirements could be fulfilled as soon as practicable once the emergency has been handled. Because the Court left in place the Ohio statute which guided the facts in this case, it is generally recognized that "as soon as practicable" means within three school days.[15] It must be noted that the Court specifically excluded procedures such as representation by counsel, presentation of witnesses, and confrontation and cross-examination of witnesses as necessary for the short-term suspension. While the *Goss* decision helped clarify the minimums for short suspensions, many questions were nonetheless left unanswered. For example, the Court said that students should be given *some kind* of notice and hearing. When can a school administrator know whether what was given meets this "some kind" standard? How informal can the informal hearing be? Do school officials need to provide procedural due process for students being removed from bus service or extracurricular activities? What process is due a student who is given an in-school suspension? Answers to these and related questions can only be gained by a careful examination of the case law since 1975. The following sections will address these questions.

Notice for Short-Term Suspensions

Without having met the requirement of notice, no due process can exist. The notice requirement has two aspects. Some clearly understood school rule must fore-warn the student that certain misbehavior might result in expulsion. The need to establish clear rules of conduct will be discussed in greater detail in the section on substantive due process.

The Court in *Goss* required that school officials provide some kind of notice and hearing before suspending a student. Unlike long-term suspensions and expulsions, there is typically no time lapse between the short-term suspension notice and the commencing of the hearing. In practice, the student is called or brought to the office where the school disciplinarian informs the student that he is about to be suspended. The hearing generally begins after this announcement. There is no requirement that parents be notified according to the Court; nevertheless, some state statutes require that parents be notified. In Illinois, for example, school officials must provide a written notice to parents by "registered or certified mail." An Illinois Association of School Boards' publication recommends that a copy of the intent-to-expel notice

15. Ohio Rev. Code § 3313.66(C)(2013).

also be sent by regular mail as a precaution against registered or certified mail being refused or otherwise not received. A question may arise concerning notice when parents are divorced: Which parent should be contacted? Generally, the custodial parent with whom the school has established a relationship should receive the notice. In cases where both parents seem to participate in the child's education, i.e., both attend conferences, volunteer for chaperoning, etc., it might be wise for school officials to contact both parents. Certainly, the school must contact both parents when joint custody exists.

In the final analysis, it appears as though the form of the notice for a short-term suspension is an oral communication which tells the student it is alleged that he/she has committed an offense which could result in a suspension. One thing is clear—unless there is a need for an emergency suspension, the suspension officer cannot simply announce that the student is suspended (even if he or she is caught "red handed"). The notice must precede the decision to suspend.

Invalid and valid scenarios might be described as follows: An invalid notice would be something like—principal witnesses a student hitting another student in the back of the head. The principal approaches the student and says, "You're suspended for fighting." This scenario lacks proper notice. A valid scenario would be something like—The principal witnesses a student hitting another student in the back of the head. The principal approaches the student and says, "You could be suspended for what you just did. Let's go over here discuss this incident." The valid notice scenario contains the element of having put the student "on notice" that he/she is about to enter into a suspension situation. Therefore, a defense can begin to be formulated in the student's mind. The principal would then proceed to the next two steps in the due process.

In *Posthumus*,[16] a Michigan student argued that his removal and deprivation were more than *de minimis* because he was barred from a once-in-a-lifetime opportunity to participate in his high school graduation ceremony as well as other extracurricular activities for the duration of the suspension. He contended that his case is an "unusual situation" as noted in *Goss:* "Nor do we put aside the possibility that in unusual situations, although involving only a short suspension, something more than the rudimentary procedures will be required."[17] Posthumus failed to cite any authority supporting his argument that exclusion from graduation or other senior events constitutes the type of "unusual situation" contemplated in *Goss* that deserves additional procedural safeguards. In the absence of such authority, the *Posthumus* court declined to hold that more formal procedures are required when a suspension includes collateral sanctions.

16. Posthumus v. Bd. of Educ. of Mona Shores Pub. Schs., 380 F. Supp. 2d 891 (W.D. Mich. 2005).
17. *Id.* at 898 (citing Goss v. Lopez, 419 U.S. 565 at 584 (1975)).

Hearing Procedures for Short-Term Suspensions

The key to the hearing procedures for suspensions of ten days or less is that they be "informal." The procedure may take place in the hall, on the school playground, in the gym, or in any number of locations. There is no requirement that a formal courtroom-like atmosphere be created for the conduct of a short-term suspension hearing. Once more, attorneys are not typically present. Their presence would indicate a formality that is inconsistent with the intent of the short-term suspension. Students do not have a right to have an attorney present for the informal hearing. All other procedural rights that are commonly recognized, such as witnesses, presentation of evidence, and record keeping, are reserved for the long-term suspension. The only procedural requirements specified by the *Goss* court were (1) oral or written notice, (2) an explanation of the evidence if the student denies the charge, and (3) an opportunity for student to tell his side of the story. Finally, there are situations where students must be notified of their *Miranda* rights. These are discussed below.

Appealing a Short-Term Suspension

Whether a suspension decision can be appealed is largely a matter of state law. There is no federal right to an appeal of a suspension decision. While it is up to state law to provide any right of appeal for a suspension decision, most states provide these procedural guarantees. A typical route for the appeal is through the office of the superintendent. Either the superintendent or a hearing officer appointed by the superintendent will hear the appeal. In some cases, the board of education assumes the responsibility for reviewing appeals from a suspension decision. Even in these cases, however, a hearing officer (usually the superintendent or someone from the superintendent's staff) will represent the board at the appeals hearing. The evidence presented at the hearing is then summarized in the form of a report to the full board. After reviewing the report, the board decides to either uphold or reverse the initial suspension.

Miranda Rights

Miranda rights must be read to persons taken into custody. "Prior to questioning, a suspect 'must be warned that he has a right to remain silent, that any statement he does make may be used as evidence against him, and that he has a right to the presence of an attorney, either retained or appointed.'"[18] Until relatively recently, these warnings seemed reserved for police interrogations. However, in 2011, the U.S.

18. J.D.B. v. North Carolina, 564 U.S. 261 (2011) (citing Miranda v. Arizona, 384 U.S. 436, 444 (1966)); *see also* Florida v. Powell, 559 U.S. 50 (2010).

Supreme Court, in *J.D.B. v. North Carolina*,[19] ruled that students held in custody at their school on a criminal investigation must be read their *Miranda* rights. [***See* Case No. 4.2.**] This requirement applies only when the investigation is criminal (rather than solely a school disciplinary issue) and when the child is in custody (i.e., believes that he does not have the right to leave).

This case involved J.D.B., a 13-year-old seventh-grade student at Smith Middle School in Chapel Hill, North Carolina, who was removed from his classroom by a uniformed police officer. The officer accompanied him to a closed-door conference room where he was questioned by police for at least half an hour. J.D.B. had been seen in the neighborhood where several items were stolen, including a digital camera, and had been questioned at home five days earlier with his grandmother/guardian. J.D.B. denied involvement; however, police later learned that a digital camera matching the description of one of the stolen items had been found at J.D.B.'s school and seen in J.D.B.'s possession. On the day of the questioning, the uniformed SRO removed J.D.B. from his social studies class and escorted him to a school conference room where he was met by Investigator DiCostanzo (the police officer assigned to this and other juvenile cases), the assistant principal, and an administrative intern. "The door to the conference room was closed. With the two police officers and the two administrators present, J.D.B. was questioned for the next 30 to 45 minutes. Prior to the commencement of questioning, J.D.B. was given neither *Miranda* warnings nor the opportunity to speak to his grandmother. Nor was he informed that he was free to leave the room."[20]

After J.D.B. was told that he might be held at a juvenile detention center before going to court, he confessed that he and a friend had stolen the missing items. He was then allowed to leave. J.D.B. was charged with one count of larceny and one count of breaking and entering. He sued, claiming that his due process rights were violated because he had not been given *Miranda* warnings before he confessed. A trial court ruled against J.D.B., stating that he was not in custody at the time of the interrogation and that the confession was voluntary. A divided panel of the state appeals court agreed with this decision.[21] Declining to take the child's age into consideration, North Carolina's Supreme Court held that J.D.B. was not in custody when he confessed. The U.S. Supreme Court reversed these lower court decisions, maintaining that the student was in custody (i.e., he did not feel he could leave), his rights were violated, and he should have been given the *Miranda* warnings prior to questioning. The Court recognized that age is a factor in reading students their rights and applied a reasonable person standard to this analysis. In other words, would a reasonable child in this situation understand his or her rights?

While seeming to ensure that students have greater due process rights, the *J.D.B.* decision has raised as many issues as it has clarified. There have been hundreds of

19. 564 U.S. 261.
20. *Id.* at 266.
21. In re J.D.B., 674 S.E.2d 795 (N.C. Ct. App. 2009).

lower court decisions either following *J.D.B.* or, in many instances, differentiating the fact patterns to say that the student was not held in custody. Furthermore, scholars and legal commentators have questioned the validity of this process, some citing research studies supporting the fact that adolescent brains are not fully developed and concluding that students may not be able to make these decisions;[22] others contending that the age of the student,[23] race,[24] and cultural[25] backgrounds could affect the reasonableness standard and how students understand or do not understand these warnings.

Our advice to educators is to make sure that you are aware of your school's policies and the laws in your state and jurisdiction on *Miranda* warnings for students as well as decisions from courts in your state and federal circuit. These should be accessible through your state's professional association and/or from your school attorney. Also, remember that *J.D.B.* only applies to criminal sanctions, so if the penalty is only a suspension or expulsion with no criminal proceedings, then you are not expected to give *Miranda* warnings unless your school policy, state statutes, or jurisdiction (federal courts) require it.

Long-Term Suspensions

Because long-term suspensions represent a higher level of deprivation for the student, additional procedural safeguards should be offered. There is no U.S. Supreme Court decision outlining what these should be; however, case law in the school district's jurisdiction as well as state statutes provide requirements specific to your own jurisdiction. Having said this, there are common elements to the long-term suspension process that hold true in most school districts. For example, most state statutes require that the notice to suspend for a long-term suspension (in excess of ten days) be in writing and sent by registered or certified mail. It is also recommended that the notice be sent by *regular* mail as a precaution against registered or certified mail being refused or otherwise not received. The notice itself should contain the following information: (1) the intent to expel the student; (2) the specific charges against the student; (3) what rule was broken; (4) the nature of the evidence supporting the charges; (5) the date, time, and place where a hearing will commence; (6) a copy of the procedures that will be followed at the hearing; and (7) a reminder of applicable rights for the student and parents, which may include right to counsel, and a copy of

22. *See, e.g.*, Emily L. Fitch & Brenda M. (Duke) Mathis, *What Did You Say?! The Changing Landscape of Juvenile Custodial Interrogations*, 107 Ill. B.J. 32 (2019).

23. *See, e.g.*, Wadad Barakat, *A Blind Spot in* Miranda *Rights: Juveniles' Lack of Understanding Regarding* Miranda *Language*, 31 St. Thomas L. Rev. 174 (2019).

24. *See* Kristin Henning, *The Reasonable Black Child: Race, Adolescence, and the Fourth Amendment*, 67 Am. U. L. Rev. 1513 (2018).

25. *See* Christy E. Lopez, *The Reasonable Latinx: A Response to Professor Henning's The Reasonable Black Child: Race, Adolescence, and the Fourth Amendment*, 68 Am. U. L. Rev. 55 (2019).

the hearing transcript, as well as presentation of witnesses and cross-examination of hostile witnesses.

Unlike short-term suspensions, a long-term suspension notice should be sent to the parents. However, sending a written notice to the student can be important when the student has reached the age of 18. The hearing that follows must be formal. The formality of the process is defined by most state statutes, but typically includes the presence of attorneys, presentation of evidence, presentation of witnesses, and a recording of the hearing. The formal hearing must be conducted by an *impartial trier of fact*. An impartial trier of fact is someone who was not involved in gathering facts or witnessing events that led to the student being brought to the hearing. For example, a principal who was personally responsible for apprehending and questioning a student who came to school with drugs would not be a good impartial trier of fact. Parents may waive their hearing rights; it is recommended, however, that the school district receive a written waiver from the parents. Unless the school knows "in writing" that the parents do not want a hearing, a hearing should be scheduled anyway.

Specialty Suspensions

Emergency Suspension

The *Goss* decision provided an exception to the notice and hearing requirements normally necessary before a student is suspended. The exception arises in the form of an emergency, when the student's presence would pose a continuing danger to person or property or disrupt the academic process. In these circumstances the student can be removed immediately, without a hearing. Even in these emergency cases, the student must be given a hearing sometime later — presumably when the danger has passed. The emergency suspension was most often applied in the 1970s when student demonstrations were viewed as disruptive to the educational environment. More recently, the emergency suspension is used to remove students who carry dangerous weapons to school.

School Bus Suspension

The leading case for the suspension of students from riding the school bus was decided in 1982 by the First Circuit Court of Appeals. In *Rose v. Nashua Board of Education*,[26] groups of New Hampshire students had committed acts of vandalism while riding the bus to and from school. Misbehaviors included slashing seats and throwing things inside the buses and at passing cars. Because the bus drivers had to watch the road, they were not able to identify specifically which students were responsible.

26. 679 F.2d 279 (1st Cir. 1982).

After several hearings to consider the problem, the board of education adopted a suspension policy for any continued acts of vandalism. No specific procedural safeguards were identified as necessary prior to the suspension decision. As the vandalism continued, several bus routes were suspended from operation for five days. This amounted to a short-term suspension. Parents of the affected bus routes brought suit in federal court, claiming that their children were not the ones causing the trouble. They further claimed that the board policy allowing for this form of mass punishment was a violation of the Fourteenth Amendment. The parents asserted that they had a constitutional right to bus transportation because New Hampshire law provides it. This right cannot be taken away without providing the same procedural due process as would be provided if a student were to be removed from school.

The court rejected the parents' arguments. In looking to *Goss* for guidance on short-term suspensions, the court saw no property or liberty interest at stake in being denied bus transportation. The procedural minimums required by *Goss* were meant for deprivation of educational opportunity. The issue at hand did not go beyond the inconvenience for parents in having to make alternative arrangements for transportation for a period of five days. The court went on to say:

> The fact that New Hampshire law guarantees free bus transportation does not seem sufficient to create a constitutionally protected interest in the *suspension-free* service that appellants seek.... [A]s previously pointed out, the deprivation itself caused only inconvenience, not loss of educational opportunity or other significant injury, we believe it is a "*de minimis*" deprivation that does not call for constitutional 'Due Process' protection.[27]

While the *Rose* case is very dated, it has yet to be overruled. Therefore, it remains the single authority on bus suspensions.[28] It should be noted that some states provide that students will be given a hearing prior to being suspended from riding the bus; however, this tends to be the exception.[29] Nonetheless, as mentioned earlier, state law or even local board policy can always extend more procedural due process for its students than would be required by federal law.

In-School Suspension

For some students, being suspended amounts to an officially sanctioned school holiday. In many families where both parents work, the supervision of those children suspended out of school can be a problem. In response, schools have turned to "in-school" suspension as an alternative to the student being physically removed from the premises. This form of suspension has given rise to the question of procedural due process. How much process, if any, is due a student who is suspended to a

27. *Id.* at 282.

28. *See also* Zehner v. Cent. Berkshire Reg'l Sch. Dist., 921 F. Supp. 850 (D. Mass.1995).

29. *See, e.g.*, ILL. REV. STAT. CH. 122, §10-22.6 (c).

special room in school? The prevailing law would suggest that as long as students have "some schoolwork" during the in-school suspension, no procedural due process is required. This would be especially true if the student is afforded the opportunity to pursue regular coursework and received instructional assistance. Perhaps one of the best descriptions of this line of thinking on in-school suspensions comes from a Fifth Circuit case.

In *Cole v. Newton Special Municipal Separate School District*,[30] Mississippi parents sued the school district when their daughter was given a six-day in-school suspension. Because notice and a hearing were not provided, the parents claimed lack of procedural due process. The school did not refute that it provided no hearing or notice. Instead, it argued that due process requirements for suspension did not apply because the student was physically present on school grounds. The court ruled for the student. The decision turned on the fact that she was not given any schoolwork during her six days of isolation from the rest of the school. The court said:

> [T]he physical presence of a student at school is not conclusive as to whether school officials are excused from according a hearing in connection with imposing in-school isolation characterized by exclusion from the classroom. . . . Under certain circumstances, in-school isolation could well constitute as much of a deprivation of education as an at-home suspension. In other words, a student could be excluded from the educational process as much by being placed in isolation as by being barred from the school grounds. The primary thrust of the educational process is classroom instruction; in both situations the student is excluded from the classroom. This is not to say that any in-detention would necessarily be equivalent to a suspension; *it would depend on the extent to which the student was deprived of instruction or the opportunity to learn.*[31]

Using the same line of thinking but ruling in opposite, the Sixth Circuit in *Laney v. Farley*[32] said that a Tennessee middle school student was not deprived of due process. Even though the student was not given a hearing for a one-day in-school suspension, the court ruled that because the student was given academic work to complete during the suspension, the educational process continued. Therefore, no property interest was implicated and consequently no hearing was required. This finding is in concert with other lower court rulings[33] where the in-school suspension was limited in time and where the student was given homework. School officials

30. 676 F. Supp. 749 (S.D. Miss. 1987).

31. *Id.* at 751–52 (emphasis added).

32. 501 F.3d 577 (6th Cir. 2007).

33. *See, e.g.*, Wise v. Pea Ridge Sch. Dist., 855 F.2d 560 (8th Cir. 1988) (reads *Goss* as not requiring procedural due process for temporary in-school suspensions); Couture v. Bd. of Educ. of Albuquerque, 535 F.3d 1243 (10th Cir. 2008) (rules that no procedural due process is required for a student with 21 timeouts over two and a half months); and Burge ex rel. Burge v. Colton Sch. Dist. 53, 100 F. Supp 3d 1057 (D. Or. 2015) (maintains that student loses no property interest for a 3½ day in-school suspension with schoolwork and adult supervision).

should, however, look to their school policies and their state's laws on school discipline as both entities could provide students with additional rights.

Some teachers, especially at the elementary school level, use "time out" areas within their classrooms. The area is typically in one corner of the room and may have several walls, usually of cardboard, surrounding the area. The purpose of the "time-out box" is to temporarily deprive the student of doing work with the others, presumably to give the student time to think about the misbehavior that precipitated the punishment.

The use of just such a time-out box was litigated in a Tennessee federal court. The case, *Dickens v. Johnson City. Board of Education*,[34] was brought by parents who objected to their son being placed in a time-out box while in the sixth grade. The parents contended that placement in the box deprived their child of his property interest in receiving a public education. Therefore, this punishment should not have been imposed without a hearing. In holding for the validity of the disciplinary measure, the court noted that not every use or even misuse of school discipline implicates the Fourteenth Amendment. It cited the *Goss* standard that due process procedures are not invoked where the student's property or liberty interest is *de minimis.* In applying this standard to the instant case, it found the time-out box to be a *de minimis* interference with the student's property and liberty interests. Therefore, the due process clause is not implicated, and notice and hearing procedures would not be required. The court's rationale bears some attention: "[T]eachers should be free to impose minor forms of classroom discipline, such as admonishing students, requiring special assignments, restricting activities, and denying certain privileges, without being subjected to the strictures of due process scrutiny."[35] It is important, however, to distinguish the facts of this case from other instances where the time-out box could be abused and constitute more than just a *de minimis* interference with the student's rights.[36]

Suspension from Extracurricular Activities

The courts generally have been unsympathetic to students who are suspended from athletics and other extracurricular activities. The constitutional problems for affected students are that the courts do not recognize extracurricular activities as part of the student's property interest. If there is no property interest, there is no process due. For example, in *Pegram v. Nelson*,[37] a high school student was charged with stealing a wallet at a basketball game. The student was afforded notice and a hearing in connection with the charges. Ultimately, the student was given a ten-day suspension and suspended from attending or participating in all extracurricular

34. 661 F. Supp. 155 (E.D. Tenn. 1987).
35. *Id.* at 157.
36. *See, e.g.*, Williams v. Fulton Cnty. Sch. Dist., 181 F. Supp. 3d 1089 (N.D. Ga. 2016).
37. 469 F. Supp. 1134 (M.D.N.C. 1979).

activities for four months. The parents did not take issue with the process given for the ten-day suspension. However, the parents did contend that the addition of a four-month suspension from extracurricular activities increased the gravity of the deprivation and therefore required more formal procedures than what was given. They contended that the additional extracurricular suspension removed the punishment from the short-term suspension category. The court held that the due process given was adequate for the deprivation. It noted that "the opportunity to participate in extracurricular activities is not, by and in itself, a property interest...."[38] Without possessing a property interest in extracurricular activities, the plaintiff would not be entitled to procedural due process.

However, the court left open the "theoretical" possibility that under certain circumstances the need for some due process might arise when a student is excluded from participation in extracurricular activities. It reasoned that this might happen because the *Goss* decision extends to the total educational process and that extracurricular activities can be considered part of the total educational process. Education is more than classroom attendance; it includes participation in athletic activities and membership in school clubs. Since *Pegram*, there have been at least 30 jurisdictions that have considered the question of due process for extracurricular-activity suspension. In all of these cases, the courts have been unwilling to grant that students have any property interests whatsoever in these activities, though most of the litigation has involved suspension from athletic activity. In addition, the Sixth Circuit applied the "no property interest" rule to a student who did not make the cheerleading squad.[39]

Indefinite Suspension

To encourage parents' participation in the discipline process, some students are suspended "indefinitely" until they bring their parents to school for a conference. A practical problem with this approach is that control is effectively taken from the school authorities and placed in the hands of the student and parents. Once the student is removed from school, how long is "indefinite"? Some parents might call the school for a conference immediately. Others might wait until they have a day off. What happens if the parents maintain that they cannot leave their work to come to school? The possibilities for practical problems occurring with the indefinite/until-your-parents-come type of suspensions are numerous. But beyond the practical issues are the legal problems. Indefinite suspensions raise constitutional questions of substantive due process. (A detailed discussion concerning substantive due process appears in a later section.)

In *Tate v. Racine Unified School District*,[40] a federal district court in Wisconsin described permanent removal as "draconian." The case dealt with a female student

38. *Id.* at 1139.

39. Brindisi v. Regano, 20 Fed. Appx. 508 (6th Cir. 2001).

40. No. 96-CV-524, 1996 WL 33322066 (E.D. Wis. Aug. 15, 1996).

who cut and wounded another student during a school event. The school district justified the permanent removal because the student was considered "dangerous." The court said: "Even if the District considers her a threat, it still has a responsibility to provide R.T. with an education. Although the District may expel a student for causing harm to another, Wisconsin also gives the District a variety of options in educating a child, including homebound education. Permanent expulsion is a Draconian penalty."[41] As an administrative and as a legal matter, indefinite suspensions are suspect.

It is sufficient to say here that substantive due process requires that the student who is subject to punishment by suspension should know ahead of time what misbehavior might lead to suspension.

Disciplinary Transfers

Another way in which school administrators have handled problematic students is by transferring them out of their school instead of suspending them. The question here becomes—is a transfer really a form of "backdoor" suspension? If so, are there any procedural requirements that must be met before a student can be transferred? Even in cases where the administration was able to show that the transfer of a student between schools of comparable quality was not meant as a punishment, some courts have held that procedural due process must be provided to a student facing transfer.[42] Given this standard, it is clear that when transferring students to less-desirable schools, notice and hearing will be required. The courts consider a transfer to a less desirable school to have occurred when the student is to be sent to a special school, such as those for behavioral problems or habitual truants. However, in some jurisdictions, reassignment to a new school with programs that will help the student (e.g., drug rehabilitation programs), has not been considered a suspension.[43] Nevertheless, for all practical and legal purposes, involuntary disciplinary transfers should be treated as suspensions. Notice and a hearing are recommended.

Related Considerations in Student Removals

Beyond the technical requirements of the procedural law for expulsions and suspensions, there are some related issues that should be examined. For example—What are the legal responsibilities of the school for the continued education of a student while out on suspension? Can the school expel or suspend a student for incidents occurring off school grounds? Finally, what are the penalties for a wrongful expulsion or suspension?

---

41. Id. at 7.

42. Everett v. Marcose, 426 F. Supp. 397 (E.D. Pa. 1977); W.A.N. v. Sch. Bd., 504 So. 2d 529 (Fla. Dist. Ct. App. 1987).

43. Martinez v. Sch. Dist. No. 60, 852 P.2d 1275 (Colo. App. 1992).

Responsibility for Alternative Education

From an educator's standpoint, providing some alternative form of schooling while the student is on suspension would be desirable. Nevertheless, the common practice is to provide no alternative schooling for the student who has been removed for disciplinary reasons. Perhaps the thinking of school officials is that the loss of schooling (examinations, extracurricular events, or even social activities) is part of the punishment. There was certainly no indication, even in *dicta*, that the *Goss* Court envisioned providing make-up work for those having been on suspension. However, states could and do provide for such compensatory education as a matter of statute. Some state courts have found that extended school removals may require compensatory education.

The personal educational deprivation that is associated with being removed from school has been an issue in several cases. In *Phillip Leon M. v. Greenbrier County Board of Education*,[44] the Supreme Court of West Virginia considered the expulsion of a student for one year for possession of a firearm. The court held that a state constitutional provision requiring a "thorough and efficient system of free schools" gave the student a right to an alternative educational program during the expulsion period. To refuse such an alternative, concluded the court, would not be "narrowly tailored" to meet the school's objective of providing a safe and secure school environment.[45]

By the same token, students have not been successful in obtaining due process prior to being removed from specific classes. In *Casey v. Newport School Commission*,[46] a high school student was misbehaving in science class. The misbehavior was chronic. The student was given fair warning. After he was removed from science class, his parents sued because he had not been afforded a due process hearing prior to removal. The court noted that he was not eligible for a due process hearing. Citing to an earlier case, the court stated, "Although it is clear that the entitlement to an education is a property interest protected by the Due Process clause of the Fourteenth Amendment, that interest does not necessarily encompass every facet of the educational program."[47] It is safe to say that students do not have to be given a hearing prior to removal from a particular course offering.

It should also be noted that the courts are split on whether they will allow schools to "automatically" reduce students' grades while on suspension. Consistent with the notion that punishing students with grades is *misrepresentation*, some courts have considered purposeful grade reductions while students are suspended as arbitrary and capricious. In those cases, the schools' actions were found to have violated the substantive due process rights of the student.[48] On the other hand, there are courts

44. 484 S.E.2d 909 (W.Va. 1996).
45. *Id.* at 914–16.
46. 13 F. Supp. 2d 242 (D.R.I. 1998).
47. *Id.* (citing Boynton v. Casey, 543 F. Supp. 995, 1001 (D. Me. 1982)).
48. *See, e.g.*, Smith v. Sch. City of Hobart, 811 F. Supp. 391 (N.D. Ind. 1993).

that have been willing to overlook grade reductions while on suspension, even when it involves a minor rule infraction.[49]

Expulsion or Suspension for Behavior off School Grounds

Whether the school has the authority to expel or suspend a student for behavior away from school may depend on the extent to which the "off-school-grounds behavior" affects what will happen in school. In other words, there needs to be a *nexus* between the off-grounds and the in-school behavior. A review of the case law also suggests that the nature of the offense committed off school grounds will play a role in determining the limits of the school board's authority. In *Killian v. Franklin Regional School District*,[50] a student was suspended for composing a lewd and vulgar message about one of his high school teachers. While the student never brought the material to school, the administration learned of the existence of the document through sources. The federal court ruled that his suspension represented an abuse of authority because there was no connection between the student expression and activities on campus. The school never argued that there might be some "on-campus" result to the student expression.

Supporting the authority of school officials to suspend students for off-school-grounds behavior is a case decided by an Arkansas federal district court. In *Smith v. Little Rock School District*,[51] an eleventh-grade student was expelled for having been charged with murder by the police. The Little Rock School District Student Conduct Code specified that a student could be suspended for "[c]riminal offenses committed away from school which may affect the school climate."[52]

The student challenged the expulsion on the grounds that the school has no authority over his actions when he is outside the bounds of school property. Once more, at the time of the expulsion, the student had not yet been convicted of any crime. The school said it made its decision to expel based on the potential harm that might be caused if the student was let in school. The principal did have some specific circumstances on which he initially recommended the expulsion. The accused had a sister in school, and the boy who was shot had a sister and brother among the student body. The principal said, "I made the judgment for the welfare of the entire student body for any type of trouble that may develop."[53] The court upheld the expulsion. In reaching its decision, the court used a balancing test. It said:

---

49. *See, e.g.*, In the Interest of T.H., 681 So. 2d 110 (Miss. 1996).

50. 136 F. Supp. 2d 446 (W.D. Pa. 2001).

51. 582 F. Supp. 159 (E.D. Ark. 1984).

52. *Id.*

53. *Id.* at 162.

> [T]he Court must balance the harm plaintiff may suffer as a result of his expulsion against the serious risk to other students which would be presented by plaintiff's presence at the school. The Court finds that the risk of harm to other students and the potential for disruption of educational processes outweigh whatever harm plaintiff Smith may suffer as a result of his expulsion.[54]

In addition, the court upheld the validity of the school policy which allowed the administration to suspend or expel based on suspicion that trouble could occur in school. This could be done even though the accused student might have only been charged with a crime. The court found it reasonable that if they were forced to wait for courtroom adjudication before acting, the rule would be meaningless.

The U.S. Circuit Court of Appeals for the Eighth Circuit ruled in *Felton v. Fayette School District*[55] that a school could consider "maintaining community support" and "off-campus program integrity" as bases for excluding a student from an off-campus vocational program. During his junior year of high school, a student was involved in the theft of auto parts. As a result, the student was confined for a short time by a state juvenile court. Although the school where the student studied auto mechanics was not the target of his thievery, the school determined that the student had violated the district's "good citizenship rule." The student's argument that the school was violating his equal protection rights because the rule discriminated against adjudicated juvenile delinquents was rejected. The court ruled against the suspension. It reasoned that there must be some connection between the off-grounds behavior and the student's role "on school premises." At the time of the occurrence, the teacher was not acting in his professional role, as would be the case if this were to happen "in school." Nor was the student acting in his role as student. Therefore, the court viewed the interaction as one between two individuals as opposed to one between a teacher and a student.

In *Martinez v. School District No. 60*,[56] a Colorado school district had suspended two high school students when they appeared intoxicated at a school dance on a Saturday night. The administration invoked a board policy which stated that students would be automatically suspended for five days for use or possession of drugs or alcohol "occurring on or off school premises." The suspended students claimed that the policy should not have applied to them because they consumed the alcohol at a private party before the dance. In ruling for the students, the court noted that there was an error in applying the policy to the students' behavior:

> [A] school district's regulation of students' conduct must bear some reasonable relationship to the educational environment; a school district cannot regulate purely private activity having no effect upon that environment....

54. *Id.*
55. 875 F.2d 191 (8th Cir. 1989).
56. 852 P. 2d 1275 (Colo. App. 1992).

> Nothing in this policy, however, suggests that it is intended to regulate a student's activities during the period before or after the school day and at purely private locations in those instances in which the student's activities have no effect upon him or her during the regular school day or at any district-sponsored function.[57]

Apparently, the court felt that appearing at a "school dance" in a state of drunkenness is different than appearing at school in the same state. However, one may question the significant distinction in reasoning between being drunk at a school dance and being drunk at school. After all, would not drunkenness at a school dance still affect the school environment?

In reviewing these cases, it appears as though school officials will be supported in punishing off-grounds behavior when the student has committed a crime and the crime is dangerous enough that the administration is concerned about the continued tranquility of the school environment if the student remains in school. However, it appears as though non-criminal behavior is more difficult for school authorities to punish. To avoid a judgment against the school, the administration would have to show a connection between the off-grounds behavior and the maintenance of in-school order. This connection is shown in more detail in our discussion of technology cases later in this chapter.

Zero Tolerance and Due Process

Zero-tolerance discipline polices are defined as mandatory disciplinary measures that are imposed for a specified offense in a school setting. Zero-tolerance discipline polices have been enacted by a variety of state and local educational agencies as a response to the growing prevalence of drugs and violence in the nation's public K-12 schools. The Columbine shootings, along with the pre- and post-related events, caused many school districts to impose zero-tolerance policies. The presence of weapons and, in many instances, drugs have been punished with suspension. Most state statutes or school district policies impose long-term suspensions of a year or more for weapons or drug possession. It should be noted, however, that in recent years, zero-tolerance policies have fallen into disfavor. Some of these concerns are connected to abuse of such zero-tolerance policies and/or over-extension into relatively minor offenses.[58] In addition, many commentators and current research connect these policies to a school-to-prison pipeline which often disproportionately affects students of color.[59] To date, however, legal challenges to school districts' zero-

---

57. *Id.* at 1279.

58. *See, e.g.*, Todd A. DeMitchell & Elyse Hambacher, *Zero Tolerance, Threats of Harm, and the Imaginary Gun: "Good Intentions Run Amuck,"* 2016 B.Y.U. EDUC. & L.J. 1 (2016).

59. *See, e.g.*, Rocio Rodriguez Ruiz, *School to Prison Pipeline: An Evaluation of Zero Tolerance Policies and Their Alternatives*, 54 HOUS. L. REV. 803 (2016); Jeremy Thompson, *Eliminating Zero Tolerance Policies in Schools: Miami-Dade County Public Schools' Approach*, 2016 B.Y.U. EDUC. &

tolerance policies have generally resulted in the court's upholding of these policies as long as the districts satisfy procedural due process requirements, namely notice and a fair hearing.

There can be both procedural and substantive due process legal issues in connection with zero-tolerance practices. Procedural due process is required regardless of the policy. A common misconception is that a zero-tolerance policy means suspension is "automatic." Of course, an automatic suspension suggests that the student is not given any due process—that because of the nature of the infraction, the situation is basically "open and shut." This is a constitutional anomaly. Regardless of the infraction, there must always be a hearing; penalties cannot be imposed absent the convening of an adjudicatory process. Even an emergency suspension as outlined by the *Goss* Court eventually comes to a hearing.

An issue of substantive due process can arise when the punishment does not fit the crime. In other words, to promote the zero-tolerance or "get-tough" policy, consequences of infractions may be overly punitive. For example, if the school were to punish tardiness or loud talking in a hallway with a semester-long suspension, substantive due process might be implicated. The issue of substantive due process is an issue of *fundamental fairness*. Do school rules exist? Are the rules graduated so that as the seriousness of the misbehavior increases, the punishment increases? In other words, does the punishment fit the crime? Another question that must be asked is whether the school has a system of rules that are clearly understood by students. The rules must be understood in such a way that students can know how to avoid being suspended. This goes to the doctrine of *fair warning*. If students cannot understand how to avoid being removed, then the system does not provide fair warning and would violate the notion of substantive due process.

An illustrative case is *Galveston Independent School District v. Boothe*.[60] In this case, a high school student was sitting in his car which was not parked on school property. He was approached by a school official and found to be in possession of a small amount of marijuana. He was suspended for one-quarter of the school year. The suspension policy stated that students could be suspended for drug possession "in our schools." The student argued that he thought that meant "in the school building." He did not believe that being in his car, off campus, with the marijuana fit the policy. The court agreed with the student. It noted that the phrasing of the policy did not provide fair warning as to the proscribed behavior. The lesson of *Boothe* is that schools should make sure that students understand the suspension policy. The importance of "correct" or legally insulating language may not be as important as student sensitive vernacular.

L.J. 325 (2016); Lydia Nussbaum, *Realizing Restorative Justice: Legal Rules and Standards for School Discipline Reform*, 69 Hastings L.J. 583 (2018).

60. 590 S.W. 2d 553 (1979).

Concluding Remarks on Student Expulsions and Suspensions

Finally, it should be noted that student suspensions, whether long-term or short-term, are administrative, not criminal, proceedings. Consequently, students' rights in schools are less than those of adults accused of crimes. Nevertheless, students have both procedural and substantive due process rights under the U.S. Constitution. Because of the existence of these rights, students may have a cause of action under 42 U.S.C. § 1983 that could result in the school district having to pay money damages. The incentive should therefore be high for school authorities to avoid errors in school suspensions, if for no other reason than to prevent a constitutional tort. (This concept of claiming money damages under 42 U.S.C. § 1983 for violation of a constitutional tort is explained in more detail in this book's chapter on liability.)

Freedom of Student Speech and Expression

The landmark U.S. Supreme Court decision that marked the inception of students' rights was also the first case to recognize students' speech rights. *Tinker v. Des Moines Independent School District*[61] [*see* **Case No. 4-3**] involved three students who were suspended for wearing black armbands to protest the Vietnam War. The Court held that wearing the armbands was symbolic expression. This expression could not be punished unless school authorities had a *reasonable forecast* that the student behavior could *materially and substantially interfere with the operation of the school or the rights of other students to learn*. The "reasonable forecast" must be more than just fear or a hunch—school officials may not punish student speech because the viewpoint is controversial. In the words of the Court, students do not "shed their constitutional rights to freedom of speech or expression at the schoolhouse gate."[62]

Lewd/Vulgar Student Speech

In 1986, the U.S. Supreme Court provided another standard for analyzing student speech issues. The legal question of whether schools may punish student speech that was not necessarily disruptive but nevertheless was vulgar, lewd, and offensive was decided in *Bethel School District No. 403 v. Fraser*.[63] [*See* **Case No. 4-4.**] In *Fraser*, a high school student delivered a nomination speech for a friend running for a student government office (Associated Student Body Vice-President). The speech included numerous sexual innuendos.[64] The student was suspended for three days

61. 393 U.S. 503 (1969).

62. *Id.* at 506.

63. 478 U.S. 675 (1986).

64. *Id.* Before a school assembly of approximately 600 people, Matthew Fraser's nomination speech for classmate Jeff Kuhlman, who was running for Associated Study Body Vice-President,

and barred from being considered as a commencement exercise speaker. Using the *Tinker* standard, lower courts had found for the student because material and substantial disruption had not been created by the speech. The Court's majority opinion also contended that Fraser had a First Amendment right to political speech under the principles of *Tinker*, which protects the vast majority of student speech that does not create a substantial disruption. However, Chief Justice Warren Burger, in writing for the Court's 7-2 majority, created a new standard that would permit schools to punish students for non-disruptive vulgar speech: "The schools, as instruments of the state, may determine that the essential lessons of civil, mature conduct cannot be conveyed in a school that tolerates lewd, indecent, or offensive speech."[65] (School officials also argued that they had a duty to protect younger students from inappropriate and sexual speech.)

School-Sponsored Speech

In 1988, the Supreme Court extended the *Fraser* student-free-speech-and-expression standard when it heard its first student publication case. Student publications such as the school newspaper are forms of student expression. Therefore, when the principal of a Missouri high school made unilateral alterations in the final copy of the paper, the students sued for a violation of their free speech.

In *Hazelwood School District v. Kuhlmeier*,[66] [***see*** **Case No. 4-5**] much of the argument concerned the issue of whether the school had created a "public forum" for free expression when it created a school newspaper. In free-speech analysis, the courts have relied on the identification of the appropriate forum before deciding how much control the government can have within that forum. The government has the least control in a "public forum," sometimes called an "open forum." Examples of open fora are public parks and streets. Only when the speech activities in a public forum violate the common law or the criminal code might the government limit speech; however, the government may apply reasonable time, place, and manner restrictions.

Another type of forum is a "limited open forum," where the government can control speech by any number of rules because the purpose of the forum is not to facilitate the free exchange of ideas; rather, it is for the orderly application of some government function. Over the years, most courts have considered the public school

---

states: "I know a man who is firm—he's firm in his pants, he's firm in his shirt, his character is firm—but most of all, his belief in you the students of Bethel, is firm. Jeff Kuhlman is a man who takes his point and pounds it in. If necessary, he'll take an issue and nail it to the wall. He doesn't attack things in spurts—he drives hard, pushing and pushing until finally—he succeeds. Jeff is a man who will go to the very end—even the climax, for each and every one of you. So please vote for Jeff Kuhlman, as he'll never come between us and the best our school can be."

65. *Id.* at 683. For example, Fraser's speech, nominating a classmate to a student elective office, referred to the student as "firm in his pants," who would take it to "the climax."

66. 494 U.S. 260 (1988).

curriculum to be a limited open forum. In the *Hazelwood* case, the Court considered the school newspaper to be a component of the curriculum. Students did receive instruction and grades for their participation in the newspaper. Because the publication was intended to be a supervised learning experience for journalism students, it held that no public forum was created.

The Court noted that educators are entitled to exercise greater control over student expression to ensure that participants learn whatever lessons the activity is designed to teach. Hence, a school may disassociate itself from speech that is, for example, ungrammatical, poorly written, inadequately researched, biased or prejudiced, vulgar, profane, or unsuitable for immature audiences. In his testimony, the principal said that he did not think the student authors had yet learned how to handle sensitively some of the subject matter being discussed in the paper. The handling of controversial material was part of the school's Journalism II class, which these students had not yet taken.

Ultimately, the Court held that educators do not offend the First Amendment by exercising editorial control over the style and content of student speech in school-sponsored expressive activities so long as their actions are reasonably related to legitimate pedagogical concerns.

Speech or Expression Promoting Illegal Drug Use Not Protected

After nearly two decades of analyzing student speech cases with the *Tinker*, *Fraser*, and *Hazelwood* tests, the U.S. Supreme Court established yet another constitutional standard, one that is easy to apply and permits school officials to punish drug-related student speech. The exception to the usual student speech analysis emanates from the 2007 U.S. Supreme Court decision in *Morse v. Frederick*.[67] [***See* Case 4-7.**] In *Morse*, high school-student Joseph Frederick and some friends unfurled a homemade sign across the street from their school during the Olympic Torch Relay as it ran through Juneau, Alaska. The sign read: "BONG HiTS 4 JESUS." The student body had been released early from school that day in order to line the relay route to show support for the Olympics. The principal suspended Frederick for ten days for promoting drug use among students.

The *Frederick* decision carved out another exception to the *Tinker* standard, with the Court ruling that student speech which contributes to the use of drugs need not be tolerated. Chief Justice John Roberts stated, "[W]e hold that schools may take steps to safeguard those entrusted to their care from speech that can reasonably be regarded as encouraging illegal drug use."[68] Reversing the Ninth Circuit's decision in favor of the student Joseph Frederick, the Supreme Court majority emphasized the

67. 551 U.S. 393.

68. *Id.* at 397.

importance of deterring drug use among students and concluded that Frederick's actions violated the school board's existing policy of prohibiting expression advocating the use of illegal drugs.[69] Interestingly, all the Justices agreed that students can be disciplined for promoting the use of illegal drugs, but disagreed on whether the "BONG HiTS 4 JESUS" banner actually did so.

Freedom to Read

What First Amendment rights do students have to read books? The short answer is that it depends on where these books originate. If the student finds the book(s) in the school library, then, absent the book being found to be obscene, the student has the right to read the book without punishment. Further, students have the right to have objectionable books remain in the school library. The leading case on this subject is *Board of Education v. Pico*.[70] [***See* Case No. 4-6.**] In this case, some community members objected to books in the school library, claiming they were "anti-American, anti-Christian, anti-Semitic, and just plain filthy."[71] The Supreme Court ruled that books cannot be removed from a school library simply because the local school board finds their content objectionable. The Court also suggested that a legal (constitutional) alternative would be to have a committee to select library books beforehand. Here, age-appropriate content as well as financial constraints may be considered.

We chose this case for further discussion because it is one of the few times that the U.S. Supreme Court has intervened in matters related to the content of what is taught in schools. Indeed, the *Pico* Court clearly stated it did not wish to interfere with the school's discretionary powers.[72] It should also be noted that this decision, rendered in 1982, was a divided one with several concurring and dissenting opinions, yet it has not been overturned. The case also raises important policy questions related to the education of children. For example, whether it is better to expose students to a wide variety of literature, even if that literature is objectionable to certain groups, or whether educators or the courts need to protect young impressionable minds by not exposing students to certain materials. If protection is the issue, then one must consider what might be appropriate at what ages or whether certain books might be inappropriate for any school-age child.

Applying Student Free Speech and Expression Standards

Since *Fraser* and *Hazelwood* were decided, the lower courts have continually struggled to apply these legal standards to a variety of free speech cases. Because *Tinker* was not overruled by either of these decisions, the courts have had to manage

69. *Id.* at 393.
70. 457 U.S. 853 (1982).
71. *Id.* at 857.
72. *Id.* at 861–62.

three different standards for student expression issues. The cases we are about to discuss all turn on which of the three standards the court applies.

The Eighth Circuit found for the school district when it applied the *Fraser* standard to a vulgar letter. In *Wildman v. Marshalltown School District*,[73] a high school female basketball player became upset when she did not make the varsity team. She wrote a letter to her teammates wherein she made disparaging references to the coach. Part of the letter included the word "bullshit." School authorities demanded an apology as a condition of the student's continued participation in basketball at any level. Relying on *Tinker*, the student argued that her speech rights were violated. In upholding the decision of the lower court which found no speech violation, the Eighth Circuit noted that *Tinker* applies only if *Fraser* or *Hazelwood* do not. A reasonable teacher, in this case a coach, would consider "bullshit" a vulgarity. The student does not have a protected right to express vulgarities—school officials have the authority to prohibit a student's expression of vulgar and offensive comments.

Accordingly, in *LaVine v. Blaine School District*,[74] a high school student, LaVine, was expelled for having written a poem containing vivid imagery of violent death and suicide and the shooting of fellow students. The student wrote the poem on his own and not in connection with any class assignment. Nevertheless, he brought the poem to school and showed several of his classmates. He also stuck the poem in with other homework that he turned into the English teacher. LaVine asked the teacher what she thought of the poem. After consulting with others, including the school guidance counselor and vice principal, the teacher handed the poem to the school principal who proceeded to expel LaVine and place documentation in his file concerning the substance of the poem.

The federal district court upheld the expulsion but ruled that placing incriminating notations in the student's file went too far. In affirming the trial court, the Ninth Circuit noted that *Fraser* did not apply as there were no vulgarities in the poem. Nor did *Hazelwood* apply as the poem was written at home with no prompt from the school district. Therefore, it could not be school-sponsored. That left *Tinker*. The court's position was that the poem did represent a reasonable forecast of material and substantial disruption; therefore, the expulsion could not be protected by the speech clause. However, it agreed with the trial court that the school's placement and maintenance of negative documentation in the student's file after the perceived threat had subsided went beyond its legitimate documentation needs.

Some years earlier, the Ninth Circuit had held that a student is protected when threatening words are used in an innocent fashion. In *Lovell v. Poway Unified School District*,[75] a high school student said, "If you don't give me this schedule change, I'm going to shoot you." The student directed this statement to her counselor after having to stand in line for a long time waiting for an anticipated course alteration. The

73. 249 F.3d 768 (8th Cir. 2001).

74. 257 F.3d 981 (9th Cir. 2001).

75. 90 F.3d 367 (9th Cir. 1996).

student testified that she immediately apologized for her inappropriate behavior. Moreover, she did not have a gun and did not appear to the counselor as though she did. The student completed the change in registration and left the office. At the end of the day, the counselor reported the incident to the assistant principal. The counselor told the administrator that she felt threatened. The student was suspended for three days. The court ruled that the student was not advancing a legitimate threat. It noted that the student was frustrated for having to spend time standing in line. Along with her lack of any physical action and her immediate apology, a reasonable person would likely not have understood her to be expressing a serious intent to harm. Applying *Tinker*, the court ruled for the student.

Student Dress Codes

In the 1960s and 1970s, students began to express themselves through how they dressed. Long hair, facial hair, and the latest fashions all seemed to become issues as school authorities sought to conform student dress to a less-distracting standard. Early on, the jurisdictions were split on the extent to which the courts were willing to consider student dress as protected speech. Most of the litigation and attempted litigation dealt with grooming issues, e.g., may schools regulate hair length and facial hair? Courts in the Fifth, Sixth, Ninth, and Tenth Circuits left school hair-grooming regulations in place.[76] On the other hand, courts in the First, Fourth, Seventh, and Eighth Circuits found that hair-length regulations violated students' speech rights.[77] Therefore, whether you could wear your hair as you pleased depended on which part of the country you were a student in. More recent decisions addressing hair have centered around whether it is discriminatory to require male athletes, such as basketball players, to keep their hair at a certain length but not have the same rule for female basketball players. A Seventh Circuit Court of Appeals[78] found that such rules are discriminatory under Title IX and violate the Equal Protection Clause; however, the Texas Supreme Court upheld a grooming policy prohibiting a third-grade boy from wearing a ponytail. The court maintained that the regulation did not deprive the student of equal educational opportunities.[79]

As to student dress, even in those areas of the country where student expression is most protected, school authorities may ban clothing that presents a health or safety issue. For example, a school might prohibit the wearing of sandals unless accompanied by socks; this regulation could be justified as a public hygiene concern. Students might be required to either cut their hair or wear a hair net as a

---

76. *See* Ferrell v. Dallas Ind. Sch. Dist., 392 F.2d 697 (5th Cir. 1968); Jackson v. Dorrier, 424 F.2d 213 (6th Cir. 1970); King v. Saddleback Junior College Dist., 445 F.2d 932 (9th Cir. 1971); and Freeman v. Flake, 448 F.2d 258 (10th Cir. 1971).

77. *See* Richards v. Thurston, 424 F.2d 1281 (1st Cir. 1971); Massie v. Henry, 455 F.2d 779 (4th Cir. 1972); Breen v. Kahl, 419 F.2d 1034 (7th Cir. 1969); and Bishop v. Colaw, 450 F.2d 1069 (8th Cir. 1971).

78. Hayden v. Greensburg Comm. Sch. Corp., 743 F.3d. 569 (7th Cir. 2014).

79. Bd. of Trs. of Bastrop Ind. Sch. Dist. v. Toungate, 958 S.W.2d 365 (Tex. 1997).

requirement for taking a shop course, as long hair could fall into a lathe or other equipment thus causing harm. Of course, in the final analysis, if whatever the student is wearing (or growing) causes a material and substantial disruption to the school operation, activities, or the rights of others, then the *Tinker* standard will apply, and the student will not be protected. In reviewing those cases where the students' rights of expression were upheld, either the schools did not have an instance of material disruption that they could point to or the expression was somewhat of a distraction but did not rise to the level of material and substantial disruption.

However, after a quick consideration of the two other standards used by the courts for student expression, *Fraser* and *Hazelwood*, the question becomes whether students' clothing can be lewd or vulgar (*Fraser*) or inconsistent with school-sponsored speech as a legitimate pedagogical interest (*Hazelwood*). The court's decision in *Chandler v. McMinnville School District*[80] is illustrative. In this case, an Oregon teachers' strike led school officials to hire replacement teachers. Two students, who had fathers among the striking teachers, wore buttons to school that read, "Do scabs bleed?" and "I'm not listening scab." The students also distributed these buttons to classmates. A temporary administrator saw the buttons that the students were wearing and asked these students to accompany him to the vice principal's office. The vice principal asked the students to remove the buttons because they were disruptive. Upon refusing to comply, the students were suspended for one day for willful disobedience.

Relying on *Fraser*, the district court found for the school district, stating that the buttons were offensive and inherently disruptive. On appeal to the Ninth Circuit, the students argued that the district court erred because *Tinker* should have been applied. They asserted that their buttons expressed a political viewpoint, not lewd speech. In reversing the lower court and holding for the students, the court of appeals outlined three distinct areas of student speech: (1) vulgar, lewd, and plainly offensive speech; (2) school-sponsored speech; and (3) speech that falls into neither of these categories. The court held that *Fraser* applies to the first category, *Hazelwood* to the second, and *Tinker* to the third. For clarification, the court pointed out that *Hazelwood* focused on two factors that distinguish *Fraser* from *Tinker*. The *Fraser* speech was vulgar, and it was given at an official school assembly. Whereas both factors were present in *Fraser*, the deferential *Fraser* standard applies when the first factor alone is present. Therefore, school officials may suppress speech that is vulgar or offensive without a showing that such speech occurred during a school-sponsored event or threatened to interfere substantially with the school's work.

The court proceeded to apply each of the three standards to the case to find the standard that should control. In looking at the *Fraser* standard (lewd or offensive speech), the court noted that the school district made no attempt to determine, nor could the court find, whether "scab" *per se* is vulgar or offensive. For the *Hazelwood* standard (school-sponsored speech), the court noted that the buttons reflected the

80. 978 F.2d 524 (9th Cir. 1992).

personal opinions of the students wearing them. They expressed a position on a local political issue that was diametrically opposed to the school district's decision to hire replacement teachers. Therefore, the complaint does not show that a reasonable person could have viewed the buttons as bearing the imprimatur of the school. This leaves the *Tinker* standard (disruptive speech). The court asked the question, did school officials have a reasonable forecast that the students' buttons would substantially disrupt, or materially interfere with, school activities? The appeals court noted that the lower court held that the "scab" buttons were inherently disruptive. However, nothing in the facts or in the analysis substantiates this conclusion. Therefore, the Ninth Circuit Court of Appeals concluded that the district court erred in holding the buttons disruptive.

A similar approach could be used to determine whether protected student speech exists in the variety of messages that students wear on shirts. Additionally, clothing such as halter tops, short-shorts, or other "revealing" clothing might fall under the *Fraser* lewd/vulgar standard. Of course, even a patriotic message might be punished under the *Tinker* standard. The *Tinker* standard does not ask for the substance of the message but only what the message produces. The *Fraser* and *Hazelwood* standards are message subject-specific. Finally, the *McMinnville* case was decided prior to the U.S. Supreme Court's opinion in *Morse v. Frederick*, which has been interpreted to prohibit student dress that promotes drug use, thus adding a third subject-specific message to this analysis. We should also add that the Supreme Court and resulting lower court decisions have been very clear that restrictions on speech must be content neutral (with the exceptions just noted). In other words, school officials must be careful not to discriminate against student speech just because they personally do not like the message being conveyed.

The last few decades have witnessed many lower court decisions focusing on student dress. In some instances, the rule is clear. To ensure school safety, students may not wear the colors or insignia of gangs, dress that reflects gang membership, or clothing designed to incite or support violence. Following the *Morse* decision, students may not wear clothing that advocates drug use. Other restrictions are not as easy. Like the grooming cases of the 1960s and 1970s mentioned above, outcomes often vary based on jurisdiction. These cases can raise sensitive, even problematic, concerns. Some courts have upheld the right of students to wear t-shirts displaying strong language aimed at certain groups or individuals. These messages are often politically and/or religiously based and are often upheld by the courts as not being vulgar or lewd (*Fraser*) and neither causing nor foreseeing material and substantial disruption (*Tinker*). For example, a number of court decisions have upheld the right of students to wear t-shirts that parody political figures or convey a religious message opposing abortion or gay rights. In response, some schools have adopted policies that prohibit the wearing of t-shirts with any messages.[81] Alternately, there have

81. Deborah M. Ahrens & Andrew M. Siegel, *Of Dress and Redress: Student Dress Restrictions in Constitutional Law and Culture*, 54 Harv. C.R.-C.L. L. Rev. 49 (2019).

also been a series of decisions in the Fourth, Fifth, Sixth, Eighth, Tenth, and Eleventh[82] Circuits disallowing Confederate flag memorabilia, insignia, and/or dress.[83] These courts based their decisions on the flag's association with a history of racial divisiveness, a forecast of material and substantial disruption as permitted under *Tinker.*

Based on the *Fraser* decision, schools may prohibit dress that is sexual or t-shirts that carry a sexual message. As mentioned above, such clothing could interfere with instruction. What is lewd? Jurisdictions differ as to whether schools may prohibit students from wearing "boobie bracelets." These bracelets, generally appearing as a wide rubber band that says, "I love (heart) boobies," were marketed as part of a breast cancer awareness campaign. In *B.H. v. Easton Area School District,*[84] the Third Circuit Court of Appeals ruled for middle school students who were punished for wearing these bracelets, stating that students have free speech rights, the bracelets were not plainly lewd, and wearing them carried an important social message. Additionally, these students had worn the bracelets for two weeks with no disturbance before the school banned them. Thus, there was no material and substantial disruption. A federal district court in Indiana[85] ruled differently. When a high school boy wore the bracelet and harassed a female student by repeating this phrase, the school banned the bracelet. A female student who had worn the bracelet for three months before the ban sued. Unlike the *B.H.* ruling, this court left the decision as to what is lewd up to the school administrators.[86]

School Uniforms

There is a difference between a "dress code" and a "uniform policy." A dress code is a list of those items that students may not wear. The list is presumed to be based on health and safety concerns. A uniform policy excludes the wearing of all clothing except for the specific items the school designates as acceptable. The uniform policy would resemble what is found in a parochial school. As we've seen, the courts are settled on the basis upon which schools may regulate (or ban) certain forms of student expression. Until the late 1990s, however, many jurisdictions were not willing to validate the ultimate control of student dress—the imposition of a school uniform.

---

82. Hardwick v. Heyward, 711 F.3d 426 (4th Cir. 2013); A.M. v. Cash, 585 F.3d 214 (5th Cir 2009); Defoe v. Spiva, 625 F.3d 324 (6th Cir. 2010); B.W.A. v. Farmington R-7 Sch. Dist., 554 F.3d 734 (8th Cir. 2009); West v. Derby Unified Sch. Dist. No. 260. 206 F.3d. 1358 (10th Cir. 2000); and Scott v. Sch. Bd. Of Alachua Cnty., 324 F.3d.1246 (11th Cir. 2003).

83. *See* Todd A. DeMitchell & Richard Fossey, *The Battle Over the Confederate Flag in Our Schools: Heritage or Oppression?* 352 EDUC. L. REP. 937 (2018).

84. B.H. v. Easton Area Sch. Dist., 725 F.3d 293 (3d Cir. 2013).

85. J.A. v. Fort Wayne Cmty. Schools, No. 1:12-CV-155 JVB, 2013 WL 4479229 (N.D. Ind. Aug. 20, 2013).

86. *See also* Mark Strasser, Tinker *Remorse on Threats, Boobies, Bullying, and Parodies,* 15 FIRST AMEND. L. REV. 1 (2017).

Most courts have upheld the right of schools to require uniforms. This notion can be illustrated by two decisions, both coming from the Fifth Circuit Court of Appeals. In the first case, *Canady v. Bossier Parish School Board*,[87] a Louisiana school district developed a uniform policy. The average uniform consisted of a choice of two colors of polo or oxford shirts and navy or khaki pants. The schools alerted parents by letter about the dress specifications, provided a list of local vendors supplying the required clothing, and displayed an example of the uniform at each school. The school district convinced the Fifth Circuit that the uniforms had an educational benefit. It said:

> The School Board's purpose for enacting the uniform policy is to increase test scores and reduce disciplinary problems throughout the school system. This purpose is in no way related to the suppression of student speech. Although students are restricted from wearing clothing of their choice at school, students remain free to wear what they want after school hours. Students may still express their views through other mediums during the school day. The uniform requirement does not bar the important "personal intercommunication among students" necessary to an effective educational process.[88]

In the second case, *Littlefield v. Forney Independent School District*,[89] parents challenged a Texas school district's mandatory uniform policy, arguing that there was no permissible basis for the restriction on their children's freedom of expression. Citing *United States v. O'Brien*,[90] the *Littlefield* court noted that:

> [T]he Supreme Court created an analytical framework to evaluate content-neutral restrictions on expressive activities. The Court held that "when 'speech' and 'non-speech' elements are combined in the same course of conduct, a sufficiently important governmental interest in regulating the non-speech element can justify incidental limitations on First Amendment freedoms." Applying *O'Brien* to the challenged governmental policy at issue, the Uniform Policy will survive Constitutional scrutiny if (1) it is within the Constitutional power of the government, (2) it furthers an important or substantial governmental interest, (3) the interest is unrelated to the suppression of student expression, and (4) the incidental restrictions on First Amendment activities are no more than is necessary to facilitate that interest.[91]

Applying this standard to the students' claims that the uniforms amounted to coerced speech and prior restraint, the *Littlefield* court had no problem ruling that the school's uniform requirement was Constitutional. Forney and the school board's desire to improve the educational process amounted to an "important and

---

87. 240 F.3d 437 (5th Cir. 2001).
88. *Id.* at 443.
89. 268 F.3d 275 (5th Cir. 2001).
90. 391 U.S. 367 (1968).
91. 268 F.3d at 286–87.

substantial [government] interest."[92] These defendants as well as the policy itself articulated specific gains that school officials anticipated by requiring uniforms ranging from instilling self-esteem, fostering confidence, and improving student achievement to reducing gang and drug-related activities.

The Ninth Circuit made an exception to this rule in *Frudden v. Pilling.*[93] Here, an elementary school required a polo shirt with the school logo and school name but also allowed students to wear uniforms of nationally recognized organizations such as the Boy Scouts or Girls Scouts on days when these groups met. One parent who was opposed to this rule sent her children to school in uniforms of a national youth soccer group even though the children were not having soccer practice on those days. The school disciplined the students, and the parent sued. The court ruled in favor of the parent, noting that allowing some exceptions and not others violated the principle of content neutrality and requiring the motto amounted to compelled speech.

Although students are restricted from wearing clothing of their choice at school, students remain free to wear what they want after school hours. Students may still express their views through other mediums during the school day. The uniform requirement does not bar the important personal intercommunication among students necessary to an effective educational process.

Students' Rights and Technology

Based on its ubiquitous nature, the internet does not fit neatly or easily into existing First Amendment legal precedents involving freedom of speech and expression, especially for children and young adults who use online forms of communication extensively. Over the past several decades, the use of technology in our society, and consequently in our schools, has grown dramatically. This growth has resulted in the need for laws and policies governing the use and possible misuse of technology, which in turn has had a profound impact on school discipline and students' other constitutional rights. For the most part, technology has affected three important areas related to the law. First, there have been issues emanating from cyber-bullying and how these problems are handled from a discipline standpoint. Second, the widespread use of technology has brought forth many questions related to students' free speech rights under the First Amendment, particularly those situations that involve social media sites, either constructed and/or distributed on or off school property. Third, when there is a search of cyber space, the Fourth Amendment (search and seizure) is generally applied. We will address the first two issues here in this section and the third later in this chapter under the Fourth Amendment.

When students use the internet to attack someone online, they often initially generate these online statements off school grounds. One major legal issue that arises is,

---

92. *Id.*

93. 742 F.3d 1199 (9th Cir. 2014).

can school officials discipline a student if the online-based statements or comments are produced off school grounds? While the law governing the legal boundaries of student cyberspeech are still evolving, a current analysis of the role of the internet on student cyberspeech can be applied to existing First Amendment precedents involving student speech and expression. For example:

1. The U.S. Supreme Court's 1986 *Bethel v. Fraser*[94] decision controls student online speech or expression that is "lewd, vulgar, or profane"; such speech can be prohibited by school officials if the language reaches students/adults in the school.
2. The U.S. Supreme Court's 1969 *Tinker v. Des Moines* ruling[95] can be applied to online speech if the speech creates a material and substantial disruption in the school.
3. Threats fall under the *Tinker* umbrella if they constitute "true threats." True threats "express a sincere intent to commit an act of unlawful violence against a particular individual or group." They need to be intentional, and the person must knowingly transmit to (or see that the threat is transmitted to) the intended recipient. Thus, school officials do not violate a student's First Amendment free speech and expression rights by suspending them, even though the student created and transmitted an online "threat" off school grounds.[96]

Cyberbullying

As today's young people spend increasingly more time online, the potential for cyberbullying, or online-based bullying and harassment, increases dramatically. Bullying has been a common disciplinary problem for centuries but has gained considerably more attention in more recent decades with the advent of the internet. In her seminal research on this topic, Shaheen Shariff observes that cyberbullying is the same as traditional bullying but with a much more expansive audience, especially among young people.[97] Additionally, cyberbullies may gain a sense of power through anonymity. The national media's spotlight on tragic teenage suicides attributed to cyberbullying combined with compelling research detailing cyberbullying's negative psychological and psychosocial effects on today's teenagers has influenced a growing number of legislators to initiate criminal anti-bullying legislation.[98] In one of the first highly publicized stories of teenage suicides connected to cyberbullying, Ryan Halligan, a 13-year old middle school student in Vermont, committed suicide. Leading

94. 478 U.S. 675 (1986).

95. 393 U.S. 503 (1969).

96. *True threat*, Black's Law Dictionary (11th ed. 2019).

97. Shaheen Shariff, Confronting Cyberbullying: What Schools Need to Know to Control Misconduct and Avoid Legal Consequences (2009).

98. *See* Kevin P. Brady, *Criminal Anti-Cyberbullying Statutes: Does Legislative Zeal Outweigh Constitutional Considerations?*, 298 Educ. Law Rep. 21 (2013).

up to his suicide, Ryan had been repeatedly harassed both at school and online off school grounds the summer before he entered eighth grade. One of Ryan's female classmates pretended to be interested in him romantically and forwarded him an instant message, or "IM." Ryan's online responses to these IMs were sent electronically to everyone in the school. When the school year began and Ryan approached the female student, "she told him he was just a loser and that she did not want anything to do with him."[99]

In April 2009, Representative Linda T. Sanchez of California sponsored H.R. 1966, more commonly referred to as the Megan Meier Cyberbullying Prevention Act (Cyberbullying Prevention Act).[100] In her congressional testimony explaining the need for federal anti-cyberbullying legislation, Representative Sanchez stated, "[C]yberbullying is always mean, ill-mannered, and cruel, but some cyberbullying is so harmful that it rises to the level of criminal activity."[101] Specifically, the proposed federal Cyberbullying Prevention Act seeks to criminalize cyberbullying by the imposition of a fine and up to two years' imprisonment for anyone who "transmits in interstate or foreign commerce any communication, with the intent to coerce, intimidate, harass, or cause substantial emotional distress to a person, using electronic means to support severe, repeated, and hostile behavior."[102] However, as of 2020, Congress has yet to pass the Megan Meier Cyberbullying Prevention Act due primarily to criticisms that the federal bill is unconstitutional and specifically violates First Amendment protections covering free speech and expression.[103] In contrast, states' legislative approaches to addressing cyberbullying vary significantly.[104] Despite wide variation among the states, it is clear that the majority of today's state legislatures view online bullying and harassment as serious issues in our

99. John Halligan, *Death by Cyber-Bully*, The Boston Globe (Aug. 17, 2005), http://www.boston.com/news/globe/editorial_ opinion/oped/articles/2005/08/17/death_by_cyber_bully/ (This article, written by Ryan Halligan's father, commended the state of Massachusetts for creating the "Safe Schools Initiative," a pilot program to prevent all forms of student harassment and hate crimes in the state's schools, including cyberbullying).

100. Megan Meier Cyberbullying Prevention Act, H.R 1966, 111th Cong. (2009).

101. Statement of Rep. Sanchez, at 22–23.

102. *Id.*

103. *See* Cyberbullying and Other Online Safety Issues for Children: Hearing Before the Subcommittee on Crime, Terrorism, and Homeland Security of the Committee on the Judiciary, House of Representatives, 111th Cong. 56–57 (2009) (statement of Harvey A. Silverplate, Attorney, Zillkind, Rodriguez, Lunt & Duncan, LLP, Cambridge, Mass.).

104. *See* Samir Hinduja & Justin W. Patchin, *State Cyberbullying Laws: A Brief Review of State Cyberbullying Laws and Policies*, Cyberbullying Res. Ctr. (July 2013), http://cyberbullying.us/Bullying_and_Cyberbullying_Laws. pdf. Only three states, Alaska, Montana, and Wyoming have anti-bullying statutes that do not specifically include the term "electronic harassment." Students who are victims of online bullying and harassment in those three states must look elsewhere for a legal cause of action, such as common law negligence. *See generally* Anne M. Payne, *Establishing Liability of a Public School District for Injuries or Damages to a Student Resulting from Bullying or Other Nonsexual Harassment by Another Student*, 105 Am. Jur. 3d Proof of Facts 93, 117–23 (2009) (discussing alternative legal avenues for young victims of bullying and harassment to bring legal claims).

nation's schools. As of 2020, 47 states and the District of Columbia have formally passed anti-bullying legislation that includes the term "electronic harassment" in its legislation.[105]

An important First Amendment constitutional consideration for states with anti-cyberbullying laws is whether the statutory language covers instances of cyberbullying originating on school grounds, off school grounds, or both. While there is existing U.S. Supreme Court precedent indicating that school officials have legal authority to regulate certain types of student speech originating on school grounds[106] and at school-sponsored activities,[107] the Court has not ruled on whether school officials have legal authority over student speech originating off school grounds. While there are a number of lower court cases involving the issue of student online speech and harassment, the legal decisions are inconsistent.

With regard to student cyberbullying incidents, it is clear that today's school officials have considerably more discretion to regulate student online speech originating from an on-campus or a school-sponsored location compared to student speech originating from an off-campus location. In terms of student online speech originating off campus, the lower courts are largely divided. For example, some lower courts require that the off-campus student online speech be "foreseeable" in order to have on-campus impact so that school officials have legal authority to regulate it.[108] Another legal split among today's lower courts involves student online speech

---

105. The 17 states that specifically include the word "cyberbullying" in their state anti-bullying statutes include: Arkansas (Ark. Code Ann. § 6-18-514 (a)(2) (2010)); California (Cal. Educ. Code § 32282(a)(1)(E) (2011)); Connecticut (Conn. Stat. Ann. § 10-222d (2012)); Florida (HB 609) (2013) (adds "cyberbullying to the anti-bullying statute and allows school officials to discipline students for their off-campus harassment, including online harassment that substantially interferes with or limits the victim's ability to participate in or benefit from the services, activities, or opportunities offered by a school or substantially disrupts the education process or orderly operation of the school."); Hawaii (Haw. Code Rev. § 8-19-13 (2012)); Kansas (Kan. Stat. Ann. § 72-8256(a)(1)(B) 2012)); Louisiana, (H.B. 1259, Act 989 ("Cyberbullying is the transmission of any electronic textual, visual, written, or oral communication with the malicious and willful intent to coerce, abuse, torment, or intimidate a person under the age of eighteen.")); Massachusetts (Mass. Gen. Laws Ann. Ch. 71§ 370 (2010)); Missouri (Mo. Rev. Stat. § 160.775(2) (2011)); Nevada (Nev. Rev. Stat. Ann. § 388.123 (2010)); New Hampshire (N.H. Rev. Stat. Ann. § 193–F:4 (2011)); North Carolina (N.C. Gen. Stat. § 115C-407.16 (2010)); Oregon (Or. Rev. Stat. § 339.356 (2010)); Tennessee (Tenn. Code Ann. § 49-6-1015–1016 (2011)); Utah (Utah Code Ann. § 53A-11A-301 (2011); Virginia (Va. Code Ann. § 22.1–279.6 (2011)); Washington (Wash. Rev. Code § 18-2C-3 (2011).

106. Hazelwood Sch. Dist. v. Kuhlmeier, 484 U.S. 260 (1988) (ruling that school officials can regulate student speech in school-sponsored newspapers); Bethel Sch. Dist. No. 403 v. Fraser, 478 U.S. 675 (1986) (holding that lewd and offensive student speech given at a school assembly can be disciplined).

107. Morse v. Frederick, 551 U.S. at 401, 408 (2007) (stating that a student "cannot stand in the midst of his fellow students, during school hours, at a school-sanctioned activity and claim he is not in school").

108. *See* Wisniewski v. Bd. of Educ. of Weedsport Central Sch. Dist., 494 F.3d 34, 38–40 (2d Cir. 2007) (indicating that *Tinker*'s student free speech "material and substantial disruption" standard

originating off-campus and whether there exists a "sufficient nexus" between the student's online speech and the school.[109]

The procedural due process requirements of notice and a right to be heard, articulated in *Goss*, still apply. Therefore, it is important that schools lay out a clear, direct policy on cyberbullying in their student handbook. In addition, all states have laws related to bullying, including cyberbullying, which must be considered in developing school policies.[110] It should be noted, however, that the North Carolina Supreme Court[111] struck down a state statute that attempted to criminalize cyberbullying, finding the law to be overbroad and not sufficiently specific.[112] Thus, it is equally important that school policies are neither overbroad nor too narrow to withstand legal scrutiny.

With this in mind, we recognize three caveats with respect to cyberbullying as opposed to traditional bullying. First, it may be much more difficult to identify the bully in a cyberbullying scenario. Second, cyberbullying is extremely difficult to ignore or avoid as it is so pervasive in our technologically dominated culture and subsequently our educational systems, thus further exacerbating an already serious situation. Third, if a student is sending these messages from home or another location outside the school, a First Amendment free speech interest or a Fourth Amendment school search issue may be at stake. These constitutional rights regarding technology are discussed below. In all bullying, there may be questions as to whether the school is liable for damages due to students being bullied. For the most part, schools are not financially responsible; however, these decisions, like most court opinions, are fact specific. In addition, if the bullying constitutes sexual harassment, then the school may well have a duty to protect. For these reasons, we strongly advise readers to consult Chapter 2 for a fuller discussion on liability.

The First Amendment and Technology

The use of technology in First Amendment school cases generally relates to text messaging and/or the creation of websites and whether or how the school can regulate such behavior, particularly if it originates away from campus. Most of these cases and their accompanying claims focus on freedom of speech guaranteed under

---

applied because it was reasonably foreseeable that the student's online speech would reach the school's campus).

109. *See* J.S. ex rel H.S. v. Bethlehem Area Sch. Dist., 807 A.2d 847 (Pa. 2002) (holding that the leading legal threshold question is whether there exists a "sufficient nexus" between the student's online speech and the school).

110. *See* Ari Ezra Waldman, *Are Anti-Bullying Laws Effective?*, 103 Cornell L. Rev. Online 135 (2018).

111. State v. Bishop, 787 S.E.2d 814 (N.C. 2016).

112. *See also* Nicholas McGuire, *Preserving the "Jewel of their Souls": How North Carolina's Common Law Could Save Cyber-Bullying Statutes*, 13 Duke J. Const. L. & Pub. Pol'y Sidebar 57 (2018); and Randall Morgan Briggs, *Criminalization of Cyberbullying: The Constitutionality of Creating an On-line Neverland for Children Under a Tinker-Bell Analysis*, 78 La. L. Rev. 1059 (2018).

the U.S. Constitution's First Amendment. Clearly, while not unlimited, students in public schools have free speech rights as evidenced by our discussion above.

On January 8, 2021, the U.S. Supreme Court granted certiorari to the Third Circuit's decision in *Mahanoy Area School District v. B.L.*,[113] a case directly involving the use of technology off school grounds. On June 23, 2021, the High Court ruled 8-1 in favor of the student. Prior to *Mahanoy*, claims related to technology were judged much the same as other student speech claims, employing standards set forth in *Tinker*, *Frasier*, *Hazelwood*, and/or *Morse*, with most lower courts relying on *Tinker*'s material and substantial-disruption test.

Just as in non-technology cases, the courts pay close attention to any behavior that may result in violence, whether it is through direct threats or cyberbullying. For example, in the Ninth Circuit case of *Wynar v. Douglas County School District*,[114] a Nevada high school student received a ten-day suspension and a 90-day expulsion after sending online text messages in which he bragged about his many weapons and threatened to shoot various classmates. Ruling for the school district, the court determined that these disciplinary procedures did not violate the student's constitutional right to free speech in that there was an identifiable threat of school violence and a material and substantial disruption to the school, even though the speech took place off campus. The court cited *LaVine*[115] (discussed earlier in this chapter), a non-technology-related ruling on whether poems that James LaVine showed his English teacher constituted a real threat. In *C.R. v. Eugene School District 4J*,[116] this same circuit ruled that a school district, this time in Oregon, could discipline a 12-year-old student for off-campus speech. The boy sexually harassed two disabled students on their way home from school. While technology was not involved, the court likened this case to that of *Wynar*,[117] where there was both a nexus and foreseeability to disruption in the school.

Similarly, in *Bell v. Itawamba County School Board*,[118] the Fifth Circuit Court of Appeals upheld the school's right to discipline a student who recorded a rap song that contained obscene language and threatened violence toward two high school coaches by name. The student recorded the song outside of school but posted it on his Facebook page. The court determined that school officials needed to act quickly when threats, intimidation, and harassment were at issue and that this student's behavior was severe enough to forecast substantial disruption in the school as required under *Tinker*. Four years later, in *Longoria v. San Benito Independent Consolidated School*

113. 964 F.3d 170 (3d Cir. 2020), *cert. granted*, Mahanoy Area Sch. Dist. v. B. L., 141 S.Ct. 976. (2021).

114. 728 F.3d 1062 (9th Cir. 2013).

115. 257 F.3d 981 (9th Cir. 2001), *rehearing en banc denied*, 279 F.3d 719 (9th Cir. 2002).

116. C.R. v. Eugene Sch. Dist. 4J, 835 F.3d 1142 (9th Cir. 2016).

117. 728 F.3d 1062 (9th Cir. 2013).

118. 799 F.3d 379 (5th Cir. 2015). *See also* Elizabeth A. Shaver, *Denying Certiorari in* Bell v. Itawamba County School Board: *A Missed Opportunity to Clarify Students' First Amendment Rights in the Digital Age*, 82 Brook. L. Rev. 1539 (2017).

District,[119] this same circuit ruled against a student who was relieved of her cheerleading duties due to remarks made on her Twitter account. The court distinguished this case from *Itawamba* because the student was merely deprived of participation in an extracurricular activity, not suspended from school; however, the court expressed concern that there was no specific rule in making these determinations and so claims of qualified immunity would always succeed because the law was not clear.

Other cases have involved student-on-student cyber bullying. In *Kowalski v. Berkeley County Schools*,[120] a West Virginia case, the Fourth Circuit Court of Appeals ruled in favor of the school district when school officials suspended a student who ridiculed (bullied) another student using vulgar criticisms on her MySpace web page. The court concluded that even though the page was constructed in the student's home, it was directed at individuals in the school and, in accordance with the *Tinker* decision, affected the school's disciplinary process.

An Eighth Circuit case, *S.J.W. v. Lee's Summit R-7 School District*,[121] involved two male high school students (twins), the Wilsons, who created a website called NorthPress, which also contained a blog. The twins used a Dutch domain site, which prevented persons in the U.S. from finding the site through a Google search. United States' users could, however, access NorthPress if they knew the website address, which was not password protected. According to the Wilsons, the purpose of the blog was to discuss, satirize, and vent about happenings at their high school. The website included racist language which mocked black students as well as sexually explicit and degrading language about female students it identified by name. Ruling for the school district, the court determined that the website was targeted at the school. It caused material and substantial disruption in that teachers had difficulty controlling their classes because of the blog, and two teachers mentioned that this had been the most difficult time in all their years of teaching. While this case addressed injunctive relief, the court was clear in stating its belief that, under *Tinker*, the school district would prevail.

Some cases have involved technology aimed specifically at challenging administrative decisions, actions, or school policies. In *Doninger v. Niehoff*,[122] there was a dispute regarding the scheduling of Jamfest, an annual event that involved a battle of the bands. Jamfest was originally scheduled for a certain date in April in the school's new auditorium. Either the Jamfest had to be moved to the school cafeteria or the date had to be changed because the teacher responsible for operating the auditorium's sound and light equipment was not available on the scheduled date. Avery Doninger, class secretary, a member of the student council, and one of the organizers of the event, was upset that the event had been changed. After not being able to reach the principal immediately, she and three other student council members accessed a computerized mailing list from one of their father's accounts using a computer from the school's

119. 942 F.3d 258 (5th Cir. 2019).
120. 652 F.3d 565 (4th Cir. 2011).
121. 696 F.3d 771 (8th Cir. 2012).
122. 642 F.3d 334 (2d Cir. 2011).

computer lab. The e-mail urged recipients to contact the central office asking that Jamfest be held in the auditorium and to pass the e-mail on to others.

As a result of this correspondence, both the school's principal, Schwartz, and the district's superintendent, Niehoff, received numerous e-mails and telephone calls. Doninger also posted information on her blog referring to Schwartz as a "dirty whore" and those who "cancelled" the event as "douchebags." Due to her actions, school authorities prohibited Avery from appearing on the ballot for senior class president. During the election, students had planned to wear "Team Avery"[123] t-shirts to a gathering in the auditorium but were not allowed. They therefore protested verbally in a non-disruptive manner. Even though Doninger won based on write-in ballots, she was denied the position and sued the school district for violation of her First Amendment free speech rights. The Second Circuit Court of Appeals upheld the school district's disciplinary actions, noting that Doninger's behavior disrupted the student government process. The court, however, determined that the students should have been allowed to wear the "Team Avery" t-shirts, as there was no reason to believe they would cause a material and substantial disruption in the school.

In a few other technology-based cases, courts have found in favor of the students. For example, in *J.S. v. Blue Mountain School District*,[124] a middle school student constructed a fictitious profile of her school principal on MySpace.com. The profile did not identify the school and gave the principal a fake name and a false location (Alabama instead of Pennsylvania). The profile described the principal as a bisexual and a pedophile and made crude derogatory remarks about him and his family. In ruling for the student, the Third Circuit Court of Appeals maintained that the website was a parody so outrageous that no one could or did take it seriously, that it was done at the student's home on her parents' computer, and that it did not cause a material and substantial disruption in the school. The student had also tried to make the website private, and it was the principal who brought the actual profile into the school by requesting a printed copy from one of the students who had access. On the same day as this decision, the Third Circuit Court ruled similarly on *Layshock v. Hermitage School District*,[125] which involved a student's using his grandmother's computer to construct a parody of the school's principal. Under a *Tinker* analysis, the court found no material and substantial disruption in the school. Notably, the court did not apply *Fraser* based on the post's vulgarity, asserting that *Fraser* did not apply to off-campus speech.

In Indiana, school officials excluded students from extracurricular activities because they had posted suggestive, but not nude, pictures of themselves on the internet. In this case, *T.V. v. Smith-Green Community School Corporation*,[126] the pictures at issue were posted off campus during summer break. They caused no material and substantial disruption in the school. The court held that parental complaints

123. *Id.* at 340–41.

124. 650 F.3d 915 (3d Cir. 2011).

125. 650 F.3d 205 (3d Cir. 2011).

126. 807 F. Supp. 2d 767 (N.D. Ind. 2011).

and claims that this behavior brought dishonor to the school were not sufficient to deprive students of their rights to free speech. The court characterized the students' behavior as juvenile and silly but not rising to a level that denied them constitutional guarantees. A California federal district court used a slightly different rationale in *J.C. v. Beverly Hills Unified School District.*[127] Here, a student-made video impugning a fellow classmate was protected speech in that, even though it was briefly posted on YouTube, it did not cause material and substantial disruption in the school.

These decisions lead us to *Mahanoy Area School District v. B.L.*[128] Because this book went to press immediately after this ruling was rendered, we were unable to include the entire decision in this text, however we strongly suggest that you read this opinion. Depending on the facts of the case, if you are in a circuit where schools tend to strictly curtail students' off-campus free speech rights or have a more expansive view of "material and substantial disruption" than *Mahanoy*, you may want to carefully consider possible legal and policy implications.

As to the facts of the case, *Mahanoy* involved a freshman high school student who had been a junior varsity (J.V.) cheerleader and was told, along with another girl, that she would need to cheer at the J.V. level for one more year, even though another freshman was allowed to cheer with the senior varsity squad. One Saturday night, at home and away from school, B.L. vented her frustrations to some 250 "friends" on Snapchat, a smartphone application in which the messages exist only temporarily and do not appear on the internet. The message showed a picture of B.L. with her middle fingers raised and the caption, "F. . k school f. . k softball, f. . k cheer F. . k everything." A classmate who had received the message took a screen shot of it and showed it to two of the cheerleading coaches. The coaches removed B.L. from the J.V. cheerleading squad, and B.L. sued based on freedom of speech. B.L. won her First Amendment claims both in district court and in the Third Circuit Court of Appeals. She also won a nominal amount on her §1983 claims. The case was then accepted by the Supreme Court, which had yet to rule.

In summary, First Amendment freedom-of-speech claims involving cyberspace are analyzed much the same as those in non-technology-related cases. The fact that these communications are initiated off campus does not seem to matter as long as the actions create a material and substantial disruption in the school or that school authorities could reasonably foresee such disruption. Six different circuit courts (mentioned above) have ruled on student free speech cases involving cyberspace. From our perspective, the outcomes from these circuits as well as other lower courts seem to be relatively consistent with what is viewed as material and substantial disruption and what can be reasonably forecast as such. The court decisions, however, are very fact specific, and circuits vary in their handling of the *Tinker* standard.

127. 711 F. Supp. 2d 1094 (C.D. Cal. 2010).

128. 964 F.3d 170 (3d Cir 2020), 141 S.Ct. 2038 (2021).

For example, in *S.J.W.*, the case involving the twins' NorthStar Press blog, the Eighth Circuit used the *Tinker* test but looked to "foreseeability," while the Fourth Circuit in *Kowalski*, the case involving the bullying of another student on a home computer, applied a "sufficient nexus" threshold. The Ninth Circuit Court has combined these two approaches.[129] The Third Circuit differs from the others in that it appears to be more protective of students' rights. If your school is in one of these circuits, it is especially important to be aware of the facts of the cases and how your federal circuit has applied *Tinker*. In all instances, threats of violence using the internet are not protected speech if they meet the test for a true threat (i.e., the person intended harm even if the action was not carried out),[130] and under *Frederick v. Morse*, language condoning drug use can likely be regulated. Finally, it is crucial to understand the reasoning of the U.S. Supreme Court's decision in *Mahanoy* in that it is now binding on the entire country and could possibly overturn some of the circuit court decisions mentioned above.

To the extent that school administrators may legally access student websites under the First Amendment, one might then turn to the Fourth Amendment to ascertain the legality of performing searches of students' cell phone content or conducting other school searches related to the use of technology. This information and relevant court decisions are included in the next section following an overview of the Fourth Amendment and how it applies to schools.

The Fourth Amendment

Search and seizure in the public schools has long been a problem for both school authorities and law enforcement officers. In addition, students have been deprived of their constitutional rights as a result of some school searches. Much of this problem stems from lack of clarity in applying the Fourth Amendment to the school setting. The myriad of lower court holdings makes certainty of the law difficult. Judicial interpretations are often locally contradictory as they could rely on school policies and/or state law as well as federal law. This situation has confounded both school authorities and law-enforcement officials. Practices and procedures that were proper yesterday may be wrong today. While it would be infeasible and impractical to provide a comprehensive view of the hundreds of, often conflicting, court decisions on search and seizure in schools, there are some basic principles that can assist educators as they make school search decisions. This section provides such guidance.

Following an overview of the sources of search and seizure law, we will describe the outcomes and standards set forth in four U.S. Supreme Court decisions as well

129. *See* Jennifer Butwin, *Children Are Crying and Dying While the Supreme Court Is Hiding: Why Public Schools Should Have Broad Authority to Regulate Off-Campus Bullying "Speech,"* 87 Fordham L. Rev. 671 (2018).

130. Virginia v. Black, 538 U.S. 343 (2003).

as illustrative examples from lower court renderings. As with other types of law, it is important to keep in mind that U.S. Supreme Court decisions apply to everyone, federal appeals court rulings only govern those in that particular jurisdiction, and state court renderings are binding only in that state. (See Chapter 1 for a review of how this system works.)

Source of Search and Seizure Law

The Fourth Amendment to the Constitution of the United States is the source of search and seizure law. This Amendment states:

> The right of the people to be secure in their persons, houses, papers, and effects, against unreasonable searches and seizures, shall not be violated, and no warrants shall issue, but upon probable cause, supported by Oath or affirmation, and particularly describing the place to be searched and the persons or things to be seized.[131]

Originally, the Fourth Amendment was thought only to protect citizens from the federal government. However, in 1961 the Supreme Court held that the Amendment's protection extends to state action through the Fourteenth Amendment.[132] The Fourth Amendment exists to protect citizens against "unreasonable searches" by the government. Therefore, a search itself may be legal if it is reasonable. Determining what is "reasonable" has been the main problem for courts ruling on search and seizure cases.

While a citizen is protected against unreasonable searches, government has a need to enforce the law. The need for government to obtain information may outweigh individuals' needs to keep their privacy. The right of privacy is not absolute; it is relative. The degree of protection may depend on the purpose of the search, the person doing the searching, the place being searched, the background or type of person being searched, the severity of the penalties resulting from the search, and the extent to which the person's privacy was invaded by the searcher.

Regarding searches of adults, courts have balanced these variables in the process of determining whether "probable cause" exists. Finding probable cause, magistrates will issue a warrant. This process represents the preferred approach to searching since the Supreme Court has ruled that warrantless searches are *per se* violative of the Fourth Amendment. However, there are exceptions to the warrant requirement. They include but are not limited to (1) consent by the person to be searched, (2) the object of the search is in plain view, (3) an emergency situation exists (exigency)

---

131. U.S. CONST. Amend. IV.

132. Mapp v. Ohio, 367 U.S. 643 (1961). The Supreme Court held the Amendment itself applicable to the states in *Wolf v. Colorado*, 338 U.S. 25 (1949), but in that case the Court held that the exclusionary rule was not applicable to the states because the rule did not derive from the explicit requirements of the Fourth Amendment. This portion was explicitly overruled in *Mapp*.

where evidence could otherwise be lost, (4) a valid arrest has been made and the search is part of the arrest (incident to arrest), and (5) the search or seizure is necessary for the safety of the searcher.[133] Consent and incident to arrest do not need probable cause. The foregoing represents the basis of search and seizure law generally. This law cannot always be directly applied in the school setting. A wide range of different approaches are used when dealing with children in school.

Privacy Rights of Students and *New Jersey v. T.L.O.*

Until the 1980s, the courts were split on the question of whether the Fourth Amendment applied at all to students. Those who thought it did not apply advanced two theories. One theory was that school authorities are "private persons." Since the Fourth Amendment protects individuals against action by the government only, these restrictions do not extend to school officials. The second theory involved the notion of *in loco parentis*. Literally translated from the Latin, "in place of parents," the doctrine states:

> The parent may also delegate part of his parental authority, during his life, to the tutor or the schoolmaster of his child; who is then *in loco parentis*, and has such a portion of power of the parent committed to his charge, *viz* that of restraint and correction, as may be necessary to answer the purposes for which he is employed.[134]

The Fourth Amendment and its probable cause requirement could be set aside if school authorities were thought to be acting "in the place of parents" and not as government officials. The position that students have no privacy rights was rejected by *New Jersey v. T.L.O.*[135] **[*See* Case No. 4-8.]**

The Case of T.L.O.

The *T.L.O.* case involved a 14-year-old female Piscataway (New Jersey) High School student. (The Court used the initials "T.L.O." to keep the identity of this minor student anonymous.) On March 7, 1980, she was caught smoking in the lavatory by a teacher. T.L.O. was with a companion student who was also apprehended. Since school rules prohibited smoking in the restroom, the teacher took both girls to the office. The girls were questioned by the assistant principal. T.L.O.'s companion admitted to the infraction but T.L.O. denied she had been smoking.

The assistant principal demanded to see T.L.O.'s purse and found a pack of cigarettes. Other suspicious material was uncovered by removing the cigarettes. He

133. *See* Illinois v. Rodriguez, 497 U.S. 177 (1990) (consent); Horton v. California, 496 U.S. 128 (1990) (plain view); Kentucky v. King, 563 U.S. 452 (2011) (exigency); Arizona v. Gant, 556 U.S. 332 (2009) (valid arrest); Terry v. Ohio, 392 U.S.1 (1968) (safety of searcher).

134. 12 William Blackstone, Commentaries at 453 (1769).

135. 469 U.S. 325 (1985).

noticed cigarette rolling papers which he assumed meant marijuana was involved. Searching further, he found marijuana, 41 dollar bills, and a pipe typically used for smoking hash. In a separate zippered compartment of the purse he found an index card with a written heading, "People who owe me money." The card contained a list of names with dollar amounts next to each name. In the separate compartment were two letters that discussed marijuana business. The assistant principal telephoned T.L.O.'s mother who drove her to the police station.

T.L.O. admitted that she sold marijuana to other students. She was then suspended for three days for smoking cigarettes in a non-smoking area and seven days for possession of marijuana. Also, she was charged by the police with delinquency based on the physical evidence submitted by the assistant principal and on her confession. At the delinquency hearing, T.L.O. contended that the search of the purse violated her Fourth Amendment privacy rights and, therefore, the evidence and her confession should be excluded. However, the juvenile court found T.L.O. delinquent. On appeal, the New Jersey Supreme Court reversed, holding that the evidence had been obtained in violation of T.L.O.'s constitutional rights.

The State of New Jersey appealed the decision to the United States Supreme Court. The state asked the Court to decide the single issue of whether the exclusionary rule applies to evidence obtained by school officials in violation of the Fourth Amendment. In other words, should a juvenile court throw out evidence seized by school authorities because it finds there was no probable cause, the standard which the police must follow? After hearing arguments, the Court decided not to rule on the issue. Instead, it ordered re-argument on whether the Fourth Amendment applies in the school setting. If it does, to what degree and by what standards does it apply?

Do Students Have a Right to Privacy?

The Supreme Court in *T.L.O.* took its position on student privacy rights as they fashioned answers to the questions posed. New Jersey had argued that the Fourth Amendment did not apply because of the *in loco parentis* doctrine. Writing for the majority, Justice White rejected the argument and maintained that school authorities are state officials, not stand-ins for parents:

> If school authorities are state actors for purposes of the constitutional guarantees of freedom of expression and due process, it is difficult to understand why they should be deemed to be exercising parental rather than public authority when conducting searches of their students.... In carrying out searches and other disciplinary functions ... school officials act as representatives of the [s]tate, not merely as surrogates for the parents, and they cannot claim the parents' immunity from the strictures of the Fourth Amendment.[136]

136. *Id.* at 336–37.

Therefore, the Fourth Amendment does indeed apply to the school setting. Its application extends to school authorities as a limitation on their search activities and to students as a protection from unreasonable searches. Having established that the Fourth Amendment applied, the Court went on to point to some of the privacy rights of students under the Constitution.

New Jersey had maintained that students have no privacy rights at all because of the special relationship between students and school authorities. The state argued that because of the high level of supervision schools must maintain over students, there is "virtually no legitimate expectation of privacy in articles of personal property 'unnecessarily' carried into a school."[137] The New Jersey argument was founded on two premises: (1) A student having an expectation of privacy is incompatible with the school trying to maintain a sound educational environment, and (2) a student has little need to bring items of personal property into the school.

Once again, the Court rejected the New Jersey argument, stating, "Both premises are severely flawed."[138] Although Justice White sympathized with the job the schools do in maintaining order, that duty is not so great as to cancel out students' privacy rights. As to students having no need to bring personal property to school, White criticized New Jersey for not being realistic. He wrote:

> Nor does the State's suggestion that children have no legitimate need to bring personal property into the schools seem well anchored in reality. Students at a minimum must bring to school not only the supplies needed for their studies, but also keys, money, and the necessaries of personal hygiene and grooming. In addition, students may carry on their persons or in purses or wallets such nondisruptive yet highly personal items as photographs, letters, and diaries. Finally, students may have perfectly legitimate reasons to carry with them articles of property needed in connection with extracurricular or recreational activities. In short, school children may find it necessary to carry with them a variety of legitimate, non-contraband items, and there is no reason to conclude that they have necessarily waived all rights to privacy in such items merely by bringing them onto school grounds.[139]

Therefore, students do have privacy rights for certain items they bring to school; however, the expectation of privacy is not limitless. Justice White stated that the Fourth Amendment does not provide privacy for contraband: "Of course the Fourth Amendment does not protect subjective expectations of privacy that are unreasonable or otherwise 'illegitimate.' To receive the protection of the Fourth Amendment, an expectation of privacy must be one that society is 'prepared to recognize as legitimate.'"[140]

137. *Id.* at 338.
138. *Id.*
139. *Id.* at 339.
140. *Id.* at 338.

Justice White returned to the discipline issue, perhaps to make sure that sufficient deference was paid to school authorities' difficult task in maintaining order. The proper perspective is to recognize that a student has some privacy rights but not to the extent where schools would be hampered in maintaining an orderly environment:

> Against the child's interest in privacy must be set the substantial interest of teachers and administrators in maintaining discipline in the classroom and on school grounds. Maintaining order in the classroom has never been easy, but in recent years, school disorder has often taken particularly ugly forms: drug use and violent crime in the schools have become major social problems. Even in schools that have been spared the most severe disciplinary problems, the preservation of order and a proper educational environment requires close supervision of school children, as well as the enforcement of rules against conduct that would be permissible if undertaken by an adult. "Events calling for discipline are frequent occurrences and sometimes require immediate effective action." Accordingly, we have recognized that maintaining security and order in the schools requires a certain degree of flexibility in school disciplinary procedures, and we have respected the value of preserving the informality of the student-teacher relationship.[141]

For the remainder of the case, the Court's task was to determine how to strike a balance between the interests of the school in maintaining order and the student in retaining some privacy rights.

The Reasonableness Standard

Attempting to strike an appropriate balance between the competing interests of the school and students, the *T.L.O.* Court proposed the reasonableness standard. It said that the higher probable cause standard which police must follow is unsuited to the school environment. School officials do not need to obtain a warrant before searching a student. The Court felt that requiring a search warrant and/or probable cause would interfere with the maintenance of the swift and informal disciplinary procedures needed in the schools. The better rule, the Court held, is that the legality of a search of a student should depend simply on the reasonableness under all the circumstances of the search. In using the reasonableness standard, a two-part analytical device was offered. First, was the search justified at its inception? In other words, did the searcher have reasonable suspicion? Second, was the search reasonable in scope—that is, was the search more intensive than it had to be? Further, was the type of search related to the object to be found? Elaboration on the use of these two analytical prongs is needed. A good beginning might be to see how the Supreme Court applied the reasonableness standard to the facts in *T.L.O.*

141. *Id.* at 339–40 (citation omitted).

Applying the Reasonableness Standard in T.L.O.

Applying the two-pronged reasonableness standard, the Court had no difficulty in upholding the search of T.L.O. The justices viewed the assistant principal as having conducted two searches: one for the cigarettes and one for the marijuana and related evidence. In the first search, the assistant principal had reasonable suspicion to enter T.L.O.'s purse. She had been caught "red handed" by a certificated teacher. T.L.O. argued that mere possession of cigarettes was not an infraction, and therefore the assistant principal had no reason to go into her purse since he could not have known that cigarettes were there. The Court responded by giving a lesson on the rules of evidence:

> But it is universally recognized that evidence, to be relevant to an inquiry, need not conclusively prove the ultimate fact in issue, but only to have any tendency to make the existence of any fact that is of consequence to the determination of the action more probable or less probable than it would be without the evidence.[142]

Therefore, the assistant principal might have been able to corroborate the teacher's report of unauthorized smoking by entering the purse. The kind of "hair-splitting" approach that New Jersey argued should have been used has no place in the school setting. Rather, the Court supported the position that school officials should simply use their good judgment in approaching the reasonable suspicion standard. Justice White wrote: "It was the sort of 'common sense conclusion[s] about human behavior' upon which 'practical people' including government officials are entitled to rely."[143] The question of reasonable scope did not enter into consideration until the second search.

The second search was also found to be reasonable (at its inception and in its scope). In picking up the pack of cigarettes, rolling papers were exposed. In the administrator's experience, the presence of rolling papers meant marijuana could be involved. After discovering the marijuana and a quantity of cash, the assistant principal was encouraged that further searching would be necessary to provide supporting evidence that T.L.O. was a drug trafficker. When he opened the zippered compartment of the purse, the Court concluded this was a reasonable extension of his previous discoveries. When the administrator found a list of names and two letters, the evidence was substantial enough to justify examination of the private correspondence. Therefore, the assistant principal had reasonable suspicion for the second search. Although T.L.O. argued that the seizing and reading of her private letters exceeded reasonable scope, the Court rejected her position by pointing to the overall reasonableness with which the assistant principal conducted the searches. The Court did not feel that reading the letters was too intrusive given the preceding evidence.

In sum, the search of T.L.O. met the reasonableness standard. First, reasonable suspicion was met because there were reasonable grounds for suspecting that

142. *Id.* at 345.

143. *Id.* at 346 (citing United States v. Cortez, 449 U.S. 411, 418 (1981)).

searching T.L.O.'s purse would turn up evidence to corroborate a teacher's report of wrongdoing. Second, the search was reasonable in scope since the measures adopted (going through the purse) were directly related to turning up evidence in support of T.L.O.'s suspected infraction.

Elaborating on the Two-Pronged Test

While the *T.L.O.* decision gave credence to the reasonableness standard, the facts of the case do not encompass all the search and seizure circumstances occurring in public schools. For example, the *T.L.O.* Court specifically stated that this decision did not apply directly to searches that are more intrusive or less intrusive than that of T.L.O., such as strip searches or locker searches. The *T.L.O.* decision also did not address the issue of police involvement in the schools and what standards apply in these situations. The issue of group searches *without* individualized suspicion was not addressed as the search in *T.L.O.* was based on individualized suspicion. Thus, the Supreme Court left in place considerable case law provided by lower courts. The *T.L.O.* Court's primary contribution was to provide an analytical framework for deciding search and seizure issues in the public schools. In the years following the decision, lower courts have applied its framework to a variety of situations, including those mentioned above.

In their monograph, *Search and Seizure in Public Schools*,[144] Rossow and Stefkovich recommend that practitioners keep several factors in mind as they apply the reasonableness standard to a search and seizure situation. In this respect, Rossow developed the **TIPS formula**. First, there must be reasonable suspicion that the search will turn up evidence. To meet this reasonableness test, the searcher should remember **TI** of the **TIPS** formula. "T" stands for *thing.* What thing (kind of contraband) are you searching for? The more dangerous the thing for which you are searching the less suspicion is required. Next, the searcher should remember "I," which stands for *information.* What information does the searcher have that the contraband exists? Who gave that information to the searcher? Does it come from a reliable source? If the searcher has a good information base, it will help in meeting the suspicion test.

After the suspicion test is met, the searcher must meet the scope test. To meet reasonable scope, the searcher should remember **PS** of the **TIPS** formula. "**P**" stands for *place or person.* Whether the searcher is searching a person or an object (place) will dictate the extent to which the expectation of privacy can be intruded upon. As the search becomes more personal, school officials should have more serious reasons for conducting the search. A highly intrusive search should not be conducted on a student's person if there is only a minor violation at stake. "**S**" stands for *search methods*. A searcher can conduct a search by asking the student to empty a pocket all the way or to take off his or her clothes, for example. The methods used in the

144. Lawrence F. Rossow & Jacqueline A. Stefkovich, Search and Seizure in Public Schools (2014), Education Law Association.

personal search should be no more intrusive than necessary to get the evidence. The searcher must keep in mind the age and sex of the student when deciding on a search method. The younger the student, the less flexibility the searcher has in using a highly intrusive method such as a sniffing dog. Also, when possible, the sex of the searcher should be the same as the student.

The Fourth Amendment and Technology

To the extent that school administrators may legally access student websites under the First Amendment, one might then turn to the Fourth Amendment and the reasonableness standard, articulated by the U.S. Supreme Court in *New Jersey v. T.L.O.*,[145] to ascertain the legality of searching through student information. In other words, was the search justified at its inception and was it reasonable in scope? Accessing content on the website or social media would then be judged much the same as any other search and/or seizure claim. To determine what is reasonable, the *T.L.O.* Court balanced the student's expectation of privacy with school officials' responsibility to maintain order and discipline. One way in which some schools have used technology to ensure safety is through use of surveillance cameras. School authorities, however, must keep in mind the purpose of these cameras and the need to ensure students' privacy. The Sixth Circuit Court's decision in *Brannum v. Overton County School Board*[146] provides some insight into this issue.

In *Brannum*, 34 middle school students sued school officials for installing and operating surveillance cameras in areas of the boys' and girls' school locker rooms designated for changing clothes. The students claimed their constitutional rights to privacy were violated when school officials viewed and retained the captured images. The district court stated that the installation of surveillance cameras for security purposes was justified but that the camera's placement and subsequent operation was inconsistent with the intended purpose of enhanced security. The Sixth Circuit Court agreed. While granting qualified immunity to school board members and others less directly involved, the appeals court denied qualified immunity to the middle school principal and assistant principal who were involved in the decision to install the cameras and who determined their location.[147] Another case, this one in Pennsylvania, resulted in the school district paying money damages related to the use of webcam information. In this instance, school officials in the Lower Merion School District monitored students at home through cameras in computers provided to students by the school.[148]

---

145. 469 U.S. 325 (1985).

146. 516 F.3d 489 (6th Cir. 2008).

147. *Id.* at 491.

148. Robbins v. Lower Merion Sch. Dist., No. 10-665, 2010 WL 3421026 (E.D. Pa. Aug. 30, 2010). *See also* Hasan v. Lower Merion Sch. Dist., No. 2:2010cv03663 (E.D. Pa. July 27, 2010) (claiming that under the April 2010 order in the *Robbins* case, which required the school district to offer students the opportunity to view images captured from their laptops, Jalil Hasan learned that the webcam

The most common types of searches involving technology have to do with cell phones owned by or in the possession of students. As may seem obvious, it is critically important that school districts have a technology-use policy and that they follow it consistently. Beyond this, seizures of cell phones and searches of the information in these phones fall under the *T.L.O.* standard for reasonableness.[149] In conducting such searches, however, educators must be aware that searching an individual's phone is a very intrusive type of search. In *Riley v. California*,[150] a 2014 U.S. Supreme Court decision addressing police searches of adults' cell phones, the Court ruled that police officers must have a warrant before searching a suspect's cell phone. A possible exception would be "fact-specific threats" of a risk indicating exigent circumstances. While this was not a school case, and school officials do not need a warrant to search students' cell phones, it is nonetheless important to understand the gravity of this type of search. In this respect, the *Riley* Court noted that every aspect of a person's life can be in their cell phone, from medical records to political affiliations, to sexual interests. Cell phones can contain much more personal information than revealed in a diary or a ransacking of one's house.

The court's decision in *Klump v. Nazareth Area School District*[151] illustrates how the *T.L.O.* standard is applied to phones. In this case, a student's cell phone rang in class, which justified confiscation of the phone, as cell phone display or use in classrooms was a violation of school policy. A federal court in the Eastern District of Pennsylvania ruled that a subsequent search of the student's cell phone, which included reviewing text messages and listening to voice mails, was not reasonable because school officials had "no reason to suspect at the outset" that such a search would reveal that the student "was violating *another* school policy."[152] This search was unreasonable at its inception and in scope.

In another lower court case, *J.W. v. Desoto County School District*,[153] a student was caught violating school policy when he opened his cell phone to read a text message during class. The teacher searched the student's cell phone and viewed several personal photos, including one photo showing another student holding a B.B. gun. Based on the discovery of this photo, the student was expelled. Applying *T.L.O.*'s two-pronged "reasonable suspicion" test, the court upheld both the school's search and seizure of the cell phone. The court surmised that it was reasonable for a school official to try to

---

on his laptop took approximately 469 photographs, at both school and home, over the course of two months. Another 543 screen shots were stored on the school district's servers.).

149. *See generally* Bernard James, T.L.O. *and Cell Phones: Student Privacy and Smart Devices After* Riley v. California, 101 Iowa L. Rev. 343 (2015); Marc C. McAllister, *Rethinking Student Cell Phone Searches*, 121 Penn St. L. Rev. 309 (2016); and Nicholas J. McGuire, *Dialing It Back: Why Courts Should Rethink Students' Privacy and Speech Rights as Cell Phone Communications Erode the "Schoolhouse Gate,"* 17 Duke L. & Tech. Rev. 1 (2018).

150. 573 U.S. 373 (2014).

151. 425 F. Supp. 2d 622 (E.D. Pa. 2006).

152. *Id.* at 640.

153. No. 2:09-cv-00155-MPM-DAS, 2010 WL 4394059 (N.D. Miss. Nov. 1, 2010).

determine why a student was improperly using his cell phone. The court distinguished this case from *Klump*, where the student unintentionally violated the school's cell phone policy; in *J.W.*, the student knowingly violated the school's cell phone policy.

N.N. v. Tunkhannock Area School District[154] demonstrates the complications and liability that can arise when school officials begin to search through a student's phone. Filed in Pennsylvania, the case involves a teacher who confiscated N.N.'s cell phone. The 17-year-old senior was using the phone in violation of a school policy that prohibited use of cell phones on school grounds. Later that day, the principal informed N.N. that he had found "explicit" photos stored on her cell phone. The photos, which were intended to be seen only by N.N. and her boyfriend, were not visible on the phone's screen and required multiple steps to locate. On September 15, 2010, the Pennsylvania branch of the American Civil Liberties Union (ACLU) reached a settlement with the school district whereby the school district denied liability for any wrongdoing but would pay the student and her lawyers $33,000 to resolve the dispute.[155]

In *Koch v. Adams*,[156] the Arkansas Supreme Court upheld a school district's confiscation of a student's cell phone. Nancy Adams, a teacher at Sylvan Hills High School (SHHS), discovered that one of her students, Anthony Koch, had his cellphone in her classroom in violation of district policy. Ms. Adams asked for Koch's cell phone. Before surrendering his phone, Koch requested that he be able to remove the phone's SIM card where he stored personal information. The teacher refused his request and Koch reluctantly handed over the phone, which was then given to the school principal where it remained in the district's possession for two weeks pursuant to district policy. Koch's parents filed suit against the district, alleging the cell phone confiscation was an "illegal taking" of the student's personal property without proper due process of law. In response, the district moved to dismiss the complaint. The Arkansas Supreme Court upheld the student's cell phone confiscation, reasoning that, in the state of Arkansas, school districts have broad discretion to direct the operation of schools, and courts have no legal authority to interfere with district operations unless there is evidence of "clear abuse" of that discretion.[157] Additionally, the court dismissed Koch's due process claim on the grounds that Koch did not support his argument. Unlike the decision in *Klump*, the *Koch* ruling maintains that the district did not exceed its legal authority by confiscating the student's cell phone. Also, Koch's cell phone was never searched while Klump's phone was searched.

G.C. v. Owensboro Public Schools[158] represents the first decision from a federal circuit court addressing the constitutionality of student cell phone searches under

---

154. 801 F. Supp. 2d 312 (M.D. Pa. 2011)

155. Press Release, *ACLU Settles Student-Cell-Phone-Search Lawsuit with Northeast Pennsylvania School District*, ACLU (Sep. 15, 2010), https://www.aclu.org/press-releases/aclu-settles-student-cell-phone-search-lawsuit-northeast-pennsylvania-school-district.

156. 361 S.W.3d 817 (Ark. 2010).

157. *Id.* at 818.

158. 711 F.3d 623 (6th Cir. 2013).

the Fourth Amendment. Here, the Sixth Circuit court held that a student cell-phone search conducted by an assistant principal resulted in an unreasonable search by failing to satisfy *T.L.O.*'s two-pronged test for reasonable suspicion.[159] G.C., a high school student attending the Owensboro Public School District, voluntarily revealed in a conversation with his assistant principal that "he used drugs and was disposed to anger and depression" and "he had a plan to take his life."[160] The assistant principal immediately notified G.C.'s parents that their son should see a mental health professional, and G.C. was taken to a mental health treatment facility the same day.

The following school year, G.C. was experiencing serious behavioral and disciplinary problems. In a meeting with the assistant principal, G.C. again voluntarily disclosed that he was experiencing suicidal thoughts. Shortly after this discussion, school officials confiscated G.C's cell phone according to school policy. The phone was given to the assistant principal, who reviewed and read multiple text messages allegedly checking for suicide-related references. In a separate incident, G.C. was disciplined by one of his teachers for texting in class in violation of school policy. His cell phone was confiscated and another assistant principal at the high school read several text messages on his cell phone to "see if there was an issue with which [she] could help [G.C.] so that [G.C.] would not do something harmful to himself or someone else."[161] The assistant principal claimed that she had prior knowledge of G.C.'s history of discussing suicidal tendencies.

Based on the second occurrence of having his cell phone confiscated, G.C., a non-resident of the district, had his privilege of attending an out-of-district school rescinded. At a formal disciplinary hearing a year later, G.C. was denied attendance at Owensboro High School. Shortly thereafter, G.C. filed a lawsuit claiming the high school violated his First, Fourth, and Fifth Amendment rights as well as state constitutional rights. More specifically, G.C. alleged that his cell phone search was unconstitutional because "it was not supported by a reasonable suspicion that would justify school officials reading his text messages."[162] In response, the school argued "the searches were limited and aimed at uncovering any evidence of illegal activity or any indication that G.C. might hurt himself."[163]

The Sixth Circuit applied the *T.L.O.* test for reasonable suspicion and cited *Brannon v. Overton*[164] in determining whether the search of G.C.'s cell phone was constitutional. The court noted that "[a] student search is justified in its inception when there are reasonable grounds for suspecting that the search will garner evidence that a student has violated or is violating the law or the rules of the school, *or is in imminent danger of injury on school premises*" (emphasis added) and that a search is

159. *Id.* at 627.
160. *Id.* at 628.
161. *Id.*
162. *Id.* at 632.
163. *Id.*
164. 516 F.3d 489 (6th Cir. 2008).

reasonable if "the measures adopted are . . . not excessively intrusive in light of the age and sex of the student and the *nature of the infraction*"[165] (emphasis original).

Next, the court turned to the lower court opinions in *J.W.*[166] and *Klump*.[167] The appeals court criticized the *J.W.* decision, which held that a district may reasonably search a student's cell phone if the student is using it in violation of school policy. According to the *G.C.* court, students' using their cell phones in violation of school policy "does not automatically trigger an essentially unlimited right enabling a school official to search any content stored on the phone that is not related either substantively or temporarily to the infraction."[168]

Instead, the Sixth Circuit judges relied on the legal analysis in *Klump*. While the court in *Klump* acknowledged that school officials were justified in confiscating a student's cell phone in violation of school policy, it also held that school officials overstepped their legal authority by searching the student's cell phone and calling other students from the student's cell phone to determine whether they had also violated school policies. According to the *Klump* decision, "the court must consider only that which the officials knew at the inception of the search."[169] As a result, the information discovered subsequent to the initial search of Klump's cell phone could not be used against the student. The Sixth Circuit's decision in *G.C.* sends a cautionary message to today's school officials by narrowing the range of circumstances in which school officials can legally conduct intrusive student cell phone searches.

Our point here is not to discourage school officials from searching students' cell phones if there is an imminent danger to other students or staff or an emergency but to indicate that a student cell-phone search is not the same as searching a student's purse, as in the *T.L.O.* decision. Rather, such searches may be more similar to student strip searches in that the level of intrusion can be quite high depending upon the intensity of a search and what potentially could be found, such as weapons or drugs. Importantly, if school officials find a lost cell phone, they may search the phone but only to ascertain its owner.

Students and Drug and Alcohol Use

There has been considerable judicial interest regarding students' use and possession of drugs. Case law in this regard takes three forms: (1) searches of individual students for drug possession, (2) drug testing of individual students, and (3) mass or random drug testing of students.

165. 711 F.3d at 633 (citing *Brannum*, 516 F.3d at 495–96).

166. J.W. v. Desoto Cty. Sch. Dist., No. 2:09-cv-00155-MPM-DAS, 2010 WL 4394059 (N.D. Miss. Nov. 1, 2010).

167. Klump v. Narareth Area Sch. Dist., 425 F. Supp. 2d 622 (E.D. Pa. 2006).

168. 711 F.3d 634.

169. *Id.* (quoting *Klump*, 425 F. Supp. 2d 622 (E.D. Pa. 2006)).

Searches of Individual Students for Drugs

A preponderance of Fourth Amendment cases dealing with public school students are aimed at suspected drug possession and confiscation of drugs or drug paraphernalia. Searches of individual students for drugs or to validate drug use are based on the two-fold standard set forth in the *New Jersey v. T.L.O.* decision discussed above, i.e., the search must be justified at its inception and reasonable in scope.

Observable symptoms have served to justify reasonable suspicion when searching for drugs. For example, in *Commonwealth v. J.B.*,[170] Singleton, a school police officer, noticed a student staggering with his eyes closed and exhibiting slurred speech. Singleton took the student to the office and ordered him to remove everything from his pockets. Finding nothing, he shook the student's pants and found a bag of marijuana. A Pennsylvania state appellate court held that it was reasonable, in view of the student's behavior, for Singleton to suspect that a search would turn up evidence of a violation of the law.

Suspicious behavior has also provided justification to search. In some of these cases, students were suspected of a lesser offense, such as cigarette smoking in violation of a school rule. For example, in a Wisconsin decision, *State v. Marola*,[171] a teacher entered the bathroom where Marola, a student, was present. Smelling smoke and considering Marola's previous citation for smoking in school, the teacher asked Marola to empty his pockets. Marola produced a large black wallet. The teacher asked Marola to open it and when he did, a bag of marijuana fell out. Marola was charged with possessing drugs within 1000 feet of school. The court held that the search was reasonable under the two-pronged *T.L.O.* standard: the initial request for the student to empty his pockets was justified, and the opening of the wallet was sufficiently related to the initial suspicion that Marola was smoking.

Another Wisconsin case, *In re David J.M.*,[172] involved a police officer on a routine bike patrol of the high school, who saw a student, David J.M., put his hand in his pocket suspiciously. Upon confrontation, David stated that he had put a cigarette in his pocket. David then pulled out a bag of marijuana, which he had tried to conceal in his hand, after the officer asked him to empty his pockets. The court held that the stop was reasonable in that the search was proportional to that stop and incident to the arrest for possession of tobacco by a minor. Because David had reason to believe he was in custody during the confrontation with the officer, this gave the officer the right to search further. Thus, the evidence should not be suppressed.

---

170. 719 A.2d 1058 (Pa. Super. 1998).

171. 582 N.W.2d 505 (Wis. Ct. App.), *cert. denied*, 585 N.W.2d 159 (Wis. 1998).

172. 587 N.W.2d 458 (Wis. Ct. App. 1998), *cert. denied*, 594 N.W.2d 384 (Wis. 1999).

Drug Testing of Individual Students

If school officials suspect an individual student of drug use, then the two-pronged test provided by the *T.L.O.* Court applies in determining the legality of the search. Generally, in these cases, the search is justified by observation of symptoms. Some cases also involve subsequent verification by a school health practitioner. *Anable v. Ford*,[173] a decision rendered shortly after *New Jersey v. T.L.O.*, employed the reasonable suspicion standard to determine whether subjecting students to either urinalysis or a breathalyzer violated the Fourth Amendment. The *Anable* court decided that the urinalysis was unreasonable. Even though school officials had reasonable suspicion to believe two students were smoking marijuana, the method of obtaining urine, which involved students stripping entirely below the waist and urinating in the presence of a same-sex monitor, was considered overly intrusive in light of the age of the students.[174] The breathalyzer test, while also subject to Fourth Amendment standards, was legal because both the student and his mother gave consent. In addition, the court pointed out that the student's erratic behavior along with the smell of alcohol on his breath was sufficient to justify punishment even without the breathalyzer results.[175]

Similarly, in *Bridgman*,[176] a male high school student exhibited what appeared to be signs of drug use. These included alleged unruly behavior, dilated pupils, bloodshot eyes, and giggling. As a result, the student was subjected to a "medical assessment" by the school's Health Service Coordinator and was searched by the school's Student Assistance Program Coordinator, who had initially noticed his behavior. The Seventh Circuit court determined that the actions the school-district personnel took were reasonable based on the student's demonstrated symptoms, that the search and ordering of a medical assessment were legal, and that the school's policy requiring written reports about student searches was constitutional.

Likewise, in *Hedges*,[177] the Third Circuit held that it was reasonable for a principal to require a female student to submit to a urinalysis. This action was based on a teacher's observation of the student's behavior and the school nurse's examination of the student which involved observation of the behavior, the taking of vital signs, and the discovery of pills of an undetermined origin in the student's purse.

Random or Mass Drug Testing of Students

The most important cases regarding students and drugs have involved random or mass drug testing. Within seven years, between 1995 and 2002, the U.S. Supreme Court rendered two decisions involving random drug testing of students

173. 653 F. Supp. 22 (W.D. Ark. 1985).
174. *Id.* at 41.
175. *Id.* at 36–37.
176. Bridgman *ex rel* Bridgman v. New Trier High Sch. Dist. No. 203, 128 F.3d 1146 (7th Cir. 1997).
177. Hedges *ex rel* C.D. v. Musco, 204 F.3d 109 (3d Cir. 2000).

in public schools. The first decision, *Vernonia Sch. Dist. 47J v. Acton*,[178] involved student athletes. The second, *Board of Education of Independent School District No. 92 of Pottawatomie County v. Earls*,[179] addressed students involved in extracurricular activities. Before examining these two Supreme Court opinions in any detail, it is important to understand the background leading up to these decisions.

The Supreme Court case of *Vernonia v. Acton* emerged from a split in two federal circuit courts. In 1988, in *Schaill v. Tippecanoe*,[180] the Seventh Circuit ruled that the school's random urine testing of student athletes was a legal search. They based their reasoning on the school's interest in preventing drug-related injuries, the fact that student athletes are role models for other school students, and because the intrusion into privacy is lessened in light of other physical examinations required of student athletes. A year later, in a case with a similar fact pattern, *Acton v. Vernonia*,[181] the Ninth Circuit struck down an Oregon school district's random drug testing program, maintaining that it was unconstitutional. The school district appealed this decision to the United States Supreme Court, which granted certiorari.

In *Vernonia School District 47J v. Acton*,[182] [***see* Case No. 4-9**] the Court ruled that drug testing of student athletes without individualized suspicion was legal under certain circumstances. Determining that the district's program was constitutional, the Court contended that there were drug problems in the school and that student athletes have a reduced expectation of privacy. Here, the Court applied a three-pronged test making the legality of the search contingent upon the need for the drug testing, the expectation of privacy of the persons to be tested, and the obtrusiveness of the search.[183] The Court did not rule explicitly on whether or how this decision might be applied to other student groups or to other types of mass searches, such as metal detector searches or random locker searches.

The Court used a test based on its earlier decisions relating to the drug testing of adults such as railroad employees[184] and customs officials.[185] First, the Court looked at the nature of the privacy interest. The justices concluded that student athletes have a decreased expectation of privacy due to regulations imposed upon them requiring routine physical examinations as well as their being subjected to communal undress in locker rooms. Second, the Court examined the character of the intrusion, noting that the searches were conducted in a manner that rendered them relatively unobtrusive. Third, the Court turned to the nature and immediacy of the

178. 515 U.S. 646 (1995).
179. 536 U.S. 822 (2002).
180. 864 F.2d 1309 (7th Cir. 1988).
181. 23 F.3d 1514 (1994).
182. 515 U.S. 646 (1995).
183. *Id.* at 648–65.
184. Skinner v. Railway Lab. Execs. Ass'n, 489 U.S. 602 (1989).
185. National Treasury Employees' Union v. Von Raab, 489 U.S. 656 (1989).

government concern and maintained that conditions in the district demonstrated a need for the drug-testing program.[186]

After *Vernonia,* lower courts grappled with cases involving a variety of fact patterns related to whether or how the *Vernonia* opinion could be extended. The majority of these cases addressed drug testing of students involved in extracurricular activities. Here, for a variety of reasons, courts were divided as to whether such programs were legal. Some courts simply maintained that the *Vernonia* standard did not apply to students involved in extracurricular activities, i.e., that such activities were somehow different than athletics. Others applied the *Vernonia* standard but found that the facts of the case did not pass *Vernonia*'s three-pronged test.

For example, in 1988, the Colorado Supreme Court in *Trinidad v. Lopez*[187] held that *Vernonia* did not apply to the drug testing of band members. Carlos Lopez, a senior band member, sued the Trinidad School District, claiming that the school's drug-testing policy which required all students in grades 6–12 participating in extracurricular activities to submit to random drug testing was unconstitutional. Citing *Vernonia,* the court held that the policy was not legal because, unlike athletic teams, participation in the band was not wholly voluntary and there was a qualitative difference in the communal undress exhibited by band members compared to athletes.

In *Brooks v. East Chambers Consolidated School District,*[188] a Texas federal district court granted a permanent injunction in the case of a student athlete who was expected to submit to urine testing. This requirement was based on a school policy requiring the test for all students who participate in extracurricular activities. The policy had been passed in light of a general societal problem, but this particular school district had not had such problems. Because there was no compelling need for the search and the search was unlikely to accomplish its objectives, the court deemed the search to be unreasonable. In an unpublished opinion handed down two years later, the Fifth Circuit affirmed the district court's opinion.[189]

Other courts have upheld such testing. In *Miller v. Wilkes,*[190] the Eighth Circuit used the *Vernonia* standard in deciding that drug testing students in all extracurricular activities was constitutional. This case addressed Cave City (Arkansas) School's drug policy which required that students give written consent to be drug tested by random selection in order to participate in extracurricular school activities. Miller refused to participate in the drug program but wanted to participate in extracurricular activities. He sought injunctive relief. The appeals court held the random drug-testing program was reasonable under the Fourth Amendment in that (a) Cave City public school students involved in extracurricular activities have a

186. 515 U.S. at 648–65.
187. 963 P.2d 1095 (Colo. 1998).
188. 730 F. Supp. 759 (S.D. Tex. 1989).
189. 930 F.2d 915 (5th Cir 1991).
190. 172 F.3d. 574 (8th Cir. 1999).

lessened expectation of privacy, (b) the school district has an important and immediate interest in discouraging drug and alcohol use, and (c) the minimal amount of intrusion is proportional to the district's interest.

Similarly, in *Todd v. Rush*,[191] the Seventh Circuit ruled that mandated drug testing for students participating in extracurricular activities in an Indiana school was legal. In this case, parents sued the Rush County Schools, claiming the district's program which required random urine testing for drugs, alcohol, and cigarettes of all high school students wanting to participate in extracurricular activities violated students' Fourth Amendment rights. Applying the test used in *Vernonia*, the court held the drug testing was reasonable.

Lower courts, however, were reluctant to extend the *Vernonia* doctrine beyond extracurricular activities. In the years after *Vernonia* but prior to *Earls*, cases involving student suspensions, students driving to school, and mass drug testing of all students were routinely struck down. For example, in *Willis v. Anderson*,[192] the Seventh Circuit held unconstitutional an Indiana school district's drug and alcohol testing policy. Here, all students who possessed or used tobacco, were truant, or were suspended for three days or more, regardless of the offense, would be drug tested. The court distinguished this case from *Todd v. Rush*, in which students participating in extracurricular activities were tested—in *Todd*, unlike *Willis*, participation was voluntary.

In a Pennsylvania case, *Theodore v. Delaware Valley School District*,[193] high school students filed suit challenging the school district's policy requiring participants in extracurricular activities and student drivers to undergo drug testing. The students brought action in the trial court, contending that the policy violated their right to privacy in violation of the prohibition against unreasonable search and seizure protected by the Pennsylvania Constitution. They also sought injunctive relief to prevent the school district from testing students. The trial court dismissed the students' action. The appellate court reversed and remanded the trial court's order, reasoning that the school district policy invaded a student's privacy rights against unreasonable searches and seizures under the state constitution. The Pennsylvania Supreme Court upheld the appellate court's decision, acknowledging the state law's greater privacy rights and asserting that there was no need in this district for the policy, i.e., there was no serious drug problem.[194]

In a case with a fact pattern similar to *Theodore*'s, the Seventh Circuit in *Joy v. Penn-Harris-Madison*[195] upheld a program that involved random drug testing of students who participated in extracurricular activities as well as students who drove

191. 983 F. Supp. 799 (S.D. Ind. 1997), *aff'd*, 133 F.3d 984 (7th Cir.), *reh'g en banc denied*, 139 F.3d 571 (7th Cir.), *cert. denied*, 525 U.S. 824 (1998).

192. 158 F.3d 415 (7th Cir. 1998), *cert. denied*, 526 U.S. 1019 (1999).

193. 761 A.2d 652 (Pa. Commw. Ct. 2000).

194. Theodore v. Delaware Valley Sch. Dist., 836 A.2d 76 (Pa. 2003).

195. 212 F.3d 1052 (7th Cir. 2000).

to work. However, the court did strike down a part of the policy that required testing for nicotine, reasoning that there was not a sufficient government interest here to invade students' privacy. On appeal, and in view of the *Linke* decision (discussed later in this text), the nicotine testing was also upheld under Indiana's state law.[196] The court asserted that this testing was for the health and safety of the students, was not punitive, and was conducted in a legal manner.

As of this writing, courts have yet to uphold drug testing of all students. The Texas Supreme Court, in *Tannahill v. Lockney*,[197] ruled against a program that would subject the entire student body to drug testing. In *Tannahill*, a student and his father brought action against the school district, claiming that the district's mandatory drug-testing policy violated the Fourth Amendment. Lockney Independent School District in Texas had implemented a mandatory drug-testing plan for all students in the district in grades 6–12. Any refusal by the student and/or parent to sign a consent form for testing would be treated as a positive test. The plaintiffs objected and refused to consent to the drug-testing policy. They followed the administrative appeals requirements of the school district, but their appeal was denied. They then filed in state court for injunctive and declaratory relief. The state court held that the drug-testing policy set forth by the Lockney Independent School District was unreasonable. It reasoned that the school district's program violated the plaintiffs' rights under the Fourth Amendment as incorporated into the Fourteenth Amendment of the U.S. Constitution in that the district failed to demonstrate a sufficient special need to justify suspicionless drug testing.

In 2002, the U.S. Supreme Court clarified issues presented in these splits among lower courts with respect to extracurricular activities. In *Board of Education v. Earls*,[198] [***see* Case No. 4-10**] Tecumseh High School had adopted a policy requiring all students participating in extracurricular activities to be included in a random urinalysis drug-testing program. The policy listed the drugs to be tested for, including alcohol and nicotine. The procedure involved students being called out of class and directed to a restroom by a faculty monitor. The monitor would stand outside the stall while the student produced the sample. The student and monitor would together seal the sample. The student would also complete a form listing all medications they had taken. Students in marching band, show choir, and academic team filed suit, claiming Fourth Amendment violations and money damages for violation of civil rights under § 1983. A federal district court granted the students a motion for summary judgment and the school district appealed.

In a 2-1 decision, the Tenth Circuit[199] ruled as unconstitutional the drug-testing program as it pertains to extracurricular activities (but not student athletes). The

196. Penn-Harris-Madison Sch. Corp. v. Joy, 768 N.E.2d 940 (Ind. Ct. App. 2002).

197. 133 F. Supp. 2d 919 (N.D. Tex. 2001).

198. 536 U.S. 822 (2002).

199. Earls v. Bd. of Educ. of Ind. Sch. Dist. No. 92 of Pottawatomie Cnty., 242 F.3d 1264 (10th Cir. 2001).

court applied *Vernonia*'s three-pronged test, first determining that unlike athletes, students involved in extracurricular activities did not have a reduced expectation of privacy.[200] Second, procedures used were "virtually identical" to those in *Vernonia;* therefore, the court expressed no concerns in this respect.[201] Third, there was little drug use among students involved in extracurricular activities. A survey administered in the mid-1990s showed that alcohol and tobacco were the most serious problems and that there was little use of illegal drugs or controlled substances.[202] This last point was pivotal in determining the court's decision.

The U.S. Supreme Court reversed the circuit court's decision, ruling that the drug-testing program was constitutional in that the students' invasion of privacy was not significant and the testing served the school's important interest in preventing, detecting, and deterring drug use. Because students voluntarily participate in such activities, they have a reduced expectation of privacy and, as noted by the Tenth Circuit, the sample collection was virtually identical to that in *Vernonia*, and thus, was legal.[203]

Following *Earls*, lower courts have been much more likely to uphold drug testing of students driving to school. In *Joye v. Hunterdon Central Regional High School Board of Education*,[204] a New Jersey high school adopted a policy for the 2000–2001 school year requiring random drug testing of pupils who parked cars on campus or were engaged in extracurricular activities. Three Hunterdon Central students filed suit in state court, alleging that the policy violated the pupils' rights to privacy under the New Jersey State Constitution. The trial court found for the plaintiffs and enjoined the school from implementing the drug-testing program. In 2002, New Jersey's appellate court overturned this lower court ruling. It maintained that, based on *Earls*, the drug-testing program in this case would not violate the U.S. Constitution. It also saw no basis for concluding that the state constitution would warrant a different approach. In 2003, New Jersey's Supreme Court affirmed the state appeals court's decision.

Similarly, in *Linke v. Northwestern School Corp.*,[205] students in Howard County, Indiana, brought an action claiming that the school's random drug-testing policy violated the Fourth Amendment. The "Extra-Curricular Activities and Student Driver Drug Testing Policy" applied to all middle and high school students (grades 7–12) participating in school athletics, extracurricular activities, and co-curricular activities, and to student drivers who wished to park their vehicles on campus. The trial court granted summary judgment in favor of the school; the state appeals court reversed. In 2002, the Indiana Supreme Court concluded that the drug-testing program was constitutional, maintaining that testing students who were at an

200. *Id.* at 1275.
201. *Id.* at 1276.
202. *Id.* at 1276–77.
203. *Id.* at 825–38.
204. 826 A.2d 624 (N.J. 2003).
205. 734 N.E.2d 252 (Ind. Ct. App. 2000).

increased risk of physical harm or who were role models and leaders was reasonably related to achieving the school's purpose in providing for the health and safety of students.[206] While some jurisdictions have permitted drug testing of students who drive to school and park on school property, this testing is not universally accepted and depends on state law and the interpretation of lower courts.

Accordingly, it is critically important that school leaders have knowledge of their district's policies and their state's laws regarding random drug testing as both entities can make rules/laws more protective of students' rights than those permitted by federal court rulings. Two state supreme court decisions, one in Washington State and the other in Wyoming, illustrate this principle. In *York v. Wahkiakum School District No. 200*,[207] a school district began random drug testing of student athletes based on a survey indicating that 50 percent of the student-athletes admitted to using drugs and/or alcohol. A lower state court upheld the district's random drug-testing policy, but the Washington State Supreme Court overturned that decision, indicating that Washington's constitution is more protective than federal law, especially regarding the need for individualized suspicion when searching students,—something the court maintained was not adequately explained in the *T.L.O.* decision.

Conversely, in the Wyoming decision, *Hageman v. Goshen County*,[208] this state's supreme court upheld random drug testing of students participating in extracurricular activities. The court acknowledged that there were state laws in Wyoming which protect students from illegal searches, however unlike Washington State, the Wyoming state statutes offers no greater protection as to random drug testing of students than federal law.

In sum, it is widely acknowledged that federal law allows public school personnel to conduct random drug testing of student athletes as well as students involved in extracurricular activities as long as there is some need for testing and that testing procedures are clearly set forth and followed commensurate with the Court's decisions in *Vernonia* and *Earls*. To date, there have been no cases allowing drug testing of the entire student body; such practices are generally considered to be illegal.

Student Strip Searches

In 2009, the U.S. Supreme Court rendered its fourth decision involving searches of students in public schools. According to the facts in *Safford v. Redding*,[209] [*see* **Case No. 4-11**] school officials in Arizona questioned Savana Redding, a 13-year-old middle school student suspected of possessing prescription-strength ibuprofen (aspirin). This search occurred after an unrelated incident where another student

206. Nw. Sch. Corp. v. Linke, 763 N.E.2d 972 (Ind. 2002).
207. 178 P.3d 995 (Wash. 2008).
208. 256 P.3d 487 (Wyo. 2011).
209. 557 U.S. 364 (2009).

became ill from ingesting aspirin at school. Savana denied any wrongdoing. After searching her personal belongings and finding nothing of interest, the school's assistant principal requested the school nurse and a female administrative assistant to search the student's clothes. Savanna sat in a chair in her bra and underwear while these individuals searched her clothing. The student was asked to pull out her bra and then do the same with her underwear, shaking them out to reveal any potentially hidden pills. This procedure resulted in exposure of Savanna's naked breasts and pelvic area.

The Court held that the searches of the student's backpack and outer clothing were legal but that the strip search violated Savanna's privacy rights. Applying the *T.L.O.* standard for reasonableness, the Court first found that the strip search was not justified at its inception as there was no reason for school officials to believe that the contraband would be in Savanna's underwear. It also found that the search was overly intrusive.

The Court then addressed whether school officials were immune under §1983. Even though the search was illegal, for school officials to be held monetarily liable requires a stricter standard, i.e., it must be clear that school officials were violating the law. Here, the justices determined that, in the absence of state law in Arizona or legal precedent in the Ninth Circuit and in light of the fact that some strip searches had been upheld in other jurisdictions, school authorities might not necessarily have known that their actions were a clear violation of the student's constitutional rights. Thus, the officials were immune.

The *Redding* Court did not determine whether Savanna's strip search would have been legal had the object of the search been more dangerous than ibuprofen, e.g., marijuana or other street drugs. In addition, the justices never ruled strip searching to be *per se* illegal. Practitioners, however, should be aware that conducting highly intrusive searches, such as strip searches, is a very serious matter. School districts may construct policies that protect students from these highly intrusive searches. Further, seven states have passed laws prohibiting school officials from conducting strip searches in public schools; these include California, Iowa, New Jersey, Oklahoma, South Carolina, Washington, and Wisconsin. If you work in one of these states, you are forbidden to strip search a student and might be personally liable for money damages. (*See* Chapter 2 on liability.) Moreover, in Wisconsin, it is a criminal offense for an educator to strip search a student in school.

If you are in a state or school district that does not prohibit strip searching, then the principles set forth in *T.L.O.* and *Safford* apply. In other words, the search must be reasonable. There are numerous court decisions related to strip searching,[210] too many to include in this brief discussion; however, *D.H. v. Clayton County School*

---

210. *See generally* Diana R. Donahoe, *Strip Searches of Students: Addressing the Undressing of Children in Schools and Redressing the Fourth Amendment Violations*, 75 Mo. L. Rev. 1123 (2010).

District,[211] an Eleventh Circuit case, provides a good illustration of how the reasonable suspicion standard applies to highly intrusive searches. Here, Mr. McDowell, an assistant principal at a public K-8 school, strip searched D.H., who was a 12-year-old seventh-grader at the time. The search was based on individualized suspicion—based on a tip from another student—that D.H. possessed marijuana at school. At the time of the search, McDowell, Deputy Redding (the school resource officer), and four other students were in Deputy Redding's office. Despite this, and despite D.H.'s request to have the search conducted in the restroom, Principal McDowell instructed D.H. to remove all of his clothes until he stood completely nude. No marijuana or other illegal contraband was found on D.H. or in his belongings. Principal McDowell later admitted that he could have performed the search in the privacy of the bathroom with Deputy Redding present.

The court applied the *T.L.O.* and *Safford* principles to this case. The court found that the assistant principal's strip search of D.H. was justified at its inception because McDowell held a "reasonable suspicion . . . of resort to underwear for hiding evidence of wrongdoing."[212] Forcing D.H. to strip fully naked in front of his peers, however, unnecessarily subjected this boy to a significantly higher level of intrusion, bore no rational relationship to the purpose of the search, and hence was unconstitutionally excessive in scope.

Because McDowell violated D.H.'s constitutional rights, the court then examined the final prong of the defense of qualified immunity: whether clearly established law put McDowell on notice of the unconstitutionality of his actions. The court concluded that a reasonable official in McDowell's position would not have believed that requiring D.H. to strip down to his fully naked body in front of several of his peers was lawful in light of the clearly established principle that a student strip search, even if justified in its inception, must be "reasonably related to the objectives of the search and not excessively intrusive in light of the age and sex of the student and the nature of the infraction."[213] Accordingly, the Eleventh Circuit affirmed the district court's denial of McDowell's motion for summary judgment based on qualified immunity. Finding that genuine issues of material fact existed and that this case should have been tried by a jury, the court remanded the case for a new trial.

While some jurisdictions have allowed strip searching of individual students with reasonable suspicion, we can say with surety that a group strip search for missing items or money with a lack of individualized suspicion is illegal.[214] In general, strip searching is highly intrusive of students' rights and should be avoided if possible. Educators should first consider less intrusive measures that might serve a similar purpose. Moreover, as mentioned previously, school districts and/or personnel

211. 830 F.3d 1306 (11th Cir. 2016).

212. *Id.* at 1317 (citing *Safford*, 557 U.S. at 386).

213. *Id.* at 1318–19 (citing *Safford* at 377) (quoting *T.L.O.* at 342).

214. *See e.g.*, Littell v. Houston Ind. Sch. Dist., 894 F.3d 616 (5th Cir. 2018).

could possibly be held liable for money damages. (See Chapter 2 on liability for more examples of strip-searching cases that address immunity.)

Student Records

A significant amount of pupil data must be collected and stored by each school. Such data include test scores, grades, grade-point averages, attendance, and lists of participants in extracurricular activities. Directory information — pupils' names, addresses, telephone numbers, parents' names, and emergency contacts — is also part of pupil data. In handling student records, the Family Educational Rights and Privacy Act (FERPA), also referred to as the Buckley Amendment, must always be followed. Some of the main provisions of the act are listed in **Figure 4-1** below.

Figure 4.1

THE FAMILY EDUCATIONAL RIGHTS AND PRIVACY ACT (FERPA)
(20 U.S.C. § 1232g; 34 C.F.R. Part 99)

(a) Conditions for availability of funds to educational agencies or institutions; inspection and review of education records; specific information to be made available; procedure for access to education records; reasonableness of time for such access; hearings; written explanations by parents; definitions.

(1)

(A) No funds shall be made available under any applicable program to any educational agency or institution which has a policy of denying, or which effectively prevents, the parents of students who are or have been in attendance at a school of such agency or at such institution, as the case may be, the right to inspect and review the education records of their children. If any material or document in the education record of a student includes information on more than one student, the parents of one of such students shall have the right to inspect and review only such part of such material or document as relates to such student or to be informed of the specific information contained in such part of such material. Each educational agency or institution shall establish appropriate procedures for the granting of a request by parents for access to the education records of their children within a reasonable period of time, but in no case more than forty-five days after the request has been made.

(B) No funds under any applicable program shall be made available to any State educational agency (whether or not that agency is an educational agency or institution under this section) that has a policy of denying, or effectively prevents, the parents of students the right to inspect and review the education records maintained by the State educational agency on their children who are or have been in attendance at any school of an educational agency or institution that is subject to the provisions of this section.

(C) The first sentence of subparagraph (A) shall not operate to make available to students in institutions of postsecondary education the following materials:

(i) financial records of the parents of the student or any information contained therein;

(ii) confidential letters and statements of recommendation, which were placed in the education records prior to January 1, 1975, if such letters or statements are not used for purposes other than those for which they were specifically intended;

(iii) if the student has signed a waiver of the student's right of access under this subsection in accordance with subparagraph (D), confidential recommendations—

(I) respecting admission to any educational agency or institution,

(II) respecting an application for employment, and

(III) respecting the receipt of an honor or honorary recognition.

(D) A student or a person applying for admission may waive his right of access to confidential statements described in clause (iii) of subparagraph (C), except that such waiver shall apply to recommendations only if (i) the student is, upon request, notified of the names of all persons making confidential recommendations and (ii) such recommendations are used solely for the purpose for which they were specifically intended. Such waivers may not be required as a condition for admission to, receipt of financial aid from, or receipt of any other services or benefits from such agency or institution.

(2) No funds shall be made available under any applicable program to any educational agency or institution unless the parents of students who are or have been in attendance at a school of such agency or at such institution are provided an opportunity for a hearing by such agency or institution, in accordance with regulations of the Secretary, to challenge the content of such student's education records, in order to insure that the records are not inaccurate, misleading, or otherwise in violation of the privacy rights of students, and to provide an opportunity for the correction or deletion of any such inaccurate, misleading, or otherwise inappropriate data contained therein and to insert into such records a written explanation of the parents respecting the content of such records.

(3) For the purposes of this section the term "educational agency or institution" means any public or private agency or institution which is the recipient of funds under any applicable program.

(4)

(A) For the purposes of this section, the term "education records" means, except as may be provided otherwise in subparagraph (B), those records, files, documents, and other materials which—

(i) contain information directly related to a student; and

(ii) are maintained by an educational agency or institution or by a person acting for such agency or institution.

(B) The term "education records" does not include—

(i) records of instructional, supervisory, and administrative personnel and educational personnel ancillary thereto which are in the sole possession of the maker thereof and which are not accessible or revealed to any other person except a substitute;

(ii) records maintained by a law enforcement unit of the educational agency or institution that were created by that law enforcement unit for the purpose of law enforcement;

(iii) in the case of persons who are employed by an educational agency or institution but who are not in attendance at such agency or institution, records made and maintained in the normal course of business which relate exclusively to such person in that person's capacity as an employee and are not available for use for any other purpose; or

(iv) records on a student who is eighteen years of age or older, or is attending an institution of postsecondary education, which are made or maintained by a physician, psychiatrist, psychologist, or other recognized professional or paraprofessional acting in his professional or paraprofessional capacity, or assisting in that capacity, and which are made, maintained, or used only in connection with the provision of treatment to the student, and are not available to anyone other than persons providing such treatment, except that such records can be personally reviewed by a physician or other appropriate professional of the student's choice.

(5)

(A) For the purposes of this section the term "directory information" relating to a student includes the following: the student's name, address, telephone listing, date and place of birth, major field of study, participation in officially recognized activities and sports, weight and height of members of athletic teams, dates of attendance, degrees and awards received, and the most recent previous educational agency or institution attended by the student.

(B) Any educational agency or institution making public directory information shall give public notice of the categories of information which it has designated as such information with respect to each student attending the institution or agency and shall allow a reasonable period of time after such notice has been given for a parent to inform the institution or agency that any or all of the information designated should not be released without the parent's prior consent.

(6) For the purposes of this section, the term "student" includes any person with respect to whom an educational agency or institution maintains education records or personally identifiable information, but does not include a person who has not been in attendance at such agency or institution.

(b) Release of education records; parental consent requirement; exceptions; compliance with judicial orders and subpoenas; audit and evaluation of Federally-supported education programs; recordkeeping.

(1) No funds shall be made available under any applicable program to any educational agency or institution which has a policy or practice of permitting the release of educational records (or personally identifiable information contained therein other than directory information, as defined in paragraph (5) of subsection (a)) of students without the written consent of their parents to any individual, agency, or organization, other than to the following—

(A) other school officials, including teachers within the educational institution or local educational agency, who have been determined by such agency or institution to have legitimate educational interests, including the educational interests of the child for whom consent would otherwise be required;

(B) officials of other schools or school systems in which the student seeks or intends to enroll, upon condition that the student's parents be notified of the transfer, receive a copy of the record if desired, and have an opportunity for a hearing to challenge the content of the record;

(C) (i) authorized representatives of (I) the Comptroller General of the United States, (II) the Secretary, or (III) State educational authorities, under the conditions set forth in paragraph (3), or (ii) authorized representatives of the Attorney General for law enforcement purposes under the same conditions as apply to the Secretary under paragraph (3);

(D) in connection with a student's application for, or receipt of, financial aid;

(E) State and local officials or authorities to whom such information is specifically allowed to be reported or disclosed pursuant to State statute adopted—

(i) before November 19, 1974, if the allowed reporting or disclosure concerns the juvenile justice system and such system's ability to effectively serve the student whose records are released, or

(ii) after November 19, 1974, if—

(I) the allowed reporting or disclosure concerns the juvenile justice system and such system's ability to effectively serve, prior to adjudication, the student whose records are released; and

(II) the officials and authorities to whom such information is disclosed certify in writing to the educational agency or institution that the information will not be disclosed to any other party except as provided under State law without the prior written consent of the parent of the student.[;]

(F) organizations conducting studies for, or on behalf of, educational agencies or institutions for the purpose of developing, validating, or administering predictive tests, administering student aid programs, and improving instruction, if such studies are conducted in such a manner as will not permit the personal identification of students and their parents by persons other than representatives of such organizations and such information will be destroyed when no longer needed for the purpose for which it is conducted;

(G) accrediting organizations in order to carry out their accrediting functions;

(H) parents of a dependent student of such parents, as defined in section 152 of the Internal Revenue Code of 1986 [26 USCS § 152];

(I) subject to regulations of the Secretary, in connection with an emergency, appropriate persons if the knowledge of such information is necessary to protect the health or safety of the student or other persons;

(J)

(i) the entity or persons designated in a Federal grand jury subpoena, in which case the court shall order, for good cause shown, the educational agency or institution (and any officer, director, employee, agent, or attorney for such agency or institution) on which the subpoena is served, to not disclose to any person the existence or contents of the subpoena or any information furnished to the grand jury in response to the subpoena; and

(ii) the entity or persons designated in any other subpoena issued for a law enforcement purpose, in which case the court or other issuing agency may order, for good cause shown, the educational agency or institution (and any officer, director, employee, agent, or attorney for such agency or institution) on which the subpoena is served, to not disclose to any person the existence or contents of the subpoena or any information furnished in response to the subpoena;

(K) the Secretary of Agriculture, or authorized representative from the Food and Nutrition Service or contractors acting on behalf of the Food and Nutrition Service, for the purposes of conducting program monitoring, evaluations, and performance measurements of State and local educational and other agencies and institutions receiving funding or providing benefits of 1 or more programs authorized under the Richard B. Russell National School Lunch Act (42 U.S.C. 1751 et seq.) or the Child Nutrition Act of 1966 (42 U.S.C. 1771 et seq.) for which the results will be reported in an aggregate form that does not identify any individual, on the conditions that—

(i) any data collected under this subparagraph shall be protected in a manner that will not permit the personal identification of students and their parents by other than the authorized representatives of the Secretary; and

(ii) any personally identifiable data shall be destroyed when the data are no longer needed for program monitoring, evaluations, and performance measurements; and

(L) an agency caseworker or other representative of a State or local child welfare agency, or tribal organization (as defined in section 4 of the Indian Self-Determination and Education Assistance Act (25 U.S.C. 450b)), who has the right to access a student's case plan, as defined and determined by the State or tribal organization, when such agency or organization is legally responsible, in accordance with State or tribal law, for the care and protection of the student, provided that the education records, or the personally identifiable information contained in such records, of the student will not be disclosed by such agency or organization, except to an individual or entity engaged in addressing the student's education needs and authorized by such agency or organization to receive such disclosure and such disclosure is consistent with the State or tribal laws applicable to protecting the confidentiality of a student's education records.

Nothing in subparagraph (E) of this paragraph shall prevent a State from further limiting the number or type of State or local officials who will continue to have access thereunder.

(2) No funds shall be made available under any applicable program to any educational agency or institution which has a policy or practice of releasing, or providing access to, any personally identifiable information in education records other than directory information, or as is permitted under paragraph (1) of this subsection unless—

(A) there is written consent from the student's parents specifying records to be released, the reasons for such release, and to whom, and with a copy of the records to be released to the student's parents and the student if desired by the parents, or

(B) except as provided in paragraph (1)(J), such information is furnished in compliance with judicial order, or pursuant to any lawfully issued subpoena, upon condition that parents and the students are notified of all such orders or subpoenas in advance of the compliance therewith by the educational institution or agency, except when a parent is a party to a court proceeding involving child abuse and neglect (as defined in section 3 of the Child Abuse Prevention and Treatment Act (42 U.S.C. 5101 note)) or dependency matters, and the order is issued in the context of that proceeding, additional notice to the parent by the educational agency or institution is not required.

(3) Nothing contained in this section shall preclude authorized representatives of (A) the Comptroller General of the United States, (B) the Secretary, or (C) State educational authorities from having access to student or other records which may be necessary in connection with the audit and evaluation of Federally-supported education programs, or in connection with the enforcement of the Federal legal requirements which relate to such programs: *Provided,* That except when collection of personally identifiable information is specifically authorized by Federal law, any data collected by such officials shall be protected in a manner which will not permit the personal identification of students and their parents by other than those officials, and such personally identifiable data shall be destroyed when no longer needed for such audit, evaluation, and enforcement of Federal legal requirements.

(4)

(A) Each educational agency or institution shall maintain a record, kept with the education records of each student, which will indicate all individuals (other than those specified in paragraph (1)(A) of this subsection), agencies, or organizations which have requested or obtained access to a student's education records maintained by such educational agency or institution, and which will indicate specifically the legitimate interest that each such person, agency, or organization has in obtaining this information. Such record of access shall be available only to parents, to the school official and his assistants who are responsible for the custody of such records, and to persons or organizations authorized in, and under the conditions of, clauses (A) and (C) of paragraph (1) as a means of auditing the operation of the system.

(B) With respect to this subsection, personal information shall only be transferred to a third party on the condition that such party will not permit any other party to have access to such information without the written consent of the parents of the student. If a third party outside the educational agency or institution permits access to information in violation of paragraph (2)(A), or fails to destroy information in violation of paragraph (1)(F), the educational agency or institution shall be prohibited from permitting access to information from education records to that third party for a period of not less than five years.

(5) Nothing in this section shall be construed to prohibit State and local educational officials from having access to student or other records which may be necessary in connection with the audit and evaluation of any federally or State supported education program or in connection with the enforcement of the Federal legal requirements which relate to any such program, subject to the conditions specified in the proviso in paragraph (3).

(6)

(A) Nothing in this section shall be construed to prohibit an institution of postsecondary education from disclosing, to an alleged victim of any crime of violence (as that term is defined in section 16 of title 18, United States Code [18 USCS § 16]), or a nonforcible sex offense, the final results of any disciplinary proceeding conducted by such institution against the alleged perpetrator of such crime or offense with respect to such crime or offense.

(B) Nothing in this section shall be construed to prohibit an institution of postsecondary education from disclosing the final results of any disciplinary proceeding conducted by such institution against a student who is an alleged perpetrator of any crime of violence (as that term is defined in section 16 of title 18 [18 USCS § 16], United States Code), or a nonforcible sex offense, if the institution determines as a result of that disciplinary proceeding that the student committed a violation of the institution's rules or policies with respect to such crime or offense.

(C) For the purpose of this paragraph, the final results of any disciplinary proceeding—

(i) shall include only the name of the student, the violation committed, and any sanction imposed by the institution on that student; and

(ii) may include the name of any other student, such as a victim or witness, only with the written consent of that other student.

(7)

(A) Nothing in this section may be construed to prohibit an educational institution from disclosing information provided to the institution under section 170101 of the Violent Crime Control and Law Enforcement Act of 1994 (42 U.S.C. 14071) concerning registered sex offenders who are required to register under such section.

(B) The Secretary shall take appropriate steps to notify educational institutions that disclosure of information described in subparagraph (A) is permitted.

(c) **Surveys or data-gathering activities; regulations.** Not later than 240 days after the date of enactment of the Improving America's Schools Act of 1994 [enacted Oct. 20, 1994], the Secretary shall adopt appropriate regulations or procedures, or identify existing regulations or procedures, which protect the rights of privacy of students and their families in connection with any surveys or data-gathering activities conducted, assisted, or authorized by the Secretary or an administrative head of an education agency. Regulations established under this subsection shall include provisions controlling the use, dissemination, and protection of such data. No survey or data-gathering activities shall be conducted by the Secretary, or an administrative head of an education agency under an applicable program, unless such activities are authorized by law.

(d) **Students' rather than parents' permission or consent.** For the purposes of this section, whenever a student has attained eighteen years of age, or is attending an institution of postsecondary education, the permission or consent required of and the rights accorded to the parents of the student shall thereafter only be required of and accorded to the student.

(e) **Informing parents or students of rights under this section.** No funds shall be made available under any applicable program to any educational agency or institution unless such agency or institution effectively informs the parents of students, or the students, if they are eighteen years of age or older, or are attending an institution of postsecondary education, of the rights accorded them by this section.

(f) **Enforcement; termination of assistance.** The Secretary shall take appropriate actions to enforce this section and to deal with violations of this section, in accordance with this Act, except that action to terminate assistance may be taken only if the Secretary finds there has been a failure to comply with this section, and he has determined that compliance cannot be secured by voluntary means.

(g) **Office and review board; creation; functions.** The Secretary shall establish or designate an office and review board within the Department for the purpose of investigating, processing, reviewing, and adjudicating violations of this section and complaints which may be filed concerning alleged violations of this section. Except for the conduct of hearings, none of the functions of the Secretary under this section shall be carried out in any of the regional offices of such Department.

(h) Certain disciplinary action information allowable. Nothing in this section shall prohibit an educational agency or institution from—

(1) including appropriate information in the education record of any student concerning disciplinary action taken against such student for conduct that posed a significant risk to the safety or well-being of that student, other students, or other members of the school community; or

(2) disclosing such information to teachers and school officials, including teachers and school officials in other schools, who have legitimate educational interests in the behavior of the student.

(i) Drug and alcohol violation disclosures.

(1) In general. Nothing in this Act or the Higher Education Act of 1965 [20 USCS §§ 1001 et seq.] shall be construed to prohibit an institution of higher education from disclosing, to a parent or legal guardian of a student, information regarding any violation of any Federal, State, or local law, or of any rule or policy of the institution, governing the use or possession of alcohol or a controlled substance, regardless of whether that information is contained in the student's education records, if—

(A) the student is under the age of 21; and

(B) the institution determines that the student has committed a disciplinary violation with respect to such use or possession.

(2) State law regarding disclosure. Nothing in paragraph (1) shall be construed to supersede any provision of State law that prohibits an institution of higher education from making the disclosure described in subsection (a).

(j) Investigation and prosecution of terrorism.

(1) In general. Notwithstanding subsections (a) through (i) or any provision of State law, the Attorney General (or any Federal officer or employee, in a position not lower than an Assistant Attorney General, designated by the Attorney General) may submit a written application to a court of competent jurisdiction for an ex parte order requiring an educational agency or institution to permit the Attorney General (or his designee) to—

(A) collect education records in the possession of the educational agency or institution that are relevant to an authorized investigation or prosecution of an offense listed in § 2332b(g)(5)(B) of title 18 United States Code [18 USCS § 232b(g)(5)(B)], or an act of domestic or international terrorism as defined in section 2331 of that title [18 USCS § 2331]; and

(B) for official purposes related to the investigation or prosecution of an offense described in paragraph (1)(A), retain, disseminate, and use (including as evidence at trial or in other administrative or judicial proceedings) such records, consistent with such guidelines as the Attorney General, after consultation with the Secretary, shall issue to protect confidentiality.

(2) Application and approval.

(A) In general. An application under paragraph (1) shall certify that there are specific and articulable facts giving reason to believe that the education records are likely to contain information described in paragraph (1)(A).

(B) The court shall issue an order described in paragraph (1) if the court finds that the application for the order includes the certification described in subparagraph (A).

(3) Protection of educational agency or institution. An educational agency or institution that, in good faith, produces education records in accordance with an order issued under this subsection shall not be liable to any person for that production.

(4) Record-keeping. Subsection (b)(4) does not apply to education records subject to a court order under this subsection.

Selected Case Law

[4-1] *Goss v. Lopez*

[4-2] *J.D.B. v. North Carolina*

[4-3] *Tinker v. Des Moines Independent Community School District*

[4-4] *Bethel School District No. 403 v. Fraser*

[4-5] *Hazelwood School District v. Kuhlmeier*

[4-6] *Board of Education, Island Trees Union Free School District No. 26 v. Pico*

[4-7] *Morse v. Frederick*

[4-8] *New Jersey v. T.L.O.*

[4-9] *Vernonia School District 47J v. Acton*

[4-10] *Board of Education of Independent School District No. 92 of Pottawatomie County v. Earls*

[4-11] *Safford Unified School District #1 v. Redding*

[Case No. 4-1]

*Public school students have a property interest in attending school.
Officials may not suspend students without first providing due process.*

Goss v. Lopez

Supreme Court of the United States
419 U.S. 565 (1975)

Mr. Justice WHITE delivered the opinion of the Court.

This appeal by various administrators of the Columbus, Ohio, Public School System (CPSS) challenges the judgment of a three-judge federal court, declaring that appellees—various high school students in the CPSS—were denied due process of law contrary to the command of the Fourteenth Amendment in that they were temporarily suspended from their high schools without a hearing either prior to suspension or within a reasonable time thereafter, and enjoining the administrators to remove all references to such suspensions from the students' records.

I

Ohio law, Rev. Code Ann. s 3313.64 (1972), provides for free education to all children between the ages of six and 21. Section 3313.66 of the Code empowers the principal of an Ohio public school to suspend a pupil for misconduct for up to 10 days or to expel him. In either case, he must notify the student's parents within 24 hours and state the reasons for his action. A pupil who is expelled, or his parents, may appeal the decision to the Board of Education and in connection therewith shall be permitted to be heard at the board meeting. The Board may reinstate in pupil following the hearing. No similar procedure is provided in s 3313.66 or any other provision of state law for a suspended student. Aside from a regulation tracking the statute, at the time of the imposition of the suspensions in this case the CPSS itself had not issued any written procedure applicable to suspensions.[215] Nor, so far as the record reflects, had any of the individual high schools involved in this case.[216] Each, however, had formally or informally described the conduct for which suspension could be imposed.

The nine named appellees, each of whom alleged that he or she had been suspended from public high school in Columbus for up to 10 days without a hearing

215. At the time of the events involved in this case, the only administrative regulation on this subject was § 1010.04 of the Administrative Guide of the Columbus Public Schools which provided: "Pupils may be suspended or expelled from school in accordance with the provisions of Section 3313.66 of the Revised Code." Subsequent to the events involved in this lawsuit, the Department of Pupil Personnel of the CPSS issued three memoranda relating to suspension procedures, dated August 16, 1971, February 21, 1973, and July 10, 1973, respectively. The first two are substantially similar to each other and require no fact-finding hearing at any time in connection with a suspension. The third, which was apparently in effect when this case was argued, places upon the principal the obligation to "investigate" "before commencing suspension procedures"; and provides as part of the procedures that the principal shall discuss the case with the pupil, so that the pupil may "be heard with respect to the alleged offense," unless the pupil is "unavailable" for such a discussion or "unwilling" to participate in it. The suspensions involved in this case occurred, and records thereof were made, prior to the effective date of these memoranda. The District Court's judgment, including its expunction order, turns on the propriety of the procedures existing at the time the suspensions were ordered and by which they were imposed.

216. According to the testimony of Phillip Fulton, the principal of one of the high schools involved in this case, there was an informal procedure applicable at the Marion-Franklin High School. It provided that in the routine case of misconduct, occurring in the presence of a teacher, the teacher would describe the misconduct on a form provided for that purpose and would send the student, with the form, to the principal's office. There, the principal would obtain the student's version of the story, and, if it conflicted with the teacher's written version, would send for the teacher to obtain the teacher's oral version — apparently in the presence of the student. Mr. Fulton testified that, if a discrepancy still existed, the teacher's version would be believed and the principal would arrive at a disciplinary decision based on it.

pursuant to s 3313.66, filed an action under 42 U.S.C. §1983 against the Columbus Board of Education and various administrators of the CPSS. The complaint sought a declaration that §3313.66 was unconstitutional in that it permitted public school administrators to deprive plaintiffs of their rights to an education without a hearing of any kind, in violation of the procedural due process component of the Fourteenth Amendment. It also sought to enjoin the public school officials from issuing future suspensions pursuant to §3313.66 and to require them to remove references to the past suspensions from the records of the students in question.[217]

The proof below established that the suspensions arose out of a period of widespread student unrest in the CPSS during February and March 1971. Six of the named plaintiffs, Rudolph Sutton, Tyrone Washington, Susan Cooper, Deborah Fox, Clarence Byars, and Bruce Harris, were students at the Marion-Franklin High School and were each suspended for 10 days[218] on account of disruptive or disobedient conduct committed in the presence of the school administrator who ordered the suspension. One of these, Tyrone Washington, was among a group of students demonstrating in the school auditorium while a class was being conducted there. He was ordered by the school principal to leave, refused to do so, and was suspended. Rudolph Sutton, in the presence of the principal, physically attacked a police officer who was attempting to remove Tyrone Washington from the auditorium. He was immediately suspended. The other four Marion-Franklin students were suspended for similar conduct. None was given a hearing to determine the operative facts underlying the suspension, but each, together with his or her parents, was offered the opportunity to attend a conference, subsequent to the effective date of the suspension, to discuss the student's future.

Two named plaintiffs, Dwight Lopez and Betty Crome, were students at the Central High School and McGuffey Junior High School, respectively. The former was suspended in connection with a disturbance in the lunchroom which involved some physical damage to school property.[219] Lopez testified that at least 75 other students

217. The plaintiffs sought to bring the action on behalf of all students of the Columbus Public Schools suspended on or after February 1971, and a class action was declared accordingly. Since the complaint sought to restrain the 'enforcement' and 'operation' of a state statute 'by restraining the action of any officer of such State in the enforcement or execution of such statute,' a three-judge court was requested pursuant to 28 U.S.C. s 2281 and convened. The students also alleged that the conduct for which they could be suspended was not adequately defined by Ohio law. This vagueness and over-breadth argument was rejected by the court below and the students have not appealed from this part of the court's decision.

218. Fox was given two separate 10-day suspensions for misconduct occurring on two separate occasions — the second following immediately upon her return to school. In addition to his suspension, Sutton was transferred to another school.

219. Lopez was actually absent from school, following his suspension, for over 20 days. This seems to have occurred because of a misunderstanding as to the length of the suspension. A letter sent to Lopez after he had been out for over 10 days purports to assume that, being over compulsory school age, he was voluntarily staying away. Upon asserting that this was not the case, Lopez was transferred to another school.

were suspended from his school on the same day. He also testified below that he was not a party to the destructive conduct but was instead an innocent bystander. Because no one from the school testified with regard to this incident, there is no evidence in the record indicating the official basis for concluding otherwise. Lopez never had a hearing.

Betty Crome was present at a demonstration at a high school other than the one she was attending. There she was arrested together with others, taken to the police station, and released without being formally charged. Before she went to school on the following day, she was notified that she had been suspended for a 10-day period. Because no one from the school testified with respect to this incident, the record does not disclose how the McGuffey Junior High School principal went about making the decision to suspend Crome, nor does it disclose on what information the decision was based. It is clear from the record that no hearing was ever held.

There was no testimony with respect to the suspension of the ninth named plaintiff, Carl Smith. The school files were also silent as to his suspension, although as to some, but not all, of the other named plaintiffs the files contained either direct references to their suspensions or copies of letters sent to their parents advising them of the suspension.

On the basis of this evidence, the three-judge court declared that plaintiffs were denied due process of law because they were 'suspended without hearing prior to suspension or within a reasonable time thereafter,' and that Ohio Rev. Code Ann. s 3313.66 (1972) and regulations issued pursuant thereto were unconstitutional in permitting such suspensions.[220] It was ordered that all references to plaintiffs' suspensions be removed from school files.

Although not imposing upon the Ohio school administrators any particular disciplinary procedures and leaving them 'free to adopt regulations providing for fair suspension procedures which are consonant with the educational goals of their schools and reflective of the characteristics of their school and locality,' the District Court declared that there were 'minimum requirements of notice and a hearing prior to suspension, except in emergency situations.' In explication, the court stated that relevant case authority would: (1) permit '(i)mmediate removal of a student whose conduct disrupts the academic atmosphere of the school, endangers fellow students, teachers or school officials, or damages property'; (2) require notice of suspension proceedings to be sent to the students' parents within 24 hours of the decision to conduct them; and (3) require a hearing to be held, with the student present, within 72 hours of his removal. Finally, the court stated that, with respect

220. In its judgment, the court stated that the statute is unconstitutional in that it provides 'for suspension . . . without first affording the student due process of law' (emphasis supplied). However, the language of the judgment must be read in light of the language in the opinion which expressly contemplates that under some circumstances students may properly be removed from school before a hearing is held, so long as the hearing follows promptly.

to the nature of the hearing, the relevant cases required that statements in support of the charge be produced, that the student and others be permitted to make statements in defense or mitigation, and that the school need not permit attendance by counsel.

The defendant school administrators have appealed the three-judge court's decision. Because the order below granted plaintiffs' request for an injunction—ordering defendants to expunge their records—this Court has jurisdiction of the appeal pursuant to 28 U.S.C. s 1253. We affirm.

II

At the outset, appellants contend that because there is no constitutional right to an education at public expense, the Due Process Clause does not protect against expulsions from the public school system. This position misconceives the nature of the issue and is refuted by prior decisions. The Fourteenth Amendment forbids the State to deprive any person of life, liberty, or property without due process of law. Protected interests in property are normally 'not created by the Constitution. Rather, they are created and their dimensions are defined' by an independent source such as state statutes or rules entitling the citizen to certain benefits. Board of Regents v. Roth, 408 U.S. 564, 577, 92 S. Ct. 2701, 2709, 33 L.Ed.2d 548 (1972).

Accordingly, a state employee who under state law, or rules promulgated by state officials, has a legitimate claim of entitlement to continued employment absent sufficient cause for discharge may demand the procedural protections of due process. Connell v. Higginbotham, 403 U.S. 207, 91 S. Ct. 1772, 29 L. Ed. 2d 418 (1971); Wieman v. Updegraff, 344 U.S. 183, 191–192, 73 S. Ct. 215, 218–219, 97 L. Ed. 216 (1952); Arnett v. Kennedy, 416 U.S. 134, 164, 94 S. Ct. 1633, 1649, 40 L. Ed. 2d 15 (Powell, J., concurring); 171, 94 S. Ct. 1652 (White, J., concurring and dissenting) (1974). So may welfare recipients who have statutory rights to welfare as long as they maintain the specified qualifications. Goldberg v. Kelly, 397 U.S. 254, 90 S. Ct. 1011, 25L. Ed. 2d 287 (1970). Morrissey v. Brewer, 408 U.S. 471, 92 S. Ct. 2593, 33 L. Ed. 2d 484 (1972), applied the limitations of the Due Process Clause to governmental decisions to revoke parole, although a parolee has no constitutional right to that status. In like vein was Wolff v. McDonnell, 418 U.S. 539, 94 S. Ct. 2963, 41 L. Ed. 2d 935 (1974), where the procedural protections of the Due Process Clause were triggered by official cancellation of a prisoner's good-time credits accumulated under state law, although those benefits were not mandated by the Constitution.

Here, on the basis of state law, appellees plainly had legitimate claims of entitlement to a public education. Ohio Rev. Code Ann. ss 3313.48 and 3313.64 (1972 and Supp.1973) direct local authorities to provide a free education to all residents between five and 21 years of age, and a compulsory-attendance law requires attendance for a school year of not less than 32 weeks. Ohio Rev. Code Ann. s 3321.04 (1972). It is true that s 3313.66 of the Code permits school principals to suspend students for up to 10 days; but suspensions may not be imposed without any grounds whatsoever.

All of the schools had their own rules specifying the grounds for expulsion or suspension. Having chosen to extend the right to an education to people of appellees' class generally, Ohio may not withdraw that right on grounds of misconduct absent, fundamentally fair procedures to determine whether the misconduct has occurred. Arnett v. Kennedy, supra, at 164, 94 S. Ct. at 1649 (Powell, J., concurring), 171, 94 S. Ct. 1652 (White, J., concurring and dissenting), 206, 94 S. Ct. 1670 (Marshall, J., dissenting).

Although Ohio may not be constitutionally obligated to establish and maintain a public school system, it has nevertheless done so and has required its children to attend. Those young people do not 'shed their constitutional rights' at the schoolhouse door. Tinker v. Des Moines Independent Community School Dist., 393 U.S. 503, 506, 89 S. Ct. 733, 736, 21 L. Ed. 2d 731 (1969). 'The Fourteenth Amendment, as now applied to the States, protects the citizen against the State itself and all of its creatures—Boards of Education not excepted.' West Virginia Board of Education v. Barnette, 319 U.S. 624, 637, 63 S. Ct. 1178, 1185, 87 L. Ed. 1628 (1943). The authority possessed by the State to prescribe and enforce standards of conduct in its schools, although concededly very broad, must be exercised consistently with constitutional safeguards. Among other things, the State is constrained to recognize a student's legitimate entitlement to a public education as a property interest which is protected by the Due Process Clause and which may not be taken away for misconduct without adherence to the minimum procedures required by that Clause.

The Due Process Clause also forbids arbitrary deprivations of liberty. 'Where a person's good name, reputation, honor, or integrity is at stake because of what the government is doing to him,' the minimal requirements of the Clause must be satisfied. Wisconsin v. Constantineau, 400 U.S. 433, 437, 91 S. Ct. 507, 510, 27 L. Ed. 2d 515 (1971); Board of Regents v. Roth, supra, 408 U.S. at 573, 92 S. Ct. at 2707. School authorities here suspended appellees from school for periods of up to 10 days based on charges of misconduct. If sustained and recorded, those charges could seriously damage the students' standing with their fellow pupils and their teachers as well as interfere with later opportunities for higher education and employment.[221] It is apparent that the claimed right of the State to determine unilaterally and

221. Appellees assert in their brief that four of 12 randomly selected Ohio colleges specifically inquire of the high school of every applicant for admission whether the applicant has ever been suspended. Brief for Appellees 34–35 and n. 40. Appellees also contend that many employers request similar information. Ibid.

Congress enacted legislation limiting access to information contained in the files of a school receiving federal funds. Section 513 of the Education Amendments of 1974, Pub.L. 93-380, 88 Stat. 571, 20 U.S.C. s 1232g (1970 ed., Supp. IV), adding s 438 to the General Education Provisions Act. That section would preclude release of 'verified reports of serious or recurrent behavior patterns' to employers without written consent of the student's parents. While subsection 513(b)(1)(B) permits release of such information to 'other schools . . . in which the student intends to enroll,' it does so only upon condition that the parent be advised of the release of the information and be given an opportunity at a hearing to challenge the content of the information to insure against inclusion of inaccurate or misleading information. The statute does not expressly state whether the parent can

without process whether that misconduct has occurred immediately collides with the requirements of the Constitution.

Appellants proceed to argue that even if there is a right to a public education protected by the Due Process Clause generally, the Clause comes into play only when the State subjects a student to a 'severe detriment or grievous loss.' The loss of 10 days, it is said, is neither severe nor grievous and the Due Process Clause is therefore of no relevance. Appellants' argument is again refuted by our prior decisions; for in determining 'whether due process requirements apply in the first place, we must look not to the 'weight' but to the nature of the interest at stake.' Board of Regents v. Roth, supra, at 570–571, 92 S. Ct. at 2705–2706. Appellees were excluded from school only temporarily, it is true, but the length and consequent severity of a deprivation, while another factor to weigh in determining the appropriate form of hearing, 'is not decisive of the basic right' to a hearing of some kind. Fuentes v. Shevin, 407 U.S. 67, 86, 92 S. Ct. 1983, 1997, 32 L. Ed. 2d 556 (1972). The Court's view has been that as long as a property deprivation is not de minimis, its gravity is irrelevant to the question whether account must be taken of the Due Process Clause. Sniadach v. Family Finance Corp., 395 U.S. 337, 342, 89 S. Ct. 1820, 1823, 23 L. Ed. 2d 349 (1969) (Harlan, J., concurring); Boddie v. Connecticut, 401 U.S. 371, 378–379, 91 S. Ct. 780, 786, 28 L. Ed. 2d 113 (1971); Board of Regents v. Roth, supra, 408 U.S., at 570 n. 8, 92 S. Ct., at 2705. A 10-day suspension from school is not de minimis in our view and may not be imposed in complete disregard of the Due Process Clause.

A short suspension is, of course, a far milder deprivation than expulsion. But, 'education is perhaps the most important function of state and local governments,' Brown v. Board of Education, 347 U.S. 483, 493, 74 S. Ct. 686, 691, 98 L. Ed. 873 (1954), and the total exclusion from the educational process for more than a trivial period, and certainly if the suspension is for 10 days, is a serious event in the life of the suspended child. Neither the property interest in educational benefits temporarily denied nor the liberty interest in reputation, which is also implicated, is so insubstantial that suspensions may constitutionally be imposed by any procedure the school chooses, no matter how arbitrary.[222]

---

contest the underlying basis for a suspension, the fact of which is contained in the student's school record.

222. Since the landmark decision of the Court of Appeals for the Fifth Circuit in Dixon v. Alabama State Board of Education, 294 F.2d 150, cert. denied, 368 U.S. 930, 82 S. Ct. 368, 7 L. Ed. 2d 193 (1961), the lower federal courts have uniformly held the Due Process Clause applicable to decisions made by tax-supported educational institutions to remove a student from the institution long enough for the removal to be classified as an expulsion. Hagopian v. Knowlton, 470 F.2d 201, 211 (CA2 1972); Wasson v. Trowbridge, 382 F.2d 807, 812 (CA2 1967); Esteban v. Central Missouri State College, 415 F.2d 1077, 1089 (CA8 1969), cert. denied, 398 U.S. 965, 90 S. Ct. 2169, 26 L. Ed. 2d 548 (1970); Vought v. Van Buren Public Schools, 306 F. Supp. 1388 (ED Mich. 1969); Whitfield v. Simpson, 312 F. Supp. 889 (ED Ill.1970); Fielder v. Board of Education of School District of Winnebago, Neb., 346 F. Supp. 722, 729 (D.C.Neb.1972); DeJesus v. Penberthy, 344 F. Supp. 70, 74 (D .C.Conn.1972); Soglin v. Kauffman, 295 F. Supp. 978, 994 (WD Wis.1968); aff'd, 418 F.2d 163 (CA7 1969); Stricklin v. Regents of University of Wisconsin, 297 F. Supp. 416, 420 (WD Wis.1969), appeal

III

'Once it is determined that due process applies, the question remains what process is due.' Morrissey v. Brewer, 408 U.S., at 481, 92 S. Ct., at 2600. We turn to that question, fully realizing as our cases regularly do that the interpretation and application of the Due Process Clause are intensely practical matters and that '(t)he very nature of due process negates any concept of inflexible procedures universally applicable to every imaginable situation.' Cafeteria Workers v. McElroy, 367 U.S. 886, 895, 81 S. Ct. 1743, 1748, 6 L. Ed. 2d 1230 (1961). We are also mindful of our own admonition: 'Judicial interposition in the operation of the public school system of the Nation raises problems requiring care and restraint.... By and large, public education in our Nation is committed to the control of state and local authorities.' Epperson v. Arkansas, 393 U.S. 97, 104, 89 S. Ct. 266, 270, 21 L. Ed. 2d 228 (1968).

There are certain bench marks to guide us, however. Mullane v. Central Hanover Trust Co., 339 U.S. 306, 70 S. Ct. 652, 94 L. Ed. 865 (1950), a case often invoked

---

dismissed, 420 F.2d 1257 (CA7 1970); Buck v. Carter, 308 F. Supp. 1246 (WD Wis.1970); General Order on Judicial Standards of Procedure and Substance in Review of Student Discipline in Tax Supported Institutions of Higher Education, 45 F.R.D. 133, 147–148 (W.D. Mo.1968) (en banc). The lower courts have been less uniform, however, on the question whether removal from school for some shorter period may ever be so trivial a deprivation as to require no process, and, if so, how short the removal must be to qualify. Courts of Appeals have held or assumed the Due Process Clause applicable to long suspensions, Pervis v. LaMarque Ind. School Dist., 466 F.2d 1054 (CA5 1972); to indefinite suspensions, Sullivan v. Houston Ind. School Dist., 475 F.2d 1071 (CA5), cert. denied, 414 U.S. 1032, 94 S. Ct. 461, 38 L. Ed. 2d 323 (1973); to the addition of a 30-day suspension to a 10-day suspension, Williams v. Dade County School Board, 441 F.2d 299 (CA5 1971); to a 10-day suspension, Black Students of North Fort Meyers Jr.-Sr. High School v. Williams, 470 F.2d 957 (CA5 1972); to 'mild' suspensions, Farrell v. Joel, 437 F.2d 160 (CA2 1971), and Tate v. Board of Education, 453 F.2d 975 (CA8 1972); and to a three-day suspension, Shanley v. Northeast Ind. School Dist., Bexar County Texas, 462 F.2d 960, 967 n. 4 (CA5 1972); but inapplicable to a seven-day suspension, Linwood v. Board of Ed. of City of Peoria, 463 F.2d 763 (CA7), cert. denied, 409 U.S. 1027, 93 S. Ct. 475, 34 L. Ed. 2d 320 (1972); to a three-day suspension, Dunn v. Tyler Ind. School Dist., 460 F.2d 137 (CA5 1972); to a suspension for not 'more than a few days,' Murray v. West Baton Rouge Parish School Board, 472 F.2d 438 (CA5 1973); and to all suspensions no matter how short, Black Coalition v. Portland School District No. 1, 484 F.2d 1040 (CA9 1973). The Federal District Courts have held the Due Process Clause applicable to an interim suspension pending expulsion proceedings in Stricklin v. Regents of University of Wisconsin, supra, and Buck v. Carter, supra; to a 10-day suspension, Banks v. Board of Public Instruction of Dade County, 314 F. Supp. 285 (SD Fla.1970), vacated, 401 U.S. 988, 91 S. Ct. 1223, 28 L. Ed. 2d 526 (1971) (for entry of a fresh decree so that a timely appeal might be taken to the Court of Appeals), aff'd, 450 F.2d 1103 (CA5 1971); to suspensions of under five days, Vail v. Board of Education of Portsmouth School Dist., 354 F. Supp. 592 (NH 1973); and to all suspensions, Mills v. Board of Education of the District of Columbia, 348 F. Supp. 866 (DC 1972), and Givens v. Poe, 346 F. Supp. 202 (WDNC 1972); and inapplicable to suspensions of 25 days, Hernandez v. School District Number One, Denver, Colorado, 315 F. Supp. 289 (D .C.Colo.1970); to suspensions of 10 days, Baker v. Downey City Board of Education, 307 F. Supp. 517 (CD Cal.1969); and to suspension of eight days, Hatter v. Los Angeles City High School District, 310 F. Supp. 1309 (CD Cal.1970), rev'd on other grounds, 452 F.2d 673 (CA9 1971). In the cases holding no process necessary in connection with short suspensions, it is not always clear whether the court viewed the Due Process Clause as inapplicable, or simply felt that the process received was 'due' even in the absence of some kind of hearing procedure.

by later opinions, said that '(m)any controversies have raged about the cryptic and abstract words of the Due Process Clause but there can be no doubt that at a minimum they require that deprivation of life, liberty or property by adjudication be preceded by notice and opportunity for hearing appropriate to the nature of the case.' Id., at 313, 70 S. Ct. at 657. 'The fundamental requisite of due process of law is the opportunity to be heard,' Grannis v. Ordean, 234 U.S. 385, 394, 34 S. Ct. 779, 783, 58 L. Ed. 1363 (1914), a right that 'has little reality or worth unless one is informed that the matter is pending and can choose for himself whether to . . . contest.' Mullane v. Central Hanover Trust Co., supra, 339 U.S. at 314, 70 S. Ct. at 657. See also Armstrong v. Manzo, 380 U.S. 545, 550, 85 S. Ct. 1187, 1190, 14 L. Ed. 2d 62 (1965); Joint Anti-Fascist Committee v. McGrath, 341 U.S. 123, 168–169, 71 S. Ct. 624, 646–647, 95 L. Ed. 817 (1951) (Frankfurter, J., concurring). At the very minimum, therefore, students facing suspension and the consequent interference with a protected property interest must be given some kind of notice and afforded some kind of hearing. 'Parties whose rights are to be affected are entitled to be heard; and in order that they may enjoy that right they must first be notified.' Baldwin v. Hale, 1 Wall. 223, 233, 17 L. Ed. 531 (1864).

It also appears from our cases that the timing and content of the notice and the nature of the hearing will depend on appropriate accommodation of the competing interests involved. Cafeteria Workers v. McElroy, supra, 367 U.S. at 895, 81 S. Ct. at 1748; Morrissey v. Brewer, supra, 408 U.S. at 481, 92 S. Ct. at 2600. The student's interest is to avoid unfair or mistaken exclusion from the educational process, with all of its unfortunate consequences. The Due Process Clause will not shield him from suspensions properly imposed, but it disserves both his interest and the interest of the State if his suspension is in fact unwarranted. The concern would be mostly academic if the disciplinary process were a totally accurate, unerring process, never mistaken and never unfair. Unfortunately, that is not the case, and no one suggests that it is. Disciplinarians, although proceeding in utmost good faith, frequently act on the reports and advice of others; and the controlling facts and the nature of the conduct under challenge are often disputed. The risk of error is not at all trivial, and it should be guarded against if that may be done without prohibitive cost or interference with the educational process.

The difficulty is that our schools are vast and complex. Some modicum of discipline and order is essential if the educational function is to be performed. Events calling for discipline are frequent occurrences and sometimes require immediate, effective action. Suspension is considered not only to be a necessary tool to maintain order but a valuable educational device. The prospect of imposing elaborate hearing requirements in every suspension case is viewed with great concern, and many school authorities may well prefer the untrammeled power to act unilaterally, unhampered by rules about notice and hearing. But it would be a strange disciplinary system in an educational institution if no communication was sought by the disciplinarian with the student in an effort to inform him of his dereliction and to let him tell his side of the story in order to make sure that an injustice is not done.

'(F)airness can rarely be obtained by secret, one-sided determination of facts decisive of rights. . . .' 'Secrecy is not congenial to truth-seeking and self-righteousness gives too slender an assurance of rightness. No better instrument has been devised for arriving at truth than to give a person in jeopardy of serious loss notice of the case against him and opportunity to meet it.' Joint Anti-Fascist Committee v. McGrath, supra, 341 U.S., at 170, 172–173, 71 S. Ct., at 647–649 (Frankfurter, J., concurring).[223]

We do not believe that school authorities must be totally free from notice and hearing requirements if their schools are to operate with acceptable efficiency. Students facing temporary suspension have interests qualifying for protection of the Due Process Clause, and due process requires, in connection with a suspension of 10 days or less, that the student be given oral or written notice of the charges against him and, if he denies them, an explanation of the evidence the authorities have and an opportunity to present his side of the story. The Clause requires at least these rudimentary precautions against unfair or mistaken findings of misconduct and arbitrary exclusion from school.[224]

There need be no delay between the time 'notice' is given and the time of the hearing. In the great majority of cases the disciplinarian may informally discuss

223. The facts involved in this case illustrate the point. Betty Crome was suspended for conduct which did not occur on school grounds, and for which mass arrests were made—hardly guaranteeing careful individualized fact finding by the police or by the school principal. She claims to have been involved in no misconduct. However, she was suspended for 10 days without ever being told what she was accused of doing or being given an opportunity to explain her presence among those arrested. Similarly, Dwight Lopez was suspended, along with many others, in connection with a disturbance in the lunchroom. Lopez says he was not one of those in the lunchroom who was involved. However, he was never told the basis for the principal's belief that he was involved, nor was he ever given an opportunity to explain his presence in the lunchroom. The school principals who suspended Crome and Lopez may have been correct on the merits, but it is inconsistent with the Due Process Clause to have made the decision that misconduct had occurred without at some meaningful time giving Crome or Lopez an opportunity to persuade the principals otherwise.

We recognize that both suspensions were imposed during a time of great difficulty for the school administrations involved. At least in Lopez' case there may have been an immediate need to send home everyone in the lunchroom in order to preserve school order and property; and the administrative burden of providing 75 'hearings' of any kind is considerable. However, neither factor justifies a disciplinary suspension without at any time gathering facts relating to Lopez specifically, confronting him with them, and giving him an opportunity to explain.

224. Appellants point to the fact that some process is provided under Ohio law by way of judicial review. Ohio Rev. Code Ann. s 2506.01 (Supp. 1973). Appellants do not cite any case in which this general administrative review statute has been used to appeal from a disciplinary decision by a school official. If it be assumed that it could be so used, it is for two reasons insufficient to save inadequate procedures at the school level. First, although new proof may be offered in a s 2506.01 proceeding, Shaker Coventry Corp. v. Shaker Heights Planning Comm'n, 18 Ohio Op.2d 272, 176 N.E.2d 332 (1961), the proceeding is not de novo. In re Locke, 33 Ohio App. 2d 177, 294 N.E.2d 230 (1972). Thus the decision by the school—even if made upon inadequate procedures—is entitled to weight in the court proceeding. Second, without a demonstration to the contrary, we must assume that delay will attend any s 2506.01 proceeding, that the suspension will not be stayed pending hearing, and that the student meanwhile will irreparably lose his educational benefits.

the alleged misconduct with the student minutes after it has occurred. We hold only that, in being given an opportunity to explain his version of the facts at this discussion, the student first be told what he is accused of doing and what the basis of the accusation is. Lower courts which have addressed the question of the nature of the procedures required in short suspension cases have reached the same conclusion. Tate v. Board of Education, 453 F.2d 975, 979 (CA8 1972); Vail v. Board of Education, 354 F.Supp. 592, 603 (NH 1973). Since the hearing may occur almost immediately following the misconduct, it follows that as a general rule notice and hearing should precede removal of the student from school. We agree with the District Court, however, that there are recurring situations in which prior notice and hearing cannot be insisted upon. Students whose presence poses a continuing danger to persons or property or an ongoing threat of disrupting the academic process may be immediately removed from school. In such cases, the necessary notice and rudimentary hearing should follow as soon as practicable, as the District Court indicated.

In holding as we do, we do not believe that we have imposed procedures on school disciplinarians which are inappropriate in a classroom setting. Instead we have imposed requirements which are, if anything, less than a fair-minded school principal would impose upon himself in order to avoid unfair suspensions. Indeed, according to the testimony of the principal of Marion-Franklin High School, that school had an informal procedure, remarkably similar to that which we now require, applicable to suspensions generally but which was not followed in this case. Similarly, according to the most recent memorandum applicable to the entire CPSS, see n. 1, supra, school principals in the CPSS are now required by local rule to provide at least as much as the constitutional minimum which we have described.

We stop short of construing the Due Process Clause to require, countrywide, that hearings in connection with short suspensions must afford the student the opportunity to secure counsel, to confront and cross-examine witnesses supporting the charge, or to call his own witnesses to verify his version of the incident. Brief disciplinary suspensions are almost countless. To impose in each such case even truncated trial-type procedures might well overwhelm administrative facilities in many places and, by diverting resources, cost more than it would save in educational effectiveness. Moreover, further formalizing the suspension process and escalating its formality and adversary nature may not only make it too costly as a regular disciplinary tool but also destroy its effectiveness as part of the teaching process.

On the other hand, requiring effective notice and informal hearing permitting the student to give his version of the events will provide a meaningful hedge against erroneous action. At least the disciplinarian will be alerted to the existence of disputes about facts and arguments about cause and effect. He may then determine himself to summon the accuser, permit cross-examination, and allow the student to present his own witnesses. In more difficult cases, he may permit counsel. In any event, his discretion will be more informed and we think the risk of error substantially reduced.

Requiring that there be at least an informal give-and-take between student and disciplinarian, preferably prior to the suspension, will add little to the fact-finding function where the disciplinarian himself has witnessed the conduct forming the basis for the charge. But things are not always as they seem to be, and the student will at least have the opportunity to characterize his conduct and put it in what he deems the proper context.

We should also make it clear that we have addressed ourselves solely to the short suspension, not exceeding 10 days. Longer suspensions or expulsions for the remainder of the school term, or permanently, may require more formal procedures. Nor do we put aside the possibility that in unusual situations, although involving only a short suspension, something more than the rudimentary procedures will be required.

IV

The District Court found each of the suspensions involved here to have occurred without a hearing, either before or after the suspension, and that each suspension was therefore invalid and the statute unconstitutional insofar as it permits such suspensions without notice or hearing. Accordingly, the judgment is *Affirmed.*

[Case No. 4-2]

If students are held in custody in school interrogations, they must be read their Miranda rights.

J.D.B. v. North Carolina

Supreme Court of the United States
564 U.S. 261 (2011)

Justice SOTOMAYOR delivered the opinion of the Court.

This case presents the question whether the age of a child subjected to police questioning is relevant to the custody analysis of Miranda v. Arizona, 384 U.S. 436, 86 S. Ct. 1602, 16 L. Ed. 2d 694 (1966). It is beyond dispute that children will often feel bound to submit to police questioning when an adult in the same circumstances would feel free to leave. Seeing no reason for police officers or courts to blind themselves to that commonsense reality, we hold that a child's age properly informs the Miranda custody analysis.

I

A

This case involved J.D.B., a 13-year-old, seventh-grade student attending class at Smith Middle School in Chapel Hill, North Carolina when he was removed from his classroom by a uniformed police officer, escorted to a closed-door conference room, and questioned by police for at least half an hour.

This was the second time that police questioned J.D.B. in the span of a week. Five days earlier, two home break-ins occurred, and various items were stolen. Police stopped and questioned J.D.B. after he was seen behind a residence in the neighborhood where the crimes occurred. That same day, police also spoke to J.D.B.'s grandmother—his legal guardian—as well as his aunt.

Police later learned that a digital camera matching the description of one of the stolen items had been found at J.D.B.'s middle school and seen in J.D.B.'s possession. Investigator DiCostanzo, the juvenile investigator with the local police force who had been assigned to the case, went to the school to question J.D.B. Upon arrival, DiCostanzo informed the uniformed police officer on detail to the school (a so-called school resource officer), the assistant principal, and an administrative intern that he was there to question J.D.B. about the break-ins. Although DiCostanzo asked the school administrators to verify J.D.B.'s date of birth, address, and parent contact information from school records, neither the police officers nor the school administrators contacted J.D.B.'s grandmother.

The uniformed officer interrupted J.D.B.'s afternoon social studies class, removed J.D.B. from the classroom, and escorted him to a school conference room.[225] There, J.D.B. was met by DiCostanzo, the assistant principal, and the administrative intern. The door to the conference room was closed. With the two police officers and the two administrators present, J.D.B. was questioned for the next 30 to 45 minutes. Prior to the commencement of questioning, J.D.B. was given neither Miranda warnings nor the opportunity to speak to his grandmother. Nor was he informed that he was free to leave the room.

Questioning began with small talk—discussion of sports and J.D.B.'s family life. DiCostanzo asked, and J.D.B. agreed, to discuss the events of the prior weekend. Denying any wrongdoing, J.D.B. explained that he had been in the neighborhood where the crimes occurred because he was seeking work mowing lawns. DiCostanzo pressed J.D.B. for additional detail about his efforts to obtain work; asked J.D.B. to explain a prior incident, when one of the victims returned home to find J.D.B. behind her house; and confronted J.D.B. with the stolen camera. The assistant principal urged J.D.B. to "do the right thing," warning J.D.B. that "the truth always comes out in the end." App. 99a, 112a.

Eventually, J.D.B. asked whether he would "still be in trouble" if he returned the "stuff." Ibid. In response, DiCostanzo explained that return of the stolen items would be helpful, but "this thing is going to court" regardless. Id., at 112a; ibid. ("[W]hat's done is done[;] now you need to help yourself by making it right"); see also id., at 99a. DiCostanzo then warned that he may need to seek a secure custody order if he believed that J.D.B. would continue to break into other homes. When J.D.B. asked

225. Although the State suggests that the "record is unclear as to who brought J.D.B. to the conference room, and the trial court made no factual findings on this specific point," Brief for Respondent 3, n. 1, the State agreed at the certiorari stage that "the SRO [school resource officer] escorted petitioner" to the room, Brief in Opposition 3.

what a secure custody order was, DiCostanzo explained that "it's where you get sent to juvenile detention before court." Id., at 112a.

After learning of the prospect of juvenile detention, J.D.B. confessed that he and a friend were responsible for the break-ins. DiCostanzo only then informed J.D.B. that he could refuse to answer the investigator's questions and that he was free to leave.[226] Asked whether he understood, J.D.B. nodded and provided further detail, including information about the location of the stolen items. Eventually J.D.B. wrote a statement, at DiCostanzo's request. When the bell rang indicating the end of the schoolday, J.D.B. was allowed to leave to catch the bus home.

B

Two juvenile petitions were filed against J.D.B., each alleging one count of breaking and entering and one count of larceny. J.D.B.'s public defender moved to suppress his statements and the evidence derived therefrom, arguing that suppression was necessary because J.D.B. had been "interrogated by police in a custodial setting without being afforded Miranda warning[s]," App. 89a, and because his statements were involuntary under the totality of the circumstances test, id., at 142a; see Schneckloth v. Bustamonte, 412 U.S. 218, 226, 93 S. Ct. 2041, 36 L. Ed. 2d 854 (1973) (due process precludes admission of a confession where "a defendant's will was overborne" by the circumstances of the interrogation). After a suppression hearing at which DiCostanzo and J.D.B. testified, the trial court denied the motion, deciding that J.D.B. was not in custody at the time of the schoolhouse interrogation and that his statements were voluntary. As a result, J.D.B. entered a transcript of admission to all four counts, renewing his objection to the denial of his motion to suppress, and the court adjudicated J.D.B. delinquent.

A divided panel of the North Carolina Court of Appeals affirmed. In re J.D.B., 196 N.C.App. 234, 674 S.E.2d 795 (2009). The North Carolina Supreme Court held, over two dissents, that J.D.B. was not in custody when he confessed, "declin[ing] to extend the test for custody to include consideration of the age . . . of an individual

226. The North Carolina Supreme Court noted that the trial court's factual findings were "uncontested and therefore . . . binding" on it. In re J.D.B., 363 N.C. 664, 668, 686 S.E.2d 135, 137 (2009). The court described the sequence of events set forth in the text. See id., at 670–671, 686 S.E.2d, at 139. ("Immediately following J.D.B.'s initial confession, Investigator DiCostanzo informed J.D.B. that he did not have to speak with him and that he was free to leave" (internal quotation marks and alterations omitted)). Though less than perfectly explicit, the trial court's order indicates a finding that J.D.B. initially confessed prior to DiCostanzo's warnings. See App. 99a.

Nonetheless, both parties' submissions to this Court suggest that the warnings came after DiCostanzo raised the possibility of a secure custody order but before J.D.B. confessed for the first time. See Brief for Petitioner 5; Brief for Respondent 5. Because we remand for a determination whether J.D.B. was in custody under the proper analysis, the state courts remain free to revisit whether the trial court made a conclusive finding of fact in this respect.

subjected to questioning by police." In re J.D.B., 363 N.C. 664, 672, 686 S.E.2d 135, 140 (2009).[227]

We granted certiorari to determine whether the Miranda custody analysis includes consideration of a juvenile suspect's age. 562 U.S. ——, 131 S. Ct. 502, 178 L. Ed. 2d 368 (2010).

II

A

Any police interview of an individual suspected of a crime has "coercive aspects to it." Oregon v. Mathiason, 429 U.S. 492, 495, 97 S. Ct. 711, 50 L. Ed. 2d 714 (1977) (per curiam). Only those interrogations that occur while a suspect is in police custody, however, "heighte[n] the risk" that statements obtained are not the product of the suspect's free choice. Dickerson v. United States, 530 U.S. 428, 435, 120 S. Ct. 2326, 147 L. Ed. 2d 405 (2000).

By its very nature, custodial police interrogation entails "inherently compelling pressures." Miranda, 384 U.S., at 467, 86 S. Ct. 1602. Even for an adult, the physical and psychological isolation of custodial interrogation can "undermine the individual's will to resist and . . . compel him to speak where he would not otherwise do so freely." Ibid. Indeed, the pressure of custodial interrogation is so immense that it "can induce a frighteningly high percentage of people to confess to crimes they never committed." Corley v. United States, 556 U.S. 303, ——, 129 S. Ct. 1558, 1570, 173 L. Ed. 2d 443 (2009) (citing Drizin & Leo, The Problem of False Confessions in the Post-DNA World, 82 N.C. L. Rev. 891, 906–907 (2004)); see also Miranda, 384 U.S., at 455, n. 23, 86 S. Ct. 1602. That risk is all the more troubling—and recent studies suggest, all the more acute—when the subject of custodial interrogation is a juvenile. See Brief for Center on Wrongful Convictions of Youth et al. as Amici Curiae 21–22 (collecting empirical studies that "illustrate the heightened risk of false confessions from youth").

Recognizing that the inherently coercive nature of custodial interrogation "blurs the line between voluntary and involuntary statements," Dickerson, 530 U.S., at 435, 120 S. Ct. 2326, this Court in Miranda adopted a set of prophylactic measures designed to safeguard the constitutional guarantee against self-incrimination. Prior to questioning, a suspect "must be warned that he has a right to remain silent, that any statement he does make may be used as evidence against him, and that he has a right to the presence of an attorney, either retained or appointed." 384 U.S., at 444, 86 S. Ct. 1602; see also Florida v. Powell, 559 U.S. ——, ——, 130 S. Ct. 1195, 1198, 175 L. Ed. 2d 1009 (2010) ("The four warnings Miranda requires are invariable, but this Court has not dictated the words in which the essential information must be

227. J.D.B.'s challenge in the North Carolina Supreme Court focused on the lower courts' conclusion that he was not in custody for purposes of Miranda v. Arizona, 384 U.S. 436, 86 S. Ct. 1602, 16 L. Ed. 2d 694 (1966). The North Carolina Supreme Court did not address the trial court's holding that the statements were voluntary, and that question is not before us.

conveyed"). And, if a suspect makes a statement during custodial interrogation, the burden is on the Government to show, as a "prerequisit[e]" to the statement's admissibility as evidence in the Government's case in chief, that the defendant "voluntarily, knowingly and intelligently" waived his rights.[228] Miranda, 384 U.S., at 444, 475–476, 86 S. Ct. 1602; Dickerson, 530 U.S., at 443–444, 120 S. Ct. 2326.

Because these measures protect the individual against the coercive nature of custodial interrogation, they are required "'only where there has been such a restriction on a person's freedom as to render him "in custody."'" Stansbury v. California, 511 U.S. 318, 322, 114 S. Ct. 1526, 128 L. Ed. 2d 293 (1994) (per curiam) (quoting Oregon v. Mathiason, 429 U.S. 492, 495, 97 S. Ct. 711, 50 L. Ed. 2d 714 (1977) (per curiam)). As we have repeatedly emphasized, whether a suspect is "in custody" is an objective inquiry.

"Two discrete inquiries are essential to the determination: first, what were the circumstances surrounding the interrogation; and second, given those circumstances, would a reasonable person have felt he or she was at liberty to terminate the interrogation and leave. Once the scene is set and the players' lines and actions are reconstructed, the court must apply an objective test to resolve the ultimate inquiry: was there a formal arrest or restraint on freedom of movement of the degree associated with formal arrest." Thompson v. Keohane, 516 U.S. 99, 112, 116 S. Ct. 457, 133 L. Ed. 2d 383 (1995) (internal quotation marks, alteration, and footnote omitted).

See also Yarborough v. Alvarado, 541 U.S. 652, 662–663, 124 S. Ct. 2140, 158 L. Ed. 2d 938 (2004); Stansbury, 511 U.S., at 323, 114 S. Ct. 1526; Berkemer v. McCarty, 468 U.S. 420, 442, and n. 35, 104 S. Ct. 3138, 82 L. Ed. 2d 317 (1984). Rather than demarcate a limited set of relevant circumstances, we have required police officers and courts to "examine all of the circumstances surrounding the interrogation," Stansbury, 511 U.S., at 322, 114 S. Ct. 1526, including any circumstance that "would have affected how a reasonable person" in the suspect's position "would perceive his or her freedom to leave," id., at 325, 114 S. Ct. 1526. On the other hand, the "subjective views harbored by either the interrogating officers or the person being questioned" are irrelevant. Id., at 323, 114 S. Ct. 1526. The test, in other words, involves no consideration of the "actual mindset" of the particular suspect subjected to police questioning. Alvarado, 541 U.S., at 667, 124 S. Ct. 2140; see also California v. Beheler, 463 U.S. 1121, 1125, n. 3, 103 S. Ct. 3517, 77 L. Ed. 2d 1275 (1983) (per curiam).

The benefit of the objective custody analysis is that it is "designed to give clear guidance to the police." Alvarado, 541 U.S., at 668, 124 S. Ct. 2140. But see Berkemer, 468 U.S., at 441, 104 S. Ct. 3138 (recognizing the "occasiona[l] . . . difficulty" that

228. Amici on behalf of J.D.B. question whether children of all ages can comprehend Miranda warnings and suggest that additional procedural safeguards may be necessary to protect their Miranda rights. Brief for Juvenile Law Center et al. as Amici Curiae 13–14, n. 7. Whatever the merit of that contention, it has no relevance here, where no Miranda warnings were administered at all.

police and courts nonetheless have in "deciding exactly when a suspect has been taken into custody"). Police must make in-the-moment judgments as to when to administer Miranda warnings. By limiting analysis to the objective circumstances of the interrogation, and asking how a reasonable person in the suspect's position would understand his freedom to terminate questioning and leave, the objective test avoids burdening police with the task of anticipating the idiosyncrasies of every individual suspect and divining how those particular traits affect each person's subjective state of mind. See id., at 430–431, 104 S. Ct. 3138 (officers are not required to "make guesses" as to circumstances "unknowable" to them at the time); Alvarado, 541 U.S., at 668, 124 S. Ct. 2140 (officers are under no duty "to consider . . . contingent psychological factors when deciding when suspects should be advised of their Miranda rights").

B

The State and its amici contend that a child's age has no place in the custody analysis, no matter how young the child subjected to police questioning. We cannot agree. In some circumstances, a child's age "would have affected how a reasonable person" in the suspect's position "would perceive his or her freedom to leave." Stansbury, 511 U.S., at 325, 114 S. Ct. 1526. That is, a reasonable child subjected to police questioning will sometimes feel pressured to submit when a reasonable adult would feel free to go. We think it clear that courts can account for that reality without doing any damage to the objective nature of the custody analysis.

A child's age is far "more than a chronological fact." Eddings v. Oklahoma, 455 U.S. 104, 115, 102 S. Ct. 869, 71 L. Ed. 2d 1 (1982); accord, Gall v. United States, 552 U.S. 38, 58, 128 S. Ct. 586, 169 L. Ed. 2d 445 (2007); Roper v. Simmons, 543 U.S. 551, 569, 125 S. Ct. 1183, 161 L. Ed. 2d 1 (2005); Johnson v. Texas, 509 U.S. 350, 367, 113 S. Ct. 2658, 125 L. Ed. 2d 290 (1993). It is a fact that "generates commonsense conclusions about behavior and perception." Alvarado, 541 U.S., at 674, 124 S. Ct. 2140 (BREYER, J., dissenting). Such conclusions apply broadly to children as a class. And, they are self-evident to anyone who was a child once himself, including any police officer or judge.

Time and again, this Court has drawn these commonsense conclusions for itself. We have observed that children "generally are less mature and responsible than adults," Eddings, 455 U.S., at 115–116, 102 S. Ct. 869; that they "often lack the experience, perspective, and judgment to recognize and avoid choices that could be detrimental to them," Bellotti v. Baird, 443 U.S. 622, 635, 99 S. Ct. 3035, 61 L. Ed. 2d 797 (1979) (plurality opinion); that they "are more vulnerable or susceptible to . . . outside pressures" than adults, Roper, 543 U.S., at 569, 125 S. Ct. 1183; and so on. See Graham v. Florida, 560 U.S. ——, ——, 130 S. Ct. 2011, 2026, 176 L. Ed. 2d 825 (2010) (finding no reason to "reconsider" these observations about the common "nature of juveniles"). Addressing the specific context of police interrogation, we have observed that events that "would leave a man cold and unimpressed can overawe and overwhelm a lad in his early teens." Haley v. Ohio, 332 U.S. 596, 599, 68 S. Ct. 302, 92 L. Ed. 224 (1948) (plurality opinion); see also Gallegos v. Colorado, 370 U.S. 49, 54, 82 S. Ct. 1209, 8 L. Ed. 2d 325 (1962) ("[N]o matter how sophisticated," a juvenile subject of police interrogation "cannot be compared" to an adult subject). Describing no one child in particular, these observations restate what "any parent knows"—indeed, what any person knows—about children generally. Roper, 543 U.S., at 569, 125 S. Ct. 1183.[229]

Our various statements to this effect are far from unique. The law has historically reflected the same assumption that children characteristically lack the capacity to exercise mature judgment and possess only an incomplete ability to understand the world around them. See, e.g., 1 W. Blackstone, Commentaries on the Laws of England *464–*465 (hereinafter Blackstone) (explaining that limits on children's legal capacity under the common law "secure them from hurting themselves by their own improvident acts"). Like this Court's own generalizations, the legal disqualifications placed on children as a class—e.g., limitations on their ability to alienate property, enter a binding contract enforceable against them, and marry without parental consent—exhibit the settled understanding that the differentiating characteristics of youth are universal.[230]

Indeed, even where a "reasonable person" standard otherwise applies, the common law has reflected the reality that children are not adults. In negligence suits, for instance, where liability turns on what an objectively reasonable person would do in the circumstances, "[a]ll American jurisdictions accept the idea that a person's childhood is a relevant circumstance" to be considered. Restatement (Third) of Torts § 10, Comment b, p. 117 (2005); see also id., Reporters' Note, pp. 121–122 (collecting cases); Restatement (Second) of Torts § 283A, Comment b, p. 15 (1963–1964)

229. Although citation to social science and cognitive science authorities is unnecessary to establish these commonsense propositions, the literature confirms what experience bears out. See, e.g., Graham v. Florida, 560 U.S. ——, ——, 130 S. Ct. 2011, 2026, 176 L. Ed. 2d 825 (2010) ("[D]evelopments in psychology and brain science continue to show fundamental differences between juvenile and adult minds").

230. See, e.g., 1 E. Farnsworth, Contracts § 4.4, p. 379, and n. 1 (1990) ("Common law courts early announced the prevailing view that a minor's contract is 'voidable' at the instance of the minor" (citing 8 W. Holdsworth, History of English Law 51 (1926))); 1 D. Kramer, Legal Rights of Children § 8.1, p. 663 (rev.2d ed. 2005) ("[W]hile minor children have the right to acquire and own property, they are considered incapable of property management" (footnote omitted)); 2 J. Kent, Commentaries on American Law *78–*79, *90 (G. Comstock ed., 11th ed. 1867); see generally id., at 233 (explaining that, under the common law, "[t]he necessity of guardians results from the inability of infants to take care of themselves . . . and this inability continues, in contemplation of law, until the infant has attained the age of [21]"); 1 Blackstone 465 ("It is generally true, that an infant can neither aliene his lands, nor do any legal act, nor make a deed, nor indeed any manner of contract, that will bind him"); Roper v. Simmons, 543 U.S. 551, 569, 125 S. Ct. 1183, 161 L. Ed. 2d 1 (2005) ("In recognition of the comparative immaturity and irresponsibility of juveniles, almost every State prohibits those under 18 years of age from voting, serving on juries, or marrying without parental consent").

("[T]here is a wide basis of community experience upon which it is possible, as a practical matter, to determine what is to be expected of [children]").

As this discussion establishes, "[o]ur history is replete with laws and judicial recognition" that children cannot be viewed simply as miniature adults. Eddings, 455 U.S., at 115–116, 102 S. Ct. 869. We see no justification for taking a different course here. So long as the child's age was known to the officer at the time of the interview, or would have been objectively apparent to any reasonable officer, including age as part of the custody analysis requires officers neither to consider circumstances "unknowable" to them, Berkemer, 468 U.S., at 430, 104 S. Ct. 3138, nor to "anticipat[e] the frailties or idiosyncrasies" of the particular suspect whom they question, Alvarado, 541 U.S., at 662, 124 S. Ct. 2140 (internal quotation marks omitted). The same "wide basis of community experience" that makes it possible, as an objective matter, "to determine what is to be expected" of children in other contexts, Restatement (Second) of Torts § 283A, at 15; see supra, at 2403, and n. 6, likewise makes it possible to know what to expect of children subjected to police questioning.

In other words, a child's age differs from other personal characteristics that, even when known to police, have no objectively discernible relationship to a reasonable person's understanding of his freedom of action. Alvarado, holds, for instance, that a suspect's prior interrogation history with law enforcement has no role to play in the custody analysis because such experience could just as easily lead a reasonable person to feel free to walk away as to feel compelled to stay in place. 541 U.S., at 668, 124 S. Ct. 2140. Because the effect in any given case would be " contingent [on the] psycholog[y]" of the individual suspect, the Court explained, such experience cannot be considered without compromising the objective nature of the custody analysis. Ibid. A child's age, however, is different. Precisely because childhood yields objective conclusions like those we have drawn ourselves — among others, that children are " most susceptible to influence," Eddings, 455 U.S., at 115, 102 S. Ct. 869, and "outside pressures," Roper, 543 U.S., at 569, 125 S. Ct. 1183 — considering age in the custody analysis in no way involves a determination of how youth "subjectively affect[s] the mindset" of any particular child, Brief for Respondent 14.[231]

In fact, in many cases involving juvenile suspects, the custody analysis would be nonsensical absent some consideration of the suspect's age. This case is a prime example. Were the court precluded from taking J.D.B.'s youth into account, it would be forced to evaluate the circumstances present here through the eyes of a reasonable person of average years. In other words, how would a reasonable adult understand his situation, after being removed from a seventh-grade social studies class by a uniformed school resource officer; being encouraged by his assistant principal to "do the right thing"; and being warned by a police investigator of the prospect

231. Thus, contrary to the dissent's protestations, today's holding neither invites consideration of whether a particular suspect is "unusually meek or compliant," post, at 2413 (opinion of Alito, J.), nor "expan[ds]" the Miranda custody analysis, post, at 2412–2413, into a test that requires officers to anticipate and account for a suspect's every personal characteristic, see post, at 2414–2415.

of juvenile detention and separation from his guardian and primary caretaker? To describe such an inquiry is to demonstrate its absurdity. Neither officers nor courts can reasonably evaluate the effect of objective circumstances that, by their nature, are specific to children without accounting for the age of the child subjected to those circumstances.

Indeed, although the dissent suggests that concerns "regarding the application of the Miranda custody rule to minors can be accommodated by considering the unique circumstances present when minors are questioned in school," post, at 2417 (opinion of ALITO, J.), the effect of the schoolhouse setting cannot be disentangled from the identity of the person questioned. A student — whose presence at school is compulsory and whose disobedience at school is cause for disciplinary action — is in a far different position than, say, a parent volunteer on school grounds to chaperone an event, or an adult from the community on school grounds to attend a basketball game. Without asking whether the person "questioned in school" is a "minor," ibid., the coercive effect of the schoolhouse setting is unknowable.

Our prior decision in Alvarado in no way undermines these conclusions. In that case, we held that a state-court decision that failed to mention a 17–year–old's age as part of the Miranda custody analysis was not objectively unreasonable under the deferential standard of review set forth by the Antiterrorism and Effective Death Penalty Act of 1996 (AEDPA), 110 Stat. 1214. Like the North Carolina Supreme Court here, see 363 N.C., at 672, 686 S.E.2d, at 140, we observed that accounting for a juvenile's age in the Miranda custody analysis "could be viewed as creating a subjective inquiry," 541 U.S., at 668, 124 S. Ct. 2140. We said nothing, however, of whether such a view would be correct under the law. Cf. Renico v. Lett, 559 U.S. ——, ——, n. 3, 130 S. Ct. 1855, 1865 n. 3, 176 L. Ed. 2d 678 (2010) ("[W]hether the [state court] was right or wrong is not the pertinent question under AEDPA"). To the contrary, Justice O'Connor's concurring opinion explained that a suspect's age may indeed "be relevant to the 'custody' inquiry." Alvarado, 541 U.S., at 669, 124 S. Ct. 2140.

Reviewing the question de novo today, we hold that so long as the child's age was known to the officer at the time of police questioning, or would have been objectively apparent to a reasonable officer, its inclusion in the custody analysis is consistent with the objective nature of that test.[232] This is not to say that a child's age will be a determinative, or even a significant, factor in every case. Cf. ibid. (O'Connor,

232. This approach does not undermine the basic principle that an interrogating officer's unarticulated, internal thoughts are never — in and of themselves — objective circumstances of an interrogation. See supra, at 2402; Stansbury v. California, 511 U.S. 318, 323, 114 S. Ct. 1526, 128 L. Ed. 2d 293 (1994) (per curiam). Unlike a child's youth, an officer's purely internal thoughts have no conceivable effect on how a reasonable person in the suspect's position would understand his freedom of action. See id., at 323–325, 114 S. Ct. 1526; Berkemer v. McCarty, 468 U.S. 420, 442, 104 S. Ct. 3138, 82 L. Ed. 2d 317 (1984). Rather than "overtur[n]" that settled principle, post, at 2415, the limitation that a child's age may inform the custody analysis only when known or knowable simply reflects our unwillingness to require officers to "make guesses" as to circumstances "unknowable" to them in deciding when to give Miranda warnings, Berkemer, 468 U.S., at 430–431, 104 S. Ct. 3138.

J., concurring) (explaining that a state-court decision omitting any mention of the defendant's age was not unreasonable under AEDPA's deferential standard of review where the defendant "was almost 18 years old at the time of his interview"); post, at 2417 (suggesting that "teenagers nearing the age of majority" are likely to react to an interrogation as would a "typical 18-year-old in similar circumstances"). It is, however, a reality that courts cannot simply ignore.

III

The State and its amici offer numerous reasons that courts must blind themselves to a juvenile defendant's age. None is persuasive.

To start, the State contends that a child's age must be excluded from the custody inquiry because age is a personal characteristic specific to the suspect himself rather than an "external" circumstance of the interrogation. Brief for Respondent 21; see also id., at 18–19 (distinguishing "personal characteristics" from "objective facts related to the interrogation itself" such as the location and duration of the interrogation). Despite the supposed significance of this distinction, however, at oral argument counsel for the State suggested without hesitation that at least some undeniably personal characteristics — for instance, whether the individual being questioned is blind — are circumstances relevant to the custody analysis. See Tr. of Oral Arg. 41. Thus, the State's quarrel cannot be that age is a personal characteristic, without more.[233]

The State further argues that age is irrelevant to the custody analysis because it "go[es] to how a suspect may internalize and perceive the circumstances of an interrogation." Brief for Respondent 12; see also Brief for United States as Amicus Curiae 21 (hereinafter U.S. Brief) (arguing that a child's age has no place in the custody analysis because it goes to whether a suspect is "particularly susceptible" to the external circumstances of the interrogation (some internal quotation marks omitted)). But the same can be said of every objective circumstance that the State agrees is relevant to the custody analysis: Each circumstance goes to how a reasonable person would "internalize and perceive" every other. See, e.g., Stansbury, 511 U.S., at 325, 114 S. Ct. 1526. Indeed, this is the very reason that we ask whether the objective circumstances "add up to custody," Keohane, 516 U.S., at 113, 116 S. Ct. 457, instead of evaluating the circumstances one by one.

In the same vein, the State and its amici protest that the "effect of . . . age on [the] perception of custody is internal," Brief for Respondent 20, or "psychological," U.S. Brief 21. But the whole point of the custody analysis is to determine whether, given the circumstances, "a reasonable person [would] have felt he or she was . . . at liberty

233. The State's purported distinction between blindness and age — that taking account of a suspect's youth requires a court "to get into the mind" of the child, whereas taking account of a suspect's blindness does not, Tr. of Oral Arg. 41–42 — is mistaken. In either case, the question becomes how a reasonable person would understand the circumstances, either from the perspective of a blind person or, as here, a 13-year-old child.

to terminate the interrogation and leave." Keohane, 516 U.S., at 112, 116 S. Ct. 457. Because the Miranda custody inquiry turns on the mindset of a reasonable person in the suspect's position, it cannot be the case that a circumstance is subjective simply because it has an "internal" or " psychological" impact on perception. Were that so, there would be no objective circumstances to consider at all.

Relying on our statements that the objective custody test is "designed to give clear guidance to the police," Alvarado, 541 U.S., at 668, 124 S. Ct. 2140, the State next argues that a child's age must be excluded from the analysis in order to preserve clarity. Similarly, the dissent insists that the clarity of the custody analysis will be destroyed unless a "one-size-fits-all reasonable-person test" applies. Post, at 2415. In reality, however, ignoring a juvenile defendant's age will often make the inquiry more artificial, see supra, at 2404–2405, and thus only add confusion. And in any event, a child's age, when known or apparent, is hardly an obscure factor to assess. Though the State and the dissent worry about gradations among children of different ages, that concern cannot justify ignoring a child's age altogether. Just as police officers are competent to account for other objective circumstances that are a matter of degree such as the length of questioning or the number of officers present, so too are they competent to evaluate the effect of relative age. Indeed, they are competent to do so even though an interrogation room lacks the "reflective atmosphere of a [jury] deliberation room," post, at 2416. The same is true of judges, including those whose childhoods have long since passed, see post, at 2416. In short, officers and judges need no imaginative powers, knowledge of developmental psychology, training in cognitive science, or expertise in social and cultural anthropology to account for a child's age. They simply need the common sense to know that a 7-year-old is not a 13-year-old and neither is an adult.

There is, however, an even more fundamental flaw with the State's plea for clarity and the dissent's singular focus on simplifying the analysis: Not once have we excluded from the custody analysis a circumstance that we determined was relevant and objective, simply to make the fault line between custodial and noncustodial "brighter." Indeed, were the guiding concern clarity and nothing else, the custody test would presumably ask only whether the suspect had been placed under formal arrest. Berkemer, 468 U.S., at 441, 104 S. Ct. 3138; see ibid. (acknowledging the "occasiona[l] . . . difficulty" police officers confront in determining when a suspect has been taken into custody). But we have rejected that "more easily administered line," recognizing that it would simply "enable the police to circumvent the constraints on custodial interrogations established by Miranda." Ibid.; see also ibid., n. 33.[234]

234. Contrary to the dissent's intimation, see post, at 2412–2413, Miranda does not answer the question whether a child's age is an objective circumstance relevant to the custody analysis. Miranda simply holds that warnings must be given once a suspect is in custody, without "paus[ing] to inquire in individual cases whether the defendant was aware of his rights without a warning being given." 384 U.S., at 468, 86 S. Ct. 1602; see also id., at 468–469, 86 S. Ct. 1602 ("Assessments

Finally, the State and the dissent suggest that excluding age from the custody analysis comes at no cost to juveniles' constitutional rights because the due process voluntariness test independently accounts for a child's youth. To be sure, that test permits consideration of a child's age, and it erects its own barrier to admission of a defendant's inculpatory statements at trial. See Gallegos, 370 U.S., at 53–55, 82 S. Ct. 1209; Haley, 332 U.S., at 599–601, 68 S. Ct. 302; see also post, at 2418 ("[C]ourts should be instructed to take particular care to ensure that [young children's] incriminating statements were not obtained involuntarily"). But Miranda 's procedural safeguards exist precisely because the voluntariness test is an inadequate barrier when custodial interrogation is at stake. See 384 U.S., at 458, 86 S. Ct. 1602 ("Unless adequate protective devices are employed to dispel the compulsion inherent in custodial surroundings, no statement obtained from the defendant can truly be the product of his free choice"); Dickerson, 530 U.S., at 442, 120 S. Ct. 2326 ("[R]eliance on the traditional totality-of-the-circumstances test raise[s] a risk of overlooking an involuntary custodial confession"); see also supra, at 2400–2401. To hold, as the State requests, that a child's age is never relevant to whether a suspect has been taken into custody—and thus to ignore the very real differences between children and adults—would be to deny children the full scope of the procedural safeguards that Miranda guarantees to adults.

The question remains whether J.D.B. was in custody when police interrogated him. We remand for the state courts to address that question, this time taking account of all of the relevant circumstances of the interrogation, including J.D.B.'s age at the time. The judgment of the North Carolina Supreme Court is reversed, and the case is remanded for proceedings not inconsistent with this opinion. *It is so ordered.*

[Case No. 4-3]

Students have speech rights and may not be punished for the exercise thereof unless school authorities can show the speech results in a material and substantial disruption.

Tinker v. Des Moines Independent Community School District

Supreme Court of the United States
393 U.S. 503 (1969)

Mr. Justice FORTAS delivered the opinion of the Court.

---

of the knowledge the defendant possessed, based on information as to age, education, intelligence, or prior contact with authorities, can never be more than speculation; a warning is a clearcut fact" (footnote omitted)). That conclusion says nothing about whether age properly informs whether a child is in custody in the first place.

Petitioner John F. Tinker, 15 years old, and petitioner Christopher Eckhardt, 16 years old, attended high schools in Des Moines, Iowa. Petitioner Mary Beth Tinker, John's sister, was a 13-year-old student in junior high school.

In December 1965, a group of adults and students in Des Moines held a meeting at the Eckhardt home. The group determined to publicize their objections to the hostilities in Vietnam and their support for a truce by wearing black armbands during the holiday season and by fasting on December 16 and New Year's Eve. Petitioners and their parents had previously engaged in similar activities, and they decided to participate in the program.

The principals of the Des Moines schools became aware of the plan to wear armbands. On December 14, 1965, they met and adopted a policy that any student wearing an armband to school would be asked to remove it, and if he refused he would be suspended until he returned without the armband. Petitioners were aware of the regulation that the school authorities adopted.

On December 16, Mary Beth and Christopher wore black armbands to their schools. John Tinker wore his armband the next day. They were all sent home and suspended from school until they would come back without their armbands. They did not return to school until after the planned period for wearing armbands had expired—that is, until after New Year's Day.

This complaint was filed in the United States District Court by petitioners, through their fathers, under *§ 1983 of Title 42 of the United States Code*. It prayed for an injunction restraining the respondent school officials and the respondent members of the board of directors of the school district from disciplining the petitioners, and it sought nominal damages. After an evidentiary hearing the District Court dismissed the complaint. It upheld the constitutionality of the school authorities' action on the ground that it was reasonable in order to prevent disturbance of school discipline. *258 F. Supp. 971 (1966)*. The court referred to but expressly declined to follow the Fifth Circuit's holding in a similar case that the wearing of symbols like the armbands cannot be prohibited unless it 'materially and substantially interfere(s) with the requirements of appropriate discipline in the operation of the school.' *Burnside v. Byars, 363 F.2d 744, 749 (1966)*.[235]

On appeal, the Court of Appeals for the Eighth Circuit considered the case en banc. The court was equally divided, and the District Court's decision was accordingly affirmed, without opinion, *383 F.2d 988 (1967)*. We granted certiorari. *390 U.S. 942, 88 S. Ct. 1050, 19 L. Ed. 2d 1130 (1968)*.

---

235. In Burnside, the Fifth Circuit ordered that high school authorities be enjoined from enforcing a regulation forbidding students to wear 'freedom buttons.' It is instructive that in *Blackwell v. Issaquena County Board of Education, 363 F.2d 749 (1966)*, the same panel on the same day reached the opposite result on different facts. It declined to enjoin enforcement of such a regulation in another high school where the students wearing freedom buttons harassed students who did not wear them and created much disturbance.

The District Court recognized that the wearing of an armband for the purpose of expressing certain views is the type of symbolic act that is within the Free Speech Clause of the First Amendment. See *West Virginia State Board of Education v. Barnette, 319 U.S. 624, 63 S. Ct. 1178, 87 L. Ed. 1628 (1943); Stromberg v. California, 283 U.S. 359, 51 S. Ct. 532, 75 L. Ed. 1117 (1931).* Cf. *Thornhill v. Alabama, 310 U.S. 88, 60 S. Ct. 736, 84 L. Ed. 1093 (1940); Edwards v. South Carolina, 372 U.S. 229, 83 S. Ct. 680, 9 L. Ed. 2d 697 (1963); Brown v. Louisiana, 383 U.S. 131, 86 S. Ct. 719, 15 L. Ed. 2d 637 (1966).* As we shall discuss, the wearing of armbands in the circumstances of this case was entirely divorced from actually or potentially disruptive conduct by those participating in it. It was closely akin to 'pure speech' which, we have repeatedly held, is entitled to comprehensive protection under the First Amendment. Cf. *Cox v. Louisiana, 379 U.S. 536, 555, 85 S. Ct. 453, 464, 13 L. Ed. 2d 471 (1965); Adderley v. Florida, 385 U.S. 39, 87 S. Ct. 242, 17 L. Ed. 2d 149 (1966).*

First Amendment rights, applied in light of the special characteristics of the school environment, are available to teachers and students. It can hardly be argued that either students or teachers shed their constitutional rights to freedom of speech or expression at the schoolhouse gate. This has been the unmistakable holding of this Court for almost 50 years. In *Meyer v. Nebraska, 262 U.S. 390, 43 S. Ct. 625, 67 L. Ed. 1042 (1923)*, and *Bartels v. Iowa, 262 U.S. 404, 43 S. Ct. 628, 67 L. Ed. 1047 (1923)*, this Court, in opinions by Mr. Justice McReynolds, held that the Due Process Clause of the Fourteenth Amendment prevents States from forbidding the teaching of a foreign language to young students. Statutes to this effect, the Court held, unconstitutionally interfere with the liberty of teacher, student, and parent.[236] See also *Pierce v. Society of Sisters, etc., 268 U.S. 510, 45 S. Ct. 571, 69 L. Ed. 1070 (1925); West Virginia State Board of Education v. Barnette, 319 U.S. 624, 63 S. Ct. 1178, 87 L. Ed. 1628 (1943); Illinois ex rel. McCollum v. Board of Education of School Dist. No. 71, 333 U.S. 203, 68 S. Ct. 461, 92 L. Ed. 649 (1948); Wieman v. Updegraff, 344 U.S. 183, 195, 73 S. Ct. 215, 220, 97 L. Ed. 216 (1952)* (concurring opinion); *Sweezy v. New Hampshire, 354 U.S. 234, 77 S. Ct. 1203, 1 L. Ed. 2d 1311 (1957); Shelton v. Tucker, 364 U.S. 479, 487, 81 S. Ct. 247, 251, 5 L. Ed. 2d 231 (1960); Engel v. Vitale, 370 U.S. 421,*

---

236. *Hamilton v. Regents of University of California, 293 U.S. 245, 55 S. Ct. 197, 79 L. Ed. 343* (1934), is sometimes cited for the broad proposition that the State may attach conditions to attendance at a state university that require individuals to violate their religious convictions. The case involved dismissal of members of a religious denomination from a land grant college for refusal to participate in military training. Narrowly viewed, the case turns upon the Court's conclusion that merely requiring a student to participate in school training in military 'science' could not conflict with his constitutionally protected freedom of conscience. The decision cannot be taken as establishing that the State may impose and enforce any conditions that it chooses upon attendance at public institutions of learning, however violative they may be of fundamental constitutional guarantees. See, e.g., *West Virginia State Board of Education v. Barnette, 319 U.S. 624, 63 S. Ct. 1178, 87 L. Ed. 1628 (1943); Dixon v. Alabama State Board of Education, 294 F.2d 150 (C.A.5th Cir. 1961); Knight v. State Board of Education, 200 F. Supp. 174 (D.C.M.D.Tenn.1961); Dickey v. Alabama State Board of Education, 273 F. Supp. 613 (D.C.M.D.Ala.1967).* See also *Note, Unconstitutional Conditions, 73 Harv. L. Rev. 1595 (1960)*; Note, Academic Freedom, 81 Harv. L. Rev. 1045 (1968).

82 S. Ct. 1261, 8 L. Ed. 2d 601 (1962); Keyishian v. Board of Regents, 385 U.S. 589, 603, 87 S. Ct. 675, 683, 17 L. Ed. 2d 629 (1967); Epperson v. Arkansas, 393 U.S. 97, 89 S. Ct. 266, 21 L. Ed. 2d 228 (1968).

In *West Virginia State Board of Education v. Barnette, supra*, this Court held that under the First Amendment, the student in public school may not be compelled to salute the flag. Speaking through Mr. Justice Jackson, the Court said: 'The Fourteenth Amendment, as now applied to the States, protects the citizen against the State itself and all of its creatures — Boards of Education not excepted. These have, of course, important, delicate, and highly discretionary functions, but none that they may not perform within the limits of the Bill of Rights. That they are educating the young for citizenship is reason for scrupulous protection of Constitutional freedoms of the individual, if we are not to strangle the free mind at its source and teach youth to discount important principles of our government as mere platitudes.' *319 U.S., at 637, 63 S. Ct. at 1185.*

On the other hand, the Court has repeatedly emphasized the need for affirming the comprehensive authority of the States and of school officials, consistent with fundamental constitutional safeguards, to prescribe and control conduct in the schools. See *Epperson v. Arkansas, supra, 393 U.S. at 104, 89 S. Ct. at 270; Meyer v. Nebraska, supra, 262 U.S. at 402, 43 S. Ct. at 627.* Our problem lies in the area where students in the exercise of First Amendment rights collide with the rules of the school authorities.

II.

The problem posed by the present case does not relate to regulation of the length of skirts or the type of clothing, to hair style, or deportment. Cf. *Ferrell v. Dallas Independent School District, 392 F.2d 697 (C.A. 5th Cir. 1968); Pugsley v. Sellmeyer, 158 Ark. 247, 250 S.W. 538, 30 A.L.R. 1212 (1923).* It does not concern aggressive, disruptive action or even group demonstrations. Our problem involves direct, primary First Amendment rights akin to 'pure speech.'

The school officials banned and sought to punish petitioners for a silent, passive expression of opinion, unaccompanied by any disorder or disturbance on the part of petitioners. There is here no evidence whatever of petitioners' interference, actual or nascent, with the schools' work or of collision with the rights of other students to be secure and to be let alone. Accordingly, this case does not concern speech or action that intrudes upon the work of the schools or the rights of other students. Only a few of the 18,000 students in the school system wore the black armbands. Only five students were suspended for wearing them. There is no indication that the work of the schools or any class was disrupted. Outside the classrooms, a few students made hostile remarks to the children wearing armbands, but there were no threats or acts of violence on school premises.

The District Court concluded that the action of the school authorities was reasonable because it was based upon their fear of a disturbance from the wearing of the armbands. But, in our system, undifferentiated fear or apprehension of disturbance is not enough to overcome the right to freedom of expression. Any departure from absolute regimentation may cause trouble. Any variation from the majority's opinion may inspire fear. Any word spoken, in class, in the lunchroom, or on the campus, that deviates from the views of another person may start an argument or cause a disturbance. But our Constitution says we must take this risk, *Terminiello v. Chicago, 337 U.S. 1, 69 S. Ct. 894, 93 L. Ed. 1131 (1949)*; and our history says that it is this sort of hazardous freedom — this kind of openness — that is the basis of our national strength and of the independence and vigor of Americans who grow up and live in this relatively permissive, often disputatious, society.

In order for the State in the person of school officials to justify prohibition of a particular expression of opinion, it must be able to show that its action was caused by something more than a mere desire to avoid the discomfort and unpleasantness that always accompany an unpopular viewpoint. Certainly where there is no finding and no showing that engaging in the forbidden conduct would 'materially and substantially interfere with the requirements of appropriate discipline in the operation of the school,' the prohibition cannot be sustained. *Burnside v. Byars, supra, 363 F.2d at 749.*In the present case, the District Court made no such finding, and our independent examination of the record fails to yield evidence that the school authorities had reason to anticipate that the wearing of the armbands would substantially interfere with the work of the school or impinge upon the rights of other students. Even an official memorandum prepared after the suspension that listed the reasons for the ban on wearing the armbands made no reference to the anticipation of such disruption.[237]

Moreover, the testimony of school authorities at trial indicates that it was not fear of disruption that motivated the regulation prohibiting the armbands; and regulation was directed against 'the principle of the demonstration' itself. School authorities simply felt that 'the schools are no place for demonstrations,' and if the students 'didn't like the way our elected officials were handling things, it should be handled with the ballot box and not in the halls of our public schools.'

On the contrary, the action of the school authorities appears to have been based upon an urgent wish to avoid the controversy which might result from the expression, even by the silent symbol of armbands, of opposition to this Nation's part in the conflagration in Vietnam.[238] It is revealing, in this respect, that the meeting at

---

237. The only suggestions of fear of disorder in the report are these:

'A former student of one of our high schools was killed in Viet Nam. Some of his friends are still in school and it was felt that if any kind of a demonstration existed, it might evolve into something which would be difficult to control.'

'Students at one of the high schools were heard to say they would wear arm bands of other colors if the black bands prevailed.'

238. The District Court found that the school authorities, in prohibiting black armbands, were influenced by the fact that '(t)he Viet Nam war and the involvement of the United States

which the school principals decided to issue the contested regulation was called in response to a student's statement to the journalism teacher in one of the schools that he wanted to write an article on Vietnam and have it published in the school paper. (The student was dissuaded.[239])

It is also relevant that the school authorities did not purport to prohibit the wearing of all symbols of political or controversial significance. The record shows that students in some of the schools wore buttons relating to national political campaigns, and some even wore the Iron Cross, traditionally a symbol of Nazism. The order prohibiting the wearing of armbands did not extend to these. Instead, a particular symbol—black armbands worn to exhibit opposition to this Nation's involvement in Vietnam—was singled out for prohibition. Clearly, the prohibition of expression of one particular opinion, at least without evidence that it is necessary to avoid material and substantial interference with schoolwork or discipline, is not constitutionally permissible.

In our system, state-operated schools may not be enclaves of totalitarianism. School officials do not possess absolute authority over their students. Students in school as well as out of school are 'persons' under our Constitution. They are possessed of fundamental rights which the State must respect, just as they themselves must respect their obligations to the State. In our system, students may not be regarded as closed-circuit recipients of only that which the State chooses to communicate. They may not be confined to the expression of those sentiments that are officially approved. In the absence of a specific showing of constitutionally valid reasons to regulate their speech, students are entitled to freedom of expression of their views. As Judge Gewin, speaking for the Fifth Circuit, said, school officials cannot suppress 'expressions of feelings with which they do not wish to contend.' *Burnside v. Byars, supra, 363 F.2d at 749.*In *Meyer v. Nebraska, supra, 262 U.S. at 402, 43 S. Ct. at 627,* Mr. Justice McReynolds expressed this Nation's repudiation of the principle that a State might so conduct its schools as to 'foster a homogeneous people.' He said: 'In order to submerge the individual and develop ideal citizens, Sparta assembled the males at seven into barracks and intrusted their subsequent education and training to official guardians. Although such measures have been deliberately approved by men of great genius, their ideas touching the relation between individual and State

---

therein has been the subject of a major controversy for some time. When the arm band regulation involved herein was promulgated, debate over the Viet Nam war had become vehement in many localities. A protest march against the war had been recently held in Washington, D.C. A wave of draft card burning incidents protesting the war had swept the country. At that time two highly publicized draft card burning cases were pending in this Court. Both individuals supporting the war and those opposing it were quite vocal in expressing their views.' *258 F. Supp., at 972–973.*

239. After the principals' meeting, the director of secondary education and the principal of the high school informed the student that the principals were opposed to publication of his article. They reported that 'we felt that it was a very friendly conversation, although we did not feel that we had convinced the student that our decision was a just one.'

were wholly different from those upon which our institutions rest; and it hardly will be affirmed that any Legislature could impose such restrictions upon the people of a state without doing violence to both letter and spirit of the Constitution.'

This principle has been repeated by this Court of numerous occasions during the intervening years. In *Keyishian v. Board of Regents, 385 U.S. 589, 603, 87 S. Ct. 675, 683, 17 L. Ed. 2d 629,* Mr. Justice Brennan, speaking for the Court, said: "The vigilant protection of constitutional freedoms is nowhere more vital than in the community of American schools.' *Shelton v. Tucker, (364 U.S. 479),* at 487 *(81 S. Ct. 247, 5 L. Ed. 2d 231).* The classroom is peculiarly the 'marketplace of ideas.' The Nation's future depends upon leaders trained through wide exposure to that robust exchange of ideas which discovers truth 'out of a multitude of tongues, (rather) than through any kind of authoritative selection."

The principle of these cases is not confined to the supervised and ordained discussion which takes place in the classroom. The principal use to which the schools are dedicated is to accommodate students during prescribed hours for the purpose of certain types of activities. Among those activities is personal intercommunication among the students.[240] This is not only an inevitable part of the process of attending school; it is also an important part of the educational process. A student's rights, therefore, do not embrace merely the classroom hours. When he is in the cafeteria, or on the playing field, or on the campus during the authorized hours, he may express his opinions, even on controversial subjects like the conflict in Vietnam, if he does so without 'materially and substantially interfer(ing) with the requirements of appropriate discipline in the operation of the school' and without colliding with the rights of others. *Burnside v. Byars, supra, 363 F.2d at 749.* But conduct by the student, in class or out of it, which for any reason — whether it stems from time, place, or type of behavior — materially disrupts classwork or involves substantial disorder or invasion of the rights of others is, of course, not immunized by the constitutional guarantee of freedom of speech. Cf. *Blackwell v. Issaquena County Board of Education, 363 F.2d 749 (C.A. 5th Cir. 1966).*

Under our Constitution, free speech is not a right that is given only to be so circumscribed that it exists in principle but not in fact. Freedom of expression would not truly exist if the right could be exercised only in an area that a benevolent government has provided as a safe haven for crackpots. The Constitution says that Congress (and the States) may not abridge the right to free speech. This provision means what it says. We properly read it to permit reasonable regulation of speech-connected

240. In *Hammond v. South Carolina State College, 272 F. Supp. 947(D.C.S.C. 1967),* District Judge Hemphill had before him a case involving a meeting on campus of 300 students to express their views on school practices. He pointed out that a school is not like a hospital or a jail enclosure. Cf. *Cox v. Louisiana, 379 U.S. 536, 85 S. Ct. 453, 13 L. Ed. 2d 471 (1965); Adderley v. Florida, 385 U.S. 39, 87 S. Ct. 242, 17 L. Ed. 2d 149 (1966).* It is a public place, and its dedication to specific uses does not imply that the constitutional rights of persons entitled to be there are to be gauged as if the premises were purely private property. Cf. *Edwards v. South Carolina, 372 U.S. 229, 83 S. Ct. 680, 9 L. Ed. 2d 697 (1963); Brown v. Louisiana, 383 U.S. 131, 86 S. Ct. 719, 15 L. Ed. 2d 637 (1966).*

activities in carefully restricted circumstances. But we do not confine the permissible exercise of First Amendment rights to a telephone booth or the four corners of a pamphlet, or to supervised and ordained discussion in a school classroom.

If a regulation were adopted by school officials forbidding discussion of the Vietnam conflict, or the expression by any student of opposition to it anywhere on school property except as part of a prescribed classroom exercise, it would be obvious that the regulation would violate the constitutional rights of students, at least if it could not be justified by a showing that the students' activities would materially and substantially disrupt the work and discipline of the school. Cf. *Hammond v. South Carolina State College, 272 F. Supp. 947 (D.C.S.C. 1967)* (orderly protest meeting on state college campus); *Dickey v. Alabama State Board of Education, 273 F. Supp. 613 (D.C.M.D. Ala. 1967)* (expulsion of student editor of college newspaper). In the circumstances of the present case, the prohibition of the silent, passive 'witness of the armbands,' as one of the children called it, is no less offensive to the constitution's guarantees.

As we have discussed, the record does not demonstrate any facts which might reasonably have led school authorities to forecast substantial disruption of or material interference with school activities, and no disturbances or disorders on the school premises in fact occurred. These petitioners merely went about their ordained rounds in school. Their deviation consisted only in wearing on their sleeve a band of black cloth, not more than two inches wide. They wore it to exhibit their disapproval of the Vietnam hostilities and their advocacy of a truce, to make their views known, and, by their example, to influence others to adopt them. They neither interrupted school activities nor sought to intrude in the school affairs or the lives of others. They caused discussion outside of the classrooms, but no interference with work and no disorder. In the circumstances, our Constitution does not permit officials of the State to deny their form of expression.

We express no opinion as to the form of relief which should be granted, this being a matter for the lower courts to determine. We reverse and remand for further proceedings consistent with this opinion.

Reversed and remanded.

[Case No. 4-4]

School authorities may punish speech that is lewd and vulgar.

Bethel School District No. 403 v. Fraser

Supreme Court of the United States
478 U.S. 675 (1986)

Chief Justice BURGER delivered the opinion of the Court.

We granted certiorari to decide whether the First Amendment prevents a school district from disciplining a high school student for giving a lewd speech at a school assembly.

I

A

On April 26, 1983, respondent Matthew N. Fraser, a student at Bethel High School in Pierce County, Washington, delivered a speech nominating a fellow student for student elective office. Approximately 600 high school students, many of whom were 14-year-olds, attended the assembly. Students were required to attend the assembly or to report to the study hall. The assembly was part of a school-sponsored educational program in self-government. Students who elected not to attend the assembly were required to report to study hall. During the entire speech, Fraser referred to his candidate in terms of an elaborate, graphic, and explicit sexual metaphor.

Two of Fraser's teachers, with whom he discussed the contents of his speech in advance, informed him that the speech was "inappropriate and that he probably should not deliver it," App. 30, and that his delivery of the speech might have "severe consequences." *Id.*, at 61.

During Fraser's delivery of the speech, a school counselor observed the reaction of students to the speech. Some students hooted and yelled; some by gestures graphically simulated the sexual activities pointedly alluded to in respondent's speech. Other students appeared to be bewildered and embarrassed by the speech. One teacher reported that on the day following the speech, she found it necessary to forgo a portion of the scheduled class lesson in order to discuss the speech with the class. *Id.*, at 41–44.

A Bethel High School disciplinary rule prohibiting the use of obscene language in the school provides: "Conduct which materially and substantially interferes with the educational process is prohibited, including the use of obscene, profane language or gestures."

The morning after the assembly, the Assistant Principal called Fraser into her office and notified him that the school considered his speech to have been a violation of this rule. Fraser was presented with copies of five letters submitted by teachers, describing his conduct at the assembly; he was given a chance to explain his conduct, and he admitted to having given the speech described and that he deliberately used sexual innuendo in the speech. Fraser was then informed that he would be suspended for three days, and that his name would be removed from the list of candidates for graduation speaker at the school's commencement exercises.

Fraser sought review of this disciplinary action through the School District's grievance procedures. The hearing officer determined that the speech given by respondent was "indecent, lewd, and offensive to the modesty and decency of many of the students and faculty in attendance at the assembly." The examiner determined that the speech fell within the ordinary meaning of "obscene," as used in the disruptive-conduct rule, and affirmed the discipline in its entirety. Fraser served two days of his suspension, and was allowed to return to school on the third day.

B

Respondent, by his father as guardian ad litem, then brought this action in the United States District Court for the Western District of Washington. Respondent alleged a violation of his First Amendment right to freedom of speech and sought both injunctive relief and monetary damages under 42 U.S.C. §1983. The District Court held that the school's sanctions violated respondent's right to freedom of speech under the First Amendment to the United States Constitution, that the school's disruptive-conduct rule is unconstitutionally vague and overbroad, and that the removal of respondent's name from the graduation speaker's list violated the Due Process Clause of the Fourteenth Amendment because the disciplinary rule makes no mention of such removal as a possible sanction. The District Court awarded respondent $278 in damages, $12,750 in litigation costs and attorney's fees, and enjoined the School District from preventing respondent from speaking at the commencement ceremonies. Respondent, who had been elected graduation speaker by a write-in vote of his classmates, delivered a speech at the commencement ceremonies on June 8, 1983.

The Court of Appeals for the Ninth Circuit affirmed the judgment of the District Court, 755 F.2d 1356 (1985), holding that respondent's speech was indistinguishable from the protest armband in *Tinker v. Des Moines Independent Community School Dist.*, 393 U.S. 503, 89 S. Ct. 733, 21 L. Ed. 2d 731 (1969). The court explicitly rejected the School District's argument that the speech, unlike the passive conduct of wearing a black armband, had a disruptive effect on the educational process. The Court of Appeals also rejected the School District's argument that it had an interest in protecting an essentially captive audience of minors from lewd and indecent language in a setting sponsored by the school, reasoning that the School District's "unbridled discretion" to determine what discourse is "decent" would "increase the risk of cementing white, middle-class standards for determining what is acceptable and proper speech and behavior in our public schools." 755 F.2d at 1363. Finally, the Court of Appeals rejected the School District's argument that, incident to its responsibility for the school curriculum, it had the power to control the language used to express ideas during a school-sponsored activity.

We granted certiorari, 474 U.S. 814, 106 S. Ct. 56, 88 L. Ed. 2d 45 (1985). We reverse.

II

This Court acknowledged in *Tinker v. Des Moines Independent Community School Dist., supra,* that students do not "shed their constitutional rights to freedom of speech or expression at the schoolhouse gate." *Id.*, 393 U.S. at 506, 89 S. Ct. at 736. The Court of Appeals read that case as precluding any discipline of Fraser for indecent speech and lewd conduct in the school assembly. That court appears to have proceeded on the theory that the use of lewd and obscene speech in order to make what the speaker considered to be a point in a nominating speech for a fellow student was essentially the same as the wearing of an armband in *Tinker* as a form of protest or the expression of a political position.

The marked distinction between the political "message" of the armbands in *Tinker* and the sexual content of respondent's speech in this case seems to have been given little weight by the Court of Appeals. In upholding the students' right to engage in a nondisruptive, passive expression of a political viewpoint in *Tinker*, this Court was careful to note that the case did "not concern speech or action that intrudes upon the work of the schools or the rights of other students." *Id.* at 508, 89 S. Ct. at 737.

It is against this background that we turn to consider the level of First Amendment protection accorded to Fraser's utterances and actions before an official high school assembly attended by 600 students.

III

The role and purpose of the American public school system were well described by two historians, who stated: "[P]ublic education must prepare pupils for citizenship in the Republic.... It must inculcate the habits and manners of civility as values in themselves conducive to happiness and as indispensable to the practice of self-government in the community and the nation." C. Beard & M. Beard, New Basic History of the United States 228 (1968). In *Ambach v. Norwick*, 441 U.S. 68, 76–77, 99 S. Ct. 1589, 1594, 60 L. Ed. 2d 49 (1979), we echoed the essence of this statement of the objectives of public education as the "inculcat[ion of] fundamental values necessary to the maintenance of a democratic political system."

These fundamental values of "habits and manners of civility" essential to a democratic society must, of course, include tolerance of divergent political and religious views, even when the views expressed may be unpopular. But these "fundamental values" must also take into account consideration of the sensibilities of others, and, in the case of a school, the sensibilities of fellow students. The undoubted freedom to advocate unpopular and controversial views in schools and classrooms must be balanced against the society's countervailing interest in teaching students the boundaries of socially appropriate behavior. Even the most heated political discourse in a democratic society requires consideration for the personal sensibilities of the other participants and audiences.

In our Nation's legislative halls, where some of the most vigorous political debates in our society are carried on, there are rules prohibiting the use of expressions offensive to other participants in the debate. The Manual of Parliamentary Practice, drafted by Thomas Jefferson and adopted by the House of Representatives to govern the proceedings in that body, prohibits the use of "impertinent" speech during debate and likewise provides that "[n]o person is to use indecent language against the proceedings of the House." Jefferson's Manual of Parliamentary Practice §§ 359, 360, reprinted in Manual and Rules of House of Representatives,

H.R.Doc. No. 97-271, pp. 158–159 (1982); see *id.*, at 111, n. *a* (Jefferson's Manual governs the House in all cases to which it applies). The Rules of Debate applicable in the Senate likewise provide that a Senator may be called to order for imputing improper motives to another Senator or for referring offensively to any state. See Senate Procedure, S.Doc. No. 97-2, Rule XIX, pp. 568–569, 588–591 (1981). Senators have been censured for abusive language directed at other Senators. See Senate Election, Expulsion and Censure Cases from 1793 to 1972, S.Doc. No. 92-7, pp. 95–98 (1972) (Sens. McLaurin and Tillman); *id.*, at 152–153 (Sen. McCarthy). Can it be that what is proscribed in the halls of Congress is beyond the reach of school officials to regulate?

The First Amendment guarantees wide freedom in matters of adult public discourse. A sharply divided Court upheld the right to express an antidraft viewpoint in a public place, albeit in terms highly offensive to most citizens. See *Cohen v. California*, 403 U.S. 15, 91 S. Ct. 1780, 29 L. Ed. 2d 284 (1971). It does not follow, however, that simply because the use of an offensive form of expression may not be prohibited to adults making what the speaker considers a political point, the same latitude must be permitted to children in a public school. In *New Jersey v. T.L.O.*, 469 U.S. 325, 340–342, 105 S. Ct. 733, 742–743, 83 L. Ed. 2d 720 (1985), we reaffirmed that the constitutional rights of students in public school are not automatically coextensive with the rights of adults in other settings. As cogently expressed by Judge Newman, "the First Amendment gives a high school student the classroom right to wear Tinker's armband, but not Cohen's jacket." *Thomas v. Board of Education, Granville Central School Dist.*, 607 F.2d 1043, 1057 (CA2 1979) (opinion concurring in result).

Surely it is a highly appropriate function of public school education to prohibit the use of vulgar and offensive terms in public discourse. Indeed, the "fundamental values necessary to the maintenance of a democratic political system" disfavor the use of terms of debate highly offensive or highly threatening to others. Nothing in the Constitution prohibits the states from insisting that certain modes of expression are inappropriate and subject to sanctions. The inculcation of these values is truly the "work of the schools." *Tinker*, 393 U.S., at 508, 89 S. Ct., at 737; see *Ambach v. Norwick, supra*. The determination of what manner of speech in the classroom or in school assembly is inappropriate properly rests with the school board.

The process of educating our youth for citizenship in public schools is not confined to books, the curriculum, and the civics class; schools must teach by example the shared values of a civilized social order. Consciously or otherwise, teachers—and indeed the older students—demonstrate the appropriate form of civil discourse and political expression by their conduct and deportment in and out of class. Inescapably, like parents, they are role models. The schools, as instruments of the state, may determine that the essential lessons of civil, mature conduct cannot be conveyed in a school that tolerates lewd, indecent, or offensive speech and conduct such as that indulged in by this confused boy.

The pervasive sexual innuendo in Fraser's speech was plainly offensive to both teachers and students—indeed to any mature person. By glorifying male sexuality, and in its verbal content, the speech was acutely insulting to teenage girl students. See App. 77–81. The speech could well be seriously damaging to its less mature audience, many of whom were only 14 years old and on the threshold of awareness of human sexuality. Some students were reported as bewildered by the speech and the reaction of mimicry it provoked.

This Court's First Amendment jurisprudence has acknowledged limitations on the otherwise absolute interest of the speaker in reaching an unlimited audience where the speech is sexually explicit and the audience may include children. In *Ginsberg v. New York,* 390 U.S. 629, 88 S. Ct. 1274, 20 L. Ed. 2d 195 (1968), this Court upheld a New York statute banning the sale of sexually oriented material to minors, even though the material in question was entitled to First Amendment protection with respect to adults. And in addressing the question whether the First Amendment places any limit on the authority of public schools to remove books from a public school library, all Members of the Court, otherwise sharply divided, acknowledged that the school board has the authority to remove books that are vulgar. *Board of Education v. Pico,* 457 U.S. 853, 871–872, 102 S. Ct. 2799, 2814–2815, 73 L. Ed. 2d 435 (1982) (plurality opinion); *id.,* at 879–881, 102 S. Ct., at 2814–2815 (BLACKMUN, J., concurring in part and in judgment); *id.,* at 918–920, 102 S. Ct., at 2834–2835 (REHNQUIST, J., dissenting). These cases recognize the obvious concern on the part of parents, and school authorities acting *in loco parentis,* to protect children—especially in a captive audience—from exposure to sexually explicit, indecent, or lewd speech.

We have also recognized an interest in protecting minors from exposure to vulgar and offensive spoken language. In *FCC v. Pacifica Foundation,* 438 U.S. 726, 98 S. Ct. 3026, 57 L. Ed. 2d 1073 (1978), we dealt with the power of the Federal Communications Commission to regulate a radio broadcast described as "indecent but not obscene." There the Court reviewed an administrative condemnation of the radio broadcast of a self-styled "humorist" who described his own performance as being in "the words you couldn't say on the public, ah, airwaves, um, the ones you definitely wouldn't say ever." *Id.,* at 729, 98 S. Ct., at 3030; see also *id.,* at 751–755, 98 S. Ct., at 3041–3043 (Appendix to opinion of the Court). The Commission concluded that "certain words depicted sexual and excretory activities in a patently offensive manner, [and] noted that they 'were broadcast at a time when children were undoubtedly in the audience.'" The Commission issued an order declaring that the radio station was guilty of broadcasting indecent language in violation of 18 U.S.C. § 1464. 438 U.S., at 732, 98 S. Ct., at 3031. The Court of Appeals set aside the Commission's determination, and we reversed, reinstating the Commission's citation of the station. We concluded that the broadcast was properly considered "obscene, indecent, or profane" within the meaning of the statute. The plurality opinion went on to reject the radio station's assertion of a First Amendment right to broadcast vulgarity:

> These words offend for the same reasons that obscenity offends. Their place in the hierarchy of First Amendment values was aptly sketched by Mr. Justice Murphy when he said: '[S]uch utterances are no essential part of any exposition of ideas, and are of such slight social value as a step to truth that any benefit that may be derived from them is clearly outweighed by the social interest in order and morality.'

Chaplinsky v. New Hampshire, 315 U.S. [568], at 572 [62 S. Ct. 766, at 769, 86 L. Ed. 1031 (1942)]." *Id.,* at 746, 98 S. Ct., at 3039.

We hold that petitioner School District acted entirely within its permissible authority in imposing sanctions upon Fraser in response to his offensively lewd and indecent speech. Unlike the sanctions imposed on the students wearing armbands in *Tinker,* the penalties imposed in this case were unrelated to any political viewpoint. The First Amendment does not prevent the school officials from determining that to permit a vulgar and lewd speech such as respondent's would undermine the school's basic educational mission. A high school assembly or classroom is no place for a sexually explicit monologue directed towards an unsuspecting audience of teenage students. Accordingly, it was perfectly appropriate for the school to disassociate itself to make the point to the pupils that vulgar speech and lewd conduct is wholly inconsistent with the "fundamental values" of public school education. Justice Black, dissenting in *Tinker,* made a point that is especially relevant in this case: "I wish therefore, . . . to disclaim any purpose . . . to hold that the Federal Constitution compels the teachers, parents, and elected school officials to surrender control of the American public school system to public school students." 393 U.S., at 526, 89 S. Ct., at 746.

IV

Respondent contends that the circumstances of his suspension violated due process because he had no way of knowing that the delivery of the speech in question would subject him to disciplinary sanctions. This argument is wholly without merit. We have recognized that "maintaining security and order in the schools requires a certain degree of flexibility in school disciplinary procedures, and we have respected the value of preserving the informality of the student-teacher relationship." *New Jersey v. T.L.O.,* 469 U.S., at 340, 105 S. Ct., at 742. Given the school's need to be able to impose disciplinary sanctions for a wide range of unanticipated conduct disruptive of the educational process, the school disciplinary rules need not be as detailed as a criminal code which imposes criminal sanctions. Cf. *Arnett v. Kennedy,* 416 U.S. 134, 161, 94 S. Ct. 1633, 1647–1648, 40 L. Ed. 2d 15 (1974) (REHNQUIST, J., concurring). Two days' suspension from school does not rise to the level of a penal sanction calling for the full panoply of procedural due process protections applicable to a criminal prosecution. Cf. *Goss v. Lopez,* 419 U.S. 565, 95 S. Ct. 729, 42 L. Ed. 2d 725 (1975). The school disciplinary rule proscribing "obscene" language and the prespeech admonitions of teachers gave adequate warning to Fraser that his lewd speech could subject him to sanctions.[241]

The judgment of the Court of Appeals for the Ninth Circuit is *Reversed.*[242]

[Case No. 4-5]

School authorities may punish student speech that is school sponsored and that which has a legitimate pedagogical interest.

Hazelwood School District v. Kuhlmeier

Supreme Court of the United States
484 U.S. 260 (1988)

Justice WHITE delivered the opinion of the Court.

This case concerns the extent to which educators may exercise editorial control over the contents of a high school newspaper produced as part of the school's journalism curriculum.

I

Petitioners are the Hazelwood School District in St. Louis County, Missouri; various school officials; Robert Eugene Reynolds, the principal of Hazelwood East High School; and Howard Emerson, a teacher in the school district. Respondents are three former Hazelwood East students who were staff members of Spectrum, the school newspaper. They contend that school officials violated their First Amendment rights by deleting two pages of articles from the May 13, 1983, issue of Spectrum.

---

241. Petitioners also challenge the ruling of the District Court that the removal of Fraser's name from the ballot for graduation speaker violated his due process rights because that sanction was not indicated as a potential punishment in the school's disciplinary rules. We agree with the Court of Appeals that this issue has become moot, since the graduation ceremony has long since passed and Fraser was permitted to speak in accordance with the District Court's injunction. No part of the damages award was based upon the removal of Fraser's name from the list, since damages were based upon the loss of two days' schooling.

242. Frasers' exact words as quoted in Justice Brennan's concurrence are as follows:

> "'I know a man who is firm—he's firm in his pants, he's firm in his shirt, his character is firm—but most . . . of all, his belief in you, the students of Bethel, is firm'". . . . "'Jeff Kuhlman is a man who takes his point and pounds it in. If necessary, he'll take an issue and nail it to the wall. He doesn't attack things in spurts—he drives hard, pushing and pushing until finally—he succeeds'". . . . "'Jeff is a man who will go to the very end—even the climax, for each and every one of you'". . . . "'So vote for Jeff for A.S.B. vice-president—he'll never come between you and the best our high school can be.'" App. 47.

Spectrum was written and edited by the Journalism II class at Hazelwood East. The newspaper was published every three weeks or so during the 1982–1983 school year. More than 4,500 copies of the newspaper were distributed during that year to students, school personnel, and members of the community.

The Board of Education allocated funds from its annual budget for the printing of Spectrum. These funds were supplemented by proceeds from sales of the newspaper. The printing expenses during the 1982–1983 school year totaled $4,668.50; revenue from sales was $1,166.84. The other costs associated with the newspaper — such as supplies, textbooks, and a portion of the journalism teacher's salary — were borne entirely by the Board.

The Journalism II course was taught by Robert Stergos for most of the 1982–1983 academic year. Stergos left Hazelwood East to take a job in private industry on April 29, 1983, when the May 13 edition of Spectrum was nearing completion, and petitioner Emerson took his place as newspaper adviser for the remaining weeks of the term.

The practice at Hazelwood East during the spring 1983 semester was for the journalism teacher to submit page proofs of each Spectrum issue to Principal Reynolds for his review prior to publication. On May 10, Emerson delivered the proofs of the May 13 edition to Reynolds, who objected to two of the articles scheduled to appear in that edition. One of the stories described three Hazelwood East students' experiences with pregnancy; the other discussed the impact of divorce on students at the school.

Reynolds was concerned that, although the pregnancy story used false names "to keep the identity of these girls a secret," the pregnant students still might be identifiable from the text. He also believed that the article's references to sexual activity and birth control were inappropriate for some of the younger students at the school. In addition, Reynolds was concerned that a student identified by name in the divorce story had complained that her father "wasn't spending enough time with my mom, my sister and I" prior to the divorce, "was always out of town on business or out late playing cards with the guys," and "always argued about everything" with her mother. App. to Pet. for Cert. 38. Reynolds believed that the student's parents should have been given an opportunity to respond to these remarks or to consent to their publication. He was unaware that Emerson had deleted the student's name from the final version of the article.

Reynolds believed that there was no time to make the necessary changes in the stories before the scheduled press run and that the newspaper would not appear before the end of the school year if printing were delayed to any significant extent. He concluded that his only options under the circumstances were to publish a four-page newspaper instead of the planned six-page newspaper, eliminating the two pages on which the offending stories appeared, or to publish no newspaper at all. Accordingly, he directed Emerson to withhold from publication the two pages containing the stories on pregnancy and divorce.[243] He informed his superiors of the decision, and they concurred.

Respondents subsequently commenced this action in the United States District Court for the Eastern District of Missouri seeking a declaration that their First Amendment rights had been violated, injunctive relief, and monetary damages. After a bench trial, the District Court denied an injunction, holding that no First Amendment violation had occurred. 607 F. Supp. 1450 (1985).

The District Court concluded that school officials may impose restraints on students' speech in activities that are "'an integral part of the school's educational function'"—including the publication of a school-sponsored newspaper by a journalism class—so long as their decision has "'a substantial and reasonable basis.'" *Id.*, at 1466 (quoting *Frasca v. Andrews,* 463 F. Supp. 1043, 1052 (EDNY 1979)). The court found that Principal Reynolds' concern that the pregnant students' anonymity would be lost and their privacy invaded was "legitimate and reasonable," given "the small number of pregnant students at Hazelwood East and several identifying characteristics that were disclosed in the article." 607 F. Supp., at 1466. The court held that Reynolds' action was also justified "to avoid the impression that [the school] endorses the sexual norms of the subjects" and to shield younger students from exposure to unsuitable material. *Ibid.* The deletion of the article on divorce was seen by the court as a reasonable response to the invasion of privacy concerns raised by the named student's remarks. Because the article did not indicate that the student's parents had been offered an opportunity to respond to her allegations, said the court, there was cause for "serious doubt that the article complied with the rules of fairness which are standard in the field of journalism and which were covered in the textbook used in the Journalism II class." *Id.*, at 1467. Furthermore, the court concluded that Reynolds was justified in deleting two full pages of the newspaper, instead of deleting only the pregnancy and divorce stories or requiring that those stories be modified to address his concerns, based on his "reasonable belief that he had to make an immediate decision and that there was no time to make modifications to the articles in question." *Id.*, at 1466.

The Court of Appeals for the Eighth Circuit reversed. 795 F.2d 1368 (1986). The court held at the outset that Spectrum was not only "a part of the school adopted curriculum," *id.*, at 1373, but also a public forum, because the newspaper was "intended to be and operated as a conduit for student viewpoint." *Id.*, at 1372. The court then concluded that Spectrum's status as a public forum precluded school officials from censoring its contents except when "'necessary to avoid material and substantial interference with school work or discipline ... or the rights of others.'" *Id.*, at 1374

243. The two pages deleted from the newspaper also contained articles on teenage marriage, runaways, and juvenile delinquents, as well as a general article on teenage pregnancy. Reynolds testified that he had no objection to these articles and that they were deleted only because they appeared on the same pages as the two objectionable articles.

(quoting *Tinker v. Des Moines Independent Community School Dist.*, 393 U.S. 503, 511, 89 S. Ct. 733, 739, 21 L. Ed. 2d 731 (1969)).

The Court of Appeals found "no evidence in the record that the principal could have reasonably forecast that the censored articles or any materials in the censored articles would have materially disrupted classwork or given rise to substantial disorder in the school." 795 F.2d, at 1375. School officials were entitled to censor the articles on the ground that they invaded the rights of others, according to the court, only if publication of the articles could have resulted in tort liability to the school. The court concluded that no tort action for libel or invasion of privacy could have been maintained against the school by the subjects of the two articles or by their families. Accordingly, the court held that school officials had violated respondents' First Amendment rights by deleting the two pages of the newspaper.

We granted certiorari, 479 U.S. 1053, 107 S. Ct. 926, 93 L. Ed. 2d 978 (1987), and we now reverse.

II

Students in the public schools do not "shed their constitutional rights to freedom of speech or expression at the schoolhouse gate." *Tinker, supra,* 393 U.S., at 506, 89 S. Ct., at 736. They cannot be punished merely for expressing their personal views on the school premises—whether "in the cafeteria, or on the playing field, or on the campus during the authorized hours," 393 U.S., at 512–513, 89 S. Ct., at 739–740—unless school authorities have reason to believe that such expression will "substantially interfere with the work of the school or impinge upon the rights of other students." *Id.*, at 509, 89 S. Ct., at 738.

We have nonetheless recognized that the First Amendment rights of students in the public schools "are not automatically coextensive with the rights of adults in other settings," *Bethel School District No. 403 v. Fraser,* 478 U.S. 675, 682, 106 S. Ct. 3159, 3164, 92 L. Ed. 2d 549 (1986), and must be "applied in light of the special characteristics of the school environment." *Tinker, supra,* 393 U.S., at 506, 89 S. Ct., at 736; cf. *New Jersey v. T.L.O.*, 469 U.S. 325, 341–343, 105 S. Ct. 733, 743–744, 83 L. Ed. 2d 720 (1985). A school need not tolerate student speech that is inconsistent with its "basic educational mission," *Fraser, supra,* 478 U.S., at 685, 106 S. Ct., at 3165, even though the government could not censor similar speech outside the school. Accordingly, we held in *Fraser* that a student could be disciplined for having delivered a speech that was "sexually explicit" but not legally obscene at an official school assembly, because the school was entitled to "disassociate itself" from the speech in a manner that would demonstrate to others that such vulgarity is "wholly inconsistent with the 'fundamental values' of public school education." 478 U.S., at 685–686, 106 S. Ct., at 3165. We thus recognized that "[t]he determination of what manner of speech in the classroom or in school assembly is inappropriate properly rests with the school board," *id.*, at 683, 106 S. Ct., at 3164, rather than with the federal courts. It is in this context that respondents' First Amendment claims must be considered.

A

We deal first with the question whether Spectrum may appropriately be characterized as a forum for public expression. The public schools do not possess all of the attributes of streets, parks, and other traditional public forums that "time out of mind, have been used for purposes of assembly, communicating thoughts between citizens, and discussing public questions." *Hague v. CIO,* 307 U.S. 496, 515, 59 S. Ct. 954, 964, 83 L. Ed. 1423 (1939). Cf. *Widmar v. Vincent,* 454 U.S. 263, 267–268, n. 5, 102 S. Ct. 269, 273, n. 5, 70 L. Ed. 2d 440 (1981). Hence, school facilities may be deemed to be public forums only if school authorities have "by policy or by practice" opened those facilities "for indiscriminate use by the general public," *Perry Education Assn. v. Perry Local Educators' Assn.,* 460 U.S. 37, 47, 103 S. Ct. 948, 956, 74 L. Ed. 2d 794 (1983), or by some segment of the public, such as student organizations. *Id.,* at 46, n. 7, 103 S. Ct., at 955, n. 7 (citing *Widmar v. Vincent*). If the facilities have instead been reserved for other intended purposes, "communicative or otherwise," then no public forum has been created, and school officials may impose reasonable restrictions on the speech of students, teachers, and other members of the school community. 460 U.S., at 46, n. 7, 103 S. Ct., at 955, n. 7. "The government does not create a public forum by inaction or by permitting limited discourse, but only by intentionally opening a nontraditional forum for public discourse." *Cornelius v. NAACP Legal Defense & Educational Fund, Inc.,* 473 U.S. 788, 802, 105 S. Ct. 3439, 3449, 87 L. Ed. 2d 567 (1985).

The policy of school officials toward Spectrum was reflected in Hazelwood School Board Policy 348.51 and the Hazelwood East Curriculum Guide. Board Policy 348.51 provided that "[s]chool sponsored publications are developed within the adopted curriculum and its educational implications in regular classroom activities." App. 22. The Hazelwood East Curriculum Guide described the Journalism II course as a "laboratory situation in which the students publish the school newspaper applying skills they have learned in Journalism I." *Id.,* at 11. The lessons that were to be learned from the Journalism II course, according to the Curriculum Guide, included development of journalistic skills under deadline pressure, "the legal, moral, and ethical restrictions imposed upon journalists within the school community," and "responsibility and acceptance of criticism for articles of opinion." *Ibid.* Journalism II was taught by a faculty member during regular class hours. Students received grades and academic credit for their performance in the course.

School officials did not deviate in practice from their policy that production of Spectrum was to be part of the educational curriculum and a "regular classroom activit[y]." The District Court found that Robert Stergos, the journalism teacher during most of the 1982–1983 school year, "both had the authority to exercise and in fact exercised a great deal of control over *Spectrum.*" 607 F. Supp., at 1453. For example, Stergos selected the editors of the newspaper, scheduled publication dates, decided the number of pages for each issue, assigned story ideas to class members, advised students on the development of their stories, reviewed the use of quotations, edited stories, selected and edited the letters to the editor, and dealt with the printing company. Many of these decisions were made without consultation with the Journalism II students. The District Court thus found it "clear that Mr. Stergos was the final authority with respect to almost every aspect of the production and publication of *Spectrum,* including its content." *Ibid.* Moreover, after each Spectrum issue had been finally approved by Stergos or his successor, the issue still had to be reviewed by Principal Reynolds prior to publication. Respondents' assertion that they had believed that they could publish "practically anything" in Spectrum was therefore dismissed by the District Court as simply "not credible." *Id.,* at 1456. These factual findings are amply supported by the record, and were not rejected as clearly erroneous by the Court of Appeals.

The evidence relied upon by the Court of Appeals in finding Spectrum to be a public forum, see 795 F.2d, at 1372–1373, is equivocal at best. For example, Board Policy 348.51, which stated in part that "[s]chool sponsored student publications will not restrict free expression or diverse viewpoints within the rules of responsible journalism," also stated that such publications were "developed within the adopted curriculum and its educational implications." App. 22. One might reasonably infer from the full text of Policy 348.51 that school officials retained ultimate control over what constituted "responsible journalism" in a school-sponsored newspaper. Although the Statement of Policy published in the September 14, 1982, issue of Spectrum declared that "*Spectrum,* as a student-press publication, accepts all rights implied by the First Amendment," this statement, understood in the context of the paper's role in the school's curriculum, suggests at most that the administration will not interfere with the students' exercise of those First Amendment rights that attend the publication of a school-sponsored newspaper. It does not reflect an intent to expand those rights by converting a curricular newspaper into a public forum.[244] Finally, that students were permitted to exercise some authority over the contents of Spectrum was fully consistent with the Curriculum Guide objective of teaching the Journalism II students "leadership responsibilities as issue and page editors." App. 11. A decision to teach leadership skills in the context of a classroom activity hardly implies a decision to relinquish school control over that activity. In sum, the evidence relied upon by the Court of Appeals fails to demonstrate the "clear intent to create a public forum," *Cornelius,* 473 U.S., at 802, 105 S. Ct., at 3449–3450, that existed in cases in which we found public forums to have been created. See *id.,* at

---

244. The Statement also cited *Tinker v. Des Moines Independent Community School Dist.,* 393 U.S. 503, 89 S. Ct. 733, 21 L. Ed. 2d 731 (1969), for the proposition that "[o]nly speech that 'materially and substantially interferes with the requirements of appropriate discipline' can be found unacceptable and therefore be prohibited." App. 26. This portion of the Statement does not, of course, even accurately reflect our holding in *Tinker.* Furthermore, the Statement nowhere expressly extended the *Tinker* standard to the news and feature articles contained in a school-sponsored newspaper. The dissent apparently finds as a fact that the Statement was published annually in Spectrum; however, the District Court was unable to conclude that the Statement appeared on more than one occasion. In any event, even if the Statement says what the dissent believes that it says, the evidence that school officials never intended to designate Spectrum as a public forum remains overwhelming.

802–803, 105 S. Ct., at 3449–3450 (citing *Widmar v. Vincent,* 454 U.S., at 267, 102 S. Ct., at 273; *Madison School District v. Wisconsin Employment Relations Comm'n,* 429 U.S. 167, 174, n. 6, 97 S. Ct. 421, 426, n. 6, 50 L. Ed. 2d 376 (1976); *Southeastern Promotions, Ltd. v. Conrad,* 420 U.S. 546, 555, 95 S. Ct. 1239, 1245, 43 L. Ed. 2d 448 (1975)). School officials did not evince either "by policy or by practice," *Perry Education Assn.,* 460 U.S., at 47, 103 S. Ct., at 956, any intent to open the pages of Spectrum to "indiscriminate use," *ibid.,* by its student reporters and editors, or by the student body generally. Instead, they "reserve[d] the forum for its intended purpos[e]," *id.,* at 46, 103 S. Ct., at 955, as a supervised learning experience for journalism students. Accordingly, school officials were entitled to regulate the contents of Spectrum in any reasonable manner. *Ibid.* It is this standard, rather than our decision in *Tinker,* that governs this case.

B

The question whether the First Amendment requires a school to tolerate particular student speech — the question that we addressed in *Tinker* — is different from the question whether the First Amendment requires a school affirmatively to promote particular student speech. The former question addresses educators' ability to silence a student's personal expression that happens to occur on the school premises. The latter question concerns educators' authority over school-sponsored publications, theatrical productions, and other expressive activities that students, parents, and members of the public might reasonably perceive to bear the imprimatur of the school. These activities may fairly be characterized as part of the school curriculum, whether or not they occur in a traditional classroom setting, so long as they are supervised by faculty members and designed to impart particular knowledge or skills to student participants and audiences.[245]

Educators are entitled to exercise greater control over this second form of student expression to assure that participants learn whatever lessons the activity is designed to teach, that readers or listeners are not exposed to material that may be inappropriate for their level of maturity, and that the views of the individual speaker are not erroneously attributed to the school. Hence, a school may in its capacity as publisher of a school newspaper or producer of a school play "disassociate itself," *Fraser,* 478 U.S., at 685, 106 S. Ct., at 3165, not only from speech that would "substantially interfere with [its] work . . . or impinge upon the rights of other students," *Tinker,* 393 U.S., at 509, 89 S. Ct., at 738, but also from speech that is, for example, ungrammatical, poorly written, inadequately researched, biased or prejudiced, vulgar or profane,

245. The distinction that we draw between speech that is sponsored by the school and speech that is not is fully consistent with *Papish v. University of Missouri Board of Curators,* 410 U.S. 667, 93 S. Ct. 1197, 35 L. Ed. 2d 618 (1973) *(per curiam),* which involved an off-campus "underground" newspaper that school officials merely had allowed to be sold on a state university campus.

or unsuitable for immature audiences.[246] A school must be able to set high standards for the student speech that is disseminated under its auspices—standards that may be higher than those demanded by some newspaper publishers or theatrical producers in the "real" world—and may refuse to disseminate student speech that does not meet those standards. In addition, a school must be able to take into account the emotional maturity of the intended audience in determining whether to disseminate student speech on potentially sensitive topics, which might range from the existence of Santa Claus in an elementary school setting to the particulars of teenage sexual activity in a high school setting. A school must also retain the authority to refuse to sponsor student speech that might reasonably be perceived to advocate drug or alcohol use, irresponsible sex, or conduct otherwise inconsistent with "the shared values of a civilized social order," *Fraser, supra,* 478 U.S., at 683, 106 S. Ct., at 3164, or to associate the school with any position other than neutrality on matters of political controversy. Otherwise, the schools would be unduly constrained from fulfilling their role as "a principal instrument in awakening the child to cultural values, in preparing him for later professional training, and in helping him to adjust normally to his environment." *Brown v. Board of Education,* 347 U.S. 483, 493, 74 S. Ct. 686, 691, 98 L. Ed. 873 (1954).

Accordingly, we conclude that the standard articulated in *Tinker* for determining when a school may punish student expression need not also be the standard for determining when a school may refuse to lend its name and resources to the dissemination of student expression.[247] Instead, we hold that educators do not offend the First Amendment by exercising editorial control over the style and content of student speech in school-sponsored expressive activities so long as their actions are reasonably related to legitimate pedagogical concerns.[248]

---

246. The dissent perceives no difference between the First Amendment analysis applied in *Tinker* and that applied in *Fraser.* We disagree. The decision in *Fraser* rested on the "vulgar," "lewd," and "plainly offensive" character of a speech delivered at an official school assembly rather than on any propensity of the speech to "materially disrup[t] classwork or involv[e] substantial disorder or invasion of the rights of others." 393 U.S., at 513, 89 S. Ct., at 740. Indeed, the *Fraser* Court cited as "especially relevant" a portion of Justice Black's dissenting opinion in *Tinker* "'disclaim[ing] any purpose ... to hold that the Federal Constitution compels the teachers, parents, and elected school officials to surrender control of the American public school system to public school students.'" 478 U.S., at 686, 106 S. Ct., at 3166 (quoting 393 U.S., at 526, 89 S. Ct., at 746). Of course, Justice Black's observations are equally relevant to the instant case.

247. We therefore need not decide whether the Court of Appeals correctly construed *Tinker* as precluding school officials from censoring student speech to avoid "invasion of the rights of others," 393 U.S., at 513, 89 S. Ct., at 740, except where that speech could result in tort liability to the school.

248. We reject respondents' suggestion that school officials be permitted to exercise prepublication control over school-sponsored publications only pursuant to specific written regulations. To require such regulations in the context of a curricular activity could unduly constrain the ability of educators to educate. We need not now decide whether such regulations are required before school officials may censor publications not sponsored by the school that students seek to distribute on school grounds. See *Baughman v. Freienmuth,* 478 F.2d 1345 (CA4 1973); *Shanley v. Northeast Independent School Dist., Bexar Cty., Tex.,* 462 F.2d 960 (CA5 1972); *Eisner v. Stamford Board of Education,* 440 F.2d 803 (CA2 1971).

This standard is consistent with our oft-expressed view that the education of the Nation's youth is primarily the responsibility of parents, teachers, and state and local school officials, and not of federal judges. *See, e.g., Board of Education of Hendrick Hudson Central School Dist. v. Rowley,* 458 U.S. 176, 208, 102 S. Ct. 3034, 3051, 73 L. Ed. 2d 690 (1982); *Wood v. Strickland,* 420 U.S. 308, 326, 95 S. Ct. 992, 1003, 43 L. Ed. 2d 214 (1975); *Epperson v. Arkansas,* 393 U.S. 97, 104, 89 S. Ct. 266, 270, 21 L. Ed. 2d 228 (1968). It is only when the decision to censor a school-sponsored publication, theatrical production, or other vehicle of student expression has no valid educational purpose that the First Amendment is so "directly and sharply implicate[d]," *ibid.,* as to require judicial intervention to protect students' constitutional rights.[249]

III

We also conclude that Principal Reynolds acted reasonably in requiring the deletion from the May 13 issue of Spectrum of the pregnancy article, the divorce article, and the remaining articles that were to appear on the same pages of the newspaper.

The initial paragraph of the pregnancy article declared that "[a]ll names have been changed to keep the identity of these girls a secret." The principal concluded that the students' anonymity was not adequately protected, however, given the other identifying information in the article and the small number of pregnant students at the school. Indeed, a teacher at the school credibly testified that she could positively identify at least one of the girls and possibly all three. It is likely that many students at Hazelwood East would have been at least as successful in identifying the girls. Reynolds therefore could reasonably have feared that the article violated whatever pledge of anonymity had been given to the pregnant students. In addition, he could reasonably have been concerned that the article was not sufficiently sensitive to the privacy interests of the students' boyfriends and parents, who were discussed in the article but who were given no opportunity to consent to its publication or to offer a response. The article did not contain graphic accounts of sexual activity. The girls did comment in the article, however, concerning their sexual histories and their use or nonuse of birth control. It was not unreasonable for the principal to have concluded that such frank talk was inappropriate in a school-sponsored publication distributed to 14-year-old freshmen and presumably taken home to be read by students' even younger brothers and sisters.

---

249. A number of lower federal courts have similarly recognized that educators' decisions with regard to the content of school-sponsored newspapers, dramatic productions, and other expressive activities are entitled to substantial deference. See, *e.g., Nicholson v. Board of Education, Torrance Unified School Dist.,* 682 F.2d 858 (CA9 1982); *Seyfried v. Walton,* 668 F.2d 214 (CA3 1981); *Trachtman v. Anker,* 563 F.2d 512 (CA2 1977), cert. denied, 435 U.S. 925, 98 S. Ct. 1491, 55 L. Ed. 2d 519 (1978); *Frasca v. Andrews,* 463 F. Supp. 1043 (EDNY 1979). We need not now decide whether the same degree of deference is appropriate with respect to school-sponsored expressive activities at the college and university level.

The student who was quoted by name in the version of the divorce article seen by Principal Reynolds made comments sharply critical of her father. The principal could reasonably have concluded that an individual publicly identified as an inattentive parent — indeed, as one who chose "playing cards with the guys" over home and family — was entitled to an opportunity to defend himself as a matter of journalistic fairness. These concerns were shared by both of Spectrum's faculty advisers for the 1982–1983 school year, who testified that they would not have allowed the article to be printed without deletion of the student's name.[250]

Principal Reynolds testified credibly at trial that, at the time that he reviewed the proofs of the May 13 issue during an extended telephone conversation with Emerson, he believed that there was no time to make any changes in the articles, and that the newspaper had to be printed immediately or not at all. It is true that Reynolds did not verify whether the necessary modifications could still have been made in the articles, and that Emerson did not volunteer the information that printing could be delayed until the changes were made. We nonetheless agree with the District Court that the decision to excise the two pages containing the problematic articles was reasonable given the particular circumstances of this case. These circumstances included the very recent replacement of Stergos by Emerson, who may not have been entirely familiar with Spectrum editorial and production procedures, and the pressure felt by Reynolds to make an immediate decision so that students would not be deprived of the newspaper altogether.

In sum, we cannot reject as unreasonable Principal Reynolds' conclusion that neither the pregnancy article nor the divorce article was suitable for publication in Spectrum. Reynolds could reasonably have concluded that the students who had written and edited these articles had not sufficiently mastered those portions of the Journalism II curriculum that pertained to the treatment of controversial issues and personal attacks, the need to protect the privacy of individuals whose most intimate concerns are to be revealed in the newspaper, and "the legal, moral, and ethical restrictions imposed upon journalists within [a] school community" that includes adolescent subjects and readers. Finally, we conclude that the principal's decision to delete two pages of Spectrum, rather than to delete only the offending articles

250. The reasonableness of Principal Reynolds' concerns about the two articles was further substantiated by the trial testimony of Martin Duggan, a former editorial page editor of the St. Louis Globe Democrat and a former college journalism instructor and newspaper adviser. Duggan testified that the divorce story did not meet journalistic standards of fairness and balance because the father was not given an opportunity to respond, and that the pregnancy story was not appropriate for publication in a high school newspaper because it was unduly intrusive into the privacy of the girls, their parents, and their boyfriends. The District Court found Duggan to be "an objective and independent witness" whose testimony was entitled to significant weight. 607 F. Supp. 1450, 1461 (ED Mo. 1985).

or to require that they be modified, was reasonable under the circumstances as he understood them. Accordingly, no violation of First Amendment rights occurred.[251]

The judgment of the Court of Appeals for the Eighth Circuit is therefore *Reversed.*

[Case No. 4-6]

School boards may not censor books once they are part of the school library.

Board of Education, Island Trees Union Free School District No. 26 v. Pico

Supreme Court of the United States
457 U.S. 853 (1982)

Justice BRENNAN announced the judgment of the Court.

The principal question presented is whether the First Amendment[252] imposes limitations upon the exercise by a local school board of its discretion to remove library books from high school and junior high school libraries.

Petitioners are the Board of Education of the Island Trees Union Free School District No. 26, in New York, and Richard Ahrens, Frank Martin, Christina Fasulo, Patrick Hughes, Richard Melchers, Richard Michaels, and Louis Nessim. When this suit was brought, Ahrens was the President of the Board, Martin was the Vice President, and the remaining petitioners were Board members. The Board is a state agency charged with responsibility for the operation and administration of the public schools within the Island Trees School District, including the Island Trees High School and Island Trees Memorial Junior High School. Respondents are Steven Pico, Jacqueline Gold, Glenn Yarris, Russell Rieger, and Paul Sochinski. When this suit was brought, Pico, Gold, Yarris, and Rieger were students at the High School, and Sochinski was a student at the Junior High School.

In September 1975, petitioners Ahrens, Martin, and Hughes attended a conference sponsored by Parents of New York United (PONYU), a politically conservative organization of parents concerned about education legislation in the State of

251. It is likely that the approach urged by the dissent would as a practical matter have far more deleterious consequences for the student press than does the approach that we adopt today. The dissent correctly acknowledges "[t]he State's prerogative to dissolve the student newspaper entirely." *Post,* at 578. It is likely that many public schools would do just that rather than open their newspapers to all student expression that does not threaten "materia[l] disrup[tion of] classwork" or violation of "rights that are protected by law," *post,* at 579, regardless of how sexually explicit, racially intemperate, or personally insulting that expression otherwise might be.

252. The Amendment provides in pertinent part that "Congress shall make no law . . . abridging the freedom of speech, or of the press." It applies to the States by virtue of the Fourteenth Amendment. *Gitlow v. New York,* 268 U.S. 652, 666 (1925); *Grosjean v. American Press Co.,* 297 U.S. 233, 244 (1936).

New York. At the conference these petitioners obtained lists of books described by Ahrens as "objectionable," App. 22, and by Martin as "improper fare for school students," *Id.*, at 101.[253] It was later determined that the High School library contained nine of the listed books, and that another listed book was in the Junior High School library.[254] In February 1976, at a meeting with the Superintendent of Schools and the Principals of the High School and Junior High School, the Board gave an "unofficial direction" that the listed books be removed from the library shelves and delivered to the Board's offices, so that Board members could read them.[255] When this directive was carried out, it became publicized, and the Board issued a press release justifying its action. It characterized the removed books as "anti-American, anti-Christian, anti-Sem[i]tic, and just plain filthy," and concluded that "[i]t is our duty, our moral obligation, to protect the children in our schools from this moral danger as surely as from physical and medical dangers." 474 F. Supp. 387, 390 (EDNY 1979).

A short time later, the Board appointed a "Book Review Committee," consisting of four Island Trees parents and four members of the Island Trees schools staff, to read the listed books and to recommend to the Board whether the books should be retained, taking into account the books' "educational suitability," "good taste," "relevance," and "appropriateness to age and grade level." In July, the Committee made its final report to the Board, recommending that five of the listed books be retained[256] and that two others be removed from the school libraries.[257] As for the remaining four books, the Committee could not agree on two,[258] took no position

253. The District Court noted, however, that petitioners "concede that the books are not obscene." 474 F. Supp. 387, 392 (EDNY 1979).

254. The nine books in the High School library were: *Slaughter House Five*, by Kurt Vonnegut, Jr.; *The Naked Ape*, by Desmond Morris; *Down These Mean Streets*, by Piri Thomas; *Best Short Stories of Negro Writers*, edited by Langston Hughes; *Go Ask Alice*, of anonymous authorship; *Laughing Boy*, by Oliver LaFarge; *Black Boy*, by Richard Wright; *A Hero Ain't Nothin' But A Sandwich*, by Alice Childress; and *Soul On Ice*, by Eldridge Cleaver. The book in the Junior High School library was *A Reader for Writers*, edited by Jerome Archer. Still another listed book, *The Fixer*, by Bernard Malamud, was found to be included in the curriculum of a twelfth-grade literature course. 474 F. Supp., at 389 and nn. 2–4.

255. The Superintendent of Schools objected to the Board's informal directive, noting:

"[W]e already have a policy . . . designed expressly to handle such problems. It calls for the Superintendent, upon receiving an objection to a book or books, to appoint a committee to study them and make recommendations. I feel it is a good policy—and it is Board policy—and that it should be followed in this instance. Furthermore, I think it can be followed quietly and in such a way as to reduce, perhaps avoid, the public furor which has always attended such issues in the past." App. 44.

The Board responded to the Superintendent's objection by repeating its directive "that *all copies* of the library books in question be removed from the libraries to the Board's office." *Id.*, at 47 (emphasis in original).

256. *The Fixer, Laughing Boy, Black Boy, Go Ask Alice,* and *Best Short Stories by Negro Writers.* 474 F. Supp., at 391, nn. 6–7.

257. *The Naked Ape* and *Down These Mean Streets.* 474 F. Supp., at 391, n. 8.

258. *Soul on Ice* and *A Hero Ain't Nothin' But A Sandwich.* 474 F. Supp., at 391, n. 9.

on one,[259] and recommended that the last book be made available to students only with parental approval.[260] The Board substantially rejected the Committee's report later that month, deciding that only one book should be returned to the High School library without restriction,[261] that another should be made available subject to parental approval,[262] but that the remaining nine books should "be removed from elementary and secondary libraries and [from] use in the curriculum." *Id.*, at 391.[263] The Board gave no reasons for rejecting the recommendations of the Committee that it had appointed.

Respondents reacted to the Board's decision by bringing the present action under 42 U.S.C. § 1983 in the United States District Court for the Eastern District of New York. They alleged that petitioners had

> "ordered the removal of the books from school libraries and proscribed their use in the curriculum because particular passages in the books offended their social, political and moral tastes and not because the books, taken as a whole, were lacking in educational value." App. 4.

Respondents claimed that the Board's actions denied them their rights under the First Amendment. They asked the court for a declaration that the Board's actions were unconstitutional, and for preliminary and permanent injunctive relief ordering the Board to return the nine books to the school libraries and to refrain from interfering with the use of those books in the schools' curricula. *Id.*, at 5–6.

The District Court granted summary judgment in favor of petitioners. 474 F. Supp. 387 (1979). In the court's view, "the parties substantially agree[d] about the motivation behind the board's actions," *Id.*, at 391—namely, that

> "the board acted not on religious principles but on its conservative educational philosophy, and on its belief that the nine books removed from the school library and curriculum were irrelevant, vulgar, immoral, and in bad taste, making them educationally unsuitable for the district's junior and senior high school students." *Id.*, at 392.

With this factual premise as its background, the court rejected respondents' contention that their First Amendment rights had been infringed by the Board's actions. Noting that statutes, history, and precedent had vested local school boards with a broad discretion to formulate educational policy,[264] the court concluded that

---

259. *A Reader for Writers.* 474 F. Supp., at 391, n. 11. The reason given for this disposition was that all members of the Committee had not been able to read the book. *Id.*, at 391.

260. *Slaughter House Five.* 474 F. Supp., at 391, n. 10.

261. *Laughing Boy.* 474 F. Supp., at 391, n. 12.

262. *Black Boy.* 474 F. Supp., at 391, n. 13.

263. As a result, the nine removed books could not be assigned or suggested to students in connection with school work. *Id.*, at 391. However, teachers were not instructed to refrain from discussing the removed books or the ideas and positions expressed in them. App. 131.

264. 474 F. Supp., at 396–397, citing Presidents Council, District 25 v. Community School Board # 25, 457 F.2d 289 (CA2 1972); James v. Board of Education, 461 F.2d 566, 573 (CA2 1972); East Hartford Educational Assn. v. Board of Education, 562 F.2d 838, 856 (CA2 1977) (en banc).

it should not intervene in "'the daily operations of school systems'" unless "'basic constitutional values'" were "'sharply implicate[d],'"[265] and determined that the conditions for such intervention did not exist in the present case. Acknowledging that the "removal [of the books] ... clearly was content-based," the court nevertheless found no constitutional violation of the requisite magnitude:

> "The board has restricted access only to certain books which the board believed to be, in essence, vulgar. While removal of such books from a school library may ... reflect a misguided educational philosophy, it does not constitute a sharp and direct infringement of any first amendment right." *Id.*, at 397.

A three-judge panel of the United States Court of Appeals for the Second Circuit reversed the judgment of the District Court, and remanded the action for a trial on respondents' allegations. 638 F.2d 404 (1980). Each judge on the panel filed a separate opinion. Delivering the judgment of the court, Judge Sifton treated the case as involving "an unusual and irregular intervention in the school libraries' operations by persons not routinely concerned with such matters," and concluded that petitioners were obliged to demonstrate a reasonable basis for interfering with respondents' First Amendment rights. *Id.*, at 414–415. He then determined that, at least at the summary judgment stage, petitioners had not offered sufficient justification for their action,[266] and concluded that respondents "should have ... been offered an opportunity to persuade a finder of fact that the ostensible justifications for [petitioners'] actions ... were simply pretexts for the suppression of free speech." *Id.*, at 417.[267] Judge Newman concurred in the result. *Id.* viewed the case as turning on the contested factual issue of whether petitioners' removal decision was motivated by a justifiable desire to remove books containing vulgarities and sexual explicitness, or rather by an impermissible desire to suppress ideas. *Id.*, at 436–437.[268] We *granted certiorari*, 454 U.S. 891, 102 S. Ct. 385, 70 L. Ed. 2d 205 (1981).

---

265. 474 F. Supp., at 395, quoting Presidents Council, District 25 v. Community School Board # 25, supra, at 291 (in turn quoting Epperson v. Arkansas, 393 U.S. 97, 104, 89 S. Ct. 266, 270, 21 L. Ed. 2d 228 (1968)).

266. After criticizing "the criteria for removal" employed by petitioners as "suffer[ing] from excessive generality and overbreadth," and the procedures used by petitioners as "erratic, arbitrary and free-wheeling," Judge Sifton observed that "precision of regulation and sensitivity to First Amendment concerns" were "hardly established" by such procedures. 638 F.2d, at 416.

267. Judge Sifton stated that it could be inferred from the record that petitioners' "political views and personal taste [were] being asserted not in the interests of the children's well-being, but rather for the purpose of establishing those views as the correct and orthodox ones for all purposes in the particular community." *Id.*, at 417.

268. Judge Mansfield dissented, *Id.*, at 419–432, based upon a distinctly different reading of the record developed in the District Court. According to Judge Mansfield, "the undisputed evidence of the motivation for the Board's action was the perfectly permissible ground that the books were indecent, in bad taste, and unsuitable for educational purposes." *Id.*, at 430. He also asserted that in reaching its decision "the Board [had] acted carefully, conscientiously and responsibly after according due process to all parties concerned." *Id.*, at 422. Judge Mansfield concluded that "the First Amendment entitles students to reasonable freedom of expression but not to freedom from what

II

We emphasize at the outset the limited nature of the substantive question presented by the case before us. Our precedents have long recognized certain constitutional limits upon the power of the State to control even the curriculum and classroom. For example, Meyer v. Nebraska, 262 U.S. 390, 43 S. Ct. 625, 67 L. Ed. 1042 (1923), struck down a state law that forbade the teaching of modern foreign languages in public and private schools, and Epperson v. Arkansas, 393 U.S. 97, 89 S. Ct. 266, 21 L. Ed. 2d 228 (1968), declared unconstitutional a state law that prohibited the teaching of the Darwinian theory of evolution in any state-supported school. But the current action does not require us to re-enter this difficult terrain, which Meyer and Epperson traversed without apparent misgiving. For as this case is presented to us, it does not involve textbooks, or indeed any books that Island Trees students would be required to read.[269] Respondents do not seek in this Court to impose limitations upon their school Board's discretion to prescribe the curricula of the Island Trees schools. On the contrary, the only books at issue in this case are *library* books, books that by their nature are optional rather than required reading. Our adjudication of the present case thus does not intrude into the classroom, or into the compulsory courses taught there. Furthermore, even as to library books, the action before us does not involve the *acquisition* of books. Respondents have not sought to compel their school Board to add to the school library shelves any books that students desire to read. Rather, the only action challenged in this case is the *removal* from school libraries of books originally placed there by the school authorities, or without objection from them.

The substantive question before us is still further constrained by the procedural posture of this case. Petitioners were *granted* summary judgment by the District Court. The Court of Appeals reversed that judgment, and remanded the action for a trial on the merits of respondents' claims. We can reverse the judgment of the Court of Appeals, and grant petitioners' request for reinstatement of the summary judgment in their favor, only if we determine that "there is no genuine issue as to any material fact," and that petitioners are "entitled to a judgment as a matter of

---

some may consider to be excessively moralistic or conservative selection by school authorities of library books to be used as educational tools." *Id.*, at 432.

269. Four of respondents' five causes of action complained of petitioners' "resolutions ordering the removal of certain books from the school libraries of the District and prohibiting the use of those books in the curriculum." App. 5. The District Court concluded that "respect for . . . the school board's substantial control over educational content . . . preclude[s] any finding of a first amendment violation arising out of removal of any of the books from use in the curriculum." 474 F. Supp., at 397. This holding is not at issue here. Respondents' fifth cause of action complained that petitioners' "resolutions prohibiting the use of certain books in the curriculum of schools in the District" had "imposed upon teachers in the District arbitrary and unreasonable restrictions upon their ability to function as teachers in violation of principles of academic freedom." App. 6. The District Court held that respondents had not proved this cause of action: "before such a claim may be sustained there must at least be a real, not an imagined controversy." 474 F. Supp., at 397. Respondents have not sought review of that holding in this Court.

law." Fed. Rule Civ. Proc. 56(c). In making our determination, any doubt as to the existence of a genuine issue of material fact must be resolved against petitioners as the moving party. Adickes v. S.H. Kress & Co., 398 U.S. 144, 157–159, 90 S. Ct. 1598, 1608–1609, 26 L. Ed. 2d 142 (1970). Furthermore, "[o]n summary judgment the inferences to be drawn from the underlying facts contained in [the affidavits, attached exhibits, and depositions submitted below] must be viewed in the light most favorable to the party opposing the motion." United States v. Diebold, Inc., 369 U.S. 654, 655, 82 S. Ct. 993, 994, 8 L. Ed. 2d 176 (1962).

In sum, the issue before us in this case is a narrow one, both substantively and procedurally. It may best be restated as two distinct questions. First, does the First Amendment impose *any* limitations upon the discretion of petitioners to remove library books from the Island Trees High School and Junior High School? Second, if so, do the affidavits and other evidentiary materials before the District Court, construed most favorably to respondents, raise a genuine issue of fact whether petitioners might have exceeded those limitations? If we answer either of these questions in the negative, then we must reverse the judgment of the Court of Appeals and reinstate the District Court's summary judgment for petitioners. If we answer both questions in the affirmative, then we must affirm the judgment below. We examine these questions in turn.

A

(1)

The Court has long recognized that local school boards have broad discretion in the management of school affairs. See, e.g., Meyer v. Nebraska, *supra*, at 402, 43 S. Ct., at 627; Pierce v. Society of Sisters, 268 U.S. 510, 534, 45 S. Ct. 571, 573, 69 L. Ed. 1070 (1925). Epperson v. Arkansas, *supra*, 393 U.S., at 104, 89 S. Ct., at 270, reaffirmed that, by and large, "public education in our Nation is committed to the control of state and local authorities," and that federal courts should not ordinarily "intervene in the resolution of conflicts which arise in the daily operation of school systems." Tinker v. Des Moines School Dist., 393 U.S. 503, 507, 89 S. Ct. 733, 736, 21 L. Ed. 2d 731 (1969), noted that we have "repeatedly emphasized . . . the comprehensive authority of the States and of school officials . . . to prescribe and control conduct in the schools." We have also acknowledged that public schools are vitally important "in the preparation of individuals for participation as citizens," and as vehicles for "inculcating fundamental values necessary to the maintenance of a democratic political system." Ambach v. Norwick, 441 U.S. 68, 76–77, 99 S. Ct. 1589, 1594, 60 L. Ed. 2d 49 (1979). We are therefore in full agreement with petitioners that local school boards must be permitted "to establish and apply their curriculum in such a way as to transmit community values," and that "there is a legitimate and substantial community interest in promoting respect for authority and traditional values be they social, moral, or political." Brief for Petitioners 10.[270]

270. Respondents also agree with these propositions. Tr. of Oral Arg. 28, 41.

At the same time, however, we have necessarily recognized that the discretion of the States and local school boards in matters of education must be exercised in a manner that comports with the transcendent imperatives of the First Amendment. In West Virginia Board of Education v. Barnette, 319 U.S. 624, 63 S. Ct. 1178, 87 L. Ed. 1628 (1943), we held that under the First Amendment a student in a public school could not be compelled to salute the flag. We reasoned:

> "Boards of Education ... have, of course, important, delicate, and highly discretionary functions, but none that they may not perform within the limits of the Bill of Rights. That they are educating the young for citizenship is reason for scrupulous protection of Constitutional freedoms of the individual, if we are not to strangle the free mind at its source and teach youth to discount important principles of our government as mere platitudes." *Id.*, at 637, 63 S. Ct. at 1185.

Later cases have consistently followed this rationale. Thus Epperson v. Arkansas, invalidated a State's anti-evolution statute as violative of the Establishment Clause, and reaffirmed the duty of federal courts "to apply the First Amendment's mandate in our educational system where essential to safeguard the fundamental values of freedom of speech and inquiry." 393 U.S., at 104, 89 S. Ct., at 270. And Tinker v. Des Moines School Dist., *supra*, held that a local school board had infringed the free speech rights of high school and junior high school students by suspending them from school for wearing black armbands in class as a protest against the Government's policy in Vietnam; we stated there that the "comprehensive authority ... of school officials" must be exercised "consistent with fundamental constitutional safeguards." 393 U.S., at 507, 89 S. Ct., at 736. In sum, students do not "shed their constitutional rights to freedom of speech or expression at the schoolhouse gate," *Id.*, at 506, 89 S. Ct., at 736, and therefore local school boards must discharge their "important, delicate, and highly discretionary functions" within the limits and constraints of the First Amendment.

The nature of students' First Amendment rights in the context of this case requires further examination. West Virginia Board of Education v. Barnette, *supra*, is instructive. There the Court held that students' liberty of conscience could not be infringed in the name of "national unity" or "patriotism." 319 U.S., at 640–641, 63 S. Ct., at 1186. We explained that

> "the action of the local authorities in compelling the flag salute and pledge transcends constitutional limitations on their power and invades the sphere of intellect and spirit which it is the purpose of the First Amendment to our Constitution to reserve from all official control." *Id.*, at 642, 63 S. Ct., at 1187.

Similarly, Tinker v. Des Moines School Dist., *supra*, held that students' rights to freedom of expression of their political views could not be abridged by reliance upon an "undifferentiated fear or apprehension of disturbance" arising from such expression:

> "Any departure from absolute regimentation may cause trouble. Any variation from the majority's opinion may inspire fear. Any word spoken, in

class, in the lunchroom, or on the campus, that deviates from the views of another person may start an argument or cause a disturbance. But our Constitution says we must take this risk, Terminiello v. Chicago, 337 U.S. 1 [69 S. Ct. 894, 93 L. Ed. 1131] (1949); and our history says that it is this sort of hazardous freedom—this kind of openness—that is the basis of our national strength and of the independence and vigor of Americans who grow up and live in this . . . often disputatious society." 393 U.S., at 508–509, 89 S. Ct., at 737.

In short, "First Amendment rights, applied in light of the special characteristics of the school environment, are available to . . . students." *Id.*, at 506, 89 S. Ct., at 736.

Of course, courts should not "intervene in the resolution of conflicts which arise in the daily operation of school systems" unless "basic constitutional values" are "directly and sharply implicate[d]" in those conflicts. Epperson v. Arkansas, 393 U.S., at 104, 89 S. Ct., at 270. But we think that the First Amendment rights of students may be directly and sharply implicated by the removal of books from the shelves of a school library. Our precedents have focused "not only on the role of the First Amendment in fostering individual self-expression but also on its role in affording the public access to discussion, debate, and the dissemination of information and ideas." First National Bank of Boston v. Bellotti, 435 U.S. 765, 783, 98 S. Ct. 1407, 1419, 55 L. Ed. 2d 707 (1978). And we have recognized that "the State may not, consistently with the spirit of the First Amendment, contract the spectrum of available knowledge." Griswold v. Connecticut, 381 U.S. 479, 482, 85 S. Ct. 1678, 1680, 14 L. Ed. 2d 510 (1965). In keeping with this principle, we have held that in a variety of contexts "the Constitution protects the right to receive information and ideas." Stanley v. Georgia, 394 U.S. 557, 564, 89 S. Ct. 1243, 1247, 22 L. Ed. 2d 542 (1969); see Kleindienst v. Mandel, 408 U.S. 753, 762–763, 92 S. Ct. 2576, 2581, 33 L. Ed. 2d 683 (1972) (citing cases). This right is an inherent corollary of the rights of free speech and press that are explicitly guar*ante*ed by the Constitution, in two senses. First, the right to receive ideas follows ineluctably from the sender's First Amendment right to send them: "The right of freedom of speech and press . . . embraces the right to distribute literature, and necessarily protects the right to receive it." Martin v. Struthers, 319 U.S. 141, 143, 63 S. Ct. 862, 863, 87 L. Ed. 1313 (1943) (citation omitted). "The dissemination of ideas can accomplish nothing if otherwise willing addressees are not free to receive and consider them. It would be a barren marketplace of ideas that had only sellers and no buyers." Lamont v. Postmaster General, 381 U.S. 301, 308, 85 S. Ct. 1493, 1497, 14 L. Ed. 2d 398 (1965) (BRENNAN, J., concurring).

More importantly, the right to receive ideas is a necessary predicate to the *recipient's* meaningful exercise of his own rights of speech, press, and political freedom. Madison admonished us:

> "A popular Government, without popular information, or the means of acquiring it, is but a Prologue to a Farce or a Tragedy; or, perhaps both. Knowledge will forever govern ignorance: And a people who mean to be

> their own Governors, must arm themselves with the power which knowledge gives." 9 Writings of James Madison 103 (G. Hunt ed. 1910).[271]

As we recognized in Tinker, students too are beneficiaries of this principle:

> "In our system, students may not be regarded as closed-circuit recipients of only that which the State chooses to communicate.... [S]chool officials cannot suppress 'expressions of feeling with which they do not wish to contend.'" 393 U.S., at 511, 89 S. Ct., at 739 (quoting Burnside v. Byars, 363 F.2d 744, 749 (CA5 1966)).

In sum, just as access to ideas makes it possible for citizens generally to exercise their rights of free speech and press in a meaningful manner, such access prepares students for active and effective participation in the pluralistic, often contentious society in which they will soon be adult members. Of course all First Amendment rights accorded to students must be construed "in light of the special characteristics of the school environment." Tinker v. Des Moines School Dist., 393 U.S., at 506, 89 S. Ct., at 736. But the special characteristics of the school library make that environment especially appropriate for the recognition of the First Amendment rights of students.

A school library, no less than any other public library, is "a place dedicated to quiet, to knowledge, and to beauty." Brown v. Louisiana, 383 U.S. 131, 142, 86 S. Ct. 719, 724, 15 L. Ed. 2d 637 (1966) (opinion of Fortas, J.). Keyishian v. Board of Regents, 385 U.S. 589, 87 S. Ct. 675, 17 L. Ed. 2d 629 (1967), observed that "'students must always remain free to inquire, to study and to evaluate, to gain new maturity and understanding.'"[272] The school library is the principal locus of such freedom. As one District Court has well put it, in the school library

> "a student can literally explore the unknown, and discover areas of interest and thought not covered by the prescribed curriculum.... Th[e] student learns that a library is a place to test or expand upon ideas presented to him,

---

271. For a modern version of this observation, see A. Meiklejohn, *Free Speech and Its Relation to Self-Government* 26 (1948):

> "Just so far as... the citizens who are to decide an issue are denied acquaintance with information or opinion or doubt or disbelief or criticism which is relevant to that issue, just so far the result must be ill-considered, ill-balanced planning, for the general good." See also Butler v. Michigan, 352 U.S. 380, 383–384, 77 S. Ct. 524, 525–526, 1 L. Ed. 2d 412 (1957); Procunier v. Martinez, 416 U.S. 396, 408–409, 94 S. Ct. 1800, 1808–1809, 40 L. Ed. 2d 224 (1974); Houchins v. KQED, Inc., 438 U.S. 1, 30, 98 S. Ct. 2588, 2604, 57 L. Ed. 2d 553 (1978) (STEVENS, J., dissenting) ("[T]he First Amendment protects not only the dissemination but also the receipt of information and ideas"); Saxbe v. Washington Post Co., 417 U.S. 843, 862–863, 94 S. Ct. 2811, 2821, 41 L. Ed. 2d 514 (1974) (POWELL, J., dissenting) ("[P]ublic debate must not only be unfettered; it must be informed. For that reason this Court has repeatedly stated that First Amendment concerns encompass the receipt of information and ideas as well as the right of free expression").

272. 385 U.S., at 603, 87 S. Ct., at 683, quoting Sweezy v. New Hampshire, 354 U.S. 234, 250, 77 S. Ct. 1203, 1211, 1 L. Ed. 2d 1311 (1957) (opinion of Warren, C. J.).

> in or out of the classroom." Right to Read Defense Committee v. School Committee, 454 F. Supp. 703, 715 (Mass.1978).

Petitioners emphasize the inculcative function of secondary education, and argue that they must be allowed *unfettered* discretion to "transmit community values" through the Island Trees schools. But that sweeping claim overlooks the unique role of the school library. It appears from the record that use of the Island Trees school libraries is completely voluntary on the part of students. Their selection of books from these libraries is entirely a matter of free choice; the libraries afford them an opportunity at self-education and individual enrichment that is wholly optional. Petitioners might well defend their claim of absolute discretion in matters of *curriculum* by reliance upon their duty to inculcate community values. But we think that petitioners' reliance upon that duty is misplaced where, as here, they attempt to extend their claim of absolute discretion beyond the compulsory environment of the classroom, into the school library and the regime of voluntary inquiry that there holds sway.

(2)

In rejecting petitioners' claim of absolute discretion to remove books from their school libraries, we do not deny that local school boards have a substantial legitimate role to play in the determination of school library content. We thus must turn to the question of the extent to which the First Amendment places limitations upon the discretion of petitioners to remove books from their libraries. In this inquiry we enjoy the guidance of several precedents. West Virginia Board of Education v. Barnette, stated:

> "If there is any fixed star in our constitutional constellation, it is that no official, high or petty, can prescribe what shall be orthodox in politics, nationalism, religion, or other matters of opinion. . . . If there are any circumstances which permit an exception, they do not now occur to us." 319 U.S., at 642, 63 S. Ct., at 1187.

This doctrine has been reaffirmed in later cases involving education. For example, Keyishian v. Board of Regents, *supra*, 385 U.S., at 603, 87 S. Ct., at 683, noted that "the First Amendment . . . does not tolerate laws that cast a pall of orthodoxy over the classroom"; see also Epperson v. Arkansas, 393 U.S., at 104–105, 89 S. Ct., at 270. And Mt. Healthy City Board of Ed. v. Doyle, 429 U.S. 274, 97 S. Ct. 568, 50 L. Ed. 2d 471 (1977), recognized First Amendment limitations upon the discretion of a local school board to refuse to rehire a nontenured teacher. The school board in Mt. Healthy had declined to renew respondent Doyle's employment contract, in part because he had exercised his First Amendment rights. Although Doyle did not have tenure, and thus "could have been discharged for no reason whatever," Mt. Healthy held that he could "nonetheless establish a claim to reinstatement if the decision not to rehire him was made by reason of his exercise of constitutionally protected First Amendment freedoms." *Id.*, at 283–284, 97 S. Ct., at 574. We held further that once Doyle had shown "that his conduct was constitutionally protected, and that this conduct was a 'substantial factor' . . . in the Board's decision not to rehire him," the school board was obliged to show "by a preponderance of the evidence that it would have reached the same decision as to respondent's reemployment even in the absence of the protected conduct." *Id.*, at 287, 97 S. Ct., at 576.

With respect to the present case, the message of these precedents is clear. Petitioners rightly possess significant discretion to determine the content of their school libraries. But that discretion may not be exercised in a narrowly partisan or political manner. If a Democratic school board, motivated by party affiliation, ordered the removal of all books written by or in favor of Republicans, few would doubt that the order violated the constitutional rights of the students denied access to those books. The same conclusion would surely apply if an all-white school board, motivated by racial animus, decided to remove all books authored by blacks or advocating racial equality and integration. Our Constitution does not permit the official suppression of *ideas*. Thus whether petitioners' removal of books from their school libraries denied respondents their First Amendment rights depends upon the motivation behind petitioners' actions. If petitioners *intended* by their removal decision to deny respondents access to ideas with which petitioners disagreed, and if this intent was the decisive factor in petitioners' decision,[273] then petitioners have exercised their discretion in violation of the Constitution. To permit such intentions to control official actions would be to encourage the precise sort of officially prescribed orthodoxy unequivocally condemned in Barnette. On the other hand, respondents implicitly concede that an unconstitutional motivation would *not* be demonstrated if it were shown that petitioners had decided to remove the books at issue because those books were pervasively vulgar. Tr. of Oral Arg. 36. And again, respondents concede that if it were demonstrated that the removal decision was based solely upon the "educational suitability" of the books in question, then their removal would be "perfectly permissible." *Id.*, at 53. In other words, in respondents' view such motivations, if decisive of petitioners' actions, would not carry the danger of an official suppression of ideas, and thus would not violate respondents' First Amendment rights.

As noted earlier, nothing in our decision today affects in any way the discretion of a local school board to choose books to *add* to the libraries of their schools. Because we are concerned in this case with the suppression of ideas, our holding today affects only the discretion to *remove* books. In brief, we hold that local school boards may not remove books from school library shelves simply because they dislike the ideas contained in those books and seek by their removal to "prescribe what shall be orthodox in politics, nationalism, religion, or other matters of opinion." West Virginia Board of Education v. Barnette, 319 U.S., at 642, 63 S. Ct., at 1187. Such purposes stand inescapably condemned by our precedents.

273. By "decisive factor" we mean a "substantial factor" in the absence of which the opposite decision would have been reached. See Mt. Healthy City Board of Ed. v. Doyle, 429 U.S. 274, 287, 97 S. Ct. 568, 576, 50 L. Ed. 2d 471 (1977).

B

We now turn to the remaining question presented by this case: Do the evidentiary materials that were before the District Court, when construed most favorably to respondents, raise a genuine issue of material fact whether petitioners exceeded constitutional limitations in exercising their discretion to remove the books from the school libraries? We conclude that the materials do raise such a question, which forecloses summary judgment in favor of petitioners.

Before the District Court, respondents claimed that petitioners' decision to remove the books "was based on [their] personal values, morals and tastes." App. 139. Respondents also claimed that petitioners objected to the books in part because excerpts from them were "anti-American." *Id.*, at 140. The accuracy of these claims was partially conceded by petitioners,[274] and petitioners' own affidavits lent further support to respondents' claims.[275] In addition, the record developed in the District Court shows that when petitioners offered their first public explanation for the removal of the books, they relied in part on the assertion that the removed books were "anti-American," and "offensive to . . . Americans in general." 474 F. Supp., at 390.[276]

Furthermore, while the Book Review Committee appointed by petitioners was instructed to make its recommendations based upon criteria that appear on their face to be permissible — the books' "educational suitability," "good taste," "relevance," and "appropriateness to age and grade level," App. 67 — the Committee's recommendations that five of the books be retained and that only two be removed were essentially rejected by petitioners, without any statement of reasons for doing so. Finally, while petitioners originally defended their removal decision with the

---

274. Petitioners acknowledged that their "evaluation of the suitability of the books was based on [their] personal values, morals, tastes and concepts of educational suitability." App. 142. But they did not accept, and thus apparently denied, respondents' assertion that some excerpts were objected to as "anti-American." *Ibid.*

275. For example, petitioner Ahrens stated:

> "I am basically a conservative in my general philosophy and feel that the community I represent as a school board member shares that philosophy. . . . I feel that it is my duty to apply my conservative principles to the decision making process in which I am involved as a board member and I have done so with regard to . . . curriculum formation and content and other educational matters." *Id.*, at 21.
>
> "We are representing the community which first elected us and re-elected us and our actions have reflected its intrinsic values and desires." *Id.*, at 27. Petitioners Fasulo, Hughes, Melchers, Michaels, and Nessim made a similar statement that they had "represented the basic values of the community in [their] actions." *Id.*, at 120.

276. When asked to give an example of "anti-Americanism" in the removed books, petitioners Ahrens and Martin both adverted to *A Hero Ain't Nothin' But A Sandwich*, which notes at one point that George Washington was a slaveholder. See A. Childress, *A Hero Ain't Nothin' But A Sandwich* 43 (1973); Deposition of Petitioner Ahrens 89; Deposition of Petitioner Martin 20–22. Petitioner Martin stated: "I believe it is anti-American to present one of the nation's heroes, the first President, . . . in such a negative and obviously one-sided life. That is one example of what I would consider anti-American." Deposition of Petitioner Martin 22.

explanation that "these books contain obscenities, blasphemies, brutality, and perversion beyond description," 474 F. Supp., at 390, one of the books, A Reader for Writers, was removed even though it contained no such language. 638 F.2d, at 428, n. 6 (Mansfield, J., dissenting).

Standing alone, this evidence respecting the substantive motivations behind petitioners' removal decision would not be decisive. This would be a very different case if the record demonstrated that petitioners had employed established, regular, and facially unbiased procedures for the review of controversial materials. But the actual record in the case before us suggests the exact opposite. Petitioners' removal procedures were vigorously challenged below by respondents, and the evidence on this issue sheds further light on the issue of petitioners' motivations.[277] Respondents alleged that in making their removal decision petitioners ignored "the advice of literary experts," the views of "librarians and teachers within the Island Trees School system," the advice of the Superintendent of Schools, and the guidance of publications that rate books for junior and senior high school students. App. 128–129. Respondents also claimed that petitioners' decision was based solely on the fact that the books were named on the PONYU list received by petitioners Ahrens, Martin, and Hughes, and that petitioners "did not undertake an independent review of other books in the [school] libraries." *Id.*, at 129–130. Evidence before the District Court lends support to these claims. The record shows that immediately after petitioners first ordered the books removed from the library shelves, the Superintendent of Schools reminded them that "we already have a policy ... designed expressly to handle such problems," and recommended that the removal decision be approached through this established channel. *See* n. 4, *supra*. But the Board disregarded the Superintendent's advice, and instead resorted to the extraordinary procedure of appointing a Book Review Committee — the advice of which was later rejected without explanation. In sum, respondents' allegations and some of the evidentiary materials presented below do not rule out the possibility that petitioners' removal procedures were highly irregular and ad hoc — the antithesis of those procedures that might tend to allay suspicions regarding petitioners' motivations.

Construing these claims, affidavit statements, and other evidentiary materials in a manner favorable to respondents, we cannot conclude that petitioners were

---

277. We have recognized in numerous precedents that when seeking to distinguish activities unprotected by the First Amendment from other, protected activities, the State must employ "sensitive tools" in order to achieve a precision of regulation that avoids the chilling of protected activities. *See, e.g.*, Speiser v. Randall, 357 U.S. 513, 525–526, 78 S. Ct. 1332, 1341–1342, 2 L. Ed. 2d 1460 (1958); NAACP v. Button, 371 U.S. 415, 433, 83 S. Ct. 328, 338, 9 L. Ed. 2d 405 (1963); Keyishian v. Board of Regents, 385 U.S. 589, 603–604, 87 S. Ct. 675, 683–684, 17 L. Ed. 2d 629 (1967); Blount v. Rizzi, 400 U.S. 410, 417, 91 S. Ct. 423, 428, 27 L. Ed. 2d 498 (1971). In the case before us, the presence of such sensitive tools in petitioners' decision-making process would naturally indicate a concern on their part for the First Amendment rights of respondents; the absence of such tools might suggest a lack of such concern. *See* 638 F.2d, at 416–417 (opinion of Sifton, J.).

"entitled to a judgment as a matter of law." The evidence plainly does not foreclose the possibility that petitioners' decision to remove the books rested decisively upon disagreement with constitutionally protected ideas in those books, or upon a desire on petitioners' part to impose upon the students of the Island Trees High School and Junior High School a political orthodoxy to which petitioners and their constituents adhered. Of course, some of the evidence before the District Court might lead a finder of fact to accept petitioners' claim that their removal decision was based upon constitutionally valid concerns. But that evidence at most creates a genuine issue of material fact on the critical question of the credibility of petitioners' justifications for their decision: On that issue, it simply cannot be said that there is no genuine issue as to any material fact.

The mandate shall issue forthwith. *Affirmed.*

[Case No. 4-7]

Public school officials held not to violate First Amendment free-speech guarantee by suspending student who refused to take down "BONG HiTS 4 JESUS" banner unfurled by the student and other students at a school-sponsored event.

Morse v. Frederick

Supreme Court of the United States
551 U.S. 393 (2007)

Chief Justice ROBERTS delivered the opinion of the Court.

At a school-sanctioned and school-supervised event, a high school principal saw some of her students unfurl a large banner conveying a message she reasonably regarded as promoting illegal drug use. Consistent with established school policy prohibiting such messages at school events, the principal directed the students to take down the banner. One student—among those who had brought the banner to the event—refused to do so. The principal confiscated the banner and later suspended the student. The Ninth Circuit held that the principal's actions violated the First Amendment, and that the student could sue the principal for damages.

Our cases make clear that students do not "shed their constitutional rights to freedom of speech or expression at the schoolhouse gate." *Tinker v. Des Moines Independent Community School Dist.*, 393 U.S. 503, 506, 89 S. Ct. 733, 21 L. Ed. 2d 731 (1969). At the same time, we have held that "the constitutional rights of students in public school are not automatically coextensive with the rights of adults in other settings," *Bethel School Dist. No. 403 v. Fraser*, 478 U.S. 675, 682, 106 S. Ct. 3159, 92 L. Ed. 2d 549 (1986), and that the rights of students "must be 'applied in light of the special characteristics of the school environment,'" *Hazelwood School Dist. v. Kuhlmeier*, 484 U.S. 260, 266, 108 S. Ct. 562, 98 L. Ed. 2d 592 (1988) (quoting *Tinker*, *supra*, at 506, 89 S. Ct. 733, 21 L. Ed. 2d 731). Consistent with these principles, we hold that schools may take steps to safeguard those entrusted to their care from speech that can reasonably be regarded as encouraging illegal drug use. We conclude that the school officials in this case did not violate the First Amendment by confiscating the pro-drug banner and suspending the student responsible for it.

I

On January 24, 2002, the Olympic Torch Relay passed through Juneau, Alaska, on its way to the winter games in Salt Lake City, Utah. The torchbearers were to proceed along a street in front of Juneau-Douglas High School (JDHS) while school was in session. Petitioner Deborah Morse, the school principal, decided to permit staff and students to participate in the Torch Relay as an approved social event or class trip. App. 22–23. Students were allowed to leave class to observe the relay from either side of the street. Teachers and administrative officials monitored the students' actions.

Respondent Joseph Frederick, a JDHS senior, was late to school that day. When he arrived, he joined his friends (all but one of whom were JDHS students) across the street from the school to watch the event. Not all the students waited patiently. Some became rambunctious, throwing plastic cola bottles and snowballs and scuffling with their classmates. As the torchbearers and camera crews passed by, Frederick and his friends unfurled a 14-foot banner bearing the phrase: "BONG HiTS 4 JESUS." App. to Pet. for Cert. 70a. The large banner was easily readable by the students on the other side of the street.

Principal Morse immediately crossed the street and demanded that the banner be taken down. Everyone but Frederick complied. Morse confiscated the banner and told Frederick to report to her office, where she suspended him for 10 days. Morse later explained that she told Frederick to take the banner down because she thought it encouraged illegal drug use, in violation of established school policy. Juneau School Board Policy No. 5520 states: "The Board specifically prohibits any assembly or public expression that ... advocates the use of substances that are illegal to minors. ..." *Id.*, at 53a. In addition, Juneau School Board Policy No. 5850 subjects "[p]upils who participate in approved social events and class trips" to the same student conduct rules that apply during the regular school program. *Id.*, at 58a.

Frederick administratively appealed his suspension, but the Juneau School District Superintendent upheld it, limiting it to time served (eight days). In a memorandum setting forth his reasons, the superintendent determined that Frederick had displayed his banner "in the midst of his fellow students, during school hours, at a school-sanctioned activity." *Id.*, at 63a. He further explained that Frederick "was not disciplined because the principal of the school 'disagreed' with his message, but because his speech appeared to advocate the use of illegal drugs." *Id.*, at 61a.

The superintendent continued: "The common-sense understanding of the phrase 'bong hits' is that it is a reference to a means of smoking marijuana. Given [Frederick's] inability or unwillingness to express any other credible meaning for the phrase, I can only agree with the principal and countless others who saw the banner as advocating the use of illegal drugs. [Frederick's] speech was not political. He was not advocating the legalization of marijuana or promoting a religious belief.

He was displaying a fairly silly message promoting illegal drug usage in the midst of a school activity, for the benefit of television cameras covering the Torch Relay. [Frederick's] speech was potentially disruptive to the event and clearly disruptive of and inconsistent with the school's educational mission to educate students about the dangers of illegal drugs and to discourage their use." *Id., at 61a–62a.*

Relying on our decision in *Fraser, supra* the superintendent concluded that the principal's actions were permissible because Frederick's banner was "speech or action that intrudes upon the work of the schools." App. to Pet. for Cert. 62a (internal quotation marks omitted). The Juneau School District Board of Education upheld the suspension.

Frederick then filed suit under 42 U.S.C. §1983, alleging that the school board and Morse had violated his First Amendment rights. He sought declaratory and injunctive relief, unspecified compensatory damages, punitive damages, and attorney's fees. The District Court granted summary judgment for the school board and Morse, ruling that they were entitled to qualified immunity and that they had not infringed Frederick's First Amendment rights. The court found that Morse reasonably interpreted the banner as promoting illegal drug use — a message that "directly contravened the Board's policies relating to drug abuse prevention." App. to Pet. for Cert. 36a–38a. Under the circumstances, the court held that "Morse had the authority, if not the obligation, to stop such messages at a school-sanctioned activity." *Id.*, at 37a.

The Ninth Circuit reversed. Deciding that Frederick acted during a "school-authorized activit[y]," and "proceed[ing] on the basis that the banner expressed a positive sentiment about marijuana use," the court nonetheless found a violation of Frederick's First Amendment rights because the school punished Frederick without demonstrating that his speech gave rise to a "risk of substantial disruption." The court further concluded that Frederick's right to display his banner was so "clearly established" that a reasonable principal in Morse's position would have understood that her actions were unconstitutional, and that Morse was therefore not entitled to qualified immunity. *Id.*, at 1123–1125.

We granted certiorari on two questions: whether Frederick had a First Amendment right to wield his banner, and, if so, whether that right was so clearly established that the principal may be held liable for damages. 549 U.S. 1075, 127 S. Ct. 722, 166 L. Ed. 2d 559 (2006). We resolve the first question against Frederick, and therefore have no occasion to reach the second.[278]

---

278. Justice Breyer would rest decision on qualified immunity without reaching the underlying First Amendment question. The problem with this approach is the rather significant one that it is inadequate to decide the case before us. Qualified immunity shields public officials from money damages only. See *Wood v. Strickland, 420 U.S. 308, 314, n. 6, 95 S. Ct. 992, 43 L. Ed. 2d 214 (1975).* In this case, Frederick asked not just for damages, but also for declaratory and injunctive relief. App. 13. Justice Breyer's proposed decision on qualified immunity grounds would dispose of the damages claims, but Frederick's other claims would remain unaddressed. To get around that problem,

II

At the outset, we reject Frederick's argument that this is not a school speech case—as has every other authority to address the question. See App. 22–23 (Principal Morse); App. to Pet. for Cert. 63a (superintendent); *id.*, at 69a (school board); *id.*, at 34a–35a (District Court); 439 F.3d at 1117 (Ninth Circuit). The event occurred during normal school hours. It was sanctioned by Principal Morse "as an approved social event or class trip," App. 22–23, and the school district's rules expressly provide that pupils in "approved social events and class trips are subject to district rules for student conduct," App. to Pet. for Cert. 58a. Teachers and administrators were interspersed among the students and charged with supervising them. The high school band and cheerleaders performed. Frederick, standing among other JDHS students across the street from the school, directed his banner toward the school, making it plainly visible to most students. Under these circumstances, we agree with the superintendent that Frederick cannot "stand in the midst of his fellow students, during school hours, at a school-sanctioned activity and claim he is not at school." *Id.*, at 63a. There is some uncertainty at the outer boundaries as to when courts should apply school speech precedents, see *Porter v. Ascension Parish School Bd.*, 393 F.3d 608, 615, n. 22 (CA5 2004), but not on these facts.

III

The message on Frederick's banner is cryptic. It is no doubt offensive to some, perhaps amusing to others. To still others, it probably means nothing at all. Frederick himself claimed "that the words were just nonsense meant to attract television cameras." 439 F.3d at 1117–1118. But Principal Morse thought the banner would be interpreted by those viewing it as promoting illegal drug use, and that interpretation is plainly a reasonable one.

As Morse later explained in a declaration, when she saw the sign, she thought that "the reference to a 'bong hit' would be widely understood by high school students and others as referring to smoking marijuana." App. 24. She further believed that "display of the banner would be construed by students, District personnel, parents and others witnessing the display of the banner, as advocating or promoting illegal drug use"—in violation of school policy. *Id.*, at 25; see *ibid.* ("I told Frederick and the other members of his group to put the banner down because I felt that it violated the [school] policy against displaying . . . material that advertises or promotes use of illegal drugs").

We agree with Morse. At least two interpretations of the words on the banner demonstrate that the sign advocated the use of illegal drugs. First, the phrase could

---

Justice Breyer hypothesizes that Frederick's suspension—the target of his request for injunctive relief—"may well be justified on non-speech-related grounds." See *post, at 433, 168 L. Ed. 2d, at 318*(opinion concurring in judgment in part and dissenting in part). That hypothesis was never considered by the courts below, never raised by any of the parties, and is belied by the record, which nowhere suggests that the suspension would have been justified solely on non-speech-related grounds.

be interpreted as an imperative: "[Take] bong hits . . ."—a message equivalent, as Morse explained in her declaration, to "smoke marijuana" or "use an illegal drug." Alternatively, the phrase could be viewed as celebrating drug use—"bong hits [are a good thing]," or "[we take] bong hits"—and we discern no meaningful distinction between celebrating illegal drug use in the midst of fellow students and outright advocacy or promotion. See *Guiles v. Marineau*, 461 F.3d 320, 328 (CA2 2006) (discussing the present case and describing the sign as "a clearly pro-drug banner").

The pro-drug interpretation of the banner gains further plausibility given the paucity of alternative meanings the banner might bear. The best Frederick can come up with is that the banner is "meaningless and funny." 439 F.3d at 1116. The dissent similarly refers to the sign's message as "curious," *post, at 434, 168 L. Ed. 2d, at 319* (opinion of Stevens, J.), "ambiguous," *ibid.*, "nonsense," *post, at 435, 168 L. Ed. 2d, at 319*, "ridiculous," *post, at 438, 168 L. Ed. 2d, at 322*, "obscure," *post, at 439, 168 L. Ed. 2d, at 322*, "silly," *post, at 444, 168 L. Ed. 2d, at 325*, "quixotic," *post, at 445, 168 L. Ed. 2d, at 326*, and "stupid," *ibid.* Gibberish is surely a possible interpretation of the words on the banner, but it is not the only one, and dismissing the banner as meaningless ignores its undeniable reference to illegal drugs.

The dissent mentions Frederick's "credible and uncontradicted explanation for the message—he just wanted to get on television." *Post, at 444, 168 L. Ed. 2d, at 325.* But that is a description of Frederick's *motive* for displaying the banner; it is not an interpretation of what the banner says. The *way* Frederick was going to fulfill his ambition of appearing on television was by unfurling a pro-drug banner at a school event, in the presence of teachers and fellow students.

Elsewhere in its opinion, the dissent emphasizes the importance of political speech and the need to foster "national debate about a serious issue," *post, at 448, 168 L. Ed. 2d, at 328*, as if to suggest that the banner is political speech. But not even Frederick argues that the banner conveys any sort of political or religious message. Contrary to the dissent's suggestion, see *post, at 446–448, 168 L. Ed. 2d, at 327–328*, this is plainly not a case about political debate over the criminalization of drug use or possession.

IV

The question thus becomes whether a principal may, consistent with the First Amendment, restrict student speech at a school event, when that speech is reasonably viewed as promoting illegal drug use. We hold that she may.

In *Tinker*, this Court made clear that "First Amendment rights, applied in light of the special characteristics of the school environment, are available to teachers and students." 393 U.S., at 506, 89 S. Ct. 733, 21 L. Ed. 2d 731. *Tinker* involved a group of high school students who decided to wear black armbands to protest the Vietnam War. School officials learned of the plan and then adopted a policy prohibiting students from wearing armbands. When several students nonetheless wore armbands to school, they were suspended. *Id.*, at 504, 89 S. Ct. 733, 21 L. Ed. 2d 731. The students sued, claiming that their First Amendment rights had been violated, and this Court agreed.

Tinker held that student expression may not be suppressed unless school officials reasonably conclude that it will "materially and substantially disrupt the work and discipline of the school." *Id.*, at 513, 89 S. Ct. 733, 21 L. Ed. 2d 731. The essential facts of *Tinker* are quite stark, implicating concerns at the heart of the First Amendment. The students sought to engage in political speech, using the armbands to express their "disapproval of the Vietnam hostilities and their advocacy of a truce, to make their views known, and, by their example, to influence others to adopt them." *Id.*, at 514, 89 S. Ct. 733, 21 L. Ed. 2d 731. Political speech, of course, is "at the core of what the First Amendment is designed to protect." *Virginia v. Black*, 538 U.S. 343, 365, 123 S. Ct. 1536, 155 L. Ed. 2d 535 (2003) (plurality opinion). The only interest the Court discerned underlying the school's actions was the "mere desire to avoid the discomfort and unpleasantness that always accompany an unpopular viewpoint," or "an urgent wish to avoid the controversy which might result from the expression." *Tinker*, 393 U.S., at 509, 510, 89 S. Ct. 733, 21 L. Ed. 2d 731. That interest was not enough to justify banning "a silent, passive expression of opinion, unaccompanied by any disorder or disturbance." *Id.*, at 508, 89 S. Ct. 733, 21 L. Ed. 2d 731.

This Court's next student speech case was *Fraser*, 478 U.S. 675, 106 S. Ct. 3159, 92 L. Ed. 2d 549. Matthew Fraser was suspended for delivering a speech before a high school assembly in which he employed what this Court called "an elaborate, graphic, and explicit sexual metaphor." *Id.*, at 678, 106 S. Ct. 3159, 92 L. Ed. 2d 549. Analyzing the case under *Tinker*, the District Court and Court of Appeals found no disruption, and therefore no basis for disciplining Fraser. 478 U.S., at 679–680, 106 S. Ct. 3159, 92 L. Ed. 2d 549. This Court reversed, holding that the "School District acted entirely within its permissible authority in imposing sanctions upon Fraser in response to his offensively lewd and indecent speech." *Id.*, at 685, 106 S. Ct. 3159, 92 L. Ed. 2d 549.

The mode of analysis employed in *Fraser* is not entirely clear. The Court was plainly attuned to the content of Fraser's speech, citing the "marked distinction between the political 'message' of the armbands in *Tinker* and the sexual content of [Fraser's] speech." *Id.*, at 680, 106 S. Ct. 3159, 92 L. Ed. 2d 549. But the Court also reasoned that school boards have the authority to determine "what manner of speech in the classroom or in school assembly is inappropriate." *Id.*, at 683, 106 S. Ct. 3159, 92 L. Ed. 2d 549. Cf. *id.*, at 689, 106 S. Ct. 3159, 92 L. Ed. 2d 549 (Brennan, J., concurring in judgment) ("In the present case, school officials sought only to ensure that a high school assembly proceed in an orderly manner. There is no suggestion that school officials attempted to regulate [Fraser's] speech because they disagreed with the views he sought to express").

We need not resolve this debate to decide this case. For present purposes, it is enough to distill from *Fraser* two basic principles. First, *Fraser*'s holding demonstrates that "the constitutional rights of students in public school are not automatically coextensive with the rights of adults in other settings." *Id.*, at 682, 106 S. Ct. 3159, 92 L. Ed. 2d 549. Had Fraser delivered the same speech in a public forum outside the school context, it would have been protected. See *Cohen v. California*, 403

U.S. 15, 91 S. Ct. 1780, 29 L. Ed. 2d 284 (1971); *Fraser, supra,* at 682–683, 106 S. Ct. 3159, 92 L. Ed. 2d 549. In school, however, Fraser's First Amendment rights were circumscribed "in light of the special characteristics of the school environment." *Tinker, supra,* at 506, 89 S. Ct. 733, 21 L. Ed. 2d 731. Second, *Fraser* established that the mode of analysis set forth in *Tinker* is not absolute. Whatever approach *Fraser* employed, it certainly did not conduct the "substantial disruption" analysis prescribed by *Tinker, supra,* at 514, 89 S. Ct. 733, 21 L. Ed. 2d 731. See *Kuhlmeier,* 484 U.S., at 271, n. 4, 108 S. Ct. 562, 98 L. Ed. 2d 592 (disagreeing with the proposition that there is "no difference between the First Amendment analysis applied in *Tinker* and that applied in *Fraser,*" and noting that the holding in *Fraser* was not based on any showing of substantial disruption).

Our most recent student speech case, *Kuhlmeier,* concerned "expressive activities that students, parents, and members of the public might reasonably perceive to bear the imprimatur of the school." 484 U.S., at 271, 108 S. Ct. 562, 98 L. Ed. 2d 592. Staff members of a high school newspaper sued their school when it chose not to publish two of their articles. The Court of Appeals analyzed the case under *Tinker,* ruling in favor of the students because it found no evidence of material disruption to classwork or school discipline. *Kuhlmeier v. Hazelwood School Dist.,* 795 F.2d 1368, 1375 (CA8 1986). This Court reversed, holding that "educators do not offend the First Amendment by exercising editorial control over the style and content of student speech in school-sponsored expressive activities so long as their actions are reasonably related to legitimate pedagogical concerns." *Kuhlmeier, supra,* 484 U.S., at 273, 108 S. Ct. 562, 98 L. Ed. 2d 592.

Kuhlmeier does not control this case because no one would reasonably believe that Frederick's banner bore the school's imprimatur. The case is nevertheless instructive because it confirms both principles cited above. *Kuhlmeier* acknowledged that schools may regulate some speech "even though the government could not censor similar speech outside the school." *Id.,* at 266, 108 S. Ct. 562, 98 L. Ed. 2d 592. And, like *Fraser,* it confirms that the rule of *Tinker* is not the only basis for restricting student speech.[279]

Drawing on the principles applied in our student speech cases, we have held in the Fourth Amendment context that "while children assuredly do not 'shed their constitutional rights ... at the schoolhouse gate,' ... the nature of those rights is what is appropriate for children in school." *Vernonia Sch. Dist. 47J v. Acton,* 515

---

279. The dissent's effort to find inconsistency between our approach here and the opinion in *Federal Election Comm'n v. Wisconsin Right to Life, Inc., 551 post p. 449, 127 S. Ct. 2652, 168 L. Ed. 2d 329, 2007 U.S. LEXIS 8515 (2007),* see *post, at 444–445, 168 L. Ed. 2d, at 325 (opinion of Stevens, J.),* overlooks what was made clear in *Tinker, Fraser, and Kuhlmeier*: Student First Amendment rights are "applied in light of the special characteristics of the school environment." *Tinker, 393 U.S., at 506, 89 S. Ct. 733, 21 L. Ed. 2d 731.* See *Fraser, 478 U.S., at 682, 106 S. Ct. 3159, 92 L. Ed. 2d 549; Kuhlmeier, 484 U.S., at 266, 108 S. Ct. 562, 98 L. Ed. 2d 592.* And, as discussed above, *supra, at 402–403, 168 L. Ed. 2d, at 299,* there is no serious argument that Frederick's banner is political speech of the sort at issue in *Wisconsin Right to Life.*

U.S. 646, 655–656, 115 S. Ct. 2386, 132 L. Ed. 2d 564 (1995) (quoting *Tinker, supra*, at 506, 89 S. Ct. 733, 21 L. Ed. 2d 731). In particular, "the school setting requires some easing of the restrictions to which searches by public authorities are ordinarily subject." *New Jersey v. T. L. O.*, 469 U.S. 325, 340, 105 S. Ct. 733, 83 L. Ed. 2d 720 (1985). See *Vernonia, supra*, at 656, 115 S. Ct. 2386, 132 L. Ed. 2d 564 ("Fourth Amendment rights, no less than First and Fourteenth Amendment rights, are different in public schools than elsewhere . . ."); *Bd. of Educ. v. Earls*, 536 U.S. 822, 829–830, 122 S. Ct. 2559, 153 L. Ed. 2d 735 (2002) ("'special needs' inhere in the public school context"; "[w]hile schoolchildren do not shed their constitutional rights when they enter the schoolhouse, Fourth Amendment rights . . . are different in public schools than elsewhere; the 'reasonableness' inquiry cannot disregard the schools' custodial and tutelary responsibility for children" (quoting *Vernonia*, 515 U.S., at 656, 115 S. Ct. 2386, 132 L. Ed. 2d 564; citation and some internal quotation marks omitted)).

Even more to the point, these cases also recognize that deterring drug use by schoolchildren is an "important — indeed, perhaps compelling" interest. *Id.*, at 661, 115 S. Ct. 2386, 132 L. Ed. 2d 564. Drug abuse can cause severe and permanent damage to the health and well-being of young people:

> "School years are the time when the physical, psychological, and addictive effects of drugs are most severe. Maturing nervous systems are more critically impaired by intoxicants than mature ones are; childhood losses in learning are lifelong and profound; children grow chemically dependent more quickly than adults, and their record of recovery is depressingly poor. And of course the effects of a drug-infested school are visited not just upon the users, but upon the entire student body and faculty, as the educational process is disrupted." *Id.*, at 661–662, 115 S. Ct. 2386, 132 L. Ed. 2d 564 (citations and internal quotation marks omitted).

Just five years ago, we wrote: "The drug abuse problem among our Nation's youth has hardly abated since *Vernonia* was decided in 1995. In fact, evidence suggests that it has only grown worse." *Earls, supra*, at 834, and n. 5, 122 S. Ct. 2559, 153 L. Ed. 2d 735.

The problem remains serious today. See generally 1 National Institute on Drug Abuse, National Institutes of Health, Monitoring the Future: National Survey Results on Drug Use, 1975–2005, Secondary School Students (2006). About half of American 12th graders have used an illicit drug, as have more than a third of 10th graders and about one-fifth of 8th graders. *Id.*, at 99. Nearly one in four 12th graders has used an illicit drug in the past month. *Id.*, at 101. Some 25% of high schoolers say that they have been offered, sold, or given an illegal drug on school property within the past year. Dept. of Health and Human Services, Centers for Disease Control and Prevention, Youth Risk Behavior Surveillance — United States, 2005, 55 Morbidity and Mortality Weekly Report, Surveillance Summaries, No. SS-5, p 19 (June 9, 2006).

Congress has declared that part of a school's job is educating students about the dangers of illegal drug use. It has provided billions of dollars to support state and local drug-prevention programs, Brief for United States as *Amicus Curiae* 1, and required that schools receiving federal funds under the Safe and Drug-Free Schools and Communities Act of 1994 certify that their drug-prevention programs "convey a clear and consistent message that . . . the illegal use of drugs [is] wrong and harmful," 20 U.S.C. § 7114(d)(6) (2000 ed., Supp. IV).

Thousands of school boards throughout the country—including JDHS—have adopted policies aimed at effectuating this message. See Pet. for Cert. 17–21. Those school boards know that peer pressure is perhaps "the single most important factor leading schoolchildren to take drugs," and that students are more likely to use drugs when the norms in school appear to tolerate such behavior. *Earls, supra,* at 840, 122 S. Ct. 2559, 153 L. Ed. 2d 735 (Breyer, J., concurring). Student speech celebrating illegal drug use at a school event, in the presence of school administrators and teachers, thus poses a particular challenge for school officials working to protect those entrusted to their care from the dangers of drug abuse.

The "special characteristics of the school environment," *Tinker,* 393 U.S., at 506, 89 S. Ct. 733, 21 L. Ed. 2d 731, and the governmental interest in stopping student drug abuse—reflected in the policies of Congress and myriad school boards, including JDHS—allow schools to restrict student expression that they reasonably regard as promoting illegal drug use. *Tinker* warned that schools may not prohibit student speech because of "undifferentiated fear or apprehension of disturbance" or "a mere desire to avoid the discomfort and unpleasantness that always accompany an unpopular viewpoint." *Id.,* at 508, 509, 89 S. Ct. 733, 21 L. Ed. 2d 731. The danger here is far more serious and palpable. The particular concern to prevent student drug abuse at issue here, embodied in established school policy, App. 92–95; App. to Pet. for Cert. 53a, extends well beyond an abstract desire to avoid controversy.

Petitioners urge us to adopt the broader rule that Frederick's speech is proscribable because it is plainly "offensive" as that term is used in *Fraser.* See Reply Brief for Petitioners 14–15. We think this stretches *Fraser* too far; that case should not be read to encompass any speech that could fit under some definition of "offensive." After all, much political and religious speech might be perceived as offensive to some. The concern here is not that Frederick's speech was offensive, but that it was reasonably viewed as promoting illegal drug use.

Although accusing this decision of doing "serious violence to the First Amendment" by authorizing "viewpoint discrimination," *post, at 435, 437, 168 L. Ed. 2d, at 319, 321,* the dissent concludes that "it might well be appropriate to tolerate some targeted viewpoint discrimination in this unique setting," *post, at 439, 168 L. Ed. 2d, at 322.* Nor do we understand the dissent to take the position that schools are required to tolerate student advocacy of illegal drug use at school events, even if that advocacy falls short of inviting "imminent" lawless action. See *Ibid.* ("[I]t is possible that our rigid imminence requirement ought to be relaxed at schools"). And even the dissent recognizes that the issues here are close enough that the principal should not be held liable in damages, but should instead enjoy qualified immunity for her actions. See *post, at 434, 168 L. Ed. 2d, at 319.* Stripped of rhetorical flourishes, then, the debate between the dissent and this opinion is less about constitutional first principles than about whether Frederick's banner constitutes promotion of illegal drug use. We have explained our view that it does. The dissent's contrary view on that relatively narrow question hardly justifies sounding the First Amendment bugle. * * *

School principals have a difficult job, and a vitally important one. When Frederick suddenly and unexpectedly unfurled his banner, Morse had to decide to act—or not act—on the spot. It was reasonable for her to conclude that the banner promoted illegal drug use—in violation of established school policy—and that failing to act would send a powerful message to the students in her charge, including Frederick, about how serious the school was about the dangers of illegal drug use. The First Amendment does not require schools to tolerate at school events student expression that contributes to those dangers.

The judgment of the United States Court of Appeals for the Ninth Circuit is reversed, and the case is remanded for further proceedings consistent with this opinion.

It is so ordered.

[Case No. 4-8]

Students have privacy rights and may not be searched absent compliance with the reasonableness standard.

New Jersey v. T.L.O.

Supreme Court of the United States
469 U.S. 325 (1985)

Justice WHITE delivered the opinion of the Court.

We granted certiorari in this case to examine the appropriateness of the exclusionary rule as a remedy for searches carried out in violation of the Fourth Amendment by public school authorities. Our consideration of the proper application of the Fourth Amendment to the public schools, however, has led us to conclude that the search that gave rise to the case now before us did not violate the Fourth Amendment. Accordingly, we here address only the questions of the proper standard for assessing the legality of searches conducted by public school officials and the application of that standard to the facts of this case.

I

On March 7, 1980, a teacher at Piscataway High School in Middlesex County, N.J., discovered two girls smoking in a lavatory. One of the two girls was the respondent T.L.O., who at that time was a 14-year-old high school freshman. Because smoking in the lavatory was a violation of a school rule, the teacher took the two girls to the Principal's office, where they met with Assistant Vice Principal Theodore Choplick. In response to questioning by Mr. Choplick, T.L.O.'s companion admitted that she had violated the rule. T.L.O., however, denied that she had been smoking in the lavatory and claimed that she did not smoke at all.

Mr. Choplick asked T.L.O. to come into his private office and demanded to see her purse. Opening the purse, he found a pack of cigarettes, which he removed from the purse and held before T.L.O. as he accused her of having lied to him. As he reached into the purse for the cigarettes, Mr. Choplick also noticed a package of cigarette rolling papers. In his experience, possession of rolling papers by high school students was closely associated with the use of marihuana. Suspecting that a closer examination of the purse might yield further evidence of drug use, Mr. Choplick proceeded to search the purse thoroughly. The search revealed a small amount of marihuana, a pipe, a number of empty plastic bags, a substantial quantity of money in one-dollar bills, an index card that appeared to be a list of students who owed T.L.O. money, and two letters that implicated T.L.O. in marihuana dealing.

Mr. Choplick notified T.L.O.'s mother and the police, and turned the evidence of drug dealing over to the police. At the request of the police, T.L.O.'s mother took her daughter to police headquarters, where T.L.O. confessed that she had been selling marihuana at the high school. On the basis of the confession and the evidence seized by Mr. Choplick, the State brought delinquency charges against T.L.O. in the Juvenile and Domestic Relations Court of Middlesex County.[280] Contending that Mr. Choplick's search of her purse violated the Fourth Amendment, T.L.O. moved to suppress the evidence found in her purse as well as her confession, which, she argued, was tainted by the allegedly unlawful search. The Juvenile Court denied the motion to suppress. *State ex rel. T.L.O.*, 178 N.J.Super. 329, 428 A.2d 1327 (1980). Although the court concluded that the Fourth Amendment did apply to searches carried out by school officials, it held that

> "a school official may properly conduct a search of a student's person if the official has a reasonable suspicion that a crime has been or is in the process of being committed, *or* reasonable cause to believe that the search is necessary to maintain school discipline or enforce school policies."

Id., 178 N.J.Super., at 341, 428 A.2d, at 1333 (emphasis in original).

Applying this standard, the court concluded that the search conducted by Mr. Choplick was a reasonable one. The initial decision to open the purse was justified by Mr. Choplick's well-founded suspicion that T.L.O. had violated the rule forbidding smoking in the lavatory. Once the purse was open, evidence of marihuana violations was in plain view, and Mr. Choplick was entitled to conduct a thorough search to determine the nature and extent of T.L.O.'s drug-related activities. *Id.*, 178 N.J.Super., at 343, 428 A.2d, at 1334. Having denied the motion to suppress, the

---

280. T.L.O. also received a 3-day suspension from school for smoking cigarettes in a nonsmoking area and a 7-day suspension for possession of marihuana. On T.L.O.'s motion, the Superior Court of New Jersey, Chancery Division, set aside the 7-day suspension on the ground that it was based on evidence seized in violation of the Fourth Amendment. *(T.L.O.) v. Piscataway Bd. of Ed.*, No. C.2865-79 (Super. Ct .N.J., Ch. Div., Mar. 31, 1980). The Board of Education apparently did not appeal the decision of the Chancery Division.

court on March 23, 1981, found T.L.O. to be a delinquent and on January 8, 1982, sentenced her to a year's probation.

On appeal from the final judgment of the Juvenile Court, a divided Appellate Division affirmed the trial court's finding that there had been no Fourth Amendment violation, but vacated the adjudication of delinquency and remanded for a determination whether T.L.O. had knowingly and voluntarily waived her Fifth Amendment rights before confessing. *State ex rel. T.L.O.*, 185 N.J.Super. 279, 448 A.2d 493 (1982). T.L.O. appealed the Fourth Amendment ruling, and the Supreme Court of New Jersey reversed the judgment of the Appellate Division and ordered the suppression of the evidence found in T.L.O.'s purse. *State ex rel. T.L.O.*, 94 N.J. 331, 463 A.2d 934 (1983).

The New Jersey Supreme Court agreed with the lower courts that the Fourth Amendment applies to searches conducted by school officials. The court also rejected the State of New Jersey's argument that the exclusionary rule should not be employed to prevent the use in juvenile proceedings of evidence unlawfully seized by school officials. Declining to consider whether applying the rule to the fruits of searches by school officials would have any deterrent value, the court held simply that the precedents of this Court establish that "if an official search violates constitutional rights, the evidence is not admissible in criminal proceedings." *Id.*, 94 N.J., at 341, 463 A.2d, at 939 (footnote omitted).

With respect to the question of the legality of the search before it, the court agreed with the Juvenile Court that a warrantless search by a school official does not violate the Fourth Amendment so long as the official "has reasonable grounds to believe that a student possesses evidence of illegal activity or activity that would interfere with school discipline and order." *Id.*, 94 N.J., at 346, 463 A.2d, at 941–942. However, the court, with two justices dissenting, sharply disagreed with the Juvenile Court's conclusion that the search of the purse was reasonable. According to the majority, the contents of T.L.O.'s purse had no bearing on the accusation against T.L.O., for possession of cigarettes (as opposed to smoking them in the lavatory) did not violate school rules, and a mere desire for evidence that would impeach T.L.O.'s claim that she did not smoke cigarettes could not justify the search. Moreover, even if a reasonable suspicion that T.L.O. had cigarettes in her purse would justify a search, Mr. Choplick had no such suspicion, as no one had furnished him with any specific information that there were cigarettes in the purse. Finally, leaving aside the question whether Mr. Choplick was justified in opening the purse, the court held that the evidence of drug use that he saw inside did not justify the extensive "rummaging" through T.L.O.'s papers and effects that followed. *Id.*, 94 N.J., at 347, 463 A.2d, at 942–943.

We granted the State of New Jersey's petition for certiorari. 464 U.S. 991, 104 S. Ct. 480, 78 L. Ed. 2d 678 (1983). Although the State had argued in the Supreme Court of New Jersey that the search of T.L.O.'s purse did not violate the Fourth Amendment, the petition for certiorari raised only the question whether the exclusionary rule should operate to bar consideration in juvenile delinquency proceedings of evidence unlawfully seized by a school official without the involvement of law enforcement officers. When this case was first argued last Term, the State conceded for the purpose of argument that the standard devised by the New Jersey Supreme Court for determining the legality of school searches was appropriate and that the court had correctly applied that standard; the State contended only that the remedial purposes of the exclusionary rule were not well served by applying it to searches conducted by public authorities not primarily engaged in law enforcement.

Although we originally granted certiorari to decide the issue of the appropriate remedy in juvenile court proceedings for unlawful school searches, our doubts regarding the wisdom of deciding that question in isolation from the broader question of what limits, if any, the Fourth Amendment places on the activities of school authorities prompted us to order reargument on that question.[281] Having heard

---

281. State and federal courts considering these questions have struggled to accommodate the interests protected by the Fourth Amendment and the interest of the States in providing a safe environment conducive to education in the public schools. Some courts have resolved the tension between these interests by giving full force to one or the other side of the balance. Thus, in a number of cases courts have held that school officials conducting in-school searches of students are private parties acting *in loco parentis* and are therefore not subject to the constraints of the Fourth Amendment. See, *e.g., D.R.C. v. State,* 646 P.2d 252 (Alaska App. 1982); *In re G.,* 11 Cal. App. 3d 1193, 90 Cal.Rptr. 361 (1970); *In re Donaldson,* 269 Cal. App. 2d 509, 75 Cal. Rptr. 220 (1969); *R.C.M. v. State,* 660 S.W.2d 552 (Tex. App. 1983); *Mercer v. State,* 450 S.W.2d 715 (Tex. Civ. App. 1970). At least one court has held, on the other hand, that the Fourth Amendment applies in full to in-school searches by school officials and that a search conducted without probable cause is unreasonable, see *State v. Mora,* 307 So. 2d 317 (La.), vacated, 423 U.S. 809, 96 S. Ct. 20, 46 L. Ed. 2d 29 (1975), on remand, 330 So. 2d 900 (La.1976); others have held or suggested that the probable-cause standard is applicable at least where the police are involved in a search, see *M. v. Board of Ed. Ball-Chatham Community Unit School Dist. No. 5,* 429 F. Supp. 288, 292 (SD Ill. 1977); *Picha v. Wielgos,* 410 F. Supp. 1214, 1219–1221 (ND Ill. 1976); *State v. Young,* 234 Ga. 488, 498, 216 S.E.2d 586, 594 (1975); or where the search is highly intrusive, see *M.M. v. Anker,* 607 F.2d 588, 589 (CA2 1979).

The majority of courts that have addressed the issue of the Fourth Amendment in the schools have, like the Supreme Court of New Jersey in this case, reached a middle position: the Fourth Amendment applies to searches conducted by school authorities, but the special needs of the school environment require assessment of the legality of such searches against a standard less exacting than that of probable cause. These courts have, by and large, upheld warrantless searches by school authorities provided that they are supported by a reasonable suspicion that the search will uncover evidence of an infraction of school disciplinary rules or a violation of the law. See, *e.g., Tarter v. Raybuck,* 742 F.2d 977 (CA6 1984); *Bilbrey v. Brown,* 738 F.2d 1462 (CA9 1984); *Horton v. Goose Creek Independent School Dist.,* 690 F.2d 470 (CA5 1982); *Bellnier v. Lund,* 438 F. Supp. 47 (NDNY 1977); *M. v. Board of Ed. Ball-Chatham Community Unit School Dist. No. 5, supra; In re W.,* 29 Cal. App. 3d 777, 105 Cal. Rptr. 775 (1973); *State v. Baccino,* 282 A.2d 869 (Del. Super.1971); *State v. D.T.W.,* 425 So. 2d 1383 (Fla. App. 1983); *State v. Young, supra; In re J.A.,* 85 Ill. App. 3d 567, 40 Ill. Dec. 755, 406 N.E.2d 958 (1980); *People v. Ward,* 62 Mich. App. 46, 233 N.W.2d 180 (1975); *Doe v. State,* 88 N.M. 347, 540 P.2d 827 (App. 1975); *People v. D.,* 34 N.Y.2d 483, 358 N.Y.S.2d 403, 315 N.E.2d 466 (1974); *State v. McKinnon,* 88 Wash. 2d 75, 558 P.2d 781 (1977); *In re L.L.,* 90 Wis. 2d 585, 280 N.W.2d 343 (App. 1979).

argument on the legality of the search of T.L.O.'s purse, we are satisfied that the search did not violate the Fourth Amendment.[282]

II

In determining whether the search at issue in this case violated the Fourth Amendment, we are faced initially with the question whether that Amendment's prohibition on unreasonable searches and seizures applies to searches conducted by public school officials. We hold that it does.

It is now beyond dispute that "the Federal Constitution, by virtue of the Fourteenth Amendment, prohibits unreasonable searches and seizures by state officers." *Elkins v. United States,* 364 U.S. 206, 213, 80 S. Ct. 1437, 1442, 4 L. Ed. 2d 1669 (1960); accord, *Mapp v. Ohio,* 367 U.S. 643, 81 S. Ct. 1684, 6 L. Ed. 2d 1081 (1961); *Wolf v. Colorado,* 338 U.S. 25, 69 S. Ct. 1359, 93 L. Ed. 1782 (1949). Equally indisputable is the proposition that the Fourteenth Amendment protects the rights of students against encroachment by public school officials:

> "The Fourteenth Amendment, as now applied to the States, protects the citizen against the State itself and all of its creatures—Boards of Education not excepted. These have, of course, important, delicate, and highly discretionary functions, but none that they may not perform within the limits of the Bill of Rights. That they are educating the young for citizenship is reason for scrupulous protection of Constitutional freedoms of the individual, if we are not to strangle the free mind at its source and teach youth to discount important principles of our government as mere platitudes." *West Virginia State Bd. of Ed. v. Barnette,* 319 U.S. 624, 637, 63 S. Ct. 1178, 1185, 87 L. Ed. 1628 (1943).

These two propositions—that the Fourth Amendment applies to the States through the Fourteenth Amendment, and that the actions of public school officials are subject to the limits placed on state action by the Fourteenth Amendment—might

---

Although few have considered the matter, courts have also split over whether the exclusionary rule is an appropriate remedy for Fourth Amendment violations committed by school authorities. The Georgia courts have held that although the Fourth Amendment applies to the schools, the exclusionary rule does not. See, *e.g., State v. Young, supra; State v. Lamb,* 137 Ga. App. 437, 224 S.E.2d 51 (1976). Other jurisdictions have applied the rule to exclude the fruits of unlawful school searches from criminal trials and delinquency proceedings. See *State v. Mora, supra; People v. D., supra.*

282. In holding that the search of T.L.O.'s purse did not violate the Fourth Amendment, we do not implicitly determine that the exclusionary rule applies to the fruits of unlawful searches conducted by school authorities. The question whether evidence should be excluded from a criminal proceeding involves two discrete inquiries: whether the evidence was seized in violation of the Fourth Amendment, and whether the exclusionary rule is the appropriate remedy for the violation. Neither question is logically antecedent to the other, for a negative answer to either question is sufficient to dispose of the case. Thus, our determination that the search at issue in this case did not violate the Fourth Amendment implies no particular resolution of the question of the applicability of the exclusionary rule.

appear sufficient to answer the suggestion that the Fourth Amendment does not proscribe unreasonable searches by school officials. On reargument, however, the State of New Jersey has argued that the history of the Fourth Amendment indicates that the Amendment was intended to regulate only searches and seizures carried out by law enforcement officers; accordingly, although public school officials are concededly state agents for purposes of the Fourteenth Amendment, the Fourth Amendment creates no rights enforceable against them.[283]

It may well be true that the evil toward which the Fourth Amendment was primarily directed was the resurrection of the pre-Revolutionary practice of using general warrants or "writs of assistance" to authorize searches for contraband by officers of the Crown. See *United States v. Chadwick,* 433 U.S. 1, 7–8, 97 S. Ct. 2476, 2481, 53 L. Ed. 2d 538 (1977); *Boyd v. United States,* 116 U.S. 616, 624–629, 6 S. Ct. 524, 528–531, 29 L. Ed. 746 (1886). But this Court has never limited the Amendment's prohibition on unreasonable searches and seizures to operations conducted by the police. Rather, the Court has long spoken of the Fourth Amendment's strictures as restraints imposed upon "governmental action"—that is, "upon the activities of sovereign authority." *Burdeau v. McDowell,* 256 U.S. 465, 475, 41 S. Ct. 574, 576, 65 L. Ed. 1048 (1921). Accordingly, we have held the Fourth Amendment applicable to the activities of civil as well as criminal authorities: building inspectors, see *Camara v. Municipal Court,* 387 U.S. 523, 528, 87 S. Ct. 1727, 1730, 18 L. Ed. 2d 930 (1967), Occupational Safety and Health Act inspectors, see *Marshall v. Barlow's Inc.,* 436 U.S. 307, 312–313, 98 S. Ct. 1816, 1820, 56 L. Ed. 2d 305 (1978), and even firemen entering privately owned premises to battle a fire, see *Michigan v. Tyler,* 436 U.S. 499, 506, 98 S. Ct. 1942, 1948, 56 L. Ed. 2d 486 (1978), are all subject to the restraints imposed by the Fourth Amendment. As we observed in *Camara v. Municipal Court, supra,* "[t]he basic purpose of this Amendment, as recognized in countless decisions of this Court, is to safeguard the privacy and security of individuals against arbitrary invasions by governmental officials." 387 U.S., at 528, 87 S. Ct., at 1730. Because the individual's interest in privacy and personal security "suffers whether the government's motivation is to investigate violations of criminal laws or breaches of other statutory or regulatory standards," *Marshall v. Barlow's, Inc., supra,* 436 U.S., at 312–313, 98 S. Ct., at 1820, it would be "anomalous to say that the individual and his private property are fully protected by the Fourth Amendment only when the individual is suspected of criminal behavior." *Camara v. Municipal Court, supra,* 387 U.S., at 530, 87 S. Ct., at 1732.

Notwithstanding the general applicability of the Fourth Amendment to the activities of civil authorities, a few courts have concluded that school officials are exempt from the dictates of the Fourth Amendment by virtue of the special nature

283. Cf. *Ingraham v. Wright,* 430 U.S. 651, 97 S. Ct. 1401, 51 L. Ed. 2d 711 (1977) (holding that the Eighth Amendment's prohibition of cruel and unusual punishment applies only to punishments imposed after criminal convictions and hence does not apply to the punishment of schoolchildren by public school officials).

of their authority over schoolchildren. See, *e.g., R.C.M. v. State,* 660 S.W.2d 552 (Tex. App.1983). Teachers and school administrators, it is said, act *in loco parentis* in their dealings with students: their authority is that of the parent, not the State, and is therefore not subject to the limits of the Fourth Amendment. *Ibid.*

Such reasoning is in tension with contemporary reality and the teachings of this Court. We have held school officials subject to the commands of the First Amendment, see *Tinker v. Des Moines Independent Community School District,* 393 U.S. 503, 89 S. Ct. 733, 21 L. Ed. 2d 731 (1969), and the Due Process Clause of the Fourteenth Amendment, see *Goss v. Lopez,* 419 U.S. 565, 95 S. Ct. 729, 42 L. Ed. 2d 725 (1975). If school authorities are state actors for purposes of the constitutional guarantees of freedom of expression and due process, it is difficult to understand why they should be deemed to be exercising parental rather than public authority when conducting searches of their students. More generally, the Court has recognized that "the concept of parental delegation" as a source of school authority is not entirely "consonant with compulsory education laws." *Ingraham v. Wright,* 430 U.S. 651, 662, 97 S. Ct. 1401, 1407, 51 L. Ed. 2d 711 (1977). Today's public school officials do not merely exercise authority voluntarily conferred on them by individual parents; rather, they act in furtherance of publicly mandated educational and disciplinary policies. See, *e.g.,* the opinion in *State ex rel. T.L.O.,* 94 N.J., at 343, 463 A.2d, at 934, 940, describing the New Jersey statutes regulating school disciplinary policies and establishing the authority of school officials over their students. In carrying out searches and other disciplinary functions pursuant to such policies, school officials act as representatives of the State, not merely as surrogates for the parents, and they cannot claim the parents' immunity from the strictures of the Fourth Amendment.

III

To hold that the Fourth Amendment applies to searches conducted by school authorities is only to begin the inquiry into the standards governing such searches. Although the underlying command of the Fourth Amendment is always that searches and seizures be reasonable, what is reasonable depends on the context within which a search takes place. The determination of the standard of reasonableness governing any specific class of searches requires "balancing the need to search against the invasion which the search entails." *Camara v. Municipal Court, supra,* 387 U.S., at 536–537, 87 S. Ct., at 1735. On one side of the balance are arrayed the individual's legitimate expectations of privacy and personal security; on the other, the government's need for effective methods to deal with breaches of public order.

We have recognized that even a limited search of the person is a substantial invasion of privacy. *Terry v. Ohio,* 392 U.S. 1, 24–25, 88 S. Ct. 1868, 1881–1882, 20 L. Ed. 2d 889 (1967). We have also recognized that searches of closed items of personal luggage are intrusions on protected privacy interests, for "the Fourth Amendment provides protection to the owner of every container that conceals its contents from plain view." *United States v. Ross,* 456 U.S. 798, 822–823, 102 S. Ct. 2157, 2171, 72 L. Ed. 2d 572 (1982). A search of a child's person or of a closed purse or other bag carried on her person,[284] no less than a similar search carried out on an adult, is undoubtedly a severe violation of subjective expectations of privacy.

Of course, the Fourth Amendment does not protect subjective expectations of privacy that are unreasonable or otherwise "illegitimate." See, *e.g., Hudson v. Palmer,* 468 U.S. 517, 104 S. Ct. 3194, 82 L. Ed. 2d 393 (1984); *Rawlings v. Kentucky,* 448 U.S. 98, 100 S. Ct. 2556, 65 L. Ed. 2d 633 (1980). To receive the protection of the Fourth Amendment, an expectation of privacy must be one that society is "prepared to recognize as legitimate." *Hudson v. Palmer, supra,* 468 U.S., at 526, 104 S. Ct., at 3200. The State of New Jersey has argued that because of the pervasive supervision to which children in the schools are necessarily subject, a child has virtually no legitimate expectation of privacy in articles of personal property "unnecessarily" carried into a school. This argument has two factual premises: (1) the fundamental incompatibility of expectations of privacy with the maintenance of a sound educational environment; and (2) the minimal interest of the child in bringing any items of personal property into the school. Both premises are severely flawed.

Although this Court may take notice of the difficulty of maintaining discipline in the public schools today, the situation is not so dire that students in the schools may claim no legitimate expectations of privacy. We have recently recognized that the need to maintain order in a prison is such that prisoners retain no legitimate expectations of privacy in their cells, but it goes almost without saying that "[t]he prisoner and the schoolchild stand in wholly different circumstances, separated by the harsh facts of criminal conviction and incarceration." *Ingraham v. Wright, supra,* 430 U.S., at 669, 97 S. Ct., at 1411. We are not yet ready to hold that the schools and the prisons need be equated for purposes of the Fourth Amendment.

Nor does the State's suggestion that children have no legitimate need to bring personal property into the schools seem well anchored in reality. Students at a minimum must bring to school not only the supplies needed for their studies,but also keys, money, and the necessaries of personal hygiene and grooming. In addition, students may carry on their persons or in purses or wallets such nondisruptive yet highly personal items as photographs, letters, and diaries. Finally, students may have perfectly legitimate reasons to carry with them articles of property needed in

284. We do not address the question, not presented by this case, whether a schoolchild has a legitimate expectation of privacy in lockers, desks, or other school property provided for the storage of school supplies. Nor do we express any opinion on the standards (if any) governing searches of such areas by school officials or by other public authorities acting at the request of school officials. Compare *Zamora v. Pomeroy,* 639 F.2d 662, 670 (CA10 1981) ("Inasmuch as the school had assumed joint control of the locker it cannot be successfully maintained that the school did not have a right to inspect it"), and *People v. Overton,* 24 N.Y.2d 522, 249 N.E.2d 366, 301 N.Y.S.2d 479 (1969) (school administrators have power to consent to search of a student's locker), with *State v. Engerud,* 94 N.J. 331, 348, 463 A.2d 934, 943 (1983) ("We are satisfied that in the context of this case the student had an expectation of privacy in the contents of his locker.... For the four years of high school, the school locker is a home away from home. In it the student stores the kind of personal 'effects' protected by the Fourth Amendment").

connection with extracurricular or recreational activities. In short, schoolchildren may find it necessary to carry with them a variety of legitimate, noncontraband items, and there is no reason to conclude that they have necessarily waived all rights to privacy in such items merely by bringing them onto school grounds.

Against the child's interest in privacy must be set the substantial interest of teachers and administrators in maintaining discipline in the classroom and on school grounds. Maintaining order in the classroom has never been easy, but in recent years, school disorder has often taken particularly ugly forms: drug use and violent crime in the schools have become major social problems. See generally 1 NIE, U.S. Dept. of Health, Education and Welfare, Violent Schools — Safe Schools: The Safe School Study Report to the Congress (1978). Even in schools that have been spared the most severe disciplinary problems, the preservation of order and a proper educational environment requires close supervision of schoolchildren, as well as the enforcement of rules against conduct that would be perfectly permissible if undertaken by an adult. "Events calling for discipline are frequent occurrences and sometimes require immediate, effective action." *Goss v. Lopez,* 419 U.S., at 580, 95 S. Ct., at 739. Accordingly, we have recognized that maintaining security and order in the schools requires a certain degree of flexibility in school disciplinary procedures, and we have respected the value of preserving the informality of the student-teacher relationship. See *id.,* at 582–583, 95 S. Ct., at 740; *Ingraham v. Wright,* 430 U.S., at 680–682, 97 S. Ct., at 1417–1418.

How, then, should we strike the balance between the schoolchild's legitimate expectations of privacy and the school's equally legitimate need to maintain an environment in which learning can take place? It is evident that the school setting requires some easing of the restrictions to which searches by public authorities are ordinarily subject. The warrant requirement, in particular, is unsuited to the school environment: requiring a teacher to obtain a warrant before searching a child suspected of an infraction of school rules (or of the criminal law) would unduly interfere with the maintenance of the swift and informal disciplinary procedures needed in the schools. Just as we have in other cases dispensed with the warrant requirement when "the burden of obtaining a warrant is likely to frustrate the governmental purpose behind the search," *Camara v. Municipal Court,* 387 U.S., at 532–533, 87 S. Ct., at 1733, we hold today that school officials need not obtain a warrant before searching a student who is under their authority.

The school setting also requires some modification of the level of suspicion of illicit activity needed to justify a search. Ordinarily, a search — even one that may permissibly be carried out without a warrant — must be based upon "probable cause" to believe that a violation of the law has occurred. See, *e.g., Almeida-Sanchez v. United States,* 413 U.S. 266, 273, 93 S. Ct. 2535, 2540, 37 L. Ed. 2d 596 (1973); *Sibron v. New York,* 392 U.S. 40, 62–66, 88 S. Ct. 1889, 1902–1904, 20 L. Ed. 2d 917 (1968). However, "probable cause" is not an irreducible requirement of a valid search. The fundamental command of the Fourth Amendment is that searches and seizures be reasonable, and although "both the concept of probable cause and the requirement of a warrant bear on the reasonableness of a search, . . . in certain limited circumstances neither is required." *Almeida-Sanchez v. United States, supra,* 413 U.S., at 277, 93 S. Ct., at 2541 (POWELL, J., concurring). Thus, we have in a number of cases recognized the legality of searches and seizures based on suspicions that, although "reasonable," do not rise to the level of probable cause. See, *e.g., Terry v. Ohio,* 392 U.S. 1, 88 S. Ct. 1868, 20 L. Ed. 2d 889 (1968); *United States v. Brignoni-Ponce,* 422 U.S. 873, 881, 95 S. Ct. 2574, 2580, 45 L. Ed. 2d 607 (1975); *Delaware v. Prouse,* 440 U.S. 648, 654–655, 99 S. Ct. 1391, 1396, 59 L. Ed. 2d 660 (1979); *United States v. Martinez-Fuerte,* 428 U.S. 543, 96 S. Ct. 3074, 49 L. Ed. 2d 1116 (1976); cf. *Camara v. Municipal Court, supra,* 387 U.S., at 534–539, 87 S. Ct., at 1733–1736. Where a careful balancing of governmental and private interests suggests that the public interest is best served by a Fourth Amendment standard of reasonableness that stops short of probable cause, we have not hesitated to adopt such a standard.

We join the majority of courts that have examined this issue[285] in concluding that the accommodation of the privacy interests of schoolchildren with the substantial need of teachers and administrators for freedom to maintain order in the schools does not require strict adherence to the requirement that searches be based on probable cause to believe that the subject of the search has violated or is violating the law. Rather, the legality of a search of a student should depend simply on the reasonableness, under all the circumstances, of the search. Determining the reasonableness of any search involves a twofold inquiry: first, one must consider "whether the . . . action was justified at its inception," *Terry v. Ohio,* 392 U.S., at 20, 88 S. Ct., at 1879; second, one must determine whether the search as actually conducted "was reasonably related in scope to the circumstances which justified the interference in the first place," *ibid.* Under ordinary circumstances, a search of a student by a teacher or other school official[286] will be "justified at its inception" when there are reasonable grounds for suspecting that the search will turn up evidence that the student has violated or is violating either the law or the rules of the school.[287] Such a search will

285. See cases cited in n. 2, *supra.*

286. We here consider only searches carried out by school authorities acting alone and on their own authority. This case does not present the question of the appropriate standard for assessing the legality of searches conducted by school officials in conjunction with or at the behest of law enforcement agencies, and we express no opinion on that question. Cf. *Picha v. Wielgos,* 410 F. Supp. 1214, 1219–1221 (ND Ill. 1976) (holding probable-cause standard applicable to searches involving the police).

287. We do not decide whether individualized suspicion is an essential element of the reasonableness standard we adopt for searches by school authorities. In other contexts, however, we have held that although "some quantum of individualized suspicion is usually a prerequisite to a constitutional search or seizure[,] . . . the Fourth Amendment imposes no irreducible requirement of such suspicion." *United States v. Martinez-Fuerte,* 428 U.S. 543, 560–561, 96 S. Ct. 3074, 3084, 49 L. Ed. 2d 1116 (1976). See also *Camara v. Municipal Court,* 387 U.S. 523, 87 S. Ct. 1727, 18 L. Ed. 2d 930 (1967). Exceptions to the requirement of individualized suspicion are generally appropriate only where the privacy interests implicated by a search are minimal and where "other safeguards" are available "to assure that the individual's reasonable expectation of privacy is not 'subject to the discretion of the official in the field.'" *Delaware v. Prouse,* 440 U.S. 648, 654–655, 99 S. Ct. 1391,

be permissible in its scope when the measures adopted are reasonably related to the objectives of the search and not excessively intrusive in light of the age and sex of the student and the nature of the infraction.[288]

This standard will, we trust, neither unduly burden the efforts of school authorities to maintain order in their schools nor authorize unrestrained intrusions upon the privacy of schoolchildren. By focusing attention on the question of reasonableness, the standard will spare teachers and school administrators the necessity of schooling themselves in the niceties of probable cause and permit them to regulate their conduct according to the dictates of reason and common sense. At the same time, the reasonableness standard should ensure that the interests of students will be invaded no more than is necessary to achieve the legitimate end of preserving order in the schools.

IV

There remains the question of the legality of the search in this case. We recognize that the "reasonable grounds" standard applied by the New Jersey Supreme Court in its consideration of this question is not substantially different from the standard that we have adopted today. Nonetheless, we believe that the New Jersey court's application of that standard to strike down the search of T.L.O.'s purse reflects a somewhat crabbed notion of reasonableness. Our review of the facts surrounding the search leads us to conclude that the search was in no sense unreasonable for Fourth Amendment purposes.[289]

1396–1397, 59 L. Ed. 2d 660 (1979) (citation omitted). Because the search of T.L.O.'s purse was based upon an individualized suspicion that she had violated school rules, see *infra,* at 745–746, we need not consider the circumstances that might justify school authorities in conducting searches unsupported by individualized suspicion.

288. Our reference to the nature of the infraction is not intended as an endorsement of Justice STEVENS' suggestion that some rules regarding student conduct are by nature too "trivial" to justify a search based upon reasonable suspicion. See *post,* at 762–765. We are unwilling to adopt a standard under which the legality of a search is dependent upon a judge's evaluation of the relative importance of various school rules. The maintenance of discipline in the schools requires not only that students be restrained from assaulting one another, abusing drugs and alcohol, and committing other crimes, but also that students conform themselves to the standards of conduct prescribed by school authorities. We have "repeatedly emphasized the need for affirming the comprehensive authority of the States and of school officials, consistent with fundamental constitutional safeguards, to prescribe and control conduct in the schools." *Tinker v. Des Moines Independent Community School District,* 393 U.S. 503, 507, 89 S. Ct. 733, 737, 21 L. Ed. 2d 731 (1969). The promulgation of a rule forbidding specified conduct presumably reflects a judgment on the part of school officials that such conduct is destructive of school order or of a proper educational environment. Absent any suggestion that the rule violates some substantive constitutional guarantee, the courts should, as a general matter, defer to that judgment and refrain from attempting to distinguish between rules that are important to the preservation of order in the schools and rules that are not.

289. Of course, New Jersey may insist on a more demanding standard under its own Constitution or statutes. In that case, its courts would not purport to be applying the Fourth Amendment when they invalidate a search.

The incident that gave rise to this case actually involved two separate searches, with the first — the search for cigarettes — providing the suspicion that gave rise to the second the search for marihuana. Although it is the fruits of the second search that are at issue here, the validity of the search for marihuana must depend on the reasonableness of the initial search for cigarettes, as there would have been no reason to suspect that T.L.O. possessed marihuana had the first search not taken place. Accordingly, it is to the search for cigarettes that we first turn our attention.

The New Jersey Supreme Court pointed to two grounds for its holding that the search for cigarettes was unreasonable. First, the court observed that possession of cigarettes was not in itself illegal or a violation of school rules. Because the contents of T.L.O.'s purse would therefore have "no direct bearing on the infraction" of which she was accused (smoking in a lavatory where smoking was prohibited), there was no reason to search her purse.[290] Second, even assuming that a search of T.L.O.'s purse might under some circumstances be reasonable in light of the accusation made against T.L.O., the New Jersey court concluded that Mr. Choplick in this particular case had no reasonable grounds to suspect that T.L.O. had cigarettes in her purse. At best, according to the court, Mr. Choplick had "a good hunch." 94 N.J., at 347, 463 A.2d, at 942.

Both these conclusions are implausible. T.L.O. had been accused of smoking, and had denied the accusation in the strongest possible terms when she stated that she did not smoke at all. Surely it cannot be said that under these circumstances, T.L.O.'s possession of cigarettes would be irrelevant to the charges against her or to her response to those charges. T.L.O.'s possession of cigarettes, once it was discovered, would both corroborate the report that she had been smoking and undermine the credibility of her defense to the charge of smoking. To be sure, the discovery of the cigarettes would not prove that T.L.O. had been smoking in the lavatory; nor would it, strictly speaking, necessarily be inconsistent with her claim that she did not smoke at all. But it is universally recognized that evidence, to be relevant to an inquiry, need not conclusively prove the ultimate fact in issue, but only have "any tendency to make the existence of any fact that is of consequence to the determination of the action more probable or less probable than it would be without the evidence." Fed.Rule

---

290. Justice STEVENS interprets these statements as a holding that enforcement of the school's smoking regulations was not sufficiently related to the goal of maintaining discipline or order in the school to justify a search under the standard adopted by the New Jersey court. See *post,* at 765. We do not agree that this is an accurate characterization of the New Jersey Supreme Court's opinion. The New Jersey court did not hold that the school's smoking rules were unrelated to the goal of maintaining discipline or order, nor did it suggest that a search that would produce evidence bearing directly on an accusation that a student had violated the smoking rules would be impermissible under the court's reasonable-suspicion standard; rather, the court concluded that any evidence a search of T.L.O.'s purse was likely to produce would not have a sufficiently direct bearing on the infraction to justify a search — a conclusion with which we cannot agree for the reasons set forth *infra,* at 745–746. JUSTICE STEVENS' suggestion that the New Jersey Supreme Court's decision rested on the perceived triviality of the smoking infraction appears to be a reflection of his own views rather than those of the New Jersey court.

Evid. 401. The relevance of T.L.O.'s possession of cigarettes to the question whether she had been smoking and to the credibility of her denial that she smoked supplied the necessary "nexus" between the item searched for and the infraction under investigation. See *Warden v. Hayden,* 387 U.S. 294, 306–307, 87 S. Ct. 1642, 1649–1650, 18 L. Ed. 2d 782 (1967). Thus, if Mr. Choplick in fact had a reasonable suspicion that T.L.O. had cigarettes in her purse, the search was justified despite the fact that the cigarettes, if found, would constitute "mere evidence" of a violation. *Ibid.*

Of course, the New Jersey Supreme Court also held that Mr. Choplick had no reasonable suspicion that the purse would contain cigarettes. This conclusion is puzzling. A teacher had reported that T.L.O. was smoking in the lavatory. Certainly this report gave Mr. Choplick reason to suspect that T.L.O. was carrying cigarettes with her; and if she did have cigarettes, her purse was the obvious place in which to find them. Mr. Choplick's suspicion that there were cigarettes in the purse was not an "inchoate and unparticularized suspicion or 'hunch,'" *Terry v. Ohio,* 392 U.S., at 27, 88 S. Ct., at 1883; rather, it was the sort of "common-sense conclusio[n] about human behavior" upon which "practical people"—including government officials—are entitled to rely. *United States v. Cortez,* 449 U.S. 411, 418, 101 S. Ct. 690, 695, 66 L. Ed. 2d 621 (1981). Of course, even if the teacher's report were true, T.L.O. *might* not have had a pack of cigarettes with her; she might have borrowed a cigarette from someone else or have been sharing a cigarette with another student. But the requirement of reasonable suspicion is not a requirement of absolute certainty: "sufficient probability, not certainty, is the touchstone of reasonableness under the Fourth Amendment. . . ." *Hill v. California,* 401 U.S. 797, 804, 91 S. Ct. 1106, 1111, 28 L. Ed. 2d 484 (1971). Because the hypothesis that T.L.O. was carrying cigarettes in her purse was itself not unreasonable, it is irrelevant that other hypotheses were also consistent with the teacher's accusation. Accordingly, it cannot be said that Mr. Choplick acted unreasonably when he examined T.L.O.'s purse to see if it contained cigarettes.[291]

Our conclusion that Mr. Choplick's decision to open T.L.O.'s purse was reasonable brings us to the question of the further search for marihuana once the pack of cigarettes was located. The suspicion upon which the search for marihuana was founded was provided when Mr. Choplick observed a package of rolling papers

---

291. T.L.O. contends that even if it was reasonable for Mr. Choplick to open her purse to look for cigarettes, it was not reasonable for him to reach in and take the cigarettes out of her purse once he found them. Had he not removed the cigarettes from the purse, she asserts, he would not have observed the rolling papers that suggested the presence of marihuana, and the search for marihuana could not have taken place. T.L.O.'s argument is based on the fact that the cigarettes were not "contraband," as no school rule forbade her to have them. Thus, according to T.L.O., the cigarettes were not subject to seizure or confiscation by school authorities, and Mr. Choplick was not entitled to take them out of T.L.O.'s purse regardless of whether he was entitled to peer into the purse to see if they were there. Such hairsplitting argumentation has no place in an inquiry addressed to the issue of reasonableness. If Mr. Choplick could permissibly search T.L.O.'s purse for cigarettes, it hardly seems reasonable to suggest that his natural reaction to finding them—picking them up—could be a constitutional violation. We find that neither in opening the purse nor in reaching into it to remove the cigarettes did Mr. Choplick violate the Fourth Amendment.

in the purse as he removed the pack of cigarettes. Although T.L.O. does not dispute the reasonableness of Mr. Choplick's belief that the rolling papers indicated the presence of marihuana, she does contend that the scope of the search Mr. Choplick conducted exceeded permissible bounds when he seized and read certain letters that implicated T.L.O. in drug dealing. This argument, too, is unpersuasive. The discovery of the rolling papers concededly gave rise to a reasonable suspicion that T.L.O. was carrying marihuana as well as cigarettes in her purse. This suspicion justified further exploration of T.L.O.'s purse, which turned up more evidence of drug-related activities: a pipe, a number of plastic bags of the type commonly used to store marihuana, a small quantity of marihuana, and a fairly substantial amount of money. Under these circumstances, it was not unreasonable to extend the search to a separate zippered compartment of the purse; and when a search of that compartment revealed an index card containing a list of "people who owe me money" as well as two letters, the inference that T.L.O. was involved in marihuana trafficking was substantial enough to justify Mr. Choplick in examining the letters to determine whether they contained any further evidence. In short, we cannot conclude that the search for marihuana was unreasonable in any respect.

Because the search resulting in the discovery of the evidence of marihuana dealing by T.L.O. was reasonable, the New Jersey Supreme Court's decision to exclude that evidence from T.L.O.'s juvenile delinquency proceedings on Fourth Amendment grounds was erroneous. Accordingly, the judgment of the Supreme Court of New Jersey is

Reversed.

[Case No. 4-9]

Drug testing of student athletes without individualized suspicion is legal under certain circumstances.

Vernonia School District 47J v. Acton

Supreme Court of the United States
515 U.S. 646 (1995)

Justice SCALIA delivered the opinion of the Court.

The Student Athlete Drug Policy adopted by School District 47J in the town of Vernonia, Oregon, authorizes random urinalysis drug testing of students who participate in the District's school athletics programs. We granted certiorari to decide whether this violates the Fourth and Fourteenth Amendments to the United States Constitution.

I

A

Petitioner Vernonia School District 47J (District) operates one high school and three grade schools in the logging community of Vernonia, Oregon. As elsewhere in small-town America, school sports play a prominent role in the town's life, and student athletes are admired in their schools and in the community.

Drugs had not been a major problem in Vernonia schools. In the mid-to-late 1980s, however, teachers and administrators observed a sharp increase in drug use. Students began to speak out about their attraction to the drug culture, and to boast that there was nothing the school could do about it. Along with more drugs came more disciplinary problems. Between 1988 and 1989 the number of disciplinary referrals in Vernonia schools rose to more than twice the number reported in the early 1980s, and several students were suspended. Students became increasingly rude during class; outbursts of profane language became common.

Not only were student athletes included among the drug users but, as the District Court found, athletes were the leaders of the drug culture. 796 F. Supp. 1354, 1357 (Ore. 1992). This caused the District's administrators particular concern, since drug use increases the risk of sports-related injury. Expert testimony at the trial confirmed the deleterious effects of drugs on motivation, memory, judgment, reaction, coordination, and performance. The high school football and wrestling coach witnessed a severe sternum injury suffered by a wrestler, and various omissions of safety procedures and misexecutions by football players, all attributable in his belief to the effects of drug use.

Initially, the District responded to the drug problem by offering special classes, speakers, and presentations designed to deter drug use. It even brought in a specially trained dog to detect drugs, but the drug problem persisted. According to the District Court:

> "[T]he administration was at its wits end and . . . a large segment of the student body, particularly those involved in interscholastic athletics, was in a state of rebellion. Disciplinary actions had reached 'epidemic proportions.' The coincidence of an almost three-fold increase in classroom disruptions and disciplinary reports along with the staff's direct observations of students using drugs or glamorizing drug and alcohol use led the administration to the inescapable conclusion that the rebellion was being fueled by alcohol and drug abuse as well as the student's misperceptions about the drug culture." *Ibid.*

At that point, District officials began considering a drug-testing program. They held a parent "input night" to discuss the proposed Student Athlete Drug Policy (Policy), and the parents in attendance gave their unanimous approval. The school board approved the Policy for implementation in the fall of 1989. Its expressed purpose is to prevent student athletes from using drugs, to protect their health and safety, and to provide drug users with assistance programs.

B

The Policy applies to all students participating in interscholastic athletics. Students wishing to play sports must sign a form consenting to the testing and must obtain the written consent of their parents. Athletes are tested at the beginning of the season for their sport. In addition, once each week of the season the names of the athletes are placed in a "pool" from which a student, with the supervision of two adults, blindly draws the names of 10% of the athletes for random testing. Those selected are notified and tested that same day, if possible.

The student to be tested completes a specimen control form which bears an assigned number. Prescription medications that the student is taking must be identified by providing a copy of the prescription or a doctor's authorization. The student then enters an empty locker room accompanied by an adult monitor of the same sex. Each boy selected produces a sample at a urinal, remaining fully clothed with his back to the monitor, who stands approximately 12 to 15 feet behind the student. Monitors may (though do not always) watch the student while he produces the sample, and they listen for normal sounds of urination. Girls produce samples in an enclosed bathroom stall, so that they can be heard but not observed. After the sample is produced, it is given to the monitor, who checks it for temperature and tampering and then transfers it to a vial.

The samples are sent to an independent laboratory, which routinely tests them for amphetamines, cocaine, and marijuana. Other drugs, such as LSD, may be screened at the request of the District, but the identity of a particular student does not determine which drugs will be tested. The laboratory's procedures are 99.94% accurate. The District follows strict procedures regarding the chain of custody and access to test results. The laboratory does not know the identity of the students whose samples it tests. It is authorized to mail written test reports only to the superintendent and to provide test results to District personnel by telephone only after the requesting official recites a code confirming his authority. Only the superintendent, principals, vice-principals, and athletic directors have access to test results, and the results are not kept for more than one year.

If a sample tests positive, a second test is administered as soon as possible to confirm the result. If the second test is negative, no further action is taken. If the second test is positive, the athlete's parents are notified, and the school principal convenes a meeting with the student and his parents, at which the student is given the option of (1) participating for six weeks in an assistance program that includes weekly urinalysis, or (2) suffering suspension from athletics for the remainder of the current season and the next athletic season. The student is then retested prior to the start of the next athletic season for which he or she is eligible. The Policy states that a second offense results in automatic imposition of option (2); a third offense in suspension for the remainder of the current season and the next two athletic seasons.

C

In the fall of 1991, respondent James Acton, then a seventh grader, signed up to play football at one of the District's grade schools. He was denied participation, however, because he and his parents refused to sign the testing consent forms. The Actons filed suit, seeking declaratory and injunctive relief from enforcement of the Policy on the grounds that it violated the Fourth and Fourteenth Amendments to the United States Constitution and Article I, § 9, of the Oregon Constitution. After a bench trial, the District Court entered an order denying the claims on the merits and dismissing the action. 796 F. Supp., at 1355. The United States Court of Appeals for the Ninth Circuit reversed, holding that the Policy violated both the Fourth and Fourteenth Amendments and Article I, § 9, of the Oregon Constitution. 23 F.3d 1514 (1994). We granted certiorari. 513 U.S. 1013, 115 S. Ct. 571, 130 L. Ed. 2d 488 (1994).

II

The Fourth Amendment to the United States Constitution provides that the Federal Government shall not violate "[t]he right of the people to be secure in their persons, houses, papers, and effects, against unreasonable searches and seizures. . . ." We have held that the Fourteenth Amendment extends this constitutional guarantee to searches and seizures by state officers, *Elkins v. United States,* 364 U.S. 206, 213, 80 S. Ct. 1437, 1441–1442, 4 L. Ed. 2d 1669 (1960), including public school officials, *New Jersey v. T.L.O.,* 469 U.S. 325, 336–337, 105 S. Ct. 733, 740, 83 L. Ed. 2d 720 (1985). In *Skinner v. Railway Labor Executives' Assn.,* 489 U.S. 602, 617, 109 S. Ct. 1402, 1413, 103 L. Ed. 2d 639 (1989), we held that state-compelled collection and testing of urine, such as that required by the Policy, constitutes a "search" subject to the demands of the Fourth Amendment. See also *Treasury Employees v. Von Raab,* 489 U.S. 656, 665, 109 S. Ct. 1384, 1390, 103 L. Ed. 2d 685 (1989).

As the text of the Fourth Amendment indicates, the ultimate measure of the constitutionality of a governmental search is "reasonableness." At least in a case such as this, where there was no clear practice, either approving or disapproving the type of search at issue, at the time the constitutional provision was enacted,[292] whether a particular search meets the reasonableness standard "'is judged by balancing its intrusion on the individual's Fourth Amendment interests against its promotion of legitimate governmental interests.'" *Skinner, supra,* at 619, 109 S. Ct., at 1414 (quoting *Delaware v. Prouse,* 440 U.S. 648, 654, 99 S. Ct. 1391, 1396, 59 L. Ed. 2d 660 (1979)). Where a search is undertaken by law enforcement officials to discover evidence of criminal wrongdoing, this Court has said that reasonableness generally requires the obtaining of a judicial warrant, *Skinner, supra,* at 619, 109 S. Ct., at 1414. Warrants cannot be issued, of course, without the showing of probable cause required by the Warrant Clause. But a warrant is not required to establish the reasonableness of *all* government searches; and when a warrant is not required (and the Warrant Clause therefore not applicable), probable cause is not invariably required either. A search unsupported by probable cause can be constitutional, we have said, "when special needs, beyond the normal need for law enforcement, make the warrant and

---

292. Not until 1852 did Massachusetts, the pioneer in the "common school" movement, enact a compulsory school-attendance law, and as late as the 1870s only 14 States had such laws. R. Butts, Public Education in the United States From Revolution to Reform 102–103 (1978); 1 Children and Youth in America 467–468 (R. Bremner ed. 1970). The drug problem, and the technology of drug testing, are of course even more recent.

probable-cause requirement impracticable." *Griffin v. Wisconsin,* 483 U.S. 868, 873, 107 S. Ct. 3164, 3168, 97 L. Ed. 2d 709 (1987) (internal quotation marks omitted).

We have found such "special needs" to exist in the public school context. There, the warrant requirement "would unduly interfere with the maintenance of the swift and informal disciplinary procedures [that are] needed," and "strict adherence to the requirement that searches be based upon probable cause" would undercut "the substantial need of teachers and administrators for freedom to maintain order in the schools." *T.L.O.,* 469 U.S., at 340, 341, 105 S. Ct., at 742. The school search we approved in *T.L.O.,* while not based on probable cause, *was* based on individualized *suspicion* of wrongdoing. As we explicitly acknowledged, however, "'the Fourth Amendment imposes no irreducible requirement of such suspicion,'" *id.,* at 342, n. 8, 105 S. Ct., at 743, n. 8 (quoting *United States v. Martinez-Fuerte,* 428 U.S. 543, 560–561, 96 S. Ct. 3074, 3084, 49 L. Ed. 2d 1116 (1976)). We have upheld suspicionless searches and seizures to conduct drug testing of railroad personnel involved in train accidents, see *Skinner, supra;* to conduct random drug testing of federal customs officers who carry arms or are involved in drug interdiction, see *Von Raab, supra;* and to maintain automobile checkpoints looking for illegal immigrants and contraband, *Martinez-Fuerte, supra,* and drunk drivers, *Michigan Dept. of State Police v. Sitz,* 496 U.S. 444, 110 S. Ct. 2481, 110 L. Ed. 2d 412 (1990).

III

The first factor to be considered is the nature of the privacy interest upon which the search here at issue intrudes. The Fourth Amendment does not protect all subjective expectations of privacy, but only those that society recognizes as "legitimate." *T.L.O.,* 469 U.S., at 338, 105 S. Ct., at 741. What expectations are legitimate varies, of course, with context, *id.,* at 337, 105 S. Ct., at 740, depending, for example, upon whether the individual asserting the privacy interest is at home, at work, in a car, or in a public park. In addition, the legitimacy of certain privacy expectations vis-a-vis the State may depend upon the individual's legal relationship with the State. For example, in *Griffin, supra,* we held that, although a "probationer's home, like anyone else's, is protected by the Fourth Amendmen[t]," the supervisory relationship between probationer and State justifies "a degree of impingement upon [a probationer's] privacy that would not be constitutional if applied to the public at large." 483 U.S., at 873, 875, 107 S. Ct., at 3168, 3169. Central, in our view, to the present case is the fact that the subjects of the Policy are (1) children, who (2) have been committed to the temporary custody of the State as schoolmaster.

Traditionally at common law, and still today, unemancipated minors lack some of the most fundamental rights of self-determination — including even the right of liberty in its narrow sense, *i.e.,* the right to come and go at will. They are subject, even as to their physical freedom, to the control of their parents or guardians. See 59 Am.Jur.2d, Parent and Child § 10 (1987). When parents place minor children in private schools for their education, the teachers and administrators of those schools stand *in loco parentis* over the children entrusted to them. In fact, the tutor or schoolmaster is the very prototype of that status. As Blackstone describes it, a parent "may . . . delegate part of his parental authority, during his life, to the tutor or schoolmaster of his child; who is then *in loco parentis,* and has such a portion of the power of the parent committed to his charge, viz. that of restraint and correction, as may be necessary to answer the purposes for which he is employed." 1 W. Blackstone, Commentaries on the Laws of England 441 (1769).

In *T.L.O.* we rejected the notion that public schools, like private schools, exercise only parental power over their students, which of course is not subject to constitutional constraints. 469 U.S., at 336, 105 S. Ct., at 740. Such a view of things, we said, "is not entirely 'consonant with compulsory education laws,'" *ibid.* (quoting *Ingraham v. Wright,* 430 U.S. 651, 662, 97 S. Ct. 1401, 1407, 51 L. Ed. 2d 711 (1977)), and is inconsistent with our prior decisions treating school officials as state actors for purposes of the Due Process and Free Speech Clauses, *T.L.O., supra,* at 336, 105 S. Ct., at 740. But while denying that the State's power over schoolchildren is formally no more than the delegated power of their parents, *T.L.O.* did not deny, but indeed emphasized, that the nature of that power is custodial and tutelary, permitting a degree of supervision and control that could not be exercised over free adults. "[A] proper educational environment requires close supervision of schoolchildren, as well as the enforcement of rules against conduct that would be perfectly permissible if undertaken by an adult." 469 U.S., at 339, 105 S. Ct., at 741. While we do not, of course, suggest that public schools as a general matter have such a degree of control over children as to give rise to a constitutional "duty to protect," see *DeShaney v. Winnebago County Dept. of Social Servs.,* 489 U.S. 189, 200, 109 S. Ct. 998, 1005–1006, 103 L. Ed. 2d 249 (1989), we have acknowledged that for many purposes "school authorities ac[t] *in loco parentis,*" *Bethel School Dist. No. 403 v. Fraser,* 478 U.S. 675, 684, 106 S. Ct. 3159, 3165, 92 L. Ed. 2d 549 (1986), with the power and indeed the duty to "inculcate the habits and manners of civility," *id.,* at 681, 106 S. Ct., at 3163 (internal quotation marks omitted). Thus, while children assuredly do not "shed their constitutional rights . . . at the schoolhouse gate," *Tinker v. Des Moines Independent Community School Dist.,* 393 U.S. 503, 506, 89 S. Ct. 733, 736, 21 L. Ed. 2d 731 (1969), the nature of those rights is what is appropriate for children in school. See, *e.g., Goss v. Lopez,* 419 U.S. 565, 581–582, 95 S. Ct. 729, 740, 42 L. Ed. 2d 725 (1975) (due process for a student challenging disciplinary suspension requires only that the teacher "informally discuss the alleged misconduct with the student minutes after it has occurred"); *Fraser, supra,* 478 U.S., at 683, 106 S. Ct., at 3164 ("[I]t is a highly appropriate function of public school education to prohibit the use of vulgar and offensive terms in public discourse"); *Hazelwood School Dist. v. Kuhlmeier,* 484 U.S. 260, 273, 108 S. Ct. 562, 571, 98 L. Ed. 2d 592 (1988) (public school authorities may censor school-sponsored publications, so long as the censorship is "reasonably related to legitimate pedagogical concerns"); *Ingraham, supra,* 430 U.S., at 682, 97 S. Ct., at 1418 ("Imposing additional administrative safeguards [upon corporal punishment] . . . would . . . entail a significant intrusion into an area of primary educational responsibility").

Fourth Amendment rights, no less than First and Fourteenth Amendment rights, are different in public schools than elsewhere; the "reasonableness" inquiry cannot disregard the schools' custodial and tutelary responsibility for children. For their own good and that of their classmates, public school children are routinely required to submit to various physical examinations, and to be vaccinated against various diseases. According to the American Academy of Pediatrics, most public schools "provide vision and hearing screening and dental and dermatological checks.... Others also mandate scoliosis screening at appropriate grade levels." Committee on School Health, American Academy of Pediatrics, School Health: A Guide for Health Professionals 2 (1987). In the 1991–1992 school year, all 50 States required public school students to be vaccinated against diphtheria, measles, rubella, and polio. U.S. Dept. of Health & Human Services, Public Health Service, Centers for Disease Control, State Immunization Requirements 1991–1992, p. 1. Particularly with regard to medical examinations and procedures, therefore, "students within the school environment have a lesser expectation of privacy than members of the population generally." *T.L.O., supra,* 469 U.S., at 348, 105 S. Ct., at 746 (Powell, J., concurring).

Legitimate privacy expectations are even less with regard to student athletes. School sports are not for the bashful. They require "suiting up" before each practice or event, and showering and changing afterwards. Public school locker rooms, the usual sites for these activities, are not notable for the privacy they afford. The locker rooms in Vernonia are typical: No individual dressing rooms are provided; shower heads are lined up along a wall, unseparated by any sort of partition or curtain; not even all the toilet stalls have doors. As the United States Court of Appeals for the Seventh Circuit has noted, there is "an element of 'communal undress' inherent in athletic participation," *Schaill by Kross v. Tippecanoe County School Corp.,* 864 F.2d 1309, 1318 (1988).

There is an additional respect in which school athletes have a reduced expectation of privacy. By choosing to "go out for the team," they voluntarily subject themselves to a degree of regulation even higher than that imposed on students generally. In Vernonia's public schools, they must submit to a preseason physical exam (James testified that his included the giving of a urine sample, App. 17), they must acquire adequate insurance coverage or sign an insurance waiver, maintain a minimum grade point average, and comply with any "rules of conduct, dress, training hours and related matters as may be established for each sport by the head coach and athletic director with the principal's approval." Record, Exh. 2, p. 30, § 8. Somewhat like adults who choose to participate in a "closely regulated industry," students who voluntarily participate in school athletics have reason to expect intrusions upon normal rights and privileges, including privacy. See *Skinner,* 489 U.S., at 627, 109 S. Ct., at 1418–1419; *United States v. Biswell,* 406 U.S. 311, 316, 92 S. Ct. 1593, 1596, 32 L. Ed. 2d 87 (1972).

IV

Having considered the scope of the legitimate expectation of privacy at issue here, we turn next to the character of the intrusion that is complained of. We recognized in *Skinner* that collecting the samples for urinalysis intrudes upon "an excretory function traditionally shielded by great privacy." 489 U.S., at 626, 109 S. Ct., at 1418.

We noted, however, that the degree of intrusion depends upon the manner in which production of the urine sample is monitored. *Ibid.* Under the District's Policy, male students produce samples at a urinal along a wall. They remain fully clothed and are only observed from behind, if at all. Female students produce samples in an enclosed stall, with a female monitor standing outside listening only for sounds of tampering. These conditions are nearly identical to those typically encountered in public restrooms, which men, women, and especially schoolchildren use daily. Under such conditions, the privacy interests compromised by the process of obtaining the urine sample are in our view negligible.

The other privacy-invasive aspect of urinalysis is, of course, the information it discloses concerning the state of the subject's body, and the materials he has ingested. In this regard it is significant that the tests at issue here look only for drugs, and not for whether the student is, for example, epileptic, pregnant, or diabetic. See *id.*, at 617, 109 S. Ct., at 1413. Moreover, the drugs for which the samples are screened are standard, and do not vary according to the identity of the student. And finally, the results of the tests are disclosed only to a limited class of school personnel who have a need to know; and they are not turned over to law enforcement authorities or used for any internal disciplinary function. 796 F. Supp., at 1364; see also 23 F.3d, at 1521.[293]

Respondents argue, however, that the District's Policy is in fact more intrusive than this suggests, because it requires the students, if they are to avoid sanctions for a falsely positive test, to identify *in advance* prescription medications they are taking. We agree that this raises some cause for concern. In *Von Raab*, we flagged as one of the salutary features of the Customs Service drug-testing program the fact that employees were not required to disclose medical information unless they tested positive, and, even then, the information was supplied to a licensed physician rather than to the Government employer. See *Von Raab*, 489 U.S., at 672–673, n. 2, 109 S. Ct., at 1394–1395, n. 2. On the other hand, we have never indicated that requiring advance disclosure of medications is *per se* unreasonable. Indeed, in *Skinner* we held that it was not "a significant invasion of privacy." 489 U.S., at 626, n. 7, 109 S. Ct., at 1418, n. 7. It can be argued that, in *Skinner*, the disclosure went only to the medical personnel taking the sample, and the Government personnel analyzing it, see *id.*, at

293. Despite the fact that, like routine school physicals and vaccinations — which the dissent apparently finds unobjectionable even though they "are both blanket searches of a sort," *post,* at 2405 — the search here is undertaken for prophylactic and distinctly *non*punitive purposes (protecting student athletes from injury, and deterring drug use in the student population), see 796 F. Supp., at 1363, the dissent would nonetheless lump this search together with "evidentiary" searches, which generally require probable cause, see *supra,* at 2390, because, from the student's perspective, the test may be "regarded" or "understood" as punishment, *post,* at 2405. In light of the District Court's findings regarding the purposes and consequences of the testing, any such perception is by definition an irrational one, which is protected nowhere else in the law. In any event, our point is not, as the dissent apparently believes, *post,* at 2405, that *since* student vaccinations and physical exams are constitutionally reasonable, student drug testing must be so as well; but rather that, by reason of those prevalent practices, public school children in general, and student athletes in particular, have a diminished expectation of privacy. See *supra,* at 2392.

609, 109 S. Ct., at 1408–1409, but see *id.*, at 610, 109 S. Ct., at 1409 (railroad personnel responsible for forwarding the sample, and presumably accompanying information, to the Government's testing lab); and that disclosure to teachers and coaches—to persons who personally *know* the student—is a greater invasion of privacy. Assuming for the sake of argument that both those propositions are true, we do not believe they establish a difference that respondents are entitled to rely on here.

The General Authorization Form that respondents refused to sign, which refusal was the basis for James's exclusion from the sports program, said only (in relevant part): "I . . . authorize the Vernonia School District to conduct a test on a urine specimen which I provide to test for drugs and/or alcohol use. I also authorize the release of information concerning the results of such a test to the Vernonia School District and to the parents and/or guardians of the student." App. 10–11. While the practice of the District seems to have been to have a school official take medication information from the student at the time of the test, see *id.*, at 29, 42, that practice is not set forth in, or required by, the Policy, which says simply: "Student athletes who . . . are or have been taking prescription medication must provide verification (either by a copy of the prescription or by doctor's authorization) prior to being tested." *Id.*, at 8. It may well be that, if and when James was selected for random testing at a time that he was taking medication, the School District would have permitted him to provide the requested information in a confidential manner—for example, in a sealed envelope delivered to the testing lab. Nothing in the Policy contradicts that, and when respondents choose, in effect, to challenge the Policy on its face, we will not assume the worst. Accordingly, we reach the same conclusion as in *Skinner*: that the invasion of privacy was not significant.

V

Finally, we turn to consider the nature and immediacy of the governmental concern at issue here, and the efficacy of this means for meeting it. In both *Skinner* and *Von Raab*, we characterized the government interest motivating the search as "compelling." *Skinner, supra*, 489 U.S., at 628, 109 S. Ct., at 1419 (interest in preventing railway accidents); *Von Raab, supra*, 489 U.S., at 670, 109 S. Ct., at 1393 (interest in insuring fitness of customs officials to interdict drugs and handle firearms). Relying on these cases, the District Court held that because the District's program also called for drug testing in the absence of individualized suspicion, the District "must demonstrate a 'compelling need' for the program." 796 F. Supp., at 1363. The Court of Appeals appears to have agreed with this view. See 23 F.3d, at 1526. It is a mistake, however, to think that the phrase "compelling state interest," in the Fourth Amendment context, describes a fixed, minimum quantum of governmental concern, so that one can dispose of a case by answering in isolation the question: Is there a compelling state interest here? Rather, the phrase describes an interest that appears *important enough* to justify the particular search at hand, in light of other factors that show the search to be relatively intrusive upon a genuine expectation of privacy. Whether that relatively high degree of government concern is necessary in this case or not, we think it is met.

That the nature of the concern is important — indeed, perhaps compelling — can hardly be doubted. Deterring drug use by our Nation's schoolchildren is at least as important as enhancing efficient enforcement of the Nation's laws against the importation of drugs, which was the governmental concern in *Von Raab, supra,* 489 U.S., at 668, 109 S. Ct., at 1392, or deterring drug use by engineers and trainmen, which was the governmental concern in *Skinner, supra,* at 628, 109 S. Ct., at 1419. School years are the time when the physical, psychological, and addictive effects of drugs are most severe. "Maturing nervous systems are more critically impaired by intoxicants than mature ones are; childhood losses in learning are lifelong and profound"; "children grow chemically dependent more quickly than adults, and their record of recovery is depressingly poor." Hawley, The Bumpy Road to Drug-Free Schools, 72 Phi Delta Kappan 310, 314 (1990). See also Estroff, Schwartz, & Hoffmann, Adolescent Cocaine Abuse: Addictive Potential, Behavioral and Psychiatric Effects, 28 Clinical Pediatrics 550 Dec. 1989); Kandel, Davies, Karus, & Yamaguchi, The Consequences in Young Adulthood of Adolescent Drug Involvement, 43 Arch. Gen. Psychiatry 746 (Aug. 1986). And of course the effects of a drug-infested school are visited not just upon the users, but upon the entire student body and faculty, as the educational process is disrupted. In the present case, moreover, the necessity for the State to act is magnified by the fact that this evil is being visited not just upon individuals at large, but upon children for whom it has undertaken a special responsibility of care and direction. Finally, it must not be lost sight of that this program is directed more narrowly to drug use by school athletes, where the risk of immediate physical harm to the drug user or those with whom he is playing his sport is particularly high. Apart from psychological effects, which include impairment of judgment, slow reaction time, and a lessening of the perception of pain, the particular drugs screened by the District's Policy have been demonstrated to pose substantial physical risks to athletes. Amphetamines produce an "artificially induced heart rate increase, [p]eripheral vasoconstriction, [b]lood pressure increase, and [m]asking of the normal fatigue response," making them a "very dangerous drug when used during exercise of any type." Hawkins, Drugs and Other Ingesta: Effects on Athletic Performance, in H. Appenzeller, Managing Sports and Risk Management Strategies 90, 90–91 (1993). Marijuana causes "[i]rregular blood pressure responses during changes in body position," "[r]eduction in the oxygen-carrying capacity of the blood," and "[i]nhibition of the normal sweating responses resulting in increased body temperature." *Id.,* at 94. Cocaine produces "[v]asoconstriction[,] [e]levated blood pressure," and "[p]ossible coronary artery spasms and myocardial infarction." *Ibid.*

As for the immediacy of the District's concerns: We are not inclined to question — indeed, we could not possibly find clearly erroneous — the District Court's conclusion that "a large segment of the student body, particularly those involved in interscholastic athletics, was in a state of rebellion," that "[d]isciplinary actions had reached 'epidemic proportions,'" and that "the rebellion was being fueled by alcohol and drug abuse as well as by the student's misperceptions about the drug culture." 796 F. Supp., at 1357. That is an immediate crisis of greater proportions than existed in *Skinner,* where we upheld the Government's drug-testing program based on findings of drug use by railroad employees nationwide, without proof that a problem existed on the particular railroads whose employees were subject to the test. See *Skinner,* 489 U.S., at 607, 109 S. Ct., at 1407–1408. And of much greater proportions than existed in *Von Raab,* where there was no documented history of drug use by any customs officials. See *Von Raab,* 489 U.S., at 673, 109 S. Ct., at 1395; *id.,* at 683, 109 S. Ct., at 1400 (SCALIA, J., dissenting).

As to the efficacy of this means for addressing the problem: It seems to us self-evident that a drug problem largely fueled by the "role model" effect of athletes' drug use, and of particular danger to athletes, is effectively addressed by making sure that athletes do not use drugs. Respondents argue that a "less intrusive means to the same end" was available, namely, "drug testing on suspicion of drug use." Brief for Respondents 45–46. We have repeatedly refused to declare that only the "least intrusive" search practicable can be reasonable under the Fourth Amendment. *Skinner, supra,* at 629, n. 9, 109 S. Ct., at 1420, n. 9 (collecting cases). Respondents' alternative entails substantial difficulties—if it is indeed practicable at all. It may be impracticable, for one thing, simply because the parents who are willing to accept random drug testing for athletes are not willing to accept accusatory drug testing for all students, which transforms the process into a badge of shame. Respondents' proposal brings the risk that teachers will impose testing arbitrarily upon troublesome but not drug-likely students. It generates the expense of defending lawsuits that charge such arbitrary imposition, or that simply demand greater process before accusatory drug testing is imposed. And not least of all, it adds to the ever-expanding diversionary duties of schoolteachers the new function of spotting and bringing to account drug abuse, a task for which they are ill prepared, and which is not readily compatible with their vocation. Cf. *Skinner, supra,* at 628, 109 S. Ct., at 1419 (quoting 50 Fed.Reg. 31526 (1985)) (a drug impaired individual "will seldom display any outward 'signs detectable by the lay person or, in many cases, even the physician.'"); *Goss,* 419 U.S., at 594, 95 S. Ct., at 746 (Powell, J., dissenting) ("There is an ongoing relationship, one in which the teacher must occupy many roles—educator, adviser, friend, and, at times, parent-substitute. It is rarely adversary in nature . . .") (footnote omitted). In many respects, we think, testing based on "suspicion" of drug use would not be better, but worse.[294]

---

294. There is no basis for the dissent's insinuation that in upholding the District's Policy we are equating the Fourth Amendment status of schoolchildren and prisoners, who, the dissent asserts, may have what it calls the "categorical protection" of a "strong preference for an individualized suspicion requirement," *post,* at 2404. The case on which it relies for that proposition, *Bell v. Wolfish,* 441 U.S. 520, 99 S. Ct. 1861, 60 L. Ed. 2d 447 (1979), displays no stronger a preference for individualized suspicion than we do today. It reiterates the proposition on which we rely, that "'elaborate less-restrictive-alternative arguments could raise insuperable barriers to the exercise of virtually all search-and-seizure powers.'" *Id.,* at 559, n. 40, 99 S. Ct., at 1884–1885, n. 40 (quoting *United States v. Martinez-Fuerte,* 428 U.S. 543, 556–557, n. 12, 96 S. Ct. 3074, 3082–3083, n. 12, 49 L. Ed. 2d 1116 (1976)). Even *Wolfish's arguendo* "assum[ption] that the existence of less intrusive alternatives is relevant to the determination of the reasonableness of the particular search method at issue,"

VI

Taking into account all the factors we have considered above — the decreased expectation of privacy, the relative unobtrusiveness of the search, and the severity of the need met by the search — we conclude Vernonia's Policy is reasonable and hence constitutional.

We caution against the assumption that suspicionless drug testing will readily pass constitutional muster in other contexts. The most significant element in this case is the first we discussed: that the Policy was undertaken in furtherance of the government's responsibilities, under a public school system, as guardian and tutor of children entrusted to its care.[295] Just as when the government conducts a search in its capacity as employer (a warrantless search of an absent employee's desk to obtain an urgently needed file, for example), the relevant question is whether that intrusion upon privacy is one that a reasonable employer might engage in, see *O'Connor v. Ortega,* 480 U.S. 709, 107 S. Ct. 1492, 94 L. Ed. 2d 714 (1987); so also when the government acts as guardian and tutor the relevant question is whether the search is one that a reasonable guardian and tutor might undertake. Given the findings of need made by the District Court, we conclude that in the present case it is.

We may note that the primary guardians of Vernonia's schoolchildren appear to agree. The record shows no objection to this district wide program by any parents other than the couple before us here — even though, as we have described, a public meeting was held to obtain parents' views. We find insufficient basis to contradict the judgment of Vernonia's parents, its school board, and the District Court, as to what was reasonably in the interest of these children under the circumstances.

* * *

The Ninth Circuit held that Vernonia's Policy not only violated the Fourth Amendment, but also, by reason of that violation, contravened Article I, § 9, of the Oregon Constitution. Our conclusion that the former holding was in error means that the latter holding rested on a flawed premise. We therefore vacate the judgment, and remand the case to the Court of Appeals for further proceedings consistent with this opinion.

It is so ordered.

---

441 U.S., at 559, n. 40, 99 S. Ct. at 1884–1885, n. 40, does not support the dissent, for the opinion ultimately rejected the hypothesized alternative (as we do) on the ground that it would impair other policies important to the institution. See *id.*, at 560, n. 40, 96 S. Ct., at 3084, n. 40 (monitoring of visits instead of conducting body searches would destroy "the confidentiality and intimacy that these visits are intended to afford").

295. The dissent devotes a few meager paragraphs of its 21 pages to this central aspect of the testing program, see *post,* at 2404–2405, in the course of which it shows none of the interest in the original meaning of the Fourth Amendment displayed elsewhere in the opinion, see *post,* at 2398–2400. Of course at the time of the framing, as well as at the time of the adoption of the Fourteenth Amendment, children had substantially fewer "rights" than legislatures and courts confer upon them today. See 1 D. Kramer, Legal Rights of Children § 1.02, p. 9 (2d ed. 1994); Wald, Children's Rights: A Framework for Analysis, 12 U.C.D. L. Rev. 255, 256 (1979).

[Case No. 4-10]

School district's policy requiring all students who participated in competitive extracurricular activities to submit to drug testing was reasonable and does not violate the Fourth Amendment.

Board of Education of Independent School District No. 92 of Pottawatomie County v. Earls

Supreme Court of the United States
536 U.S. 822 (2002)

Justice THOMAS delivered the opinion of the Court.

The Student Activities Drug Testing Policy implemented by the Board of Education of Independent School District No. 92 of Pottawatomie County (School District) requires all students who participate in competitive extracurricular activities to submit to drug testing. Because this Policy reasonably serves the School District's important interest in detecting and preventing drug use among its students, we hold that it is constitutional.

I

The city of Tecumseh, Oklahoma, is a rural community located approximately 40 miles southeast of Oklahoma City. The School District administers all Tecumseh public schools. In the fall of 1998, the School District adopted the Student Activities Drug Testing Policy (Policy), which requires all middle and high school students to consent to drug testing in order to participate in any extracurricular activity. In practice, the Policy has been applied only to competitive extracurricular activities sanctioned by the Oklahoma Secondary Schools Activities Association, such as the Academic Team, Future Farmers of America, Future Homemakers of America, band, choir, pom pon, cheerleading, and athletics. Under the Policy, students are required to take a drug test before participating in an extracurricular activity, must submit to random drug testing while participating in that activity, and must agree to be tested at any time upon reasonable suspicion. The urinalysis tests are designed to detect only the use of illegal drugs, including amphetamines, marijuana, cocaine, opiates, and barbituates, not medical conditions or the presence of authorized prescription medications.

At the time of their suit, both respondents attended Tecumseh High School. Respondent Lindsay Earls was a member of the show choir, the marching band, the Academic Team, and the National Honor Society. Respondent Daniel James sought to participate in the Academic Team.[296] Together with their parents, Earls and James

296. The District Court noted that the School District's allegations concerning Daniel James called his standing to sue into question because his failing grades made him ineligible to participate in any interscholastic competition. See 115 F. Supp. 2d 1281, 1282, n. 1 (W.D.Okla.2000). The court noted, however, that the dispute need not be resolved because Lindsay Earls had standing, and therefore the court was required to address the constitutionality of the drug testing policy. See

brought a 42 U.S.C. § 1983 action against the School District, challenging the Policy both on its face and as applied to their participation in extracurricular activities.[297] They alleged that the Policy violates the Fourth Amendment as incorporated by the Fourteenth Amendment and requested injunctive and declarative relief. They also argued that the School District failed to identify a special need for testing students who participate in extracurricular activities, and that the "Drug Testing Policy neither addresses a proven problem nor promises to bring any benefit to students or the school." App. 9.

Applying the principles articulated in *Vernonia School Dist. 47J v. Acton,* 515 U.S. 646, 115 S. Ct. 2386, 132 L. Ed. 2d 564 (1995), in which we upheld the suspicionless drug testing of school athletes, the United States District Court for the Western District of Oklahoma rejected respondents' claim that the Policy was unconstitutional and granted summary judgment to the School District. The court noted that "special needs" exist in the public school context and that, although the School District did "not show a drug problem of epidemic proportions," there was a history of drug abuse starting in 1970 that presented "legitimate cause for concern." 115 F. Supp. 2d1281, 1287 (2000). The District Court also held that the Policy was effective because "[i]t can scarcely be disputed that the drug problem among the student body is effectively addressed by making sure that the large number of students participating in competitive, extracurricular activities do not use drugs." *Id.,* at 1295.

The United States Court of Appeals for the Tenth Circuit reversed, holding that the Policy violated the Fourth Amendment. The Court of Appeals agreed with the District Court that the Policy must be evaluated in the "unique environment of the school setting," but reached a different conclusion as to the Policy's constitutionality. 242 F.3d 1264, 1270 (2001). Before imposing a suspicionless drug testing program, the Court of Appeals concluded that a school "must demonstrate that there is some identifiable drug abuse problem among a sufficient number of those subject to the testing, such that testing that group of students will actually redress its drug problem." *Id.,* at 1278. The Court of Appeals then held that because the School District failed to demonstrate such a problem existed among Tecumseh students participating in competitive extracurricular activities, the Policy was unconstitutional. We granted certiorari, 534 U.S. 1015, 122 S. Ct. 509, 151 L. Ed. 2d 418 (2001), and now reverse.

II

The Fourth Amendment to the United States Constitution protects "[t]he right of the people to be secure in their persons, houses, papers, and effects, against unreasonable searches and seizures." Searches by public school officials, such as the collection of urine samples, implicate Fourth Amendment interests. See *Vernonia, supra,* at 652, 115 S. Ct. 2386; cf. *New Jersey v. T.L.O.,* 469 U.S. 325, 334, 105 S. Ct. 733, 83 L.

---

ibid. Because we are likewise satisfied that Earls has standing, we need not address whether James also has standing.

297. The respondents did not challenge the Policy either as it applies to athletes or as it provides for drug testing upon reasonable, individualized suspicion. See App. 28.

Ed. 2d 720 (1985). We must therefore review the School District's Policy for "reasonableness," which is the touchstone of the constitutionality of a governmental search.

In the criminal context, reasonableness usually requires a showing of probable cause. See, *e.g., Skinner v. Railway Labor Executives' Assn.,* 489 U.S. 602, 619, 109 S. Ct. 1402, 103 L. Ed. 2d 639 (1989). The probable-cause standard, however, "is peculiarly related to criminal investigations" and may be unsuited to determining the reasonableness of administrative searches where the "Government seeks to *prevent* the development of hazardous conditions." *Treasury Employees v. Von Raab,* 489 U.S. 656, 667–668, 109 S. Ct. 1384, 103 L. Ed. 2d 685 (1989) (internal quotation marks and citations omitted) (collecting cases). The Court has also held that a warrant and finding of probable cause are unnecessary in the public school context because such requirements "'would unduly interfere with the maintenance of the swift and informal disciplinary procedures [that are] needed.'" *Vernonia, supra,* at 653, 115 S. Ct. 2386 (quoting *T.L.O., supra,* at 340–341, 105 S. Ct. 733).

Given that the School District's Policy is not in any way related to the conduct of criminal investigations, see Part II-B, *infra,* respondents do not contend that the School District requires probable cause before testing students for drug use. Respondents instead argue that drug testing must be based at least on some level of individualized suspicion. See Brief for Respondents 12–14. It is true that we generally determine the reasonableness of a search by balancing the nature of the intrusion on the individual's privacy against the promotion of legitimate governmental interests. See *Delaware v. Prouse,* 440 U.S. 648, 654, 99 S. Ct. 1391, 59 L. Ed. 2d 660 (1979). But we have long held that "the Fourth Amendment imposes no irreducible requirement of [individualized] suspicion." *United States v. Martinez-Fuerte,* 428 U.S. 543, 561, 96 S. Ct. 3074, 49 L. Ed. 2d 1116 (1976). "[I]n certain limited circumstances, the Government's need to discover such latent or hidden conditions, or to prevent their development, is sufficiently compelling to justify the intrusion on privacy entailed by conducting such searches without any measure of individualized suspicion." *Von Raab, supra,* at 668, 109 S. Ct. 1384; see also *Skinner, supra,* at 624, 109 S. Ct. 1402. Therefore, in the context of safety and administrative regulations, a search unsupported by probable cause may be reasonable "when 'special needs, beyond the normal need for law enforcement, make the warrant and probable-cause requirement impracticable.'" *Griffin v. Wisconsin,* 483 U.S. 868, 873, 107 S. Ct. 3164, 97 L. Ed. 2d 709 (1987) (quoting *T.L.O., supra,* at 351, 105 S. Ct. 733 (Blackmun, J., concurring in judgment)); see also *Vernonia, supra,* at 653, 115 S. Ct. 2386; *Skinner, supra,* at 619, 109 S. Ct. 1402.

Significantly, this Court has previously held that "special needs" inhere in the public school context. See *Vernonia, supra,* at 653, 115 S. Ct. 2386; *T.L.O., supra,* at 339–340, 105 S. Ct. 733. While schoolchildren do not shed their constitutional rights when they enter the schoolhouse, see *Tinker v. Des Moines Independent Community School Dist.,* 393 U.S. 503, 506, 89 S. Ct. 733, 21 L. Ed. 2d 731 (1969), "Fourth Amendment rights . . . are different in public schools than elsewhere; the 'reasonableness' inquiry cannot disregard the schools' custodial and tutelary responsibility for children." *Vernonia, supra,* at 656, 115 S. Ct. 2386. In particular, a finding of individualized suspicion may not be necessary when a school conducts drug testing.

In *Vernonia,* this Court held that the suspicionless drug testing of athletes was constitutional. The Court, however, did not simply authorize all school drug testing, but rather conducted a fact-specific balancing of the intrusion on the children's Fourth Amendment rights against the promotion of legitimate governmental interests. See 515 U.S., at 652–653, 115 S. Ct. 2386. Applying the principles of *Vernonia* to the somewhat different facts of this case, we conclude that Tecumseh's Policy is also constitutional.

A

We first consider the nature of the privacy interest allegedly compromised by the drug testing. See *id.,* at 654, 115 S. Ct. 2386. As in *Vernonia,* the context of the public school environment serves as the backdrop for the analysis of the privacy interest at stake and the reasonableness of the drug testing policy in general. See *ibid.* ("Central . . . is the fact that the subjects of the Policy are (1) children, who (2) have been committed to the temporary custody of the State as schoolmaster"); see also *id.,* at 665, 115 S. Ct. 2386 ("The most significant element in this case is the first we discussed: that the Policy was undertaken in furtherance of the government's responsibilities, under a public school system, as guardian and tutor of children entrusted to its care"); *ibid.* ("[W]hen the government acts as guardian and tutor the relevant question is whether the search is one that a reasonable guardian and tutor might undertake").

A student's privacy interest is limited in a public school environment where the State is responsible for maintaining discipline, health, and safety. Schoolchildren are routinely required to submit to physical examinations and vaccinations against disease. See *id.,* at 656, 115 S. Ct. 2386. Securing order in the school environment sometimes requires that students be subjected to greater controls than those appropriate for adults. See *T.L.O., supra,* at 350, 105 S. Ct. 733 (Powell, J., concurring) ("Without first establishing discipline and maintaining order, teachers cannot begin to educate their students. And apart from education, the school has the obligation to protect pupils from mistreatment by other children, and also to protect teachers themselves from violence by the few students whose conduct in recent years has prompted national concern").

Respondents argue that because children participating in nonathletic extracurricular activities are not subject to regular physicals and communal undress, they have a stronger expectation of privacy than the athletes tested in *Vernonia.* See Brief for Respondents 18–20.[298] This distinction, however, was not essential to our deci-

298. Justice GINSBURG argues that *Vernonia School Dist. 47J v. Acton,* 515 U.S. 646, 115 S. Ct. 2386, 132 L. Ed. 2d 564 (1995), depended on the fact that the drug testing program applied only to student athletes. But even the passage cited by the dissent manifests the supplemental nature of this factor, as the Court in *Vernonia* stated that "[l]egitimate privacy expectations are *even less* with regard to student athletes." See *post,* at 45 (citing *Vernonia,* 515 U.S., at 657, 115 S. Ct. 2386) (emphasis added). In upholding the drug testing program in *Vernonia,* we considered the school

sion in *Vernonia,* which depended primarily upon the school's custodial responsibility and authority.

In any event, students who participate in competitive extracurricular activities voluntarily subject themselves to many of the same intrusions on their privacy as do athletes.[299] Some of these clubs and activities require occasional off-campus travel and communal undress. All of them have their own rules and requirements for participating students that do not apply to the student body as a whole. 115 F. Supp. 2d, at 1289–1290. For example, each of the competitive extracurricular activities governed by the Policy must abide by the rules of the Oklahoma Secondary Schools Activities Association, and a faculty sponsor monitors the students for compliance with the various rules dictated by the clubs and activities. See *id.,* at 1290. This regulation of extracurricular activities further diminishes the expectation of privacy among schoolchildren. Cf. *Vernonia, supra,* at 657, 115 S. Ct. 2386 ("Somewhat like adults who choose to participate in a closely regulated industry, students who voluntarily participate in school athletics have reason to expect intrusions upon normal rights and privileges, including privacy" (internal quotation marks omitted)). We therefore conclude that the students affected by this Policy have a limited expectation of privacy.

B

Next, we consider the character of the intrusion imposed by the Policy. See *Vernonia, supra,* at 658, 115 S. Ct. 2386. Urination is "an excretory function traditionally shielded by great privacy." *Skinner,* 489 U.S., at 626, 109 S. Ct. 1402. But the "degree of intrusion" on one's privacy caused by collecting a urine sample "depends upon the manner in which production of the urine sample is monitored." *Vernonia, supra,* at 658, 115 S. Ct. 2386.

Under the Policy, a faculty monitor waits outside the closed restroom stall for the student to produce a sample and must "listen for the normal sounds of urination in order to guard against tampered specimens and to insure an accurate chain of custody." App. 199. The monitor then pours the sample into two bottles that are sealed and placed into a mailing pouch along with a consent form signed by the student. This procedure is virtually identical to that reviewed in *Vernonia,* except that it additionally protects privacy by allowing male students to produce their samples behind a closed stall. Given that we considered the method of collection in *Vernonia* a "negligible" intrusion, 515 U.S., at 658, 115 S. Ct. 2386, the method here is even less problematic.

---

context "[c]entral" and "[t]he most significant element." 515 U.S., at 654, 665, 115 S. Ct. 2386. This hefty weight on the side of the school's balance applies with similar force in this case even though we undertake a separate balancing with regard to this particular program.

299. Justice GINSBURG's observations with regard to extracurricular activities apply with equal force to athletics. See *post,* at 4 ("Participation in such [extracurricular] activities is a key component of school life, essential in reality for students applying to college, and, for all participants, a significant contributor to the breadth and quality of the educational experience").

In addition, the Policy clearly requires that the test results be kept in confidential files separate from a student's other educational records and released to school personnel only on a "need to know" basis. Respondents nonetheless contend that the intrusion on students' privacy is significant because the Policy fails to protect effectively against the disclosure of confidential information and, specifically, that the school "has been careless in protecting that information: for example, the Choir teacher looked at students' prescription drug lists and left them where other students could see them." Brief for Respondents 24. But the choir teacher is someone with a "need to know," because during off-campus trips she needs to know what medications are taken by her students. Even before the Policy was enacted the choir teacher had access to this information. See App. 132. In any event, there is no allegation that any other student did see such information. This one example of alleged carelessness hardly increases the character of the intrusion.

Moreover, the test results are not turned over to any law enforcement authority. Nor do the test results here lead to the imposition of discipline or have any academic consequences. Cf. *Vernonia, supra,* at 658, and n. 2, 115 S. Ct. 2386. Rather, the only consequence of a failed drug test is to limit the student's privilege of participating in extracurricular activities. Indeed, a student may test positive for drugs twice and still be allowed to participate in extracurricular activities. After the first positive test, the school contacts the student's parent or guardian for a meeting. The student may continue to participate in the activity if within five days of the meeting the student shows proof of receiving drug counseling and submits to a second drug test in two weeks. For the second positive test, the student is suspended from participation in all extracurricular activities for 14 days, must complete four hours of substance abuse counseling, and must submit to monthly drug tests. Only after a third positive test will the student be suspended from participating in any extracurricular activity for the remainder of the school year, or 88 school days, whichever is longer. See App. 201–202.

Given the minimally intrusive nature of the sample collection and the limited uses to which the test results are put, we conclude that the invasion of students' privacy is not significant.

C

Finally, this Court must consider the nature and immediacy of the government's concerns and the efficacy of the Policy in meeting them. See *Vernonia,* 515 U.S., at 660, 115 S. Ct. 2386. This Court has already articulated in detail the importance of the governmental concern in preventing drug use by schoolchildren. See *id.,* at 661–662, 115 S. Ct. 2386. The drug abuse problem among our Nation's youth has hardly abated since *Vernonia* was decided in 1995. In fact, evidence suggests that it has only grown worse.[300] As in *Vernonia,* "the necessity for the State to act is mag-

300. For instance, the number of 12th graders using any illicit drug increased from 48.4 percent in 1995 to 53.9 percent in 2001. The number of 12th graders reporting they had used marijuana jumped from 41.7 percent to 49.0 percent during that same period. See Department of Health and

nified by the fact that this evil is being visited not just upon individuals at large, but upon children for whom it has undertaken a special responsibility of care and direction." *Id.*, at 662, 115 S. Ct. 2386. The health and safety risks identified in *Vernonia* apply with equal force to Tecumseh's children. Indeed, the nationwide drug epidemic makes the war against drugs a pressing concern in every school.

Additionally, the School District in this case has presented specific evidence of drug use at Tecumseh schools. Teachers testified that they had seen students who appeared to be under the influence of drugs and that they had heard students speaking openly about using drugs. See, *e.g.*, App. 72 (deposition of Dean Rogers); *id.*, at 115 (deposition of Sheila Evans). A drug dog found marijuana cigarettes near the school parking lot. Police officers once found drugs or drug paraphernalia in a car driven by a Future Farmers of America member. And the school board president reported that people in the community were calling the board to discuss the "drug situation." See 115 F. Supp. 2d, at 1285–1286. We decline to second-guess the finding of the District Court that "[v]iewing the evidence as a whole, it cannot be reasonably disputed that the [School District] was faced with a 'drug problem' when it adopted the Policy." *Id.*, at 1287.

Respondents consider the proffered evidence insufficient and argue that there is no "real and immediate interest" to justify a policy of drug testing nonathletes. Brief for Respondents 32. We have recognized, however, that "[a] demonstrated problem of drug abuse . . . [is] not in all cases necessary to the validity of a testing regime," but that some showing does "shore up an assertion of special need for a suspicionless general search program." *Chandler v. Miller*, 520 U.S. 305, 319, 117 S. Ct. 1295, 137 L. Ed. 2d 513 (1997). The School District has provided sufficient evidence to shore up the need for its drug testing program.

Furthermore, this Court has not required a particularized or pervasive drug problem before allowing the government to conduct suspicionless drug testing. For instance, in *Von Raab* the Court upheld the drug testing of customs officials on a purely preventive basis, without any documented history of drug use by such officials. See 489 U.S., at 673, 109 S. Ct. 1384. In response to the lack of evidence relating to drug use, the Court noted generally that "drug abuse is one of the most serious problems confronting our society today," and that programs to prevent and detect drug use among customs officials could not be deemed unreasonable. *Id.*, at 674, 109 S. Ct. 1384; cf. *Skinner*, 489 U.S., at 607, and n. 1, 109 S. Ct. 1402 (noting nationwide studies that identified on-the-job alcohol and drug use by railroad employees). Likewise, the need to prevent and deter the substantial harm of childhood drug use provides the necessary immediacy for a school testing policy. Indeed, it would make little sense to require a school district to wait for a substantial portion of its

---

Human Services, Monitoring the Future: National Results on Adolescent Drug Use, Overview of Key Findings (2001) (Table 1).

students to begin using drugs before it was allowed to institute a drug testing program designed to deter drug use.

Given the nationwide epidemic of drug use, and the evidence of increased drug use in Tecumseh schools, it was entirely reasonable for the School District to enact this particular drug testing policy. We reject the Court of Appeals' novel test that "any district seeking to impose a random suspicionless drug testing policy as a condition to participation in a school activity must demonstrate that there is some identifiable drug abuse problem among a sufficient number of those subject to the testing, such that testing that group of students will actually redress its drug problem." 242 F.3d, at 1278. Among other problems, it would be difficult to administer such a test. As we cannot articulate a threshold level of drug use that would suffice to justify a drug testing program for schoolchildren, we refuse to fashion what would in effect be a constitutional quantum of drug use necessary to show a "drug problem."

Respondents also argue that the testing of nonathletes does not implicate any safety concerns, and that safety is a "crucial factor" in applying the special needs framework. Brief for Respondents 25–27. They contend that there must be "surpassing safety interests," *Skinner, supra,* at 634, 109 S. Ct. 1402, or "extraordinary safety and national security hazards," *Von Raab, supra,* at 674, 109 S. Ct. 1384, in order to override the usual protections of the Fourth Amendment. See Brief for Respondents 25–26. Respondents are correct that safety factors into the special needs analysis, but the safety interest furthered by drug testing is undoubtedly substantial for all children, athletes and nonathletes alike. We know all too well that drug use carries a variety of health risks for children, including death from overdose.

We also reject respondents' argument that drug testing must presumptively be based upon an individualized reasonable suspicion of wrongdoing because such a testing regime would be less intrusive. See *id.*, at 12–16. In this context, the Fourth Amendment does not require a finding of individualized suspicion, see *supra,* at 5, and we decline to impose such a requirement on schools attempting to prevent and detect drug use by students. Moreover, we question whether testing based on individualized suspicion in fact would be less intrusive. Such a regime would place an additional burden on public school teachers who are already tasked with the difficult job of maintaining order and discipline. A program of individualized suspicion might unfairly target members of unpopular groups. The fear of lawsuits resulting from such targeted searches may chill enforcement of the program, rendering it ineffective in combating drug use. See *Vernonia,* 515 U.S., at 663–664, 115 S. Ct. 2386 (offering similar reasons for why "testing based on 'suspicion' of drug use would not be better, but worse"). In any case, this Court has repeatedly stated that reasonableness under the Fourth Amendment does not require employing the least intrusive means, because "[t]he logic of such elaborate less-restrictive-alternative arguments could raise insuperable barriers to the exercise of virtually all search-and-seizure powers." *Martinez-Fuerte,* 428 U.S., at 556–557, n. 12, 96 S. Ct. 3074; see also *Skinner, supra,* at 624, 109 S. Ct. 1402 ("[A] showing of individualized suspicion is not a constitutional floor, below which a search must be presumed unreasonable").

Finally, we find that testing students who participate in extracurricular activities is a reasonably effective means of addressing the School District's legitimate concerns in preventing, deterring, and detecting drug use. While in *Vernonia* there might have been a closer fit between the testing of athletes and the trial court's finding that the drug problem was "fueled by the 'role model' effect of athletes' drug use," such a finding was not essential to the holding. 515 U.S., at 663, 115 S. Ct. 2386; cf. *id.,* at 684–685, 115 S. Ct. 2386 (O'CONNOR, J., dissenting) (questioning the extent of the drug problem, especially as applied to athletes). *Vernonia* did not require the school to test the group of students most likely to use drugs, but rather considered the constitutionality of the program in the context of the public school's custodial responsibilities. Evaluating the Policy in this context, we conclude that the drug testing of Tecumseh students who participate in extracurricular activities effectively serves the School District's interest in protecting the safety and health of its students.

III

Within the limits of the Fourth Amendment, local school boards must assess the desirability of drug testing schoolchildren. In upholding the constitutionality of the Policy, we express no opinion as to its wisdom. Rather, we hold only that Tecumseh's Policy is a reasonable means of furthering the School District's important interest in preventing and deterring drug use among its schoolchildren. Accordingly, we reverse the judgment of the Court of Appeals.

It is so ordered.

[Case No. 4-11]

Public school officials' search of middle school student's underwear for banned pills violated student's Fourth Amendment rights; school officials had qualified immunity from liability.

Safford Unified School District #1 v. Redding

Supreme Court of the United States
557 U.S. 364 (2009)

Justice SOUTER delivered the opinion of the Court.

The issue here is whether a 13-year-old student's Fourth Amendment right was violated when she was subjected to a search of her bra and underpants by school officials acting on reasonable suspicion that she had brought forbidden prescription and over-the-counter drugs to school. Because there were no reasons to suspect the drugs presented a danger or were concealed in her underwear, we hold that the search did violate the Constitution, but because there is reason to question the clarity with which the right was established, the official who ordered the unconstitutional search is entitled to qualified immunity from liability.

I

The events immediately prior to the search in question began in 13-year-old Savana Redding's math class at Safford Middle School one October day in 2003. The assistant principal of the school, Kerry Wilson, came into the room and asked Savana to go to his office. There, he showed her a day planner, unzipped and open flat on his desk, in which there were several knives, lighters, a permanent marker, and a cigarette. Wilson asked Savana whether the planner was hers; she said it was, but that a few days before she had lent it to her friend, Marissa Glines. Savana stated that none of the items in the planner belonged to her.

Wilson then showed Savana four white prescription-strength ibuprofen 400-mg pills, and one over-the-counter blue naproxen 200-mg pill, all used for pain and inflammation but banned under school rules without advance permission. He asked Savana if she knew anything about the pills. Savana answered that she did not. Wilson then told Savana that he had received a report that she was giving these pills to fellow students; Savana denied it and agreed to let Wilson search her belongings. Helen Romero, an administrative assistant, came into the office, and together with Wilson they searched Savana's backpack, finding nothing.

At that point, Wilson instructed Romero to take Savana to the school nurse's office to search her clothes for pills. Romero and the nurse, Peggy Schwallier, asked Savana to remove her jacket, socks, and shoes, leaving her in stretch pants and a T-shirt (both without pockets), which she was then asked to remove. Finally, Savana was told to pull her bra out and to the side and shake it, and to pull out the elastic on her underpants, thus exposing her breasts and pelvic area to some degree. No pills were found.

Savana's mother filed suit against Safford Unified School District #1, Wilson, Romero, and Schwallier for conducting a strip search in violation of Savana's Fourth Amendment rights. The individuals (hereinafter petitioners) moved for summary judgment, raising a defense of qualified immunity. The District Court for the District of Arizona granted the motion on the ground that there was no Fourth Amendment violation, and a panel of the Ninth Circuit affirmed. 504 F.3d 828 (2007).

A closely divided Circuit sitting en banc, however, reversed. Following the two-step protocol for evaluating claims of qualified immunity, see Saucier v. Katz, 533 U.S. 194, 200, 121 S. Ct. 2151, 150 L. Ed. 2d 272 (2001), the Ninth Circuit held that the strip search was unjustified under the Fourth Amendment test for searches of children by school officials set out in New Jersey v. T. L. O., 469 U.S. 325, 105 S. Ct. 733, 83 L. Ed. 2d 720 (1985). 531 F.3d 1071, 1081–1087 (2008). The Circuit then applied the test for qualified immunity, and found that Savana's right was clearly established at the time of the search: "'[t]hese notions of personal privacy are "clearly established" in that they inhere in all of us, particularly middle school teenagers, and are inherent in the privacy component of the Fourth Amendment's proscription against unreasonable searches.'" Id., at 1088–1089 (quoting Brannum v. Overton Cty. School Bd., 516 F.3d 489, 499 (CA6 2008)). The upshot was reversal of summary judgment as to Wilson, while affirming the judgments in favor of Schwallier, the school nurse, and Romero, the administrative assistant, since they had not acted as independent decisionmakers. 531 F.3d at 1089.

We granted certiorari, 555 U.S. 1130, 129 S. Ct. 987, 173 L. Ed. 2d 171 (2009), and now affirm in part, reverse in part, and remand.

II

The Fourth Amendment "right of the people to be secure in their persons ... against unreasonable searches and seizures" generally requires a law enforcement officer to have probable cause for conducting a search. "Probable cause exists where 'the facts and circumstances within [an officer's] knowledge and of which [he] had reasonably trustworthy information [are] sufficient in themselves to warrant a man of reasonable caution in the belief that' an offense has been or is being committed," Brinegar v. United States, 338 U.S. 160, 175–176, 69 S. Ct. 1302, 93 L. Ed. 1879 (1949) (quoting Carroll v. United States, 267 U.S. 132, 162, 45 S. Ct. 280, 69 L. Ed. 543 (1925)), and that evidence bearing on that offense will be found in the place to be searched.

In T. L. O., we recognized that the school setting "requires some modification of the level of suspicion of illicit activity needed to justify a search," 469 U.S., at 340, 105 S. Ct. 733, 83 L. Ed. 2d 720, and held that for searches by school officials "a careful balancing of governmental and private interests suggests that the public interest is best served by a Fourth Amendment standard of reasonableness that stops short of probable cause," id., at 341, 105 S. Ct. 733, 83 L. Ed. 2d 720. We have thus applied a standard of reasonable suspicion to determine the legality of a school administrator's search of a student, id., at 342, 345, 105 S. Ct. 733, 83 L. Ed. 2d 720, and have held that a school search "will be permissible in its scope when the measures adopted are reasonably related to the objectives of the search and not excessively intrusive in light of the age and sex of the student and the nature of the infraction," id., at 342, 105 S. Ct. 733, 83 L. Ed. 2d 720.

A number of our cases on probable cause have an implicit bearing on the reliable knowledge element of reasonable suspicion, as we have attempted to flesh out the knowledge component by looking to the degree to which known facts imply prohibited conduct, see, e.g., Adams v. Williams, 407 U.S. 143, 148, 92 S. Ct. 1921, 32 L. Ed. 2d 612 (1972); id., at 160, n. 9, 92 S. Ct. 1921, 32 L. Ed. 2d 612 (Marshall, J., dissenting), the specificity of the information received, see, e.g., Spinelli v. United States, 393 U.S. 410, 416–417, 89 S. Ct. 584, 21 L. Ed. 2d 637 (1969), and the reliability of its source, see, e.g., Aguilar v. Texas, 378 U.S. 108, 114, 84 S. Ct. 1509, 12 L. Ed. 2d 723 (1964). At the end of the day, however, we have realized that these factors cannot rigidly control, Illinois v. Gates, 462 U.S. 213, 230, 103 S. Ct. 2317, 76 L. Ed. 2d

527 (1983), and we have come back to saying that the standards are "fluid concepts that take their substantive content from the particular contexts" in which they are being assessed, Ornelas v. United States, 517 U.S. 690, 696, 116 S. Ct. 1657, 134 L. Ed. 2d 911 (1996).

Perhaps the best that can be said generally about the required knowledge component of probable cause for a law enforcement officer's evidence search is that it raise a "fair probability," Gates, 462 U.S., at 238, 103 S. Ct. 2317, 76 L. Ed. 2d 527, or a "substantial chance," id., at 244, n. 13, 103 S. Ct. 2317, 76 L. Ed. 2d 527, of discovering evidence of criminal activity. The lesser standard for school searches could as readily be described as a moderate chance of finding evidence of wrongdoing.

III

A

In this case, the school's policies strictly prohibit the nonmedical use, possession, or sale of any drug on school grounds, including "'[a]ny prescription or over-the-counter drug, except those for which permission to use in school has been granted pursuant to Board policy.'" App. to Pet. for Cert. 128a.[301] A week before Savana was searched, another student, Jordan Romero (no relation of the school's administrative assistant), told the principal and Assistant Principal Wilson that "certain students were bringing drugs and weapons on campus," and that he had been sick after taking some pills that "he got from a classmate." App. 8a. On the morning of October 8, the same boy handed Wilson a white pill that he said Marissa Glines had given him. He told Wilson that students were planning to take the pills at lunch.

Wilson learned from Peggy Schwallier, the school nurse, that the pill was Ibuprofen 400 mg, available only by prescription. Wilson then called Marissa out of class. Outside the classroom, Marissa's teacher handed Wilson the day planner, found within Marissa's reach, containing various contraband items. Wilson escorted Marissa back to his office.

In the presence of Helen Romero, Wilson requested Marissa to turn out her pockets and open her wallet. Marissa produced a blue pill, several white ones, and a razor blade. Wilson asked where the blue pill came from, and Marissa answered, "'I guess

301. When the object of a school search is the enforcement of a school rule, a valid search assumes, of course, the rule's legitimacy. But the legitimacy of the rule usually goes without saying as it does here. The Court said plainly in New Jersey v. T. L. O., 469 U.S. 325, 342, n. 9, 105 S. Ct. 733, 83 L. Ed. 2d 720 (1985), that standards of conduct for schools are for school administrators to determine without second-guessing by courts lacking the experience to appreciate what may be needed. Except in patently arbitrary instances, Fourth Amendment analysis takes the rule as a given, as it obviously should do in this case. There is no need here either to explain the imperative of keeping drugs out of schools, or to explain the reasons for the school's rule banning all drugs, no matter how benign, without advance permission. Teachers are not pharmacologists trained to identify pills and powders, and an effective drug ban has to be enforceable fast. The plenary ban makes sense, and there is no basis to claim that the search was unreasonable owing to some defect or shortcoming of the rule it was aimed at enforcing.

it slipped in when she gave me the IBU 400s.'" Id., at 13a. When Wilson asked whom she meant, Marissa replied, "'Savana Redding.'" Ibid. Wilson then enquired about the day planner and its contents; Marissa denied knowing anything about them. Wilson did not ask Marissa any followup questions to determine whether there was any likelihood that Savana presently had pills: neither asking when Marissa received the pills from Savana nor where Savana might be hiding them.

Schwallier did not immediately recognize the blue pill, but information provided through a poison control hotline[302] indicated that the pill was a 200-mg dose of an antiinflammatory drug, generically called naproxen, available over the counter. At Wilson's direction, Marissa was then subjected to a search of her bra and underpants by Romero and Schwallier, as Savana was later on. The search revealed no additional pills.

It was at this juncture that Wilson called Savana into his office and showed her the day planner. Their conversation established that Savana and Marissa were on friendly terms: while she denied knowledge of the contraband, Savana admitted that the day planner was hers and that she had lent it to Marissa. Wilson had other reports of their friendship from staff members, who had identified Savana and Marissa as part of an unusually rowdy group at the school's opening dance in August, during which alcohol and cigarettes were found in the girls' bathroom. Wilson had reason to connect the girls with this contraband, for Wilson knew that Jordan Romero had told the principal that before the dance, he had been at a party at Savana's house where alcohol was served. Marissa's statement that the pills came from Savana was thus sufficiently plausible to warrant suspicion that Savana was involved in pill distribution.

This suspicion of Wilson's was enough to justify a search of Savana's backpack and outer clothing.[303] If a student is reasonably suspected of giving out contraband pills, she is reasonably suspected of carrying them on her person and in the carryall that has become an item of student uniform in most places today. If Wilson's reasonable suspicion of pill distribution were not understood to support searches of outer clothes and backpack, it would not justify any search worth making. And the look into Savana's bag, in her presence and in the relative privacy of Wilson's office, was not excessively intrusive, any more than Romero's subsequent search of her outer clothing.

---

302. Poison control centers across the country maintain 24-hour help hotlines to provide "immediate access to poison exposure management instructions and information on potential poisons." American Association of Poison Control Centers, online at http://www.aapcc.org/dnn/About/tabid/74/Default.aspx (all Internet materials as visited June 19, 2009, and available in Clerk of Court's case file).

303. There is no question here that justification for the school officials' search was required in accordance with the T. L. O. standard of reasonable suspicion, for it is common ground that Savana had a reasonable expectation of privacy covering the personal things she chose to carry in her backpack, cf. 469 U.S., at 339, 105 S. Ct. 733, 83 L. Ed. 2d 720, and that Wilson's decision to look through it was a "search" within the meaning of the Fourth Amendment.

B

Here it is that the parties part company, with Savana's claim that extending the search at Wilson's behest to the point of making her pull out her underwear was constitutionally unreasonable. The exact label for this final step in the intrusion is not important, though strip search is a fair way to speak of it. Romero and Schwallier directed Savana to remove her clothes down to her underwear, and then "pull out" her bra and the elastic band on her underpants. Id., at 23a. Although Romero and Schwallier stated that they did not see anything when Savana followed their instructions, App. to Pet. for Cert. 135a, we would not define strip search and its Fourth Amendment consequences in a way that would guarantee litigation about who was looking and how much was seen. The very fact of Savana's pulling her underwear away from her body in the presence of the two officials who were able to see her necessarily exposed her breasts and pelvic area to some degree, and both subjective and reasonable societal expectations of personal privacy support the treatment of such a search as categorically distinct, requiring distinct elements of justification on the part of school authorities for going beyond a search of outer clothing and belongings.

Savana's subjective expectation of privacy against such a search is inherent in her account of it as embarrassing, frightening, and humiliating. The reasonableness of her expectation (required by the Fourth Amendment standard) is indicated by the consistent experiences of other young people similarly searched, whose adolescent vulnerability intensifies the patent intrusiveness of the exposure. See Brief for National Association of Social Workers et al. as Amici Curiae 6–14; Hyman & Perone, The Other Side of School Violence: Educator Policies and Practices that may Contribute to Student Misbehavior, 36 J. School Psychology 7, 13 (1998) (strip search can "result in serious emotional damage"). The common reaction of these adolescents simply registers the obviously different meaning of a search exposing the body from the experience of nakedness or near undress in other school circumstances. Changing for gym is getting ready for play; exposing for a search is responding to an accusation reserved for suspected wrongdoers and fairly understood as so degrading that a number of communities have decided that strip searches in schools are never reasonable and have banned them no matter what the facts may be, see, e.g., New York City Dept. of Education, Reg. No. A-432, p 2 (2005).... ("Under no circumstances shall a strip-search of a student be conducted").

The indignity of the search does not, of course, outlaw it, but it does implicate the rule of reasonableness as stated in T. L. O., that "the search as actually conducted [be] reasonably related in scope to the circumstances which justified the interference in the first place." 469 U.S., at 341, 105 S. Ct. 733, 83 L. Ed. 2d 720 (internal quotation marks omitted). The scope will be permissible, that is, when it is "not excessively intrusive in light of the age and sex of the student and the nature of the infraction." Id., at 342, 105 S. Ct. 733, 83 L. Ed. 2d 720.

Here, the content of the suspicion failed to match the degree of intrusion. Wilson knew beforehand that the pills were prescription-strength ibuprofen and over-the-counter naproxen, common pain relievers equivalent to two Advil, or one Aleve.[304] He must have been aware of the nature and limited threat of the specific drugs he was searching for, and while just about anything can be taken in quantities that will do real harm, Wilson had no reason to suspect that large amounts of the drugs were being passed around, or that individual students were receiving great numbers of pills.

Nor could Wilson have suspected that Savana was hiding common painkillers in her underwear. Petitioners suggest, as a truth universally acknowledged, that "students ... hid[e] contraband in or under their clothing," Reply Brief for Petitioners 8, and cite a smattering of cases of students with contraband in their underwear, id., at 8–9. But when the categorically extreme intrusiveness of a search down to the body of an adolescent requires some justification in suspected facts, general background possibilities fall short; a reasonable search that extensive calls for suspicion that it will pay off. But nondangerous school contraband does not raise the specter of stashes in intimate places, and there is no evidence in the record of any general practice among Safford Middle School students of hiding that sort of thing in underwear; neither Jordan nor Marissa suggested to Wilson that Savana was doing that, and the preceding search of Marissa that Wilson ordered yielded nothing. Wilson never even determined when Marissa had received the pills from Savana; if it had been a few days before, that would weigh heavily against any reasonable conclusion that Savana presently had the pills on her person, much less in her underwear.

In sum, what was missing from the suspected facts that pointed to Savana was any indication of danger to the students from the power of the drugs or their quantity, and any reason to suppose that Savana was carrying pills in her underwear. We think that the combination of these deficiencies was fatal to finding the search reasonable.

In so holding, we mean to cast no ill reflection on the assistant principal, for the record raises no doubt that his motive throughout was to eliminate drugs from his school and protect students from what Jordan Romero had gone through. Parents are known to overreact to protect their children from danger, and a school official with responsibility for safety may tend to do the same. The difference is that the Fourth Amendment places limits on the official, even with the high degree of deference that courts must pay to the educator's professional judgment.

We do mean, though, to make it clear that the T. L. O. concern to limit a school search to reasonable scope requires the support of reasonable suspicion of danger or of resort to underwear for hiding evidence of wrongdoing before a search can reasonably make the quantum leap from outer clothes and backpacks to exposure of intimate parts. The meaning of such a search, and the degradation its subject may

304. An Advil tablet, caplet, or gel caplet, contains 200 mg ibuprofen. See 2007 Physicians' Desk Reference for Nonprescription Drugs, Dietary Supplements, and Herbs 674 (28th ed. 2006). An Aleve caplet contains 200 mg naproxen and 20 mg sodium. See id., at 675.

reasonably feel, place a search that intrusive in a category of its own demanding its own specific suspicions.

IV

A school official searching a student is "entitled to qualified immunity where clearly established law does not show that the search violated the Fourth Amendment." Pearson v. Callahan, 555 U.S. 223, 243–244, 129 S. Ct. 808, 822, 172 L. Ed. 2d 565, 580 (2009). To be established clearly, however, there is no need that "the very action in question [have] previously been held unlawful." Wilson v. Layne, 526 U.S. 603, 615, 119 S. Ct. 1692, 143 L. Ed. 2d 818 (1999). The unconstitutionality of outrageous conduct obviously will be unconstitutional, this being the reason, as Judge Posner has said, that "[t]he easiest cases don't even arise." K. H. v. Morgan, 914 F.2d 846, 851 (CA7 1990). But even as to action less than an outrage, "officials can still be on notice that their conduct violates established law . . . in novel factual circumstances." Hope v. Pelzer, 536 U.S. 730, 741, 122 S. Ct. 2508, 153 L. Ed. 2d 666 (2002).

T. L. O. directed school officials to limit the intrusiveness of a search, "in light of the age and sex of the student and the nature of the infraction," 469 U.S., at 342, 105 S. Ct. 733, 83 L. Ed. 2d 720, and as we have just said at some length, the intrusiveness of the strip search here cannot be seen as justifiably related to the circumstances. But we realize that the lower courts have reached divergent conclusions regarding how the T. L. O. standard applies to such searches.

A number of judges have read T. L. O. as the en banc minority of the Ninth Circuit did here. The Sixth Circuit upheld a strip search of a high school student for a drug, without any suspicion that drugs were hidden next to her body. Williams v. Ellington, 936 F.2d 881, 882–883, 887 (1991). And other courts considering qualified immunity for strip searches have read T. L. O. as "a series of abstractions, on the one hand, and a declaration of seeming deference to the judgments of school officials, on the other," Jenkins v. Talladega City Bd. of Ed., 115 F.3d 821, 828 (CA11 1997) (en banc), which made it impossible "to establish clearly the contours of a Fourth Amendment right . . . [in] the wide variety of possible school settings different from those involved in T. L. O." itself, ibid. See also Thomas v. Roberts, 323 F.3d 950 (CA11 2003) (granting qualified immunity to a teacher and police officer who conducted a group strip search of a fifth grade class when looking for a missing $26).

We think these differences of opinion from our own are substantial enough to require immunity for the school officials in this case. We would not suggest that entitlement to qualified immunity is the guaranteed product of disuniform views of the law in the other federal, or state, courts, and the fact that a single judge, or even a group of judges, disagrees about the contours of a right does not automatically render the law unclear if we have been clear. That said, however, the cases viewing school strip searches differently from the way we see them are numerous enough, with well-reasoned majority and dissenting opinions, to counsel doubt that we were sufficiently clear in the prior statement of law. We conclude that qualified immunity is warranted.

V

The strip search of Savana Redding was unreasonable and a violation of the Fourth Amendment, but petitioners Wilson, Romero, and Schwallier are nevertheless protected from liability through qualified immunity. Our conclusions here do not resolve, however, the question of the liability of petitioner Safford Unified School District #1 under Monell v. Dep't of Soc. Servs., 436 U.S. 658, 694, 98 S. Ct. 2018, 56 L. Ed. 2d 611 (1978), a claim the Ninth Circuit did not address. The judgment of the Ninth Circuit is therefore affirmed in part and reversed in part, and this case is remanded for consideration of the Monell claim.

It is so ordered.

Chapter 5

Special Education

Introduction

In the United States, the inclusion of students with disabilities in public schools took considerable time to develop. The earliest known schools for students with disabilities were established in the early nineteenth century. In 1817, Thomas Hopkins Gallaudet founded the American Asylum for the Education of the Deaf and Dumb (later renamed the American School for the Deaf).[1] Today, approximately 6 million students are considered eligible to receive some type of special education or related service(s), representing nearly 14 percent of the total student population enrolled in United States public schools.[2] Of the total number of school-age children and youth receiving special education and related services, approximately 63 percent spend 80 percent or more of their day in a general education classroom alongside students without disabilities.[3] The most significant legal advancements involving students with disabilities did not occur until the late 1960s and early 1970s. Historically, students with disabilities were either routinely placed in unregulated and ill-equipped state institutions or did not attend school at all.

On November 29, 1975, President Gerald R. Ford signed into law the inaugural *Education for All Handicapped Children Act* (EAHCA), which has been subsequently amended in 1978, 1983, 1986, 1990, 1997, and 2004.[4] The EAHCA was later renamed the Individuals with Disabilities Education Act (IDEA) in 1990 to reflect substantive changes in the federal law, including a change in references from "handicapped children" to "children with disabilities." The most recent reauthorization, or revision, to the IDEA federal statute was passed by Congress on November 19, 2004, and is currently referred to as the Individuals with Disabilities Education Improvement Act of 2004 (hereafter called the IDEA). Former President George Bush signed the IDEA into law on December 3, 2004, and the federal statute went officially into effect on July 1, 2005. While the EAHCA statute has been amended and renamed

1. *See* Donald F. Moores, Educating the deaf: Psychology, Principles, and Practices (Boston: Houghton Muffin, 1978).

2. U.S. Dep't of Educ., Office of Special Educ. & Rehab. Serv., *41st Annual Report to Congress on the Implementation of the Individuals with Disabilities Act, 2019* (Oct. 2019), https://www2.ed.gov/about/reports/annual/osep/2019/parts-b-c/41st-arc-for-idea.pdf.

3. *Id.*

4. Pub. L. 101-46, 104 Stat. 1103 (1975).

numerous times since its initial enactment in 1975, four original purposes of this federal statute remain, including:

1. To assure the rights of all students with disabilities to a free appropriate public education.
2. To protect the rights of the students and their parents in securing such an education.
3. To assist state and local agencies to provide for the education of those students.
4. To assess and assure the effectiveness of state and local efforts to educate those students.[5]

Early Landmark Legal Cases Involving Students with Disabilities

The legal movement to advance equal educational opportunities for students with disabilities gained notable momentum during the late 1960s and early 1970s.[6] In 1972, two separate federal class action lawsuits were litigated, leaving a profound legal impact and legacy on the access of students with disabilities in public schools. Both cases, *Pennsylvania Association for Retarded Children (PARC) v. Commonwealth of Pennsylvania*[7] and *Mills v. Board of Education of the District of Columbia*,[8] marked significant turning points in establishing formal constitutional rights for students with disabilities.

In *PARC*, a class action lawsuit was initiated on behalf of a group of students between the ages of six and 21 with intellectual disabilities who were excluded from public schools. Local school officials justified the exclusion of these students based on four Pennsylvania statutes. One statute relieved public school officials from any legal obligation to educate a child who was certified, in the terminology of that time, as "uneducable and untrainable." A second statute permitted any child who had not attained a mental age of five years to have his admission to public school postponed indefinitely. A third statute excused from compulsory school attendance any child deemed by a psychologist as "unable to profit" from education. Finally, a fourth statute postponed the admissions of intellectually disabled children until eight years of age or legally permitted these students to be removed from the public school system at age 17.

The *PARC* case was legally resolved by means of a consent agreement between the parties and endorsed by a federal trial court. In language that preceded the Individuals with Disabilities Education Act (IDEA), the agreement stipulated that

---

5. Pub. L. 94–142, 20 U.S.C. §1400(d) (1975).

6. *See* Legal Issues in Special Education: Principles, Policies, and Practices (Kevin P. Brady, Charles J. Russo, Cynthia A. Dieterich, & Allan G. Osborne, Jr., eds. 2020).

7. 343 F. Supp. 279 (E.D. Pa. 1972).

8. 348 F. Supp. 866 (D.D.C. 1972).

no "mentally retarded" child, or child thought to be "mentally retarded," could be assigned to a special education program or be excluded from the public schools without due process. The consent agreement established that school systems in Pennsylvania had the obligation to provide all mentally retarded children with a free appropriate public education and training programs appropriate to their capacities. Even though *PARC* was a consent decree, thereby arguably limiting its legal value beyond the immediate parties, there is no doubt that it helped usher in significant positive change protecting the educational rights and protections of students with disabilities. *PARC* helped establish that students who were classified as "mentally retarded" (now referred to as having an "intellectual disability") were legally entitled to receive a free appropriate public education (FAPE).

In *Mills*, a class action lawsuit was brought on behalf of children who were excluded from the public schools in Washington, D.C., after they were classified as having "behavior problems" and being "mentally retarded, emotionally disturbed, and hyperactive."[9] In fact, in an egregious oversight, the plaintiffs estimated that approximately 18,000 out of 22,000 students with disabilities in the Washington, D.C., Public School District were not receiving special education services. The plaintiff class sought a declaration of rights and an order directing the school board to provide a publicly supported education to all students with disabilities, either within its system of public schools or at alternative programs at public expense. School officials responded that while the board had the responsibility to provide a publicly supported education to meet the needs of all children within its boundaries and that it had failed to do so, it was impossible to afford the plaintiff class the relief it sought due to a lack of funds. Additionally, school personnel admitted that they had not provided the plaintiffs with due process prior to their exclusion.

Entering legal judgment in favor of the plaintiff-students, the federal trial court pointed out that the United States Constitution, the District of Columbia Code, and its own regulations required the local school board to provide a publicly supported education to all children, including those students with disabilities. The court explained that the local school board had to expend its available funds equitably so that all students would receive a publicly funded education consistent with their needs and abilities. If sufficient funds were not available, the court asserted that existing funds would have to be distributed in such a manner that no child was entirely excluded, and the inadequacies could not be allowed to bear more heavily on one class of students. In so ruling, the court directed the board to provide due process safeguards before any children were excluded from the public schools, reassigned, or had their special education services terminated. At the same time, as part of its opinion, the court outlined elaborate due process procedures that it expected the school board to follow. These procedures later formed the foundation for the due process safeguards that were mandated in the federal special education statute. As a result of the *Mills* decision, the Washington, D.C., Public Schools were required to:

9. *Id.*

1. Admit all children regardless of their disability.
2. Provide immediate and adequate educational facilities in the public schools or provide for an alternative placement at the school system's expense.
3. Provide an individualized education plan for each child.
4. Provide detailed due-process procedures before placing a child in special education and before altering a child's special-education program.

Taken together, the *PARC* and *Mills* cases firmly established that students with disabilities have recognized constitutional rights and may not be misclassified or excluded from the nation's public schools. They are considered landmark legal decisions because they greatly influenced historic federal legislation that would shortly follow.

Major Federal Legislation Impacting Students with Disabilities

Due to increasing awareness of the unequal access and treatment of students with disabilities in public schools resulting from the *PARC* and *Mills* legal decisions, Congress moved quickly to develop comprehensive federal legislation and to supply funding aimed at educating and providing individualized services for students with disabilities. The initial result was the federal Education for All Handicapped Children Act of 1975 (EAHCA), which applied to all eligible children with disabilities between the ages of 3 and 21.[10] The most important three federal laws related to the legal rights of children with disabilities include:

1. Individuals with Disabilities Education Act (IDEA)[11]
2. Section 504 of the Rehabilitation Act of 1973[12]
3. Americans with Disabilities Act (ADA)[13]

While these three federal statutes offer many similar legal guarantees and protections to students with disabilities, there are important differences and distinctions among them.

---

10. Pub. L. 101-46, 104 Stat. 1103 (1975). The original Education for All Handicapped Children Act (EAHCA) was signed into law on November 29, 1975, by President Gerald R. Ford. The EAHCA was amended in 1978, 1983, 1990, 1997, and most recently in 2004. In 1990, the federal law was renamed the Individuals with Disabilities Education Act (IDEA) and in 2004 the law received another name change by inserting the word "improvement," resulting in the Individuals with Disabilities Education Improvement Act (IDEIA). In this book, the federal statute will be consistently referred to as the IDEA.

11. *Id.*

12. 29 U.S.C. §794.

13. 42 U.S.C. §12101.

Individuals with Disabilities Education Act (IDEA)

Educational rights for children with disabilities originated with the passage of the Education for All Handicapped Children Act of 1975 (EAHCA).[14] Since 1975, additional developments and innovations in special education and services provided to children and youth with disabilities have given rise to its reauthorization and renaming in 1997 to the Individuals with Disabilities Education Act of 1997.[15] The most recent reauthorization, or revision, to the IDEA added the word "improvement," so the current legislation is now known as the Individuals with Disabilities Education Improvement Act of 2004 (IDEIA).[16] Contrary to some perceptions, gifted/talented education is not covered under IDEA. Therefore, any state wishing to provide services for the gifted must do so at their own expense. Likewise, the rules governing services under IDEA do not apply to education for gifted students. Similar to its federal statutory predecessor, the Education for All Handicapped Children Act, the most recent version of the IDEA is divided into four major sections: Parts A through D [*see* **Table 5.1**].

The primary purposes of the IDEA include:

> (1)(A) To ensure that all children with disabilities have available to them a free appropriate public education that emphasizes special education and related services designed to meet their unique needs and prepare them for further education, employment, and independent living;
>
> (B) to ensure that the rights of children with disabilities and parents of such children are protected; and
>
> (C) to assist States, localities, educational service agencies, and Federal agencies to provide for the education of all children with disabilities;
>
> (2) to assist States in the implementation of a statewide, comprehensive, coordinated, multidisciplinary, and interagency system of early intervention services for infants and toddlers with disabilities and their families;
>
> (3) to ensure that educators and parents have the necessary tools to improve educational results for children with disabilities by supporting system improvement activities; coordinated research and personnel preparation; coordinated technical assistance, dissemination, and support; and technology development and media services; and
>
> (4) to assess, and ensure the effectiveness of, efforts to educate children with disabilities.[17]

14. *Id.*
15. *Id.*
16. *Id.*
17. 20 U.S.C. § 1400 (d).

Table 5-1. Basic Structure of the IDEA

Part A	Part B	Part C	Part D
General Provisions • States congressional findings and purposes of the law. • Contains all relevant definitions used in the statute.	**Assistance to States for All Children with Disabilities** • Covers ages 3 through 21. • Authorizes federal funds to be distributed to individual states which submit plans that detail how a state will ensure a free appropriate public education (FAPE) to qualified children and youth. • Details legal rights for parents and children with disabilities and establishes the procedural due process system.	**Infants and Toddlers with Disabilities** • Provides categorical grants to states providing appropriate special education services to infants and toddlers with disabilities.	**National Activities to Improve Education of Children with Disabilities** • Provides federal grant monies that support the implementation of the IDEA, including the support of personnel preparation and research projects that support effective early intervention strategies.

The four parts, or components, of the current IDEA include:

(1.) Part A — General Provisions[18]

Part A of the IDEA 2004 is a mandatory component of the federal statute and includes Sections 1400 through 1409 of Title 20 of the United States Code (U.S.C.). The three primary purposes of Part A include:

1. The major terms and definitions used throughout the IDEA 2004 federal statute.
2. Congress' primary findings and purposes of the IDEA 2004 law.
3. Establishing that the U.S. Department of Education's Office of Special Education Programs (OSEP) has the direct legal authority to implement as well as oversee the statute.[19]

(2.) Part B — Assistance for Education of All Children with Disabilities[20]

Comparable to Part A, Part B of the IDEA 2004 is a mandatory component of the federal statute. Part B of the IDEA 2004 primarily governs special education and

18. 20 U.S.C. §§ 1400–1409.
19. 20 U.S.C. § 1400(d).
20. 20 U.S.C. §§ 1411–1419.

related services for children with disabilities between the ages of three and 21. For those interested in familiarizing themselves with the IDEA statute, the most important sections of Part B are Sections 1412, 1414, and 1415. These three sections of the IDEA encompass the following topics:

1. ***Section 1412: State Eligibility.*** Often called the "Catch-All" statute because it covers so many diverse topics under the IDEA, including provisions related to child find, free appropriate public education, children with disabilities who attend private or religiously affiliated schools, least restrictive environment, mandatory medication prohibition provision, over-identification of minority children and youth with disabilities, qualifications of special education teachers, unilateral placements, tuition reimbursements, and state and district assessments.
2. ***Section 1414: Evaluations, Eligibility, Individualized Education Programs, and Educational Placements.*** Describes both the process and requirements covering initial student evaluations, parental consent, re-evaluations, student eligibility, individualized education programs (IEPs), and educational placements.
3. ***Section 1415: Procedural Safeguards.*** Details the various procedural safeguards designed to protect both the rights of children and youth with disabilities and their parents. Under the IDEA, the number of parental responsibilities has been expanded. More specifically, procedural safeguards include the right to examine a student with disabilities' educational records and obtain an independent educational evaluation (IEE) as well as numerous legal requirements associated with acquiring prior written notice, due process hearings, mediation, attorneys' fees, and disciplinary provisions.

(3.) Part C—Infants and Toddlers with Disabilities[21]

While the IDEA statute focuses primarily on children and youth with disabilities aged three years and older, Part C of the IDEA was developed in 1986 in response to the need for special education services for children with developmental disabilities beginning at birth to three years of age. More specifically, Part C governs early intervention special education programs and services for infants and toddlers under the age of three. In many respects, the statutory structure of Part C aligns closely with the structure found in Part B. Unlike Part B, Part C of the IDEA recognizes the unique needs of infants and toddlers with disabilities and places increased emphasis on providing special education services within home and community settings instead of schools and mandates family involvement in the process. Since compliance with Part C is non-mandatory, the U.S. Department of Education authorizes grants to individual states to incentivize the improvement of special education programs and services serving infants and toddlers with identified disabilities. The decision whether to comply with the Part C provisions is at the discretion of individual states.

21. 20 U.S.C. §§1431–1444.

(4.) Part D — National Activities to Improve Education of Children with Disabilities[22]

Congress has made noteworthy changes to Part D of the IDEA statute. Specifically, Section 1450: Findings expressly details a major theme of this book—namely the critical need for appropriately trained school personnel, including school administrators, general education and special education teachers, and other school personnel, as well as "high quality, comprehensive professional development programs . . . to ensure that the persons responsible for the education or transition of children with disabilities possess the skills and knowledge necessary to address the needs of those children."[23] In addition to a focus on improving professional development for today's educators to improve special education programs and services for children and youth with disabilities, Congress has emphasized the invaluable role parents play in the education of their children with disabilities. As such, Congress created Parent Training and Information Centers (PTI) and Parent Resource Centers (CPRC). These centers aim to help parents learn more about their child's disabilities and unique educational needs, understand their and their child's legal rights and responsibilities in the special education process, learn how to more effectively communicate with school personnel, and learn how to more actively participate in the educational decision-making process involving their child.[24]

While the IDEA has been revised numerous times, the original and primary goal of this federal law helping students with disabilities remains unchanged, primarily that individual states and local school districts must offer IDEA-eligible students a free and appropriate public education (FAPE) in the least restrictive environment (LRE), as much as possible. As evidence of the importance of FAPE, Congress' stated primary purpose for the IDEA is "to ensure that all children with disabilities have available to them a free appropriate public education that emphasizes special education and related services designed to meet their unique needs and prepare them for further education, employment, and independent living"[25] and to "ensure that the rights of children with disabilities and parents of such children are protected."[26] Additionally, the IDEA federal statute and regulations contain important legal principles and provisions that help ensure all eligible students with disabilities receive FAPE. There are six key principles associated with the IDEA 2004:

1. Zero Reject, or Child Find Principle
2. Nondiscriminatory Evaluation and Appropriate Student Eligibility Practices
3. Individualized Education Program (IEP)
4. Least Restrictive Environment (LRE)

22. 20 U.S.C. §§1450–1482.
23. 20 U.S.C. §1450(6).
24. 20 U.S.C. §1471.
25. 20 U.S.C. §1401(d)(d)(1)(A).
26. 20 U.S.C. §1401(d)(d)(1)(B).

5. Parental and Student Participation in the Decision-Making Process
6. Procedural Due Process and Safeguards

These six core IDEA legal principles are described below.

Zero Reject (Child Find Provision)

Under the IDEA, the principle of zero reject legally prohibits schools from excluding any student with an eligible disability from receiving a free appropriate public education. This applies to children and youth ranging in age from three to 21, regardless of the severity of their disability. Relatedly, the IDEA statute contains a "child find" mandate, which is a term used interchangeably with the zero-reject principle requiring all states to "identify, locate, and evaluate" all resident children and youth with disabilities regardless of the severity of their disability(ies) or whether they attend public or private schools. Under the IDEA, the zero-reject principle applies to all states; public school districts; private schools (if the public system places a student into a private school); state-operated programs, including schools for students with visual or hearing impairments; psychiatric hospitals; and institutions for people with other disabilities. Simply stated, the zero-reject principle requires that all eligible children with disabilities be provided with a free appropriate public education. This principle is implemented by conducting a child-find program on an annual basis to locate, identify, and evaluate all children with disabilities who reside within the jurisdiction of each public agency. If local agencies comply with this principle, they become eligible to receive federal funds based upon the number of children being served, not to exceed 12 percent of the school population. In addition to providing an education to children with disabilities, the public agency must ensure that they have the same opportunities as non-disabled children to participate in nonacademic and extracurricular services, including physical education which must be provided to every student with a disability.

Principle of Nondiscriminatory Evaluation and Appropriate Student Eligibility Practices

The IDEA legally requires that a child or youth with a disability (or suspected disability) must receive a full individualized evaluation prior to placement in a special education program. A student placement decision should be made by a group of persons knowledgeable about the child or youth, the meaning of the evaluation data, and the available placement options. The placement recommendation may be suggested by the evaluation team and finalized by a committee which has the responsibility for writing the Individual Educational Plan. All children with disabilities must be completely re-evaluated every three years.

Presently, the IDEA has extensive and detailed rules involving evaluation procedures to determine student eligibility. Evaluation of a child or youth suspected of having a disability is a crucial part of the special education process since it is the primary mechanism not only for establishing student eligibility for special education and related services but also for determining the specific nature of necessary special education and related services.[27] When conducting an evaluation to determine IDEA eligibility, a school district must ensure that they satisfy the following requirements:

1. Adopt a variety of assessment tools and strategies to gather relevant functional, developmental, and academic information, including information provided by the parent, that may assist in determining whether the child is a child with a disability; and the content of the child's individualized education program, including information related to enabling the child to be involved in and progress in the general curriculum, or, for preschool children, to participate in appropriate activities;
2. Not use any single measure or assessment as the sole criterion for determining whether a child is a child with a disability or determining an appropriate educational program for the child; and
3. Use technically sound instruments that may assess the relative contribution of cognitive and behavioral factors, in addition to physical or developmental factors.[28]

Under the IDEA, fair and accurate evaluation practices are legally required for the proper and most beneficial placement of students with disabilities. The IDEA requires the establishment of policies, practices, and procedures ensuring that all children with disabilities who reside within a particular state or local educational agency (LEA) are "identified, located, and evaluated."[29] It is the legal responsibility of local public school districts to determine if a particular student is eligible for special education services under the IDEA by conducting an initial evaluation, which should determine if the student has a qualifying disability under the IDEA as well as both the type and level of specific service(s) the student needs. In fact, no provision of special education programs or services may take place unless the student receives a full evaluation of their unique, individualized educational needs.[30]

School officials should not initiate an evaluation of a student for potential special education eligibility under the IDEA without receiving the informed, written consent of the parent(s) or designated legal guardian(s).[31] In some circumstances, school officials may explain, in writing, the reasons why they believe a student does not have an eligible disability and does not require an initial evaluation, satisfying the requirement of notifying parents when they refuse to perform a requested evaluation.[32] If parents are dissatisfied with an evaluation of their child performed by a local school system, the IDEA provides the parent(s) or designated legal guardian(s)

27. 20 U.S.C. § 1414(a)(1)(C).
28. 20 U.S.C. § 1414(b)(2).
29. 20 U.S.C. § 1412(a)(3).
30. 20 U.S.C. § 1412(a)(3).
31. 20 U.S.C. § 1414(a)(1)(D).
32. 34 C.F.R. § 300.503.

the legal right to an independent educational evaluation, commonly referred to an IEE. Moreover, if the parents disagree with a school's refusal to have a student evaluated for potential IDEA eligibility, the parent can request a due process hearing to dispute the school's decision.

Currently, the IDEA has established a 60-day time period in which a student evaluation for student eligibility under the IDEA must be completed after initial parental or legal guardian consent has been received by the school district.[33] For example, the 2006 IDEA regulations provide further details and establish that an individualized education plan, or IEP meeting, must be held within a 30-day period of a student's eligibility determination, and strongly suggest that the student's actual IEP be implemented as soon as possible after its initial development.[34]

After an initial evaluation or re-evaluation has been completed, a local school system must compile and review all the student's evaluation data to determine if the child or youth meets the criteria for a "child with a disability" and is eligible for special education and related services under the IDEA. Under the IDEA, the definition of eligibility for special education and related services contains three primary considerations which are required to establish student eligibility, including:

1. The age of the student at the period she or he is seeking eligibility;
2. the student's specified disability; and
3. the determined "need(s)" for special education and related services.[35]

Under the IDEA, two necessary criteria are required to establish student eligibility. First, a student over the age of nine must be determined to have one or more of the present 13 eligibility categories under the IDEA (*see* Table 5.1). Second, the student's disability(ies) must be shown by academic and functional performance data to adversely affect the student's educational performance.[36] In terms of student eligibility under the IDEA, it is crucial that educational practitioners and those working closely with students with disabilities understand that establishing eligibility under the IDEA is not satisfied when a student merely meets one or more of the current 13 IDEA disability categories found in the federal regulations. In other words, satisfying one or more of the 13 disability categories alone does not establish IDEA eligibility. Instead, a child or youth determined to have one or more of the current 13 disability conditions must also show evidence that the disabling condition adversely impact(s) their educational performance.[37] Additionally, individual states may develop definitions of disabilities that differ from those listed by IDEA. The principal is required to follow the state's outline if it is not less comprehensive

33. 20 U.S.C. § 1414(a)(1)(C)(i).
34. 34 C.F.R. § 300.323(c).
35. 34 C.F.R. § 300.7(a)(2).
36. 20 U.S.C. § 1401(3)(A)(2).
37. 20 U.S.C. § 1401(3)(A).

than IDEA. States may always voluntarily provide more benefits or guarantees for their citizens than is required by the federal government.

The current 13 disability categories under the IDEA include:

1. Autism
2. Deaf-blindness
3. Deafness
4. Emotional disturbance
5. Hearing impairment
6. Intellectual disability
7. Multiple disabilities
8. Orthopedic impairment
9. Other health impairment (OHI)
10. Specific learning disability (SLD)
11. Speech or language impairment
12. Traumatic brain injury
13. Visual impairment

Table 5-2. IDEA Disability Eligibility Classification Definitions

Disability Category	IDEA Regulatory Definition
Autism	(1) (i) *Autism* means a developmental disability significantly affecting verbal and nonverbal communication and social interaction, generally evident before age 3, that adversely affects a child's educational performance. Other characteristics often associated with autism are engagement in repetitive activities and stereotyped movements, resistance to environmental change or change in daily routines, and unusual responses to sensory experiences. (ii) Autism does not apply if a child's educational performance is adversely affected primarily because the child has an emotional disturbance, as defined in . . . this section. (iii) A child who manifests the characteristics of "autism" after age 3 could be diagnosed as having "autism" if the criteria in paragraph (c)(1)(i) . . . are satisfied.[38]
Deaf-Blindness	The IDEA regulations define this disability as concomitant hearing and visual impairments, the combination of which causes such severe communication and other developmental and educational needs that they cannot be accommodated in special education programs solely for children with deafness or children with blindness.[39]

38. 34 C.F.R. § 300.8(c).
39. 34 C.F.R. § 300.8 (c)(2).

Disability Category	IDEA Regulatory Definition
Deafness	The IDEA regulations define this disability as a hearing impairment that is so severe that the child is impaired in processing linguistic information through hearing, with or without amplification, that adversely affects a child's educational performance.[40]
Emotional Disturbance (ED)	The IDEA regulations define this disability as: (i) a condition exhibiting one or more of the following characteristics over a long period of time and to a marked degree that adversely affects a child's educational performance: (a) An inability to learn that cannot be explained by intellectual, sensory, or health factors, (b) An inability to build or maintain satisfactory interpersonal relationships with peers and teachers, (c) Inappropriate types of behavior or feelings under normal circumstances, (d) A general pervasive mood of unhappiness or depression, (e) A tendency to develop physical symptoms or fears associated with personal or school problems (34 § CFR 300.8 (c)(4)(i), (ii) Emotional disturbance includes schizophrenia.[41]
Hearing Impairment	The IDEA regulations define this disability as: "an impairment in hearing, whether permanent or fluctuating, that adversely affects a child's educational performance but that is not included under the definition of deafness in this section."[42]
Intellectual Disability	The IDEA regulations define this disability as: "significantly subaverage general intellectual functioning, existing concurrently with deficits in adaptive behavior and manifested during the developmental period that adversely affects a child's educational performance."[43]
Multiple Disabilities	The IDEA regulations define this disability as: "concomitant impairments (such as mental retardation [intellectual disability]-blindness or mental retardation [intellectual disability]-orthopedic impairment), the combination of which causes such severe educational needs that they cannot be accommodated in special education programs solely for one of the impairments. Multiple disabilities does not include deaf-blindness."[44] **Note:* The term "mental retardation" has been replaced in brackets with the term now used in the IDEA regulations, "intellectual disability."

40. 34 C.F.R. § 300.8.
41. 34 C.F.R. § 300.8 (c)(4)(ii).
42. 34 C.F.R. § 300.8 (c)(5).
43. 34 C.F.R. § 300.8 (c) (6).
44. 34 C.F.R. § 300.8 (c)(7).

Disability Category	IDEA Regulatory Definition
Orthopedic Impairment	The IDEA regulations define this disability as: ". . . a severe orthopedic impairment that adversely affects a child's educational performance caused by a congenital anomaly, impairments caused by disease (e.g., poliomyelitis, bone tuberculosis), and impairments from other causes (e.g., cerebral palsy, amputations, and fractures or burns that cause contractures."[45]
Other Heath Impairment (OHI)	The IDEA regulations define this disability as: ". . . a student with OHI having limited strength, vitality, or alertness, including a heightened alertness to environmental stimuli, that results in limited alertness with respect to the educational environment, that is due to chronic or acute health problems such as asthma, attention deficit disorder or attention deficit hyperactivity disorder, diabetes, epilepsy, a heart condition, hemophilia, lead poisoning, leukemia, nephritis, rheumatic fever, sickle cell anemia, and Tourette syndrome."[46]
Specific Learning Disability (SLD)	The IDEA regulations define this disability as: ". . . a disorder in one or more of the basic psychological processes involved in understanding or in using language, spoken or written, that may manifest itself in the imperfect ability to listen, think, speak, read, write, spell, or to do mathematical calculations, including conditions such as perceptual disabilities, brain injury, minimal brain dysfunction, dyslexia, and developmental aphasia." The term does not include learning problems that are primarily the result of visual, hearing, or motor disabilities, of intellectual disability, of emotional disturbance, or of environmental, cultural, or economic disadvantage.[47]
Speech or Language Impairment	The IDEA regulations define this disability as: ". . . a communication disorder, such as stuttering, impaired articulation, a language impairment, or a voice impairment, that adversely affects a child's educational performance."[48]
Traumatic Brain Injury	The IDEA regulations define traumatic brain injury as: ". . . an acquired injury to the brain caused by an external physical force, resulting in total or partial functional disability or psychosocial impairment or both, that adversely affects a child's educational performance. The term applies to open or closed head injuries resulting in impairments in one or more areas, such as cognition; language; memory; attention; reasoning; abstract thinking; judgment; problem-solving; sensory, perceptual, and motor abilities; psychosocial behavior; physical functions; information processing; and speech. The term does not apply to brain injuries that are congenital or degenerative, or to brain injuries induced by birth trauma."[49]

45. 34 C.F.R. § 300.8 (c)(8).
46. 34 C.F.R. § 300.8 (c)(9).
47. 34 C.F.R. § 300.8 (c)(10).
48. 34 C.F.R. § 300.8 (c)(11).
49. 34 C.F.R. § 300.8 (c)(12).

Disability Category	IDEA Regulatory Definition
Visual Impairment (Including Blindness)	The IDEA regulations define this disability as: ". . . an impairment in vision that, even with correction, adversely affects a child's educational performance. The term includes both partial sight and blindness."[50]

*Note: When Congress reauthorized the IDEA in 1997, it provided states flexibility in using the "developmental delay" disability category to children aged three through nine under Part B of the IDEA. The IDEA gives discretion to individual states and LEAs to potentially include children ages three through nine who do not meet the other eligibility requirements if a child experiences a "developmental delay" in their physical, cognitive, communication, social/emotional, or adaptive development that results in a possible need for special education and related services.

In addition to being entitled to receive special education, the IDEA also specifies that eligible students may be legally entitled to receive certain "related services" considered necessary for the child or youth to derive educational and functional benefit(s) from special education.[51] These "related services" may potentially include one or more of the following:

1. Speech pathology
2. Audiology
3. Psychological services
4. Physical and occupational therapy
5. Recreation (including therapeutic recreation)
6. Counseling services (including rehabilitation counseling)
7. Medical services for diagnostic or evaluation purposes)
8. School health services
9. Social work services
10. Free transportation related to early identification and assessment of disabilities
11. Parent counseling and training[52]

This list of related services is not inclusive. As the field of special education continues to grow, the ability to identify children and youth with special needs increases. Schools now serve children and youth with varying degrees of severity of disability. The increase in the number of children with unique needs has led to greater demands upon schools to provide related services. Disagreements between parents and schools regarding the definition of related services continue to be debated by the courts. When such disagreements are litigated, it is often because the related service(s) requested by the parents is not specifically defined by law and is therefore

50. *Id.*
51. *Id.*
52. 20 U.S.C. §1401(17).

subject to interpretation. The most precarious legal question involves the distinction between services that fall into the medical and school health-service categories. If the proposed related service is considered medical, the school may not be required to provide the service. The law requires only that the schools provide medical services as they relate to diagnosis and evaluation. Medical service is now defined in the law as services provided by a licensed physician. School health-related services are those provided by a qualified school nurse or other qualified person(s).[53] Today's schools must provide related services only when those services are required for the student to benefit directly from special education and individualized related services.

Individualized Education Programs (IEPs)

The IDEA ensures that special education programs and related and supplemental services are individually tailored to the unique needs of students with disabilities by mandating the development of individualized education plans, commonly referred to as IEPs, for all IDEA eligible students. School personnel, acting collaboratively with parents, must develop IEPs before providing students with special education and related services. Furthermore, IEPs must be in effect at the beginning of each school year.[54] The specific content of IEPs may vary by state, but most contain some of the same basic elements. For example, the IDEA does not require benchmarks and short-term objectives for children with disabilities, other than for those who take alternate assessments aligned to alternate achievement standards.[55] Even so, some state laws require IEPs to include benchmarks and short-term objectives. Thus, it is important for educators and parents to be familiar with their own states' laws and regulations regarding the required content of IEPs.

One of the IDEA's overriding themes is that IEPs must be individualized to the unique needs of each student. This means that IEPs must be customized for each child, taking into consideration the child's unique, individual circumstances and disabilities.[56] [***See* Case No. 5-2.**] In accordance with this theme, courts have consistently invalidated IEPs that are not individualized to the unique needs and disabilities of students. The IEP must include statements of the student's present level of academic achievement and functional performance; measurable annual goals, including academic and functional goals; how the child's progress will be measured and when progress reports will be provided; the special education, related services, and supplementary aids and services to be provided; the extent, if any, to which the child will not participate in regular classes; accommodations necessary for state and district-wide assessments; the projected date for the beginning of services, and the anticipated frequency, location, and duration of those services; and (for students 16

53. Irving Indep. Sch. Dist. v. Tatro, 468 U.S. 883, 892 (1984).

54. 34 C.F.R. § 300.323.

55. 20 U.S.C. § 1414(d)(1)(A)(I).

56. *See* Endrew F. v. Douglas Cty. Sch. Dist. RE-1, 137 S. Ct. 988 (2017).

and over) transition goals and services.[57] At a minimum, a student's IEP must contain the following eight components:

1. A statement detailing a student's present level of academic achievement and functional performance.
2. A discussion of measurable annual goals for the student.
3. A statement containing an explanation of progress monitoring, or how progress toward the student's academic and functional goals and objectives will be measured. It should also describe how that information will be reported to parents.
4. Documentation of the special education services to be provided.
5. Time(s) the student will spend in special education and related services.
6. A statement containing transition for the student no later than a student's 16th birthday. Transitional goals and services focus on instruction and support services needed to help the student move from the school environment and into a job, vocational program, or other program designed to promote independent living. The goals should also prepare a student to advocate for herself in college.
7. Date(s) for initiating service and anticipated duration.
8. Evaluation procedures and schedules for determining mastery of the objectives.[58]

Members required to be in attendance at a student's IEP meeting include the following:

1. The parent(s) or legal guardian(s) of the student;
2. not less than one regular education teacher of the student (if the student is, or may be, participating in the regular education environment);
3. not less than one special education teacher of the student, or where appropriate, not less than one special education provider of the student;
4. a representative of the public agency who is qualified to provide, or supervise the provision of, specially designed instruction to meet the unique needs of students with disabilities; is knowledgeable about the general education curriculum; and is knowledgeable about the availability of resources of the public agency;
5. an individual who can interpret the instructional implications of evaluation results;
6. other individuals who have knowledge or special expertise regarding the student, including related services personnel as appropriate (invited at the discretion of the parent or the local educational agency); and
7. the student with the disability(ies) (where appropriate).[59]

57. 20 U.S.C. § 1414(d)(1)(A).
58. *Id.*
59. *Id.*

Least Restrictive Environment (LRE)

Over the last several decades, one of the primary objectives of the IDEA has been to ensure that all placements for eligible students with disabilities are in the least restrictive environment, often simply referred to as LRE, as much as possible. Under the LRE provision of the IDEA, students with disabilities can be removed from general educational environments only to the extent necessary for them to be provided with special education services. This does not, however, mean that students with disabilities can never be placed in restrictive settings in educational environments. Rather, the basic principle is that each student should be placed in the setting that is least restrictive for that individual child based on their unique needs and disabilities. When developing IEPs for students with disabilities, today's school personnel must balance the student's individualized needs for special education and related services against the nonacademic benefits gained from the inclusion of students with disabilities alongside their nondisabled student peers in regular classrooms.[60]

Consistent with the IDEA statute, school districts must establish procedures to ensure that students with disabilities are educated with children who do not have disabilities to the maximum extent appropriate. As a result, the IDEA allows local school boards to place children with disabilities in special classes and/or separate facilities or remove them from the general education environment only when either the nature or severity of their disabilities is such that instruction in general education classes cannot be achieved satisfactorily, even with supplementary aids and services. These provisions apply to students in private schools, institutions, and other care facilities as well as to students in public schools and facilities.

The terms *mainstreaming*, *inclusion*, and *least restrictive environment*, while often used interchangeably, are distinct. The difference between inclusion and mainstreaming is one of degree. *Mainstreaming* refers to the practice of placing special education class students in general education classes for a portion of the school day. *Inclusion*, on the other hand, refers to a philosophy where students with disabilities are enrolled in general education classes and are removed only when necessary to receive special education services. In many situations, special education services are provided within the general education environment so that students are not removed at all. *Least restrictive environment* is the legal term used in the IDEA. The IDEA federal statute does not legally require inclusion in every situation, but it does mandate that all students be educated in educational environments that are the least restrictive possible and that removal from the general education classroom setting should occur only when necessary. Thus, to the maximum extent possible, children and youth with disabilities should be educated alongside students who do not have disabilities. The removal of students with disabilities to special classes and separate facilities should occur only when the nature or severity of their disability prevents them from successfully being educated alongside students in general education classes with the use(s) of supplementary aids and services.

60. U.S.C. § 1412(a)(5).

Parental and Student Participation in the Decision-Making Process

Since the inception of the Education for All Handicapped Children Act (EAHCA) in 1975, parental participation has and continues to be a major component of the law, now known as the IDEA. Congress included significant and numerous parental rights in the IDEA statute to ensure that parents could advocate and fully participate in the IDEA process on behalf of their children. For example, the IDEA requires local education agencies, often referred to as LEAs, to develop and monitor parental notice and participation requirements. These parental notice and participation provisions are integral components of the IDEA and impact significant aspects of the special education process, ranging from the initial identification to post-high school transition of students with disabilities. They strongly encourage parents (or designated legal guardians) to become integral partners in the education of their children.

The IDEA has expanded the definition of a parent. According to the IDEA, the term *parent* now means a natural, adoptive, or foster parent of a child (unless a foster parent is prohibited by state law from serving as a parent); a guardian (but not the state if the child is a ward of the state); an individual acting in the place of a natural or adoptive parent (including a grandparent, stepparent, or other relative) with whom the child lives, or an individual who is legally responsible for the child's welfare; or an individual assigned to be a surrogate parent.[61]

An illustrative case detailing the significance of parental participation in the special education process under the IDEA is a 2013 decision from the Ninth Circuit, *Doug C. v. Hawaii Department of Education*.[62] In this case, the court held that a parent's right to participate in their child's IEP meeting was more important than the Hawaii Department of Education's need to meet an existing IEP annual review deadline. The parent, Doug C., had initially e-mailed the special education coordinator of his child's school district the day of his son's IEP meeting indicating he was unable to attend the meeting because he was ill. The parent offered to reschedule the IEP meeting for the following week, which was a few days past Hawaii's annual IEP review date set by the state's education department. In response, the district's special education coordinator attempted to convince the parent to participate in his son's IEP meeting the same morning by phone, but the parent indicated he was not feeling well and wanted to participate in-person at his son's IEP meeting. The special education coordinator went ahead with the IEP meeting without any parent present. At the meeting, the IEP team decided to change the student's existing placement from a private special education facility to a public high school workshop readiness program. The parent rejected the changes made to his son's IEP because it was created without his participation and requested a due process hearing. Initially, the special education hearing officer and the district court ruled in favor of the school district. On appeal, the Ninth Circuit ruled in favor of the parent, rejecting the argument that the IEP meeting needed to be held by the state's annual IEP review deadline. The court

61. 20 U.S.C. §1402(23).
62. 720 F.3d 1038 (9th Cir. 2013).

maintained the state education officials could have continued to provide the student with special education and related services after the state's review date had passed. It also indicated that the importance of parental participation in their child's IEP was more important than the state's IEP review date deadline. The *Doug C.* decision reinforces the importance of parental participation in the special education process, especially if school officials are considering adjusting or changing a student's existing IEP.

Procedural Due Process and Safeguards

The IDEA was specifically developed to provide both parents and school officials opportunities to work together collaboratively to develop individualized education programs for students with disabilities. Yet, in recognizing that parents and educators may not agree in all situations, Congress also included specific dispute-resolution provisions in the IDEA law including mediation, due process complaint(s), resolution processes, and state administrative complaint(s).[63] Since disagreements, including those involving student evaluation, eligibility, or placement, may arise during the special education process, the IDEA provides a variety of dispute-resolution processes in which parents and school officials can seek third-party administrative review.[64]

By definition, due process is a procedure(s) which seeks to ensure the fairness of educational decisions. It can also be viewed as a system of checks and balances concerning the identification, evaluation, and provision of services regarding students with disabilities. It may be initiated by either the parent or state or local educational agency as an impartial forum for presenting legal complaints regarding the child's identification, evaluation, and placement, or for challenging decisions made by another party. Under the IDEA, due process hearings are strongly encouraged as the primary method for resolving legal disputes between the parents of students with disabilities and school districts. The filing of lawsuits is often adversarial, timely, and costly. Thus, in most instances, it is believed that lawsuits do not serve the best interests of students with disabilities.[65] Due process hearings address a wide range of special education conflicts, including the identification, evaluation, placement, or provision of FAPE to students with disabilities.[66] Parents of students with disabilities may request mediation or due process hearings if they disagree with any actions of school officials regarding proposed IEPs or of the provision of FAPE for their children. Once they exhaust administrative remedies, parents may seek judicial review in federal or state courts.[67]

---

63. 20 U.S.C. § 1415.

64. *Id.*

65. *See* Sasha Pudelski, Rethinking Special Education Due Process: A Proposal for the Next Reauthorization of the Individuals with Disabilities in Education Act (2016).

66. 34 C.F.R. § 300.507.

67. 20 U.S.C. § 1415(i)(2)(A).

When attempting to understand legal issues surrounding special education, it is beneficial to think in terms of the major areas where legal issues and problems often arise. These areas include providing eligible students with a *free appropriate public education,* ensuring placements are in the *least restrictive environment,* providing *related and supplemental services,* and various aspects of *discipline.*

Free Appropriate Public Education (FAPE)

A free appropriate public education, or FAPE, is considered the legal cornerstone of the provision of special education to eligible students. That is, when Congress recognized that millions of special needs students were being excluded from schools nationwide, the prime objective was to get these students back in the school environment. Therefore, free appropriate public education, is at its core, the legal rights that all students have, including students with disabilities, to a free public K-12 education. When parents have concerns that eventually lead to a due process hearing or litigation, it is quite common for the issue to be related to a "lack of FAPE" for a particular student with disabilities. In essence, it means that the parents are arguing for a different approach to the education of their child than what the school district has or has not been providing. Does FAPE for a special needs child provide a right to the best education possible? Does it mean that whatever education is provided must be to maximize the student's potential?

The U.S. Supreme Court in *Board of Education of Hendrick Hudson Central School District v. Rowley*[68] [***see*** **Case No. 5-1**] answered these questions with a resounding "no." In *Rowley,* a kindergarten student with a diagnosed hearing impairment was provided with a sign-language interpreter by her neighborhood public school district. After it became evident that the student, Amy Rowley, was well above grade level in her academic performance, the district changed the assistance she was receiving to a voice projection device worn by the teacher. This assistive technology device was much less costly to the school district. The projection device allowed the student to continue to academically achieve above her grade level, although her report card grades dropped below her previous grades. The parents argued that the school district was legally obligated to return to the sign-language interpreter because it allowed Amy to academically achieve at a higher level. The parents' position was that FAPE meant that the district must do all it reasonably could to maximize the potential of all students. Ruling for the school district, the *Rowley* Court noted that Congress had not specifically defined FAPE. The Court viewed FAPE as only requiring that the district provide *a basic floor of opportunity* for the student to achieve. The measure of whether FAPE exists is evidenced by the student's promotion from grade to grade. The standard is not the maximization of an individual student's academic potential.

68. 458 U.S. 176 (1982).

Clarifying Rowley's *FAPE Provision: The Legal Significance of* Endrew F.

While the defining legal case addressing the term "appropriate" under FAPE continues to be *Rowley*, a 2017 U.S. Supreme Court decision attempted to clarify the existing *Rowley* legal standard related to the IDEA's FAPE provision.

In *Endrew F. v. Douglas County School District RE-1*,[69] [*see* **Case No. 5-2**] the Court issued a unanimous ruling in which it found that the lower *de minimis* ("slightly more than trivial") educational benefit standard is inappropriate for successfully conferring FAPE for eligible students receiving special education and related services. As stated by Chief Justice Roberts, who wrote the unanimous opinion, "[A] student offered an educational program providing merely more than *de minimis* progress from year to year can hardly be said to have been offered an education at all."[70] Essentially, the Court rejected the *de minimis* test as being inconsistent with the existing *Rowley* decision's focus on a student's IEP to produce adequate educational benefits.

The *Endrew F.* case was brought by parents on behalf of their son Endrew, a student diagnosed with autism spectrum disorder (ASD) and attention deficit/hyperactivity disorder (ADHD), who attended the Douglas County School District from preschool to the fourth grade. Endrew's parents claimed their son was not provided appropriate special education programming as legally required under the IDEA. More specifically, Endrew's parents believed the strategies used by the school district to address his challenging behaviors did not improve his learning. Endrew's concerning behaviors included screaming in class, climbing over furniture and other students, and occasionally running away from school. Additionally, Endrew had phobias to things such as such as flies, spills, and public restrooms. According to his parents, "Endrew's [Individualized Education Programs (IEPs)] largely carried over the same basic goals and objectives from one year to the next, indicating that he was failing to make meaningful progress toward his aims."[71] At the end of fourth grade, when the school district failed to change Endrew's goals and objectives, his parents enrolled him in a private school, Firefly Autism, which specialized in working with students with autism. Within only one month, Endrew's parents noticed major differences in their child allowing him to make significant academic improvements that never occurred while he was enrolled in public school.

Prior to *Endrew F.* coming before the Supreme Court, the school district legally prevailed at all levels, including the U.S. Court of Appeals for the Tenth Circuit. In each instance, the court ruled that the educational benefit mandated by an IDEA must be "more than *de minimis*,"[72] and so Endrew's IEP met the existing IDEA's FAPE requirement. Yet the Supreme Court mandated a far more robust,

69. 137 S. Ct. 988 (2017).

70. *Id.*

71. *Id.* at 996.

72. *Id.* at 1338.

outcome-oriented FAPE standard in *Endrew F.*, clarifying that FAPE is legally required to be "appropriately ambitious in light of [a student with disabilities'] circumstances" and "markedly more demanding than the 'merely more than *de minimis*' test" and should be designed with parents and school officials working collaboratively throughout the IEP process to "fully air their respective opinions."[73]

For over three decades, the nation's courts have struggled to legally define what FAPE means for eligible students with disabilities under the IDEA. As a result of this lack of legal clarity and guidance, today's school personnel and parents of students with disabilities are placed in challenging situations of trying to interpret the FAPE standard under the IDEA with limited guidance. It is important to understand that the *Endrew F.* decision has clarified but not replaced the existing *Rowley* legal standard for satisfying the IDEA's FAPE provision. More specifically, *Endrew F.* did clarify that a student's progress on their IEP must be considerably more demanding than the "merely *de minimis*" standard previously applied by many courts across the country. An important legal takeaway from the *Endrew F.* ruling is that any review of a student's IEP must directly address the issue of whether the IEP is reasonable, and that determination must be made on an individual student case-by-case basis. In making these important determinations for every IDEA-eligible student, the *Endrew F.* Court stressed that noticeably more deference must be given to today's local school officials, who use evidence-based practices (EBP), including timely data and assessments of their students, to accurately determine students with disabilities' individualized, appropriate level of academic and functional progress.

Related Services Under the IDEA

It is not enough that a school district provide special education; it must also provide related services so the child can benefit from that special education. For example, it would do no good to provide a program of special education for a child that had a physical impairment if the child had no specialized transportation to get to school. IDEA lists areas of possible related services, but the list is not exhaustive. Any service that is necessary to deliver special education must be provided no matter how novel. The primary exception to providing related services is the medical exception. That is, the school is not required to provide ongoing medical service beyond what is needed for an initial diagnosis of the student's exceptionality. The question of what an excepted medical service is was brought before the Supreme Court in *Irving Independent School District v. Tatro.*[74] [***See* Case No. 5-3.**]

In *Tatro*, an elementary school student had spina bifida, a physical disability which required that she receive a specialized procedure during school hours. As a result of her condition, she suffered from orthopedic and speech impairments and a neurogenic bladder. She needed to be catheterized every three to four hours to avoid injury to her kidneys. The school district refused to provide the service, arguing that

73. *Id.* at 993.

74. 468 U.S. 883 (1984).

it was a medical service specifically excluded by federal statute. The parents argued that the procedure need not be provided by a medical doctor. The school nurse or any of the school personnel could be trained to provide the clean intermittent catheterization (CIC).

The Court ruled for the parents. It interpreted the medical exception statute as applying to those services that could *only* be provided by a medical doctor. The fact that the CIC was not an exclusive M.D. procedure ruled out the application of the medical service exception. Therefore, the CIC was indeed a covered related service that the district was required to provide.

A second argument was advanced by the school district regarding the nature of the related service. It noted that the CIC was something the student had to get regardless of whether she was in school or not. Therefore, the procedure was not education-related. In rejecting this argument, the Court said that the purpose of related services was to ensure that a student could benefit from the special education. In this case, the student needed the CIC every three to four hours. This time interval meant that the student would be in school at a time when the procedure was to be provided. Without the procedure the student could not be in school. The only way to provide the CIC and special education is to administer the CIC during school hours. Thus, the CIC is a covered related service.

The *Tatro* legal standard has been applied to a whole host of related services. What about hearing aids, eyeglasses, or wheelchairs? Who pays for these health aids? The answer is, it depends. In the first instance, IDEA does not require the school district to pay any expense that is covered by the parents' insurance. Beyond the insurance provider, however, the question must be asked — is the device necessary for being in school and learning? In the final analysis, it is likely that anything the evaluation team discovers is necessary for the student to benefit from special education will be a related service expense to be borne by the school district.

Discipline of Students with Disabilities

Special Education Disproportionality in Disciplinary Practices

In 2019, the U.S. Commission on Civil Rights (USCCR) released a comprehensive and alarming report highlighting a plethora of research studies investigating disciplinary incident data involving students with disabilities.[75] A majority of these studies revealed significant disparities in exclusionary disciplinary practices, including out-of-school suspension and expulsion rates, most notably involving racial and ethnic minority students with disabilities compared to other groups of students with disabilities and the overall student population.[76] The Civil Rights Data Col-

75. U.S. Comm. on Civil Rights, Beyond Suspensions: Examining School Discipline Policies and Connections to the School-to-Prison Pipeline for Students of Color with Disabilities (2019), https://www.usccr.gov/pubs/2019/07-23-Beyond-Suspensions.pdf.

76. *Id.*

lection (CRDC) survey also revealed that while students with disabilities represent approximately 12% of the overall student population nationwide, they are also more than twice as likely to receive exclusionary disciplinary practices compared to their student peers in general education.[77] During the 2018–19 school year, for example, 17.89% of students with disabilities in the U.S. were identified as Black and 1.35% of students with disabilities were identified as American Indian or Alaska Native.[78] A study revealed that Black students with disabilities are approximately 2.8 times more likely compared to their student peers with disabilities to receive some form of exclusionary discipline in response to alleged problem behavior(s).[79] There are growing concerns involving the use of exclusionary disciplinary practices throughout the nation's schools, particularly students with disabilities who are identified as Black, Indigenous, or from other underrepresented communities.[80]

Interestingly and ironically, the IDEA was originally created to redress inequities encountered by students with disabilities, including biased and discriminatory referral, assessment, identification, and evaluation procedures. Unfortunately, however, it was not until the 1997 reauthorization of the IDEA that it first included any statutory provisions addressing the existence of racial disproportionality in special education.[81] During the 1997 reauthorization of the IDEA, Congress recognized that "greater efforts are needed to prevent the intensification of problems connected to mislabeling . . . among minority children with disabilities."[82] Based on these needs, the 1997 amendment added a specific provision addressing racial disproportionality in special education, stating:

> Each State that receives assistance under this part, and the Secretary of the Interior, shall provide for the collection and examination of data to determine if significant disproportionality based on race is occurring in the State with respect to: (A) the identification of children as children with disabilities, including the identification of children as children with disabilities in accordance with a particular impairment described in section 602(3); and (B) the placement in particular educational settings of such children.[83]

---

77. U.S. Dep't of Educ., Office of Civil Rights, *Civil Rights Data Collection Data Snapshot: School Discipline* (Issue Brief No. 1) (2014).

78. U.S. Dep't of Educ., Office of Spec. Educ. Programs (OSEP), *OSEP Fast Facts* (Aug. 2020).

79. Russell J. Skiba et al., *CCBD's Position Summary on Federal Policy on Disproportionality in Special Education*. 38 Behav. Disorders 108 (2013).

80. Kaitlin P. Anderson & Gary W. Ritter. *Disparate Use of Exclusionary Discipline: Evidence from Inequities in School Discipline from a U.S. State*. 25 Educ. Pol'y Analysis Archives 49 (2017) (finding schools in Arkansas with larger non-white student populations tend to deliver longer and more severe punishments in the form of out-of-school suspensions and expulsions).

81. Individuals with Disabilities Education Improvement Act of 1997 (IDEA), 20 U.S.C. § 1418(c).

82. IDEA, 20 U.S.C. § 1400(c)(12)(A).

83. IDEA, 20 U.S.C. § 1400(c)(12)(A).

In 2004, Congress once again reauthorized the IDEA and "prioritized the problem of racial disproportionality, [in part] because neither the 1997 amendments nor [the Office of Civil Rights] appeared to have had much impact on the problem."[84] During the IDEA's 2004 reauthorization, Congress recognized racial and ethnic disproportionality in special education as one of its three priority areas and delegated direct authority in the areas of monitoring and enforcement to individual states.[85] Consequently, the IDEA now focused on state monitoring and enforcement practices with a particular concentration on the adoption of numerical criteria to evaluate potential inequitable disproportionality practices involving students of color eligible for special education under the IDEA.[86] Specifically, the IDEA statute implemented two requirements for states to comply with as a precondition of receiving federal funding:

> (1.) The "state has in effect policies and procedures . . . designed to prevent the inappropriate overidentification or disproportionate representation by race and ethnicity of children as children with disabilities. . . .[87]
>
> (2.) States must monitor local school districts for "significant discrepancies" in disciplinary practices, including racial and ethnic disparities, long-term suspensions, and expulsions among students with disabilities.[88]

Under the current IDEA, states are now required to monitor the special education outcomes of their local school systems based on a total of 20 qualitative and quantitative indicators, known as State Performance Plan (SPP) indicators.[89] Three of these 20 SPP indicators focus specifically on issues related to student racial disproportionality in special education:

1. *Indicator 4:* (Two Components)

   Indicator 4A: requires individual states to monitor the rates of suspension for students with disabilities, identifying the percentage of local school districts having a "significant discrepancy in the rates of suspension and expulsion of children with Individualized Education Plans (IEP's) for greater than 10 days in a school year."[90]

   Indicator 4B: requires individual states to monitor the percentage of local school districts exhibiting those same discrepancies by "race and ethnicity."[91]

---

84. *Id.* at 15.

85. 20 U.S.C. § 1416(a)(3)(C).

86. *Id.*

87. 20 U.S.C. § 1412(a)(24).

88. 20 U.S.C. § 1412(a)(22). Under the IDEA, significant disproportionality has been identified based on three factors, including (1) overrepresentation in special education and a specific disability; (2) overrepresentation in special education placement; and (3) the duration, intensity, and type of specific suspensions in special education.

89. *Id.*

90. 20 U.S.C. § 1416(a)(3)(A).

91. *Id.*

2. *Indicator 9:* requires individual states to identify the proportion of local school districts exhibiting "this proportionate representation of racial and ethnic groups in special education and related services, to the extent the representation is the result of inappropriate identification."[92]

3. *Indicator 10:* requires individual states to identify the percentage of local school districts in the state with "disproportionate representation of racial and ethnic groups in specific disability categories that is the result of inappropriate identification."[93]

The IDEA's most recent attempt at addressing racial disproportionality involving students with disabilities has resulted in two unintended but significantly different definitions of racial disproportionality in special education.[94] First, significant racial disproportionality is defined under the IDEA as a numerical threshold determined by each individual state, and this definition serves to alert a particular state whether it has a disproportionate outcome based on the overrepresentation of specific ethnic or racial student subgroups in their local school districts statewide. There are multiple methods or measures by which an individual state could potentially identify racial disproportionality. Three of the most commonly used methods are the composition index, risk index, or risk ratio.[95] The current IDEA requires that every state collect and examine special education data based on student race and ethnicity at the school district level, and when an individual state finds that a local education agency has "significant" or ethnic disproportionality involving a student's identification or restrictiveness of the educational setting, the LEA must spend 15 percent of its Part B funds on uncoordinated early intervention services.

Even with this background detailing the continued existence of racial and ethnic disproportionality in disciplinary practices between students with and without disabilities, there are currently no legal restrictions on how to handle the misbehavior of special education students short of suspension. However, disciplinary measures should be spelled out in each student's IEP; if they are not, then approaches such as time-out or staying after school should be considered a change in the student's educational program. The teacher or principal may not change a special education student's program. Only the multidisciplinary team that initially developed the IEP may change the student's IEP.

When the misbehavior of a special education student becomes severe enough that suspension or expulsion is contemplated, the principal must be aware that several restrictions will apply. In 1990, the Supreme Court addressed the issue of suspension

92. 20 U.S.C. § 1416(a)(3)(C).

93. *Id.*

94. *Id.*

95. *See* Michael J. Boneshefski & Timothy J. Runge, *Addressing Disproportionality Discipline Practices Within a School-Wide Positive Behavioral Interventions and Supports Framework: A Practical Guide for Calculating and Using Disproportionality Rates,* 16 J. of Positive Behav. Interventions 149 (2014).

of special education students in *Honig v. Doe.*[96] [*See* **Case No. 5-4.**] In this case, two special education students were suspended for 39 days during which they had no educational services. The Court ruled that the federal law (specifically the "stay-put provision") does not permit a "change in placement" unless and until the multidisciplinary team decides that the IEP should reflect this change. Any removal of a child with an IEP for more than ten days is a change in placement. The following provides the basic guidance for principals in the discipline of children with disabilities:

1. A child is protected under the procedural safeguards of IDEA by having an IEP. This is true regardless of the child's disability and what misbehavior the child engaged in. Therefore, no child with an IEP can be suspended for more than ten days by the principal. After ten days, it is considered a change in placement. Only the multidisciplinary team can decide to extend the time of suspension and then only if it would appropriate for the child's benefit.

2. As provided in *Honig*, if the special education child needs to be "out of school" for more than ten days and there is disagreement on the multidisciplinary team regarding the alternative placement for the child, the school district can obtain an order from the appropriate U.S. district court to extend the time beyond ten days.

In the aftermath of *Honig*, a legal question arose. Is the ten-day maximum consecutive or cumulative? The answer to consecutive is clear. A student with an IEP cannot be suspended for more than ten consecutive school days without a change in placement. However, could a school district suspend a special education student for any number of days as long as it was not ten in a row? In other words, nine days here, eight days there, and so on. The Office for Civil Rights (OCR) of the U.S. Department of Education issued a letter shortly after the *Honig* ruling addressing this question. The DOE's advice was that it depended on the number of days per incident as well as the number of days in between incidents. For example, if a special education student was suspended for nine days in September, it might not be a violation of the *Honig* standard if the student were not suspended again until April or May even though the spring suspension was for two or three days. Thus, the cumulative number of days might exceed ten if there is sufficient spacing between suspension events.

Drugs and Weapons Suspensions Involving Students with Disabilities

One significant change in the discipline of students with IEPs has been the latitude given by Congress to school administrators to remove special education students who either (1) knowingly possess or use illegal drugs or sell or solicit the sale of a controlled substance while at school or a school function, or (2) carry a weapon to school or to a school function. As a result, school officials have the authority to transfer students with disabilities to appropriate interim alternative placements for up to forty-five school days for weapon, drug, or alcohol violations.

96. 484 U.S. 305 (1988).

For purposes of deciding what is an illegal drug, school districts must be guided by the federal controlled-substance statutes. The term "illegal drug" would not include a substance that is legally possessed or used under the supervision of a licensed healthcare professional. For weapons or drug offenses, school officials may suspend special education students for up to 45 days.[97] This would be 45 days available to the administration in excess of the ten days normally available for a removal.

Other Disciplinary Removals

If the need to remove the student with an IEP does not fall specifically under the drugs or weapons category, the student might still be removed by order of an IDEA due process hearing officer. For example, the IDEA now allows school officials to remove students to interim alternative placements for up to forty-five school days for inflicting serious bodily injuries.[98] The IDEA's definition of serious bodily injury may involve an injury with a substantial risk of death; extreme physical pain; protracted and obvious disfigurement; or protracted loss or impairment of the function of a bodily member, organ, or mental faculty.[99]The IDEA provides that a hearing officer may order a change in the placement of a child with a disability to an appropriate interim alternative educational setting for not more than 45 days if the hearing officer—

> **(A)** determines that the public agency has demonstrated by substantial evidence that maintaining the current placement of such child is substantially likely to result in injury to the child or to others;
>
> **(B)** considers the appropriateness of the child's current placement;
>
> **(C)** considers whether the public agency has made reasonable efforts to minimize the risk of harm in the child's current placement, including the use of supplementary aids and services; and
>
> **(D)** determines that the interim alternative educational setting meets the requirements of paragraph (3)(B).[100]

It should be noted that the Interim Alternative Educational Placement, or IAEP, is not simply forced home schooling. While homebound placement might be considered, it would be the last resort because homebound placement is the most restrictive placement on the continuum. Because of need within the regular student population as well as special education, some school districts have developed "alternative schools." These schools are used to temporarily provide students a place to go while being disciplined. Instead of removing students by suspension, the student might be sent to the alternative school for a specified number of days/months. If these schools also provide special education services, they can be used as an IAEP

97. 20 U.S.C. §1415(k)(1)(G)(i)-(ii).
98. 20 U.S.C. §1415(k)(1)(G)(iii).
99. 18 U.S.C. §1365(h)(3)).
100. 20 U.S.C. §1415(k)(1)(G)(i).

for students with IEPs who are removed to the regular education setting for up to 45 days.

The Americans with Disabilities Act (ADA)

Unlike the IDEA, which requires today's school officials to identify, assess, and serve eligible students with disabilities, the Americans with Disability Act (ADA) is a federal anti-discrimination statute that prohibits school officials from offering unequal access and opportunities to qualified students. This law is commonly referred to as the ADA. It applies to all facets of activity in the United States. Public access, employment, and educational issues are covered. Prior to its passage in 1990, individuals with handicaps were covered under Section 504 of the Vocational Rehabilitation Act of 1973. The ADA incorporates all of Section 504 and expands the areas of protection for those with disabilities. It includes all entities (e.g., public and private schools) regardless of whether federal funds are received by that entity. While there are several important definitions in the ADA, the one which applies directly to schools describes who is "qualified." According to the ADA, the term "qualified individual with a disability" means an individual with a disability who, with or without modifications to rules, policies, or practices, the removal of architectural, communication, or transportation barriers, or the provision of auxiliary aids and services, meets the essential eligibility requirements for the receipt of services or the participation in programs or activities provided by a public entity.[101]

The purpose of the ADA is to eliminate discrimination on the basis of disability. A disability is:

> **(A)** a physical or mental impairment that substantially limits one or more major life activities of such individual;
>
> **(B)** a record of such an impairment; or
>
> **(C)** being regarded as having such an impairment.[102]

A "major life activity" is a phenomenon such as walking, breathing, talking, or seeing. An individual need not currently have the disability in order to qualify. It is enough that the individual has had the disability in the past. In addition, the individual need not actually have or have had a disability. It is enough that the individual is "regarded" as having the disability. For example, an individual with a temporary skin rash that looks like leprosy may be qualified under the ADA because the public regards the individual as a leper.[103]

The ADA is important for schools because it may cover those students with disabilities that do not qualify under the IDEA for special education. If the child is able to be promoted from grade to grade, it is not likely that IDEA will apply even

101. 42 U.S.C.A. § 12131(2).
102. 42 U.S.C.A. § 12102(1).
103. *See id.* at (2)(A).

though the child has an obvious disability. This is where the ADA takes over. A child who is doing well in school may be covered under the ADA if the child is provided with reasonable accommodation in order to take "regular" advantage of school regardless of the disability. Of particular note is the coverage that the ADA provides children with acquired immune deficiency syndrome (AIDS). A child may not be excluded from school for having AIDS as long as they do not threaten the health or safety of others. AIDS is considered by the U.S. Department of Health as being non-communicable; although it is contagious, it is not communicable in the school setting. Simple safety precautions on the part of school personnel reduces the disease from the threat category. Instances of students with AIDS being removed are traceable to the student being in such an advanced stage of the disease that they were a threat to themselves by remaining in school.

Interestingly, some areas of modern life which society may once have recognized as disabilities have been specifically excluded from protection: transvestitism, homosexuality, bisexuality, transsexualism, pedophilia, exhibitionism, voyeurism, gender identity disorders not resulting from physical impairments, and other sexual disorders, as well as compulsive gambling, kleptomania, pyromania, or psychoactive substance use disorders resulting from illegal drug use.[104]

Section 504 of the Rehabilitation Act of 1973 (Section 504)

Many school districts in the U.S. have significant numbers of students who qualify to receive a "reasonable accommodation" to assist them in their schoolwork under Section 504. Section 504 is a federal anti-discrimination statute applicable to all public institutions that receive federal aid. Section 504 states, "[n]o otherwise qualified individual with a disability. . . shall, solely by reason of her or his disability, be excluded from participation in, be denied the benefits of, or be subjected to discrimination under any program or activity receiving Federal financial assistance" (29 U.S.C. § 794). Section 504 effectively prohibits recipients of federal financial assistance, public and nonpublic, from discriminating against individuals with disabilities in the provision of services or employment.

Section 504 defines an individual with a disability as a person "who (i) has a physical or mental impairment which substantially limits one or more of such person's major life activities, (ii) has a record of such an impairment, or (iii) is regarded as having such an impairment" (29 U.S.C.A. § 706(7)(B)). The Section 504 regulations define physical or mental impairments as including the following: (a.) any physiological disorder or condition, cosmetic disfigurement, or anatomical loss affecting one or more of the following body systems: neurological; musculoskeletal; special sense organs; respiratory, including speech organs; cardiovascular; reproductive,

104. 42 U.S.C.A. § 511.

digestive, genito-urinary; hemic and lymphatic; skin; and endocrine; or (b.) any mental or psychological disorder, such as mental retardation, organic brain syndrome, emotional or mental illness, and specific learning disorders (45 C.F.R. § 84.3(j)(2)(i),34 C.F.R. § 104.3(j)(2)(i)).

Once a student is identified, they receive an accommodation plan that describes what the school will provide in order that the handicapping condition might not prevent the student from doing quality work in the school setting. The plans describe accommodations, including sitting closer to the front of class and being given more time to complete tasks including tests.[105] In making accommodations and modifications for Section 504 eligible students, school officials must provide aid, benefits, and/or services that are currently comparable to those students who do not have disabilities.

Parental Rights Involving the Special Education Process

The IDEA requires that a special education student's parents be involved in every step of the educational process of their child. Parents have the following five basic procedural due process rights throughout the special education process involving their child, including:

1. When the student is first suspected of having a problem requiring special education, parents' permission must be obtained before the student can be assessed (tested).
2. Parents have the right to have the results of the assessment explained to them and to be informed about whether their child could benefit from special education.
3. Parents have the right to participate in the development of an IEP for their child as a result of the assessment.
4. They have a right to receive written notice in advance, and in their native language, of any meeting that will deal with their child's special education program.
5. Parents have the right of access to their child's records; otherwise, confidentiality of the records must be maintained.

In addition to the procedural due process rights just mentioned, parents have the right to formally disagree with any decision that the school attempts to make regarding their child. If parents disagree with a decision, they must request a due process hearing. At the hearing, a state-sponsored presiding officer hears both sides of the issue and renders a decision. If the parents are dissatisfied with the decision, they may appeal to the chief state school officer. Parents may take legal action if they

105. 29 U.S.C.A. §701 *et seq.*

are not satisfied with the chief school officer's decision. Parents have the following procedural rights at due process hearing:

1. The right to be represented by counsel.
2. The right to present evidence.
3. The right to present witnesses.
4. The right to cross-examine the school's witnesses.
5. The right to obtain a transcript of the proceedings.
6. The right to an appeal of the hearing officer's decision, provided the appeal request is filed within 30 days of receipt of the initial decision.

Students may not be required to undergo a psychiatric examination for which the primary purpose is to gain information about any of the following:

1. Political affiliation;
2. mental and psychological problems potentially embarrassing to the student or his or her family;
3. sexual behavior and attitudes;
4. illegal, anti-social, self-incriminating, and demeaning behavior;
5. critical appraisals of other individuals with whom respondents have close family relationships;
6. legally recognized privileged and analogous relationships, such as those of lawyers, physicians, and ministers; or
7. income, under certain circumstances.[106]

The Impact of the COVID-19 Global Pandemic on the Provision of Special Education

Throughout most of 2020, the coronavirus (COVID-19) pandemic had an unprecedented impact on the provision of special education and related services for the nation's students with disabilities. By early March 2020, the extremely contagious COVID-19 virus had spread into an alarming and deadly international pandemic, and by April 2020, every U.S. state had mandated the closure of its K-12 public schools. Shortly after the closure of the nation's public schools, many schools also began operating largely or exclusively remotely, which required increased online access to technology and high-speed internet connectivity by students and their families to maintain acceptable student learning and communication levels with school leaders, teachers, and other relevant staff. In this new, radically different, and possibly long-term remote or hybrid educational landscape, there were

106. Family Rights and Privacy Act (Buckley Amendment), 20 U.S.C.A.A. §1232 (h) and 34 C.F.R. §300.500–517.

many unique, additional, and enduring challenges presented to the nation's most vulnerable student populations, including students with disabilities. At the onset of school closures, local school officials desperately needed federal guidance regarding the provision of special education and related services to eligible students during the coronavirus pandemic.

At its initial peak in Spring 2020, COVID-19 resulted in "a near-total shutdown of school buildings" as well as "an historic upheaval of K-12 schooling in the United States."[107] It is reported that the closures affected at least 55.1 million students across 124,000 U.S. public and private schools.[108] Nearly every state in the country either ordered or recommended that schools remain closed through the end of the 2020 school year.[109] This sudden and extreme shift in the provision of special education and related services to eligible students resulted in monumental and never-before-encountered issues and decisions for school leaders, educators, and special education students, as well as federal, state, and local officials. As of the time of this writing, these issues continue to persist as the nation ponders the constantly changing landscape of whether and how schools will reopen safely, in the absence of a widely available COVID-19 vaccine.

The coronavirus pandemic has "forced a sudden and widespread shift to online learning" which, according to Pew Research Center, "has been especially challenging for the nation's nearly 7 million disabled students."[110] Instruction and support for many special education students are arguably not as easily transferred to online-learning teaching modalities. Even students who were previously enrolled in or attending online programs faced changes to the delivery of certain related services and face-to-face services as a result of state-mandated quarantine and "shut-down" orders. These changes have resulted in new challenges and opportunities for school entities, parents, and students with disabilities.[111]

Federal Guidelines for the Provision of Special Education During COVID-19

While it is important to point out that guidance documents issued by the U.S. Department of Education (DOE) are neither legally binding nor have the force of law, these documents often serve as invaluable resources for today's educational

107. *Map: Coronavirus and School Closures*, Educ. Week (updated Sept. 15, 2020), https://www.edweek.org/ew/section/multimedia/map-coronavirus-and-school-closures.html.

108. *Id.*

109. *Id.*

110. *See* Katherine Schaeffer, *As Schools Shift to Online Learning Amid Pandemic, Here's What We Know About Disabled Students in the U.S.*, Pew Res. Ctr. (Apr. 23, 2020), https://www.pewresearch.org/fact-tank/2020/04/23/as-schools-shift-to-online-learning-amid-pandemic-heres-what-we-know-about-disabled-students-in-the-u-s/.

111. *Id.*

practitioners, parents, and others who work closely with students with disabilities because of their ability to convey existing special education legal mandates in a concise and readable format. Shortly after the nationwide closure of public schools, on March 12, 2020, the DOE issued its first of two detailed statements providing an interpretation of federal special education law in light of the special circumstances imposed by the COVID-19 pandemic.[112] This fact sheet stressed the importance of meeting the specified legal mandates required of the Individuals with Disabilities Education Act during the new shift to remote learning necessitated by the coronavirus pandemic. Specifically, the DOE's question-and-answer document stated:

> If a [local educational agency, typically a school district (LEA)] continues to provide educational opportunities to the general student population during a school closure [i.e., by providing online learning], the school must ensure that students with disabilities also have equal access to the same opportunities, including the provision of [free appropriate public education].

Unfortunately, the DOE's March 12 statement was misinterpreted by some state and local education agencies across the country as meaning that public schools should not offer online learning opportunities for any students based on the schools' perceived inability to meet the legal requirements of both IDEA and the ADA. Some school district officials reasoned that they could alleviate themselves of the legal obligation requiring that schools provide a free and appropriate public education to all eligible students with disabilities if they withheld instruction, including online instruction, from the general student population.[113] Basically, the DOE document advised state and local school agencies that if student learning was interrupted for general education students in a school district due to COVID-19, then the same school district had no legal obligation to provide Individualized Education Plan services to eligible students with disabilities. Moreover, if a school district was unable to provide special education and related services, once school resumed, compensatory education would be due to the students with disabilities. The term "compensatory services" is a legal remedy that ensures a particular student remains where they would have been educationally but for the interruption and disruption caused by the pandemic and the closure of public schools. Based on this interpretation, some public school students with and without disabilities were not receiving any educational services during all of part of the time schools were closed. Additionally, the fact sheet indicated that IEP teams were not required to meet in person while schools were closed and, where evaluations required face-to-face assessment or observation, the evaluation would need to be delayed until the school building reopened.[114]

112. Julie Weatherly, Phyllis Wolfram, & Suzanne E. Eckes, *Special Education and FAPE in the Age of COVID-19* (Sept. 2020), https://www.nassp.org/publication/principal-leadership/volume-21-2020-2021/principal-leadership-september-2020/legal-matters-september-2020/.

113. *Id.*

114. *Id.*

To address growing confusion among state and local school officials resulting from the March 12 guidance document, the DOE along with the Office of Civil Rights and the Office of Special Education and Rehabilitative Services (OSERS) jointly issued a statement attempting to clarify the DOE's earlier interpretation of federal special education law, stating:

> A serious misunderstanding . . . has recently circulated within the educational community. As school districts nationwide take necessary steps to protect the health and safety of their students, many are moving to virtual or online education (distance instruction). Some educators, however, have been reluctant to provide any distance instruction because they believe that federal disability law presents insurmountable barriers to remote education. This is simply not true. To be clear: ensuring compliance with [federal special education law] . . . should not prevent any school from offering educational programs through distance instruction.[115]

In this March 21 memo, the DOE explicitly indicated that even in the time of COVID-19, school "districts must provide a [FAPE] consistent with the need to protect the health and safety of students with disabilities and those individuals providing education, specialized instruction, and related services to these students." The March 21 document also expressly afforded school officials considerable flexibility in making determinations regarding how best to meet the individualized needs of students with disabilities and that the "determination of how FAPE is to be provided may need to be different in this time of unprecedented national emergency."[116]

The COVID-19 Pandemic Education Relief Act of 2020, included as Title III-B of the CARES Act, provided for waivers primarily related to the Elementary and Secondary Education Act (ESEA). Section 3511 of the CARES Act allows the Secretary, upon request of a state educational agency (SEA), local educational agency (LEA), or Indian tribe, to grant waivers of various statutory or regulatory provisions if the Secretary determines that such a waiver is necessary and appropriate due to the coronavirus pandemic.

The Department did not request waiver authority for any core tenets of the IDEA or Section 504 of the Rehabilitation Act of 1973, most notably a free appropriate public education in the least restrictive environment. The Department's position was based on the principles that schools can, and must, provide education to all students, including children with disabilities; the health and safety of children, students, educators, and service providers must be the first consideration; the needs and best interests of the individual student, not any system, should guide decisions and expenditures; parents or recipients of services must be informed of and be involved in decisions relating to the provision of services; and services typically provided in

115. U.S. Dep't of Educ., *Supplemental Fact Sheet Addressing the Risk of COVID-19 in Preschool, Elementary and Secondary Schools While Serving Children with Disabilities* (March 21, 2020).

116. *Id.*

person may now need to be provided through alternative methods requiring creative and innovative approaches.

Litigation Resulting from COVID-19 and Providing Special Education Services

Even as the COVID-19 pandemic is still unfolding as of the time of this writing, class action lawsuits related to the coronavirus have already begun. On March 13, 2020, for example, Pennsylvania Governor Tom Wolf ordered the statewide closure of Pennsylvania's public schools. On March 19, 2020, Governor Wolf issued another Executive Order preventing business from operating in Pennsylvania which are not "life-sustaining" in the midst of the COVID pandemic. In *Benner v. Wolf*,[117] parents claimed that the governor's school closure order denied all Pennsylvania school-age children the right to a public education, as Pennsylvanians have the right to a public education provided by the Commonwealth under Pennsylvania's Constitution: "The General Assembly shall provide for the maintenance and support of a thorough and efficient system of public education to serve the needs of the Commonwealth."[118] The parents admitted that their school children were receiving education from their schools via distance learning during the pandemic; however, they argued that "this [was] not a thorough or efficient education." On May 21, 2020, U.S. District Judge John E. Jones III denied the plaintiffs' request for a temporary restraining order, stating: "It is not the place of this Court to question the reasonable motives of elected officials, nor can we grant petitioners' motion based largely upon their political disagreements with the same."[119]

Another legal complaint filed on May 18, 2020, in the U.S. District Court for the Eastern District of Pennsylvania on behalf of two students, alleged that the Pennsylvania DOE "intentionally and/or with deliberate indifference has failed to ensure that the students of the Plaintiff Class II have received a free appropriate public education, or FAPE, and were free from discrimination on the basis of their disabilities."[120] The legal suit requested class action status to represent the "hundreds if not thousands" of nonverbal and partially verbal students who received augmented or alternative communication supports in public schools in Pennsylvania. The complaint admitted that the named students' teachers and therapists in the Central Bucks School District made "heroic efforts" to offer students with disabilities online learning after the school system closed to in-person classes on March 16, 2020. Both students named in the complaint had allegedly had their instruction and therapy reduced following the district's transition to online learning. Plaintiffs in this matter were asking the Court to require that the governor classify in-person education as a "life-sustaining"

117. 461 F. Supp. 3d 154 (M.D. Pa. 2020).
118. PA. CONST. ART. 3, § 14.
119. 461 F. Supp. 3d at 168.
120. Doe v. Wolf, *et. al.*, No. 20-CV-02320 (E.D. Pa. May 18, 2020).

activity and to award compensatory damages and reasonable costs and expenses pursuant to 34 C.F.R. §330.517, 29 U.S.C. §794a(b), 42 U.S.C §12205, and Fed. R. Civ. Proc. 23(h). However, on June 10, 2020 the plaintiffs voluntarily withdrew their complaint as moot and the court dismissed the case without prejudice.

On April 13, 2020, a legal complaint was filed representing a class of roughly 30,000 special needs children in Hawaii who were eligible for services under IDEA and Section 504 of the Rehabilitation Act of 1974.[121] The federal suit named the Hawaii Department of Education and alleged that students were being denied a free and appropriate public education due to school closures. The requested relief included a court-ordered process to determine the compensatory education a child needs to make up for lost educational services during school shutdowns. The suit alleged the Hawaii DOE and the Hawaiian courts would be flooded with due process complaints from parents after the shutdown ended. At issue were the alleged issues with distance learning for special education students and the implementation of a student's IEP. At an August 14, 2020, scheduling conference, the parties held a discussion concerning the possibility of formulating a specific process to assess the educational needs of proposed class members and to tailor educational plans that might resolve the dispute.

On May 19, 2020, the Chicago Teachers Union filed suit in the Northern District of Illinois against U.S. Secretary of Education Betsy DeVos and the Chicago Board of Education, claiming the lack of waivers or requested flexibility under IDEA and Section 504 of the Rehabilitation Action of 1973 "impose[d] unnecessary or impossible burdens" on union members.[122] Among the requested relief, the union asked the court to grant it an injunction against the Chicago Board of Education and the Department of Education, so that it would not be required to strictly follow IEP and Section 504 guidelines during the 2020 pandemic's remote learning period. On June 19, 2020, the union's request for a preliminary injunction was denied.

On August 7, 2020, a nationwide group of parents of students identified as students with disabilities qualifying for services under the Individuals with Disabilities Act filed a class action lawsuit naming every public school district in the country.[123] The plaintiffs sought a court order to either reopen schools to provide students with disabilities in-person services or to provide "pendency vouchers" or compensatory education for services unable to be rendered during the pandemic. This case was filed in the Federal District Court of the Southern District of New York and named as lead defendants the Mayor of New York City and the Chancellor of New York City's Department of Education. While the facts recited by the plaintiffs follow the school closure actions taken by politicians in New York City and New York state, the plaintiffs alleged that similar actions were taken all over the country following

121. W.G. v. Kishimoto, No. 20-CV- 00154, (D. Haw. April 13, 2020).

122. Chi. Teachers. Union v. DeVos., No. 1:20-cv-02958 (N.D. Illinois, May 19, 2020).

123. J.T., et al. v. Bill de Blasio, et al., No. 20 Civ. 5878 (CM), 2020 U.S. Dist. LEXIS 212663 (S.D.N.Y. Nov. 13, 2020).

New York's lead. They did not, however, detail those actions nor state what services plaintiffs should have received but did not receive due to the school shutdowns.

After the legal complaint was filed, the court, without being prompted by a party to the action, issued a "Rule to Show Cause" expressing doubt that it had jurisdiction over school districts in the 49 states other than New York and requested that the plaintiffs write a brief on why the complaint should not be dismissed against school districts outside of New York City. On October 14, 2020, the Court ordered a stay pending decision on outstanding motions to dismiss the case.

Selected Case Law

[5-1] *Board of Education of the Hendrick Hudson Central School District v. Rowley*

[5-2] *Endrew F. v. Douglas County School District*

[5-3] *Irving Independent School District v. Tatro*

[5-4] *Honig v. Doe*

[Case No. 5-1]

The Free and Appropriate Public Education (FAPE) clause of the IDEA does not require a state to maximize the potential of each child with a disability.

Board of Education of the Hendrick Hudson Central School District v. Rowley

Supreme Court of the United States
458 U.S. 176 (1982)

Justice REHNQUIST delivered the opinion of the Court.

This case presents a question of statutory interpretation. Petitioners contend that the Court of Appeals and the District Court misconstrued the requirements imposed by Congress upon States which receive federal funds under the Education of the Handicapped Act. We agree and reverse the judgment of the Court of Appeals.

I

The Education of the Handicapped Act (Act) [now IDEA] . . . provides federal money to assist state and local agencies in educating handicapped children, and conditions such funding upon a State's compliance with extensive goals and procedures. The Act represents an ambitious federal effort to promote the education of handicapped children, . . . The Act's evolution and major provisions shed light on the question of statutory interpretation which is at the heart of this case. . . .

In order to qualify for federal financial assistance under the Act, a State must demonstrate that it "has in effect a policy that assures all handicapped children the right to a free appropriate public education." . . .

The "free appropriate public education" required by the Act is tailored to the unique needs of the handicapped child by means of an "individualized educational program" (IEP).... The IEP, which is prepared at a meeting between a qualified representative of the local educational agency, the child's teacher, the child's parents or guardian, and, where appropriate, the child, consists of a written document....

II

This case arose in connection with the education of Amy Rowley, a deaf student at the Furnace Woods School in the Hendrick Hudson Central School District, Peekskill, N.Y. Amy has minimal residual hearing and is an excellent lipreader. During the year before she began attending Furnace Woods, a meeting between her parents and school administrators resulted in a decision to place her in a regular kindergarten class in order to determine what supplemental services would be necessary to her education. Several members of the school administration prepared for Amy's arrival by attending a course in sign-language interpretation, and a teletype machine was installed in the principal's office to facilitate communication with her parents who are also deaf. At the end of the trial period it was determined that Amy should remain in the kindergarten class, but that she should be provided with an FM hearing aid which would amplify words spoken into a wireless receiver by the teacher or fellow students during certain classroom activities. Amy successfully completed her kindergarten year.

As required by the Act, an IEP was prepared for Amy during the fall of her first-grade year. The IEP provided that Amy should be educated in a regular classroom at Furnace Woods, should continue to use the FM hearing aid, and should receive instruction from a tutor for the deaf for one hour each day and from a speech therapist for three hours each week. The Rowleys agreed with parts of the IEP, but insisted that Amy also be provided a qualified sign-language interpreter in all her academic classes in lieu of the assistance proposed in other parts of the IEP. Such an interpreter had been placed in Amy's kindergarten class for a 2-week experimental period, but the interpreter had reported that Amy did not need his services at that time. The school administrators likewise concluded that Amy did not need such an interpreter in her first-grade classroom. They reached this conclusion after consulting the school district's Committee on the Handicapped, which had received expert evidence from Amy's parents on the importance of a sign-language interpreter, received testimony from Amy's teacher and other persons familiar with her academic and social progress, and visited a class for the deaf.

When their request for an interpreter was denied, the Rowleys demanded and received a hearing before an independent examiner. After receiving evidence from both sides, the examiner agreed with the administrators' determination that an interpreter was not necessary because "Amy was achieving educationally, academically, and socially" without such assistance.... The examiner's decision was affirmed on appeal by the New York Commissioner of Education on the basis of substantial evidence in the record.... Pursuant to the Act's provision for judicial review, the Rowleys then brought an action in the United States District Court for the Southern District of New York, claiming that the administrators' denial of the sign-language interpreter constituted a denial of the "free appropriate public education" guaranteed by the Act.

The District Court found that Amy "is a remarkably well-adjusted child" who interacts and communicates well with her classmates and has "developed an extraordinary rapport" with her teachers.... It also found that "she performs better than the average child in her class and is advancing easily from grade to grade," but "that she understands considerably less of what goes on in class than she could if she were not deaf" and thus "is not learning as much, or performing as well academically, as she would without her handicap," This disparity between Amy's achievement and her potential led the court to decide that she was not receiving a "free appropriate public education," which the court defined as "an opportunity to achieve [her] full potential commensurate with the opportunity provided to other children." ... According to the District Court, such a standard "requires that the potential of the handicapped child be measured and compared to his or her performance, and that the resulting differential or 'shortfall' be compared to the shortfall experienced by nonhandicapped children." The District Court's definition arose from its assumption that the responsibility for "giv[ing] content to the requirement of an 'appropriate education'" had "been left entirely to the [federal] courts and the hearing officers." ...

A divided panel of the United States Court of Appeals for the Second Circuit affirmed. The Court of Appeals "agree[d] with the [D]istrict [C]ourt's conclusions of law," and held that its "findings of fact [were] not clearly erroneous." ...

We granted certiorari to review the lower courts' interpretation of the Act.... Such review requires us to consider two questions: What is meant by the Act's requirement of a "free appropriate public education"? And what is the role of state and federal courts in exercising the review granted by [the Act]? We consider these questions separately.

III

A

This is the first case in which this Court has been called upon to interpret any provision of the Act. As noted previously, the District Court and the Court of Appeals concluded that "[t]he Act itself does not define 'appropriate education,'" ... but leaves "to the courts and the hearing officers" the responsibility of "giv[ing] content to the requirement of an 'appropriate education....'" Petitioners contend that the definition of the phrase "free appropriate public education" used by the courts below overlooks the definition of that phrase actually found in the Act. Respondents agree that the Act defines "free appropriate public education," but contend that the statutory definition is not "functional" and thus "offers judges no guidance in their consideration of controversies involving 'the identification, evaluation, or educational placement of the child or the provision of a free appropriate public education....'" The United States, appearing as *amicus curiae* on behalf of respondents, states that "[a]lthough the Act includes definitions of a 'free appropriate public education' and other related terms, the statutory definitions do not adequately explain what is meant by 'appropriate.' . . ."

We are loath to conclude that Congress failed to offer any assistance in defining the meaning of the principal substantive phrase used in the Act. It is beyond dispute that, contrary to the conclusions of the courts below, the Act does expressly define "free appropriate public education":

> "The term 'free appropriate public education' means *special education* and *related services* which (A) have been provided at public expense, under public supervision and direction, and without charge, (B) meet the standards of the State educational agency, (C) include an appropriate preschool, elementary, or secondary school education in the State involved, and (D) are provided in conformity with the individualized education program required under [this Act]."
>
> "Special education," as referred to in this definition, means "specially designed instruction, at no cost to parents or guardians, to meet the unique needs of a handicapped child, including classroom instruction, instruction in physical education, home instruction, and instruction in hospitals and institutions." . . "Related services" are defined as "transportation, and such developmental, corrective, and other supportive services . . . as may be required to assist a handicapped child to benefit from special education."

Like many statutory definitions, this one tends toward the cryptic rather than the comprehensive, but that is scarcely a reason for abandoning the quest for legislative intent.

According to the definitions contained in the Act, a "free appropriate public education" consists of educational instruction specially designed to meet the unique needs of the handicapped child, supported by such services as are necessary to permit the child "to benefit" from the instruction. Almost as a checklist for adequacy under the Act, the definition also requires that such instruction and services be provided at public expense and under public supervision, meet the State's educational standards, approximate the grade levels used in the State's regular education, and comport with the child's IEP. Thus, if personalized instruction is being provided with sufficient supportive services to permit the child to benefit from the instruction, and the other items on the definitional checklist are satisfied, the child is receiving a "free appropriate public education" as defined by the Act.

Other portions of the statute also shed light upon congressional intent. Congress found that of the roughly eight million handicapped children in the United States at the time of enactment, one million were "excluded entirely from the public school system" and more than half were receiving an inappropriate education. . . . When these express statutory findings and priorities are read together with the Act's extensive procedural requirements and its definition of "free appropriate public education," the face of the statute evinces a congressional intent to bring previously excluded handicapped children into the public education systems of the States and to require the States to adopt *procedures* which would result in individualized consideration of and instruction for each child.

Noticeably absent from the language of the statute is any substantive standard prescribing the level of education to be accorded handicapped children. Certainly the language of the statute contains no requirement like the one imposed by the lower courts-that States maximize the potential of handicapped children "commensurate with the opportunity provided to other children." ... That standard was expounded by the District Court without reference to the statutory definitions or even to the legislative history of the Act. Although we find the statutory definition of "free appropriate public education" to be helpful in our interpretation of the Act, there remains the question of whether the legislative history indicates a congressional intent that such education meet some additional substantive standard. For an answer, we turn to that history.

B

(i)

... By passing the Act, Congress sought primarily to make public education available to handicapped children. But in seeking to provide such access to public education, Congress did not impose upon the States any greater substantive educational standard than would be necessary to make such access meaningful. Indeed, Congress expressly "recognize[d] that in many instances the process of providing special education and related services to handicapped children is not guaranteed to produce any particular outcome." ... Thus, the intent of the Act was more to open the door of public education to handicapped children on appropriate terms than to guarantee any particular level of education once inside.

Both the House and the Senate Reports attribute the impetus for the Act and its predecessors to two federal-court judgments rendered in 1971 and 1972. As the Senate Report states, passage of the Act "followed a series of landmark court cases establishing in law the right to education for all handicapped children." ... The first case, *Pennsylvania Assn. for Retarded Children v. Commonwealth* (*PARC*), was a suit on behalf of retarded children challenging the constitutionality of a Pennsylvania statute which acted to exclude them from public education and training. The case ended in a consent decree which enjoined the State from "deny[ing] to any mentally retarded child *access* to a free public program of education and training." ...

PARC was followed by *Mills v. Board of Education of District of Columbia*, ... a case in which the plaintiff handicapped children had been excluded from the District of Columbia public schools. The court's judgment ... provided that

> "no [handicapped] child eligible for a publicly supported education in the District of Columbia public schools shall be *excluded* from a regular school assignment by a Rule, policy, or practice of the Board of Education of the District of Columbia or its agents unless such child is provided (a) *adequate* alternative educational services suited to the child's needs, which may include special education or tuition grants, and (b) a constitutionally

adequate prior hearing and periodic review of the child's status, progress, and the *adequacy* of any educational alternative." . . .

Mills and *PARC* both held that handicapped children must be given *access* to an adequate, publicly supported education. Neither case purports to require any particular substantive level of education. Rather, like the language of the Act, the cases set forth extensive procedures to be followed in formulating personalized educational programs for handicapped children. . . . The fact that both *PARC* and *Mills* are discussed at length in the legislative Reports suggests that the principles which they established are the principles which, to a significant extent, guided the drafters of the Act. Indeed, immediately after discussing these cases the Senate Report describes the 1974 statute as having "incorporated the major principles of the right to education cases." . . . Those principles in turn became the basis of the Act, which itself was designed to effectuate the purposes of the 1974 statute. . . .

That the Act imposes no clear obligation upon recipient States beyond the requirement that handicapped children receive some form of specialized education is perhaps best demonstrated by the fact that Congress, in explaining the need for the Act, equated an "appropriate education" to the receipt of some specialized educational services. . . .

(ii)

Respondents contend that "the goal of the Act is to provide each handicapped child with an equal educational opportunity." . . . We think, however, that the requirement that a State provide specialized educational services to handicapped children generates no additional requirement that the services so provided be sufficient to maximize each child's potential "commensurate with the opportunity provided other children . . ." and the United States correctly note that Congress sought "to provide assistance to the States in carrying out their responsibilities under . . . the Constitution of the United States to provide equal protection of the laws." . . . But we do not think that such statements imply a congressional intent to achieve strict equality of opportunity or services.

The educational opportunities provided by our public school systems undoubtedly differ from student to student, depending upon a myriad of factors that might affect a particular student's ability to assimilate information presented in the classroom. The requirement that States provide "equal" educational opportunities would thus seem to present an entirely unworkable standard requiring impossible measurements and comparisons. Similarly, furnishing handicapped children with only such services as are available to nonhandicapped children would in all probability fall short of the statutory requirement of "free appropriate public education"; to require, on the other hand, the furnishing of every special service necessary to maximize each handicapped child's potential is, we think, further than Congress intended to go. Thus to speak in terms of "equal" services in one instance gives less than what is required by the Act and in another instance more. The theme of the Act is "free appropriate public education," a phrase which is too complex to be captured by the word "equal" whether one is speaking of opportunities or services.

The legislative conception of the requirements of equal protection was undoubtedly informed by the two District Court decisions referred to above. But cases such as *Mills* and *PARC* held simply that handicapped children may not be excluded entirely from public education. In *Mills,* the District Court said:

> "If sufficient funds are not available to finance all of the services and programs that are needed and desirable in the system then the available funds must be expended equitably in such a manner that no child is entirely excluded from a publicly supported education consistent with his needs and ability to benefit therefrom." . . .

The *PARC* court used similar language, saying "[i]t is the commonwealth's obligation to place each mentally retarded child in a free, public program of education and training appropriate to the child's capacity." . . . The right of access to free public education enunciated by these cases is significantly different from any notion of absolute equality of opportunity regardless of capacity. To the extent that Congress might have looked further than these cases which are mentioned in the legislative history, at the time of enactment of the Act this Court had held at least twice that the Equal Protection Clause of the Fourteenth Amendment does not require States to expend equal financial resources on the education of each child. . . .

In explaining the need for federal legislation, the House Report noted that "no congressional legislation has required a precise guarantee for handicapped children, i.e. a basic floor of opportunity that would bring into compliance all school districts with the constitutional right of equal protection with respect to handicapped children." Assuming that the Act was designed to fill the need identified in the House Report-that is, to provide a "basic floor of opportunity" consistent with equal protection-neither the Act nor its history persuasively demonstrates that Congress thought that equal protection required anything more than equal access. Therefore, Congress' desire to provide specialized educational services, even in furtherance of "equality," cannot be read as imposing any particular substantive educational standard upon the States.

The District Court and the Court of Appeals thus erred when they held that the Act requires New York to maximize the potential of each handicapped child commensurate with the opportunity provided nonhandicapped children. Desirable though that goal might be, it is not the standard that Congress imposed upon States which receive funding under the Act. Rather, Congress sought primarily to identify and evaluate handicapped children, and to provide them with access to a free public education.

(iii)

Implicit in the congressional purpose of providing access to a "free appropriate public education" is the requirement that the education to which access is provided be sufficient to confer some educational benefit upon the handicapped child. It would do little good for Congress to spend millions of dollars in providing access to a public education only to have the handicapped child receive no benefit from that education. The statutory definition of "free appropriate public education," in addition to requiring that States provide each child with "specially designed instruction," expressly requires the provision of "such . . . supportive services . . . as may be required to assist a handicapped child *to benefit* from special education." . . . We therefore conclude that the "basic floor of opportunity" provided by the Act consists of access to specialized instruction and related services which are individually designed to provide educational benefit to the handicapped child. . . .

The determination of when handicapped children are receiving sufficient educational benefits to satisfy the requirements of the Act presents a more difficult problem. The Act requires participating States to educate a wide spectrum of handicapped children, from the marginally hearing-impaired to the profoundly retarded and palsied. It is clear that the benefits obtainable by children at one end of the spectrum will differ dramatically from those obtainable by children at the other end, with infinite variations in between. One child may have little difficulty competing successfully in an academic setting with nonhandicapped children while another child may encounter great difficulty in acquiring even the most basic of self-maintenance skills. We do not attempt today to establish any one test for determining the adequacy of educational benefits conferred upon all children covered by the Act. Because in this case we are presented with a handicapped child who is receiving substantial specialized instruction and related services, and who is performing above average in the regular classrooms of a public school system, we confine our analysis to that situation.

The Act requires participating States to educate handicapped children with nonhandicapped children whenever possible. When that "mainstreaming" preference of the Act has been met and a child is being educated in the regular classrooms of a public school system, the system itself monitors the educational progress of the child. Regular examinations are administered, grades are awarded, and yearly advancement to higher grade levels is permitted for those children who attain an adequate knowledge of the course material. The grading and advancement system thus constitutes an important factor in determining educational benefit. Children who graduate from our public school systems are considered by our society to have been "educated" at least to the grade level they have completed, and access to an "education" for handicapped children is precisely what Congress sought to provide in the Act.

C

When the language of the Act and its legislative history are considered together, the requirements imposed by Congress become tolerably clear. Insofar as a State is required to provide a handicapped child with a "free appropriate public education," we hold that it satisfies this requirement by providing personalized instruction with sufficient support services to permit the child to benefit educationally from that instruction. Such instruction and services must be provided at public expense, must meet the State's educational standards, must approximate the grade levels used in the State's regular education, and must comport with the child's IEP. In addition, the IEP, and therefore the personalized instruction, should be formulated in accordance with the requirements of the Act and, if the child is being educated in the regular classrooms of the public education system, should be reasonably calculated to enable the child to achieve passing marks and advance from grade to grade. . . .

IV

A

As mentioned in Part I, the Act permits "[a]ny party aggrieved by the findings and decision" of the state administrative hearings "to bring a civil action" in "any State court of competent jurisdiction or in a district court of the United States without regard to the amount in controversy." The complaint, and therefore the civil action, may concern "any matter relating to the identification, evaluation, or educational placement of the child, or the provision of a free appropriate public education to such child." . . . In reviewing the complaint, the Act provides that a court "shall receive the record of the [state] administrative proceedings, shall hear additional evidence at the request of a party, and, basing its decision on the preponderance of the evidence, shall grant such relief as the court determines is appropriate." . . .

The parties disagree sharply over the meaning of these provisions, petitioners contending that courts are given only limited authority to review for state compliance with the Act's procedural requirements and no power to review the substance of the state program, and respondents contending that the Act requires courts to exercise *de novo* review over state educational decisions and policies. We find petitioners' contention unpersuasive, for Congress expressly rejected provisions that would have so severely restricted the role of reviewing courts. In substituting the current language of the statute for language that would have made state administrative findings conclusive if supported by substantial evidence, the Conference Committee explained that courts were to make "independent decision[s] based on a preponderance of the evidence." . . .

But although we find that this grant of authority is broader than claimed by petitioners, we think the fact that it is found in § 1415, which is entitled "Procedural safeguards," is not without significance. When the elaborate and highly specific procedural safeguards embodied in § 1415 are contrasted with the general and somewhat imprecise substantive admonitions contained in the Act, we think that the importance Congress attached to these procedural safeguards cannot be gainsaid. It seems to us no exaggeration to say that Congress placed every bit as much emphasis upon compliance with procedures giving parents and guardians a large measure of participation at every stage of the administrative process, . . . as it did upon the measurement of the resulting IEP against a substantive standard. We think that the congressional emphasis upon full participation of concerned parties throughout the development of the IEP, as well as the requirements that state and local plans be submitted to the Secretary for approval, demonstrates the legislative conviction that adequate compliance with the procedures prescribed would in most cases assure much if not all of what Congress wished in the way of substantive content in an IEP.

Thus the provision that a reviewing court base its decision on the "preponderance of the evidence" is by no means an invitation to the courts to substitute their own notions of sound educational policy for those of the school authorities which they review. The very importance which Congress has attached to compliance with certain procedures in the preparation of an IEP would be frustrated if a court were permitted simply to set state decisions at nought. The fact that § 1415(e) requires that the reviewing court "receive the records of the [state] administrative proceedings" carries with it the implied requirement that due weight shall be given to these proceedings. And we find nothing in the Act to suggest that merely because Congress was rather sketchy in establishing substantive requirements, as opposed to procedural requirements for the preparation of an IEP, it intended that reviewing courts should have a free hand to impose substantive standards of review which cannot be derived from the Act itself. In short, the statutory authorization to grant "such relief as the court determines is appropriate" cannot be read without reference to the obligations, largely procedural in nature, which are imposed upon recipient States by Congress.

Therefore, a court's inquiry in suits brought under [the Act] is twofold. First, has the State complied with the procedures set forth in the Act? And second, is the individualized educational program developed through the Act's procedures reasonably calculated to enable the child to receive educational benefits? If these requirements are met, the State has complied with the obligations imposed by Congress and the courts can require no more.

B

In assuring that the requirements of the Act have been met, courts must be careful to avoid imposing their view of preferable educational methods upon the States. The primary responsibility for formulating the education to be accorded a handicapped child, and for choosing the educational method most suitable to the child's needs, was left by the Act to state and local educational agencies in cooperation with the parents or guardian of the child....

We previously have cautioned that courts lack the "specialized knowledge and experience" necessary to resolve "persistent and difficult questions of educational policy." ... We think that Congress shared that view when it passed the Act. As already demonstrated, Congress' intention was not that the Act displace the primacy of States in the field of education, but that States receive funds to assist them in extending their educational systems to the handicapped. Therefore, once a court determines that the requirements of the Act have been met, questions of methodology are for resolution by the States.

V

Entrusting a child's education to state and local agencies does not leave the child without protection. Congress sought to protect individual children by providing for parental involvement in the development of state plans and policies ... and in the formulation of the child's individual educational program.... As this very case demonstrates, parents and guardians will not lack ardor in seeking to ensure that handicapped children receive all of the benefits to which they are entitled by the Act.

VI

Applying these principles to the facts of this case, we conclude that the Court of Appeals erred in affirming the decision of the District Court. Neither the District Court nor the Court of Appeals found that petitioners had failed to comply with the procedures of the Act, and the findings of neither court would support a conclusion that Amy's educational program failed to comply with the substantive requirements of the Act. On the contrary, the District Court found that the "evidence firmly establishes that Amy is receiving an 'adequate' education, since she performs better than the average child in her class and is advancing easily from grade to grade." . . . In light of this finding, and of the fact that Amy was receiving personalized instruction and related services calculated by the Furnace Woods school administrators to meet her educational needs, the lower courts should not have concluded that the Act requires the provision of a sign-language interpreter. Accordingly, the decision of the Court of Appeals is reversed, and the case is remanded for further proceedings consistent with this opinion.

So ordered.

[Case No. 5-2]

Clarified existing FAPE standard requiring that a school district must offer an Individual Education Plan (IEP) that is "reasonably calculated to enable a child to make progress in light of the child's circumstances."

Endrew F. v. Douglas County School District

Supreme Court of the United States
137 S. Ct. 988 (2017)

Chief Justice ROBERTS delivered the opinion of the Court.

Thirty-five years ago, this Court held that the Individuals with Disabilities Education Act establishes a substantive right to a "free appropriate public education" for certain children with disabilities. *Board of Ed. of Hendrick Hudson Central School Dist., Westchester Cty. v. Rowley*, 458 U.S. 176 (1982). We declined, however, to endorse any one standard for determining "when handicapped children are receiving sufficient educational benefits to satisfy the requirements of the Act." *Id.*, at 202, 102 S. Ct. 3034. That "more difficult problem" is before us today.

I

A

The Individuals with Disabilities Education Act (IDEA or Act) offers States federal funds to assist in educating children with disabilities. In exchange for the funds, a State pledges to comply with a number of statutory conditions. Among them, the State must provide a free appropriate public education—a FAPE, for short—to all eligible children.

A FAPE, as the Act defines it, includes both "special education" and "related services. "Special education" is "specially designed instruction . . . to meet the unique needs of a child with a disability"; "related services" are the support services "required to assist a child . . . to benefit from" that instruction. A State covered by the IDEA must provide a disabled child with such special education and related services "in conformity with the [child's] individualized education program," or IEP.

. . .

The IDEA requires that every IEP include "a statement of the child's present levels of academic achievement and functional performance," describe "how the child's disability affects the child's involvement and progress in the general education curriculum," and set out "measurable annual goals, including academic and functional goals," along with a "description of how the child's progress toward meeting" those goals will be gauged. The IEP must also describe the "special education and related services . . . that will be provided" so that the child may "advance appropriately toward attaining the annual goals" and, when possible, "be involved in and make progress in the general education curriculum."

B

In view of Amy Rowley's excellent progress and the "substantial" suite of specialized instruction and services offered in her IEP, we concluded that her program satisfied the FAPE requirement. But we went no further. Instead, we expressly "confine[d] our analysis" to the facts of the case before us. Observing that the Act requires States to "educate a wide spectrum" of children with disabilities and that "the benefits obtainable by children at one end of the spectrum will differ dramatically from those obtainable by children at the other end," we declined "to establish any one test for determining the adequacy of educational benefits conferred upon all children covered by the Act."

C

Petitioner Endrew F. was diagnosed with autism at age two. Autism is a neurodevelopmental disorder generally marked by impaired social and communicative skills, "engagement in repetitive activities and stereotyped movements, resistance to environmental change or change in daily routines, and unusual responses to sensory experiences. A child with autism qualifies as a "[c]hild with a disability" under the IDEA, and Colorado (where Endrew resides) accepts IDEA funding. Endrew is therefore entitled to the benefits of the Act, including a FAPE provided by the State.

Endrew attended school in respondent Douglas County School District from preschool through fourth grade. Each year, his IEP Team drafted an IEP addressed to his educational and functional needs. By Endrew's fourth grade year, however, his parents had become dissatisfied with his progress. Although Endrew displayed a number of strengths—his teachers described him as a humorous child with a "sweet disposition" who "show[ed] concern[ ] for friends"—he still "exhibited multiple behaviors that inhibited his ability to access learning in the classroom." Endrew would scream in class, climb over furniture and other students, and occasionally run away from school. He was afflicted by severe fears of commonplace things like flies, spills, and public restrooms. As Endrew's parents saw it, his academic and functional progress had essentially stalled: Endrew's IEPs largely carried over the same basic goals and objectives from one year to the next, indicating that he was failing to make meaningful progress toward his aims. His parents believed that only a thorough overhaul of the school district's approach to Endrew's behavioral problems could reverse the trend. But in April 2010, the school district presented Endrew's parents with a proposed fifth grade IEP that was, in their view, pretty much the same as his past ones. So his parents removed Endrew from public school and enrolled him at Firefly Autism House, a private school that specializes in educating children with autism.

Endrew did much better at Firefly. The school developed a "behavioral intervention plan" that identified Endrew's most problematic behaviors and set out particular strategies for addressing them. Firefly also added heft to Endrew's academic goals. Within months, Endrew's behavior improved significantly, permitting him to make a degree of academic progress that had eluded him in public school.

In November 2010, some six months after Endrew started classes at Firefly, his parents again met with representatives of the Douglas County School District. The district presented a new IEP. Endrew's parents considered the IEP no more adequate than the one proposed in April, and rejected it. They were particularly concerned that the stated plan for addressing Endrew's behavior did not differ meaningfully from the plan in his fourth grade IEP, despite the fact that his experience at Firefly suggested that he would benefit from a different approach.

Endrew's parents sought review in Federal District Court. Giving "due weight" to the decision of the ALJ, the District Court affirmed. The court acknowledged that Endrew's performance under past IEPs "did not reveal immense educational growth." But it concluded that annual modifications to Endrew's IEP objectives were "sufficient to show a pattern of, at the least, minimal progress." Because Endrew's previous IEPs had enabled him to make this sort of progress, the court reasoned, his latest, similar IEP was reasonably calculated to do the same thing. In the court's view, that was all *Rowley* demanded. The Tenth Circuit affirmed. The Court of Appeals recited language from *Rowley* stating that the instruction and services furnished to children with disabilities must be calculated to confer "*some* educational benefit." The court noted that it had long interpreted this language to mean that a child's IEP is adequate as long as it is calculated to confer an "educational benefit [that is] merely . . . more than *de minimis*." Applying this standard, the Tenth Circuit held that Endrew's IEP had been "reasonably calculated to enable [him] to make *some* progress." Accordingly, he had not been denied a FAPE.

We granted certiorari.

II

A

The Court in *Rowley* declined "to establish any one test for determining the adequacy of educational benefits conferred upon all children covered by the Act." The school district, however, contends that *Rowley* nonetheless established that "an IEP need not promise any particular *level* of benefit," so long as it is "'reasonably calculated' to provide *some* benefit, as opposed to *none*."

The district relies on several passages from *Rowley* to make its case. It points to our observation that "any substantive standard prescribing the level of education to be accorded" children with disabilities was "[n]oticeably absent from the language of the statute." The district also emphasizes the Court's statement that the Act requires States to provide access to instruction "sufficient to confer *some* educational benefit," reasoning that any benefit, however minimal, satisfies this mandate.). Finally, the district urges that the Court conclusively adopted a "some educational benefit" standard when it wrote that "the intent of the Act was more to open the door of public education to handicapped children ... than to guarantee any particular level of education."

These statements in isolation do support the school district's argument. But the district makes too much of them. Our statement that the face of the IDEA imposed no explicit substantive standard must be evaluated alongside our statement that a substantive standard was "implicit in the Act." Similarly, we find little significance in the Court's language concerning the requirement that States provide instruction calculated to "confer some educational benefit." The Court had no need to say anything more particular, since the case before it involved a child whose progress plainly demonstrated that her IEP was designed to deliver more than adequate educational benefits. The Court's principal concern was to correct what it viewed as the surprising rulings below: that the IDEA effectively empowers judges to elaborate a federal common law of public education, and that a child performing *better* than most in her class had been denied a FAPE. The Court was not concerned with precisely articulating a governing standard for closer cases. And the statement that the Act did not "guarantee any particular level of education" simply reflects the unobjectionable proposition that the IDEA cannot and does not promise "any particular [educational] outcome." No law could do that—for any child.

More important, the school district's reading of these isolated statements runs headlong into several points on which *Rowley* is crystal clear. For instance—just after saying that the Act requires instruction that is "sufficient to confer some educational benefit"—we noted that "[t]he determination of when handicapped children are receiving *sufficient* educational benefits ... presents a ... difficult problem." And then we expressly declined "to establish any one test for determining the *adequacy* of educational benefits" under the Act. It would not have been "difficult" for us to say when educational benefits are sufficient if we had just said that *any* educational benefit was enough. And it would have been strange to refuse to set out a test for the adequacy of educational benefits if we had just done exactly that. We cannot accept the school district's reading of *Rowley*.

B

While *Rowley* declined to articulate an overarching standard to evaluate the adequacy of the education provided under the Act, the decision and the statutory language point to a general approach: To meet its substantive obligation under the IDEA, a school must offer an IEP reasonably calculated to enable a child to make progress appropriate in light of the child's circumstances. The "reasonably calculated" qualification reflects a recognition that crafting an appropriate program of education requires a prospective judgment by school officials. The Act contemplates that this fact-intensive exercise will be informed not only by the expertise of school officials, but also by the input of the child's parents or guardians. Any review of an IEP must appreciate that the question is whether the IEP is *reasonable*, not whether the court regards it as ideal.

The IEP must aim to enable the child to make progress. After all, the essential function of an IEP is to set out a plan for pursuing academic and functional advancement. This reflects the broad purpose of the IDEA, an "ambitious" piece of legislation enacted "in response to Congress' perception that a majority of handicapped children in the United States 'were either totally excluded from schools or [were] sitting idly in regular classrooms awaiting the time when they were old enough to "drop out." A substantive standard not focused on student progress would do little to remedy the pervasive and tragic academic stagnation that prompted Congress to act. That the progress contemplated by the IEP must be appropriate in light of the child's circumstances should come as no surprise. A focus on the particular child is at the core of the IDEA. The instruction offered must be "*specially* designed" to meet a child's "*unique* needs" through an "[*i*]*ndividualized* education program." An IEP is not a form document. It is constructed only after careful consideration of the child's present levels of achievement, disability, and potential for growth. As we observed in *Rowley*, the IDEA "requires participating States to educate a wide spectrum of handicapped children," and "the benefits obtainable by children at one end of the spectrum will differ dramatically from those obtainable by children at the other end, with infinite variations in between." *Rowley* sheds light on what appropriate progress will look like in many cases. There, the Court recognized that the IDEA requires that children with disabilities receive education in the regular classroom "whenever possible." When this preference is met, "the system itself monitors the educational progress of the child." "Regular examinations are administered, grades are awarded, and yearly advancement to higher grade levels is permitted for those children who attain an adequate knowledge of the course material." Progress through this system is what our society generally means by an "education." And access to an "education" is what the IDEA promises. Accordingly, for a child fully integrated in the regular classroom, an IEP typically should, as *Rowley* put it, be "reasonably calculated to enable the child to achieve passing marks and advance from grade to grade."

This guidance is grounded in the statutory definition of a FAPE. One of the components of a FAPE is "special education," defined as "specially designed instruction . . . to meet the unique needs of a child with a disability." In determining what it means to "meet the unique needs" of a child with a disability, the provisions governing the IEP development process are a natural source of guidance: It is through the IEP that "[t]he 'free appropriate public education' required by the Act is tailored to the unique needs of" a particular child.

Rowley had no need to provide concrete guidance with respect to a child who is not fully integrated in the regular classroom and not able to achieve on grade level. That case concerned a young girl who was progressing smoothly through the regular curriculum. If that is not a reasonable prospect for a child, his IEP need not aim for grade-level advancement. But his educational program must be appropriately ambitious in light of his circumstances, just as advancement from grade to grade is appropriately ambitious for most children in the regular classroom. The goals may differ, but every child should have the chance to meet challenging objectives. Of course, this describes a general standard, not a formula. But whatever else can be said about it, this standard is markedly more demanding than the "merely more than *de minimis*" test applied by the Tenth Circuit. It cannot be the case that the Act typically aims for grade-level advancement for children with disabilities who can be educated in the regular classroom, but is satisfied with barely more than *de minimis* progress for those who cannot.

When all is said and done, a student offered an educational program providing "merely more than *de minimis*" progress from year to year can hardly be said to have been offered an education at all. For children with disabilities, receiving instruction that aims so low would be tantamount to "sitting idly . . . awaiting the time when they were old enough to 'drop out.' The IDEA demands more. It requires an educational program reasonably calculated to enable a child to make progress appropriate in light of the child's circumstances.

C

Endrew's parents argue that the Act goes even further. In their view, a FAPE is "an education that aims to provide a child with a disability opportunities to achieve academic success, attain self-sufficiency, and contribute to society that are substantially equal to the opportunities afforded children without disabilities."

This standard is strikingly similar to the one the lower courts adopted in *Rowley*, and it is virtually identical to the formulation advanced by Justice Blackmun in his separate writing in that case. Mindful that Congress (despite several intervening amendments to the IDEA) has not materially changed the statutory definition of a FAPE since *Rowley* was decided, we decline to interpret the FAPE provision in a manner so plainly at odds with the Court's analysis in that case.

D

We will not attempt to elaborate on what "appropriate" progress will look like from case to case. It is in the nature of the Act and the standard we adopt to resist such an effort: The adequacy of a given IEP turns on the unique circumstances of the child for whom it was created. This absence of a bright-line rule, however, should not be mistaken for "an invitation to the courts to substitute their own notions of sound educational policy for those of the school authorities which they review."

At the same time, deference is based on the application of expertise and the exercise of judgment by school authorities. The Act vests these officials with responsibility for decisions of critical importance to the life of a disabled child. The nature of the IEP process, from the initial consultation through state administrative proceedings, ensures that parents and school representatives will fully air their respective opinions on the degree of progress a child's IEP should pursue. By the time any dispute reaches court, school authorities will have had a complete opportunity to bring their expertise and judgment to bear on areas of disagreement. A reviewing court may fairly expect those authorities to be able to offer a cogent and responsive explanation for their decisions that shows the IEP is reasonably calculated to enable the child to make progress appropriate in light of his circumstances.

The judgment of the United States Court of Appeals for the Tenth Circuit is vacated, and the case is remanded for further proceedings consistent with this opinion.

[Case No. 5-3]

Under the IDEA, intermittent catherization for a child with spina bifida and who cannot urinate normally falls within the legal definition of a related service and is not considered a medical service.

Irving Independent School District v. Tatro

Supreme Court of the United States
468 U.S. 883 (1984)

Chief Justice BURGER delivered the opinion of the Court.

We granted certiorari to determine whether the Education of the Handicapped Act or the Rehabilitation Act of 1973 requires a school district to provide a handicapped child with clean intermittent catheterization during school hours.

I

Amber Tatro is an 8-year-old girl born with a defect known as spina bifida. As a result, she suffers from orthopedic and speech impairments and a neurogenic bladder, which prevents her from emptying her bladder voluntarily. Consequently, she must be catheterized every three or four hours to avoid injury to her kidneys. In accordance with accepted medical practice, clean intermittent catheterization (CIC), a procedure involving the insertion of a catheter into the urethra to drain the bladder, has been prescribed. The procedure is a simple one that may be performed in a few minutes by a layperson with less than an hour's training. Amber's parents, babysitter, and teenage brother are all qualified to administer CIC, and Amber soon will be able to perform this procedure herself.

In 1979 petitioner Irving Independent School District agreed to provide special education for Amber, who was then three and one-half years old. In consultation with her parents, who are respondents here, petitioner developed an individualized education program for Amber under the requirements of the Education of the Handicapped Act, 84 Stat. 175, as amended significantly by the Education for All Handicapped Children Act of 1975, 89 Stat. 773, 20 U.S.C. §§1401(19), 1414(a)(5). The individualized education program provided that Amber would attend early childhood development classes and receive special services such as physical and occupational therapy. That program, however, made no provision for school personnel to administer CIC.

Respondents unsuccessfully pursued administrative remedies to secure CIC services for Amber during school hours.[124] In October 1979 respondents brought the present action in District Court against petitioner, the State Board of Education, and others. See §1415(e)(2). They sought an injunction ordering petitioner to provide Amber with CIC and sought damages and attorney's fees. First, respondents invoked the Education of the Handicapped Act. Because Texas received funding under that statute, petitioner was required to provide Amber with a "free appropriate public education," §§1412(1), 1414(a)(1)(C)(ii), which is defined to include "related services," §1401(18). Respondents argued that CIC is one such "related service."[125] Second, respondents invoked §504 of the Rehabilitation Act of 1973, 87 Stat. 394, as amended, 29 U.S.C. §794, which forbids an individual, by reason of a handicap, to be "excluded from the participation in, be denied the benefits of, or be subjected to discrimination under" any program receiving federal aid.

The District Court denied respondents' request for a preliminary injunction. Tatro v. Texas, 481 F. Supp. 1224 (ND Tex. 1979). That court concluded that CIC was not a "related service" under the Education of the Handicapped Act because it did not serve a need arising from the effort to educate. It also held that §504 of the Rehabilitation Act did not require "the setting up of governmental health care for people seeking to participate" in federally funded programs. Id., at 1229.

The Court of Appeals reversed. Tatro v. Texas, 625 F.2d 557 (CA5 1980) (Tatro I). First, it held that CIC was a "related service" under the Education of the Handicapped

124. The Education of the Handicapped Act's procedures for administrative hearings are set out in 20 U.S.C. §1415. In this case a hearing officer ruled that the Education of the Handicapped Act did require the school to provide CIC, and the Texas Commissioner of Education adopted the hearing officer's decision. The State Board of Education reversed, holding that the Act did not require petitioner to provide CIC.

125. As discussed more fully later, the Education of the Handicapped Act defines "related services" to include "supportive services (including . . . medical and counseling services, except that such medical services shall be for diagnostic and evaluation purposes only) as may be required to assist a handicapped child to benefit from special education" 20 U.S.C. §1401(17).

Act, 20 U.S.C. §1401(17), because without the procedure Amber could not attend classes and benefit from special education. Second, it held that petitioner's refusal to provide CIC effectively excluded her from a federally funded educational program in violation of §504 of the Rehabilitation Act. The Court of Appeals remanded for the District Court to develop a factual record and apply these legal principles.

On remand petitioner stressed the Education of the Handicapped Act's explicit provision that "medical services" could qualify as "related services" only when they served the purpose of diagnosis or evaluation. See n. 2, supra. The District Court held that under Texas law a nurse or other qualified person may administer CIC without engaging in the unauthorized practice of medicine, provided that a doctor prescribes and supervises the procedure. The District Court then held that, because a doctor was not needed to administer CIC, provision of the procedure was not a "medical service" for purposes of the Education of the Handicapped Act. Finding CIC to be a "related service" under that Act, the District Court ordered petitioner and the State Board of Education to modify Amber's individualized education program to include provision of CIC during school hours. It also awarded compensatory damages against petitioner. Tatro v. Texas, 516 F. Supp. 968 (ND Tex. 1981).[126]

On the authority of Tatro I, the District Court then held that respondents had proved a violation of §504 of the Rehabilitation Act. Although the District Court did not rely on this holding to authorize any greater injunctive or compensatory relief, it did invoke the holding to award attorney's fees against petitioner and the State Board of Education.[127] 516 F. Supp., at 968; App. to Pet. for Cert. 55a–63a. The Rehabilitation Act, unlike the Education of the Handicapped Act, authorizes prevailing parties to recover attorney's fees. See 29 U.S.C. §794a.

The Court of Appeals affirmed. Tatro v. Texas, 703 F.2d 823 (CA5 1983) (Tatro II). That court accepted the District Court's conclusion that state law permitted qualified persons to administer CIC without the physical presence of a doctor, and it affirmed the award of relief under the Education of the Handicapped Act. In affirming the award of attorney's fees based on a finding of liability under the Rehabilitation Act, the Court of Appeals held that no change of circumstances since Tatro I justified a different result. We granted certiorari, 464 U.S. 1007, 104 S. Ct. 523, 78 L. Ed. 2d 707 (1983), and we affirm in part and reverse in part.

II

This case poses two separate issues. The first is whether the Education of the Handicapped Act requires petitioner to provide CIC services to Amber. The second

126. The District Court dismissed the claims against all defendants other than petitioner and the State Board, though it retained the members of the State Board "in their official capacities for the purpose of injunctive relief" 516 F. Supp., at 972–974.

127. The District Court held that §505 of the Rehabilitation Act, 29 U.S.C. §794a, which authorizes attorney's fees as a part of a prevailing party's costs, abrogated the State Board's immunity under the Eleventh Amendment. See App. to Pet. for Cert. 56a–60a. The State Board did not petition for certiorari, and the Eleventh Amendment issue is not before us.

is whether § 504 of the Rehabilitation Act creates such an obligation. We first turn to the claim presented under the Education of the Handicapped Act.

States receiving funds under the Act are obliged to satisfy certain conditions. A primary condition is that the state implement a policy "that assures all handicapped children the right to a free appropriate public education." 20 U.S.C. § 1412(1). Each educational agency applying to a state for funding must provide assurances in turn that its program aims to provide "a free appropriate public education to all handicapped children." § 1414(a)(1)(C)(ii).

A "free appropriate public education" is explicitly defined as "special education and related services." § 1401(18).[128] The term "special education" means "specially designed instruction, at no cost to parents or guardians, to meet the unique needs of a handicapped child, including classroom instruction, instruction in physical education, home instruction, and instruction in hospitals and institutions." § 1401(16).

"Related services" are defined as "transportation, and such developmental, corrective, and other supportive services (including speech pathology and audiology, psychological services, physical and occupational therapy, recreation, and medical and counseling services, except that such medical services shall be for diagnostic and evaluation purposes only) as may be required to assist a handicapped child to benefit from special education, and includes the early identification and assessment of handicapping conditions in children." § 1401(17) (emphasis added).

The issue in this case is whether CIC is a "related service" that petitioner is obliged to provide to Amber. We must answer two questions: first, whether CIC is a "supportive servic[e] . . . required to assist a handicapped child to benefit from special education"; and second, whether CIC is excluded from this definition as a "medical servic[e]" serving purposes other than diagnosis or evaluation.

A

The Court of Appeals was clearly correct in holding that CIC is a "supportive servic[e] . . . required to assist a handicapped child to benefit from special education."[129] It is clear on this record that, without having CIC services available during the school day, Amber cannot attend school and thereby "benefit from

128. Specifically, the "special education and related services" must "(A) have been provided at public expense, under public supervision and direction, and without charge, (B) meet the standards of the State educational agency, (C) include an appropriate preschool, elementary, or secondary school education in the State involved, and (D) [be] provided in conformity with the individualized education program required under section 1414(a)(5) of this title" § 1401(18).

129. Petitioner claims that courts deciding cases arising under the Education of the Handicapped Act are limited to inquiring whether a school district has followed the requirements of the state plan and has followed the Act's procedural requirements. However, we held in Board of Education of Hendrick Hudson Central School District v. Rowley, 458 U.S. 176, 206, n. 27, 102 S. Ct. 3034, 3051, n. 27 (1982), that a court is required "not only to satisfy itself that the State has adopted the state plan, policies, and assurances required by the Act, but also to determine that the State has created an [individualized education plan] for the child in question which conforms with the requirements of § 1401(19) [defining such plans]." Judicial review is equally appropriate in this case,

special education." CIC services therefore fall squarely within the definition of a "supportive service."[130]

As we have stated before, "Congress sought primarily to make public education available to handicapped children" and "to make such access meaningful." Board of Education of Hendrick Hudson Central School District v. Rowley, 458 U.S. 176, 192, 102 S. Ct. 3034, 3043, 73 L. Ed. 2d 690 (1982). A service that enables a handicapped child to remain at school during the day is an important means of providing the child with the meaningful access to education that Congress envisioned. The Act makes specific provision for services, like transportation, for example, that do no more than enable a child to be physically present in class, see 20 U.S.C. § 1401(17); and the Act specifically authorizes grants for schools to alter buildings and equipment to make them accessible to the handicapped, § 1406; see S.Rep. No. 94-168, p. 38 (1975), U.S.Code Cong. & Admin.News 1975, p. 1425; 121 Cong.Rec. 19483–19484 (1975) (remarks of Sen. Stafford). Services like CIC that permit a child to remain at school during the day are no less related to the effort to educate than are services that enable the child to reach, enter, or exit the school.

We hold that CIC services in this case qualify as a "supportive servic[e] ... required to assist a handicapped child to benefit from special education."[131]

B

We also agree with the Court of Appeals that provision of CIC is not a "medical servic[e]," which a school is required to provide only for purposes of diagnosis or evaluation. See 20 U.S.C. § 1401(17). We begin with the regulations of the Department of Education, which are entitled to deference.[132] See, e.g., Blum v. Bacon, 457 U.S. 132, 141, 102 S. Ct. 2355, 2361, 72 L. Ed. 2d 728 (1982). The regulations define

---

which presents the legal question of a school's substantive obligation under the "related services" requirement of § 1401(17).

130. The Department of Education has agreed with this reasoning in an interpretive ruling that specifically found CIC to be a "related service" 46 Fed. Reg. 4912 (1981). Accord, Tokarcik v. Forest Hills School District, 665 F.2d 443 (CA3 1981), cert. denied sub nom. Scanlon v. Tokarcik, 458 U.S. 1121, 102 S. Ct. 3508, 73 L. Ed. 2d 1383 (1982). The Secretary twice postponed temporarily the effective date of this interpretive ruling, see 46 Fed. Reg. 12495 (1981); id., at 18975, and later postponed it indefinitely, id., at 25614. But the Department presently does view CIC services as an allowable cost under Part B of the Act. Ibid.

131. The obligation to provide special education and related services is expressly phrased as a "conditio[n]" for a state to receive funds under the Act. See 20 U.S.C. § 1412; see also S. Rep. No. 94-168, p. 16 (1975). This refutes petitioner's contention that the Act did not "impos[e] an obligation on the States to spend state money to fund certain rights as a condition of receiving federal moneys" but "spoke merely in precatory terms," Pennhurst State School and Hospital v. Halderman, 451 U.S. 1, 18, 101 S. Ct. 1531, 1540, 67 L. Ed. 2d 694 (1981).

132. The Secretary of Education is empowered to issue such regulations as may be necessary to carry out the provisions of the Act. 20 U.S.C. § 1417(b). This function was initially vested in the Commissioner of Education of the Department of Health, Education, and Welfare, who promulgated the regulations in question. This function was transferred to the Secretary of Education when Congress created that position, see Department of Education Organization Act, §§ 301(a)(1), (2)(H), 93 Stat. 677, 20 U.S.C. §§ 3441(a)(1), (2)(H).

"related services" for handicapped children to include "school health services," 34 CFR § 300.13(a) (1983), which are defined in turn as "services provided by a qualified school nurse or other qualified person," § 300.13(b)(10). "Medical services" are defined as "services provided by a licensed physician." § 300.13(b)(4).[133] Thus, the Secretary has determined that the services of a school nurse otherwise qualifying as a "related service" are not subject to exclusion as a "medical service," but that the services of a physician are excludable as such.

This definition of "medical services" is a reasonable interpretation of congressional intent. Although Congress devoted little discussion to the "medical services" exclusion, the Secretary could reasonably have concluded that it was designed to spare schools from an obligation to provide a service that might well prove unduly expensive and beyond the range of their competence.[134] From this understanding of congressional purpose, the Secretary could reasonably have concluded that Congress intended to impose the obligation to provide school nursing services.

Congress plainly required schools to hire various specially trained personnel to help handicapped children, such as "trained occupational therapists, speech therapists, psychologists, social workers and other appropriately trained personnel." S. Rep. No. 94-168, supra, at 33, U.S. Code Cong. & Admin. News 1975, p. 1457. School nurses have long been a part of the educational system, and the Secretary could therefore reasonably conclude that school nursing services are not the sort of burden that Congress intended to exclude as a "medical service." By limiting the "medical services" exclusion to the services of a physician or hospital, both far more expensive, the Secretary has given a permissible construction to the provision. Petitioner's contrary interpretation of the "medical services" exclusion is unconvincing. In petitioner's view, CIC is a "medical service," even though it may be provided by a nurse or trained layperson; that conclusion rests on its reading of Texas law that confines CIC to uses in accordance with a physician's prescription and under a physician's ultimate supervision. Aside from conflicting with the Secretary's reasonable interpretation of congressional intent, however, such a rule would be anomalous. Nurses in petitioner School District are authorized to dispense oral medications and administer emergency injections in accordance with a physician's prescription. This kind of service for nonhandicapped children is difficult to distinguish from the provision of CIC to the handicapped.[135] It would be strange indeed if Congress, in attempting to extend

133. The regulations define only those "medical services" that are owed to handicapped children: "services provided by a licensed physician to determine a child's medically related handicapping condition which results in the child's need for special education and related services" 34 C.F.R. § 300.13(b)(4) (1983). Presumably this means that "medical services" not owed under the statute are those "services by a licensed physician" that serve other purposes.

134. Children with serious medical needs are still entitled to an education. For example, the Act specifically includes instruction in hospitals and at home within the definition of "special education." See 20 U.S.C. § 1401(16).

135. Petitioner attempts to distinguish the administration of prescription drugs from the administration of CIC on the ground that Texas law expressly limits the liability of school personnel performing the former, see Tex. Educ. Code Ann. § 21.914(c) (Supp. 1984), but not the latter.

special services to handicapped children, were unwilling to guarantee them services of a kind that are routinely provided to the nonhandicapped.

To keep in perspective the obligation to provide services that relate to both the health and educational needs of handicapped students, we note several limitations that should minimize the burden petitioner fears. First, to be entitled to related services, a child must be handicapped so as to require special education. See 20 U.S.C. § 1401(1); 34 CFR § 300.5 (1983). In the absence of a handicap that requires special education, the need for what otherwise might qualify as a related service does not create an obligation under the Act. See 34 CFR § 300.14, Comment (1) (1983).

Second, only those services necessary to aid a handicapped child to benefit from special education must be provided, regardless how easily a school nurse or layperson could furnish them. For example, if a particular medication or treatment may appropriately be administered to a handicapped child other than during the school day, a school is not required to provide nursing services to administer it. Third, the regulations state that school nursing services must be provided only if they can be performed by a nurse or other qualified person, not if they must be performed by a physician. See 34 CFR §§ 300.13(a), (b)(4), (b)(10) (1983). It bears mentioning that here not even the services of a nurse are required; as is conceded, a layperson with minimal training is qualified to provide CIC. See also, e.g., Department of Education of Hawaii v. Katherine D., 727 F.2d 809 (CA9 1983).

Finally, we note that respondents are not asking petitioner to provide equipment that Amber needs for CIC. Tr. of Oral Arg. 18–19. They seek only the services of a qualified person at the school.

We conclude that provision of CIC to Amber is not subject to exclusion as a "medical service," and we affirm the Court of Appeals' holding that CIC is a "related service" under the Education of the Handicapped Act.[136]

This distinction, however, bears no relation to whether CIC is a "related service." The introduction of handicapped children into a school creates numerous new possibilities for injury and liability. Many of these risks are more serious than that posed by CIC, which the courts below found is a safe procedure even when performed by a 9-year-old girl. Congress assumed that states receiving the generous grants under the Act were up to the job of managing these new risks. Whether petitioner decides to purchase more liability insurance or to persuade the State to extend the limitation on liability, the risks posed by CIC should not prove to be a large burden.

136. We need not address respondents' claim that CIC, in addition to being a "related service," is a "supplementary ai[d] and servic[e]" that petitioner must provide to enable Amber to attend classes with nonhandicapped students under the Act's "mainstreaming" directive. See 20 U.S.C. § 1412(5)(B). Respondents have not sought an order prohibiting petitioner from educating Amber with handicapped children alone. Indeed, any request for such an order might not present a live controversy. Amber's present individualized education program provides for regular public school classes with nonhandicapped children. And petitioner has admitted that it would be far more costly to pay for Amber's instruction and CIC services at a private school, or to arrange for home tutoring, than to provide CIC at the regular public school placement provided in her current individualized education program. Tr. of Oral Arg. 12.

III

Respondents sought relief not only under the Education of the Handicapped Act but under §504 of the Rehabilitation Act as well.[137] After finding petitioner liable to provide CIC under the former, the District Court proceeded to hold that petitioner was similarly liable under §504 and that respondents were therefore entitled to attorney's fees under §505 of the Rehabilitation Act, 29 U.S.C. §794a. We hold today, in Smith v. Robinson, 468 U.S. 992, 104 S. Ct. 345, 82 L. Ed. 2d 746 (1984), that §504 is inapplicable when relief is available under the Education of the Handicapped Act to remedy a denial of educational services. Respondents are therefore not entitled to relief under §504, and we reverse the Court of Appeals' holding that respondents are entitled to recover attorney's fees. In all other respects, the judgment of the Court of Appeals is affirmed.

It is so ordered.

[Case No. 5-4]

Special education students may not be suspended for more than ten days unless a court orders differently.

Honig v. Doe

Supreme Court of the United States
484 U.S. 305 (1988)

Justice BRENNAN delivered the opinion of the Court.

As a condition of federal financial assistance, the Education of the Handicapped Act requires States to ensure a "free appropriate public education" for all disabled children within their jurisdictions. In aid of this goal, the Act establishes a comprehensive system of procedural safeguards designed to ensure parental participation in decisions concerning the education of their disabled children and to provide administrative and judicial review of any decisions with which those parents disagree. Among these safeguards is the so-called "stay-put" provision, which directs that a disabled child "shall remain in [his or her] then current educational placement" pending completion of any review proceedings, unless the parents and

---

137. The "Statement of the Questions Presented" in the petition for certiorari reads as follows:

"1. Whether 'medical treatment' such as clean intermittent catherization is a 'related service' required under the Education for All Handicapped Children Act and, therefore, required to be provided to the minor Respondent.

"2. Is a public school required to provide and perform the medical treatment prescribed by the physician of a handicapped child by the Education of All Handicapped Children Act or the Rehabilitation Act of 1973?

"3. Whether the Fifth Circuit Court of Appeals misconstrued the opinions of this Court in Southeastern Community College v. Davis, Pennhurst State School & Hospital v. Halderman, and State Board of Education v. Rowley." Pet. for Cert.

Because the Court does not hold that the Court of Appeals answered any of these questions incorrectly, it is not justified in reversing in part the judgment of that court.

state or local educational agencies otherwise agree. 20 U.S.C. §1415(e)(3). Today we must decide whether, in the face of this statutory proscription, state or local school authorities may nevertheless unilaterally exclude disabled children from the classroom for dangerous or disruptive conduct growing out of their disabilities. In addition, we are called upon to decide whether a district court may, in the exercise of its equitable powers, order a State to provide educational services directly to a disabled child when the local agency fails to do so.

In the Education of the Handicapped Act (EHA or the Act), 84 Stat. 175, as amended, 20 U.S.C. §1400 *et seq.*, Congress sought "to assure that all handicapped children have available to them . . . a free appropriate public education which emphasizes special education and related services designed to meet their unique needs, [and] to assure that the rights of handicapped children and their parents or guardians are protected." §1400(c). When the law was passed in 1975, Congress had before it ample evidence that such legislative assurances were sorely needed: 21 years after this Court declared education to be "perhaps the most important function of state and local governments," *Brown v. Board of Education*, 347 U.S. 483, 493, 74 S. Ct. 686, 691, 98 L. Ed. 873 (1954), congressional studies revealed that better than half of the Nation's 8 million disabled children were not receiving appropriate educational services. §1400(b)(3). Indeed, one out of every eight of these children was excluded from the public school system altogether, §1400(b)(4); many others were simply "warehoused" in special classes or were neglectfully shepherded through the system until they were old enough to drop out. See H.R. Rep. No. 94-332, p. 2 (1975). Among the most poorly served of disabled students were emotionally disturbed children: Congressional statistics revealed that for the school year immediately preceding passage of the Act, the educational needs of 82 percent of all children with emotional disabilities went unmet. See S. Rep. No. 94-168, p. 8 (1975), U.S. Code Cong. & Admin. News 1975, p. 1425 (hereinafter S. Rep.).

Although these educational failings resulted in part from funding constraints, Congress recognized that the problem reflected more than a lack of financial resources at the state and local levels. Two federal-court decisions, which the Senate Report characterized as "landmark," see *id.*, at 6, U.S.Code Cong. & Admin. News 1430, demonstrated that many disabled children were excluded pursuant to state statutes or local rules and policies, typically without any consultation with, or even notice to, their parents. See *Mills v. Board of Education of District of Columbia*, 348 F. Supp. 866 (DC 1972); *Pennsylvania Assn. for Retarded Children v. Pennsylvania*, 334 F. Supp. 1257 (ED Pa. 1971), and 343 F. Supp. 279 (1972) (*PARC*). Indeed, by the time of the EHA's enactment, parents had brought legal challenges to similar exclusionary practices in 27 other States. See S. Rep., at 6.

In responding to these problems, Congress did not content itself with passage of a simple funding statute. Rather, the EHA confers upon disabled students an enforceable substantive right to public education in participating States, see *Board of Education of Hendrick Hudson Central School Dist. v. Rowley*, 458 U.S. 176, 102 S. Ct. 3034, 73 L. Ed. 2d 690 (1982), and conditions federal financial assistance upon a State's compliance with the substantive and procedural goals of the Act. Accordingly, States seeking to qualify for federal funds must develop policies assuring all disabled children the "right to a free appropriate public education," and must file with the Secretary of Education formal plans mapping out in detail the programs, procedures, and timetables under which they will effectuate these policies. 20 U.S.C. §§ 1412(1), 1413(a). Such plans must assure that, "to the maximum extent appropriate," States will "mainstream" disabled children, *i.e.*, that they will educate them with children who are not disabled, and that they will segregate or otherwise remove such children from the regular classroom setting "only when the nature or severity of the handicap is such that education in regular classes ... cannot be achieved satisfactorily." § 1412(5).

The primary vehicle for implementing these congressional goals is the "individualized educational program" (IEP), which the EHA mandates for each disabled child. Prepared at meetings between a representative of the local school district, the child's teacher, the parents or guardians, and, whenever appropriate, the disabled child, the IEP sets out the child's present educational performance, establishes annual and short-term objectives for improvements in that performance, and describes the specially designed instruction and services that will enable the child to meet those objectives. § 1401(19). The IEP must be reviewed and, where necessary, revised at least once a year in order to ensure that local agencies tailor the statutorily required "free appropriate public education" to each child's unique needs. § 1414(a)(5).[138]

Envisioning the IEP as the centerpiece of the statute's education delivery system for disabled children, and aware that schools had all too often denied such children appropriate educations without in any way consulting their parents, Congress repeatedly emphasized throughout the Act the importance and indeed the necessity of parental participation in both the development of the IEP and any subsequent assessments of its effectiveness. See §§ 1400(c), 1401(19), 1412(7), 1415(b)(1)(A), (C), (D), (E), and 1415(b)(2). Accordingly, the Act establishes various procedural safeguards that guarantee parents both an opportunity for meaningful input into all decisions affecting their child's education and the right to seek review of any decisions they

138. Congress' earlier efforts to ensure that disabled students received adequate public education had failed in part because the measures it adopted were largely hortatory. In the 1966 amendments to the Elementary and Secondary Education Act of 1965, Congress established a grant program "for the purpose of assisting the States in the initiation, expansion, and improvement of programs and projects ... for the education of handicapped children." Pub. L. 89-750, § 161, 80 Stat. 1204. It repealed that program four years later and replaced it with the original version of the Education of the Handicapped Act, Pub. L. 91-230, 84 Stat. 175, Part B of which contained a similar grant program. Neither statute, however, provided specific guidance as to how States were to use the funds, nor did they condition the availability of the grants on compliance with any procedural or substantive safeguards. In amending the EHA to its present form, Congress rejected its earlier policy of "merely establish[ing] an unenforceable goal requiring all children to be in school." 121 Cong. Rec. 37417 (1975) (remarks of Sen. Schweiker). Today, all 50 States and the District of Columbia receive funding assistance under the EHA. U.S. Dept. of Education, Ninth Annual Report to Congress on Implementation of Education of the Handicapped Act (1987).

think inappropriate. These safeguards include the right to examine all relevant records pertaining to the identification, evaluation, and educational placement of their child; prior written notice whenever the responsible educational agency proposes (or refuses) to change the child's placement or program; an opportunity to present complaints concerning any aspect of the local agency's provision of a free appropriate public education; and an opportunity for "an impartial due process hearing" with respect to any such complaints. §§ 1415(b)(1), (2).

At the conclusion of any such hearing, both the parents and the local educational agency may seek further administrative review and, where that proves unsatisfactory, may file a civil action in any state or federal court. §§ 1415(c), (e)(2). In addition to reviewing the administrative record, courts are empowered to take additional evidence at the request of either party and to "grant such relief as [they] determine[ ] is appropriate." § 1415(e)(2). The "stay-put" provision at issue in this case governs the placement of a child while these often lengthy review procedures run their course. It directs that: "During the pendency of any proceedings conducted pursuant to [§ 1415], unless the State or local educational agency and the parents or guardian otherwise agree, the child shall remain in the then current educational placement of such child. . . ." § 1415(e)(3).

The present dispute grows out of the efforts of certain officials of the San Francisco Unified School District (SFUSD) to expel two emotionally disturbed children from school indefinitely for violent and disruptive conduct related to their disabilities. In November 1980, respondent John Doe assaulted another student at the Louise Lombard School, a developmental center for disabled children. Doe's April 1980 IEP identified him as a socially and physically awkward 17-year-old who experienced considerable difficulty controlling his impulses and anger. Among the goals set out in his IEP was "[i]mprovement in [his] ability to relate to [his] peers [and to] cope with frustrating situations without resorting to aggressive acts." App. 17. Frustrating situations, however, were an unfortunately prominent feature of Doe's school career: physical abnormalities, speech difficulties, and poor grooming habits had made him the target of teasing and ridicule as early as the first grade, *id.*, at 23; his 1980 IEP reflected his continuing difficulties with peers, noting that his social skills had deteriorated and that he could tolerate only minor frustration before exploding. *Id.*, at 15–16.

On November 6, 1980, Doe responded to the taunts of a fellow student in precisely the explosive manner anticipated by his IEP: he choked the student with sufficient force to leave abrasions on the child's neck, and kicked out a school window while being escorted to the principal's office afterwards. *Id.*, at 208. Doe admitted his misconduct and the school subsequently suspended him for five days. Thereafter, his principal referred the matter to the SFUSD Student Placement Committee (SPC or Committee) with the recommendation that Doe be expelled. On the day the suspension was to end, the SPC notified Doe's mother that it was proposing to exclude her child permanently from SFUSD and was therefore extending his suspension until such time as the expulsion proceedings were completed.[139] The Committee further advised her that she was entitled to attend the November 25 hearing at which it planned to discuss the proposed expulsion.

After unsuccessfully protesting these actions by letter, Doe brought this suit against a host of local school officials and the State Superintendent of Public Instructions. Alleging that the suspension and proposed expulsion violated the EHA, he sought a temporary restraining order canceling the SPC hearing and requiring school officials to convene an IEP meeting. The District Judge granted the requested injunctive relief and further ordered defendants to provide home tutoring for Doe on an interim basis; shortly thereafter, she issued a preliminary injunction directing defendants to return Doe to his then current educational placement at Louise Lombard School pending completion of the IEP review process. Doe reentered school on December 15, 5 1/2 weeks, and 24 school-days, after his initial suspension.

John Doe's case, the Committee scheduled a hearing and extended the suspension indefinitely pending a final disposition in the matter. On November 28, Smith's counsel protested these actions on grounds essentially identical to those raised by Doe, and the SPC agreed to cancel the hearing and to return Smith to a half-day program at A.P. Giannini or to provide home tutoring. Smith's grandparents chose the latter option and the school began home instruction on December 10; on January 6, 1981, an IEP team convened to discuss alternative placements.

After learning of Doe's action, Smith sought and obtained leave to intervene in the suit. The District Court subsequently entered summary judgment in favor of respondents on their EHA claims and issued a permanent injunction. In a series of decisions, the District Judge found that the proposed expulsions and indefinite suspensions of respondents for conduct attributable to their disabilities deprived them of their congressionally mandated right to a free appropriate public education, as well as their right to have that education provided in accordance with the procedures set out in the EHA. The District Judge therefore permanently enjoined the school district from taking any disciplinary action other than a 2- or 5-day suspension against any disabled child for disability-related misconduct, or from effecting any other change in the educational placement of any such child without parental consent pending completion of any EHA proceedings. In addition, the judge barred the State from authorizing unilateral placement changes and directed it to establish an EHA compliance-monitoring system or, alternatively, to enact guidelines governing local school responses to disability-related misconduct. Finally, the judge ordered the State to provide services directly to disabled children when, in any individual case, the State determined that the local educational agency was unable or unwilling to do so.

---

139. California law at the time empowered school principals to suspend students for no more than five consecutive schooldays, Cal. Educ. Code Ann. § 48903(a) (West 1978), but permitted school districts seeking to expel a suspended student to "extend the suspension until such time as [expulsion proceedings were completed]; provided, that [it] has determined that the presence of the pupil at the school or in an alternative school placement would cause a danger to persons or property or a threat of disrupting the instructional process." § 48903(h). The State subsequently amended the law to permit school districts to impose longer initial periods of suspension. See n. 3, *infra*.

On appeal, the Court of Appeals for the Ninth Circuit affirmed the orders with slight modifications. *Doe v. Maher,* 793 F.2d 1470 (1986). Agreeing with the District Court that an indefinite suspension in aid of expulsion constitutes a prohibited "change in placement" under § 1415(e)(3), the Court of Appeals held that the stay-put provision admitted of no "dangerousness" exception and that the statute therefore rendered invalid those provisions of the California Education Code permitting the indefinite suspension or expulsion of disabled children for misconduct arising out of their disabilities. The court concluded, however, that fixed suspensions of up to 30 schooldays did not fall within the reach of § 1415(e)(3), and therefore upheld recent amendments to the state Education Code authorizing such suspensions.[140] Lastly, the court affirmed that portion of the injunction requiring the State to provide services directly to a disabled child when the local educational agency fails to do so.

Petitioner Bill Honig, California Superintendent of Public Instruction,[141] sought review in this Court, claiming that the Court of Appeals' construction of the stay-put provision conflicted with that of several other Courts of Appeals which had recognized a dangerousness exception, compare *Doe v. Maher, supra,* (case below), with *Jackson v. Franklin County School Board,* 765 F.2d 535, 538 (CA5 1985); *Victoria L. v. District School Bd. of Lee County, Fla.,* 741 F.2d 369, 374 (CA11 1984); *S-1 v. Turlington,* 635 F.2d 342, 348, n. 9 (CA5), cert. denied, 454 U.S. 1030, 102 S. Ct. 566, 70 L. Ed. 2d 473 (1981), and that the direct services ruling placed an intolerable burden on the State. We granted certiorari to resolve these questions, 479 U.S. 1084, 107 S. Ct. 1284, 94 L. Ed. 2d 142 (1987), and now affirm.

II

At the outset, we address the suggestion, raised for the first time during oral argument, that this case is moot.[142] Under Article III of the Constitution this Court may only adjudicate actual, ongoing controversies. *Nebraska Press Assn v. Stuart,* 427 U.S. 539, 546, 96 S. Ct. 2791, 2796, 49 L. Ed. 2d 683 (1976); *Preiser v. Newkirk,* 422 U.S. 395, 401, 95 S. Ct. 2330, 2334, 45 L. Ed. 2d 272 (1975). That the dispute between the parties was very much alive when suit was filed, or at the time the Court of Appeals rendered its judgment, cannot substitute for the actual case or controversy that an exercise of this Court's jurisdiction requires. *Steffel v. Thompson,* 415 U.S. 452, 459, n. 10, 94 S. Ct. 1209, 1216, n. 10, 39 L. Ed. 2d 505 (1974); *Roe v. Wade,* 410 U.S. 113, 125, 93 S. Ct. 705, 713, 35 L. Ed. 2d 147 (1973). In the present case, we have jurisdiction if there is a reasonable likelihood that respondents will again suffer the

---

140. In 1983, the State amended its Education Code to permit school districts to impose initial suspensions of 20, and in certain circumstances, 30 schooldays. Cal. Educ. Code Ann. §§ 48912(a), 48903 (West Supp. 1988). The legislature did not alter the indefinite suspension authority which the SPC exercised in this case, but simply incorporated the earlier provision into a new section. See § 48911(g).

141. At the time respondent Doe initiated this suit, Wilson Riles was the California Superintendent of Public Instruction. Petitioner Honig succeeded him in office.

142. We note that both petitioner and respondents believe that this case presents a live controversy. See Tr. of Oral Arg. 6, 27–31. Only the United States, appearing as *amicus curiae,* urges that the case is presently nonjusticiable. *Id.,* at 21.

deprivation of EHA-mandated rights that gave rise to this suit. We believe that, at least with respect to respondent Smith, such a possibility does in fact exist and that the case therefore remains justiciable.

Respondent John Doe is now 24 years old and, accordingly, is no longer entitled to the protections and benefits of the EHA, which limits eligibility to disabled children between the ages of 3 and 21. See 20 U.S.C. § 1412(2)(B). It is clear, therefore, that whatever rights to state educational services he may yet have as a ward of the State, see Tr. of Oral Arg. 23, 26, the Act would not govern the State's provision of those services, and thus the case is moot as to him. Respondent Jack Smith, however, is currently 20 and has not yet completed high school. Although at present he is not faced with any proposed expulsion or suspension proceedings, and indeed no longer even resides within the SFUSD, he remains a resident of California and is entitled to a "free appropriate public education" within that State. His claims under the EHA, therefore, are not moot if the conduct he originally complained of is "'capable of repetition, yet evading review.'" *Murphy v. Hunt,* 455 U.S. 478, 482, 102 S. Ct. 1181, 1183, 71 L. Ed. 2d 353 (1982). Given Smith's continued eligibility for educational services under the EHA,[143] the nature of his disability, and petitioner's insistence that

---

143. Notwithstanding respondent's undisputed right to a free appropriate public education in California, Justice SCALIA argues in dissent that there is no "demonstrated probability" that Smith will actually avail himself of that right because his counsel was unable to state affirmatively during oral argument that her client would seek to reenter the state school system. See *post,* at 611. We believe the dissent overstates the stringency of the "capable of repetition" test. Although Justice SCALIA equates "reasonable expectation" with "demonstrated probability," the very case he cites for this proposition described these standards in the disjunctive, see *Murphy v. Hunt,* 455 U.S., at 482, 102 S. Ct., at 1183, 1184 ("[T]here must be a 'reasonable expectation' *or* a 'demonstrated probability' that the same controversy will recur" (emphasis added)), and in numerous cases decided both before and since *Hunt* we have found controversies capable of repetition based on expectations that, while reasonable, were hardly demonstrably probable. See, *e.g., Burlington Northern R. Co. v. Maintenance of Way Employees,* 481 U.S. 429, 436, n. 4, 107 S. Ct. 1841, 1846, n. 4, 95 L. Ed. 2d 381 (1987) (parties "reasonably likely" to find themselves in future disputes over collective-bargaining agreement); *California Coastal Comm'n v. Granite Rock Co.,* 480 U.S. 572, 578, 107 S. Ct. 1419, 1424, 94 L. Ed. 2d 577 (1987) (O'CONNOR, J.) ("likely" that respondent would again submit mining plans that would trigger contested state permit requirement); *Press-Enterprise Co. v. Superior Court of Cal., Riverside County,* 478 U.S. 1, 6, 106 S. Ct. 2735, 2739, 92 L. Ed. 2d 1 (1986) ("It can reasonably be assumed" that newspaper publisher will be subjected to similar closure order in the future); *Globe Newspaper Co. v. Superior Court of Norfolk County,* 457 U.S. 596, 603, 102 S. Ct. 2613, 2618, 73 L. Ed. 2d 248 (1982) (same); *United States Parole Comm'n v. Geraghty,* 445 U.S. 388, 398, 100 S. Ct. 1202, 1210, 63 L. Ed. 2d 479 (1980) (case not moot where litigant "faces some likelihood of becoming involved in same controversy in the future") (dicta). Our concern in these cases, as in all others involving potentially moot claims, was whether the controversy was *capable* of repetition and not, as the dissent seems to insist, whether the claimant had demonstrated that a recurrence of the dispute was more probable than not. Regardless, then, of whether respondent has established with mathematical precision the likelihood that he will enroll in public school during the next two years, we think there is at the very least a reasonable expectation that he will exercise his rights under the EHA. In this regard, we believe respondent's actions over the course of the last seven years speak louder than his counsel's momentary equivocation during oral argument. Since 1980, he has sought to vindicate his right to an appropriate public education that is not only free of charge, but also free from the threat that school officials will unilaterally change his placement or

all local school districts retain residual authority to exclude disabled children for dangerous conduct, we have little difficulty concluding that there is a "reasonable expectation," *ibid.*, that Smith would once again be subjected to a unilateral "change in placement" for conduct growing out of his disabilities were it not for the state-wide injunctive relief issued below.

Our cases reveal that, for purposes of assessing the likelihood that state authorities will reinflict a given injury, we generally have been unwilling to assume that the party seeking relief will repeat the type of misconduct that would once again place him or her at risk of that injury. See *Los Angeles v. Lyons*, 461 U.S. 95, 105–106, 103 S. Ct. 1660, 1666–1667, 75 L. Ed. 2d 675 (1983) (no threat that party seeking injunction barring police use of chokeholds would be stopped again for traffic violation or other offense, or would resist arrest if stopped); *Murphy v. Hunt*, *supra*, 455 U.S., at 484, 102 S. Ct., at 1184 (no reason to believe that party challenging denial of pre-trial bail "will once again be in a position to demand bail"); *O'Shea v. Littleton*, 414 U.S. 488, 497, 94 S. Ct. 669, 676, 38 L. Ed. 2d 674 (1974) (unlikely that parties challenging discriminatory bond-setting, sentencing, and jury-fee practices would again violate valid criminal laws). No such reluctance, however, is warranted here. It is respondent Smith's very inability to conform his conduct to socially acceptable norms that renders him "handicapped" within the meaning of the EHA. See 20 U.S.C. § 1401(1); 34 CFR § 300.5(b)(8) (1987). As noted above, the record is replete with evidence that Smith is unable to govern his aggressive, impulsive behavior — indeed, his notice of suspension acknowledged that "Jack's actions seem beyond his control." App. 152. In the absence of any suggestion that respondent has overcome his earlier difficulties, it is certainly reasonable to expect, based on his prior history of behavioral problems, that he will again engage in classroom misconduct. Nor is it reasonable to suppose that Smith's future educational placement will so perfectly suit his emotional and academic needs that further disruptions on his part are improbable. Although Justice SCALIA suggests in his dissent, *post*, at 3, that school officials are unlikely to place Smith in a setting where they cannot control his misbehavior, any efforts to ensure such total control must be tempered by the school system's statutory obligations to provide respondent with a free appropriate public education in "the least restrictive environment," 34 CFR § 300.552(d) (1987); to educate him, "to the maximum extent appropriate," with children who are not disabled, 20 U.S.C. § 1412(5); and to consult with his parents or guardians, and presumably with respondent himself, before choosing a placement. §§ 1401(19), 1415(b). Indeed, it is only by ignoring these mandates, as well as Congress' unquestioned desire to wrest from school

---

exclude him from class altogether. As a disabled young man, he has as at least as great a need of a high school education and diploma as any of his peers, and his counsel advises us that he is awaiting the outcome of this case to decide whether to pursue his degree. Tr. Oral Arg. 23–24. Under these circumstances, we think it not only counterintuitive but also unreasonable to assume that respondent will forgo the exercise of a right that he has for so long sought to defend. Certainly we have as much reason to expect that respondent will re-enter the California school system as we had to assume that Jane Roe would again both have an unwanted pregnancy and wish to exercise her right to an abortion. See *Roe v. Wade*, 410 U.S. 113, 125, 93 S. Ct. 705, 713, 35 L. Ed. 2d 147 (1973).

officials their former unilateral authority to determine the placement of emotionally disturbed children, see *infra,* at 15–16, that the dissent can so readily assume that respondent's future placement will satisfactorily prevent any further dangerous conduct on his part. Overarching these statutory obligations, moreover, is the inescapable fact that the preparation of an IEP, like any other effort at predicting human behavior, is an inexact science at best. Given the unique circumstances and context of this case, therefore, we think it reasonable to expect that respondent will again engage in the type of misconduct that precipitated this suit.

We think it equally probable that, should he do so, respondent will again be subjected to the same unilateral school action for which he initially sought relief. In this regard, it matters not that Smith no longer resides within the SFUSD. While the actions of SFUSD officials first gave rise to this litigation, the District Judge expressly found that the lack of a state policy governing local school responses to disability-related misconduct had led to, and would continue to result in, EHA violations, and she therefore enjoined the state defendant from authorizing, among other things, unilateral placement changes. App. 247–248. She of course also issued injunctions directed at the local defendants, but they did not seek review of those orders in this Court. Only petitioner, the State Superintendent of Public Instruction, has invoked our jurisdiction, and he now urges us to hold that local school districts retain unilateral authority under the EHA to suspend or otherwise remove disabled children for dangerous conduct. Given these representations, we have every reason to believe that were it not for the injunction barring petitioner from authorizing such unilateral action, respondent would be faced with a real and substantial threat of such action in any California school district in which he enrolled. Cf. *Los Angeles v. Lyons, supra,* 461 U.S., at 106, 103 S. Ct., at 1667 (respondent lacked standing to seek injunctive relief because he could not plausibly allege that police officers choked all persons whom they stopped, or that the city "*authorized* police officers to act in such manner" (emphasis added)). Certainly, if the SFUSD's past practice of unilateral exclusions was at odds with state policy and the practice of local school districts generally, petitioner would not now stand before us seeking to defend the right of all local school districts to engage in such aberrant behavior.[144]

We have previously noted that administrative and judicial review under the EHA is often "ponderous," *Burlington School Committee v. Massachusetts Dept. of Education,* 471 U.S. 359, 370, 105 S. Ct. 1996, 2003, 85 L. Ed. 2d 385 (1985), and this case, which has taken seven years to reach us, amply confirms that observation. For obvious reasons, the misconduct of an emotionally disturbed or otherwise disabled child

144. Petitioner concedes that the school district "made a number of procedural mistakes in its eagerness to protect other students from Doe and Smith." Reply Brief for Petitioner 6. According to petitioner, however, unilaterally excluding respondents from school was not among them; indeed, petitioner insists that the SFUSD acted properly in removing respondents and urges that the stay-put provision "should not be interpreted to require a school district to maintain such dangerous children with other children." *Id.,* at 6–7.

who has not yet reached adolescence typically will not pose such a serious threat to the well-being of other students that school officials can only ensure classroom safety by excluding the child. Yet, the adolescent student improperly disciplined for misconduct that does pose such a threat will often be finished with school or otherwise ineligible for EHA protections by the time review can be had in this Court. Because we believe that respondent Smith has demonstrated both "a sufficient likelihood that he will again be wronged in a similar way," *Los Angeles v. Lyons,* 461 U.S., at 111, 103 S. Ct., at 1670, and that any resulting claim he may have for relief will surely evade our review, we turn to the merits of his case.

III

The language of § 1415(e)(3) is unequivocal. It states plainly that during the pendency of any proceedings initiated under the Act, unless the state or local educational agency and the parents or guardian of a disabled child otherwise agree, "the child *shall* remain in the then current educational placement." § 1415(e)(3) (emphasis added). Faced with this clear directive, petitioner asks us to read a "dangerousness" exception into the stay-put provision on the basis of either of two essentially inconsistent assumptions: first, that Congress thought the residual authority of school officials to exclude dangerous students from the classroom too obvious for comment; or second, that Congress inadvertently failed to provide such authority and this Court must therefore remedy the oversight. Because we cannot accept either premise, we decline petitioner's invitation to rewrite the statute.

Petitioner's arguments proceed, he suggests, from a simple, commonsense proposition: Congress could not have intended the stay-put provision to be read literally, for such a construction leads to the clearly unintended, and untenable, result that school districts must return violent or dangerous students to school while the often lengthy EHA proceedings run their course. We think it clear, however, that Congress very much meant to strip schools of the *unilateral* authority they had traditionally employed to exclude disabled students, particularly emotionally disturbed students, from school. In so doing, Congress did not leave school administrators powerless to deal with dangerous students; it did, however, deny school officials their former right to "self-help," and directed that in the future the removal of disabled students could be accomplished only with the permission of the parents or, as a last resort, the courts.

As noted above, Congress passed the EHA after finding that school systems across the country had excluded one out of every eight disabled children from classes. In drafting the law, Congress was largely guided by the recent decisions in *Mills v. Board of Education of District of Columbia,* 348 F. Supp. 866 (1972), and *PARC,* 343 F. Supp. 279 (1972), both of which involved the exclusion of hard-to-handle disabled students. *Mills* in particular demonstrated the extent to which schools used disciplinary measures to bar children from the classroom. There, school officials had labeled four of the seven minor plaintiffs "behavioral problems," and had excluded them from classes without providing any alternative education to them or any notice to their parents. 348 F. Supp., at 869–870. After finding that this practice was not limited to the named plaintiffs but affected in one way or another an estimated class of 12,000 to 18,000 disabled students, *id.*, at 868–869, 875, the District Court enjoined future exclusions, suspensions, or expulsions "on grounds of discipline." *Id.*, at 880.

Congress attacked such exclusionary practices in a variety of ways. It required participating States to educate *all* disabled children, regardless of the severity of their disabilities, 20 U.S.C. § 1412(2)(C), and included within the definition of "handicapped" those children with serious emotional disturbances. § 1401(1). It further provided for meaningful parental participation in all aspects of a child's educational placement, and barred schools, through the stay-put provision, from changing that placement over the parent's objection until all review proceedings were completed. Recognizing that those proceedings might prove long and tedious, the Act's drafters did not intend § 1415(e)(3) to operate inflexibly, see 121 Cong.Rec. 37412 (1975) (remarks of Sen. Stafford), and they therefore allowed for interim placements where parents and school officials are able to agree on one. Conspicuously absent from § 1415(e)(3), however, is any emergency exception for dangerous students. This absence is all the more telling in light of the injunctive decree issued in *PARC,* which permitted school officials unilaterally to remove students in "'extraordinary circumstances.'" 343 F. Supp., at 301. Given the lack of any similar exception in *Mills,* and the close attention Congress devoted to these "landmark" decisions, see S.Rep., at 6, U.S.Code Cong. & Admin.News p. 1430, we can only conclude that the omission was intentional; we are therefore not at liberty to engraft onto the statute an exception Congress chose not to create.

Our conclusion that § 1415(e)(3) means what it says does not leave educators hamstrung. The Department of Education has observed that, "[w]hile the [child's] placement may not be changed [during any complaint proceeding], this does not preclude the agency from using its normal procedures for dealing with children who are endangering themselves or others." Comment following 34 CFR § 300.513 (1987). Such procedures may include the use of study carrels, timeouts, detention, or the restriction of privileges. More drastically, where a student poses an immediate threat to the safety of others, officials may temporarily suspend him or her for up to 10 schooldays.[145] This authority, which respondent in no way disputes, not

---

145. The Department of Education has adopted the position first espoused in 1980 by its Office of Civil Rights that a suspension of up to 10 school-days does not amount to a "change in placement" prohibited by § 1415(e)(3). U.S. Dept. of Education, Office of Special Education Programs, Policy Letter (Feb. 26, 1987), Ed. for Handicapped L.Rep. 211:437 (1987). The EHA nowhere defines the phrase "change in placement," nor does the statute's structure or legislative history provide any guidance as to how the term applies to fixed suspensions. Given this ambiguity, we defer to the construction adopted by the agency charged with monitoring and enforcing the statute. See *INS v. Cardoza-Fonseca,* 480 U.S. 421, 448, 107 S. Ct. 1207, 1221, 94 L. Ed. 2d 434 (1987). Moreover, the agency's position comports fully with the purposes of the statute: Congress sought to prevent schools from permanently and unilaterally excluding disabled children by means of indefinite suspensions and expulsions; the power to impose fixed suspensions of short duration does not carry the potential for total exclusion that Congress found so objectionable. Indeed, despite its broad

only ensures that school administrators can protect the safety of others by promptly removing the most dangerous of students, it also provides a "cooling down" period during which officials can initiate IEP review and seek to persuade the child's parents to agree to an interim placement. And in those cases in which the parents of a truly dangerous child adamantly refuse to permit any change in placement, the 10-day respite gives school officials an opportunity to invoke the aid of the courts under § 1415(e)(2), which empowers courts to grant any appropriate relief.

Petitioner contends, however, that the availability of judicial relief is more illusory than real, because a party seeking review under § 1415(e)(2) must exhaust time-consuming administrative remedies, and because under the Court of Appeals' construction of § 1415(e)(3), courts are as bound by the stay-put provision's "automatic injunction," 793 F.2d, at 1486, as are schools.[146] It is true that judicial review is normally not available under § 1415(e)(2) until all administrative proceedings are completed, but as we have previously noted, parents may bypass the administrative process where exhaustion would be futile or inadequate. See *Smith v. Robinson,* 468 U.S. 992, 1014, n. 17, 104 S. Ct. 3457, 3469, 82 L. Ed. 2d 746 (1984) (citing cases); see also 121 Cong. Rec. 37416 (1975) (remarks of Sen. Williams) ("[E]xhaustion ... sould not be required ... in cases where such exhaustion would be futile either as a legal or practical matter"). While many of the EHA's procedural safeguards protect the rights of parents and children, schools can and do seek redress through the administrative review process, and we have no reason to believe that Congress meant to require schools alone to exhaust in all cases, no matter how exigent the circumstances. The burden in such cases, of course, rests with the school to demonstrate the futility or inadequacy of administrative review, but nothing in § 1415(e)(2) suggests that schools are completely barred from attempting to make such a showing. Nor do we think that § 1415(e)(3) operates to limit the equitable powers of district courts such that they cannot, in appropriate cases, temporarily enjoin a dangerous disabled child from attending school. As the EHA's legislative history makes clear, one of the evils Congress sought to remedy was the unilateral exclusion of disabled

---

injunction, the District Court in *Mills v. Board of Education of District of Columbia,* 348 F. Supp. 866 (DC 1972), recognized that school officials could suspend disabled children on a short-term, temporary basis. See *id,* at 880. Cf. *Goss v. Lopez,* 419 U.S. 565, 574–576, 95 S. Ct. 729, 736–737, 42 L. Ed. 2d 725 (1975) (suspension of 10 schooldays or more works a sufficient deprivation of property and liberty interests to trigger the protections of the Due Process Clause). Because we believe the agency correctly determined that a suspension in excess of 10 days does constitute a prohibited "change in placement," we conclude that the Court of Appeals erred to the extent it approved suspensions of 20 and 30 days' duration.

146. Petitioner also notes that in California, schools may not suspend any given student for more than a total of 20, and in certain special circumstances 30, school days in a single year, see Cal. Educ. Code Ann. § 48903 (West Supp. 1988); he argues, therefore, that a school district may not have the option of imposing a 10-day suspension when dealing with an obstreperous child whose previous suspensions for the year total 18 or 19 days. The fact remains, however, that state law does not define the scope of § 1415(e)(3). There may be cases in which a suspension that is otherwise valid under the stay-put provision would violate local law. The effect of such a violation, however, is a question of state law upon which we express no view.

children by *schools*, not courts, and one of the purposes of § 1415(e)(3), therefore, was "to prevent *school* officials from removing a child from the regular public school classroom over the parents' objection pending completion of the review proceedings." *Burlington School Committee v. Massachusetts Dept. of Education,* 471 U.S., at 373, 105 S. Ct., at 2004 (emphasis added). The stay-put provision in no way purports to limit or pre-empt the authority conferred on courts by § 1415(e)(2), see *Doe v. Brookline School Committee,* 722 F.2d 910, 917 (CA1 1983); indeed, it says nothing whatever about judicial power.

In short, then, we believe that school officials are entitled to seek injunctive relief under § 1415(e)(2) in appropriate cases. In any such action, § 1415(e)(3) effectively creates a presumption in favor of the child's current educational placement which school officials can overcome only by showing that maintaining the child in his or her current placement is substantially likely to result in injury either to himself or herself, or to others. In the present case, we are satisfied that the District Court, in enjoining the state and local defendants from indefinitely suspending respondent or otherwise unilaterally altering his then current placement, properly balanced respondent's interest in receiving a free appropriate public education in accordance with the procedures and requirements of the EHA against the interests of the state and local school officials in maintaining a safe learning environment for all their students.[147]

IV

We believe the courts below properly construed and applied § 1415(e)(3), except insofar as the Court of Appeals held that a suspension in excess of 10 schooldays does not constitute a "change in placement."[148] We therefore affirm the Court of Appeals' judgment on this issue as modified herein. Because we are equally divided on the question whether a court may order a State to provide services directly to a disabled child where the local agency has failed to do so, we affirm the Court of Appeals' judgment on this issue as well.

Affirm

---

147. We therefore reject the United States' contention that the District Judge abused her discretion in enjoining the local school officials from indefinitely suspending respondent pending completion of the expulsion proceedings. Contrary to the Government's suggestion, the District Judge did not view herself bound to enjoin any and all violations of the stay-put provision, but rather, consistent with the analysis we set out above, weighed the relative harms to the parties and found that the balance tipped decidedly in favor of respondent. App. 222–223. We of course do not sit to review the factual determinations underlying that conclusion. We do note, however, that in balancing the parties' respective interests, the District Judge gave proper consideration to respondent's rights under the EHA. While the Government complains that the District Court indulged an improper presumption of irreparable harm to respondent, we do not believe that school officials can escape the presumptive effect of the stay-put provision simply by violating it and forcing parents to petition for relief. In any suit brought by parents seeking injunctive relief for a violation of § 1415(e)(3), the burden rests with the school district to demonstrate that the educational status quo must be altered.

148. See n.8, *supra.*

Chapter 6

Church/State/Education Relationships

The First Amendment to the U.S. Constitution states, in part, "Congress shall make no law respecting an establishment of religion or prohibiting the free exercise thereof." Therefore, federal and state governments can neither promote nor prohibit religion. Public schools are agents of the state and are therefore part of government. The restrictions and freedoms embodied in the religion clause apply directly to public schools. For the most part, legal analysis cannot make use of a religion clause. The religion clause has relevance for history as well as political science; however, legal analysis requires that they be bifurcated. Those separate parts are the Establishment Clause and the Free Exercise Clause. Both have a distinct jurisprudence, and both have separate "tests" for determining constitutional violations.

Brief History of the Religion Clause

Americans recall that the Pilgrims landed on Plymouth Rock in 1620. Thus began the immigration of those leaving their European homes in search of a better life. Elementary school history books emphasize that these Pilgrims were religious people wishing to be free of religious persecution in England. To be more accurate, the Pilgrims were a sect of Protestants called Puritans. They opposed the English state religion (the Anglican Church) because they thought it was too much like Roman Catholicism. The Puritans also took exception to England adopting an official state religion. The Book of Common Prayer was approved by Parliament. Of course, the Puritans, not being Anglican, were not members of the "right" church.[1]

Given the situation, it can be concluded that the Pilgrims were not only in search of freedom from religious persecution but from civil persecution as well. Not being a member of the Anglican Church could bring disadvantages in the life of the citizen. The Puritans were a type of "second class citizen" because they practiced the "wrong" religion. It is little wonder that when the Framers began writing the First Amendment, the religion clause appeared first; the business of religious oppression had to be dealt with first if liberty was to be genuine in America. They did not want

1. John J. Meng & E.J. Gergely, American History 52–53 (1959).

what they had in England. The idea of worshiping in the religion of choice, without government interference, was paramount.

Ironically, the colonists' behavior for the first hundred years or so did not conform to their ideals. By the time the Puritans were joined in the colonies by other churches, all took up rather exclusive control over certain areas. The English Puritans in New England, the Dutch Reformed in New Amsterdam, and the Anglicans in Virginia assumed the pattern that they knew. That is, religious uniformity would by necessity be perpetuated in America.[2] They saw that religious uniformity to some degree was required for political unity. The favored churches were granted various tax exemptions. Those people living in areas where a church other than their own was favored were not given any tax advantages. Indeed, those "non-favored" churchgoers were subject to certain civil penalties. During the 1600s to mid-1700s, government authorities did exercise control over certain church affairs; however, it must be remembered that at this time America was not yet independent.

From the mid-1700s up to the writing of the First Amendment (signed into law in 1791), there were major changes in the "church turf" approach used earlier. There became an interest in *disestablishing* churches as a necessary part of the movement to gain independence from England. According to some historians, the disestablishment took hold because of the convergence of two dissimilar movements.[3] One of these movements is known as the "Great Awakening." This was a religious revival that swept through the colonies beginning in the 1740s. It was largely comprised of Baptist and Presbyterian members. The Great Awakening captured the interests of the average citizen and therefore could easily be called a mass movement. The revival focused, in part, on an antiestablishment of the churches. The movement was fueled when clergy of the established churches attempted to use their influence to quash the movement. While the Great Awakening motivated the masses, so-called Enlightenment liberal rationalists like Thomas Jefferson, James Madison, and Patrick Henry provided the intellectual component in support of disestablishment.

Jefferson, Madison, and Henry felt that human reason could decide what religion was best for each individual. Doctrines held by the churches that had been in control were believed to be unnecessary or even dangerous for the public order. Therefore, religion should be separated from the government and made a matter of private choice.[4] As the two movements came together in 1776, the disestablishment of the Anglican Church in Virginia came first. The Virginia legislature repealed tax and other privileges that had been given the church. In 1778, Patrick Henry introduced a General Assessment Bill that required there be no government-established church. Shortly thereafter, James Madison introduced the famous *Memorial and*

---

2. Sidney E. Mead, The Lively Experiment 17 (1963).

3. Stephan V. Monsma & J. Christopher Soper, The Challenge of Pluralism 18–46 (1997).

4. *Id.*

Remonstrance against Religious Assessments.[5] In the *Remonstrance*, he argued that the same authority that would require a citizen to pay money to an established church could also require that citizen to conform to any other establishment.[6] Finally, in 1785, the Virginia legislature enacted a bill written by Thomas Jefferson. The *Bill for Establishing Religious Freedom* provided that "no man shall be compelled to frequent or support any religious worship, place, or ministry whatsoever . . . but all men shall be free to profess, and by argument to maintain, their opinions in matters of religion, and that the same shall in no wise diminish, enlarge, or affect their civil capacities."[7]

Thereafter, other states with laws creating official colonial churches repealed them one after another. In 1833, Massachusetts became the last of the 13 colonies to repeal the law establishing an official state church. The elimination of these state laws which disestablished churches was primarily the result of the application of a democratic ideal. While early interpretations of the religion clause believed it prohibited the federal government from establishing an official "Church of the United States," its interpretation as a prohibition on the establishment of a state church did not come until later. In fact, the disestablishment of any official government-sanctioned church as a matter of law did not occur until the passage of the Fourteenth Amendment to the U.S. Constitution. Because of the Fourteenth Amendment, all the guarantees of the Bill of Rights apply to a person's relationships with state government, not just the federal government.

In 1985, Alabama still insisted that the prohibitions of the religion clause were not applicable to the sovereign State of Alabama. In *Wallace v. Jaffree*,[8] the state argued that it could validly apply a state statute requiring "school prayer" because it could promote religion if it wanted. Only the federal government was prohibited from setting up an official church. The Alabama legislature, it averred, could promote religion. The U.S. Supreme Court gave Alabama a civics lesson in ruling that the Alabama statute requiring school prayer violated the Establishment Clause. It reminded Alabama that all parts of the Bill of Rights applied to the states through the Fourteenth Amendment.

Relationship Between the Free Exercise Clause and the Establishment Clause

As discussed above, for the most part, there is no direct relationship between the two clauses as they relate to the fundamental freedom of the individual as can be argued in the law. The jurisprudence of the two clauses has taken different routes

5. James Madison, *Memorial and Remonstrance Against Religious Assessments, in* The Supreme Court on Church and State 19–20 (Robert S. Alley ed., 1988).

6. *Id.*

7. Thomas Jefferson, *Bill for Establishing Religious Freedom, in* The Supreme Court on Church and State 26..

8. 472 U.S. 38 (1985).

throughout the case law. The Free Exercise Clause is the source of what is sometimes referred to in the broader literature as *freedom of religion* or *religious liberty.* In plain words, the Free Exercise Clause requires that the government not *prohibit* religion. On the other hand, the Establishment Clause is the source of what is commonly referred to as the *separation of church and state.* It requires that the government not *promote* religion. Therefore, the government is stuck in the middle—it cannot prohibit, and it cannot promote. If the government is seen doing anything proactive with regard to religion, it needs to take steps to reestablish *neutrality.*

There are times when the two clauses conflict with one another. Take, for example, the job of the military chaplain. The chaplain is paid by the government to provide religion. That certainly is a form of religious promotion. However, if the military did not provide the service, it would be prohibiting religion. It is not always workable for military personnel to leave their post to attend a religious service. In fact, the serviceperson would be subject to a severe penalty for abandoning their post even for religious purposes. As a result, the government has opted to promote religion in order to avoid prohibiting it. The bottom line, of course, is that one be able to worship as one pleases without penalty from government.

So why is the Establishment Clause necessary? The Pilgrims were practical people who had the experience of worshiping the "wrong religion" in England. It was hard for them to "freely exercise" their religion because the government had "established" an official religion. They seemed to understand that if they did not keep their new government from establishing an official religion, before long they might not be able to freely exercise their own—in other words, what might be the right religion today could be the wrong religion tomorrow. The Pilgrims decided that keeping government out of religion altogether would be the best way to ensure their own free exercise of religion.

The ultimate goal is to freely exercise. So in the doctrinal sense, the Free Exercise Clause has preeminence over the Establishment Clause if ever a decision of one or the other is required. Fortunately, there have been few times when the government has had to make this choice.

The Free Exercise Clause in Education

The tests used by the U.S. Supreme Court over the last century for free exercise issues have varied. The tests themselves are not distinct but instead build upon one another and have become more complex over time as the number of variables has increased. These evolving tests, beginning with *Reynolds v. United States*,[9] decided in 1878, and continuing through *Employment Division v. Smith*,[10] decided in 1990, could be summed up as follows: (1) The belief-conduct distinction, (2) balance of

9. 98 U.S. 145 (1878).
10. 110 S. Ct. 1595 (1990).

competing interests, and (3) balance of competing interests with restricted application tests.

Much of what is known concerning free exercise jurisprudence has grown out of issues in education. Whether students can be punished for exercising their religion continues to be a serious question for school administration, and the guidance of the courts continues to evolve. The earliest case to provide a constitutional test for a free exercise issue grew out a polygamy law before the turn of the century.

The Belief-Conduct Distinction Test

In *Reynolds v. United States*,[11] the Court introduced the earliest free exercise test, known as the belief-conduct distinction. The Court affirmed a conviction of a member of the Church of Jesus Christ of Latter-Day Saints in the Territory of Utah under a federal law that made bigamy a crime in the territories. Mr. Reynolds argued that his religion "required" him to have multiple wives. To deny him the right to be legally married to more than one wife was to deny him his rights under the Free Exercise Clause. The Court was faced with the question of just what the government is prohibited from doing regarding religion. Could any behavior be exempt from regulation by a citizen raising a shield of religion?

Reynolds v. United States[12]

In *Reynolds*, a man was prosecuted in the Territory of Utah for violating a statute banning polygamy. The plaintiff claimed that he was a member of the Church of Jesus Christ of Latter-Day Saints, and that it was the duty of male members of the church to practice polygamy. The question before the Court was whether the statute under consideration violated the Free Exercise Clause of the First Amendment, and if so, whether those who practiced polygamy for religious purposes were exempted from prosecution.

The Court held that the statute was within Congress' legislative power and that those who practiced polygamy as a religious duty were not exempt from prosecution. The Constitution does not grant Congress the power to interfere with religious belief or opinion, but it does grant that power with respect to religious actions or practices. To allow exemption from prosecution could lead to future crimes, such as murder, and the government has the right to prevent such crimes and to protect future victims.

In writing for the majority, Chief Justice Waite drew a sharp *belief-conduct distinction* in affirming the conviction of Mr. Reynolds. He wrote, "Laws are made for the government of actions, and while they cannot interfere with mere religious belief and opinions, they may with practices."[13]

11. 98 U.S. 145.
12. 98 U.S. 145 (1878).
13. *Id.* at 166.

To put it plainly, the government cannot require the conformity of a religiously oriented citizen to a certain belief. The government can, however, require that citizens conform their actions. Reynolds claimed that his polygamy was a belief. The Court viewed it as conduct. Therefore, the question a court would need to answer if applying the belief-conduct distinction to determine whether a free exercise violation took place would be whether a claimant's belief was being regulated. If it is simply the behavior, the conduct, or the action that is being regulated, then there is no free exercise violation. The belief-conduct distinction allows government to control conduct, even religious conduct. For example, for a church to pass out fliers on Main Street calling for an end to violence around the world could be regulated. The content of the flier could not be regulated (belief in peace) but the fact that the distribution of the fliers might violate other laws such as public nuisance or illegal vending could be regulated. The church would likely have little success in claiming a free exercise right to pass out the fliers if the distribution violated some other law.

Mr. Reynolds could have espoused or even promoted the idea of polygamy. That would have been his right under the Free Exercise Clause to hold that religious belief. However, when Mr. Reynolds married the women, he engaged in conduct.

In the final analysis, under the belief-conduct distinction, citizens can expect to be protected in their beliefs but not protected when the beliefs turn into specific observable "actions." Ultimately, the remedy for a free exercise violation is to grant the claimant an exemption from the regulation. It should not be expected that the regulation itself would be ruled as unconstitutional; rather, it would be unconstitutional as applied to a particular claimant and others similarly situated. For example, Jehovah's Witnesses receiving a court-ruled exemption from reciting the Pledge of Allegiance in school does not mean that all religious people would be given the same exemption. Each religion or church would have to show how the regulation punishes his or her beliefs.

Balance of Competing Interests Test

The belief-conduct distinction served well for nearly 100 years as a viable test for deciding free exercise issues. However, when it becomes difficult to determine where belief leaves off and conduct begins, the belief-conduct distinction test breaks down because it relies on being able to discern a difference between the two.

It took a religion as austere as the Amish faith to bring an end to the exclusive use of the belief-conduct distinction. With the Amish, it cannot be readily observed what constitutes conduct and what constitutes belief because in many respects, their actions *are* their beliefs. Their religious beliefs require a certain way of living that is integrated into their faith. The realization that a new test for free exercise issues was needed arose in 1972 with a small Amish community in Green County, Wisconsin. The case, *Wisconsin v. Yoder*,[14] [*see* **Case No. 6-1**] used the balance of competing

14. 406 U.S. 205 (1972).

interests test, which had been previously employed by the Court in cases dealing with other fundamental freedoms such as free speech. In *Yoder*, the Amish objected to Wisconsin's compulsory education law for their high-school aged children. In Wisconsin, as in most states, children are required to be in school until age 16 at a minimum. Starting at age 14, however, the Amish need to begin their education at home and in community apprentice programs. This is essential to the perpetuation of the Amish way of life. To send their children to high school would mean the destruction of the apprenticeships and therefore the Amish faith.

The State of Wisconsin has a compelling interest in requiring the education of children. To determine whether the Amish should be given an exemption to the law based on the Free Exercise Clause, the Court employed the balance of competing interests test. That is, the Court compared the magnitude of the state's interest in requiring children to go to school against the level of coercion the Amish would experience in being forced to comply with the law to decide which had the greater interest.

In *Yoder*, the Supreme Court was convinced that the Amish could not survive in their faith if they were forced to comply with Wisconsin's compulsory education law, so it ruled for the Amish and thus required Wisconsin to give the Amish an exemption. The Wisconsin exemption of course applies to all states and to all Amish communities throughout the United States. As a result of this case, several states amended their compulsory education law statutes to provide for a general exemption from high school for all Amish. These general exemptions are known as the Amish Acts.

Threshold Requirement for the Claimant: A Sincerely Held Religious Belief

The *Yoder* decision established another requirement: for a court to apply the balance of competing interests test, the free exercise claimant must "qualify" as a person who has a *sincerely held religious belief*. This is a threshold requirement; if it is not met, there will be no balancing of competing interests and the claim for relief will be denied. Having a sincerely held personal or philosophical belief does not meet this threshold requirement.

The question now becomes, what is a sincerely held religious belief? In many respects, the Amish set the standard. For the next 20 years, no cases were decided without the free exercise claimant being able to show elements of religious sincerity such as membership in a church and/or specific scriptural or otherwise dogmatic documentation. So much were the courts requiring this form of evidence that only mainline organized religion stood much chance of meeting the threshold requirement. The case of an unemployed clerical worker was about to change that trend.

In *Frazee v. Illinois Department of Employment* Security,[15] Mr. Frazee had been laid off from his clerical job. He qualified for unemployment compensation as long

15. 489 U.S. 829 (1989).

as he did not refuse to accept work in a job for which he was qualified. After receiving unemployment benefits for some time, he was offered a job through the Illinois Employment Division to perform clerical work in a department store. The job required that he work Sundays because it was one of the busiest days for business. Frazee refused the job because of this requirement. He claimed that it was against his religion to work on Sunday. Both the Illinois trial court and the appeals court ruled that Frazee did not meet the threshold requirement, concluding that because Frazee was not a member of any church, he could not possibly have a sincerely held religious belief. Reversing the Illinois courts, the U.S. Supreme Court held that being a member of a church is not the only way to establish that the claimant has a sincerely held religious belief. Frazee believed that the Bible taught that he should not work on Sunday. He cited to Exodus 20 from a Christian Holy Bible, which says, "Remember to keep holy the Sabbath day. Six days you may labor and do all your work, but the seventh day is the Sabbath of the Lord, your God."[16]

While it may be more difficult to determine whether a claimant has met the threshold requirement without traditional indicators such as official church membership, it has never been a requirement that one belong to a church to have a sincerely held religious belief.[17]

Threshold Requirement for the State: Least Restrictive Means

In 1981 the U.S. Supreme Court decided *Thomas v. Review Board*.[18] The case dealt with a Jehovah's Witness who quit his job at a foundry that made turrets for military tanks. Mr. Thomas claimed that his religion did not allow him to participate in the production of weapons. When Thomas applied for unemployment compensation, it was denied because he did not have "good cause [arising] in connection with [his] work."[19] In federal courts he argued that his free exercise right entitled him to an exemption to what otherwise might be a valid application of the Indiana statute. Both at trial and on appeal the courts ruled that Thomas had no sincerely held religious belief. While he claimed that his belief required his pacifism, the courts noted that other members of the Jehovah's Witness faith did not feel that the church required non-participation in weapons' construction.

The U.S. Supreme Court reversed. It noted that not all members of a particular church need to share in the same beliefs. That others in the Jehovah's Witness faith could be found who did not share in Thomas' belief did not mean that he was disqualified. Therefore, Thomas met the Free Exercise claimant threshold requirement of having a sincerely held religious belief. Once it was determined that Thomas was

16. *Exodus* 20: 8–10.
17. 489 U.S. at 835.
18. 450 U.S. 707 (1981).
19. *Id.*

indeed a qualified Free Exercise claimant, the Court then turned to the balance of competing interests test. Before the Court will determine whether the state's level of compelling interest outweighs the claimant's coercion, the Court must see that the state has applied the law with *the least restrictive means.* Indiana had a compelling state interest in ensuring that workers were not taking advantage of the unemployment system. It could do so by applying the law to those who quit their jobs because of purely personal reasons. It was not a requirement to apply the law to those quitting because of a free exercise of religion reason. Therefore, by applying the law to religious-based and personal-based reasons alike, it was not applying the law with the least restrictive means.

The ruling in *Thomas* suggests that the claimant is not the only one who has a threshold requirement. Before the state can deny an exemption based on a free exercise claim, it must show that it has used the least restrictive (to religion) means of applying a law. An interesting early case shows how the least restrictive means requirement might fit in free exercise and education. In *New Life Baptist Church Academy v. Town of East Longmeadow,*[20] a local school sought to acquire state accreditation. However, the local board that would oversee the accreditation process on behalf of the state required that the religiously affiliated school go through the same process as any other school. The process required that the state make on-site visits and observe school activities. The school objected to the process as applied to their school. At trial, the school argued that their right under the Free Exercise Clause required that the state employ the least restrictive means of applying the accreditation process. The school contended that the state's normal procedure was overly invasive and not necessary for the collection of needed data. The court ruled for the school, stating that the school having offered the results of their school-wide standardized tests would have been the least restrictive means of gathering data. On appeal, the First Circuit reversed. It found no offense to the Free Exercise Clause in gathering information. Collecting standardized test scores would not have required state examiners to go on-site and would have satisfied the least restrictive means requirement. However, the least restrictive means must also comply with the law, and as it stood, simply collecting test score data did not supply the state with all the information it would have needed to make an accreditation decision.

In the final analysis, it is suggested that a least restrictive means challenge from a free exercise claimant can be successfully defended if the state shows that the means chosen are necessary to inform the state of compliance with a regulation.

The Modified Balance of Interest Test: Targeting Required

In 1990, the use of the *Yoder* balance of interests test along with its threshold requirement became severely restricted as a free exercise test when the Court decided *Employment Division, Department of Human Resources of Oregon v.*

20. 885 F.2d 940 (1st Cir. 1989).

Smith.[21] In *Smith*, two state-employed drug counselors were terminated for work-related misconduct. The employees had been ingesting peyote, which was illegal in Oregon. The employees' use of the peyote only took place as part of a religious ceremony in the Native American Church. Nevertheless, Oregon provided no exception for peyote use for sacramental purposes. On the state-controlled substance statute, peyote remained as an illegal hallucinogen. Therefore, when the counselors took peyote, they were violating the criminal code. Both at trial and on appeal, the courts ruled for the counselors. They noted that the counselors had a free exercise right which outweighed the state's interest in applying the controlled-substance statute "without exception." It recognized that the majority of U.S. states exempt peyote use for sacramental purposes from its controlled-substance statutes, and the federal controlled-substance statutes exempt peyote as well.

The reinstatement of the drug counselors, however, was not to last long. Writing for the majority, Justice Scalia reversed the lower court decisions. The Court held that the balance of interests test should only be used when there is evidence that the free exercise claimant was *targeted* by the state. The majority held that the balance of interests test was overly burdensome on states in their attempt to require compliance with statutes of general applicability. The place for a free exercise claim is in the state house, not the federal court. The Court expects that the individual citizen wishing to achieve a free exercise exemption from a generally applicable law should engage the political process.

With the burden now on free exercise claimants to show that the state is targeting their religious belief(s), the number of free exercise cases making it to federal court has been greatly reduced.

Congress Reacts to Oregon v. Smith*: The Religious Freedom Restoration Act*

On the heels of *Oregon v. Smith*, a bill was quickly introduced in the United States Congress which attempted to "legislatively" restore the original application of the balance of competing interests test without requiring the claimant to show *targeting*.

Known as The Religious Freedom Restoration Act of 1993 (RFRA),[22] the act is essentially what the Congress used as a cure for a Supreme Court decision it did not agree with. According to Congress, the *Smith* decision would all but end all free exercise claims because most governments do not commit targeting of religious groups. From 1993 forward, many of the free exercise cases were decided for claimants relying on RFRA.

21. 494 U.S. 872 (1990).

22. 42 U.S.C.A. § bb-1.

Figure 6.1

UNITED STATES CODE ANNOTATED
TITLE 42. THE PUBLIC HEALTH AND WELFARE
CHAPTER 21B — RELIGIOUS FREEDOM RESTORATION

§ 2000bb-1. Free exercise of religion protected

(a) In general

Government shall not substantially burden a person's exercise of religion even if the burden results from a rule of general applicability, except as provided in subsection (b) of this section.

(b) Exception

Government may substantially burden a person's exercise of religion only if it demonstrates that application of the burden to the person —

(1) is in furtherance of a compelling governmental interest; and

(2) is the least restrictive means of furthering that compelling governmental interest?

(c) Judicial relief

A person whose religious exercise has been burdened in violation of this section may assert that violation as a claim or defense in a judicial proceeding and obtain appropriate relief against a government. Standing to assert a claim or defense under this section shall be governed by the general rules of standing under Article III of the Constitution.

The viability of continuing to rely on RFRA as a source of free exercise freedom was about to end. One municipality, the City of Boerne, Texas, decided it would challenge the constitutionality of RFRA when it denied the Catholic Archdiocese of San Antonio a permit to build an addition on to an existing church.

In *City of Boerne v. Flores*,[23] the local Catholic church was experiencing overcrowding in the rapidly growing community of Boerne, just outside San Antonio. Many Sundays, people could not get into church because of the shortage of space. When the Archdiocese applied for a building permit to add onto the existing church building, it was told by the city that it could not build because the area was now considered an historic site. The archbishop sued in federal court under RFRA. He argued that the city could not show that it had a compelling interest that outweighed the church's rights. Once more, it argued that the city did not apply least restrictive means in carrying out the intent of the ordinance. The church had offered to

23. 521 U.S. 507 (1997).

make the addition architecturally identical to the existing building. This offer was rejected.

The response of the City of Boerne was that the church could not show targeting as the ordinance would be applied to all. Therefore, the city maintained it met the requirements consistent with *Oregon v. Smith*, which it believed controlled the issue, not RFRA. It argued that in the face of *Smith*, RFRA was unconstitutional. This set up a separation of powers issue, which the U.S. Supreme Court did hear.

Ruling for the City of Boerne, the Court considered RFRA to be overbroad and not consistent with the Enforcement Clause of the Fourteenth Amendment. Other congressional enactments passed to enforce those civil rights, such as the Civil Rights Act and the Voters Rights Act, were valid because of the history of various states refusing to recognize rights under the federal Bill of Rights. A situation of widespread free exercise deprivations following the *Smith* ruling was not recognized by the Court; therefore, the necessary predicate for Congress' invoking of the Enforcement Clause and passing RFRA did not exist. The scope of RFRA was considered too broad because it required all levels of government — local, state, and federal — to comply. Therefore, the Court ruled that RFRA was unconstitutional as applied to the states but still controlled the free exercise relationship between citizens and the federal government.

Except for the federal Department of Defense schools, all public schools in the United States are a function of state government. Therefore, RFRA does not apply generally to public schools. *Smith* controls free exercise issues within the school setting. As a practical matter, if a school patron were to have interest in a free exercise exemption, it is not likely the federal court would provide relief. To have any success, the patron, most often a parent, would need to show that the school was specifically targeting them for coercive effects. It is not likely that the school chose textbooks or holiday activities with certain religious groups in mind — groups that the school wanted to coerce because it knew the parents had religious beliefs to the contrary. This would be the parent's burden given the *Smith* holding.

However, that is not to say parents could not "lobby" the school board for a free exercise exemption. They may feel they need exemptions from offensive reading materials, pagan rituals, or teachings that run contrary to their religion. Those exemptions, which in the past were gained by federal court victories, would now have to be political victories. The *Smith* holding also provided this avenue: "Values that are protected against government interference through enshrinement in the Bill of Rights are not thereby banished from the political process . . . religious belief can be expected to be solicitous of that value in its legislation as well."[24]

Given the evolution of the constitutional tests for deciding free exercise issues, it is safe to say that there are few opportunities for court-imposed rights under the Clause. There are political rights to be gained, however. Once legislation is in place

---

24. 494 U.S. 872 at 890.

to provide for a free exercise exemption, the courts can be used to settle issues as to whether a state agent is complying with legislation.

In May 2017, President Donald Trump issued Executive Order 13798, Promoting Free Speech and Religious Liberty.[25] This order reinforced the administration's commitment to respect and protect religious and political speech, suggesting amended regulations to address conscience-based objections to the preventive-care mandate promulgated under the Affordable Care Act and directing the Attorney General to issue guidance interpreting religious liberty protections in federal law. This order could be interpreted as a response to many topics in the national conversation but is most directly supportive of the 2014 case of *Burwell v. Hobby Lobby Stores, Inc.*,[26] which split the Supreme Court 5-4. In *Burwell*, the Court determined that regulations promulgated by the Department of Health and Human Services requiring employers to provide their female employees with no-cost access to contraception violated RFRA.

Shortly after this directive, the Supreme Court decided *Masterpiece Cakeshop v. Colorado Civil Rights Commission*,[27] ruling that the Colorado Civil Rights Commission's conduct in its evaluation of a cake shop owner's reasons for declining to make a wedding cake for a same-sex couple violated the Free Exercise Clause. As of the date of this publication, over 20 states have enacted state religious freedom laws. More than ten others have established these protections through state court precedents.[28]

Free Exercise and Home Schooling

As noted earlier in the chapter, several states passed Amish Acts in the aftermath of the *Yoder* decision. State statutes which required compulsory school attendance up to age 16, without exception, were amended to exempt the Amish from high school attendance. Sometime after the Amish were provided these exemptions, other churches tested the limits of the application of the judicially won Amish exemptions to their own faiths. In the beginning, the requests for school attendance exemptions based on the free exercise of religion were relatively few. Distinctions as to whether the requests came from the Amish or some other faith-based group were not strenuously challenged in many states.

Little by little, the rationale for keeping school-age children at home for religious purposes became generalized. Parents were keeping their children at home based on

---

25. Exec. Order No. 13798, 82 F.R. 21675 (May 4, 2017).

26. 573 U.S. 682 (2014).

27. 138 S. Ct. 1719 (2018).

28. *See* State Religious Freedom Restoration Acts, Nat'l Conf. St. Legislatures (May 4, 2017), http://www.ncsl.org/research/civil-and-criminal-justice/state-rfra-statutes.aspx; , and Juliet Elperin, *31 States Have Heightened Religious Freedom Protections*, Wash. Post (Mar. 1, 2014), https://www.washingtonpost.com/news/the-fix/wp/2014/03/01/where-in-the-u-s-are-there-heightened-protections-for-religious-freedom/

any number of dissatisfactions with the public schools; these reasons may or may not have had anything to do with the free exercise of religion. In 2002, LaMorte estimated that there were over 1.5 million students being home schooled in the United States. The percentage of children is growing at a rate of 12 percent per year.[29] (See Chapter 1 for a general discussion of home schooling and updated statistics on the number of children educated at home.)

The conditions under which states grant school attendance exemptions vary widely from state to state. All states grant some form of attendance exemption. There are states that are "hard" on home schooling and those which are quite accommodating. Home-school parents, for example, challenged a Michigan state statute that in effect required that the home school parent be a certified teacher.[30] The statute was upheld. A Virginia statute requiring home-school parents to be qualified teachers was also upheld.[31] Expanding its control of home schooling even further, West Virginia law rendered children ineligible for home schooling if their standardized test score composites fell below the 40th percentile.[32]

On the other hand, Massachusetts went too far by requiring parents to allow visits to the home by the local school superintendent. The Supreme Court of Massachusetts ruled that the visitation statute was invalid because it was not necessary to further the state's interest in a quality education. There were other "less invasive" means available to support the government's interest. The state could have simply required parents to show how they were qualified. It could require parents to submit lesson plans for approval as well as the curricula and materials to be used for teaching.[33] The states have been less successful in requiring that conditions be met for home schooling when parents have articulated a religious reason.

The highest court to consider a home-schooling issue so far is the U.S. Court of Appeals for the Tenth Circuit. In *Swanson v. Guthrie Independent School District No. I-1*,[34] a home-schooling family in Oklahoma decided that they did not have the capability of teaching their high school-aged child the subject of physics. The purpose of their home schooling had always been largely based in religion. When it became necessary to teach this advanced subject, the parents requested that their child be allowed to attend regular high school just for this one course. Aside from the one course, the child would remain home schooled. The Guthrie, Oklahoma, school district refused. It told the parents that their child was welcome to return to school as a regular full-time attendee or remain a full-time home schooler. The purpose of their position was based on funding. The State of Oklahoma did not support with any state aid the partial enrollment of students. Because the child was being

29. Michael W. LaMorte, School Law Cases and Concepts 25 (7th ed., 2002).
30. People v. Bennett, 501 N.W.2d 106 (Mich. 1993).
31. Grigg v. Virginia, 297 S.E.2d 799 (Va. 1982).
32. *See* Null v. Bd. of Educ., 815 F. Supp. 937 (S.D.W. Va. 1993).
33. Brunelle v. Lynn Pub. Sch., 702 N.E.2d 1182 (Mass. 1998).
34. 135 F.3d 694 (10th Cir. 1998).

home schooled, the school district was not claiming any state aid for that child, but at least the district did not have to absorb the cost of instruction for that child in addition to the loss of state aid. If the child were to attend on a part-time basis, the district would assume the cost of instruction for that attendance and still not receive state aid.

At trial, the parents argued that they had a right under the Free Exercise Clause to be free from the coercive aspects of such a school-district policy. They should not have to choose between their religious beliefs and the sound education of their child. The trial court ruled for the school district. Affirming on appeal, the Tenth Circuit noted that the parents could not meet the *targeting* requirement of *Oregon v. Smith*. The school district had a generally applicable law based on the preservation of funding that would apply to all home schoolers regardless of religion. Therefore, the parents failed to show the district passed this policy with a purpose of coercing them.

The *Swanson* case stands for the proposition that school districts cannot be forced, based on free exercise, to allow home schoolers to use school facilities or attend courses as they please. On the other hand, state legislatures or even local school districts might decide to forego funding problems and allow any number of permissive arrangements for home schoolers to attend on an as-wanted basis. Some states such as Florida, Idaho, and Oregon have such permissive participation statutes for home-schooled students.

Course Requirements and Religious Objections

Wishing to remain in the system rather than be home schooled, parents and students of various faiths have objected to the inclusion of certain courses or activities in the curriculum. In *Grove v. Mead School District No. 354*,[35] parents objected to the classroom use of a sophomore-level English book called *The Learning Tree*. The book has as its theme the experience of racism from the perspective of a teenage boy in a working-class black family. The Ninth Circuit court noted that although the book contains some reference to religion, it is minor. Nevertheless, the parents, who were fundamentalist Christians, claimed that requiring their child to read the book had the effect of inhibiting their religious beliefs. The court found no validity to the parents' free exercise claim. It reasoned as follows:

> The state interest in providing well-rounded public education would be critically impeded by accommodation of Grove's wishes. If we are to eliminate everything that is objectionable to any of [the religious bodies existing in the United States] or inconsistent with any of their doctrines, we will leave public education in shreds.[36]

35. 753 F.2d 1528 (9th Cir. 1985).

36. *Id.* at 1533.

The leading case in terms of free exercise objections is *Mozert v. Hawkins County Board of Education*,[37] decided by the Court of Appeals for the Sixth Circuit. In *Mozert*, a Tennessee family claimed religious interference because their elementary school children used the Holt Reading Series, which contained content the parents found objectionable on account of their born-again Christian beliefs. The mother testified "the word of God as found in the Christian Bible is the totality of my beliefs."[38]

The children's father had found objectionable passages in the readings that dealt with magic, role reversal, or role elimination, particularly biographical material about women who have been recognized for achievements outside their homes and an emphasis on one world or a planetary society. Both parents testified under cross-examination. They objected to passages that expose their children to other forms of religion and to the feelings, attitudes, and values of other students that contradict the plaintiffs' religious views without a statement that the other views are incorrect and that the plaintiffs' religious views are the correct ones.

In deciding for the school district, the court reasoned, "[A]ctions that merely offend or cast doubt on religious beliefs do not on that account violate Free Exercise. An actual burden on the profession or exercise of religion is required."[39] In short, distinctions must be drawn between those governmental actions that actually interfere with the exercise of religion and those that merely require or result in exposure to attitudes and outlooks at odds with perspectives prompted by religion.

More recently, in *Wood v. Arnold*,[40] the Fourth Circuit ruled that a world history course that covered a unit on "The Muslim World" alongside units on the Renaissance, the Reformation, and the Enlightenment period did not impermissibly endorse any religion and did not compel a student to profess any belief. In the unit, students were presented with a "fill in the blank" worksheet which asked them to complete information related to the "Five Pillars" of Islam. Among statements with blanks to fill was "There is no god but Allah and Muhammad is the messenger of Allah."

By now it should be clear that students or parents must do more than claim a religious objection if a student is to be excused from an activity. One commentator summarized the issues of parents' religious objections as follows:

> While the free-exercise clause may permit students to manifest their religious beliefs in the school setting, their claims must be religious in origin and based on an aversion to an activity that goes to the heart of the basic tenets of an organized and historically established faith.... Courts also have expressed concern that these personal attitudes and values not be allowed to stifle the free exchange of ideas in classrooms so necessary for the education of citizens.[41]

---

37. 827 F.2d 1058 (6th Cir. 1987).
38. *Id.* at 1061.
39. *Id.* at 1068.
40. 915 F.3d 308 (4th Cir. 2019).
41. Bruce Beezer, *The Rights of Students to Be Informed*, 45 Educ. Forum 443, 443–44 (1981).

The Establishment Clause in Education

The Establishment Clause requires that schools do nothing to promote religion. Generally, the courts have disallowed activities such as praying, Bible reading, and religious discussion in the classroom. The "tests" for Establishment Clause violations have evolved over the years. The early cases were decided by what was essentially a two-pronged test. The court would inquire whether the challenged school activity had (1) a secular purpose and (2) a primary effect that neither advanced nor prohibited religion. So, from the end of WWII until the early 1970s, the courts' use of this two-pronged test did not allow much religious activity in the public schools, although transportation and textbook provisions were exceptions.

The Early Cases: Child-Benefit Theory and the Two-Pronged Test

The doctrines laid out in the early cases are still good law today; however, they are not enough. A modern-day court deciding an issue concerning a school's violation of the Establishment Clause may require up to four different tests. Nevertheless, the early cases are helpful in providing groundwork for what followed in later years. The basic approach used by the Court was what might be described as strict separation. There should be strict separation unless an exception need be made to directly benefit a child. Ironically, the source of the strict separation doctrine came in a school case where ultimately the Court provided an exception.

In *Everson v. Board of Education*,[42] the Court considered whether the New Jersey statute that allowed school districts to provide reimbursements to parents for bus transportation to parochial schools promoted religion and thus violated the Establishment Clause. Before deciding that there was no violation, the Court made it clear what it believed to be the requirements of the Establishment Clause.

> The Establishment Clause of the First Amendment means at least this: Neither a state nor the Federal government can set up a church. Neither can pass laws which aid one religion, aid all religions, or prefer one religion to another. Neither can force nor influence a person to go to or to remain away from church against his will or force him to profess a belief or disbelief in any religion. No person can be punished for entertaining or professing religious beliefs or disbeliefs, for church attendance or non-attendance. No tax in any amount, large or small, can be levied to support any religious activities or institutions, whatever they may be called, or whatever they may adopt to teach or practice religion. Neither a state nor the federal government can, openly or secretly, participate in the affairs of any religious organizations or groups and vice versa. In the words of Jefferson, the clause against establishment of religion by law was intended to erect "a wall of separation between Church and State."[43]

42. 330 U.S. 1 (1947).
43. *Id.* at 15–16.

While the Court reminded us of the wall, it nevertheless ruled that the tax money going to support bus transportation reimbursements was for the direct benefit of children. It took note that the New Jersey legislature's intent was for all children to be able to go to and from school without having to cross busy intersections or otherwise be placed in harm's way. In terms of the two-pronged test, the purpose of the enactment was secular (child safety). The primary effect of the statute did not advance religion—*directly.* It is true that some *indirect* benefit might accrue to the budgets of parochial schools by having more children now be able to attend. The Court saw no offense to the Establishment Clause unless *direct* aid was being provided to the institution of the church. The New Jersey law avoided direct contact with the church altogether. Reimbursement money was sent directly to parents. The fact that the parents had a religious affiliation is not an Establishment Clause problem.

In *Board of Education of Central School District No. 1 v. Allen*,[44] the Court extended its child-benefit exception regarding textbooks. The State of New York provided free textbooks for children attending public schools, but the provision for free textbooks did not exclude children attending parochial schools. A challenge to the statute was taken in federal court. It was argued that allowing parochial schools to be included in the free textbook program would promote religion and thus violate the Establishment Clause. Once again, the Court used the child-benefit theory to uphold the statute. It saw the textbooks as going *directly* to benefit school children. While it was true that the program allowed parochial school officials or parents to benefit, the benefit was considered *indirect.* In terms of the two-pronged test, the purpose of the statute was considered secular: (1) It was intended to benefit all children of the state, and (2) the primary effect was to benefit children directly. The benefit to the church was considered indirect. (This distinction between direct and indirect aid will become important later in this chapter when we consider the constitutionality of school vouchers.)

More recently, the Supreme Court considered the participation of a church-affiliated pre-school center in a statewide program run through Missouri's Department of Natural Resources in which reimbursement grants were issued to qualifying nonprofit organizations that installed playground surfaces made from recycled tires. In *Trinity Lutheran Church of Columbia, Inc. v. Comer*,[45] by strict and express policy, the grant-issuing department denied grants to all entities affiliated with religious institutions. This policy was established to avoid conflict with a provision in their state constitution by which the state could not provide financial assistance directly to a church.

Although Trinity Lutheran's grant application received a high rating, their application was summarily denied. In their federal lawsuit, Trinity Lutheran alleged that the disqualification made solely on the basis of the religious aspect of the institution

44. 392 U.S. 236 (1968).
45. 137 S. Ct. 2012 (2017).

was a violation of the Free Exercise Clause. The Supreme Court evaluated the case and keeping in line with its repeated confirmation that "denying a generally available benefit solely on account of religious identity imposes a penalty on the free exercise of religion,"[46] ruled that such a policy triggers the most exacting scrutiny. The state's interest in staying far afield of Establishment Clause concerns was an insufficient state interest to justify the policy at issue. The Court ruled that disqualifying otherwise eligible recipients from a public benefit "solely because of their religious character" imposes "a penalty on the free exercise of religion that triggers the most exacting scrutiny." The Missouri Department of Natural Resources had violated the Establishment Clause "by denying the Church an otherwise available public benefit on account of its religious status."[47]

The Teaching of Creationism versus Evolution

While the two-pronged test was still in use, the Court heard a case whose topic was thought to be just part of history. The case, *Epperson v. Arkansas*,[48] dealt with an Arkansas anti-evolution statute. The issue of evolution versus creationism first became a heated debate in 1925 with the famous "Scopes Monkey Trial," which focused the country's attention on the extent to which evolution or Darwinism was taught in the public schools.[49] In that case, John Scopes was found guilty of teaching evolution in violation of a Tennessee statute that forbade any teaching that humans descended from apes. Fast forward to the 1960s, where the Arkansas law being challenged in *Epperson* required the teaching of the origin of humankind but demanded that the only permissible theory to be taught was *creationism*. In other words, evolution could not be taught, but creationism, a biblically based "theory" maintaining that the Old Testament's account of Adam and Eve accurately describes the origin of humankind's existence, was required to be taught in the public schools of Arkansas.

The Court did not need two prongs to decide this case. It was clear that the *purpose* of the Arkansas legislature in banning the teaching of evolution while requiring the teaching of creationism was anything other than secular. The Court ruled that requiring creationism be taught was to require that religion be taught because creationism is a Bible-based theory. If a government enactment cannot pass the first prong, the enactment is an invalid promotion of religion prohibited by the Establishment Clause. The remedy, as in all Establishment Clause cases, involved enjoining the government from applying the statute or policy. All practices associated with the enactment must immediately end.

---

46. *Id.* at 2015.
47. *Id.* at 2015–16.
48. 393 U.S. 97 (1968).
49. *See generally* Ruth C. Stern & J. Herbie DiFonzo, *Dogging Darwin: America's Revolt Against The Teaching of Evolution*, 36 N. Ill. U. L. Rev. 33 (2016).

The Three-Pronged *Lemon* Test

In 1971, when the U.S. Supreme Court decided *Lemon v. Kurtzman*,[50] **[see Case No. 6-2]** a third prong was added to the Establishment Clause test. The case considered whether certain states permitting parochial schools to receive salary supplements violated the Establishment Clause. Among the conditions for the parochial school to receive the funds was that the instruction being supported could only be for secular subjects. In ruling that the program was invalid, the Court did not spend much time with what had been the two-pronged test. Instead, it jumped to a new third prong called *excessive entanglement.*

As a result, the question before federal courts should not only be whether there is a secular purpose and a primary effect that does not advance religion but also whether the challenged program excessively entangles government with religion. In the *Lemon* case, the answer was that a program of salary supplements would excessively entangle the two. To carry out the salary-supplement program, agents of the state would need to audit the parochial school. The only way to accurately determine that the salary supplements were supporting reported secular subjects would be to sit in on the classes. This would further require that the government be able to tell the difference between a secular and a sectarian presentation. The Court considered that the practical aspects of carrying out this program would require surveillance at a level which could only be described as *excessive entanglement.* The government must not get in the position of making value judgments about how a church conducts business as a predicate for the distribution of resources. All three prongs together—secular purpose, primary effect, and excessive entanglement—became known as the *Lemon* test.

The *Lemon* test remains today as the most often used constitutional test for Establishment Clause issues in the federal courts. However, the excessive entanglement described here is only one of two types of excessive entanglement. When a government program excessively entangles because of what is required to implement and run the program, it is called *administrative excessive entanglement.* In the case itself, the Court did describe another form of excessive entanglement which it called *political excessive entanglement.*

In simple terms, *political excessive entanglement* takes place when citizens feel pressure to make political decisions along religious lines. In *Lemon*, the Court had concerns that voters would support the salary supplement measure because they perceived it would help their particular church. Opponents to the church or the perceived favoritism that might incur would use the ballot box to defeat the measure. In plain words, *political excessive entanglement* can exist when voters use the ballot box to support a religious position. It further has the potential to cause churches to behave in ways they might not ordinarily behave just to get civic benefits. For

50. 403 U.S. 602 (1971).

example, in *Lemon*, might the Catholic Church have felt pressure to offer fewer religious subjects and more secular subjects because the plan allowed financial benefits for the latter but not the former? The policy placed the government in the position of coercing religious institutions to behave in non-religious ways. The third prong of the *Lemon* test disallows both administrative and political excessive entanglement.

Creationism Revisited

Following the time that the third prong (excessive entanglement) was added to the test for Establishment Clause issues, interest in teaching creationism continued. In *Edwards v. Aguillard*,[51] the Court ruled that the purpose of Louisiana's Balanced Treatment Act was to advance religion and that it was therefore unconstitutional under the Establishment Clause. The Balanced Treatment Act essentially mandated that whenever evolution was taught in the public schools of Louisiana, "equal time" had to be given to creationism. On the surface this might seem fair, but the statute's basic problem was that creationism is religion. Whether by direct mandate or by some equal-time fairness approach, a Bible-based account of the origin of humans is a religious teaching. Up to the time of the *Edwards* case, there had been some movement to legitimize creationism as an alternative theory to evolution. Since *Edwards*, however, formal attempts at the state level to promote creationism and diminish the teaching of evolution have quieted.

In *Freiler v. Tangipahoa Parish Board of Education*,[52] a local school district in Louisiana tried to affect the teaching of evolution by passing a board policy that required a verbal evolution "disclaimer." The school district directed that before any instructor begin teaching about the origins of humankind, they recite the following: "It is further recognized by the Board of Education that it is the basic right and privilege of each student to form his/her own opinion *or* maintain beliefs taught by parents on this very important matter of the origin of life and matter."[53] The Court of Appeals for the Fifth Circuit held that: (1) the disclaimer did not further the articulated objective of encouraging informed freedom of belief or critical thinking by students; (2) the disclaimer furthered the purposes of disclaiming orthodoxy of belief and of reducing offense to the sensibilities of any student or parent, and those were permissible secular objectives for purposes of the secular purpose prong of the *Lemon* test; (3) and the primary effect of the disclaimer was to protect and maintain a particular religious viewpoint, thereby violating the second prong of the *Lemon* test as well. It did not use the third prong.

Attempts to use disclaimers at the state level have occurred in several states, by various methods. Some of these attempts include requiring "equal time" for creation

51. 482 U.S. 578 (1987).
52. 185 F.3d 337 (5th Cir. 1999).
53. *Id.* at 344.

science and inclusion of creationism in the curriculum. One popular approach includes placing supposedly neutral disclaimers in science textbooks.

In 2006, the Eleventh Circuit Court of Appeals took up a case from the Federal District Court for the Northern District of Georgia in *Selman v. Cobb County School District.*[54] The controversy surrounded the issue of a science textbook disclaimer that stated, in part:

> This textbook contains material on evolution. Evolution is a theory, not a fact, regarding the origin of living things. This material should be approached with an open mind, studied carefully, and critically considered.

In evaluating the action of the school board, the district court found that the sticker, while possibly misleading and inaccurate, was neutral on its face and contained no religious content. Further, nothing in the spotty record clearly established sectarian purpose or intent on the part of any of the state actors involved, specifically the school board. However, the court found there to be a material issue of fact as to whether the sticker had the primary effect of protecting and maintaining a particular religious viewpoint. In reviewing the third prong of the *Lemon* test, the court stated that "the practical effect of students being encouraged to consider and discuss alternatives to evolution could implicate excessive entanglement concerns."[55] However, The Eleventh Circuit found the record to be so riddled with evidential uncertainties and factual problems that it sent the case back to the district court, stressing that "factual context is everything."[56]

The case returned to the district court, where the parties settled out of court in favor of the plaintiffs. While we can infer the eventual holding, this and similar cases where settlements preceded concrete court rulings have left room for some to feel that the continuation of similar practices are not clearly unlawful. In one of the more blatant examples, Alabama upped the ante in their longstanding practice of placing disclaimers in textbooks dating back to 1996. In 2016, the Alabama State Board of Education issued a resolution stating:

> The word "theory" has many meanings. Theories are defined as systematically organized knowledge, abstract reasoning, a speculative idea or plan, or a systematic statement of principles. Scientific theories are based on both observations of the natural world and assumptions about the natural world. They are always subject to change in view of new and confirmed observations.
>
> Many scientific theories have been developed over time. The value of scientific work is not only the development of theories but also what is learned from the development process. The Alabama Course of Study: Science

54. 449 F.3d 1320 (11th Cir. 2006).

55. *Id.* at 1329.

56. *Id.* at 1338.

> includes many theories and studies of scientists' work. The work of Copernicus, Newton, and Einstein, to name a few, has provided a basis of our knowledge of the world today.
>
> The theory of evolution by natural selection is a controversial theory that is included in this textbook. It is controversial because it states that natural selection provides the basis for the modern scientific explanation for the diversity of living things. Since natural selection has been observed to play a role in influencing small changes in a population, it is assumed that it produces large changes, even though this has not been directly observed. Because of its importance and implications, students should understand the nature of evolutionary theories. They should learn to make distinctions between the multiple meanings of evolution, to distinguish between observations and assumptions used to draw conclusions, and to wrestle with the unanswered questions and unresolved problems still faced by evolutionary theory.
>
> There are many unanswered questions about the origin of life. With the explosion of new scientific knowledge in biochemical and molecular biology and exciting new fossil discoveries, Alabama students may be among those who use their understanding and skills to contribute to knowledge and to answer many unanswered questions. Instructional material associated with controversy should be approached with an open mind, studied carefully, and critically considered.

Unquestionably, there was backlash in the media. But the State Board of Education was not alone in supporting such disclaimers. In 2017, the Alabama legislature affirmed its support for the State Board of Education by issuing a joint resolution that reads, in part:

> (a) The State Board of Education, public elementary and secondary school governing authorities, directors of schools, school system administrators, and public elementary and secondary school principals and administrators and teachers should endeavor to create an environment within public elementary and secondary schools that encourages students to explore scientific questions, develop critical thinking skills, analyze the scientific strengths and weaknesses of scientific explanations, and respond appropriately and respectfully to differences of opinion about scientific subjects required to be taught under the curriculum framework developed by the State Board of Education.
>
> (b) The State Board of Education, public elementary or secondary school governing authorities, directors of, school system administrators, and public elementary or secondary school principals and administrators should refrain from prohibiting any teacher in a public school system of this state from helping students understand, analyze, critique, and review in an

> objective manner the scientific strengths and scientific weaknesses of existing scientific theories covered in the course being taught within the curriculum framework developed by the State Board of Education.[57]

To date, the practice has not been formally litigated.

Intelligent Design

Another attempt to introduce creationism into the curriculum came by way of "intelligent design."[58] In the case *Kitzmiller v. Dover Area School District*,[59] parents of school-aged children and members of the high school science faculty brought action against the school district and school board, challenging the constitutionality of the district's policy on teaching intelligent design in the high school's biology class. This policy required students to hear a statement mentioning intelligent design as an alternative to Darwin's theory of evolution. The theory, put simply, is that creation must have had an "intelligent designer" to come together. This intelligent designer can be thought of as God.

The federal district court ruled that the school district's policy on teaching intelligent design in the high school's biology class, which required students to hear a statement mentioning intelligent design as an alternative to Darwin's theory of evolution, amounted to an endorsement of religion in violation of the Establishment Clause; this policy imposed a religious view of biological origins into the biology course.

The Modified *Lemon* Test

Over the years, accommodationist pressures have attempted to erode the viability of the *Lemon* test. One of the earliest moves to minimize the use of *Lemon* came in 1984 when Warren Burger wrote for the majority in *Lynch v. Donnelly*.[60] Chief Justice Burger suggested that *Lemon* had been over-used by the lower courts and that it was never meant to be a universal test for Establishment Clause issues. According to Justice Burger, the doctrine of the separation of church and state described by a "wall" is a "useful figure of speech probably deriving from views of Thomas Jefferson. The metaphor has served as a reminder that the Establishment Clause forbids an established church or anything approaching it. But the metaphor itself is not a wholly accurate description of the practical aspects of the relationship that in fact exists between church and state."[61] The primary concern for Establishment

57. H.J.R. 78, 2017 Reg. Sess., (Ala. 2017).

58. *See generally* Roger L. Tarbutton, *Evolution, Intelligent Design, and the Establishment Clause*, 19 Rutgers J.L. & Religion 25 (2017).

59. 400 F. Supp. 2d 707 (M.D. Pa. 2005).

60. 465 U.S. 668 (1984).

61. *Id.* at 673.

Clause purposes is whether the government conduct "establishes a religion or religious faith or tends to do so." Therefore, no violation exists if the government is not attempting to set up a *state church*.

Therefore, the five-person majority decided *Lynch* by using a substitute for *Lemon*, though it should be noted that *Lemon* was not overruled. As if to kill *Lemon* by benign neglect, the majority decided it would uphold the City of Pawtucket's Christmas crèche display without the three-pronged test. The case involved a challenge to the city's 40-year use of a Christmas manger scene on display at a city park. The ACLU argued that the display promoted religion. Using the *Lemon* test, the lower courts agreed that the display violated the Establishment Clause. In reversing the lower courts, the U.S. Supreme Court noted that (1) the purpose of the crèche was not entirely sectarian as there were some elements representing symbolically the secular aspects of Christmas, i.e., wrapped presents, Santa Claus. Unless the scene was totally sectarian, which it was not, it could not be said to violate the purposes of the Establishment Clause. Thus, the majority did not say the purpose-prong of *Lemon* should be overruled. However, its application is such that unless the Court can find a purpose entirely motivated by sectarian views, there should be no violation. (2) Instead of the primary-effect prong as typically used by the federal courts, the majority noted that the United States has Judeo-Christian roots. It is only natural that many public secular holidays *merely coincide* with the tenets of some religions. According to the Court, Christmas is one of those holidays. Therefore, any government promotion of such a holiday should not violate any Establishment Clause considerations. (3) In terms of excessive entanglement, the majority focused on the political entanglement aspect of the analysis. For the majority, there was no excessive political entanglement because of the immediate litigation. There was no evidence of any prolonged divisiveness. For the Court to find a violation of the excessive entanglement prong it would have to have evidence of a *whole history* of entanglement. With the version of the *Lemon* test as proposed by the *Lynch* majority, many government activities that had been invalidated might now pass constitutional muster. This accommodationist approach is best summarized by the Court when it said:

> It has never been thought either possible or desirable to enforce a regime of total separation.... Nor does the Constitution require complete separation of church and state; it affirmatively mandates accommodation, not merely tolerance, of all religions, and forbids hostility toward any.[62]

Nevertheless, the "new and improved" accommodationist approach has yet to be utilized by any other court in its entirety.

Interestingly, it was Justice O'Connor's concurrence in *Lynch* that gained popularity as a means of "modifying" *Lemon* for certain Establishment Clause issues. O'Connor proposed that a more appropriate test for Establishment Clause issues

62. *Id.* (citing Comm. for Pub. Educ. & Religious Liberty v. Nyquist, 413 U.S. 756, 760 (1973)).

should center on whether a government activity sends a message of endorsement of religion. This doctrine has become known as the *Endorsement Test.* In the words of Justice O'Connor:

> The Establishment Clause prohibits government from making adherence to a religion relevant in any way to a person's standing in the political community. Government can run afoul of that prohibition in two principal ways. One is excessive entanglement with religious institutions, which may interfere with the independence of the institutions, give the institutions access to government or governmental powers not fully shared by nonadherents of the religion, and foster the creation of political constituencies defined along religious lines. *E.g., Larkin v. Grendel's Den, 459 U.S. 116, 103 S. Ct. 505, 74 L. Ed. 2d 297 (1982).* The second and more direct infringement is government endorsement or disapproval of religion. Endorsement sends a message to nonadherents that they are outsiders, not full members of the political community, and an accompanying message to adherents that they are insiders, favored members of the political community. Disapproval sends the opposite message. See generally *Abington School District v. Schempp, 374 U.S. 203, 83 S. Ct. 1560, 10 L. Ed. 2d 844 (1963).*[63]

The test can be viewed as two-pronged. In the first prong, the court would ask, "what message was intended" by the government. If the government intended to send a message that it "favors" religion or religiously oriented citizens, then the prong has failed. It constitutes an Establishment Clause violation. If the court concludes that the message intended was neutral, then it will move to the next prong. In the second prong, the question for the court will be "what message was received" by citizens about the government endorsement or disfavoring of religion. Regardless of the government's intent, if the message received is that government favors or disfavors religion, then the prong fails, and an Establishment Clause violation exists. For the challenged government activity to stand, both prongs of the endorsement test must be passed.

Especially for education cases involving the promotion of religious activity in schools, the lower courts have used the *Lemon* test modified by the second prong of the *endorsement* test. Put succinctly, the modified *Lemon* test features three prongs: (1) secular purpose, (2) message received (instead of primary effect), and (3) excessive entanglement. This test first made its appearance in *Bell v. Little Axe*,[64] where the Tenth Circuit found that the school district was promoting religion when it conducted prayer meetings, among other things. The court applied the second prong of the endorsement test (message received) instead of the primary-effect prong of *Lemon*. Indeed, the court held that the school's activities were invalid because students received a message that officials "favored" religion. The modified *Lemon* test

63. *Id.* at 688.

64. 766 F.2d 1391 (10th Cir. 1985).

became the federal courts' test of choice when the issue dealt with the more psychological aspects of school events as they relate to religious activities. The traditional *Lemon* test continued to be used for those school Establishment Clause challenges dealing with government aid.

Prayers at School Board Meetings

A particularly unsettled part of the law regarding schools and one that has been and is still actively litigated in the lower courts is the legality of prayers at school board meetings.[65] After *Marsh v. Chambers*,[66] a Supreme Court decision that upheld prayers by chaplains at legislative meetings, federal appeals courts in the Third,[67] Sixth,[68] and Ninth[69] Circuits struck down prayers at school board meetings as violating the *Lemon* test. They noted that the *Marsh* exception did not apply to school board meetings because, unlike legislative meetings, the audience often included students, who may be there to receive awards, address disciplinary infractions, or as student representatives to the board. The Fifth Circuit[70] appeared to be leaning in a similar direction, but upon rehearing determined that the plaintiffs lacked standing.

In 2014, however, 31 years after *Marsh*, the issue became much less clear with the Supreme Court's decision in *Town of Greece v. Galloway*.[71] This most recent Court ruling on ceremonial prayer concerned prayers conducted at town board meetings in Greece, New York. In addition to the roll call and Pledge of Allegiance, the town board meetings included a prayer offered by a member of the clergy representing various (in fact almost all) congregations listed in a local directory. While the program was facially open to all creeds, nearly all local congregations were Christian. Therefore, almost all those offering prayers at town meetings represented some sect of Christianity. Citizens who attended the meetings to speak on local issues filed suit, alleging the town board was in violation of the Establishment Clause of the First Amendment because of their preference for Christianity over other faiths and by sponsoring sectarian prayer.

The complainants sought to limit the ceremonial prayer to "inclusive and ecumenical prayers" that referred to only a "generic God." The district court found no impermissible preference for Christianity but rather saw the faiths represented as reflective of the whole community. However, the Second Circuit Court of Appeals

---

65. *See* Martha McCarthy, *School Board Meeting Prayers: A Moving Target*, 358 Educ. L. Rep. 751 (2018).

66. 463 U.S. 783 (1983).

67. Doe v. Indian River Sch. Dist., 653 F.3d 256 (3d Cir. 2011).

68. Coles v. Cleveland Bd. of Educ., 171 F.3d 369 (6th Cir. 1999).

69. Bacus v. Palo Verde Unified Sch. Dist., 11 F. Supp. 2d 1192 (C.D. Cal. 1998), *rev'd*, 52 F. Appx. 355 (9th Cir. 2002).

70. Doe v. Tangipahoa Par. Sch. Bd., 473 F.3d 188 (5th Cir. 2006), *vacated on reh'g en banc*, 494 F.3d 494 (5th Cir. 2007).

71. 572 U.S. 565 (2014).

reversed, finding that, viewed in its totality by a reasonable observer, the town board's message was one of endorsing Christianity. "The town's failure to promote the prayer opportunity to the public, or to invite ministers from congregations outside the town limits, all but 'ensured a Christian viewpoint.'"[72]

The U.S. Supreme Court, given prior history, considered whether the practice in the town of Greece fit within the ceremonial traditions long followed in Congress and the state legislatures.

> The First Amendment is not a majority rule, and government may not seek to define permissible categories of religious speech. Once it invites prayer into the public sphere, government must permit a prayer giver to address his or her own God or gods as conscience dictates, unfettered by what an administrator or judge considers to be nonsectarian.[73]

It ruled that so long as the town maintains a policy of nondiscrimination, the Constitution does not require it to search beyond its borders for non-Christian prayer givers in an effort to achieve religious balancing.[74] The quest to promote "a 'diversity' of religious views" would require the town to make inappropriate judgments about the number of religions it should sponsor and how often each should be given the opportunity, a form of government entanglement with religion that it considered to be far more troublesome than Greece's approach.[75] In upholding the policy, the Court also noted that an observer's feelings of offense are not tantamount to government coercion.

Implications for School Boards

Following *Town of Greece*, federal courts have grappled with its application in school settings. While many jurisdictions are still balancing ceremonial prayer in school settings, the aftermath of two major cases in different federal court districts illustrates that this remains a very fact-specific area of inquiry.

The Fifth Circuit Court evaluated prayer at school board meetings in *American Humanist Association v. McCarty*.[76] In this case, a Texas school board modified its longstanding policies surrounding elementary and middle school students reciting the Pledge of Allegiance and making statements, which could, and often did include, a form of prayer.[77] Until early 2015, student presenters were selected by merit, and the board referred to these student presentations as "invocations." at which point the board changed the selection process from one based on a merit

72. *Id.* at 574.
73. *Id.* at 572.
74. *Id.* at 567.
75. *Id.* at 586.
76. 851 F.3d 521 (5th Cir. 2017).
77. *Id.*

system to one of random selection and also began referring to the presentations as "student expressions." The board also noted that the views expressed by the students did not reflect those of the board. These changes were made in response to complaints by the American Humanist Association (AHA).

The AHA nevertheless remained displeased and sued the district and its board members, alleging the board maintained a "policy, practice, and custom of permitting, promoting, and endorsing prayers delivered by school-selected students" at board meetings, in violation of the Establishment Clause.[78] In its evaluation, the court determined that prayer at a school board meeting was more akin to legislative prayer than school prayer, despite the presence of school children. Ruling in favor of the school district, the court stated, "[A]lthough it is possible to imagine a school-board student-expression practice that offends the Establishment Clause, this one, under its specific facts, does not."[79] Upon appeal, the U.S. Supreme Court denied the AHA's petition for certiorari.

Meanwhile, the Ninth Circuit Court of Appeals evaluated prayer in another school board meeting session. In *Freedom from Religion Foundation v. Chino Valley Unified School District*,[80] the school board in question typically began their meetings in confidential closed session. The open session of the meetings started with a report of the closed meeting, moved into a portion of the meeting where a member of the community (which could include a student) led the recitation of the Pledge of Allegiance, the Junior ROTC presented the colors, and then a prayer was led by a member of the clergy, a board member, or a member of the audience. It was not unusual for board members to make ad hoc statements about the invocation, their personal Christian faith, or biblical teachings during this time. This portion of the meeting was followed by a student showcase, often a student or class performance, and a time for the recognizing students for all manner of achievement, meritorious service, and accomplishment. The board then moved into formal business and closed its meetings with public comment.

The Freedom from Religion Foundation brought suit against the board and the district, alleging the board's policy and custom of opening board meetings with prayer, as well as its policy and custom of including Bible reading and preaching in meetings, violated the Establishment Clause, the Fourteenth Amendment's Equal Protection Clause, and the California Constitution.[81] Given the circumstances, the court determined the schoolchildren who attended these meetings either to participate or be recognized were not truly there voluntarily and that the prayer at the board meetings fell outside the legislative prayer tradition. Therefore, the *Lemon* test applied.[82] As such,

78. *Id.* at 525.
79. *Id.* at 529–30.
80. 896 F.3d 1132 (9th Cir. 2018).
81. *Id.* at 1141.
82. *Id.* at 1142.

the court held the prayer policy lacked a secular legislative purpose, the principal or primary effect of the prayers could not be said to neither advance nor inhibit religion, and the policy fostered an "excessive government entanglement" with religion.[83]

The Prayer Clubs Cases

In the early 1980s, there was an influx of student clubs wanting to meet for religious purposes. The U.S. Supreme Court addressed this issue in *Widmar v. Vincent*,[84] where administrators at the University of Missouri–Kansas City denied a registered religious student group access to university facilities based on a regulation prohibiting the use of university buildings or grounds for religious worship or religious teaching. Members of the student group challenged this regulation as a violation of their right to free exercise of religion, equal protection, and free speech.

The High Court held that this policy violated the fundamental principle that state regulation of speech must be content-neutral. The university had argued that a content-neutral policy would violate the Establishment Clause and that the university had a compelling state interest to satisfy the Clause. The Court applied the *Lemon* test to determine whether a content-neutral policy would violate the Establishment Clause. Under the first prong of the *Lemon* test, the Court said the challenged regulation did not have a secular purpose because it specifically targeted religious groups. On the other hand, an open-forum policy would be secular and satisfy the first prong. The policy would be content-neutral, so it would not violate the Establishment Clause.

An open-forum policy would also satisfy the second prong of the test because it would not have the principal effect of advancing religion. The Court reasoned that any effects or benefits resulting from equal access to the university facilities would be merely incidental. It was unlikely that religious groups would dominate the open forum if given general benefits. The Court also said that the university atmosphere would not be considered religious under an open-forum policy any more than it could be considered socialist by allowing a student socialist group to meet.

As to religious clubs in public schools, all except one circuit court distinguished *Widmar* because it took place on a college campus. The cases upholding a school's compelling interest in avoiding an Establishment Clause violation took place in high schools. The courts have noted that, unlike college students, high school adolescents are not sufficiently mature to be able to perceive religious neutrality.[85] One empirical

83. *Id.* at 1143–52.

84. 454 U.S. 263 (1981).

85. *See, e.g.*, Brandon v. Bd. of Educ. of the Guilderland Cent. Sch. Dist., 635 F.2d 971 (2d Cir. 1980); Lubbock Civil Liberties Union v. Lubbock Indep. Sch. Dist., 669 F.2d 1038 (5th Cir. 1982); Bender v. Williamsport Area Sch. Dist., 741 F.2d 538 (3d Cir. 1984).

study showed that high school students could not perceive their school acting in a neutral manner if allowing a prayer club to meet.[86]

The prayer club cases make for an interesting use of both free exercise and Establishment Clause tests. Strictly speaking, the prayer club cases are free exercise cases which depend upon Establishment Clause analysis. In other words, when the students sued, their argument was that they had a free exercise right because they experienced coercion that outweighed the compelling interest of the state. But what was the compelling state interest? The schools argued that permitting student prayer clubs to meet would violate the modified *Lemon* test; therefore, the compelling state interest was "avoiding an Establishment Clause violation." To determine whether an Establishment Clause violation would occur and thus provide the compelling interest, the circuit courts needed to apply the test. In each of the cases, the courts ruled that the primary-effect prong of the *Lemon* test or the message-received prong of the modified *Lemon* test would fail because the primary effect/message received by high schoolers was that the school endorsed religion by permitting the clubs. The potential violation of the Establishment Clause outweighed any free exercise coercion. The courts observed that students could pray at home or at their churches. Not being able to pray at school amounted to little or no coercion.

The Equal Access Act

In the face of the circuit courts decisions that student prayer clubs constituted an Establishment Clause violation for those high schools that would permit them, Congress passed the Equal Access Act (EAA).[87] [*See* **Figure 6-2.**] In contrast to the courts making it unconstitutional for schools to recognize prayer clubs, the Act affirmatively requires that secondary schools recognize religious, political, or philosophical clubs, provided several conditions exist in that school.

Figure 6.2. Equal Access Act

§ 4071. Denial of equal access prohibited

(a) Restriction of limited open forum on basis of religious, political, philosophical, or other speech content prohibited

It shall be unlawful for any public secondary school which receives Federal financial assistance and which has a limited open forum to deny equal access or a fair opportunity to, or discriminate against, any students who wish to conduct

86. Lawrence F. Rossow & Nancy D. Rossow, *Student Initiated Religious Activity: Constitutional Argument or Psychological Inquiry,* 19 J.L. & Educ. 207 (1990).

87. 20 U.S.C.A. §§ 4071 & 4072.

a meeting within that limited open forum on the basis of the religious, political, philosophical, or other content of the speech at such meetings.

(b) "Limited open forum" defined

A public secondary school has a limited open forum whenever such school grants an offering to or opportunity for one or more noncurriculum related student groups to meet on school premises during noninstructional time.

(c) Fair opportunity criteria

Schools shall be deemed to offer a fair opportunity to students who wish to conduct a meeting within its limited open forum if such school uniformly provides that—

(1) the meeting is voluntary and student-initiated;

(2) there is no sponsorship of the meeting by the school, the government, or its agents or employees;

(3) employees or agents of the school or government are present at religious meetings only in a nonparticipatory capacity;

(4) the meeting does not materially and substantially interfere with the orderly conduct of educational activities within the school; and

(5) nonschool persons may not direct, conduct, control, or regularly attend activities of student groups.

(d) Construction of subchapter with respect to certain rights

Nothing in this subchapter shall be construed to authorize the United States or any State or political subdivision thereof—

(1) to influence the form or content of any prayer or other religious activity;

(2) to require any person to participate in prayer or other religious activity;

(3) to expend public funds beyond the incidental cost of providing the space for student-initiated meetings;

(4) to compel any school agent or employee to attend a school meeting if the content of the speech at the meeting is contrary to the beliefs of the agent or employee;

(5) to sanction meetings that is otherwise unlawful;

(6) to limit the rights of groups of students which are not of a specified numerical size; or

(7) to abridge the constitutional rights of any person.

(e) Federal financial assistance to schools unaffected

Notwithstanding the availability of any other remedy under the Constitution or the laws of the United States, nothing in this subchapter shall be construed to authorize the United States to deny or withhold Federal financial assistance to any school.

(f) Authority of schools with respect to order, discipline, well-being, and attendance concerns

Nothing in this subchapter shall be construed to limit the authority of the school, its agents or employees, to maintain order and discipline on school premises, to protect the well being of students and faculty, and to assure that attendance of students at meetings is voluntary.

§ 4072. Definitions

As used in this subchapter—

(1) The term "secondary school" means a public school, which provides secondary education as determined by State law.

(2) The term "sponsorship" includes the act of promoting, leading, or participating in a meeting. The assignment of a teacher, administrator, or other school employee to a meeting for custodial purposes does not constitute sponsorship of the meeting.

(3) The term "meeting" includes those activities of student groups, which are permitted under a school's limited open forum and are not directly related to the school curriculum.

(4) The term "noninstructional time" means time set aside by the school before actual classroom instruction begins or after actual classroom instruction ends.

To be sure, the right of high school students to form an official prayer club was not necessarily widespread due to the number of conditions that had to be met. To begin, the school must have at least one non-curricular club to trigger the Act. If every club in the school is somehow related to the curriculum, one of the primary conditions of the Act is not met. Unlike other extracurricular clubs, a religion club, meeting under the auspices of EAA, cannot have a faculty sponsor. If insurance requirements dictate that there must be a school employee at the club meetings, then the employee can attend but not participate. The club cannot be given a budget. It is arguable whether the school can even allow the prayer club to use school resources to promote it for fear that it might violate the "no sponsorship" provision of the statute.

The Eighth Circuit decided it would split from the other circuits when it decided for a student prayer club in Omaha, Nebraska. The club was denied recognition because the school claimed all of the clubs were curriculum related, and therefore EAA did not apply. The students argued that at least 10 of the 30 extracurricular clubs were not curriculum related. They said that the school simply "made up" and articulated curricular connections to avoid having to comply with EAA. For example, the school said the Chess Club was related to mathematics because one had to use logic and thinking to play chess. In its defense, the school argued that it was entirely up to school authorities to define curricular/noncurricular as it saw fit. Besides, the school argued, the EAA is unconstitutional because the vast majority of federal circuits have held that student prayer clubs violate the Establishment Clause. In ruling for the students, the Eighth Circuit agreed that the school could not simply define its way of out compliance. It noted that any reasonable observation of perhaps up to a dozen extracurricular clubs showed that they were not related to the curriculum; therefore, the EAA should apply. The students' prayer club should be recognized.[88] Regarding the constitutional question, the court opined that the purpose of the Act was to promote free speech, not promote religion.

Affirming the Eighth Circuit's decision, the U.S. Supreme Court ruled on two issues in *Board of Education of Westside Community Schools. v. Mergens.*[89] [***See* Case No. 6-3.**] First, whether the EAA applies to any public secondary school will depend on whether that school has any noncurricular clubs. The school cannot simply develop its own definition of curricular. The majority laid down three criteria for "curricular." If every club in the school applies to at least one of these criteria, then it will indeed have all curricular clubs and the EAA will not apply:

1. The subject matter of the club is taught or will be taught as a course in the school curriculum (i.e., French Club is curricular because the school offers French courses).
2. The subject matter of the club relates to the general school curriculum (i.e., National Honor Society or Student Council).
3. The club is required as part of an academic course (i.e., student newspaper required for Journalism IV or Marching Band required for Music III).
4. The club carries actual course credit (i.e., Football or Band will appear on the transcript as a course credit).

If a school cannot get every club to meet one of these criteria, then a noncurricular club exists and the EAA will apply. The majority opinion written by Justice O'Connor used the modified *Lemon* test to rule that the EAA is constitutional. It states that in the first instance the *purpose* of the EAA was secular. That is, on its face, the intention of Congress was to guarantee that all students had the right to freedom of expression within the extracurricular environment. Second, it was noted that Congress in its hearings on the act concluded that high school students were sufficiently mature to be able to perceive that the school would not be endorsing religion by permitting a prayer club. Thus, the *message received* by the students would be one of neutrality. In terms of *excessive entanglement*, the Court noted that the act requires that teachers not participate if they attend the club meetings. In addition, the Act specifically prohibits any sponsorship (promotion) of the clubs. Therefore, the third prong is satisfied.

Avoiding the Equal Access Act

"Beware that you may get that for which you wish." Not every school district in the United States is particularly excited about opening the school to Equal Access type clubs. Recall that the act is not just for the right of students wishing to form

88. Mergens v. Bd. of Educ. of the Westside Cmty. Schs., 867 F.2d 1076 (8th Cir. 1989).
89. 496 U.S. 226 (1990).

prayer clubs. Equal Access clubs include *political* and *philosophical* clubs. Junior versions of the American Nazis or the Ku Klux Klan are also provided the right to form given the political or philosophical orientation of those groups. Virtually any controversial or even hate group could demand recognition under EAA as long as that group is otherwise lawful. Therefore, for those school districts that fear the formation of student hate groups and the like, it is important to consider how they might legally avoid the EAA.

The majority elaborated on the topic of "avoidance" as means of assuring it was not removing local control from schools.[90] Schools are completely free to structure their extracurricular offerings so as to eliminate any club that does not fall within the *Mergens* definition of curricular. In so doing, the EAA would not apply. In addition to the Act not applying because of the total curricular environment, schools could also alter club meeting times. The Act only applies if clubs are meeting *before* and *after* school.[91] It is possible, then, for school districts to move all club meeting times to the *interior* of the school day. Even if clubs have been meeting at a time that is considered "before school," for example, 7:30 a.m., the board of education would have to resolve to officially begin its school day at 7:30 a.m. This approach is sometimes called the creation of a "zero hour." The same alterations in the schedule could happen for the end of the day as well. It should also be noted that junior high school or middle school students could not invoke rights under the EAA unless the school district considers those levels of education to be "secondary." Whatever the school district or, in some cases, state departments of education decide is secondary school, there the *EAA* could apply. It is entirely possible for an eighth grader to be part of a recognized prayer club in one part of a state, but then move to another part of the state where eighth grade is not considered secondary and have no equal access in the new location. The reverse could also be possible.

Gernetzke v. Kenosha Unified School District No. 1[92]

Since the U.S. Supreme Court ruled that the EAA was constitutional, there has been scant legal activity. One notable exception, however, is *Gernetzke v. Kenosha Unified School District No. 1*. In *Gernetzke*, members of the school Bible Club challenged the principal's decision to remove the display of a cross contained in a mural. The students claimed that based on the Equal Access Act, they should be permitted to include the cross in a mural that they created on behalf of the Bible Club. The mural also contained other religious symbols.

The Seventh Circuit, in an opinion by Judge Posner, upheld the school principal's decision to remove the cross from the mural, reasoning that there was no evidence

90. *Id.* at 241.

91. *Id.* at 236. While the direct language of the EAA refers to "noninstructional time," *Mergens* interprets this to mean *before* and *after* the school day.

92. 274 F.3d 464 (7th Cir. 2001).

of discrimination against the Bible Club. Rather, the principal forbade the inclusion of the large cross because of litigation concerns and fears that the cross could lead to conflict and disruption in the school, particularly by the school's well-recognized neo-Nazi population. Significantly, the principal had banned selected content from other murals, including the name of a brand of beer from a mural created by the Students Against Drunk Driving. The court reasoned that the Equal Access Act states that nothing in the act should limit the authority of the school to maintain order and discipline on school premises. It also found that order and discipline are part of any high school's basic educational mission.

More recently, in *Carver Middle School Gay-Straight Alliance v. School Board. of Lake County,*[93] the school board refused to recognize the Gay Straight Alliance as a school-sponsored club for the 2013–14 school year. The complainants argued that the school board's unwillingness to recognize the club constituted a violation of the Equal Access Act and/or a violation of their rights under the First Amendment. In 2015, judgment was entered in favor of the school board, noting that the claim was not ripe and was moot, or alternatively that the Equal Access Act did not apply to Carver Middle School because the court did not consider it a secondary school, and that there was no First Amendment violation.

Upon appeal, the appeals court found that the EAA *was* applicable to Carver Middle School. As such, the appellate court directed the district court to determine whether the EAA provided a private right of action and whether the GSA had organizational standing to pursue a claim. On remand, the district court determined that Carver Middle School, as a public secondary educational institution, was subject to the EAA. The GSA was awarded nominal damages of $1, and the school board was ultimately responsible for just over $200,000 in the GSA's attorneys' fees and litigation costs associated with the legal dispute.

Religious Materials in School

Shortly after the Supreme Court ruled in 1962 that nondenominational prayer at the beginning of the school day was unconstitutional, regardless of whether participation was voluntary,[94] challenges began to arise questioning religious materials used in schools. Perhaps the earliest case dealing with the presence of religious material in public school, although not directly, was *School District of Abington Township v. Schempp.*[95] While this case is famous for "putting an end to school prayer," a less recognized element in the case, perhaps because it was in *dicta*, concerned the use of the Bible in school. The Court concluded that, while official school

93. 249 F. Supp. 3d 1286 (M.D. Fla. 2017).

94. Engel v. Vitale, 370 U.S. 421 (1962). *See also* John Dayton, Karen Bryant & Jami Royal Berry, *Protected Prayer or Unlawful Religious Coercion? Guarding Everyone's Religious Freedom in Public Schools by Understanding and Respecting the Difference*, 358 Ed. Law Rep. 673 (2018).

95. 374 U.S. 203 (1963).

prayer may not have a place in the public school, the Establishment Clause did not preclude the use of Bibles. The only caveat is that the Bible must only be used for its historical or literary contribution and not the teaching of values. To date, very few school districts in the United States offer courses in "Bible as History." Nevertheless, the distribution of Bibles has been litigated. In *Berger v. Rensselear Central School Corporation*,[96] an Indiana school district was enjoined from allowing the Gideons to distribute Bibles to middle school students. Even though school agents themselves did not pass out the Bibles, the Gideons were present with the approval of school authorities. According to the Seventh Circuit, the activity gave an impermissible message to students that the school endorsed religion.

In contrast, however, the Fourth Circuit upheld a school district policy that allowed Bibles to be placed on a "give-away" table in a school hall once a year. In *Peck v. Upshur County Board of Education*,[97] a West Virginia school district had a policy that prohibited the "distribution" of Bibles. However, it interpreted distribution to mean a person handing out the Bibles. The district concluded that displaying Bibles on tables once a year alongside a written disclaimer that students were not required to take a Bible would not be unconstitutional. The court agreed. It viewed the policy as neutral and not endorsing religion. It should be noted, however, that a number of neutral "precautions" accompanied the table display. For instance, no one was allowed to enter classrooms to announce the availability of the religious or political material, or to stand at the tables to encourage or pressure students to take the material. No school announcement or assembly was allowed to mark the availability of the Bibles or any other religious or political material. School principals were charged with ensuring strict compliance with these guidelines.[98] It should also be noted that the court ruled unconstitutional the display of Bibles in the district's elementary schools because elementary age children would receive a message that the school endorsed religion regardless of the neutral safeguards employed.

In *Roark v. South Iron R-1 School District*,[99] school officials in Iron County, Missouri, had permitted members of the Gideon faith to distribute Bibles to fifth grade students for 30 years. The distributions would take place in the classroom during the school day in the presence of a teacher or school administrator. In 2006, several parents sued, complaining the practice violated the Establishment Clause.

In 2005, the superintendent warned the board that several attorneys, including the district's attorney and that of the school's insurer, had advised the district to cease the practice. The board voted to "pretend this meeting never happened, and to continue to allow the Gideons to distribute Bibles as we have done in the past."[100] A month later they decided to delay the distribution pending further legal advice.

---

96. 982 F.2d 1169 (7th Cir. 1993).
97. 155 F.3d 274 (4th Cir. 1998).
98. *Id.* at 276.
99. 573 F.3d 556 (8th Cir. 2009).
100. *Id.* at 559.

In September, after again being told the practice was unconstitutional, the board sought a middle ground that would allow schoolchildren to distribute the Bibles to their peers. When told by a representative from the Gideons that only Gideons may distribute their Bibles, the board voted to allow the Gideons to distribute Bibles to fifth graders. When the district's attorney asked the board to reconsider this action, the board refused, and the superintendent immediately resigned. In October, the elementary school principal met with two board members, then accompanied two Gideons to the fifth-grade classrooms and observed as they distributed Bibles.

A lawsuit was immediately filed. On the eve of the preliminary injunction hearing, the board adopted a new policy mandating that those seeking to distribute printed materials to students must submit the materials in advance to the superintendent. The board was to approve all requests unless they were libelous, obscene, unlawful, advertised products or services, endorsed a political candidate; promoted drugs, alcohol, tobacco, or illegal activities, or was likely to cause a substantial disruption.

The district court ultimately permanently enjoined the district from distributing Bibles to elementary school children on school property during the school day. This was upheld by the appellate court. However, the Eighth Circuit ruled that the updated but not yet implemented policy could not be shut down based on analysis weighing past practice. It must instead be independently evaluated using the *Lemon* criteria.

Over the years, display of the Ten Commandments in schools has been an issue. As far back as 1980, the U.S. Supreme Court in *Stone v. Graham*[101] ruled that a Kentucky statute could not require the posting of the Ten Commandments in every classroom without violating the Establishment Clause. The Ten Commandments were considered religious in nature, so a required posting would have the primary effect of advancing religion. In *Diloreto v. Downey Unified School District Board of Education*,[102] the Ninth Circuit ruled that a California school district could disallow a local patron from using the fence around the school baseball field for advertising the Ten Commandments. The court held that (1) the fence was a "nonpublic forum" open for a limited purpose, and the district could exclude subjects from posting thereon that would be disruptive to the educational purpose of the school; (2) the district's concerns regarding disruption and potential controversy were legitimate reasons for restricting the content of the advertisements on the fence by excluding ads on certain subjects, including religion; (3) precluding plaintiff's sign was pursuant to a permissible, content-based limitation on the forum, and not viewpoint discrimination; and (4) the fact that the district chose to close the forum rather than post plaintiff's advertisement and risk further disruption or litigation did not constitute viewpoint discrimination.

101. 449 U.S. 39 (1980).

102. 196 F.3d 958 (9th Cir. 1999).

The Third Establishment Clause Test: Coercion Analysis

Establishment Clause analysis began with a two-pronged test in the 1940s. That test was replaced by the *Lemon* test in the 1970s. Then the *modified Lemon* test emerged in the 1980s. Then, in 1992, the U.S. Supreme Court added yet another test, which has become known as *coercion analysis.* This test was born out of a case dealing with prayer at a junior high school graduation ceremony. In *Lee v. Weisman,*[103] [*see* **Case No. 6-4**] parents objected to a rabbi giving an invocation at the beginning of the graduation program. They argued that the prayer violated the Establishment Clause because the students received a message that the school officially endorsed religion. Both the trial and the appeals court ruled for the parents, finding that the activity failed the modified *Lemon* test.

The Bush administration had directed Solicitor General Ken Starr to submit an *amicus* brief, but to no avail—the Supreme Court affirmed the decision of the lower courts. In the brief, the administration asked the Court to overrule the *Lemon* test, urging it adopt a more accommodationist position. It asked the Court to use something called *liberty focused inquiry.* Under this approach, the proper question would be whether the activity of government "coerces" individuals to behave in religious ways contrary to their beliefs. In its brief, the government argued that it should not be prevented from accommodating religion unless it seeks to use its power to penalize individuals for failure to comply with a religious event.[104]

Writing for the majority in *Lee,* Justice Kennedy specifically declined the Bush administration's request. The Court did not overrule *Lemon*; it did, however, decide the case without it. The Court emphasized coercion, asking that there be sensitivity to what it called "psychological coercion," that is, coercion that must be observed even if it is *incidental.* The Court was not very clear in detailing how courts should apply this new *coercion analysis.*

Nevertheless, the Supreme Court remanded *Jones v. Clear Creek Independent School District,*[105] a Fifth Circuit opinion, and requested this lower court to apply the coercion analysis. The case involved a Clear Creek, Texas, high school graduation prayer policy which allowed students to choose whether they wanted a prayer to be read at their graduation. In deciding the policy was constitutional, it used the new coercion analysis provided by *Lee.*

The Fifth Circuit found that coercion analysis could be reduced to three specific prongs. A federal court should ask the following: (1) Are the students directing the prayer event? (2) Is the event low on religiosity? and (3) Is student participation voluntary? If the court finds that the event is student-led, low on religiosity, and truly voluntary, then the activity will not violate the Establishment Clause. Determining that the policy was not a violation of the Establishment Clause, the Fifth Circuit

---

103. 505 U.S. 577 (1992).

104. Brief for the United States as amicus curiae supporting petitioners, No. 90-1014.

105. 977 F.2d 963 (5th Cir. 1992).

looked both to *Lemon* and to *Lee*. Applying *Lemon*, the judges determined that there was a secular purpose to the policy, that the policy did not have the primary effect of advancing religion, and that there was no excessive entanglement between government and religion. The court also found that there was no endorsement of religion in the policy. In determining whether the policy was coercive, the Fifth Circuit found that none of these three factors was violated by the policy.

Prayer at School Events

Whether schools may offer a prayer at graduation exercises seems to have been settled by the *Lee* decision. As an original presentation in *Lee*, coercion analysis was a bit cryptic. However, the Fifth Circuit in *Jones* made a useful contribution by identifying three prongs to follow in conducting coercion analysis. Since the *Lee* decision, the three-pronged coercion analysis has been applied to several school prayer events.

As if to forget all but the "student directness" of a prayer event, one school district in Santa Fe, Texas, found itself before the U.S. Supreme Court. In *Santa Fe Independent School District v. Doe*,[106] [*see* **Case No. 6-5**] the Court considered whether a student-led prayer before the high school's football games violated the Establishment Clause. The school district argued that it complied with *Lee* because students led the prayer. Once more, the prayer took place at the stadium (low religiosity) and of course students were free to attend the game or not, meaning that it was not a required activity. The Supreme Court disagreed with the school district. While it may have been student-led and low in religiosity, it was not genuinely voluntary. The Court reasoned that students in that small town in Texas are very much inclined if not peer pressured into attending "the big game." To suggest that students could take it or leave it is to deny the reality of the importance of social activities to the average adolescent in America.

Therefore, prayer before the football game sends an impermissible message that the school endorses religion. While the prayer at the game passes the first and second prongs of coercion analysis, it violates the third prong of the test because the football game is not truly a voluntary event. Much attention has been focused on ensuring that school prayer activities are student-directed, but the "student-directed" prong of the analysis is only one of three necessary elements. Coercion analysis was used in the next case to find an Establishment Clause violation.

Doe v. Beaumont Independent School District[107]

In *Doe v. Beaumont Independent School District*, the Beaumont School District initiated a "clergy in schools" program that was "open only to clergymen," and "invite[d] individual members of the local clergy to provide volunteer counseling

106. 530 U.S. 290 (2000).

107. 173 F.3d 274 (5th Cir. 1999).

to students at the schools during school hours." Parents brought an Establishment Clause claim against the school district. In finding the program to be unconstitutional, the circuit court looked to the *Lemon* test, the *Lee* test, and the endorsement test. In looking to *Lemon,* the court made no determination as to whether the program had a primarily secular purpose, since it found that it violated the second two prongs of the standard. The court found *Lee*'s coercion test was violated. Since the clergy was the focus of the entire program (thereby constituting a formal religious exercise), there was "no dispute that [the school district] directed the Program" (direction) and providing students a choice between participating or offending school officials was essentially no choice (participation). Finally, the Fifth Circuit found the program failed the endorsement test since the "palpably ubiquitous involvement" of the school district "and its highest officials — superintendent, school principals, and counselors — conveys the unmistakable message that religion is favored, preferred, and even promoted, over other beliefs."

Adler v. Duval County School Board[108]

In *Adler v. Duval County School Board*, the first post-*Santa Fe* decision, the Eleventh Circuit considered the legality of a Florida school district policy that allowed graduating high school seniors to decide if they wanted to have a graduating student speaker at commencement, and if so, who the speaker would be. The policy granted the speaking student the ability to deliver a message without control by the school administration and potentially including religious speech. In finding this policy to be constitutionally acceptable, the court determined that it did not violate the requirements of *Lemon* or *Lee*. The policy was facially neutral and there was no coercion (no school control). The court distinguished *Adler* from *Santa Fe* because the Florida policy was entirely student-directed.

Lassonde v. Pleasanton[109]

In *Lassonde v. Pleasanton,* one of a high school's two salutatorians crafted a graduation speech quoting extensively from the Bible. The student made clear "[his] desire for [his] fellow graduates to develop a personal relationship with God through faith in Christ in order to better their lives."[110] Upon review, considering the Establishment Clause implications and with the advice of legal counsel, the principal advised the student that statements concerning his personal beliefs would be allowed, but statements considered to be proselytizing must be removed. The student offered to issue a disclaimer that his views did not represent those of the school but was rejected. In the end, the student delivered the speech modified as requested

108. 250 F.3d 1330 (11th Cir. 2001).

109. 320 F.3d 979 (9th Cir. 2003).

110. *Id* at 981.

by the administration, stated his planned speech had been censored, and indicated the speech in its planned entirety would be provided in paper form outside the ceremony and presented in full at his church the following Sunday. The student sued the district and its administration for violation of his First Amendment rights. The Ninth Circuit determined that had the school not intervened, his delivering the speech as drafted would have resulted in a violation of the Establishment Clause and any issuance of a disclaimer would not have cured the violation.

In the final analysis, it seems possible for a school district to allow a prayer at a school event. School authorities would need to avoid the temptation of attempting to control the content of the prayer event. Advising or reviewing the prayer ahead of time might be evidence of the school "directing" the event, thus violating the first prong of coercion analysis. Once more, inviting clergy to deliver prayer invocations or benedictions could indicate the presence of "religiosity." Also, the event, or at least the students' participation in that part of the event (where the prayer takes place) must be truly voluntary.

It should be noted that many of the post-*Lee* and post-*Santa Fe* decisions continue to use a *Lemon* or modified *Lemon* test along with coercion analysis. Perhaps because the *Lemon* tests have been used for almost five decades the courts feel comfort in applying them as part of their Establishment Clause analysis. It may take more than suggested alternatives or even benign neglect to stop the courts from using *Lemon*. In the future, the U.S. Supreme Court may need to clearly overrule *Lemon* as it has done with other longstanding doctrines before the lower courts will let go of its use.

Very popular school prayer events such as baccalaureates or "See You at the Pole" have yet to be challenged as Establishment Clause violations at the appellate level. These events are rarely uniform, even among schools in the same state. Judicial interpretations of these events are very fact specific, and school districts seem to have a difficult time finding a balance between endorsing no religion and protecting the rights of their students and staff.[111]

Free Exercise as Speech

Opponents of the *Lee* and *Santa Fe* decisions such as Pat Robertson's The American Center for Law and Justice have identified restrictions on religious speech as censorship. That is, religious speech becomes relegated to second-class speech when students are not permitted to pray at school. The difficulty with this argument is that the intentions of the Free Speech Clause and the Free Exercise Clause are different. If the Framers intended for religion to be protected as speech, they would not have crafted the Free Exercise Clause. Commentators might agree that the purpose of the Free Speech Clause was to protect political discourse among citizens—that

111. *See generally* Doe v. Wilson Cnty. Sch. Sys., 564 F. Supp. 2d 766 (M.D. Tenn. 2008); Gold v. Wilson Cnty. Sch. Bd. of Educ., 632 F. Supp. 2d 771 (M.D. Tenn. 2009); and Doe v. Sch. Bd. for Santa Rosa Cnty., 264 F.R.D. 670 (N.D. Fla. 2010).

is, to keep government from deciding which political views could be punished and which it approved of. The Free Exercise Clause is not about the expression of political views. It is about the protection of sincerely held religious beliefs from coercion by government. To the extent that religion often uses prayer to express itself, it might be thought that if one clause doesn't work (Free Exercise), the other might (Speech). This thinking is clouded. Religious speech will not be protected because it is religious speech unless the Free Exercise Clause protects it. Religious speech might be protected under the Free Speech Clause as a result of the religious speech being protected under forum analysis. This, of course, needs more explanation.

Classical forum analysis involves recognition of the "speech forum" the government has established for citizens. One forum is the *open* or *public* forum. In this forum citizens may express themselves on whatever topic they wish. This is because the government has designated the open forum for a free exchange of ideas. Examples of the open forum are public parks or sidewalks. There are no natural open fora in schools. Once the bell rings in the morning until it rings again at the end of the school day, school authorities dictate the content for students. Students are not free to say whatever they want whenever they want in school because school is not an open forum. The school would have to purposely create an open forum. For example, a teacher giving a creative writing assignment with no limits as to form or topic comes close to an open forum. Recess or lunchtime comes close to an open forum. But even there, the school would have to suspend the rules of expression during that time and let the students know it. When students have argued that an open forum exists, they have not been successful. Schools are not the place of traditional open fora.[112]

A *closed* forum is the opposite of the *public* forum. In a closed forum the government is entirely in control of the content of the speech. Examples in the education setting would be the principal's office or the faculty lounge. This forum does not allow a citizen or, in the case of education, a student or parent or teacher to say whatever they wish. A parent, for example, could not claim a right to recite poetry in the principal's office because it happens to be a "public building."

The forum that applies in the school setting most of the time is the *limited public forum*. In this forum the government controls the content of the speech, no matter how the content is made known to citizens. Its designation is clear to the public. For example, a student would not have a speech right to talk about linear equations in a literature class. An example of a limited public forum in the school setting would be the curriculum.

The leading case on the issue of school speech fora is *Lamb's Chapel v. Center Moriches Union Free School District*.[113] [*See* **Case No. 6-6.**] In *Lamb's Chapel*, a group of parents wanted to use the school district's facilities to have a meeting and

112. *See* Perry Educ. Assn. v. Perry Local Educators Assn., 460 U.S. 37 (1983).

113. 508 U.S. 384 (1993).

show a film on Christian parenting. The parents got this idea from a previous group that had presented on secular parenting. The school-use policy did not permit religious use of facilities. The school considered this group of parents to have violated the policy, and so it denied the access to them. The U.S. Supreme Court ruled that the school had created a limited public forum when it permitted parents to use the facilities. The only difference in the second group of parents is that their expression would include some aspects of religious beliefs. The Court maintained that this religious aspect violated the conditions of the limited public forum and constituted viewpoint discrimination.

The principle of *Lamb's Chapel* is that schools may not control the views being expressed by patrons once those individuals meet the conditions of the limited public forum. The parents in the second group qualified to use the facilities for expressive purposes because the policy allowed parents access generally. The only way for the school to have disallowed the second group of religiously oriented parents would have been to create an initial policy that did not allow *any* parents to use facilities. Therefore, in effect, the religious speech of the parents was protected under the Free Speech Clause but not because the speech was religious. It was protected because the school differentiated on the basis of the viewpoint being expressed. For example, the second group of parents would have been just as protected if they decided they wanted to present a gay parenting film or a film on single parenting. Therefore, if any speech had been protected, then it would also include any religious speech.

In *Good News Club v. Milford Central School*,[114] two questions were before the Court. The first question was whether Milford Central School violated the free speech rights of the Good News Club when it excluded the club from meeting after hours at the school. The second question was whether any such violation was justified by Milford's concern that permitting the club's activities would violate the Establishment Clause. The Court concluded that Milford's restriction violated the club's free speech rights and that no Establishment Clause concern justified that violation.

Moment of Silence, Meditation, or Prayer

When states have sought "to return religion" to the schools, attempts to create mandatory prayer statutes have failed. In *Wallace v. Jaffree*,[115] the State of Alabama resolved to amend its existing "moment of silent mediation" statute to include the word "prayer." The U.S. Supreme Court observed that Alabama was unabashed in its purpose to have prayer in its schools. In applying the *Lemon* test, the Court concluded that the secular purpose prong failed. The state's argument was that the Establishment Clause did not apply to Alabama. If Alabama wished to establish a state church or religion in its schools, it may do so because the First Amendment

114. 533 U.S. 98 (2001).
115. 472 U.S. 38 (1985).

only prohibited the federal government from promoting religion. In the form of a mini civics lesson, the Court reminded Alabama that the Bill of Rights applied to the states through the Fourteenth Amendment. While most challenges to state promotion of religion do not turn on the purpose prong of the *Lemon* test, when a legislative body admits to having a sectarian purpose behind its enactment, courts will invalidate the action on the first prong. Failing the first prong of *Lemon* will allow the court to end its analysis there. It is of no consequence that the second or the third prongs might pass. Government action that does not have a secular purpose cannot be valid under the Establishment Clause. This would seem to hold true whether a court uses *Lemon*, modified *Lemon*, or coercion analysis.

Given the example laid down in *Wallace*, for the state to apply a valid "moment" statute it would need to avoid avowing a religious purpose. In fact, Justice O'Connor in her concurrence in *Wallace* pointed out that the decision did not invalidate existing state statutes that may use the word "prayer" in a moment of silence. In *Brown v. Gilmore*,[116] the Fourth Circuit upheld a Virginia statute which allowed students to have a moment of silence at the beginning of each school day. The statute included the possibility that the students might pray during this time.

Brown v. Gilmore[117]

In 2000, the Commonwealth of Virginia amended a statute that previously authorized "a minute of silence" so that "each pupil may, in the exercise of his or her individual choice, meditate, pray, or engage in any other silent activity which does not interfere with, distract, or impede other pupils in the like exercise of individual choice." The newly amended statute required the minute of silence, rather than merely authorizing it, and was challenged by students and parents.

In upholding the new law, the Fourth Circuit held that the First Amendment's Establishment Clause requires that government must sometimes accommodate religious practices so that it does not promote the absence of religion over the practice of religion. The court looked to the *Lemon* test and found that all three prongs were met, focusing its analysis heavily upon the first prong. It reasoned that because the minute of silence could be used for any purpose, the primary purpose of the statute was secular, even if there was also a competing religious purpose in the statute. The court did analyze the other two *Lemon* prongs but did not dwell upon them, arguing that because the challenge was facial, there was no evidence of the statute's effect.

Finally, the court separated its case from *Wallace v. Jaffree*.[118] In *Wallace*, it was clear that the primary purpose of enacting several statutes was religious. This difference in purpose distinguished the two nearly identical fact patterns, according to the Fourth Circuit.

116. 258 F.3d 265 (4th Cir. 2001).
117. *Id.* at 270 (citing VA. CODE ANN. § 22.1-203).
118. 472 U.S. 38 (1985).

In contrast to the Fourth Circuit, the Fifth Circuit decided three months later that a Louisiana moment of silence statute was invalid. In *Doe v. School Board of Ouachita Parish*,[119] the Louisiana legislature amended a statute to allow students and teachers to observe a brief time in prayer or meditation. School children and parents brought suit against the statute. In finding the statute to be unconstitutional, the court looked to the *Lemon* test and determined that the first prong of the *Lemon* test was unconditionally violated: there was no secular purpose in enacting the statute. The Fifth Circuit found that if the statute was not enacted for religious purposes, then the statute must have been enacted for no purpose. The court refused to find the statute had no purpose, reasoning that such intent would be inconsistent with the commonsense presumption that statutes are enacted to change existing law.

Illinois' legislative history with moments of silence goes back as far as 1969. There were modifications over the years with little fanfare. However, in 2007, the wording of what had been most recently known as the "Silent Reflection and Student Prayer Act" had been changed from "the teacher in charge may observe a brief period of silence" to "the teacher in charge *shall* observe a brief period of silence" (emphasis original) with the participation of all students at the beginning of every school day.[120] It was specified as "an opportunity for silent prayer or for silent reflection on the anticipated activities of the day."[121]

The measure was not without controversy. Then-Governor Blagojevich vetoed the bill but was overturned by the legislature. Fifteen days from the law's effective date, parents sued. The district court held in favor of the parents; however, the U.S. Court of Appeals for the Seventh Circuit found that, unlike other cases in its progeny, there was no legislative record of a goal to return prayer to school on the part of the members voting to enact the law. Further, the law specifically stated that the moment of silence "shall not be conducted as a religious exercise."[122] In upholding the practice, the court concluded that a moment-of-silence law can constitutionally include a "prayer" option, it need not include a phrase specifically permitting any other silent activity,[123] and a teacher's facilitation of such a practice does not foster excessive entanglement with religion.

Kennedy v. Bremerton School District[124] is an important case to watch in that it involves a coach who chose to pray silently on the high school field immediately after school football games. He started out praying alone, but he was doing this in the presence of others who were leaving the game, under the field's bright lights, while wearing a jacket or shirt with the school's insignia. His own students and some from the other team began joining him. Concerned that these prayers might

---

119. 274 F.3d 289 (5th Cir. 2001).

120. Sherman v. Koch, 623 F.3d 501 (7th Cir. 2010).

121. *Id.* at 505.

122. *Id.* at 515.

123. *Id.* at 516.

124. 443 F. Supp. 3d 1223 (W.D. Wash. 2020).

appear to be school sponsored and thus pose an Establishment Clause problem, the school district prohibited Coach Kennedy from continuing this practice. Despite two notices in writing from the school superintendent, the coach did not stop and was put on paid administrative leave. When his one-year contract came up for renewal, he did not reapply. Kennedy sued the school, claiming that his right to free speech had been abridged and that he had been subject to retaliation in violation of Title VI of the Civil Rights Act. Kennedy lost his suit at both the district court and Ninth Circuit Court of Appeals. While the Supreme Court refused to hear the case, Justice Alito, joined by Justices Thomas, Gorsuch, and Kavanaugh, wrote a memorandum opinion stating that even though Kennedy lost on Free Speech and Title VI, he still had live claims based on the First Amendment's Free Exercise of Religion and Title VII of the Civil Rights Act of 1964.[125] At the time of this writing, the case was wending its way through the courts with these new claims. (See Chapter 3 for a fuller discussion of how limitations on leading prayer in school-sponsored fora affect the rights of teachers.)

Curriculum as an Establishment Clause Issue

When parents have objected to certain elements of the curriculum as advancing "secular humanism," it has failed. For example, in *Smith v. Board of School Commissioners of Mobile County*,[126] parents objected to the absence of any reference to God in the curriculum. It was argued that the absence of God represented a commitment to the religion of secular humanism. While the federal district court agreed, the Eleventh Circuit reversed, finding that secular humanism was not a religion. Therefore, even if the school district was promoting something called secular humanism, it did not violate the Establishment Clause because it is not a religion. In *Fleischfresser v. Directors of School District 200*,[127] an Establishment Clause challenge was raised because the *Impressions* reading series by Holt, Reinhart, and Winston used in the elementary school had sections dealing with witchcraft and Satanism. It was argued that these ideas form the basis of a religion, and therefore the school could not promote it. Once again, the Seventh Circuit did not recognize these forms of thought as a religion. The same argument was made in California that same year, where the Ninth Circuit also found that witchcraft was not a religion for Establishment Clause purposes.[128]

In *Nurre v. Whitehead*,[129] a school district attempted to prevent future disputes and still got sued in federal court. The large school district in Washington State received a number of public and private complaints about a musical selection performed by a student choir at one of its high school graduation ceremonies that

125. 139 S. Ct. 634 (2019).
126. 827 F.2d 684 (11th Cir. 1987).
127. 15 F.3d 680 (7th Cir. 1994).
128. Brown v. Woodland Joint Unified Sch. Dist., 27 F.3d 1373 (9th Cir. 1994).
129. 580 F.3d 1087 (9th Cir. 2009).

included lyrics referring to "God," "heaven," and "angels." The following year, the principal reviewed the musical selections proposed by the student performance groups. Recognizing the instrumental "Ave Maria" as a religious piece, he forwarded the list to the associate superintendent for review. District administrators determined that the title and meaning of the song would cause attendees to easily recognize the religious connotations of the song and asked the group to make a different selection. An email to all principals explained that, while district policy typically permitted the performance of religious music selected for artistic value and performed alongside equal numbers of non-religious works, music for graduation should be purely secular in nature. A student sued, arguing that the school violated the students' rights under the First Amendment and Equal Protection Clause.

Upon appeal, the Ninth Circuit Court of Appeals limited its analysis "to the narrow conclusion that when there is a captive audience at a graduation ceremony, which spans a finite amount of time, and during which the demand for equal time is so great that comparable non-religious musical works might not be presented, it is reasonable for a school official to prohibit the performance of an obviously religious piece."[130] While the court made clear that it "does not hold that the performance of music, even 'Ave Maria, would necessarily violate the Establishment Clause," it concluded that the district's action was reasonable in light of the circumstances and therefore did not violate the student's right to free speech.[131]

While most published cases revolve around the alleged advancement or inhibition of Christian religious viewpoints, the court in *Jock v. Ransom*[132] considered the Mohawk language Thanksgiving Address. The address embodies Mohawk tradition, history, and culture, and is spoken at the openings and closings of political, ceremonial, and sporting events. For a period of two to two-and-a-half-years, the Salmon River School District employed an English language translation of an abridged version of the address, which acknowledged People, Mother Earth, Plants, Fruits, Grasses, Water, Fish, Medicine, Animals, Trees, Birds, Grandfather Thunders, Four Winds, Elder Brother Sun, Grandmother Moon, Four Beings, and Creator, in a recitation over the school's public address system on Monday mornings and Friday afternoons, and at other events.

When a non-Mohawk parent and board member complained that the address could be a prayer, the school consulted its attorney. The attorney advised that a court would likely determine the practice to be a violation of the Establishment Clause, and that a way to protect the rights of both those who choose to participate and those who do not would be to allow student-initiated recitations outside the school day. The school responded in accordance with this advice and discontinued the use of the address over the public address system, at pep rallies, and at lacrosse games. A

---

130. *Id.* at 1095.

131. *See generally* Frederick B. Jonassen, *The "Ava Maria" Effect*, 54 IDAHO L. REV. 729 (2018).

132. No. 7:05-cv-1108, 2007 WL 1879717 (N.D.N.Y. June 28, 2007), *affirmed*, No. 07-3162-cv, 2009 WL 742193 (2d Cir. Mar. 20, 2009).

group of dissatisfied parents sued, claiming the district violated their rights to Equal Protection. While the plaintiffs argued that the Mohawk address should be viewed similarly to the Pledge of Allegiance and that they were receiving disparate treatment, the court decided it need not opine whether the address qualified as a prayer. The district court determined, and the Second Circuit Court of Appeals affirmed, that the decision to remove the address from public address system and school events was made on the basis of factors other than discriminatory intent toward plaintiffs' race or national origin.

School Vouchers and the Establishment Clause

As discussed in Chapter 1, the idea of school vouchers is not new. Decades ago, the Nobel Prize winning economist Milton Friedman developed a plan that would allow parents to choose where to send their children to school. The plan provided that parents would get back an amount of tax money equivalent to an amount they had paid in property taxes. Thus, parents would receive a voucher worth a certain amount of money that they could use to pay for education. The voucher would allow the child to enter what would have been the local public school, tuition or cost free. If the parent wished to send their child to a neighboring community's school or even a private school, then they might have to make up the difference between the cost of instruction and the amount of the voucher they held. The idea of the voucher program was to induce competition among schools and thus provide for improvement.

The constitutional problem for the voucher plan would develop if the plan allowed parents to use the voucher for private, religiously affiliated schooling. In effect, tax dollars would go toward promoting private religious education. Just such a problem occurred when the Cleveland, Ohio, voucher program included parochial schools. The Sixth Circuit held that including religiously affiliated schools violated the second prong of the *Lemon* test. The voucher plan would be providing *direct aid* to the schools. The U.S. Supreme Court reversed. In *Zelman v. Simmons-Harris*,[133] the Court ruled that there was no violation of the Establishment Clause. In large part, the problems of the *effect* prong were seen to have been avoided by the practical aspects of the Cleveland program. Parents received payments directly, not parochial schools. However, to ensure that the money would indeed be spent on education, the voucher/payment could only be used if endorsed over to a school. Thus, the problem of direct versus indirect aid is avoided.

In early summer of 2020, the Supreme Court issued its opinion in *Espinoza v. Montana Dept. of Revenue*.[134] [***See* Case No. 6-7.**] The Montana legislature established a program that granted tax credits to those who donate to organizations that award scholarships for private school tuition. To prevent any violation of their state constitution which barred aid to religious schools (aka a "no aid" provision), the

133. 536 U.S. 639 (2002).
134. 140 S. Ct. 2246 (2020).

Montana Department of Revenue issued a rule by which families were prohibited from using the scholarships at religious schools. The parents of children attending religious private schools sued, arguing the rule discriminated against them on the basis of their religious views and the religiosity of the school they chose for their children. Relying heavily on *Trinity Lutheran*,[135] the court again stated that any state action excluding religious schools from public benefits solely because of religious status must be reviewed with the strictest scrutiny.[136] The ruling found that the no-aid provision discriminated against religious schools and the families whose children attend or hope to attend them in violation of the Free Exercise Clause.

Considerations for Parochial Schools

Private and parochial schools are typically exempt from many federal laws about education mostly because they do not receive federal funding. For example, students do not usually have the right to free expression or to be free of unreasonable search and seizure in private schools because the schools are not government actors and do not operate on government funds. An exception, historically, has been the Civil Rights Act of 1964 or Title VII of the U.S. Code. Nevertheless, upon passage, the Civil Rights Act specifically allowed religiously affiliated employers to consider religion in some of their employment decisions, allowing employers to favor those of their faith in hiring decisions.[137] Courts have long established that this provision does not give employers wide latitude to violate Title VII's nondiscrimination protections but serves as a narrow carve-out for religiously affiliated employers.

The school in *Hosanna-Tabor Evangelical Lutheran Church & School v. Equal Employment Opportunity Commission*,[138] employed both lay teachers and what they designated "called teachers," or teachers who held both the formal title of "Minister of Religion, Commissioned" and teacher. As a called teacher, the individual on whose behalf the EEOC brought suit taught secular subjects in addition to a religion class, led her students in daily prayer and devotional exercises and took her students to a weekly school-wide chapel service. She also led the chapel service twice a year.

After a term of disability leave, the teacher was terminated and brought a claim of discrimination to the EEOC. The Supreme Court, siding with the school, held firmly to what it called a "ministerial exception" to the employment provisions of the Civil Rights Act. It held the Establishment and Free Exercise clauses bar suits brought on behalf of ministers against their churches claiming termination in violation of employment discrimination laws. "The interest of society in the enforcement of employment discrimination statutes is undoubtedly important. But so too is the

135. 137 S. Ct. 2012 (2017).

136. 140 S. Ct. at 2256–57.

137. Title VII, Section 702, 42 U.S.C. § 2000e-1.

138. 565 U.S. 171 (2012).

interest of religious groups in choosing who will preach their beliefs, teach their faith, and carry out their mission."[139]

Eight years later, two teachers without specific ministerial designation or duties brought similar suits that were combined in *Our Lady of Guadalupe School v. Morrissey-Berru*.[140] One teacher's employment was not renewed shortly after disclosing she was undergoing treatment for breast cancer. She sued for disability discrimination. Another sued for age discrimination after her employment was terminated at the age of 64. They claimed that, because they held no "ministerial duties," their employers were not exempted from civil rights laws in relation to their employment.

In denying both claims, the Supreme Court dismissed any idea of a rigid test to determine whether a church or religious school employee conducts ministerial duties.

> When a school with a religious mission entrusts a teacher with the responsibility of educating and forming students in the faith, judicial intervention into disputes between the school and the teacher threatens the school's independence in a way that the First Amendment does not allow.[141]

Final Thoughts on Accommodation

The continued vitality of the *Lemon* test or those related Establishment Clause tests remains to be seen. On the one hand, the lower courts have had several decades of experience in applying the *Lemon* test to a variety of establishment issues. Therefore, from one perspective, unless the U.S. Supreme Court clearly overrules the *Lemon* test, it is likely to continue to make an appearance among trial and appellate courts. On the other hand, the U.S. Supreme Court seems less willing to hold on to *Lemon*. While not overruling it, the Court continues to find ways to decide establishment issues without the *Lemon* test. For example, in *Mitchell v. Helms*,[142] it was argued that Louisiana could not include religiously affiliated schools in a statewide program to provide computers to pupils because doing so would violate the Establishment Clause. The Supreme Court fell back on an old doctrine, the Child Benefit Theory, to decide that there was no violation. The Court determined that the computers were intended to directly benefit children in all schools, not to benefit institutions; therefore, when the state seeks to benefit children directly, it may do so without violating the Establishment Clause even though a program may include those children attending parochial schools.

---

139. *Id* at 196.
140. 140 S. Ct. 2049 (2020).
141. *Id.* at 2069.
142. 530 U.S. 793 (2000).

Selected Case Law

[6-1] *Wisconsin v. Yoder*

[6-2] *Lemon v. Kurtzman*

[6-3] *Board of Education of the Westside Community Schools v. Mergens*

[6-4] *Lee v. Weisman*

[6-5] *Santa Fe Independent School District v. Doe*

[6-6] *Lamb's Chapel v. Center Moriches Union Free School District*

[6-7] *Espinoza v. Montana Department of Revenue*

[Case No. 6-1]

The Amish are exempt from universal compulsory high school attendance policy as its application would violate their sincerely held religious beliefs.

Wisconsin v. Yoder

Supreme Court of the United States
406 U.S. 205 (1972)

Mr. Chief Justice BURGER delivered the opinion of the Court.

On petition of the State of Wisconsin, we granted the writ of certiorari in this case to review a decision of the Wisconsin Supreme Court holding that respondents' convictions for violating the State's compulsory school-attendance law were invalid under the Free Exercise Clause of the First Amendment to the United States Constitution made applicable to the States by the Fourteenth Amendment. For the reasons hereafter stated we affirm the judgment of the Supreme Court of Wisconsin.

Respondents Jonas Yoder and Wallace Miller are members of the Old Order Amish religion, and respondent Adin Yutzy is a member of the Conservative Amish Mennonite Church. They and their families are residents of Green County, Wisconsin. Wisconsin's compulsory school-attendance law required them to cause their children to attend public or private school until reaching age 16 but the respondents declined to send their children, ages 14 and 15, to public school after they complete the eighth grade.[143] The children were not enrolled in any private school, or within any recognized exception to the compulsory-attendance law,[144] and they are conceded to be subject to the Wisconsin statute.

---

143. The children, Frieda Yoder, aged 15, Barbara Miller, aged 15, and Vernon Yutzy, aged 14, were all graduates of the eighth grade of public school.

144. Wis. Stat. s 118.15 (1969) provides in pertinent part:

'118.15 Compulsory school attendance

'(1)(a) Unless the child has a legal excuse or has graduated from high school, any person having under his control a child who is between the ages of 7 and 16 years shall cause such child to attend school regularly during the full period and hours, religious holidays excepted, that the public or private school in which such child should be enrolled is in

On complaint of the school district administrator for the public schools, respondents were charged, tried, and convicted of violating the compulsory-attendance law in Green County Court and were fined the sum of $5 each.[145] Respondents defended on the ground that the application of the compulsory-attendance law violated their rights under the First and Fourteenth Amendments.[146] The trial testimony showed that respondents believed, in accordance with the tenets of Old Order Amish communities generally, that their children's attendance at high school, public or private, was contrary to the Amish religion and way of life. They believed that by sending their children to high school, they would not only expose themselves to the danger of the censure of the church community, but, as found by the county court, also endanger their own salvation and that of their children. The State stipulated that respondents' religious beliefs were sincere.

In support of their position, respondents presented as expert witnesses scholars on religion and education whose testimony is uncontradicted. They expressed their opinions on the relationship of the Amish belief concerning school attendance to the more general tenets of their religion, and described the impact that compulsory high school attendance could have on the continued survival of Amish communities

---

session until the end of the school term, quarter or semester of the school year in which he becomes 16 years of age.

'(3) This section does not apply to any child who is not in proper physical or mental condition to attend school, to any child exempted for good cause by the school board of the district in which the child resides or to any child who has completed the full 4-year high school course. The certificate of a reputable physician in general practice shall be sufficient proof that a child is unable to attend school.

'(4) Instruction during the required period elsewhere than at school may be substituted for school attendance. Such instruction must be approved by the state superintendent as substantially equivalent to instruction given to children of like ages in the public or private schools where such children reside.

'(5) Whoever violates this section . . . may be fined not less than $5 nor more than $50 or imprisoned not more than 3 months or both.'

145. Prior to trial, the attorney for respondents wrote the State Superintendent of Public Instruction in an effort to explore the possibilities for a compromise settlement. Among other possibilities, he suggested that perhaps the State Superintendent could administratively determine that the Amish could satisfy the compulsory-attendance law by establishing their own vocational training plan similar to one that has been established in Pennsylvania. Supp. App. 6. Under the Pennsylvania plan, Amish children of high school age are required to attend an Amish vocational school for three hours a week, during which time they are taught such subjects as English, mathematics, health, and social studies by an Amish teacher. For the balance of the week, the children perform farm and household duties under parental supervision, and keep a journal of their daily activities. The major portion of the curriculum is home projects in agriculture and homemaking. See generally J. Hostetler & G. Huntington, Children in Amish Society: Socialization and Community Education, c. 5 (1971). A similar program has been instituted in Indiana. Ibid. See also Iowa Code s 299.24 (1971); Kan. Stat. Ann. s 72-1111 (Supp. 1971).

The Superintendent rejected this proposal on the ground that it would not afford Amish children 'substantially equivalent education' to that offered in the schools of the area. Supp. App. 6.

146. The First Amendment provides: 'Congress shall make no law respecting an establishment of religion, or prohibiting the free exercise thereof. . . .'

as they exist in the United States today. The history of the Amish sect was given in some detail, beginning with the Swiss Anabaptists of the 16th century who rejected institutionalized churches and sought to return to the early, simple, Christian life de-emphasizing material success, rejecting the competitive spirit, and seeking to insulate themselves from the modern world. As a result of their common heritage, Old Order Amish communities today are characterized by a fundamental belief that salvation requires life in a church community separate and apart from the world and worldly influence. This concept of life aloof from the world and its values is central to their faith.

A related feature of Old Order Amish communities is their devotion to a life in harmony with nature and the soil, as exemplified by the simple life of the early Christian era that continued in America during much of our early national life. Amish beliefs require members of the community to make their living by farming or closely related activities. Broadly speaking, the Old Order Amish religion pervades and determines the entire mode of life of its adherents. Their conduct is regulated in great detail by the Ordnung, or rules, of the church community. Adult baptism, which occurs in late adolescence, is the time at which Amish young people voluntarily undertake heavy obligations, not unlike the Bar Mitzvah of the Jews, to abide by the rules of the church community.[147]

Amish objection to formal education beyond the eighth grade is firmly grounded in these central religious concepts. They object to the high school, and higher education generally, because the values they teach are in marked variance with Amish values and the Amish way of life; they view secondary school education as an impermissible exposure of their children to a 'worldly' influence in conflict with their beliefs. The high school tends to emphasize intellectual and scientific accomplishments, self-distinction, competitiveness, worldly success, and social life with other students. Amish society emphasizes informal learning-through-doing; a life of 'goodness,' rather than a life of intellect; wisdom, rather than technical knowledge, community welfare, rather than competition; and separation from, rather than integration with, contemporary worldly society.

Formal high school education beyond the eighth grade is contrary to Amish beliefs, not only because it places Amish children in an environment hostile to Amish beliefs with increasing emphasis on competition in class work and sports and with pressure to conform to the styles, manners, and ways of the peer group, but also because it takes them away from their community, physically and emotionally, during the crucial and formative adolescent period of life. During this period, the children must acquire Amish attitudes favoring manual work and self-reliance and the specific skills needed to perform the adult role of an Amish farmer or housewife.

147. See generally J. Hostetler, Amish Society (1968); J. Hostetler & G. Huntington, Children in Amish Society (1971); Littell, Sectarian Protestantism and the Pursuit of Wisdom: Must Technological Objectives Prevail?, in Public Controls for Nonpublic Schools 61 (G. Erickson ed. 1969).

They must learn to enjoy physical labor. Once a child has learned basic reading, writing, and elementary mathematics, these traits, skills, and attitudes admittedly fall within the category of those best learned through example and 'doing' rather than in a classroom. And, at this time in life, the Amish child must also grow in his faith and his relationship to the Amish community if he is to be prepared to accept the heavy obligations imposed by adult baptism. In short, high school attendance with teachers who are not of the Amish faith—and may even be hostile to it—interposes a serious barrier to the integration of the Amish child into the Amish religious community. Dr. John Hostetler, one of the experts on Amish society, testified that the modern high school is not equipped, in curriculum or social environment, to impart the values promoted by Amish society.

The Amish do not object to elementary education through the first eight grades as a general proposition because they agree that their children must have basic skills in the 'three R's' in order to read the Bible, to be good farmers and citizens, and to be able to deal with non-Amish people when necessary in the course of daily affairs. They view such a basic education as acceptable because it does not significantly expose their children to worldly values or interfere with their development in the Amish community during the crucial adolescent period. While Amish accept compulsory elementary education generally, wherever possible they have established their own elementary schools in many respects like the small local schools of the past. In the Amish belief higher learning tends to develop values they reject as influences that alienate man from God.

On the basis of such considerations, Dr. Hostetler testified that compulsory high school attendance could not only result in great psychological harm to Amish children, because of the conflicts it would produce, but would also, in his opinion, ultimately result in the destruction of the Old Order Amish church community as it exists in the United States today. The testimony of Dr. Donald A. Erickson, an expert witness on education, also showed that the Amish succeed in preparing their high school age children to be productive members of the Amish community. He described their system of learning through doing the skills directly relevant to their adult roles in the Amish community as 'ideal' and perhaps superior to ordinary high school education. The evidence also showed that the Amish have an excellent record as law-abiding and generally self-sufficient members of society.

Although the trial court in its careful findings determined that the Wisconsin compulsory school-attendance law 'does interfere with the freedom of the Defendants to act in accordance with their sincere religious belief' it also concluded that the requirement of high school attendance until age 16 was a 'reasonable and constitutional' exercise of governmental power, and therefore denied the motion to dismiss the charges. The Wisconsin Circuit Court affirmed the convictions. The Wisconsin Supreme Court, however, sustained respondents' claim under the Free Exercise Clause of the First Amendment and reversed the convictions. A majority of the court was of the opinion that the State had failed to make an adequate showing that its interest in 'establishing and maintaining an educational system overrides the defendants' right to the free exercise of their religion.' 49 Wis. 2d 430, 447, 182 N.W.2d 539, 547 (1971).

I

There is no doubt as to the power of a State, having a high responsibility for education of its citizens, to impose reasonable regulations for the control and duration of basic education. See, e.g., Pierce v. Society of Sisters, 268 U.S. 510, 534, 45 S. Ct. 571, 573, 69 L. Ed. 1070 (1925). Providing public schools ranks at the very apex of the function of a State. Yet even this paramount responsibility was, in Pierce, made to yield to the right of parents to provide an equivalent education in a privately operated system. There the Court held that Oregon's statute compelling attendance in a public school from age eight to age 16 unreasonably interfered with the interest of parents in directing the rearing of their off-spring, including their education in church-operated schools. As that case suggests, the values of parental direction of the religious upbringing and education of their children in their early and formative years have a high place in our society. See also Ginsberg v. New York, 390 U.S. 629, 639, 88 S. Ct. 1274, 1280, 20 L. Ed. 2d 195 (1968); Meyer v. Nebraska, 262 U.S. 390, 43 S. Ct. 625, 67 L. Ed. 1042 (1923); cf. Rowan v. United States Post Office Dept., 397 U.S. 728, 90 S. Ct. 1484, 25 L. Ed. 2d 736 (1970). Thus, a State's interest in universal education, however highly we rank it, is not totally free from a balancing process when it impinges on fundamental rights and interests, such as those specifically protected by the Free Exercise Clause of the First Amendment, and the traditional interest of parents with respect to the religious upbringing of their children so long as they, in the words of Pierce, 'prepare (them) for additional obligations.' 268 U.S., at 535, 45 S. Ct., at 573.

It follows that in order for Wisconsin to compel school attendance beyond the eighth grade against a claim that such attendance interferes with the practice of a legitimate religious belief, it must appear either that the State does not deny the free exercise of religious belief by its requirement, or that there is a state interest of sufficient magnitude to override the interest claiming protection under the Free Exercise Clause. Long before there was general acknowledgment of the need for universal formal education, the Religion Clauses had specifically and firmly fixed the right to free exercise of religious beliefs, and buttressing this fundamental right was an equally firm, even if less explicit, prohibition against the establishment of any religion by government. The values underlying these two provisions relating to religion have been zealously protected, sometimes even at the expense of other interests of admittedly high social importance. The invalidation of financial aid to parochial schools by government grants for a salary subsidy for teachers is but one example of the extent to which courts have gone in this regard, notwithstanding that such aid programs were legislatively determined to be in the public interest and the service of sound educational policy by States and by Congress. Lemon v. Kurtzman, 403 U.S. 602, 91 S. Ct. 2105, 29 L. Ed. 2d 745 (1971); Tilton v. Richardson, 403 U.S. 672, 91 S. Ct.

2091, 29 L. Ed. 2d 790 (1971). See also Everson v. Board of Education, 330 U.S. 1, 18, 67 S. Ct. 504, 513, 91 L. Ed. 711 (1947).

The essence of all that has been said and written on the subject is that only those interests of the highest order and those not otherwise served can overbalance legitimate claims to the free exercise of religion. We can accept it as settled, therefore, that, however strong the State's interest in universal compulsory education, it is by no means absolute to the exclusion or subordination of all other interests. E.g., Sherbert v. Verner, 374 U.S. 398, 83 S. Ct. 1790, 10 L. Ed. 2d 965 (1963); McGowan v. Maryland, 366 U.S. 420, 459, 81 S. Ct. 1101, 1122, 6 L. Ed. 2d 393 (1961) (separate opinion of Frankfurter, J.); Prince v. Massachusetts, 321 U.S. 158, 165, 64 S. Ct. 438, 441, 88 L. Ed. 645 (1944).

II

We come then to the quality of the claims of the respondents concerning the alleged encroachment of Wisconsin's compulsory school-attendance statute on their rights and the rights of their children to the free exercise of the religious beliefs they and their forbears have adhered to for almost three centuries. In evaluating those claims we must be careful to determine whether the Amish religious faith and their mode of life are, as they claim, inseparable and interdependent. A way of life, however virtuous and admirable, may not be interposed as a barrier to reasonable state regulation of education if it is based on purely secular considerations; to have the protection of the Religion Clauses, the claims must be rooted in religious belief. Although a determination of what is a 'religious' belief or practice entitled to constitutional protection may present a most delicate question,[148] the very concept of ordered liberty precludes allowing every person to make his own standards on matters of conduct in which society as a whole has important interests. Thus, if the Amish asserted their claims because of their subjective evaluation and rejection of the contemporary secular values accepted by the majority, much as Thoreau rejected the social values of his time and isolated himself at Walden Pond, their claims would not rest on a religious basis. Thoreau's choice was philosophical and personal rather than religious, and such belief does not rise to the demands of the Religion Clauses.

Giving no weight to such secular considerations, however, we see that the record in this case abundantly supports the claim that the traditional way of life of the Amish is not merely a matter of personal preference, but one of deep religious conviction, shared by an organized group, and intimately related to daily living. That the Old Order Amish daily life and religious practice stem from their faith is shown by the fact that it is in response to their literal interpretation of the Biblical injunction from the Epistle of Paul to the Romans, 'be not conformed to this

148. See Welsh v. United States, 398 U.S. 333, 351–361, 90 S. Ct. 1792, 1802–1807, 26 L. Ed. 2d 308 (1970) (Harlan, J., concurring in result); United States v. Ballard, 322 U.S. 78, 64 S. Ct. 882, 88 L. Ed. 1148 (1944).

world. . . .' This command is fundamental to the Amish faith. Moreover, for the Old Order Amish, religion is not simply a matter of theocratic belief. As the expert witnesses explained, the Old Order Amish religion pervades and determines virtually their entire way of life, regulating it with the detail of the Talmudic diet through the strictly enforced rules of the church community.

The record shows that the respondents' religious beliefs and attitude toward life, family, and home have remained constant—perhaps some would say static—in a period of unparalleled progress in human knowledge generally and great changes in education.[149] The respondents freely concede, and indeed assert as an article of faith, that their religious beliefs and what we would today call 'life style' have not altered in fundamentals for centuries. Their way of life in a church-oriented community, separated from the outside world and 'worldly' influences, their attachment to nature and the soil, is a way inherently simple and uncomplicated, albeit difficult to preserve against the pressure to conform. Their rejection of telephones, automobiles, radios, and television, their mode of dress, of speech, their habits of manual work do indeed set them apart from much of contemporary society; these customs are both symbolic and practical.

As the society around the Amish has become more populous, urban, industrialized, and complex, particularly in this century, government regulation of human affairs has correspondingly become more detailed and pervasive. The Amish mode of life has thus come into conflict increasingly with requirements of contemporary society exerting a hydraulic insistence on conformity to majoritarian standards. So long as compulsory education laws were confined to eight grades of elementary basic education imparted in a nearby rural schoolhouse, with a large proportion of students of the Amish faith, the Old Order Amish had little basis to fear that school attendance would expose their children to the worldly influence they reject. But modern compulsory secondary education in rural areas is now largely carried on in a consolidated school, often remote from the student's home and alien to his daily home life. As the record so strongly shows, the values and programs of the modern secondary school are in sharp conflict with the fundamental mode of life mandated by the Amish religion; modern laws requiring compulsory secondary education have accordingly engendered great concern and conflict.[150] The conclusion is inescapable that secondary schooling, by exposing Amish children to worldly influences in terms of attitudes, goals, and values contrary to beliefs, and by substantially interfering with the religious development of the Amish child and his integration into the way of life of the Amish faith community at the crucial adolescent stage of development, contravenes the basic religious tenets and practice of the Amish faith, both as to the parent and the child.

---

149. See generally R. Butts & L. Cremin, A History of Education in American Culture (1953); L. Cremin, The Transformation of the School (1961).

150. Hostetler, supra, n. 5, c. 9; Hostetler & Huntington, supra, n. 5.

The impact of the compulsory-attendance law on respondents' practice of the Amish religion is not only severe, but inescapable, for the Wisconsin law affirmatively compels them, under threat of criminal sanction, to perform acts undeniably at odds with fundamental tenets of their religious beliefs. See Braunfeld v. Brown, 366 U.S. 599, 605, 81 S. Ct. 1144, 1147, 6 L. Ed. 2d 563 (1961). Nor is the impact of the compulsory-attendance law confined to grave interference with important Amish religious tenets from a subjective point of view. It carries with it precisely the kind of objective danger to the free exercise of religion that the First Amendment was designed to prevent. As the record shows, compulsory school attendance to age 16 for Amish children carries with it a very real threat of undermining the Amish community and religious practice as they exist today; they must either abandon belief and be assimilated into society at large, or be forced to migrate to some other and more tolerant region.[151]

In sum, the unchallenged testimony of acknowledged experts in education and religious history, almost 300 years of consistent practice, and strong evidence of a sustained faith pervading and regulating respondents' entire mode of life support the claim that enforcement of the State's requirement of compulsory formal education after the eighth grade would gravely endanger if not destroy the free exercise of respondents' religious beliefs.

III

Neither the findings of the trial court nor the Amish claims as to the nature of their faith are challenged in this Court by the State of Wisconsin. Its position is that the State's interest in universal compulsory formal secondary education to age 16 is so great that it is paramount to the undisputed claims of respondents that their mode of preparing their youth for Amish life, after the traditional elementary education, is an essential part of their religious belief and practice. Nor does the State undertake to meet the claim that the Amish mode of life and education is inseparable from and a part of the basic tenets of their religion—indeed, as much a part of their religious belief and practices as baptism, the confessional, or a sabbath may be for others.

Wisconsin concedes that under the Religion Clauses religious beliefs are absolutely free from the State's control, but it argues that 'actions,' even though religiously grounded, are outside the protection of the First Amendment.[152] But our

151. Some States have developed working arrangements with the Amish regarding high school attendance. See n. 3, supra. However, the danger to the continued existence of an ancient religious faith cannot be ignored simply because of the assumption that its adherents will continue to be able, at considerable sacrifice, to relocate in some more tolerant State or country or work out accommodations under threat of criminal prosecution. Forced migration of religious minorities was an evil that lay at the heart of the Religion Clauses. See, e.g., Everson v. Board of Education, 330 U.S. 1, 9–10, 67 S. Ct. 504, 508–509, 91 L. Ed. 711 (1947); Madison, Memorial and Remonstrance Against Religious Assessments, 2 Writings of James Madison 183 (G. Hunt ed. 1901).

152. That has been the apparent ground for decision in several previous state cases rejecting claims for exemption similar to that here. See, e.g., State v. Garber, 197 Kan. 567, 419 P.2d 896 (1966),

decisions have rejected the idea that religiously grounded conduct is always outside the protection of the Free Exercise Clause. It is true that activities of individuals, even when religiously based, are often subject to regulation by the States in the exercise of their undoubted power to promote the health, safety, and general welfare, or the Federal Government in the exercise of its delegated powers. See, e.g., Gillette v. United States, 401 U.S. 437, 91 S. Ct. 828, 28 L. Ed. 2d 168 (1971); Braunfeld v. Brown, 366 U.S. 599, 81 S. Ct. 1144, 6 L. Ed. 2d 563 (1961); Prince v. Massachusetts, 321 U.S. 158, 64 S. Ct. 438, 88 L. Ed. 645 (1944); Reynolds v. United States, 98 U.S. 145, 25 L. Ed. 244 (1879). But to agree that religiously grounded conduct must often be subject to the broad police power of the State is not to deny that there are areas of conduct protected by the Free Exercise Clause of the First Amendment and thus beyond the power of the State to control, even under regulations of general applicability. E.g., Sherbert v. Verner, 374 U.S. 398, 83 S. Ct. 1790, 10 L. Ed. 2d 965 (1963); Murdock v. Pennsylvania, 319 U.S. 105, 63 S. Ct. 870, 87 L. Ed. 1292 (1943); Cantwell v. Connecticut, 310 U.S. 296, 303–304, 60 S. Ct. 900, 903, 84 L. Ed. 1213 (1940). This case, therefore, does not become easier because respondents were convicted for their 'actions' in refusing to send their children to the public high school; in this context belief and action cannot be neatly confined in logic-tight compartments. Cf. Lemon v. Kurtzman, 403 U.S., at 612, 91 S. Ct., at 2111, 29 L. Ed. 2d 745.

Nor can this case be disposed of on the grounds that Wisconsin's requirement for school attendance to age 16 applies uniformly to all citizens of the State and does not, on its face, discriminate against religions or a particular religion, or that it is motivated by legitimate secular concerns. A regulation neutral on its face may, in its application, nonetheless offend the constitutional requirement for governmental neutrality if it unduly burdens the free exercise of religion. Sherbert v. Verner, supra; cf. Walz v. Tax Commission, 397 U.S. 664, 90 S. Ct. 1409, 25 L. Ed. 2d 697 (1970). The Court must not ignore the danger that an exception from a general obligation of citizenship on religious grounds may run afoul of the Establishment Clause, but that danger cannot be allowed to prevent any exception no matter how vital it may be to the protection of values promoted by the right of free exercise. By preserving doctrinal flexibility and recognizing the need for a sensible and realistic application of the Religion Clauses 'we have been able to chart a course that preserved the autonomy and freedom of religious bodies while avoiding any semblance of established religion. This is a 'tight rope' and one we have successfully traversed.' Walz v. Tax Commission, supra, at 672, 90 S. Ct., at 1413.

We turn, then, to the State's broader contention that its interest in its system of compulsory education is so compelling that even the established religious practices of the Amish must give way. Where fundamental claims of religious freedom are at stake, however, we cannot accept such a sweeping claim; despite its admitted validity in the generality of cases, we must searchingly examine the interests that the

---

cert. denied, 389 U.S. 51, 88 S. Ct. 236, 19 L. Ed. 2d 50 (1967); State v. Hershberger, 103 Ohio App. 188, 144 N.E.2d 693 (1955); Commonwealth v. Beiler, 168 Pa. Super. 462, 79 A.2d 134 (1951).

State seeks to promote by its requirement for compulsory education to age 16, and the impediment to those objectives that would flow from recognizing the claimed Amish exemption. See, e.g., Sherbert v. Verner, supra; Martin v. City of Struthers, 319 U.S. 141, 63 S. Ct. 862, 87 L. Ed. 1313 (1943); Schneider v. State, 308 U.S. 147, 60 S. Ct. 146, 84 L. Ed. 155 (1939).

The State advances two primary arguments in support of its system of compulsory education. It notes, as Thomas Jefferson pointed out early in our history, that some degree of education is necessary to prepare citizens to participate effectively and intelligently in our open political system if we are to preserve freedom and independence. Further, education prepares individuals to be self-reliant and self-sufficient participants in society. We accept these propositions.

However, the evidence adduced by the Amish in this case is persuasively to the effect that an additional one or two years of formal high school for Amish children in place of their long-established program of informal vocational education would do little to serve those interests. Respondents' experts testified at trial, without challenge, that the value of all education must be assessed in terms of its capacity to prepare the child for life. It is one thing to say that compulsory education for a year or two beyond the eighth grade may be necessary when its goal is the preparation of the child for life in modern society as the majority live, but it is quite another if the goal of education be viewed as the preparation of the child for life in the separated agrarian community that is the keystone of the Amish faith. See Meyer v. Nebraska, 262 U.S., at 400, 43 S. Ct., at 627, 67 L. Ed. 1042.

The State attacks respondents' position as one fostering 'ignorance' from which the child must be protected by the State. No one can question the State's duty to protect children from ignorance but this argument does not square with the facts disclosed in the record. Whatever their idiosyncrasies as seen by the majority, this record strongly shows that the Amish community has been a highly successful social unit within our society, even if apart from the conventional 'mainstream.' Its members are productive and very law-abiding members of society; they reject public welfare in any of its usual modern forms. The Congress itself recognized their self-sufficiency by authorizing exemption of such groups as the Amish from the obligation to pay social security taxes.[153]

---

153. Title 26 U.S.C. s 1402(h) authorizes the Secretary of Health, Education, and Welfare to exempt members of 'a recognized religious sect' existing at all times since December 31, 1950, from the obligation to pay social security taxes if they are, by reason of the tenets of their sect, opposed to receipt of such benefits and agree to waive them, provided the Secretary finds that the sect makes reasonable provision for its dependent members. The history of the exemption shows it was enacted with the situation of the Old Order Amish specifically in view. H.R. Rep. No. 213, 89th Cong., 1st Sess., 101–102 (1965).

The record in this case establishes without contradiction that the Green County Amish had never been known to commit crimes, that none had been known to receive public assistance, and that none were unemployed.

It is neither fair nor correct to suggests that the Amish are opposed to education beyond the eighth grade level. What this record shows is that they are opposed to conventional formal education of the type provided by a certified high school because it comes at the child's crucial adolescent period of religious development. Dr. Donald Erickson, for example, testified that their system of learning-by-doing was an 'ideal system' of education in terms of preparing Amish children for life as adults in the Amish community, and that 'I would be inclined to say they do a better job in this than most of the rest of us do.' As he put it, 'These people aren't purporting to be learned people, and it seems to me the self-sufficiency of the community is the best evidence I can point to — whatever is being done seems to function well.'[154]

We must not forget that in the Middle Ages important values of the civilization of the Western World were preserved by members of religious orders who isolated themselves from all worldly influences against great obstacles. There can be no assumption that today's majority is 'right' and the Amish and others like them are 'wrong.' A way of life that is odd or even erratic but interferes with no rights or interests of others is not to be condemned because it is different.

The State, however, supports its interest in providing an additional one or two years of compulsory high school education to Amish children because of the possibility that some such children will choose to leave the Amish community, and that if this occurs they will be ill-equipped for life. The State argues that if Amish children leave their church they should not be in the position of making their way in the world without the education available in the one or two additional years the State requires. However, on this record, that argument is highly speculative. There is no specific evidence of the loss of Amish adherents by attrition, nor is there any showing that upon leaving the Amish community Amish children, with their practical agricultural training and habits of industry and self-reliance, would become burdens on society because of educational shortcomings. Indeed, this argument of the State appears to rest primarily on the State's mistaken assumption, already noted, that the Amish do not provide any education for their children beyond the eighth grade, but allow them to grow in 'ignorance.' To the contrary, not only do the Amish accept the necessity for formal schooling through the eighth grade level, but continue to provide what has been characterized by the undisputed testimony of expert educators as an 'ideal' vocational education for their children in the adolescent years.

There is nothing in this record to suggest that the Amish qualities of reliability, self-reliance, and dedication to work would fail to find ready markets in today's

---

154. Dr. Erickson had previously written: 'Many public educators would be elated if their programs were as successful in preparing students for productive community life as the Amish system seems to be. In fact, while some public schoolmen strive to outlaw the Amish approach, others are being forced to emulate many of its features.' Erickson, Showdown at an Amish Schoolhouse: A Description and Analysis of the Iowa Controversy, in Public Controls for Nonpublic Schools 15, 53 (D. Erickson ed. 1969). And see Littell, supra, n. 5, at 61.

society. Absent some contrary evidence supporting the State's position, we are unwilling to assume that persons possessing such valuable vocational skills and habits are doomed to become burdens on society should they determine to leave the Amish faith, nor is there any basis in the record to warrant a finding that an additional one or two years of formal school education beyond the eighth grade would serve to eliminate any such problem that might exist.

Insofar as the State's claim rests on the view that a brief additional period of formal education is imperative to enable the Amish to participate effectively and intelligently in our democratic process, it must fall. The Amish alternative to formal secondary school education has enabled them to function effectively in their day-to-day life under self-imposed limitations on relations with the world, and to survive and prosper in contemporary society as a separate, sharply identifiable and highly self-sufficient community for more than 200 years in this country. In itself this is strong evidence that they are capable of fulfilling the social and political responsibilities of citizenship without compelled attendance beyond the eighth grade at the price of jeopardizing their free exercise of religious belief.[155] When Thomas Jefferson emphasized the need for education as a bulwark of a free people against tyranny, there is nothing to indicate he had in mind compulsory education through any fixed age beyond a basic education. Indeed, the Amish communities singularly parallel and reflect many of the virtues of Jefferson's ideal of the 'sturdy yeoman' who would form the basis of what he considered as the ideal of a democratic society.[156] Even their idiosyncratic separateness exemplifies the diversity we profess to admire and encourage.

The requirement for compulsory education beyond the eighth grade is a relatively recent development in our history. Less than 60 years ago, the educational requirements of almost all of the States were satisfied by completion of the elementary grades, at least where the child was regularly and lawfully employed.[157] The independence and successful social functioning of the Amish community for a

155. All of the children involved in this case are graduates of the eighth grade. In the county court, the defense introduced a study by Dr. Hostetler indicating that Amish children in the eighth grade achieved comparably to non-Amish children in the basic skills. Supp. App. 9–11. See generally Hostetler & Huntington, supra, n. 5, at 88–96.

156. While Jefferson recognized that education was essential to the welfare and liberty of the people, he was reluctant to directly force instruction of children 'in opposition to the will of the parent.' Instead he proposed that state citizenship be conditioned on the ability to 'read readily in some tongue, native or acquired.' Letter from Thomas Jefferson to Joseph Cabell, Sept. 9, 1817, in 17 Writings of Thomas Jefferson 417, 423–424 (Mem. ed. 1904). And it is clear that, so far as the mass of the people were concerned, he envisaged that a basic education in the 'three R's' would sufficiently meet the interests of the State. He suggested that after completion of elementary school, 'those destined for labor will engage in the business of agriculture, or enter into apprenticeships to such handicraft art as may be their choice.' Letter from Thomas Jefferson to Peter Carr, Sept. 7, 1814, in Thomas Jefferson and Education in a Republic 93–106 (Arrowood ed. 1930). See also id., at 60–64, 70, 83, 136–137.

157. See Dept. of Interior, Bureau of Education, Bulletin No. 47, Digest of State Laws Relating to Public Education 527–559 (1916); Joint Hearings on S. 2475 and H.R. 7200 before the Senate

period approaching almost three centuries and more than 200 years in this country are strong evidence that there is at best a speculative gain, in terms of meeting the duties of citizenship, from an additional one or two years of compulsory formal education. Against this background it would require a more particularized showing from the State on this point to justify the severe interference with religious freedom such additional compulsory attendance would entail.

We should also note that compulsory education and child labor laws find their historical origin in common humanitarian instincts, and that the age limits of both laws have been coordinated to achieve their related objectives.[158] In the context of this case, such considerations, if anything, support rather than detract from respondents' position. The origins of the requirement for school attendance to age 16, an age falling after the completion of elementary school but before completion of high school, are not entirely clear. But to some extent such laws reflected the movement to prohibit most child labor under age 16 that culminated in the provisions of the Federal Fair Labor Standards Act of 1938.[159] It is true, then, that the 16-year child labor age limit may to some degree derive from a contemporary impression that children should be in school until that age. But at the same time, it cannot be denied that, conversely, the 16-year education limit reflects, in substantial measure, the concern that children under that age not be employed under conditions hazardous to their health, or in work that should be performed by adults.

The requirement of compulsory schooling to age 16 must therefore be viewed as aimed not merely at providing educational opportunities for children, but as

---

Committee on Education and Labor and the House Committee on Labor, 75th Cong., 1st Sess., pt. 2, p. 416.

Even today, an eighth grade education fully satisfies the educational requirements of at least six States. See Ariz. Rev. Stat. Ann. s 15-321, subsec. B, par. 4 (1956); Ark. Stat. Ann. s 80–1504 (1947); Iowa Code s 299.2 (1971); S.D.Comp.Laws Ann. s 13-27-1 (1967); Wyo. Stat. Ann. s 21.1-48 (Supp. 1971). (Mississippi has no compulsory education law.) A number of other States have flexible provisions permitting children aged 14 or having completed the eighth grade to be excused from school in order to engage in lawful employment. E.g., Colo. Rev. Stat. Ann. ss 123-20-5, 80-6-1 to 80-6-12 (1963); Conn. Gen. Stat. Rev. ss 10-184, 10–189 (1964); D.C. Code Ann. ss 31-202, 36-201 to 36–228 (1967); Ind. Ann. Stat. ss 28-505 to 28-506, 28–519 (1948); Mass. Gen. Laws Ann., c. 76, s 1 (Supp. 1972) and c. 149, s 86 (1971); Mo. Rev. Stat. ss 167.031, 294.051 (1969); Nev. Rev. Stat. s 392.110 (1968); N.M. Stat. Ann. s 77-10-6 (1968). An eighth grade education satisfied Wisconsin's formal education requirements until 1933. See Wis. Laws 1927, c. 425, s 97; Laws 1933, c. 143. (Prior to 1933, provision was made for attendance at continuation or vocational schools by working children past the eighth grade, but only if one was maintained by the community in question.) For a general discussion of the early development of Wisconsin's compulsory education and child labor laws, see F. Ensign, Compulsory School Attendance and Child Labor 203–230 (1921).

158. See, e.g., Joint Hearings, supra, n. 15, pt. 1, at 185–187 (statement of Frances Perkins, Secretary of Labor), pt. 2, at 381–387 (statement of Katherine Lenroot, Chief, Children's Bureau, Department of Labor); National Child Labor Committee, 40th Anniversary Report, The Long Road (1944); 1 G. Abbott, The Child and the State 259–269, 566 (Greenwood reprint 1968); L. Cremin, The Transformation of the School, c. 3 (1961); A. Steinhilber & C. Sokolowski, State Law on Compulsory Attendance 3–4 (Dept. of Health, Education, and Welfare 1966).

159. 52 Stat. 1060, as amended, 29 U.S.C. ss 201–219.

an alternative to the equally undesirable consequence of unhealthful child labor displacing adult workers, or, on the other hand, forced idleness.[160] The two kinds of statutes — compulsory school attendance and child labor laws — tend to keep children of certain ages off the labor market and in school; this regimen in turn provides opportunity to prepare for a livelihood of a higher order than that which children could pursue without education and protects their health in adolescence.

In these terms, Wisconsin's interest in compelling the school attendance of Amish children to age 16 emerges as somewhat less substantial than requiring such attendance for children generally. For, while agricultural employment is not totally outside the legitimate concerns of the child labor laws, employment of children under parental guidance and on the family farm from age 14 to age 16 is an ancient tradition that lies at the periphery of the objectives of such laws.[161] There is no intimation that the Amish employment of their children on family farms is in any way deleterious to their health or that Amish parents exploit children at tender years. Any such inference would be contrary to the record before us. Moreover, employment of Amish children on the family farm does not present the undesirable economic aspects of eliminating jobs that might otherwise be held by adults.

IV

Finally, the State, on authority of Prince v. Massachusetts, argues that a decision exempting Amish children from the State's requirement fails to recognize the substantive right of the Amish child to a secondary education, and fails to give due regard to the power of the State as parens patriae to extend the benefit of secondary education to children regardless of the wishes of their parents. Taken at its broadest sweep, the Court's language in Prince, might be read to give support to the State's position. However, the Court was not confronted in Prince with a situation comparable to that of the Amish as revealed in this record; this is shown by the Court's severe characterization of the evils that it thought the legislature could legitimately associate with child labor, even when performed in the company of an adult. 321 U.S., at 169–170, 64 S. Ct., at 443–444. The Court later took great care to confine Prince to a narrow scope in Sherbert v. Verner, when it stated: 'On the other hand, the Court has rejected challenges under the Free Exercise Clause to governmental regulation of certain overt acts prompted by religious beliefs or principles, for 'even when the action is in accord with one's religious convictions, (it) is not totally free from legislative restrictions.' Braunfeld v. Brown, 366 U.S. 599, 603, 81 S. Ct. 1144, 1146, 6 L. Ed. 2d 563. The conduct or actions so regulated have invariably posed

160. See materials cited n. 16, supra; Casad, Compulsory Education and Individual Rights, in 5 Religion and the Public Order 51, 82 (D. Giannella ed. (1969).

161. See, e.g., Abbott, supra, n. 16 at 266. The Federal Fair Labor Standards Act of 1938 excludes from its definition of '(o)ppressive child labor' employment of a child under age 16 by 'a parent ... employing his own child ... in an occupation other than manufacturing or mining or an occupation found by the Secretary of Labor to be particularly hazardous for the employment of children between the ages of sixteen and eighteen years or detrimental to their health or well-being.' 29 U.S.C. s 203(l).

some substantial threat to public safety, peace or order. See, e.g., Reynolds v. United States, 98 U.S. 145, 25 L. Ed. 244; Jacobson v. Massachusetts, 197 U.S. 11, 25 S. Ct. 358, 49 L. Ed. 643; Prince v. Massachusetts, 321 U.S. 158, 64 S. Ct. 438, 88 L. Ed. 645. . . .' 374 U.S., at 402–403, 83 S. Ct., at 1793.

This case, of course, is not one in which any harm to the physical or mental health of the child or to the public safety, peace, order, or welfare has been demonstrated or may be properly inferred.[162] The record is to the contrary, and any reliance on that theory would find no support in the evidence.

Contrary to the suggestion of the dissenting opinion of Mr. Justice DOUGLAS, our holding today in no degree depends on the assertion of the religious interest of the child as contrasted with that of the parents. It is the parents who are subject to prosecution here for failing to cause their children to attend school, and it is their right of free exercise, not that of their children, that must determine Wisconsin's power to impose criminal penalties on the parent. The dissent argues that a child who expresses a desire to attend public high school in conflict with the wishes of his parents should not be prevented from doing so. There is no reason for the Court to consider that point since it is not an issue in the case. The children are not parties to this litigation. The State has at no point tried this case on the theory that respondents were preventing their children from attending school against their expressed desires, and indeed the record is to the contrary.[163] The State's position from the outset has been that it is empowered to apply its compulsory-attendance law to Amish parents in the same manner as to other parents—that is, without regard to the wishes of the child. That is the claim we reject today.

Our holding in no way determines the proper resolution of possible competing interests of parents, children, and the State in an appropriate state court proceeding in which the power of the State is asserted on the theory that Amish parents are preventing their minor children from attending high school despite their expressed desires to the contrary. Recognition of the claim of the State in such a proceeding would, of course, call into question traditional concepts of parental control over the religious upbringing and education of their minor children recognized in this Court's past decisions. It is clear that such an intrusion by a State into family decisions in the area of religious training would give rise to grave questions of religious freedom comparable to those raised here and those presented in Pierce v. Society of

162. Cf. e.g., Jacobson v. Massachusetts, 197 U.S. 11, 25 S. Ct. 358, 49 L. Ed. 643 (1905); Wright v. DeWitt School District, 238 Ark. 906, 385 S.W.2d 644 (1965); Application of President and Directors of Georgetown College, Inc., 118 U.S. App. D.C. 80, 87–90, 331 F.2d 1000, 1007–1010 (1964) (in-chambers opinion), cert. denied, 377 U.S. 978, 84 S. Ct. 1883, 12 L. Ed. 2d 746 (1964).

163. The only relevant testimony in the record is to the effect that the wishes of the one child who testified corresponded with those of her parents. Testimony of Frieda Yoder, Tr. 92–94, to the effect that her personal religious beliefs guided her decision to discontinue school attendance after the eighth grade. The other children were not called by either side.

Sisters, 268 U.S. 510, 45 S. Ct. 571, 69 L. Ed. 1070 (1925). On this record we neither reach nor decide those issues.

The State's argument proceeds without reliance on any actual conflict between the wishes of parents and children. It appears to rest on the potential that exemption of Amish parents from the requirements of the compulsory-education law might allow some parents to act contrary to the best interests of their children by foreclosing their opportunity to make an intelligent choice between the Amish way of life and that of the outside world. The same argument could, of course, be made with respect to all church schools short of college. There is nothing in the record or in the ordinary course of human experience to suggest that non-Amish parents generally consult with children of ages 14–16 if they are placed in a church school of the parents' faith.

Indeed it seems clear that if the State is empowered, as parens patriae, to 'save' a child from himself or his Amish parents by requiring an additional two years of compulsory formal high school education, the State will in large measure influence, if not determine, the religious future of the child. Even more markedly than in Prince, therefore, this case involves the fundamental interest of parents, as contrasted with that of the State, to guide the religious future and education of their children. The history and culture of Western civilization reflect a strong tradition of parental concern for the nurture and upbringing of their children. This primary role of the parents in the upbringing of their children is now established beyond debate as an enduring American tradition. If not the first, perhaps the most significant statements of the Court in this area are found in Pierce v. Society of Sisters, in which the Court observed:

> 'Under the doctrine of Meyer v. Nebraska, 262 U.S. 390, 43 S. Ct. 625, 67 L. Ed. 1042, 29 A.L.R. 1146, we think it entirely plain that the Act of 1922 unreasonably interferes with the liberty of parents and guardians to direct the upbringing and education of children under their control. As often heretofore pointed out, rights guaranteed by the Constitution may not be abridged by legislation which has no reasonable relation to some purpose within the competency of the State. The fundamental theory of liberty upon which all governments in this Union repose excludes any general power of the State to standardize its children by forcing them to accept instruction from public teachers only. The child is not the mere creature of the State; those who nurture him and direct his destiny have the right, coupled with the high duty, to recognize and prepare him for additional obligations.'

268 U.S., at 534–535, 45 S. Ct., at 573.

The duty to prepare the child for 'additional obligations,' referred to by the Court, must be read to include the inculcation of moral standards, religious beliefs, and elements of good citizenship. Pierce, of course, recognized that where nothing more than the general interest of the parent in the nurture and education of his children is involved, it is beyond dispute that the State acts 'reasonably' and constitutionally in requiring education to age 16 in some public or private school meeting the standards prescribed by the State.

However read, the Court's holding in Pierce stands as a charter of the rights of parents to direct the religious upbringing of their children. And, when the interests of parenthood are combined with a free exercise claim of the nature revealed by this record, more than merely a 'reasonable relation to some purpose within the competency of the State' is required to sustain the validity of the State's requirement under the First Amendment. To be sure, the power of the parent, even when linked to a free exercise claim, may be subject to limitation under Prince if it appears that parental decisions will jeopardize the health or safety of the child, or have a potential for significant social burdens. But in this case, the Amish have introduced persuasive evidence undermining the arguments the State has advanced to support its claims in terms of the welfare of the child and society as a whole. The record strongly indicates that accommodating the religious objections of the Amish by forgoing one, or at most two, additional years of compulsory education will not impair the physical or mental health of the child, or result in an inability to be self-supporting or to discharge the duties and responsibilities of citizenship, or in any other way materially detract from the welfare of society.

In the fact of our consistent emphasis on the central values underlying the Religion Clauses in our constitutional scheme of government, we cannot accept a parens patriae claim of such all-encompassing scope and with such sweeping potential for broad and unforeseeable application as that urged by the State.

V

For the reasons stated we hold, with the Supreme Court of Wisconsin, that the First and Fourteenth Amendments prevent the State from compelling respondents to cause their children to attend formal high school to age 16.[164] Our disposition of this case, however, in no way alters our recognition of the obvious fact that courts

164. What we have said should meet the suggestion that the decision of the Wisconsin Supreme Court recognizing an exemption for the Amish from the State's system of compulsory education constituted an impermissible establishment of religion. In Walz v. Tax Commission, the Court saw the three main concerns against which the Establishment Clause sought to protect as 'sponsorship, financial support, and active involvement of the sovereign in religious activity.' 397 U.S. 664, 668, 90 S. Ct. 1409, 1411, 25 L. Ed. 2d 697 (1970). Accommodating the religious beliefs of the Amish can hardly be characterized as sponsorship or active involvement. The purpose and effect of such an exemption are not to support, favor, advance, or assist the Amish, but to allow their centuries-old religious society, here long before the advent of any compulsory education, to survive free from the heavy impediment compliance with the Wisconsin compulsory-education law would impose. Such an accommodation 'reflects nothing more than the governmental obligation of neutrality in the face of religious differences, and does not represent that involvement of religious with secular institutions which it is the object of the Establishment Clause to forestall.' Sherbert v. Verner, 374 U.S. 398, 409, 83 S. Ct. 1790, 1797, 10 L. Ed. 2d 965 (1963).

are not school boards or legislatures, and are ill-equipped to determine the 'necessity' of discrete aspects of a State's program of compulsory education. This should suggest that courts must move with great circumspection in performing the sensitive and delicate task of weighing a State's legitimate social concern when faced with religious claims for exemption from generally applicable education requirements. It cannot be overemphasized that we are not dealing with a way of life and mode of education by a group claiming to have recently discovered some 'progressive' or more enlightened process for rearing children for modern life.

Aided by a history of three centuries as an identifiable religious sect and a long history as a successful and self-sufficient segment of American society, the Amish in this case have convincingly demonstrated the sincerity of their religious beliefs, the interrelationship of belief with their mode of life, the vital role that belief and daily conduct play in the continued survival of Old Order Amish communities and their religious organization, and the hazards presented by the State's enforcement of a statute generally valid as to others. Beyond this, they have carried the even more difficult burden of demonstrating the adequacy of their alternative mode of continuing informal vocational education in terms of precisely those overall interests that the State advances in support of its program of compulsory high school education. In light of this convincing showing, one that probably few other religious groups or sects could make, and weighing the minimal difference between what the State would require and what the Amish already accept, it was incumbent on the State to show with more particularity how its admittedly strong interest in compulsory education would be adversely affected by granting an exemption to the Amish. Sherbert v. Verner, supra.

Nothing we hold is intended to undermine the general applicability of the State's compulsory school-attendance statutes or to limit the power of the State to promulgate reasonable standards that, while not impairing the free exercise of religion, provide for continuing agricultural vocational education under parental and church guidance by the Old Order Amish or others similarly situated. The States have had a long history of amicable and effective relationships with church-sponsored schools, and there is no basis for assuming that, in this related context, reasonable standards cannot be established concerning the content of the continuing vocational education of Amish children under parental guidance, provided always that state regulations are not inconsistent with what we have said in this opinion.[165]

Affirmed.

165. Several States have now adopted plans to accommodate, Amish religious beliefs through the establishment of an 'Amish vocational school.' See n. 3, supra. These are not schools in the traditional sense of the word. As previously noted, respondents attempted to reach a compromise with the State of Wisconsin patterned after the Pennsylvania plan, but those efforts were not productive. There is no basis to assume that Wisconsin will be unable to reach a satisfactory accommodation with the Amish in light of what we now hold, so as to serve its interests without impinging on respondents' protected free exercise of their religion.

[Case No. 6-2]

Government aid to religiously affiliated schools through salary supplements violates the Establishment Clause unless provided without excessive entanglement between church and state.

Lemon v. Kurtzman

Supreme Court of the United States
403 U.S. 602 (1971)

Mr. Chief Justice BURGER delivered the opinion of the Court.

These two appeals raise questions as to Pennsylvania and Rhode Island statutes providing state aid to church-related elementary and secondary schools. Both statutes are challenged as violative of the Establishment and Free Exercise Clauses of the First Amendment and the Due Process Clause of the Fourteenth Amendment.

Pennsylvania has adopted a statutory program that provides financial support to nonpublic elementary and secondary schools by way of reimbursement for the cost of teachers' salaries, textbooks, and instructional materials in specified secular subjects. Rhode Island has adopted a statute under which the State pays directly to teachers in nonpublic elementary schools a supplement of 15% of their annual salary. Under each statute state aid has been given to church-related educational institutions. We hold that both statutes are unconstitutional.

I

The Rhode Island Statute

The Rhode Island Salary Supplement Act[166] was enacted in 1969. It rests on the legislative finding that the quality of education available in nonpublic elementary schools has been jeopardized by the rapidly rising salaries needed to attract competent and dedicated teachers. The Act authorizes state officials to supplement the salaries of teachers of secular subjects in nonpublic elementary schools by paying directly to a teacher an amount not in excess of 15% of his current annual salary. As supplemented, however, a nonpublic school teacher's salary cannot exceed the maximum paid to teachers in the State's public schools, and the recipient must be certified by the state board of education in substantially the same manner as public school teachers.

In order to be eligible for the Rhode Island salary supplement, the recipient must teach in a nonpublic school at which the average per-pupil expenditure on secular education is less than the average in the State's public schools during a specified period. Appellant State Commissioner of Education also requires eligible schools to submit financial data. If this information indicates a per-pupil expenditure in excess

166. R.I. Pen. Laws Ann. s 16-51-1 et seq. (Supp. 1970).

of the statutory limitation, the records of the school in question must be examined in order to assess how much of the expenditure is attributable to secular education and how much to religious activity.[167]

The Act also requires that teachers eligible for salary supplements must teach only those subjects that are offered in the State's public schools. They must use 'only teaching materials which are used in the public schools.' Finally, any teacher applying for a salary supplement must first agree in writing 'not to teach a course in religion for so long as or during such time as he or she receives any salary supplements' under the Act.

Appellees are citizens and taxpayers of Rhode Island. They brought this suit to have the Rhode Island Salary Supplement Act declared unconstitutional and its operation enjoined on the ground that it violates the Establishment and Free Exercise Clauses of the First Amendment. Appellants are state officials charged with administration of the Act, teachers eligible for salary supplements under the Act, and parents of children in church-related elementary schools whose teachers would receive state salary assistance.

A three-judge federal court was convened pursuant to 28 U.S.C. ss 2281, 2284. It found that Rhode Island's nonpublic elementary schools accommodated approximately 25% of the State's pupils. About 95% of these pupils attended schools affiliated with the Roman Catholic church. To date some 250 teachers have applied for benefits under the Act. All of them are employed by Roman Catholic schools.

The court held a hearing at which extensive evidence was introduced concerning the nature of the secular instruction offered in the Roman Catholic schools whose teachers would be eligible for salary assistance under the Act. Although the court found that concern for religious values does not necessarily affect the content of secular subjects, it also found that the parochial school system was 'an integral part of the religious mission of the Catholic Church.'

The District Court concluded that the Act violated the Establishment Clause, holding that it fostered 'excessive entanglement' between government and religion. In addition two judges thought that the Act had the impermissible effect of giving 'significant aid to a religious enterprise.' 316 F. Supp. 112. We affirm.

The Pennsylvania Statute

Pennsylvania has adopted a program that has some but not all of the features of the Rhode Island program. The Pennsylvania Nonpublic Elementary and Secondary Education Act[168] was passed in 1968 in response to a crisis that the Pennsylvania

167. The District Court found only one instance in which this breakdown between religious and secular expenses was necessary. The school in question was not affiliated with the Catholic church. The court found it unlikely that such determinations would be necessary with respect to Catholic schools because their heavy reliance on nuns kept their wage costs substantially below those of the public schools.

168. Pa. Stat. Ann., Tit. 24, ss 5601–5609 (Supp. 1971).

Legislature found existed in the State's nonpublic schools due to rapidly rising costs. The statute affirmatively reflects the legislative conclusion that the State's educational goals could appropriately be fulfilled by government support of 'those purely secular educational objectives achieved through nonpublic education * * *.'

The statute authorizes appellee state Superintendent of Public Instruction to 'purchase' specified 'secular educational services' from nonpublic schools. Under the 'contracts' authorized by the statute, the State directly reimburses nonpublic schools solely for their actual expenditures for teachers' salaries, textbooks, and instructional materials. A school seeking reimbursement must maintain prescribed accounting procedures that identify the 'separate' cost of the 'secular educational service.' These accounts are subject to state audit. The funds for this program were originally derived from a new tax on horse and harness racing, but the Act is now financed by a portion of the state tax on cigarettes.

There are several significant statutory restrictions on state aid. Reimbursement is limited to courses 'presented in the curricula of the public schools.' It is further limited 'solely' to courses in the following 'secular' subjects: mathematics, modern foreign languages,[169] physical science, and physical education. Textbooks and instructional materials included in the program must be approved by the state Superintendent of Public Instruction. Finally, the statute prohibits reimbursement for any course that contains 'any subject matter expressing religious teaching, or the morals or forms of worship of any sect.'

The Act went into effect on July 1, 1968, and the first reimbursement payments to schools were made on September 2, 1969. It appears that some $5 million has been expended annually under the Act. The State has now entered into contracts with some 1,181 nonpublic elementary and secondary schools with a student population of some 535,215 pupils — more than 20% of the total number of students in the State. More than 96% of these pupils attend church-related schools, and most of these schools are affiliated with the Roman Catholic church.

Appellants brought this action in the District Court to challenge the constitutionality of the Pennsylvania statute. The organizational plaintiffs-appellants are associations of persons resident in Pennsylvania declaring belief in the separation of church and state; individual plaintiffs-appellants are citizens and taxpayers of Pennsylvania. Appellant Lemon, in addition to being a citizen and a taxpayer, is a parent of a child attending public school in Pennsylvania. Lemon also alleges that he purchased a ticket at a race track and thus had paid the specific tax that supports the expenditures under the Act. Appellees are state officials who have the responsibility for administering the Act. In addition seven church-related schools are defendants-appellees.

A three-judge federal court was convened pursuant to 28 U.S.C. ss 2281, 2284. The District Court held that the individual plaintiffs-appellants had standing to

169. Latin, Hebrew, and classical Greek are excluded.

challenge the Act, 310 F. Supp. 42. The organizational plaintiffs-appellants were denied standing under Flast v. Cohen, 392 U.S. 83, 99, 101, 88 S. Ct. 1942, 1952, 1953, 20 L. Ed. 2d 947 (1968).

The court granted appellees' motion to dismiss the complaint for failure to state a claim for relief.[170] 310 F. Supp. 35. It held that the Act violated neither the Establishment nor the Free Exercise Clause, Chief Judge Hastie dissenting. We reverse.

II

In Everson v. Board of Education, 330 U.S. 1, 67 S. Ct. 504, 91 L. Ed. 711 (1947), this Court upheld a state statute that reimbursed the parents of parochial school children for bus transportation expenses. There Mr. Justice Black, writing for the majority, suggested that the decision carried to 'the verge' of forbidden territory under the Religion Clauses. Id., at 16, 67 S. Ct., at 511. Candor compels acknowledgment, moreover, that we can only dimly perceive the lines of demarcation in this extraordinarily sensitive area of constitutional law.

The language of the Religion Clauses of the First Amendment is at best opaque, particularly when compared with other portions of the Amendment. Its authors did not simply prohibit the establishment of a state church or a state religion, an area history shows they regarded as very important and fraught with great dangers. Instead they commanded that there should be 'no law respecting an establishment of religion.' A law may be one 'respecting' the forbidden objective while falling short of its total realization. A law 'respecting' the proscribed result, that is, the establishment of religion, is not always easily identifiable as one violative of the Clause. A given law might not establish a state religion but nevertheless be one 'respecting' that end in the sense of being a step that could lead to such establishment and hence offend the First Amendment.

In the absence of precisely stated constitutional prohibitions, we must draw lines with reference to the three main evils against which the Establishment Clause was intended to afford protection: 'sponsorship, financial support, and active involvement of the sovereign in religious activity.' Walz v. Tax Commission, 397 U.S. 664, 668, 90 S. Ct. 1409, 1411, 25 L. Ed. 2d 697 (1970).

Every analysis in this area must begin with consideration of the cumulative criteria developed by the Court over many years. Three such tests may be gleaned from our cases. First, the statute must have a secular legislative purpose; second, its principal or primary effect must be one that neither advances nor inhibits religion, Board of Education v. Allen, 392 U.S. 236, 243, 88 S. Ct. 1923, 1926, 20 L. Ed. 2d 1060

170. Plaintiffs-appellants also claimed that the Act violated the Equal Protection Clause of the Fourteenth Amendment by providing state assistance to private institutions that discriminated on racial and religious grounds in their admissions and hiring policies. The court unanimously held that no plaintiff had standing to raise this claim because the complaint did not allege that the child of any plaintiff had been denied admission to any nonpublic school on racial or religious grounds. Our decision makes it unnecessary for us to reach this issue.

(1968); finally, the statute must not foster 'an excessive government entanglement with religion.' Walz, supra, at 674, 90 S. Ct., at 1414.

Inquiry into the legislative purposes of the Pennsylvania and Rhode Island statutes affords no basis for a conclusion that the legislative intent was to advance religion. On the contrary, the statutes themselves clearly state that they are intended to enhance the quality of the secular education in all schools covered by the compulsory attendance laws. There is no reason to believe the legislatures meant anything else. A State always has a legitimate concern for maintaining minimum standards in all schools it allows to operate. As in Allen, we find nothing here that undermines the stated legislative intent; it must therefore be accorded appropriate deference.

In Allen the Court acknowledged that secular and religious teachings were not necessarily so intertwined that secular textbooks furnished to students by the State were in fact instrumental in the teaching of religion. 392 U.S., at 248, 88 S. Ct., at 1929. The legislatures of Rhode Island and Pennsylvania have concluded that secular and religious education are identifiable and separable. In the abstract we have no quarrel with this conclusion.

The two legislatures, however, have also recognized that church-related elementary and secondary schools have a significant religious mission and that a substantial portion of their activities is religiously oriented. They have therefore sought to create statutory restrictions designed to guarantee the separation between secular and religious educational functions and to ensure that State financial aid supports only the former. All these provisions are precautions taken in candid recognition that these programs approached, even if they did not intrude upon, the forbidden areas under the Religion Clauses. We need not decide whether these legislative precautions restrict the principal or primary effect of the programs to the point where they do not offend the Religion Clauses, for we conclude that the cumulative impact of the entire relationship arising under the statutes in each State involves excessive entanglement between government and religion.

III

In Walz v. Tax Commission, supra, the Court upheld state tax exemptions for real property owned by religious organizations and used for religious worship. That holding, however, tended to confine rather than enlarge the area of permissible state involvement with religious institutions by calling for close scrutiny of the degree of entanglement involved in the relationship. The objective is to prevent, as far as possible, the intrusion of either into the precincts of the other.

Our prior holdings do not call for total separation between church and state; total separation is not possible in an absolute sense. Some relationship between government and religious organizations is inevitable. Zorach v. Clauson, 343 U.S. 306, 312, 72 S. Ct. 679, 683, 96 L. Ed. 954 (1952); Sherbert v. Verner, 374 U.S. 398, 422, 83 S. Ct. 1790, 1803, 10 L. Ed. 2d 965 (1963) (Harlan, J., dissenting). Fire inspections, building and zoning regulations, and state requirements under compulsory school-attendance laws are examples of necessary and permissible contacts. Indeed, under the statutory exemption before us in Walz, the State had a continuing burden to ascertain that the exempt property was in fact being used for religious worship. Judicial caveats against entanglement must recognize that the line of separation, far from being a 'wall,' is a blurred, indistinct, and variable barrier depending on all the circumstances of a particular relationship.

This is not to suggest, however, that we are to engage in a legalistic minuet in which precise rules and forms must govern. A true minuet is a matter of pure form and style, the observance of which is itself the substantive end. Here we examine the form of the relationship for the light that it casts on the substance.

In order to determine whether the government entanglement with religion is excessive, we must examine the character and purposes of the institutions that are benefited, the nature of the aid that the State provides, and the resulting relationship between the government and the religious authority. Mr. Justice Harlan, in a separate opinion in Walz, supra, echoed the classic warning as to 'programs, whose very nature is apt to entangle the state in details of administration. * * *' Id., at 695, 90 S. Ct., at 1425. Here we find that both statutes foster an impermissible degree of entanglement.

(a) Rhode Island program

The District Court made extensive findings on the grave potential for excessive entanglement that inheres in the religious character and purpose of the Roman Catholic elementary schools of Rhode Island, to date the sole beneficiaries of the Rhode Island Salary Supplement Act.

The church schools involved in the program are located close to parish churches. This understandably permits convenient access for religious exercises since instruction in faith and morals is part of the total educational process. The school buildings contain identifying religious symbols such as crosses on the exterior and crucifixes, and religious paintings and statutes either in the classrooms or hallways. Although only approximately 30 minutes a day are devoted to direct religious instruction, there are religiously oriented extracurricular activities. Approximately two-thirds of the teachers in these schools are nuns of various religious orders. Their dedicated efforts provide an atmosphere in which religious instruction and religious vocations are natural and proper parts of life in such schools. Indeed, as the District Court found, the role of teaching nuns in enhancing the religious atmosphere has led the parochial school authorities to attempt to maintain a one-to-one ratio between nuns and lay teachers in all schools rather than to permit some to be staffed almost entirely by lay teachers.

On the basis of these findings the District Court concluded that the parochial schools constituted 'an integral part of the religious mission of the Catholic Church.' The various characteristics of the schools make them 'a powerful vehicle for transmitting the Catholic faith to the next generation.' This process of inculcating religious doctrine is, of course, enhanced by the impressionable age of the pupils, in primary schools particularly. In short, parochial schools involve substantial religious activity and purpose.[171]

The substantial religious character of these church-related schools gives rise to entangling church-state relationships of the kind the Religion Clauses sought to avoid. Although the District Court found that concern for religious values did not inevitably or necessarily intrude into the content of secular subjects, the considerable religious activities of these schools led the legislature to provide for careful governmental controls and surveillance by state authorities in order to ensure that state aid supports only secular education.

The dangers and corresponding entanglements are enhanced by the particular form of aid that the Rhode Island Act provides. Our decisions from Everson to Allen have permitted the States to provide church-related schools with secular, neutral, or nonideological services, facilities, or materials. Bus transportation, school lunches, public health services, and secular textbooks supplied in common to all students were not thought to offend the Establishment Clause. We note that the dissenters in Allen seemed chiefly concerned with the pragmatic difficulties involved in ensuring the truly secular content of the textbooks provided at state expense.

In Allen the Court refused to make assumptions, on a meager record, about the religious content of the textbooks that the State would be asked to provide. We cannot, however, refuse here to recognize that teachers have a substantially different ideological character from books. In terms of potential for involving some aspect of faith or morals in secular subjects, a textbook's content is ascertainable, but a teacher's handling of a subject is not. We cannot ignore the danger that a teacher under religious control and discipline poses to the separation of the religious from the purely secular aspects of precollege education. The conflict of functions inheres in the situation.

In our view the record shows these dangers are present to a substantial degree. The Rhode Island Roman Catholic elementary schools are under the general supervision of the Bishop of Providence and his appointed representative, the Diocesan Superintendent of Schools. In most cases, each individual parish, however, assumes the ultimate financial responsibility for the school, with the parish priest authorizing the allocation of parish funds. With only two exceptions, school principals are nuns appointed either by the Superintendent or the Mother Provincial of the order whose members staff the school. By 1969 lay teachers constituted more than a third of all teachers in the parochial elementary schools, and their number is growing. They are first interviewed by the superintendent's office and then by the school principal. The

171. See, e.g., J. Fichter, Parochial School: A Sociological Study 77–108 (1958); Giannella, Religious Liberty, Nonestablishment, and Doctrinal Development, pt. II, The Nonestablishment Principle, 81 Harv. L .Rev. 513, 574 (1968).

contracts are signed by the parish priest, and he retains some discretion in negotiating salary levels. Religious authority necessarily pervades the school system.

The schools are governed by the standards set forth in a 'Handbook of School Regulations,' which has the force of synodal law in the diocese. It emphasizes the role and importance of the teacher in parochial schools: 'The prime factor for the success or the failure of the school is the spirit and personality, as well as the professional competency, of the teacher * * *.' The Handbook also states that: 'Religious formation is not confined to formal courses; nor is it restricted to a single subject area.' Finally, the Handbook advises teachers to stimulate interest in religious vocations and missionary work. Given the mission of the church school, these instructions are consistent and logical.

Several teachers testified, however, that they did not inject religion into their secular classes. And the District Court found that religious values did not necessarily affect the content of the secular instruction. But what has been recounted suggests the potential if not actual hazards of this form of state aid. The teacher is employed by a religious organization, subject to the direction and discipline of religious authorities, and works in a system dedicated to rearing children in a particular faith. These controls are not lessened by the fact that most of the lay teachers are of the Catholic faith. Inevitably some of a teacher's responsibilities hover on the border between secular and religious orientation.

We need not and do not assume that teachers in parochial schools will be guilty of bad faith or any conscious design to evade the limitations imposed by the statute and the First Amendment. We simply recognize that a dedicated religious person, teaching in a school affiliated with his or her faith and operated to inculcate its tenets, will inevitably experience great difficulty in remaining religiously neutral. Doctrines and faith are not inculcated or advanced by neutrals. With the best of intentions such a teacher would find it hard to make a total separation between secular teaching and religious doctrine. What would appear to some to be essential to good citizenship might well for others border on or constitute instruction in religion. Further difficulties are inherent in the combination of religious discipline and the possibility of disagreement between teacher and religious authorities over the meaning of the statutory restrictions.

We do not assume, however, that parochial school teachers will be unsuccessful in their attempts to segregate their religious beliefs from their secular educational responsibilities. But the potential for impermissible fostering of religion is present. The Rhode Island Legislature has not, and could not, provide state aid on the basis of a mere assumption that secular teachers under religious discipline can avoid conflicts. The State must be certain, given the Religion Clauses, that subsidized teachers do not inculcate religion—indeed the State here has undertaken to do so. To ensure that no trespass occurs, the State has therefore carefully conditioned its aid with pervasive restrictions. An eligible recipient must teach only those courses that are offered in the public schools and use only those texts and materials that are found in the public schools. In addition the teacher must not engage in teaching any course in religion.

A comprehensive, discriminating, and continuing state surveillance will inevitably be required to ensure that these restrictions are obeyed and the First Amendment otherwise respected. Unlike a book, a teacher cannot be inspected once so as to determine the extent and intent of his or her personal beliefs and subjective acceptance of the limitations imposed by the First Amendment. These prophylactic contacts will involve excessive and enduring entanglement between state and church.

There is another area of entanglement in the Rhode Island program that gives concern. The statute excludes teachers employed by nonpublic schools whose average per-pupil expenditures on secular education equal or exceed the comparable figures for public schools. In the event that the total expenditures of an otherwise eligible school exceed this norm, the program requires the government to examine the school's records in order to determine how much of the total expenditures is attributable to secular education and how much to religious activity. This kind of state inspection and evaluation of the religious content of a religious organization is fraught with the sort of entanglement that the Constitution forbids. It is a relationship pregnant with dangers of excessive government direction of church schools and hence of churches. The Court noted 'the hazards of government supporting churches' in Walz v. Tax Commission, supra, 397 U.S., at 675, 90 S. Ct., at 1414, and we cannot ignore here the danger that pervasive modern governmental power will ultimately intrude on religion and thus conflict with the Religion Clauses.

(b) Pennsylvania program

The Pennsylvania statute also provides state aid to church-related schools for teachers' salaries. The complaint describes an educational system that is very similar to the one existing in Rhode Island. According to the allegations, the church-related elementary and secondary schools are controlled by religious organizations, have the purpose of propagating and promoting a particular religious faith, and conduct their operations to fulfill that purpose. Since this complaint was dismissed for failure to state a claim for relief, we must accept these allegations as true for purposes of our review.

As we noted earlier, the very restrictions and surveillance necessary to ensure that teachers play a strictly non-ideological role give rise to entanglements between church and state. The Pennsylvania statute, like that of Rhode Island, fosters this kind of relationship. Reimbursement is not only limited to courses offered in the public schools and materials approved by state officials, but the statute excludes 'any subject matter expressing religious teaching, or the morals or forms of worship of any sect.' In addition, schools seeking reimbursement must maintain accounting procedures that require the State to establish the cost of the secular as distinguished from the religious instruction.

The Pennsylvania statute, moreover, has the further defect of providing state financial aid directly to the church-related schools. This factor distinguishes both

Everson and Allen, for in both those cases the Court was careful to point out that state aid was provided to the student and his parents—not to the church-related school. Board of Education v. Allen, supra, 392 U.S., at 243–244, 88 S. Ct., at 1926–1927; Everson v. Board of Education, supra, 330 U.S., at 18, 67 S. Ct., at 512. In Walz v. Tax Commission, supra, 397 U.S., at 675, 90 S. Ct., at 1414, the Court warned of the dangers of direct payments to religious organizations: 'Obviously a direct money subsidy would be a relationship pregnant with involvement and, as with most governmental grant programs, could encompass sustained and detailed administrative relationships for enforcement of statutory or administrative standards * * *.'

The history of government grants of a continuing cash subsidy indicates that such programs have almost always been accompanied by varying measures of control and surveillance. The government cash grants before us now provide no basis for predicting that comprehensive measures of surveillance and controls will not follow. In particular the government's post-audit power to inspect and evaluate a church-related school's financial records and to determine which expenditures are religious and which are secular creates an intimate and continuing relationship between church and state.

IV

A broader base of entanglement of yet a different character is presented by the divisive political potential of these state programs. In a community where such a large number of pupils are served by church-related schools, it can be assumed that state assistance will entail considerable political activity. Partisans of parochial schools, understandably concerned with rising costs and sincerely dedicated to both the religious and secular educational missions of their schools, will inevitably champion this cause and promote political action to achieve their goals. Those who oppose state aid, whether for constitutional, religious, or fiscal reasons, will inevitably respond and employ all of the usual political campaign techniques to prevail. Candidates will be forced to declare and voters to choose. It would be unrealistic to ignore the fact that many people confronted with issues of this kind will find their votes aligned with their faith.

Ordinarily political debate and division, however vigorous or even partisan, are normal and healthy manifestations of our democratic system of government, but political division along religious lines was one of the principal evils against which the First Amendment was intended to protect. Freund, Comment, Public Aid to Parochial Schools, 82 Harv.L.Rev. 1680, 1692 (1969). The potential divisiveness of such conflict is a threat to the normal political process. Walz v. Tax Commission, supra, at 695, 90 S. Ct., at 1424. (separate opinion of Harlan, J.). See also Board of Education v. Allen, 392 U.S., at 249, 88 S. Ct., at 1929 (Harlan, J., concurring); Abington School District v. Schempp, 374 U.S. 203, 307, 83 S. Ct. 1560, 1616, 10 L. Ed. 2d 844 (1963) (Goldberg, J., concurring). To have States or communities divide on the issues presented by state aid to parochial schools would tend to confuse and obscure other issues of great urgency. We have an expanding array of vexing issues, local and national, domestic and international, to debate and divide on. It conflicts with our whole history and tradition to permit questions of the Religion Clauses to assume such importance in our legislatures and in our elections that they could divert attention from the myriad issues and problems that confront every level of government. The highways of church and state relationships are not likely to be one-way streets, and the Constitution's authors sought to protect religious worship from the pervasive power of government. The history of many countries attests to the hazards of religion's intruding into the political arena or of political power intruding into the legitimate and free exercise of religious belief.

Of course, as the Court noted in Walz, '(a)dherents of particular faiths and individual churches frequently take strong positions on public issues.' Walz v. Tax Commission, supra, at 670, 90 S. Ct., at 1412. We could not expect otherwise, for religious values pervade the fabric of our national life. But in Walz we dealt with a status under state tax laws for the benefit of all religious groups. Here we are confronted with successive and very likely permanent annual appropriations that benefit relatively few religious groups. Political fragmentation and divisiveness on religious lines are thus likely to be intensified.

The potential for political divisiveness related to religious belief and practice is aggravated in these two statutory programs by the need for continuing annual appropriations and the likelihood of larger and larger demands as costs and populations grow. The Rhode Island District Court found that the parochial school system's 'monumental and deepening financial crisis' would 'inescapably' require larger annual appropriations subsidizing greater percentages of the salaries of lay teachers. Although no facts have been developed in this respect in the Pennsylvania case, it appears that such pressures for expanding aid have already required the state legislature to include a portion of the state revenues from cigarette taxes in the program.

V

In Walz it was argued that a tax exemption for places of religious worship would prove to be the first step in an inevitable progression leading to the establishment of state churches and state religion. That claim could not stand up against more than 200 years of virtually universal practice imbedded in our colonial experience and continuing into the present.

The progression argument, however, is more persuasive here. We have no long history of state aid to church-related educational institutions comparable to 200 years of tax exemption for churches. Indeed, the state programs before us today represent something of an innovation. We have already noted that modern governmental programs have self-perpetuating and self-expanding propensities. These internal pressures are only enhanced when the schemes involve institutions whose legitimate needs are growing and whose interests have substantial political support. Nor can we fail to see that in constitutional adjudication some steps, which when taken were thought to approach 'the verge,' have become the platform for yet further steps. A certain momentum develops in constitutional theory and it can be a 'downhill thrust' easily set in motion but difficult to retard or stop. Development by momentum is not invariably bad; indeed, it is the way the common law has grown, but it is a force to be recognized and reckoned with. The dangers are increased by the difficulty of perceiving in advance exactly where the 'verge' of the precipice lies. As well as constituting an independent evil against which the Religion Clauses were intended to protect, involvement or entanglement between government and religion serves as a warning signal.

Finally, nothing we have said can be construed to disparage the role of church-related elementary and secondary schools in our national life. Their contribution has been and is enormous. Nor do we ignore their economic plight in a period of rising costs and expanding need. Taxpayers generally have been spared vast sums by the maintenance of these educational institutions by religious organizations, largely by the gifts of faithful adherents.

The merit and benefits of these schools, however, are not the issue before us in these cases. The sole question is whether state aid to these schools can be squared with the dictates of the Religion Clauses. Under our system the choice has been made that government is to be entirely excluded from the area of religious instruction and churches excluded from the affairs of government. The Constitution decrees that religion must be a private matter for the individual, the family, and the institutions of private choice, and that while some involvement and entanglement are inevitable, lines must be drawn.

The judgment of the Rhode Island District Court in No. 569 and No. 570 is affirmed. The judgment of the Pennsylvania District Court in No. 89 is reversed, and the case is remanded for further proceedings consistent with this opinion.

[Case No. 6-3]

The Equal Access Act, which provides for official recognition of secondary school student prayer clubs, is constitutional.

Board of Education of the Westside Community Schools v. Mergens

Supreme Court of the United States
496 U.S. 226 (1990)

Justice O'CONNOR delivered the opinion of the Court, except as to Part III.

This case requires us to decide whether the Equal Access Act, 98 Stat. 1302, 20 U.S.C. §§ 4071–4074, prohibits Westside High School from denying a student religious group permission to meet on school premises during noninstructional time, and if so, whether the Act, so construed, violates the Establishment Clause of the First Amendment.

I

Respondents are current and former students at Westside High School, a public secondary school in Omaha, Nebraska. At the time this suit was filed, the school enrolled about 1,450 students and included grades 10 to 12; in the 1987–1988 school year, ninth graders were added. Westside High School is part of the Westside Community Schools system, an independent public school district. Petitioners are the Board of Education of Westside Community Schools (District 66); Wayne W. Meier, the president of the school board; James E. Findley, the principal of Westside High School; Kenneth K. Hanson, the superintendent of schools for the school district; and James A. Tangdell, the associate superintendent of schools for the school district.

Students at Westside High School are permitted to join various student groups and clubs, all of which meet after school hours on school premises. The students may choose from approximately 30 recognized groups on a voluntary basis. A list of student groups, together with a brief description of each provided by the school, appears in the Appendix to this opinion.

School Board Policy 5610 concerning "Student Clubs and Organizations" recognizes these student clubs as a "vital part of the total education program as a means of developing citizenship, wholesome attitudes, good human relations, knowledge and skills." App. 488. Board Policy 5610 also provides that each club shall have faculty sponsorship and that "clubs and organizations shall not be sponsored by any political or religious organization, or by any organization which denies membership on the basis of race, color, creed, sex or political belief." App. 488. Board Policy 6180 on "Recognition of Religious Beliefs and Customs" requires that "[s]tudents adhering to a specific set of religious beliefs or holding to little or no belief shall be alike respected." App. 462. In addition, Board Policy 5450 recognizes its students' "Freedom of Expression," consistent with the authority of the board. App. 489.

There is no written school board policy concerning the formation of student clubs. Rather, students wishing to form a club present their request to a school official who determines whether the proposed club's goals and objectives are consistent with school board policies and with the school district's "Mission and Goals"—a broadly worded "blueprint" that expresses the district's commitment to teaching academic, physical, civic, and personal skills and values. *Id.*, at 473–478.

In January 1985, respondent Bridget Mergens met with Westside's Principal, Dr. Findley, and requested permission to form a Christian club at the school. The proposed club would have the same privileges and meet on the same terms and conditions as other Westside student groups, except that the proposed club would not have a faculty sponsor. According to the students' testimony at trial, the club's purpose would have been, among other things, to permit the students to read and discuss the Bible, to have fellowship, and to pray together. Membership would have been voluntary and open to all students regardless of religious affiliation.

Findley denied the request, as did Associate Superintendent Tangdell. In February 1985, Findley and Tangdell informed Mergens that they had discussed the matter with Superintendent Hanson and that he had agreed that her request should be denied. The school officials explained that school policy required all student clubs to have a faculty sponsor, which the proposed religious club would not or could not have, and that a religious club at the school would violate the Establishment Clause. In March 1985, Mergens appealed the denial of her request to the board of education, but the board voted to uphold the denial.

Respondents, by and through their parents as next friends, then brought this suit in the United States District Court for the District of Nebraska seeking declaratory and injunctive relief. They alleged that petitioners' refusal to permit the proposed club to meet at Westside violated the Equal Access Act, 20 U.S.C. §§4071–4074, which prohibits public secondary schools that receive federal financial assistance and that maintain a "limited open forum" from denying "equal access" to students who wish to meet within the forum on the basis of the content of the speech at such meetings, §4071(a). Respondents further alleged that petitioners' actions denied them their First and Fourteenth Amendment rights to freedom of speech, association, and the free exercise of religion. Petitioners responded that the Equal Access Act did not apply to Westside and that, if the Act did apply, it violated the Establishment Clause of the First Amendment and was therefore unconstitutional. The United States intervened in the action pursuant to 28 U.S.C. §2403 to defend the constitutionality of the Act.

The District Court entered judgment for petitioners. The court held that the Act did not apply in this case because Westside did not have a "limited open forum" as defined by the Act—all of Westside's student clubs, the court concluded, were curriculum-related and tied to the educational function of the school. The court rejected respondents' constitutional claims, reasoning that Westside did not have a limited public forum as set forth in *Widmar v. Vincent,* 454 U.S. 263, 102 S. Ct. 269, 70 L. Ed. 2d 440 (1981), and that Westside's denial of respondents' request was reasonably related to legitimate pedagogical concerns, see *Hazelwood School Dist. v. Kuhlmeier,* 484 U.S. 260, 273, 108 S. Ct. 562, 571, 98 L. Ed. 2d 592 (1988).

The United States Court of Appeals for the Eighth Circuit reversed. 867 F.2d 1076 (1989). The Court of Appeals held that the District Court erred in concluding that all the existing student clubs at Westside were curriculum related. The Court of Appeals noted that the "broad interpretation" advanced by the Westside school officials "would make the [Equal Access Act] meaningless" and would allow any school to "arbitrarily deny access to school facilities to any unfavored student club on the basis of its speech content," which was "exactly the result that Congress sought to prohibit by enacting the [Act]." *Id.,* at 1078. The Court of Appeals instead found that "[m]any of the student clubs at WHS, including the chess club, are noncurriculum-related." *Id.,* at 1079. Accordingly, because it found that Westside maintained a limited open forum under the Act, the Court of Appeals concluded that the Act applied to "forbi[d] discrimination against [respondents'] proposed club on the basis of its religious content." *Ibid.*

The Court of Appeals then rejected petitioners' contention that the Act violated the Establishment Clause. Noting that the Act extended the decision in *Widmar v. Vincent, supra,* to public secondary schools, the Court of Appeals concluded that "[a]ny constitutional attack on the [Act] must therefore be predicated on the difference between secondary school students and university students." 867 F.2d, at 1080 (footnote omitted). Because "Congress considered the difference in the maturity level of secondary students and university students before passing the [Act]," the Court of Appeals held, on the basis of Congress' factfinding, that the Act did not violate the Establishment Clause. *Ibid.*

We granted certiorari, 492 U.S. 917, 109 S. Ct. 3240, 106 L. Ed. 2d 587 (1989), and now affirm.

II

A

In *Widmar v. Vincent, supra,* we invalidated, on free speech grounds, a state university regulation that prohibited student use of school facilities "'for purposes of religious worship or religious teaching.'" *Id.*, at 265, 102 S. Ct., at 272. In doing so, we held that an "equal access" policy would not violate the Establishment Clause under our decision in *Lemon v. Kurtzman,* 403 U.S. 602, 612–613, 91 S. Ct. 2105, 2111, 29 L. Ed. 2d 745 (1971). In particular, we held that such a policy would have a secular purpose, would not have the primary effect of advancing religion, and would not result in excessive entanglement between government and religion. *Widmar,* 454 U.S., at 271–274, 102 S. Ct., at 275–76. We noted, however, that "[u]niversity students are, of course, young adults. They are less impressionable than younger students and should be able to appreciate that the University's policy is one of neutrality toward religion." *Id.,* at 274, n. 14, 102 S. Ct., at 276–77, n. 14.

In 1984, Congress extended the reasoning of *Widmar* to public secondary schools. Under the Equal Access Act, a public secondary school with a "limited open forum" is prohibited from discriminating against students who wish to conduct a meeting within that forum on the basis of the "religious, political, philosophical, or other content of the speech at such meetings." 20 U.S.C. §§ 4071(a) and (b). Specifically, the Act provides:

> "It shall be unlawful for any public secondary school which receives Federal financial assistance and which has a limited open forum to deny equal access or a fair opportunity to, or discriminate against, any students who wish to conduct a meeting within that limited open forum on the basis of the religious, political, philosophical, or other content of the speech at such meetings."

§ 4071(a).

A "limited open forum" exists whenever a public secondary school "grants an offering to or opportunity for one or more noncurriculum related student groups to meet on school premises during noninstructional time." § 4071(b). "Meeting" is defined to include "those activities of student groups which are permitted under a school's limited open forum and are not directly related to the school curriculum." § 4072(3). "Noninstructional time" is defined to mean "time set aside by the school before actual classroom instruction begins or after actual classroom instruction ends." § 4072(4). Thus, even if a public secondary school allows only one "noncurriculum related student group" to meet, the Act's obligations are triggered and the school may not deny other clubs, on the basis of the content of their speech, equal access to meet on school premises during noninstructional time.

The Act further specifies that a school "shall be deemed to offer a fair opportunity to students who wish to conduct a meeting within its limited open forum" if the school uniformly provides that the meetings are voluntary and student-initiated; are not sponsored by the school, the government, or its agents or employees; do not materially and substantially interfere with the orderly conduct of educational activities within the school; and are not directed, controlled, conducted, or regularly attended by "nonschool persons." §§ 4071(c)(1), (2), (4), and (5). "Sponsorship" is defined to mean "the act of promoting, leading, or participating in a meeting. The assignment of a teacher, administrator, or other school employee to a meeting for custodial purposes does not constitute sponsorship of the meeting." § 4072(2). If the meetings are religious, employees or agents of the school or government may attend only in a "nonparticipatory capacity." § 4071(c)(3). Moreover, a State may not influence the form of any religious activity, require any person to participate in such activity, or compel any school agent or employee to attend a meeting if the content of the speech at the meeting is contrary to that person's beliefs. §§ 4071(d)(1), (2), and (4).

Finally, the Act does not "authorize the United States to deny or withhold Federal financial assistance to any school," § 4071(e), or "limit the authority of the school, its agents or employees, to maintain order and discipline on school premises, to protect the well-being of students and faculty, and to assure that attendance of students at meetings is voluntary," § 4071(f).

B

The parties agree that Westside High School receives federal financial assistance and is a public secondary school within the meaning of the Act. App. 57–58. The Act's obligation to grant equal access to student groups is therefore triggered if Westside maintains a "limited open forum"—*i.e.*, if it permits one or more "noncurriculum related student groups" to meet on campus before or after classes.

Unfortunately, the Act does not define the crucial phrase "noncurriculum related student group." Our immediate task is therefore one of statutory interpretation. We begin, of course, with the language of the statute. See, *e.g.*, *Mallard v. District Court, Southern District of Iowa*, 490 U.S. 296, 300, 109 S. Ct. 1814, 1818, 104 L. Ed. 2d 318 (1989); *United States v. James*, 478 U.S. 597, 604, 106 S. Ct. 3116, 3120, 92 L. Ed. 2d 483 (1986). The common meaning of the term "curriculum" is "the whole body of courses offered by an educational institution or one of its branches." Webster's Third New International Dictionary 557 (1976); see also Black's Law Dictionary 345 (5th ed. 1979) ("The set of studies or courses for a particular period, designated by a school or branch of a school"). Cf. *Hazelwood School Dist. v. Kuhlmeier,* 484 U.S., at 271, 108 S. Ct., at 570 (high school newspaper produced as part of the school's journalism class was part of the curriculum). Any sensible interpretation of "noncurriculum related student group" must therefore be anchored in the notion that such student groups are those that are not related to the body of courses offered by the school. The difficult question is the degree of "unrelatedness to the curriculum" required for a group to be considered "noncurriculum related."

The Act's definition of the sort of "meeting[s]" that must be accommodated under the statute, § 4071(a), sheds some light on this question. "The term 'meeting' includes those activities of student groups which are . . . not *directly related* to the school curriculum." § 4072(3) (emphasis added). Congress' use of the phrase "directly related" implies that student groups directly related to the subject matter of courses offered by the school do not fall within the "noncurriculum related" category and would therefore be considered "curriculum related."

The logic of the Act also supports this view, namely, that a curriculum-related student group is one that has more than just a tangential or attenuated relationship to courses offered by the school. Because the purpose of granting equal access is to prohibit discrimination between religious or political clubs on the one hand and other noncurriculum-related student groups on the other, the Act is premised on the notion that a religious or political club is itself likely to be a noncurriculum-related student group. It follows, then, that a student group that is "curriculum related" must at least have a more direct relationship to the curriculum than a religious or political club would have.

Although the phrase "noncurriculumrelated student group" nevertheless remains sufficiently ambiguous that we might normally resort to legislative history, see, *e.g., James, supra,* 478 U.S., at 606, 106 S. Ct., at 3121, we find the legislative history on this issue less than helpful. Because the bill that led to the Act was extensively rewritten in a series of multilateral negotiations after it was passed by the House and reported out of committee by the Senate, the Committee Reports shed no light on the language actually adopted. During congressional debate on the subject, legislators referred to a number of different definitions, and thus both petitioners and respondents can cite to legislative history favoring their interpretation of the phrase. Compare 130 Cong. Rec. 19223 (1984) (statement of Sen. Hatfield) (curriculum-related clubs are those that are "really a kind of extension of the classroom"), with *ibid.* (statement of Sen. Hatfield) (in response to question whether school districts would have full authority to decide what was curriculum related, "[w]e in no way seek to limit that discretion"). See Laycock, Equal Access and Moments of Silence: The Equal Status of Religious Speech by Private Speakers, 81 Nw.U.L.Rev. 1, 37–39 (1986).

We think it significant, however, that the Act, which was passed by wide, bipartisan majorities in both the House and the Senate, reflects at least some consensus on a broad legislative purpose. The Committee Reports indicate that the Act was intended to address perceived widespread discrimination against religious speech in public schools, see H.R.Rep. No. 98-710, p. 4 (1984); S.Rep. No. 98-357, pp. 10–11 (1984), and, as the language of the Act indicates, its sponsors contemplated that the Act would do more than merely validate the status quo. The Committee Reports also show that the Act was enacted in part in response to two federal appellate court decisions holding that student religious groups could not, consistent with the Establishment Clause, meet on school premises during noninstructional time. See H.R.Rep. No. 98-710, *supra,* at 3–6 (discussing *Lubbock Civil Liberties Union v. Lubbock Independent School Dist.,* 669 F.2d 1038, 1042–1048 (CA5 1982), cert. denied, 459 U.S. 1155–1156, 103 S. Ct. 800, 74 L. Ed. 2d 1003 (1983), and *Brandon v. Guilderland Bd. of Ed.,* 635 F.2d 971 (CA2 1980), cert. denied, 454 U.S. 1123, 102 S. Ct. 970, 71 L. Ed. 2d 109 (1981)); S.Rep. No. 98-357, *supra,* at 6–9, 11–14 (same). A broad reading of the Act would be consistent with the views of those who sought to end discrimination by allowing students to meet and discuss religion before and after classes.

In light of this legislative purpose, we think that the term "noncurriculum related student group" is best interpreted broadly to mean any student group that does not *directly* relate to the body of courses offered by the school. In our view, a student group directly relates to a school's curriculum if the subject matter of the group is actually taught, or will soon be taught, in a regularly offered course; if the subject matter of the group concerns the body of courses as a whole; if participation in the group is required for a particular course; or if participation in the group results in academic credit. We think this limited definition of groups that directly relate to the curriculum is a commonsense interpretation of the Act that is consistent with Congress' intent to provide a low threshold for triggering the Act's requirements.

For example, a French club would directly relate to the curriculum if a school taught French in a regularly offered course or planned to teach the subject in the near future. A school's student government would generally relate directly to the curriculum to the extent that it addresses concerns, solicits opinions, and formulates proposals pertaining to the body of courses offered by the school. If participation in a school's band or orchestra were required for the band or orchestra classes, or resulted in academic credit, then those groups would also directly relate to the curriculum. The existence of such groups at a school would not trigger the Act's obligations.

On the other hand, unless a school could show that groups such as a chess club, a stamp collecting club, or a community service club fell within our description of groups that directly relate to the curriculum, such groups would be "noncurriculum related student groups" for purposes of the Act. The existence of such groups would create a "limited open forum" under the Act and would prohibit the school from denying equal access to any other student group on the basis of the content of that group's speech. Whether a specific student group is a "noncurriculum related student group" will therefore depend on a particular school's curriculum, but such determinations would be subject to factual findings well within the competence of trial courts to make.

Petitioners contend that our reading of the Act unduly hinders local control over schools and school activities, but we think that schools and school districts nevertheless retain a significant measure of authority over the type of officially recognized activities in which their students participate. See, *e.g.*, *Hazelwood School Dist. v. Kuhlmeier,* 484 U.S. 260, 108 S. Ct. 562, 98 L. Ed. 2d 592 (1988); *Bethel School Dist. No. 403 v. Fraser,* 478 U.S. 675, 106 S. Ct. 3159, 92 L. Ed. 2d 549 (1986). First, schools and school districts maintain their traditional latitude to determine appropriate subjects of instruction. To the extent that a school chooses to structure its course offerings and existing student groups to avoid the Act's obligations, that result is not prohibited by the Act. On matters of statutory interpretation, "[o]ur task is to apply the text, not to improve on it." *Pavelic & LeFlore v. Marvel Entertainment Group,* 493 U.S. 120, 126, 110 S. Ct. 456, 460, 107 L. Ed. 2d 438 (1989). Second, the Act expressly does not limit a school's authority to prohibit meetings that would "materially and substantially interfere with the orderly conduct of educational activities within the school." § 4071(c)(4); cf. *Tinker v. Des Moines Independent Community School Dist.,* 393 U.S. 503, 509, 89 S. Ct. 733, 738, 21 L. Ed. 2d 731 (1969). The Act also preserves "the authority of the school, its agents or employees, to maintain order and discipline on school premises, to protect the well-being of students and faculty, and to assure that attendance of students at meetings is voluntary." § 4071(f). Finally, because the Act applies only to public secondary schools that receive federal financial assistance, § 4071(a), a school district seeking to escape the statute's obligations could simply forgo federal funding. Although we do not doubt that in some cases this may be an unrealistic option, Congress clearly sought to prohibit schools from discriminating on the basis of the content of a student group's speech, and that obligation is the price a federally funded school must pay if it opens its facilities to noncurriculum-related student groups.

The dissent suggests that "an extracurricular student organization is 'noncurriculum related' if it has as its purpose (or as part of its purpose) the advocacy of partisan theological, political, or ethical views." *Post,* at 2385; see also *post,* at 2383, 2393 (Act is triggered only if school permits "controversial" or "distasteful" groups to use its facilities); *post,* at 2393 ("noncurriculum" subjects are those that "'cannot properly be included in a public school curriculum'"). This interpretation of the Act, we are told, is mandated by Congress' intention to "track our own Free Speech Clause jurisprudence," *post,* at 2387, n. 10, by incorporating *Widmar*'s notion of a "limited public forum" into the language of the Act. *Post,* at 2383–2384.

This suggestion is flawed for at least two reasons. First, the Act itself neither uses the phrase "limited public forum" nor so much as hints that that doctrine is somehow "incorporated" into the words of the statute. The operative language of the statute, 20 U.S.C. § 4071(a), of course, refers to a "limited open forum," a term that is specifically defined in the next subsection, § 4071(b). Congress was presumably aware that "limited public forum," as used by the Court, is a term of art, see, *e.g., Perry Ed. Assn. v. Perry Local Educators' Assn.*, 460 U.S. 37, 45–49, 103 S. Ct. 948, 954–57, 74 L. Ed. 2d 794 (1983), and had it intended to import that concept into the Act, one would suppose that it would have done so explicitly. Indeed, Congress' deliberate choice to use a different term—and to define that term—can only mean that it intended to establish a standard different from the one established by our free speech cases. See Laycock, 81 Nw.U.L.Rev., at 36 ("The statutory 'limited open forum' is an artificial construct, and comparisons with the constitutional ['limited public forum'] cases can be misleading"). To paraphrase the dissent, "[i]f Congress really intended to [incorporate] *Widmar* for reasons of administrative clarity, Congress kept its intent well hidden, both in the statute and in the debates preceding its passage." *Post,* at 2388, n. 15.

Second, and more significant, the dissent's reliance on the legislative history to support its interpretation of the Act shows just how treacherous that task can be. The dissent appears to agree with our view that the legislative history of the Act, even if relevant, is highly unreliable, see, *e.g., post,* at 2385, n. 5, and 2388, n. 15, yet the interpretation it suggests rests solely on a few passing, general references by legislators to our decision in *Widmar,* see *post,* at 2384–2385, and n. 4. We think that reliance on legislative history is hazardous at best, but where "'not even the sponsors of the bill knew what it meant,'" *post,* at 2388, n. 15 (quoting Laycock, *supra,* at 38 (citation omitted)), such reliance cannot form a reasonable basis on which to interpret the text of a statute. For example, the dissent appears to place great reliance on a comment by Senator Levin that the Act extends the rule in *Widmar* to secondary schools, see *post,* at 2384–2385, n. 4, but Senator Levin's understanding of the "rule," expressed in the same breath as the statement on which the dissent relies, fails to support the dissent's reading of the Act. See 130 Cong. Rec. 19236 (1984) ("The pending amendment will allow students equal access to secondary schools student-initiated religious meetings before and after school where the school *generally* allows groups of secondary school students to meet during those times") (emphasis added). Moreover, a number of Senators, during the same debate, warned that some of the views stated did not reflect their own views. See, *e.g., ibid.* ("I am troubled with the legislative history that you are making here") (statement of Sen. Chiles); *id.,* at 19237 ("[T]here have been a number of statements made on the floor today which may be construed as legislative history modifying what my understanding was or what anyone's understanding might be of this bill") (statement of Sen. Denton). The only thing that can be said with any confidence is that *some* Senators *may* have thought that the obligations of the Act would be triggered only when a school permits advocacy groups to meet on school premises during noninstructional time. That conclusion, of course, cannot bear the weight the dissent places on it.

C

The parties in this case focus their dispute on 10 of Westside's approximately 30 voluntary student clubs: Interact (a service club related to Rotary International);

Chess Club; Subsurfers (a club for students interested in scuba diving); National Honor Society; Photography Club; Welcome to Westside Club (a club to introduce new students to the school); Future Business Leaders of America; Zonta Club (the female counterpart to Interact); Student Advisory Board (student government); and Student Forum (student government). App. 60. Petitioners contend that all of these student activities are curriculum related because they further the goals of particular aspects of the school's curriculum. The Welcome to Westside Club, for example, helps "further the School's overall goal of developing effective citizens by requiring student members to contribute to their fellow students." Brief for Petitioners 16. The student government clubs "advance the goals of the School's political science classes by providing an understanding and appreciation of government processes." *Id.*, at 17. Subsurfers furthers "one of the essential goals of the Physical Education Department—enabling students to develop lifelong recreational interests." *Id.*, at 18. The Chess Club "supplement[s] math and science courses because it enhances students' ability to engage in critical thought processes." *Id.*, at 18–19. Participation in Interact and the Zonta Club "promotes effective citizenship, a critical goal of the WHS curriculum, specifically the Social Studies Department." *Id.*, at 19.

To the extent that petitioners contend that "curriculum related" means anything remotely related to abstract educational goals, however, we reject that argument. To define "curriculum related" in a way that results in almost no schools having limited open fora, or in a way that permits schools to evade the Act by strategically describing existing student groups, would render the Act merely hortatory. See 130 Cong. Rec. 19222 (1984) (statement of Sen. Leahy) ("[A] limited open forum should be triggered by what a school does, not by what it says"). As the court below explained:

> "Allowing such a broad interpretation of 'curriculum-related' would make the [Act] meaningless. A school's administration could simply declare that it maintains a closed forum and choose which student clubs it wanted to allow by tying the purposes of those student clubs to some broadly defined educational goal. At the same time the administration could arbitrarily deny access to school facilities to any unfavored student club on the basis of its speech content. This is exactly the result that Congress sought to prohibit by enacting the [Act]. A public secondary school cannot simply declare that it maintains a closed forum and then discriminate against a particular student group on the basis of the content of the speech of that group."

867 F.2d, at 1078.

See also *Garnett v. Renton School Dist. No. 403*, 874 F.2d 608, 614 (CA9 1989) ("Complete deference [to the school district] would render the Act meaningless because school boards could circumvent the Act's requirements simply by asserting that all student groups are curriculum related").

Rather, we think it clear that Westside's existing student groups include one or more "noncurriculum related student groups." Although Westside's physical education classes apparently include swimming, see Record, Tr. of Preliminary Injunction Hearing 25, counsel stated at oral argument that scuba diving is not taught in any regularly offered course at the school, Tr. of Oral Arg. 6. Based on Westside's own description of the group, Subsurfers does not directly relate to the curriculum as a whole in the same way that a student government or similar group might. App. 485–486. Moreover, participation in Subsurfers is not required by any course at the school and does not result in extra academic credit. *Id.*, at 170–171, 236. Thus, Subsurfers is a "noncurriculum related student group" for purposes of the Act. Similarly, although math teachers at Westside have encouraged their students to play chess, *id.*, at 442–444, chess is not taught in any regularly offered course at the school, Tr. of Oral Arg. 6, and participation in the Chess Club is not required for any class and does not result in extra credit for any class, App. 302–304. The Chess Club is therefore another "noncurriculum related student group" at Westside. Moreover, Westside's principal acknowledged at trial that the Peer Advocates program — a service group that works with special education classes — does not directly relate to any courses offered by the school and is not required by any courses offered by the school. *Id.*, at 231–233; see also *id.*, at 198–199 (participation in Peer Advocates is not required for any course and does not result in extra credit in any course). Peer Advocates would therefore also fit within our description of a "noncurriculum related student group." The record therefore supports a finding that Westside has maintained a limited open forum under the Act.

Although our definition of "noncurriculum related student activities" looks to a school's actual practice rather than its stated policy, we note that our conclusion is also supported by the school's own description of its student activities. As reprinted in the Appendix to this opinion, the school states that Band "is included in our regular curriculum"; Choir "is a course offered as part of the curriculum"; Distributive Education "is an extension of the Distributive Education class"; International Club is "developed through our foreign language classes"; Latin Club is "designed for those students who are taking Latin as a foreign language"; Student Publications "includes classes offered in preparation of the yearbook (Shield) and the student newspaper (Lance)"; Dramatics "is an extension of a regular academic class"; and Orchestra "is an extension of our regular curriculum." These descriptions constitute persuasive evidence that these student clubs directly relate to the curriculum. By inference, however, the fact that the descriptions of student activities such as Subsurfers and chess do not include such references strongly suggests that those clubs do not, by the school's own admission, directly relate to the curriculum. We therefore conclude that Westside permits "one or more noncurriculum related student groups to meet on school premises during noninstructional time," § 4071(b). Because Westside maintains a "limited open forum" under the Act, it is prohibited from discriminating, based on the content of the students' speech, against students who wish to meet on school premises during noninstructional time.

The remaining statutory question is whether petitioners' denial of respondents' request to form a religious group constitutes a denial of "equal access" to the school's limited open forum. Although the school apparently permits respondents to meet informally after school, App. 315–316, respondents seek equal access in the form of official recognition by the school. Official recognition allows student clubs to be part of the student activities program and carries with it access to the school newspaper, bulletin boards, the public address system, and the annual Club Fair. *Id.*, at 434–435. Given that the Act explicitly prohibits denial of "equal access . . . to . . . any students who wish to conduct a meeting within [the school's] limited open forum" on the basis of the religious content of the speech at such meetings, § 4071(a), we hold that Westside's denial of respondents' request to form a Christian club denies them "equal access" under the Act.

Because we rest our conclusion on statutory grounds, we need not decide — and therefore express no opinion on — whether the First Amendment requires the same result.

III

Petitioners contend that even if Westside has created a limited open forum within the meaning of the Act, its denial of official recognition to the proposed Christian club must nevertheless stand because the Act violates the Establishment Clause of the First Amendment, as applied to the States through the Fourteenth Amendment. Specifically, petitioners maintain that because the school's recognized student activities are an integral part of its educational mission, official recognition of respondents' proposed club would effectively incorporate religious activities into the school's official program, endorse participation in the religious club, and provide the club with an official platform to proselytize other students.

We disagree. In *Widmar,* we applied the three-part *Lemon* test to hold that an "equal access" policy, at the university level, does not violate the Establishment Clause. See 454 U.S., at 271–275, 102 S. Ct., at 275–77 (applying *Lemon,* 403 U.S., at 612–613, 91 S. Ct., at 2111). We concluded that "an open-forum policy, including nondiscrimination against religious speech, would have a secular purpose," 454 U.S., at 271, 102 S. Ct., at 275 (footnotes omitted), and would in fact *avoid* entanglement with religion. See *id.*, at 272, n. 11, 102 S. Ct., at 275, n. 11 ("[T]he University would risk greater 'entanglement' by attempting to enforce its exclusion of 'religious worship' and 'religious speech'"). We also found that although incidental benefits accrued to religious groups who used university facilities, this result did not amount to an establishment of religion. First, we stated that a university's forum does not "confer any imprimatur of state approval on religious sects or practices." *Id.*, at 274, 102 S. Ct., at 276. Indeed, the message is one of neutrality rather than endorsement; if a State refused to let religious groups use facilities open to others, then it would demonstrate not neutrality but hostility toward religion. "The Establishment Clause does not license government to treat religion and those who teach or practice it, simply by virtue of their status as such, as subversive of American ideals and therefore subject to unique disabilities." *McDaniel v. Paty,* 435 U.S. 618, 641, 98 S. Ct. 1322, 1335, 55 L. Ed. 2d 593 (1978) (BRENNAN, J., concurring in judgment). Second, we noted that "[t]he [University's] provision of benefits to [a] broad . . . spectrum of groups" — both nonreligious and religious speakers — was "an important index of secular effect." 454 U.S., at 274, 102 S. Ct., at 277.

We think the logic of *Widmar* applies with equal force to the Equal Access Act. As an initial matter, the Act's prohibition of discrimination on the basis of "political, philosophical, or other" speech as well as religious speech is a sufficient basis for meeting the secular purpose prong of the *Lemon* test. See *Edwards v. Aguillard,* 482 U.S. 578, 586, 107 S. Ct. 2573, 2579, 96 L. Ed. 2d 510 (1987) Court "is normally deferential to a [legislative] articulation of a secular purpose"); *Mueller v. Allen,* 463 U.S. 388, 394–395, 103 S. Ct. 3062, 3066–67, 77 L. Ed. 2d 721 (1983) (Court is "reluctan[t] to attribute unconstitutional motives to the States, particularly when a plausible secular purpose for the State's program may be discerned from the face of the statute"). Congress' avowed purpose — to prevent discrimination against religious and other types of speech — is undeniably secular. See *Corporation of Presiding Bishop of Church of Jesus Christ of Latter-day Saints v. Amos,* 483 U.S. 327, 335–336, 107 S. Ct. 2862, 2868–2869, 97 L. Ed. 2d 273 (1987); *Committee for Public Education & Religious Liberty v. Nyquist,* 413 U.S. 756, 773, 93 S. Ct. 2955, 2965, 37 L. Ed. 2d 948 (1973). Cf. 42 U.S.C. § 2000e-2(a) (prohibiting employment discrimination on grounds of race, color, religion, sex, or national origin). Even if some legislators were motivated by a conviction that religious speech in particular was valuable and worthy of protection, that alone would not invalidate the Act, because what is relevant is the legislative *purpose* of the statute, not the possibly religious *motives* of the legislators who enacted the law. Because the Act on its face grants equal access to both secular and religious speech, we think it clear that the Act's purpose was not to "'endorse or disapprove of religion,'" *Wallace v. Jaffree,* 472 U.S. 38, 56, 105 S. Ct. 2479, 2489, 86 L. Ed. 2d 29 (1985) (quoting *Lynch v. Donnelly,* 465 U.S. 668, 690, 104 S. Ct. 1355, 1368, 79 L. Ed. 2d 604 (1984) (O'CONNOR, J., concurring)).

Petitioners' principal contention is that the Act has the primary effect of advancing religion. Specifically, petitioners urge that, because the student religious meetings are held under school aegis, and because the State's compulsory attendance laws bring the students together (and thereby provide a ready-made audience for student evangelists), an objective observer in the position of a secondary school student will perceive official school support for such religious meetings. See *County of Allegheny v. American Civil Liberties Union, Greater Pittsburgh Chapter,* 492 U.S. 573, 593, 109 S. Ct. 3086, 3101, 106 L. Ed. 2d 472 (1989) (Establishment Clause inquiry is whether the government "'convey[s] or attempt[s] to convey a message that religion or a particular religious belief is favored or preferred'") (quoting *Wallace v. Jaffree, supra,* 472 U.S., at 70, 105 S. Ct., at 2497 (O'CONNOR, J., concurring in part and concurring in judgment)).

We disagree. First, although we have invalidated the use of public funds to pay for teaching state-required subjects at parochial schools, in part because of the risk of creating "a crucial symbolic link between government and religion, thereby enlisting — at least in the eyes of impressionable youngsters — the powers of government to the support of the religious denomination operating the school," *School Dist. of*

Grand Rapids v. Ball, 473 U.S. 373, 385, 105 S. Ct. 3216, 3223, 87 L. Ed. 2d 267 (1985), there is a crucial difference between *government* speech endorsing religion, which the Establishment Clause forbids, and *private* speech endorsing religion, which the Free Speech and Free Exercise Clauses protect. We think that secondary school students are mature enough and are likely to understand that a school does not endorse or support student speech that it merely permits on a nondiscriminatory basis. Cf. *Tinker v. Des Moines Independent Community School Dist.*, 393 U.S. 503, 89 S. Ct. 733, 21 L. Ed. 2d 731 (1969) (no danger that high school students' symbolic speech implied school endorsement); *West Virginia State Bd. of Ed. v. Barnette*, 319 U.S. 624, 63 S. Ct. 1178, 87 L. Ed. 1628 (1943) (same). See generally Note, 92 Yale L.J. 499, 507–509 (1983) (summarizing research in adolescent psychology). The proposition that schools do not endorse everything they fail to censor is not complicated. "[P]articularly in this age of massive media information . . . the few years difference in age between high school and college students [does not] justif[y] departing from *Widmar*." *Bender v. Williamsport Area School Dist.*, 475 U.S. 534, 556, 106 S. Ct. 1326, 1339, 89 L. Ed. 2d 501 (1986) (Powell, J., dissenting).

Indeed, we note that Congress specifically rejected the argument that high school students are likely to confuse an equal access policy with state sponsorship of religion. See S.Rep. No. 98-357, p. 8 (1984); *id.*, at 35 ("[S]tudents below the college level are capable of distinguishing between State-initiated, school sponsored, or teacher-led religious speech on the one hand and student-initiated, student-led religious speech on the other"). Given the deference due "the duly enacted and carefully considered decision of a coequal and representative branch of our Government," *Walters v. National Assn. of Radiation Survivors*, 473 U.S. 305, 319, 105 S. Ct. 3180, 3188, 87 L. Ed. 2d 220 (1985); see also *Rostker v. Goldberg*, 453 U.S. 57, 64, 101 S. Ct. 2646, 2651, 69 L. Ed. 2d 478 (1981), we do not lightly second-guess such legislative judgments, particularly where the judgments are based in part on empirical determinations.

Second, we note that the Act expressly limits participation by school officials at meetings of student religious groups, §§ 4071(c)(2) and (3), and that any such meetings must be held during "noninstructional time," § 4071(b). The Act therefore avoids the problems of "the students' emulation of teachers as role models" and "mandatory attendance requirements," *Edwards v. Aguillard*, 482 U.S., at 584, 107 S. Ct., at 2578; see also *Illinois ex rel. McCollum v. Board of Ed. of School Dist. No. 71, Champaign County*, 333 U.S. 203, 209–210, 68 S. Ct. 461, 464, 92 L. Ed. 649 (1948) (release time program invalid where students were "released in part from their legal duty [to attend school] upon the condition that they attend the religious classes"). To be sure, the possibility of *student* peer pressure remains, but there is little if any risk of official state endorsement or coercion where no formal classroom activities are involved and no school officials actively participate. Moreover, petitioners' fear of a mistaken inference of endorsement is largely self-imposed, because the school itself has control over any impressions it gives its students. To the extent a school makes clear that its recognition of respondents' proposed club is not an endorsement of the views of the club's participants, see *Widmar*, 454 U.S., at 274, n. 14, 102 S. Ct., at 277, n. 14

(noting that university student handbook states that the university's name will not be identified with the aims, policies, or opinions of any student organization or its members), students will reasonably understand that the school's official recognition of the club evinces neutrality toward, rather than endorsement of, religious speech.

Third, the broad spectrum of officially recognized student clubs at Westside, and the fact that Westside students are free to initiate and organize additional student clubs, see App. 221–222, counteract any possible message of official endorsement of or preference for religion or a particular religious belief. See *Widmar,* 454 U.S., at 274, 102 S. Ct., at 277 ("The provision of benefits to so broad a spectrum of groups is an important index of secular effect"). Although a school may not itself lead or direct a religious club, a school that permits a student-initiated and student-led religious club to meet after school, just as it permits any other student group to do, does not convey a message of state approval or endorsement of the particular religion. Under the Act, a school with a limited open forum may not lawfully deny access to a Jewish students' club, a Young Democrats club, or a philosophy club devoted to the study of Nietzsche. To the extent that a religious club is merely one of many different student-initiated voluntary clubs, students should perceive no message of government endorsement of religion. Thus, we conclude that the Act does not, at least on its face and as applied to Westside, have the primary effect of advancing religion. See *id.,* at 275, 102 S. Ct., at 277 ("At least in the absence of empirical evidence that religious groups will dominate [the university's] open forum, . . . the advancement of religion would not be the forum's 'primary effect'").

Petitioners' final argument is that by complying with the Act's requirements, the school risks excessive entanglement between government and religion. The proposed club, petitioners urge, would be required to have a faculty sponsor who would be charged with actively directing the activities of the group, guiding its leaders, and ensuring balance in the presentation of controversial ideas. Petitioners claim that this influence over the club's religious program would entangle the government in day-to-day surveillance of religion of the type forbidden by the Establishment Clause.

Under the Act, however, faculty monitors may not participate in any religious meetings, and nonschool persons may not direct, control, or regularly attend activities of student groups. §§ 4071(c)(3) and (5). Moreover, the Act prohibits school "sponsorship" of any religious meetings, § 4071(c)(2), which means that school officials may not promote, lead, or participate in any such meeting, § 4072(2). Although the Act permits "[t]he assignment of a teacher, administrator, or other school employee to a meeting for custodial purposes," *ibid.,* such custodial oversight of the student-initiated religious group, merely to ensure order and good behavior, does not impermissibly entangle government in the day-to-day surveillance or administration of religious activities. See *Tony and Susan Alamo Foundation v. Secretary of Labor,* 471 U.S. 290, 305–306, 105 S. Ct. 1953, 1963–64, 85 L. Ed. 2d 278 (1985). Indeed, as the Court noted in *Widmar,* a denial of equal access to religious speech might well create greater entanglement problems in the form of invasive monitoring to prevent religious speech at meetings at which such speech might occur. See 454 U.S., at 272, n. 11, 102 S. Ct., at 275, n. 11.

Accordingly, we hold that the Equal Access Act does not on its face contravene the Establishment Clause. Because we hold that petitioners have violated the Act, we do not decide respondents' claims under the Free Speech and Free Exercise Clauses. For the foregoing reasons, the judgment of the Court of Appeals is affirmed.

It is so ordered.

[Case No. 6-4]

Officially endorsed prayer at a school graduation ceremony violates the Establishment Clause.

Lee v. Weisman

Supreme Court of the United States
505 U.S. 577 (1992)

Justice KENNEDY delivered the opinion of the Court.

School principals in the public school system of the city of Providence, Rhode Island, are permitted to invite members of the clergy to offer invocation and benediction prayers as part of the formal graduation ceremonies for middle schools and for high schools. The question before us is whether including clerical members who offer prayers as part of the official school graduation ceremony is consistent with the Religion Clauses of the First Amendment, provisions the Fourteenth Amendment makes applicable with full force to the States and their school districts.

I

A

Deborah Weisman graduated from Nathan Bishop Middle School, a public school in Providence, at a formal ceremony in June 1989. She was about 14 years old. For many years it has been the policy of the Providence School Committee and the Superintendent of Schools to permit principals to invite members of the clergy to give invocations and benedictions at middle school and high school graduations. Many, but not all, of the principals elected to include prayers as part of the graduation ceremonies. Acting for himself and his daughter, Deborah's father, Daniel Weisman, objected to any prayers at Deborah's middle school graduation, but to no avail. The school principal, petitioner Robert E. Lee, invited a rabbi to deliver prayers at the graduation exercises for Deborah's class. Rabbi Leslie Gutterman, of the Temple Beth El in Providence, accepted.

It has been the custom of Providence school officials to provide invited clergy with a pamphlet entitled "Guidelines for Civic Occasions," prepared by the National Conference of Christians and Jews. The Guidelines recommend that public prayers at nonsectarian civic ceremonies be composed with "inclusiveness and sensitivity," though they acknowledge that "[p]rayer of any kind may be inappropriate on some civic occasions." App. 20–21. The principal gave Rabbi Gutterman the pamphlet before the graduation and advised him the invocation and benediction should be nonsectarian. Agreed Statement of Facts ¶ 17, *id.*, at 13.

Rabbi Gutterman's prayers were as follows:

> "INVOCATION
>
> "God of the Free, Hope of the Brave:
>
> "For the legacy of America where diversity is celebrated and the rights of minorities are protected, we thank You. May these young men and women grow up to enrich it.
>
> "For the liberty of America, we thank You. May these new graduates grow up to guard it.
>
> "For the political process of America in which all its citizens may participate, for its court system where all may seek justice we thank You. May those we honor this morning always turn to it in trust.
>
> "For the destiny of America we thank You. May the graduates of Nathan Bishop Middle School so live that they might help to share it.
>
> "May our aspirations for our country and for these young people, who are our hope for the future, be richly fulfilled.
>
> AMEN"
>
> "BENEDICTION
>
> "O God, we are grateful to You for having endowed us with the capacity for learning which we have celebrated on this joyous commencement.
>
> "Happy families give thanks for seeing their children achieve an important milestone. Send Your blessings upon the teachers and administrators who helped prepare them.
>
> "The graduates now need strength and guidance for the future, help them to understand that we are not complete with academic knowledge alone. We must each strive to fulfill what You require of us all: To do justly, to love mercy, to walk humbly.
>
> "We give thanks to You, Lord, for keeping us alive, sustaining us and allowing us to reach this special, happy occasion.
>
> AMEN"

Id., at 22–23.

The record in this case is sparse in many respects, and we are unfamiliar with any fixed custom or practice at middle school graduations, referred to by the school district as "promotional exercises." We are not so constrained with reference to high schools, however. High school graduations are such an integral part of American cultural life that we can with confidence describe their customary features, confirmed by aspects of the record and by the parties' representations at oral argument.

In the Providence school system, most high school graduation ceremonies are conducted away from the school, while most middle school ceremonies are held on school premises. Classical High School, which Deborah now attends, has conducted its graduation ceremonies on school premises. Agreed Statement of Facts ¶ 37, *id.*, at 17. The parties stipulate that attendance at graduation ceremonies is voluntary. Agreed Statement of Facts ¶ 41, *id.*, at 18. The graduating students enter as a group in a processional, subject to the direction of teachers and school officials, and sit together, apart from their families. We assume the clergy's participation in any high school graduation exercise would be about what it was at Deborah's middle school ceremony. There the students stood for the Pledge of Allegiance and remained standing during the rabbi's prayers. Tr. of Oral Arg. 38. Even on the assumption that there was a respectful moment of silence both before and after the prayers, the rabbi's two presentations must not have extended much beyond a minute each, if that. We do not know whether he remained on stage during the whole ceremony, or whether the students received individual diplomas on stage, or if he helped to congratulate them.

The school board (and the United States, which supports it as *amicus curiae*) argued that these short prayers and others like them at graduation exercises are of profound meaning to many students and parents throughout this country who consider that due respect and acknowledgment for divine guidance and for the deepest spiritual aspirations of our people ought to be expressed at an event as important in life as a graduation. We assume this to be so in addressing the difficult case now before us, for the significance of the prayers lies also at the heart of Daniel and Deborah Weisman's case.

B

Deborah's graduation was held on the premises of Nathan Bishop Middle School on June 29, 1989. Four days before the ceremony, Daniel Weisman, in his individual capacity as a Providence taxpayer and as next friend of Deborah, sought a temporary restraining order in the United States District Court for the District of Rhode Island to prohibit school officials from including an invocation or benediction in the graduation ceremony. The court denied the motion for lack of adequate time to consider it. Deborah and her family attended the graduation, where the prayers were recited. In July 1989, Daniel Weisman filed an amended complaint seeking a permanent injunction barring petitioners, various officials of the Providence public schools, from inviting the clergy to deliver invocations and benedictions at future graduations. We find it unnecessary to address Daniel Weisman's taxpayer standing, for a live and justiciable controversy is before us. Deborah Weisman is enrolled as a student at Classical High School in Providence and from the record it appears likely, if not certain, that an invocation and benediction will be conducted at her high school graduation. Agreed Statement of Facts ¶ 38, App. 17.

The case was submitted on stipulated facts. The District Court held that petitioners' practice of including invocations and benedictions in public school graduations violated the Establishment Clause of the First Amendment, and it enjoined petitioners from continuing the practice. 728 F. Supp. 68 (1990). The court applied the three-part Establishment Clause test set forth in *Lemon v. Kurtzman,* 403 U.S. 602, 91 S. Ct. 2105, 29 L. Ed. 2d 745 (1971). Under that test as described in our past cases, to satisfy the Establishment Clause a governmental practice must (1) reflect a clearly secular purpose; (2) have a primary effect that neither advances nor inhibits religion; and (3) avoid excessive government entanglement with religion. *Committee for Public Ed. & Religious Liberty v. Nyquist,* 413 U.S. 756, 773, 93 S. Ct. 2955, 2965, 37 L. Ed. 2d 948 (1973). The District Court held that petitioners' actions violated the second part of the test, and so did not address either the first or the third. The court decided, based on its reading of our precedents, that the effects test of *Lemon* is violated whenever government action "creates an identification of the state with a religion, or with religion in general," 728 F. Supp., at 71, or when "the effect of the governmental action is to endorse one religion over another, or to endorse religion in general." *Id.,* at 72. The court determined that the practice of including invocations and benedictions, even so-called nonsectarian ones, in public school graduations creates an identification of governmental power with religious practice, endorses religion, and violates the Establishment Clause. In so holding the court expressed the determination not to follow *Stein v. Plainwell Community Schools,* 822 F.2d 1406 (1987), in which the Court of Appeals for the Sixth Circuit, relying on our decision in *Marsh v. Chambers,* 463 U.S. 783, 103 S. Ct. 3330, 77 L. Ed. 2d 1019 (1983), held that benedictions and invocations at public school graduations are not always unconstitutional. In *Marsh* we upheld the constitutionality of the Nebraska State Legislature's practice of opening each of its sessions with a prayer offered by a chaplain paid out of public funds. The District Court in this case disagreed with the Sixth Circuit's reasoning because it believed that *Marsh* was a narrow decision, "limited to the unique situation of legislative prayer," and did not have any relevance to school prayer cases. 728 F. Supp., at 74.

On appeal, the United States Court of Appeals for the First Circuit affirmed. The majority opinion by Judge Torruella adopted the opinion of the District Court. 908 F.2d 1090 (1990). Judge Bownes joined the majority, but wrote a separate concurring opinion in which he decided that the practices challenged here violated all three parts of the *Lemon* test. Judge Bownes went on to agree with the District Court that *Marsh* had no application to school prayer cases and that the *Stein* decision was flawed. He concluded by suggesting that under Establishment Clause rules no prayer, even one excluding any mention of the Deity, could be offered at a public school graduation ceremony. 908 F.2d, at 1090–1097. Judge Campbell dissented, on the basis of *Marsh* and *Stein.* He reasoned that if the prayers delivered were nonsectarian, and if school officials ensured that persons representing a variety of beliefs and ethical systems were invited to present invocations and benedictions, there was no violation of the Establishment Clause. 908 F.2d, at 1099. We granted certiorari, 499 U.S. 918, 111 S. Ct. 1305, 113 L. Ed. 2d 240 (1991), and now affirm.

II

These dominant facts mark and control the confines of our decision: State officials direct the performance of a formal religious exercise at promotional and graduation ceremonies for secondary schools. Even for those students who object to the religious exercise, their attendance and participation in the state-sponsored religious activity are in a fair and real sense obligatory, though the school district does not require attendance as a condition for receipt of the diploma.

This case does not require us to revisit the difficult questions dividing us in recent cases, questions of the definition and full scope of the principles governing the extent of permitted accommodation by the State for the religious beliefs and practices of many of its citizens. See *County of Allegheny v. American Civil Liberties Union, Greater Pittsburgh Chapter,* 492 U.S. 573, 109 S. Ct. 3086, 106 L. Ed. 2d 472 (1989); *Wallace v. Jaffree,* 472 U.S. 38, 105 S. Ct. 2479, 86 L. Ed. 2d 29 (1985); *Lynch v. Donnelly,* 465 U.S. 668, 104 S. Ct. 1355, 79 L. Ed. 2d 604 (1984). For without reference to those principles in other contexts, the controlling precedents as they relate to prayer and religious exercise in primary and secondary public schools compel the holding here that the policy of the city of Providence is an unconstitutional one. We can decide the case without reconsidering the general constitutional framework by which public schools' efforts to accommodate religion are measured. Thus we do not accept the invitation of petitioners and *amicus* the United States to reconsider our decision in *Lemon v. Kurtzman, supra.* The government involvement with religious activity in this case is pervasive, to the point of creating a state-sponsored and state-directed religious exercise in a public school. Conducting this formal religious observance conflicts with settled rules pertaining to prayer exercises for students, and that suffices to determine the question before us.

The principle that government may accommodate the free exercise of religion does not supersede the fundamental limitations imposed by the Establishment Clause. It is beyond dispute that, at a minimum, the Constitution guarantees that government may not coerce anyone to support or participate in religion or its exercise, or otherwise act in a way which "establishes a [state] religion or religious faith, or tends to do so." *Lynch, supra,* at 678, 104 S. Ct., at 1361; see also *County of Allegheny, supra,* 492 U.S., at 591, 109 S. Ct., at 3100, quoting *Everson v. Board of Ed. of Ewing,* 330 U.S. 1, 15–16, 67 S. Ct. 504, 511–512, 91 L. Ed. 711 (1947). The State's involvement in the school prayers challenged today violates these central principles.

That involvement is as troubling as it is undenied. A school official, the principal, decided that an invocation and a benediction should be given; this is a choice attributable to the State, and from a constitutional perspective it is as if a state statute decreed that the prayers must occur. The principal chose the religious participant, here a rabbi, and that choice is also attributable to the State. The reason for the choice of a rabbi is not disclosed by the record, but the potential for divisiveness over the choice of a particular member of the clergy to conduct the ceremony is apparent.

Divisiveness, of course, can attend any state decision respecting religions, and neither its existence nor its potential necessarily invalidates the State's attempts to accommodate religion in all cases. The potential for divisiveness is of particular relevance here though, because it centers around an overt religious exercise in a secondary school environment where, as we discuss below, see *infra,* at 2659, subtle coercive pressures exist and where the student had no real alternative which would have allowed her to avoid the fact or appearance of participation.

The State's role did not end with the decision to include a prayer and with the choice of a clergyman. Principal Lee provided Rabbi Gutterman with a copy of the "Guidelines for Civic Occasions," and advised him that his prayers should be nonsectarian. Through these means the principal directed and controlled the content of the prayers. Even if the only sanction for ignoring the instructions were that the rabbi would not be invited back, we think no religious representative who valued his or her continued reputation and effectiveness in the community would incur the State's displeasure in this regard. It is a cornerstone principle of our Establishment Clause jurisprudence that "it is no part of the business of government to compose official prayers for any group of the American people to recite as a part of a religious program carried on by government," *Engel v. Vitale,* 370 U.S. 421, 425, 82 S. Ct. 1261, 1264, 8 L. Ed. 2d 601 (1962), and that is what the school officials attempted to do.

Petitioners argue, and we find nothing in the case to refute it, that the directions for the content of the prayers were a good-faith attempt by the school to ensure that the sectarianism which is so often the flashpoint for religious animosity be removed from the graduation ceremony. The concern is understandable, as a prayer which uses ideas or images identified with a particular religion may foster a different sort of sectarian rivalry than an invocation or benediction in terms more neutral. The school's explanation, however, does not resolve the dilemma caused by its participation. The question is not the good faith of the school in attempting to make the prayer acceptable to most persons, but the legitimacy of its undertaking that enterprise at all when the object is to produce a prayer to be used in a formal religious exercise which students, for all practical purposes, are obliged to attend.

We are asked to recognize the existence of a practice of nonsectarian prayer, prayer within the embrace of what is known as the Judeo-Christian tradition, prayer which is more acceptable than one which, for example, makes explicit references to the God of Israel, or to Jesus Christ, or to a patron saint. There may be some support, as an empirical observation, to the statement of the Court of Appeals for the Sixth Circuit, picked up by Judge Campbell's dissent in the Court of Appeals in this case, that there has emerged in this country a civic religion, one which is tolerated when sectarian exercises are not. *Stein,* 822 F.2d, at 1409; 908 F.2d 1090, 1098–1099 (CA1 1990) (Campbell, J., dissenting) (case below); see also Note, Civil Religion and the Establishment Clause, 95 Yale L.J. 1237 (1986). If common ground can be defined which permits once conflicting faiths to express the shared conviction that there is an ethic and a morality which transcend human invention, the sense of community and purpose sought by all decent societies might be advanced. But though the First Amendment does not allow the government to stifle prayers which aspire to these ends, neither does it permit the government to undertake that task for itself.

The First Amendment's Religion Clauses mean that religious beliefs and religious expression are too precious to be either proscribed or prescribed by the State. The design of the Constitution is that preservation and transmission of religious beliefs and worship is a responsibility and a choice committed to the private sphere, which itself is promised freedom to pursue that mission. It must not be forgotten then, that while concern must be given to define the protection granted to an objector or a dissenting nonbeliever, these same Clauses exist to protect religion from government interference. James Madison, the principal author of the Bill of Rights, did not rest his opposition to a religious establishment on the sole ground of its effect on the minority. A principal ground for his view was: "[E]xperience witnesseth that ecclesiastical establishments, instead of maintaining the purity and efficacy of Religion, have had a contrary operation." Memorial and Remonstrance Against Religious Assessments (1785), in 8 Papers of James Madison 301 (W. Rachal, R. Rutland, B. Ripel, & F. Teute eds. 1973).

These concerns have particular application in the case of school officials, whose effort to monitor prayer will be perceived by the students as inducing a participation they might otherwise reject. Though the efforts of the school officials in this case to find common ground appear to have been a good-faith attempt to recognize the common aspects of religions and not the divisive ones, our precedents do not permit school officials to assist in composing prayers as an incident to a formal exercise for their students. *Engel v. Vitale, supra,* 370 U.S., at 425, 82 S. Ct., at 1264. And these same precedents caution us to measure the idea of a civic religion against the central meaning of the Religion Clauses of the First Amendment, which is that all creeds must be tolerated and none favored. The suggestion that government may establish an official or civic religion as a means of avoiding the establishment of a religion with more specific creeds strikes us as a contradiction that cannot be accepted.

The degree of school involvement here made it clear that the graduation prayers bore the imprint of the State and thus put school-age children who objected in an untenable position. We turn our attention now to consider the position of the students, both those who desired the prayer and she who did not.

To endure the speech of false ideas or offensive content and then to counter it is part of learning how to live in a pluralistic society, a society which insists upon open discourse towards the end of a tolerant citizenry. And tolerance presupposes some mutuality of obligation. It is argued that our constitutional vision of a free society requires confidence in our own ability to accept or reject ideas of which we do not approve, and that prayer at a high school graduation does nothing more than offer a choice. By the time they are seniors, high school students no doubt have been required to attend classes and assemblies and to complete assignments exposing them to ideas they find distasteful or immoral or absurd or all of these. Against this background, students may consider it an odd measure of justice to be subjected during the course of their educations to ideas deemed offensive and irreligious, but to be denied a brief, formal prayer ceremony that the school offers in return. This argument cannot prevail, however. It overlooks a fundamental dynamic of the Constitution.

The First Amendment protects speech and religion by quite different mechanisms. Speech is protected by ensuring its full expression even when the government participates, for the very object of some of our most important speech is to persuade the government to adopt an idea as its own. *Meese v. Keene,* 481 U.S. 465, 480–481, 107 S. Ct. 1862, 1870–1871, 95 L. Ed. 2d 415 (1987); see also *Keller v. State Bar of California,* 496 U.S. 1, 10–11, 110 S. Ct. 2228, 2234–2235, 110 L. Ed. 2d 1 (1990); *Abood v. Detroit Bd. of Ed.,* 431 U.S. 209, 97 S. Ct. 1782, 52 L. Ed. 2d 261 (1977). The method for protecting freedom of worship and freedom of conscience in religious matters is quite the reverse. In religious debate or expression the government is not a prime participant, for the Framers deemed religious establishment antithetical to the freedom of all. The Free Exercise Clause embraces a freedom of conscience and worship that has close parallels in the speech provisions of the First Amendment, but the Establishment Clause is a specific prohibition on forms of state intervention in religious affairs with no precise counterpart in the speech provisions. *Buckley v. Valeo,* 424 U.S. 1, 92–93, and n. 127, 96 S. Ct. 612, 669–670, and n. 127, 46 L. Ed. 2d 659 (1976) (*per curiam*). The explanation lies in the lesson of history that was and is the inspiration for the Establishment Clause, the lesson that in the hands of government what might begin as a tolerant expression of religious views may end in a policy to indoctrinate and coerce. A state-created orthodoxy puts at grave risk that freedom of belief and conscience which are the sole assurance that religious faith is real, not imposed.

The lessons of the First Amendment are as urgent in the modern world as in the 18th century when it was written. One timeless lesson is that if citizens are subjected to state-sponsored religious exercises, the State disavows its own duty to guard and respect that sphere of inviolable conscience and belief which is the mark of a free people. To compromise that principle today would be to deny our own tradition and forfeit our standing to urge others to secure the protections of that tradition for themselves.

As we have observed before, there are heightened concerns with protecting freedom of conscience from subtle coercive pressure in the elementary and secondary public schools. See, *e.g., School Dist. of Abington v. Schempp,* 374 U.S. 203, 307, 83 S. Ct. 1560, 1616, 10 L. Ed. 2d 844 (1963) (Goldberg, J., concurring); *Edwards v. Aguillard,* 482 U.S. 578, 584, 107 S. Ct. 2573, 2578, 96 L. Ed. 2d 510 (1987); *Board of Ed. of Westside Community Schools (Dist. 66) v. Mergens,* 496 U.S. 226, 261–262, 110 S. Ct. 2356, 2377–2378, 110 L. Ed. 2d 191 (1990) (KENNEDY, J., concurring). Our decisions in *Engel v. Vitale,* 370 U.S. 421, 82 S. Ct. 1261, 8 L. Ed. 2d 601 (1962), and *School Dist. of Abington, supra,* recognize, among other things, that prayer exercises in public schools carry a particular risk of indirect coercion. The concern may not be limited to the context of schools, but it is most pronounced there. See *County of Allegheny v. American Civil Liberties Union, Greater Pittsburgh Chapter,* 492 U.S., at 661, 109 S. Ct., at 3137 (KENNEDY, J., concurring in judgment in part and dissenting in part). What to most believers may seem nothing more than a reasonable request that the nonbeliever respect their religious practices, in a school context may appear to the nonbeliever or dissenter to be an attempt to employ the machinery of the State to enforce a religious orthodoxy.

We need not look beyond the circumstances of this case to see the phenomenon at work. The undeniable fact is that the school district's supervision and control of a high school graduation ceremony places public pressure, as well as peer pressure, on attending students to stand as a group or, at least, maintain respectful silence during the invocation and benediction. This pressure, though subtle and indirect, can be as real as any overt compulsion. Of course, in our culture standing or remaining silent can signify adherence to a view or simple respect for the views of others. And no doubt some persons who have no desire to join a prayer have little objection to standing as a sign of respect for those who do. But for the dissenter of high school age, who has a reasonable perception that she is being forced by the State to pray in a manner her conscience will not allow, the injury is no less real. There can be no doubt that for many, if not most, of the students at the graduation, the act of standing or remaining silent was an expression of participation in the rabbi's prayer. That was the very point of the religious exercise. It is of little comfort to a dissenter, then, to be told that for her the act of standing or remaining in silence signifies mere respect, rather than participation. What matters is that, given our social conventions, a reasonable dissenter in this milieu could believe that the group exercise signified her own participation or approval of it.

Finding no violation under these circumstances would place objectors in the dilemma of participating, with all that implies, or protesting. We do not address whether that choice is acceptable if the affected citizens are mature adults, but we think the State may not, consistent with the Establishment Clause, place primary and secondary school children in this position. Research in psychology supports the common assumption that adolescents are often susceptible to pressure from their peers towards conformity, and that the influence is strongest in matters of social convention. Brittain, Adolescent Choices and Parent-Peer Cross-Pressures, 28 Am.Sociological Rev. 385 (June 1963); Clasen & Brown, The Multidimensionality of Peer Pressure in Adolescence, 14 J. of Youth and Adolescence 451 (Dec. 1985); Brown, Clasen, & Eicher, Perceptions of Peer Pressure, Peer Conformity Dispositions, and Self-Reported Behavior Among Adolescents, 22 Developmental Psychology 521 (July 1986). To recognize that the choice imposed by the State constitutes an unacceptable constraint only acknowledges that the government may no more use social pressure to enforce orthodoxy than it may use more direct means.

The injury caused by the government's action, and the reason why Daniel and Deborah Weisman object to it, is that the State, in a school setting, in effect required participation in a religious exercise. It is, we concede, a brief exercise during which the individual can concentrate on joining its message, meditate on her own religion, or let her mind wander. But the embarrassment and the intrusion of the religious exercise cannot be refuted by arguing that these prayers, and similar ones to be said in the future, are of a *de minimis* character. To do so would be an affront to the rabbi who offered them and to all those for whom the prayers were an essential and profound recognition of divine authority. And for the same reason, we think that the intrusion is greater than the two minutes or so of time consumed for prayers like these. Assuming, as we must, that the prayers were offensive to the student and the parent who now object, the intrusion was both real and, in the context of a secondary school, a violation of the objectors' rights. That the intrusion was in the course of promulgating religion that sought to be civic or nonsectarian rather than pertaining to one sect does not lessen the offense or isolation to the objectors. At best it narrows their number, at worst increases their sense of isolation and affront. See *supra*, at 2658.

There was a stipulation in the District Court that attendance at graduation and promotional ceremonies is voluntary. Agreed Statement of Facts ¶ 41, App. 18. Petitioners and the United States, as *amicus*, made this a center point of the case, arguing that the option of not attending the graduation excuses any inducement or coercion in the ceremony itself. The argument lacks all persuasion. Law reaches past formalism. And to say a teenage student has a real choice not to attend her high school graduation is formalistic in the extreme. True, Deborah could elect not to attend commencement without renouncing her diploma; but we shall not allow the case to turn on this point. Everyone knows that in our society and in our culture high school graduation is one of life's most significant occasions. A school rule which excuses attendance is beside the point. Attendance may not be required by official decree, yet it is apparent that a student is not free to absent herself from the graduation exercise in any real sense of the term "voluntary," for absence would require forfeiture of those intangible benefits which have motivated the student through youth and all her high school years. Graduation is a time for family and those closest to the student to celebrate success and express mutual wishes of gratitude and respect, all to the end of impressing upon the young person the role that it is his or her right and duty to assume in the community and all of its diverse parts.

The importance of the event is the point the school district and the United States rely upon to argue that a formal prayer ought to be permitted, but it becomes one of the principal reasons why their argument must fail. Their contention, one of considerable force were it not for the constitutional constraints applied to state action, is that the prayers are an essential part of these ceremonies because for many persons an occasion of this significance lacks meaning if there is no recognition, however brief, that human achievements cannot be understood apart from their spiritual essence. We think the Government's position that this interest suffices to force students to choose between compliance or forfeiture demonstrates fundamental inconsistency in its argumentation. It fails to acknowledge that what for many of Deborah's classmates and their parents was a spiritual imperative was for Daniel and Deborah Weisman religious conformance compelled by the State. While in some societies the wishes of the majority might prevail, the Establishment Clause of the First Amendment is addressed to this contingency and rejects the balance urged upon us. The Constitution forbids the State to exact religious conformity from a student as the price of attending her own high school graduation. This is the calculus the Constitution commands.

The Government's argument gives insufficient recognition to the real conflict of conscience faced by the young student. The essence of the Government's position is that with regard to a civic, social occasion of this importance it is the objector, not the majority, who must take unilateral and private action to avoid compromising religious scruples, hereby electing to miss the graduation exercise. This turns conventional First Amendment analysis on its head. It is a tenet of the First Amendment that the State cannot require one of its citizens to forfeit his or her rights and benefits as the price of resisting conformance to state-sponsored religious practice. To say that a student must remain apart from the ceremony at the opening invocation and closing benediction is to risk compelling conformity in an environment analogous to the classroom setting, where we have said the risk of compulsion is especially high. See *supra*, at 2658–2659. Just as in *Engel v. Vitale*, 370 U.S., at 430, 82 S. Ct., at 1266, and *School Dist. of Abington v. Schempp*, 374 U.S., at 224–225, 83 S. Ct., at 1572–1573, where we found that provisions within the challenged legislation permitting a student to be voluntarily excused from attendance or participation in the daily prayers did not shield those practices from invalidation, the fact that attendance at the graduation ceremonies is voluntary in a legal sense does not save the religious exercise.

Inherent differences between the public school system and a session of a state legislature distinguish this case from *Marsh v. Chambers*, 463 U.S. 783, 103 S. Ct. 3330, 77 L. Ed. 2d 1019 (1983). The considerations we have raised in objection to the invocation and benediction are in many respects similar to the arguments we considered in *Marsh*. But there are also obvious differences. The atmosphere at the opening of a session of a state legislature where adults are free to enter and leave with little comment and for any number of reasons cannot compare with the constraining potential of the one school event most important for the student to attend. The influence and force of a formal exercise in a school graduation are far greater than the prayer exercise we condoned in *Marsh*. The *Marsh* majority in fact gave specific recognition to this distinction and placed particular reliance on it in upholding the prayers at issue there. 463 U.S., at 792, 103 S. Ct., at 3336. Today's case is different. At a high school graduation, teachers and principals must and do retain a high degree of control over the precise contents of the program, the speeches, the timing, the movements, the dress, and the decorum of the students. *Bethel School Dist. No. 403 v. Fraser*, 478 U.S. 675, 106 S. Ct. 3159, 92 L. Ed. 2d 549 (1986). In this atmosphere the state-imposed character of an invocation and benediction by clergy selected by the school combine to make the prayer a state-sanctioned religious exercise in which the student was left with no alternative but to submit. This is different from *Marsh* and suffices to make the religious exercise a First Amendment violation. Our Establishment Clause jurisprudence remains a delicate and fact-sensitive one, and we cannot accept the parallel relied upon by petitioners and the United States between the facts of *Marsh* and the case now before us. Our decisions in *Engel v. Vitale, supra*, and *School Dist. of Abington v. Schempp, supra*, require us to distinguish the public school context.

We do not hold that every state action implicating religion is invalid if one or a few citizens find it offensive. People may take offense at all manner of religious as well as nonreligious messages, but offense alone does not in every case show a violation. We know too that sometimes to endure social isolation or even anger may be the price of conscience or nonconformity. But, by any reading of our cases, the conformity required of the student in this case was too high an exaction to withstand the test of the Establishment Clause. The prayer exercises in this case are especially improper because the State has in every practical sense compelled attendance and participation in an explicit religious exercise at an event of singular importance to every student, one the objecting student had no real alternative to avoid.

> Our jurisprudence in this area is of necessity one of line-drawing, of determining at what point a dissenter's rights of religious freedom are infringed by the State.
>
> "The First Amendment does not prohibit practices which by any realistic measure create none of the dangers which it is designed to prevent and which do not so directly or substantially involve the state in religious exercises or in the favoring of religion as to have meaningful and practical impact. It is of course true that great consequences can grow from small beginnings, but the measure of constitutional adjudication is the ability and willingness to distinguish between real threat and mere shadow."

School Dist. of Abington v. Schempp, supra, 374 U.S., at 308, 83 S. Ct., at 1616 (Goldberg, J., concurring).

Our society would be less than true to its heritage if it lacked abiding concern for the values of its young people, and we acknowledge the profound belief of adherents to many faiths that there must be a place in the student's life for precepts of a morality higher even than the law we today enforce. We express no hostility to those aspirations, nor would our oath permit us to do so. A relentless and all-pervasive attempt to exclude religion from every aspect of public life could itself become inconsistent with the Constitution. See *School Dist. of Abington, supra,* at 306, 83 S. Ct., at 1615 (Goldberg, J., concurring). We recognize that, at graduation time and throughout the course of the educational process, there will be instances when religious values, religious practices, and religious persons will have some interaction with the public schools and their students. See *Board of Ed. of Westside Community Schools (Dist. 66) v. Mergens,* 496 U.S. 226, 110 S. Ct. 2356, 110 L. Ed. 2d 191 (1990). But these matters, often questions of accommodation of religion, are not before us. The sole question presented is whether a religious exercise may be conducted at a graduation ceremony in circumstances where, as we have found, young graduates who object are induced to conform. No holding by this Court suggests that a school can persuade or compel a student to participate in a religious exercise. That is being done here, and it is forbidden by the Establishment Clause of the First Amendment.

For the reasons we have stated, the judgment of the Court of Appeals is *Affirmed.*

[Case No. 6-5]

Permitting high school students to recite prayers over the public address system at a football game violates the Establishment Clause.

Santa Fe Independent School District v. Doe

Supreme Court of the United States
530 U.S. 290 (2000)

Justice STEVENS delivered the opinion of the Court.

Prior to 1995, the Santa Fe High School student who occupied the school's elective office of student council chaplain delivered a prayer over the public address system before each varsity football game for the entire season. This practice, along with others, was challenged in District Court as a violation of the Establishment Clause of the First Amendment. While these proceedings were pending in the District Court, the school district adopted a different policy that permits, but does not require, prayer initiated and led by a student at all home games. The District Court entered an order modifying that policy to permit only nonsectarian, nonproselytizing prayer. The Court of Appeals held that, even as modified by the District Court, the football prayer policy was invalid. We granted the school district's petition for certiorari to review that holding.

I

The Santa Fe Independent School District (District) is a political subdivision of the State of Texas, responsible for the education of more than 4,000 students in a small community in the southern part of the State. The District includes the Santa Fe High School, two primary schools, an intermediate school and the junior high school. Respondents are two sets of current or former students and their respective mothers. One family is Mormon and the other is Catholic. The District Court permitted respondents (Does) to litigate anonymously to protect them from intimidation or harassment.[172]

---

172. A decision, the Fifth Circuit Court of Appeals noted, that many District officials "apparently neither agreed with nor particularly respected." 168 F.3d 806, 809, n. 1 (C.A.5 1999). About a month after the complaint was filed, the District Court entered an order that provided, in part:

> "[A]ny further attempt on the part of District or school administration, officials, counsellors, teachers, employees or servants of the School District, parents, students or anyone else, overtly or covertly to ferret out the identities of the Plaintiffs in this cause, by means of bogus petitions, questionnaires, individual interrogation, or downright 'snooping', will cease immediately. ANYONE TAKING ANY ACTION ON SCHOOL PROPERTY, DURING SCHOOL HOURS, OR WITH SCHOOL RESOURCES OR APPROVAL FOR PURPOSES OF ATTEMPTING TO ELICIT THE NAMES OR IDENTITIES OF THE PLAINTIFFS IN THIS CAUSE OF ACTION, BY OR ON BEHALF OF ANY OF THESE INDIVIDUALS, WILL FACE THE HARSHEST POSSIBLE CONTEMPT SANCTIONS FROM THIS COURT, AND MAY ADDITIONALLY FACE CRIMINAL LIABILITY. The Court wants these proceedings addressed on their merits, and not on the basis of intimidation or harassment of the participants on either side." App. 34–35.

Respondents commenced this action in April 1995 and moved for a temporary restraining order to prevent the District from violating the Establishment Clause at the imminent graduation exercises. In their complaint the Does alleged that the District had engaged in several proselytizing practices, such as promoting attendance at a Baptist revival meeting, encouraging membership in religious clubs, chastising children who held minority religious beliefs, and distributing Gideon Bibles on school premises. They also alleged that the District allowed students to read Christian invocations and benedictions from the stage at graduation ceremonies,[173] and to deliver overtly Christian prayers over the public address system at home football games.

On May 10, 1995, the District Court entered an interim order addressing a number of different issues.[174] With respect to the impending graduation, the order provided that "non-denominational prayer" consisting of "an invocation and/or benediction" could be presented by a senior student or students selected by members of the graduating class. The text of the prayer was to be determined by the students, without scrutiny or preapproval by school officials. References to particular religious figures "such as Mohammed, Jesus, Buddha, or the like" would be permitted "as long as the general thrust of the prayer is non-proselytizing." App. 32.

In response to that portion of the order, the District adopted a series of policies over several months dealing with prayer at school functions. The policies enacted in May and July for graduation ceremonies provided the format for the August and October policies for football games. The May policy provided:

> "'The board has chosen to permit the graduating senior class, with the advice and counsel of the senior class principal or designee, to elect by secret ballot to choose whether an invocation and benediction shall be part

---

173. At the 1994 graduation ceremony the senior class president delivered this invocation:

> "Please bow your heads.
>
> "Dear heavenly Father, thank you for allowing us to gather here safely tonight. We thank you for the wonderful year you have allowed us to spend together as students of Santa Fe. We thank you for our teachers who have devoted many hours to each of us. Thank you, Lord, for our parents and may each one receive the special blessing. We pray also for a blessing and guidance as each student moves forward in the future. Lord, bless this ceremony and give us all a safe journey home. In Jesus' name we pray." *Id.*, at 19.

174. For example, it prohibited school officials from endorsing or participating in the baccalaureate ceremony sponsored by the Santa Fe Ministerial Alliance, and ordered the District to establish policies to deal with

> "manifest First Amendment infractions of teachers, counsellors, or other District or school officials or personnel, such as ridiculing, berating or holding up for inappropriate scrutiny or examination the beliefs of any individual students. Similarly, the School District will establish or clarify existing procedures for excluding overt or covert sectarian and proselytizing religious teaching, such as the use of blatantly denominational religious terms in spelling lessons, denominational religious songs and poems in English or choir classes, denominational religious stories and parables in grammar lessons and the like, while at the same time allowing for frank and open discussion of moral, religious, and societal views and beliefs, which are non-denominational and non-judgmental." *Id.*, at 34.

> of the graduation exercise. If so chosen the class shall elect by secret ballot, from a list of student volunteers, students to deliver nonsectarian, nonproselytizing invocations and benedictions for the purpose of solemnizing their graduation ceremonies.'"

168 F.3d 806, 811 (C.A.5 1999) (emphasis deleted).

The parties stipulated that after this policy was adopted, "the senior class held an election to determine whether to have an invocation and benediction at the commencement [and that the] class voted, by secret ballot, to include prayer at the high school graduation." App. 52. In a second vote the class elected two seniors to deliver the invocation and benediction.[175]

In July, the District enacted another policy eliminating the requirement that invocations and benedictions be "nonsectarian and nonproselytising," but also providing that if the District were to be enjoined from enforcing that policy, the May policy would automatically become effective.

The August policy, which was titled "Prayer at Football Games," was similar to the July policy for graduations. It also authorized two student elections, the first to determine whether "invocations" should be delivered, and the second to select the spokesperson to deliver them. Like the July policy, it contained two parts, an initial statement that omitted any requirement that the content of the invocation be "nonsectarian and nonproselytising," and a fallback provision that automatically added that limitation if the preferred policy should be enjoined. On August 31, 1995, according to the parties' stipulation: "[T]he district's high school students voted to determine whether a student would deliver prayer at varsity football games. . . . The students chose to allow a student to say a prayer at football games." *Id.*, at 65. A week later, in a separate election, they selected a student "to deliver the prayer at varsity football games." *Id.*, at 66.

The final policy (October policy) is essentially the same as the August policy, though it omits the word "prayer" from its title, and refers to "messages" and "statements" as well as "invocations."[176] It is the validity of that policy that is before us.[177]

---

175. The student giving the invocation thanked the Lord for keeping the class safe through 12 years of school and for gracing their lives with two special people and closed: "Lord, we ask that You keep Your hand upon us during this ceremony and to help us keep You in our hearts through the rest of our lives. In God's name we pray. Amen." *Id.*, at 53. The student benediction was similar in content and closed: "Lord, we ask for Your protection as we depart to our next destination and watch over us as we go our separate ways. Grant each of us a safe trip and keep us secure throughout the night. In Your name we pray. Amen." *Id.*, at 54.

176. Despite these changes, the school did not conduct another election, under the October policy, to supersede the results of the August policy election.

177. It provides:

"STUDENT ACTIVITIES:

"PRE-GAME CEREMONIES AT FOOTBALL GAMES

"The board has chosen to permit students to deliver a brief invocation and/ or message to be delivered during the pre-game ceremonies of home varsity football games to

The District Court did enter an order precluding enforcement of the first, open-ended policy. Relying on our decision in *Lee v. Weisman,* 505 U.S. 577, 112 S. Ct. 2649, 120 L. Ed. 2d 467 (1992), it held that the school's "action must not 'coerce anyone to support or participate in' a religious exercise." App. to Pet. for Cert. E7. Applying that test, it concluded that the graduation prayers appealed "to distinctively Christian beliefs,"[178] and that delivering a prayer "over the school's public address system prior to each football and baseball game coerces student participation in religious events."[179] Both parties appealed, the District contending that the enjoined portion of the October policy was permissible and the Does contending that both alternatives violated the Establishment Clause. The Court of Appeals majority agreed with the Does.

The decision of the Court of Appeals followed Fifth Circuit precedent that had announced two rules. In *Jones v. Clear Creek Independent School Dist.,* 977 F.2d 963 (C.A.5 1992), that court held that student-led prayer that was approved by a vote of the students and was nonsectarian and nonproselytizing was permissible at high school graduation ceremonies. On the other hand, in later cases the Fifth Circuit made it clear that the *Clear Creek* rule applied only to high school graduations and that school-encouraged prayer was constitutionally impermissible at school-related

---

solemnize the event, to promote good sportsmanship and student safety, and to establish the appropriate environment for the competition.

"Upon advice and direction of the high school principal, each spring, the high school student council shall conduct an election, by the high school student body, by secret ballot, to determine whether such a statement or invocation will be a part of the pre-game ceremonies and if so, shall elect a student, from a list of student volunteers, to deliver the statement or invocation. The student volunteer who is selected by his or her classmates may decide what message and/ or invocation to deliver, consistent with the goals and purposes of this policy.

"If the District is enjoined by a court order from the enforcement of this policy, then and only then will the following policy automatically become the applicable policy of the school district.

"The board has chosen to permit students to deliver a brief invocation and/ or message to be delivered during the pre-game ceremonies of home varsity football games to solemnize the event, to promote good sportsmanship and student safety, and to establish the appropriate environment for the competition.

"Upon advice and direction of the high school principal, each spring, the high school student council shall conduct an election, by the high school student body, by secret ballot, to determine whether such a message or invocation will be a part of the pre-game ceremonies and if so, shall elect a student, from a list of student volunteers, to deliver the statement or invocation. The student volunteer who is selected by his or her classmates may decide what statement or invocation to deliver, consistent with the goals and purposes of this policy. Any message and/ or invocation delivered by a student must be nonsectarian and nonproselytizing." *Id.,* at 104–105.

178. "The graduation prayers at issue in the instant case, in contrast, are infused with explicit references to Jesus Christ and otherwise appeal to distinctively Christian beliefs. The Court accordingly finds that use of these prayers during graduation ceremonies, considered in light of the overall manner in which they were delivered, violated the Establishment Clause." App. to Pet. for Cert. E8.

179. *Id.,* at E8–E9.

sporting events. Thus, in *Doe v. Duncanville Independent School Dist.*, 70 F.3d 402 (C.A.5 1995), it had described a high school graduation as "a significant, once in-a-lifetime event" to be contrasted with athletic events in "a setting that is far less solemn and extraordinary." *Id.*, at 406–407.[180]

In its opinion in this case, the Court of Appeals explained:

> "The controlling feature here is the same as in *Duncanville:* The prayers are to be delivered *at football games*—hardly the sober type of annual event that can be appropriately solemnized with prayer. The distinction to which [the District] points is simply one without difference. Regardless of whether the prayers are selected by vote or spontaneously initiated at these frequently-recurring, informal, school-sponsored events, school officials are present and have the authority to stop the prayers. Thus, as we indicated in *Duncanville,* our decision in *Clear Creek II* hinged on the singular context and singularly serious nature of a graduation ceremony. Outside that nurturing context, a Clear Creek Prayer Policy cannot survive. We therefore reverse the district court's holding that [the District's] alternative Clear Creek Prayer Policy can be extended to football games, irrespective of the presence of the nonsectarian, nonproselytizing restrictions."

168 F.3d, at 823.

The dissenting judge rejected the majority's distinction between graduation ceremonies and football games. In his opinion the District's October policy created a limited public forum that had a secular purpose[181] and provided neutral accommodation of noncoerced, private, religious speech.[182]

We granted the District's petition for certiorari, limited to the following question: "Whether petitioner's policy permitting student-led, student-initiated prayer at football games violates the Establishment Clause." 528 U.S. 1002, 120 S. Ct. 494, 145 L. Ed. 2d 381 (1999). We conclude, as did the Court of Appeals, that it does.

---

180. Because the dissent overlooks this case, it incorrectly assumes that a "prayer-only policy" at football games was permissible in the Fifth Circuit. See *post,* at 2286 (opinion of REHNQUIST, C.J.).

181. "There are in fact several secular reasons for allowing a brief, serious message before football games—some of which [the District] has listed in its policy. At sporting events, messages and/ or invocations can promote, among other things, honest and fair play, clean competition, individual challenge to be one's best, importance of team work, and many more goals that the majority could conceive would it only pause to do so.

"Having again relinquished all editorial control, [the District] has created a limited public forum for the students to give brief statements or prayers concerning the value of those goals and the methods for achieving them." 168 F.3d, at 835.

182. "The majority fails to realize that what is at issue in this *facial challenge* to this school policy is the neutral accommodation of non-coerced, private, religious speech, which allows students, selected by students, to express their personal viewpoints. The state is not involved. The school board has neither scripted, supervised, endorsed, suggested, nor edited these personal viewpoints. Yet the majority imposes a judicial curse upon sectarian religious speech." *Id.*, at 836.

II

The first Clause in the First Amendment to the Federal Constitution provides that "Congress shall make no law respecting an establishment of religion, or prohibiting the free exercise thereof." The Fourteenth Amendment imposes those substantive limitations on the legislative power of the States and their political subdivisions. *Wallace v. Jaffree,* 472 U.S. 38, 49–50, 105 S. Ct. 2479, 86 L. Ed. 2d 29 (1985). In *Lee v. Weisman,* 505 U.S. 577, 112 S. Ct. 2649, 120 L. Ed. 2d 467 (1992), we held that a prayer delivered by a rabbi at a middle school graduation ceremony violated that Clause. Although this case involves student prayer at a different type of school function, our analysis is properly guided by the principles that we endorsed in *Lee.*

As we held in that case:

> "The principle that government may accommodate the free exercise of religion does not supersede the fundamental limitations imposed by the Establishment Clause. It is beyond dispute that, at a minimum, the Constitution guarantees that government may not coerce anyone to support or participate in religion or its exercise, or otherwise act in a way which 'establishes a [state] religion or religious faith, or tends to do so.'"

Id., at 587, 112 S. Ct. 2649 (citations omitted) (quoting *Lynch v. Donnelly,* 465 U.S. 668, 678, 104 S. Ct. 1355, 79 L. Ed. 2d 604 (1984)).

In this case the District first argues that this principle is inapplicable to its October policy because the messages are private student speech, not public speech. It reminds us that "there is a crucial difference between *government* speech endorsing religion, which the Establishment Clause forbids, and *private* speech endorsing religion, which the Free Speech and Free Exercise Clauses protect." *Board of Ed. of Westside Community Schools (Dist.66) v. Mergens,* 496 U.S. 226, 250, 110 S. Ct. 2356, 110 L. Ed. 2d 191 (1990) (opinion of O'CONNOR, J.). We certainly agree with that distinction, but we are not persuaded that the pregame invocations should be regarded as "private speech."

These invocations are authorized by a government policy and take place on government property at government-sponsored school-related events. Of course, not every message delivered under such circumstances is the government's own. We have held, for example, that an individual's contribution to a government-created forum was not government speech. See *Rosenberger v. Rector and Visitors of Univ. of Va.,* 515 U.S. 819, 115 S. Ct. 2510, 132 L. Ed. 2d 700 (1995). Although the District relies heavily on *Rosenberger* and similar cases involving such forums,[183] it is clear

183. See, *e.g.,* Brief for Petitioner 44–48, citing *Rosenberger v. Rector and Visitors of Univ. of Va.,* 515 U.S. 819, 115 S. Ct. 2510, 132 L. Ed. 2d 700 (1995) (limited public forum); *Widmar v. Vincent,* 454 U.S. 263, 102 S. Ct. 269, 70 L. Ed. 2d 440 (1981) (limited public forum); *Capitol Square Review and Advisory Bd. v. Pinette,* 515 U.S. 753, 115 S. Ct. 2440, 132 L. Ed. 2d 650 (1995) (traditional public forum); *Lamb's Chapel v. Center Moriches Union Free School Dist.,* 508 U.S. 384, 113 S. Ct. 2141,

that the pregame ceremony is not the type of forum discussed in those cases.[184] The Santa Fe school officials simply do not "evince either 'by policy or by practice,' any intent to open the [pregame ceremony] to 'indiscriminate use,' . . . by the student body generally." *Hazelwood School Dist. v. Kuhlmeier,* 484 U.S. 260, 270, 108 S. Ct. 562, 98 L. Ed. 2d 592 (1988) (quoting *Perry Ed. Assn. v. Perry Local Educators' Assn.,* 460 U.S. 37, 47, 103 S. Ct. 948, 74 L. Ed. 2d 794 (1983)). Rather, the school allows only one student, the same student for the entire season, to give the invocation. The statement or invocation, moreover, is subject to particular regulations that confine the content and topic of the student's message, see *infra,* at 2277–2278, 2278–2279. By comparison, in *Perry* we rejected a claim that the school had created a limited public forum in its school mail system despite the fact that it had allowed far more speakers to address a much broader range of topics than the policy at issue here.[185] As we concluded in *Perry,* "selective access does not transform government property into a public forum." 460 U.S., at 47, 103 S. Ct. 948.

Granting only one student access to the stage at a time does not, of course, necessarily preclude a finding that a school has created a limited public forum. Here, however, Santa Fe's student election system ensures that only those messages deemed "appropriate" under the District's policy may be delivered. That is, the majoritarian process implemented by the District guarantees, by definition, that minority candidates will never prevail and that their views will be effectively silenced.

Recently, in *Board of Regents of Univ. of Wis. System v. Southworth,* 529 U.S. 217, 120 S. Ct. 1346, 146 L. Ed. 2d 193 (2000), we explained why student elections that determine, by majority vote, which expressive activities shall receive or not receive school benefits are constitutionally problematic:

> "To the extent the referendum substitutes majority determinations for viewpoint neutrality it would undermine the constitutional protection the program requires. The whole theory of viewpoint neutrality is that minority views are treated with the same respect as are majority views. Access to a public forum, for instance, does not depend upon majoritarian consent. That principle is controlling here."

Id., at 235, 120 S. Ct. 1346.

---

124 L. Ed. 2d 352 (1993) (limited public forum). Although the District relies on these public forum cases, it does not actually argue that the pregame ceremony constitutes such a forum.

184. A conclusion that the District had created a public forum would help shed light on whether the resulting speech is public or private, but we also note that we have never held the mere creation of a public forum shields the government entity from scrutiny under the Establishment Clause. See, *e.g., Pinette,* 515 U.S., at 772, 115 S. Ct. 2440 (O'CONNOR, J., concurring in part and concurring in judgment) ("I see no necessity to carve out . . . an exception to the endorsement test for the public forum context").

185. The school's internal mail system in *Perry* was open to various private organizations such as "[l]ocal parochial schools, church groups, YMCA's, and Cub Scout units." 460 U.S., at 39, n. 2, 103 S. Ct. 948.

Like the student referendum for funding in *Southworth,* this student election does nothing to protect minority views but rather places the students who hold such views at the mercy of the majority.[186] Because "fundamental rights may not be submitted to vote; they depend on the outcome of no elections," *West Virginia Bd. of Ed. v. Barnette,* 319 U.S. 624, 638, 63 S. Ct. 1178, 87 L. Ed. 1628 (1943), the District's elections are insufficient safeguards of diverse student speech.

In *Lee,* the school district made the related argument that its policy of endorsing only "civic or nonsectarian" prayer was acceptable because it minimized the intrusion on the audience as a whole. We rejected that claim by explaining that such a majoritarian policy "does not lessen the offense or isolation to the objectors. At best it narrows their number, at worst increases their sense of isolation and affront." 505 U.S., at 594, 112 S. Ct. 2649. Similarly, while Santa Fe's majoritarian election might ensure that *most* of the students are represented, it does nothing to protect the minority; indeed, it likely serves to intensify their offense.

Moreover, the District has failed to divorce itself from the religious content in the invocations. It has not succeeded in doing so, either by claiming that its policy is "'one of neutrality rather than endorsement'"[187] or by characterizing the individual student as the "circuit-breaker"[188] in the process. Contrary to the District's repeated assertions that it has adopted a "hands-off" approach to the pregame invocation, the realities of the situation plainly reveal that its policy involves both perceived and actual endorsement of religion. In this case, as we found in *Lee,* the "degree of school involvement" makes it clear that the pregame prayers bear "the imprint of the State and thus put school-age children who objected in an untenable position." *Id.,* at 590, 112 S. Ct. 2649.

The District has attempted to disentangle itself from the religious messages by developing the two-step student election process. The text of the October policy, however, exposes the extent of the school's entanglement. The elections take place at all only because the school "board *has chosen to permit* students to deliver a brief invocation and/or message." App. 104 (emphasis added). The elections thus "shall" be conducted "by the high school student council" and "[u]pon advice and direction of the high school principal." *Id.,* at 104–105. The decision whether to deliver a

186. If instead of a choice between an invocation and no pregame message, the first election determined whether a political speech should be made, and the second election determined whether the speaker should be a Democrat or a Republican, it would be rather clear that the public address system was being used to deliver a partisan message reflecting the viewpoint of the majority rather than a random statement by a private individual.

The fact that the District's policy provides for the election of the speaker only after the majority has voted on her message identifies an obvious distinction between this case and the typical election of a "student body president, or even a newly elected prom king or queen." *Post,* at 2285.

187. Brief for Petitioner 19 (quoting *Board of Ed. of Westside Community Schools (Dist.66) v. Mergens,* 496 U.S. 226, 248, 110 S. Ct. 2356, 110 L. Ed. 2d 191 (1990) (plurality opinion)).

188. Tr. of Oral Arg. 7.

message is first made by majority vote of the entire student body, followed by a choice of the speaker in a separate, similar majority election. Even though the particular words used by the speaker are not determined by those votes, the policy mandates that the "statement or invocation" be "consistent with the goals and purposes of this policy," which are "to solemnize the event, to promote good sportsmanship and student safety, and to establish the appropriate environment for the competition." *Ibid.*

In addition to involving the school in the selection of the speaker, the policy, by its terms, invites and encourages religious messages. The policy itself states that the purpose of the message is "to solemnize the event." A religious message is the most obvious method of solemnizing an event. Moreover, the requirements that the message "promote good sportsmanship" and "establish the appropriate environment for competition" further narrow the types of message deemed appropriate, suggesting that a solemn, yet nonreligious, message, such as commentary on United States foreign policy, would be prohibited.[189] Indeed, the only type of message that is expressly endorsed in the text is an "invocation"—a term that primarily describes an appeal for divine assistance.[190] In fact, as used in the past at Santa Fe High School, an "invocation" has always entailed a focused religious message. Thus, the expressed purposes of the policy encourage the selection of a religious message, and that is precisely how the students understand the policy. The results of the elections described in the parties' stipulation[191] make it clear that the students understood that the central question before them was whether prayer should be a part of the pregame ceremony.[192] We recognize the important role that public worship plays in many communities, as well as the sincere desire to include public prayer as a part of various occasions so as to mark those occasions' significance. But such religious activity in public schools, as elsewhere, must comport with the First Amendment.

The actual or perceived endorsement of the message, moreover, is established by factors beyond just the text of the policy. Once the student speaker is selected and the message composed, the invocation is then delivered to a large audience assembled as part of a regularly scheduled, school-sponsored function conducted on school property. The message is broadcast over the school's public address system, which

---

189. THE CHIEF JUSTICE's hypothetical of the student body president asked by the school to introduce a guest speaker with a biography of her accomplishments, see *post,* at 2287–2288 (dissenting opinion), obviously would pose no problems under the Establishment Clause.

190. See, *e.g.,* Webster's Third New International Dictionary 1190 (1993) (defining "invocation" as "a prayer of entreaty that is usu[ally] a call for the divine presence and is offered at the beginning of a meeting or service of worship").

191. See *supra,* at 2272–2273, and n. 4.

192. Even if the plain language of the October policy were facially neutral, "the Establishment Clause forbids a State to hide behind the application of formally neutral criteria and remain studiously oblivious to the effects of its actions." *Capitol Square Review and Advisory Bd. v. Pinette,* 515 U.S., at 777, 115 S. Ct. 2440 (O'CONNOR, J., concurring in part and concurring in judgment); see also *Church of Lukumi Babalu Aye, Inc. v. Hialeah,* 508 U.S. 520, 534–535, 113 S. Ct. 2217, 124 L. Ed. 2d 472 (1993) (making the same point in the Free Exercise Clause context).

remains subject to the control of school officials. It is fair to assume that the pregame ceremony is clothed in the traditional indicia of school sporting events, which generally include not just the team, but also cheerleaders and band members dressed in uniforms sporting the school name and mascot. The school's name is likely written in large print across the field and on banners and flags. The crowd will certainly include many who display the school colors and insignia on their school T-shirts, jackets, or hats and who may also be waving signs displaying the school name. It is in a setting such as this that "[t]he board has chosen to permit" the elected student to rise and give the "statement or invocation."

In this context the members of the listening audience must perceive the pregame message as a public expression of the views of the majority of the student body delivered with the approval of the school administration. In cases involving state participation in a religious activity, one of the relevant questions is "whether an objective observer, acquainted with the text, legislative history, and implementation of the statute, would perceive it as a state endorsement of prayer in public schools." *Wallace,* 472 U.S., at 73, 76, 105 S. Ct. 2479 (O'CONNOR, J., concurring in judgment); see also *Capitol Square Review and Advisory Bd. v. Pinette,* 515 U.S. 753, 777, 115 S. Ct. 2440, 132 L. Ed. 2d 650 (1995) (O'CONNOR, J., concurring in part and concurring in judgment). Regardless of the listener's support for, or objection to, the message, an objective Santa Fe High School student will unquestionably perceive the inevitable pregame prayer as stamped with her school's seal of approval.

The text and history of this policy, moreover, reinforce our objective student's perception that the prayer is, in actuality, encouraged by the school. When a governmental entity professes a secular purpose for an arguably religious policy, the government's characterization is, of course, entitled to some deference. But it is nonetheless the duty of the courts to "distinguis[h] a sham secular purpose from a sincere one." *Wallace,* 472 U.S., at 75, 105 S. Ct. 2479 (O'CONNOR, J., concurring in judgment).

According to the District, the secular purposes of the policy are to "foste[r] free expression of private persons . . . as well [as to] solemniz[e] sporting events, promot[e] good sportsmanship and student safety, and establis[h] an appropriate environment for competition." Brief for Petitioner 14. We note, however, that the District's approval of only one specific kind of message, an "invocation," is not necessary to further any of these purposes. Additionally, the fact that only one student is permitted to give a content-limited message suggests that this policy does little to "foste[r] free expression." Furthermore, regardless of whether one considers a sporting event an appropriate occasion for solemnity, the use of an invocation to foster such solemnity is impermissible when, in actuality, it constitutes prayer sponsored by the school. And it is unclear what type of message would be both appropriately "solemnizing" under the District's policy and yet nonreligious.

Most striking to us is the evolution of the current policy from the long-sanctioned office of "Student Chaplain" to the candidly titled "Prayer at Football Games" regulation. This history indicates that the District intended to preserve the practice of prayer before football games. The conclusion that the District viewed the October policy simply as a continuation of the previous policies is dramatically illustrated by the fact that the school did not conduct a new election, pursuant to the current policy, to replace the results of the previous election, which occurred under the former policy. Given these observations, and in light of the school's history of regular delivery of a student-led prayer at athletic events, it is reasonable to infer that the specific purpose of the policy was to preserve a popular "state-sponsored religious practice." *Lee,* 505 U.S., at 596, 112 S. Ct. 2649.

School sponsorship of a religious message is impermissible because it sends the ancillary message to members of the audience who are nonadherents "that they are outsiders, not full members of the political community, and an accompanying message to adherents that they are insiders, favored members of the political community." *Lynch,* 465 U.S., at 688, 104 S. Ct. 1355 (O'CONNOR, J., concurring). The delivery of such a message — over the school's public address system, by a speaker representing the student body, under the supervision of school faculty, and pursuant to a school policy that explicitly and implicitly encourages public prayer — is not properly characterized as "private" speech.

III

The District next argues that its football policy is distinguishable from the graduation prayer in *Lee* because it does not coerce students to participate in religious observances. Its argument has two parts: first, that there is no impermissible government coercion because the pregame messages are the product of student choices; and second, that there is really no coercion at all because attendance at an extracurricular event, unlike a graduation ceremony, is voluntary.

The reasons just discussed explaining why the alleged "circuit-breaker" mechanism of the dual elections and student speaker do not turn public speech into private speech also demonstrate why these mechanisms do not insulate the school from the coercive element of the final message. In fact, this aspect of the District's argument exposes anew the concerns that are created by the majoritarian election system. The parties' stipulation clearly states that the issue resolved in the first election was "whether a student would deliver prayer at varsity football games," App. 65, and the controversy in this case demonstrates that the views of the students are not unanimous on that issue.

One of the purposes served by the Establishment Clause is to remove debate over this kind of issue from governmental supervision or control. We explained in *Lee* that the "preservation and transmission of religious beliefs and worship is a responsibility and a choice committed to the private sphere." 505 U.S., at 589, 112 S. Ct. 2649. The two student elections authorized by the policy, coupled with the debates that presumably must precede each, impermissibly invade that private sphere. The election mechanism, when considered in light of the history in which the policy in question evolved, reflects a device the District put in place that determines whether religious messages will be delivered at home football games. The mechanism encourages divisiveness along religious lines in a public school setting, a result at odds with the Establishment Clause. Although it is true that the ultimate choice of student speaker is "attributable to the students," Brief for Petitioner 40, the District's decision to hold the constitutionally problematic election is clearly "a choice attributable to the State," *Lee,* 505 U.S., at 587, 112 S. Ct. 2649.

The District further argues that attendance at the commencement ceremonies at issue in *Lee* "differs dramatically" from attendance at high school football games, which it contends "are of no more than passing interest to many students" and are "decidedly extracurricular," thus dissipating any coercion. Brief for Petitioner 41. Attendance at a high school football game, unlike showing up for class, is certainly not required in order to receive a diploma. Moreover, we may assume that the District is correct in arguing that the informal pressure to attend an athletic event is not as strong as a senior's desire to attend her own graduation ceremony.

There are some students, however, such as cheerleaders, members of the band, and, of course, the team members themselves, for whom seasonal commitments mandate their attendance, sometimes for class credit. The District also minimizes the importance to many students of attending and participating in extracurricular activities as part of a complete educational experience. As we noted in *Lee,* "[l]aw reaches past formalism." 505 U.S., at 595, 112 S. Ct. 2649. To assert that high school students do not feel immense social pressure, or have a truly genuine desire, to be involved in the extracurricular event that is American high school football is "formalistic in the extreme." *Ibid.* We stressed in *Lee* the obvious observation that "adolescents are often susceptible to pressure from their peers towards conformity, and that the influence is strongest in matters of social convention." *Id.,* at 593, 112 S. Ct. 2649. High school home football games are traditional gatherings of a school community; they bring together students and faculty as well as friends and family from years present and past to root for a common cause. Undoubtedly, the games are not important to some students, and they voluntarily choose not to attend. For many others, however, the choice between attending these games and avoiding personally offensive religious rituals is in no practical sense an easy one. The Constitution, moreover, demands that the school may not force this difficult choice upon these students for "[i]t is a tenet of the First Amendment that the State cannot require one of its citizens to forfeit his or her rights and benefits as the price of resisting conformance to state-sponsored religious practice." *Id.,* at 596, 112 S. Ct. 2649.

Even if we regard every high school student's decision to attend a home football game as purely voluntary, we are nevertheless persuaded that the delivery of a pregame prayer has the improper effect of coercing those present to participate in an act of religious worship. For "the government may no more use social pressure to enforce orthodoxy than it may use more direct means." *Id.,* at 594, 112 S. Ct. 2649. As in *Lee,* "[w]hat to most believers may seem nothing more than a reasonable request that the nonbeliever respect their religious practices, in a school context may appear to the nonbeliever or dissenter to be an attempt to employ the machinery of the State to enforce a religious orthodoxy." *Id.*, at 592, 112 S. Ct. 2649. The constitutional command will not permit the District "to exact religious conformity from a student as the price" of joining her classmates at a varsity football game.[193]

The Religion Clauses of the First Amendment prevent the government from making any law respecting the establishment of religion or prohibiting the free exercise thereof. By no means do these commands impose a prohibition on all religious activity in our public schools. See, *e.g., Lamb's Chapel v. Center Moriches Union Free School Dist.*, 508 U.S. 384, 395, 113 S. Ct. 2141, 124 L. Ed. 2d 352 (1993); *Board of Ed. of Westside Community Schools (Dist.66) v. Mergens,* 496 U.S. 226, 110 S. Ct. 2356, 110 L. Ed. 2d 191 (1990); *Wallace,* 472 U.S., at 59, 105 S. Ct. 2479. Indeed, the common purpose of the Religion Clauses "is to secure religious liberty." *Engel v. Vitale,* 370 U.S. 421, 430, 82 S. Ct. 1261, 8 L. Ed. 2d 601 (1962). Thus, nothing in the Constitution as interpreted by this Court prohibits any public school student from voluntarily praying at any time before, during, or after the schoolday. But the religious liberty protected by the Constitution is abridged when the State affirmatively sponsors the particular religious practice of prayer.

IV

Finally, the District argues repeatedly that the Does have made a premature facial challenge to the October policy that necessarily must fail. The District emphasizes, quite correctly, that until a student actually delivers a solemnizing message under the latest version of the policy, there can be no certainty that any of the statements or invocations will be religious. Thus, it concludes, the October policy necessarily survives a facial challenge.

This argument, however, assumes that we are concerned only with the serious constitutional injury that occurs when a student is forced to participate in an act of religious worship because she chooses to attend a school event. But the Constitution also requires that we keep in mind "the myriad, subtle ways in which Establishment Clause values can be eroded," *Lynch,* 465 U.S., at 694, 104 S. Ct. 1355 (O'CONNOR, J., concurring), and that we guard against other different, yet equally important, constitutional injuries. One is the mere passage by the District of a policy that has the purpose and perception of government establishment of religion. Another is the implementation of a governmental electoral process that subjects the issue of prayer to a majoritarian vote.

---

193. "We think the Government's position that this interest suffices to force students to choose between compliance or forfeiture demonstrates fundamental inconsistency in its argumentation. It fails to acknowledge that what for many of Deborah's classmates and their parents was a spiritual imperative was for Daniel and Deborah Weisman religious conformance compelled by the State. While in some societies the wishes of the majority might prevail, the Establishment Clause of the First Amendment is addressed to this contingency and rejects the balance urged upon us. The Constitution forbids the State to exact religious conformity from a student as the price of attending her own high school graduation. This is the calculus the Constitution commands." *Lee,* 505 U.S., at 595–596, 112 S. Ct. 2649.

The District argues that the facial challenge must fail because "Santa Fe's Football Policy cannot be invalidated on the basis of some 'possibility or even likelihood' of an unconstitutional application." Brief for Petitioner 17 (quoting *Bowen v. Kendrick,* 487 U.S. 589, 613, 108 S. Ct. 2562, 101 L. Ed. 2d 520 (1988)). Our Establishment Clause cases involving facial challenges, however, have not focused solely on the possible applications of the statute, but rather have considered whether the statute has an unconstitutional purpose. Writing for the Court in *Bowen,* THE CHIEF JUSTICE concluded that "[a]s in previous cases involving facial challenges on Establishment Clause grounds, *e.g., Edwards v. Aguillard,* [482 U.S. 578, 107 S. Ct. 2573, 96 L. Ed. 2d 510 (1987)]; *Mueller v. Allen,* 463 U.S. 388, 103 S. Ct. 3062, 77 L. Ed. 2d 721 (1983), we assess the constitutionality of an enactment by reference to the three factors first articulated in *Lemon v. Kurtzman,* 403 U.S. 602, 612, 91 S. Ct. 2105, 29 L. Ed. 2d 745 (1971) . . . , which guides '[t]he general nature of our inquiry in this area,' *Mueller v. Allen, supra,* at 394, 103 S. Ct. 3062." 487 U.S., at 602, 108 S. Ct. 2562. Under the *Lemon* standard, a court must invalidate a statute if it lacks "a secular legislative purpose." *Lemon v. Kurtzman,* 403 U.S. 602, 612, 91 S. Ct. 2105, 29 L. Ed. 2d 745 (1971). It is therefore proper, as part of this facial challenge, for us to examine the purpose of the October policy.

As discussed, *supra,* at 2277–2278, 2278–2279, the text of the October policy alone reveals that it has an unconstitutional purpose. The plain language of the policy clearly spells out the extent of school involvement in both the election of the speaker and the content of the message. Additionally, the text of the October policy specifies only one, clearly preferred message—that of Santa Fe's traditional religious "invocation." Finally, the extremely selective access of the policy and other content restrictions confirm that it is not a content-neutral regulation that creates a limited public forum for the expression of student speech. Our examination, however, need not stop at an analysis of the text of the policy.

This case comes to us as the latest step in developing litigation brought as a challenge to institutional practices that unquestionably violated the Establishment Clause. One of those practices was the District's long-established tradition of sanctioning student-led prayer at varsity football games. The narrow question before us is whether implementation of the October policy insulates the continuation of such prayers from constitutional scrutiny. It does not. Our inquiry into this question not only can, but must, include an examination of the circumstances surrounding its enactment. Whether a government activity violates the Establishment Clause is "in large part a legal question to be answered on the basis of judicial interpretation of social facts. . . . Every government practice must be judged in its unique circumstances. . . ." *Lynch,* 465 U.S., at 693–694, 104 S. Ct. 1355 (O'CONNOR, J., concurring). Our discussion in the previous sections, *supra,* at 2277–2279, demonstrates that in this case the District's direct involvement with school prayer exceeds constitutional limits.

The District, nevertheless, asks us to pretend that we do not recognize what every Santa Fe High School student understands clearly—that this policy is about prayer.

The District further asks us to accept what is obviously untrue: that these messages are necessary to "solemnize" a football game and that this single-student, year-long position is essential to the protection of student speech. We refuse to turn a blind eye to the context in which this policy arose, and that context quells any doubt that this policy was implemented with the purpose of endorsing school prayer.

Therefore, the simple enactment of this policy, with the purpose and perception of school endorsement of student prayer, was a constitutional violation. We need not wait for the inevitable to confirm and magnify the constitutional injury. In *Wallace,* for example, we invalidated Alabama's as yet unimplemented and voluntary "moment of silence" statute based on our conclusion that it was enacted "for the sole purpose of expressing the State's endorsement of prayer activities for one minute at the beginning of each school day." 472 U.S., at 60, 105 S. Ct. 2479; see also *Church of Lukumi Babalu Aye, Inc. v. Hialeah,* 508 U.S. 520, 532, 113 S. Ct. 2217, 124 L. Ed. 2d 472 (1993). Therefore, even if no Santa Fe High School student were ever to offer a religious message, the October policy fails a facial challenge because the attempt by the District to encourage prayer is also at issue. Government efforts to endorse religion cannot evade constitutional reproach based solely on the remote possibility that those attempts may fail.

This policy likewise does not survive a facial challenge because it impermissibly imposes upon the student body a majoritarian election on the issue of prayer. Through its election scheme, the District has established a governmental electoral mechanism that turns the school into a forum for religious debate. It further empowers the student body majority with the authority to subject students of minority views to constitutionally improper messages. The award of that power alone, regardless of the students' ultimate use of it, is not acceptable.[194] Like the referendum in *Board of Regents of Univ. of Wis. System v. Southworth,* 529 U.S. 217, 120 S. Ct. 1346, 146 L. Ed. 2d 193 (2000), the election mechanism established by the District undermines the essential protection of minority viewpoints. Such a system encourages divisiveness along religious lines and threatens the imposition of coercion upon those students not desiring to participate in a religious exercise. Simply by establishing this school-related procedure, which entrusts the inherently nongovernmental subject of religion to a majoritarian vote, a constitutional violation has occurred.[195] No further injury is required for the policy to fail a facial challenge.

---

194. THE CHIEF JUSTICE accuses us of "essentially invalidat[ing] all student elections," see *post,* at 2285. This is obvious hyperbole. We have concluded that the resulting religious message under this policy would be attributable to the school, not just the student, see *supra,* at 2275–2279. For this reason, we now hold only that the District's decision to allow the student majority to control whether students of minority views are subjected to a school-sponsored prayer violates the Establishment Clause.

195. THE CHIEF JUSTICE contends that we have "misconstrue[d] the nature . . . [of] the policy as being an election on 'prayer' and 'religion,'" *post,* at 2285. We therefore reiterate that the District has stipulated to the facts that the most recent election was held "to determine whether a student would deliver *prayer* at varsity football games," that the "students chose to allow a student to say

To properly examine this policy on its face, we "must be deemed aware of the history and context of the community and forum," *Pinette,* 515 U.S., at 780, 115 S. Ct. 2440 (O'CONNOR, J., concurring in part and concurring in judgment). Our examination of those circumstances above leads to the conclusion that this policy does not provide the District with the constitutional safe harbor it sought. The policy is invalid on its face because it establishes an improper majoritarian election on religion, and unquestionably has the purpose and creates the perception of encouraging the delivery of prayer at a series of important school events.

The judgment of the Court of Appeals is, accordingly, *affirmed.*

[Case No. 6-6]

Parent group using school premises for a presentation with a religious message were protected under a limited public forum established by the school district.

Lamb's Chapel v. Center Moriches Union Free School District

Supreme Court of the United States (1993)
508 U.S. 384

Justice WHITE delivered the opinion of the Court.

New York Educ. Law § 414 (McKinney 1988 and Supp.1993) authorizes local school boards to adopt reasonable regulations for the use of school property for 10 specified purposes when the property is not in use for school purposes. Among the permitted uses is the holding of "social, civic and recreational meetings and entertainments, and other uses pertaining to the welfare of the community; but such meetings, entertainment and uses shall be non-exclusive and shall be open to the general public." § 414(1)(c).[196] The list of permitted uses does not include meetings for religious purposes, and a New York appellate court in *Trietley v. Board of Ed. of Buffalo,* 65 A.D.2d 1, 409 N.Y.S.2d 912, 915 (1978), ruled that local boards could not allow student bible clubs to meet on school property because "[r]eligious purposes are not included in the enumerated purposes for which a school may be used under section 414." In *Deeper Life Christian Fellowship, Inc. v. Sobol,* 948 F.2d 79, 83–84 (1991), the Court of Appeals for the Second Circuit accepted *Trietley* as an

---

a *prayer* at football games," and that a second election was then held "to determine which student would deliver the *prayer.*" App. 65–66 (emphases added). Furthermore, the policy was titled "*Prayer* at Football Games." *Id.,* at 99 (emphasis added). Although the District has since eliminated the word "prayer" from the policy, it apparently viewed that change as sufficiently minor as to make holding a new election unnecessary.

196. Section 414(1)(e) authorizes the use of school property "[f]or polling places for holding primaries and elections and for the registration of voters and for holding political meetings. But no meetings sponsored by political organizations shall be permitted unless authorized by a vote of a district meeting, held as provided by law, or, in cities by the board of education thereof."

authoritative interpretation of state law. Furthermore, the Attorney General of New York supports *Trietley* as an appropriate approach to deciding this case.

Pursuant to § 414's empowerment of local school districts, the Board of Center Moriches Union Free School District (District) has issued rules and regulations with respect to the use of school property when not in use for school purposes. The rules allow only 2 of the 10 purposes authorized by § 414: social, civic, or recreational uses (Rule 10) and use by political organizations if secured in compliance with § 414 (Rule 8). Rule 7, however, consistent with the judicial interpretation of state law, provides that "[t]he school premises shall not be used by any group for religious purposes." App. to Pet. for Cert. 57a.

The issue in this case is whether, against this background of state law, it violates the Free Speech Clause of the First Amendment, made applicable to the States by the Fourteenth Amendment, to deny a church access to school premises to exhibit for public viewing and for assertedly religious purposes, a film series dealing with family and child-rearing issues faced by parents today.

I

Petitioners (Church) are Lamb's Chapel, an evangelical church in the community of Center Moriches, and its pastor John Steigerwald. Twice the Church applied to the District for permission to use school facilities to show a six-part film series containing lectures by Doctor James Dobson.[197] A brochure provided on request of the District identified Dr. Dobson as a licensed psychologist, former associate clinical professor of pediatrics at the University of Southern California, best-selling author, and radio commentator.

The brochure stated that the film series would discuss Dr. Dobson's views on the undermining influences of the media that could only be counterbalanced by returning to traditional, Christian family values instilled at an early stage. The brochure went on to describe the contents of each of the six parts of the series.[198] The District

197. Shortly before the first of these requests, the Church had applied for permission to use school rooms for its Sunday morning services and for Sunday School. The hours specified were 9 a.m. to 1 p.m. and the time period one year beginning in the next month. 959 F.2d 381, 383 (CA2 1992). Within a few days the District wrote petitioner that the application "requesting use of the high school for your Sunday services" was denied, citing both N.Y. Educ. Law § 414 and the District's Rule 7 barring uses for religious purposes. The Church did not challenge this denial in the courts and the validity of this denial is not before us.

198. "*Turn Your Heart Toward Home* is available now in a series of six discussion-provoking films:

> "1) A FATHER LOOKS BACK emphasizes how swiftly time passes and appeals to all parents to 'turn their hearts toward home' during the all-important child-rearing years. (*60 minutes.*)
>
> "2) POWER IN PARENTING: THE YOUNG CHILD begins by exploring the inherent nature of power, and offers many practical helps for facing the battlegrounds in child-rearing—bedtime, mealtime and other confrontations so familiar to parents. Dr. Dobson also takes a look at areas of conflict in marriage and other adult relationships. (*60 minutes.*)

denied the first application, saying that "[t]his film does appear to be church related and therefore your request must be refused." App. 84. The second application for permission to use school premises for showing the film series, which described it as a "Family oriented movie—from a Christian perspective," *id.*, at 91, was denied using identical language.

The Church brought suit in the District Court, challenging the denial as a violation of the Freedom of Speech and Assembly Clauses, the Free Exercise Clause, and the Establishment Clause of the First Amendment, as well as the Equal Protection Clause of the Fourteenth Amendment. As to each cause of action, the Church alleged that the actions were undertaken under color of state law, in violation of 42 U.S.C. § 1983. The District Court granted summary judgment for respondents, rejecting all the Church's claims. With respect to the free-speech claim under the First Amendment, the District Court characterized the District's facilities as a "limited public forum." The court noted that the enumerated purposes for which § 414 allowed access to school facilities did not include religious worship or instruction, that Rule 7 explicitly proscribes using school facilities for religious purposes, and that the Church had conceded that its showing of the film series would be for religious purposes. *770 F. Supp. 91, 92, 98–99 (E.D.N.Y.1991).* The District Court stated that once a limited public forum is opened to a particular type of speech, selectively denying access to other activities of the same genre is forbidden. *Id.,* at 99. Noting that the District had not opened its facilities to organizations similar to Lamb's Chapel for religious purposes, the District Court held that the denial in this case was viewpoint neutral and, hence, not a violation of the Freedom of Speech Clause. *Ibid.* The District Court also rejected the assertion by the Church that denying its application demonstrated a hostility to religion and advancement of nonreligion not justified under the Establishment of Religion Clause of the First Amendment. *736 F. Supp. 1247, 1253 (1990).*

"3) POWER IN PARENTING: THE ADOLESCENT discusses father/ daughter and mother/ son relationships, and the importance of allowing children to grow to develop as individuals. Dr. Dobson also encourages parents to free themselves of undeserved guilt when their teenagers choose to rebel. (*45 minutes.*)

"4) THE FAMILY UNDER FIRE views the family in the context of today's society, where a "civil war of values" is being waged. Dr. Dobson urges parents to look at the effects of governmental interference, abortion and pornography, and to get involved. To preserve what they care about most—their own families! (*52 minutes.*)

Note: This film contains explicit information regarding the pornography industry. Not recommended for young audiences.

"5) OVERCOMING A PAINFUL CHILDHOOD includes Shirley Dobson's intimate memories of a difficult childhood with her alcoholic father. Mrs. Dobson recalls the influences which brought her to a loving God who saw her personal circumstances and heard her cries for help. (*40 minutes.*)

"6) THE HERITAGE presents Dr. Dobson's powerful closing remarks. Here he speaks clearly and convincingly of our traditional values which, if properly employed and defended, can assure happy, healthy, strengthened homes and family relationships in the years to come. (*60 minutes.*)" App. 87–88.

The Court of Appeals affirmed the judgment of the District Court "in all respects." 959 F.2d 381, 389 (CA2 1992). It held that the school property, when not in use for school purposes, was neither a traditional nor a designated public forum; rather, it was a limited public forum open only for designated purposes, a classification that "allows it to remain non-public except as to specified uses." *Id.*, at 386. The court observed that exclusions in such a forum need only be reasonable and viewpoint neutral, *ibid.*, and ruled that denying access to the Church for the purpose of showing its film did not violate this standard. Because the holding below was questionable under our decisions, we granted the petition for certiorari, 506 U.S. 813, 113 S. Ct. 51, 121 L. Ed. 2d 20 (1992), which in principal part challenged the holding below as contrary to the Free Speech Clause of the First Amendment.[199]

II

There is no question that the District, like the private owner of property, may legally preserve the property under its control for the use to which it is dedicated. *Cornelius v. NAACP Legal Defense & Ed. Fund, Inc.*, 473 U.S. 788, 800, 105 S. Ct. 3439, 3448, 87 L. Ed. 2d 567 (1985); *Perry Ed. Assn. v. Perry Local Educators' Assn.*, 460 U.S. 37, 46, 103 S. Ct. 948, 955, 74 L. Ed. 2d 794 (1983); *Postal Service v. Council of Greenburgh Civic Assns.*, 453 U.S. 114, 129–130, 101 S. Ct. 2676, 2685, 69 L. Ed. 2d 517 (1981); *Greer v. Spock*, 424 U.S. 828, 836, 96 S. Ct. 1211, 1216, 47 L. Ed. 2d 505 (1976); *Adderley v. Florida*, 385 U.S. 39, 47, 87 S. Ct. 242, 247, 17 L. Ed. 2d 149 (1966). It is also common ground that the District need not have permitted after-hours use of its property for any of the uses permitted by N.Y. Educ. Law § 414. The District, however, did open its property for 2 of the 10 uses permitted by § 414. The Church argued below that because under Rule 10 of the rules issued by the District, school property could be used for "social, civic, and recreational" purposes, the District had opened its property for such a wide variety of communicative purposes that restrictions on communicative uses of the property were subject to the same constitutional limitations as restrictions in traditional public forums such as parks and sidewalks. Hence, its view was that subject matter or speaker exclusions on District property were required to be justified by a compelling state interest and to be narrowly drawn to achieve that end. See *Perry, supra*, 460 U.S. at 45, 103 S. Ct., at 955; *Cornelius, supra*, 473 U.S. at 800, 105 S. Ct., at 3448. Both the District Court and the Court of Appeals rejected this submission, which is also presented to this Court. The argument has considerable force, for the District's property is heavily used by a wide variety of private organizations, including some that presented a "close question," which the Court of Appeals resolved in the District's favor, as to whether the District had in fact already opened its property for religious uses.

199. The petition also presses the claim by the Church, rejected by both courts below, that the rejection of its application to exhibit its film series violated the Establishment Clause because it and Rule 7's categorical refusal to permit District property to be used for religious purposes demonstrate hostility to religion. Because we reverse on another ground, we need not decide what merit this submission might have.

959 F.2d, at 387.[200] We need not rule on this issue, however, for even if the courts below were correct in this respect — and we shall assume for present purposes that they were — the judgment below must be reversed.

With respect to public property that is not a designated public forum open for indiscriminate public use for communicative purposes, we have said that "[c]ontrol over access to a nonpublic forum can be based on subject matter and speaker identity so long as the distinctions drawn are reasonable in light of the purpose served by the forum and are viewpoint neutral." *Cornelius,* 473 U.S., at 806, 105 S. Ct., at 3451, citing *Perry Education Assn., supra,* 460 U.S., at 49, 103 S. Ct., at 957. The Court of Appeals appeared to recognize that the total ban on using District property for religious purposes could survive First Amendment challenge only if excluding this category of speech was reasonable and viewpoint neutral. The court's conclusion in

---

200. The petition also presses the claim by the Church, rejected by both courts below, that the rejection of its application to exhibit its film series violated the Establishment Clause because it and Rule 7's categorical refusal to permit District property to be used for religious purposes demonstrate hostility to religion. Because we reverse on another ground, we need not decide what merit this submission might have. In support of its case in the District Court, the Church presented the following sampling of the uses that had been permitted under Rule 10 in 1987 and 1988:

"A New Age religious group known as the 'Mind Center'
Southern Harmonize Gospel Singers Salvation Army Youth Band
Hampton Council of Churches' Billy Taylor Concert
Center Moriches Co-op Nursery School's Quilting Bee
Manorville Humane Society's Chinese Auction
Moriches Bay Power Squadron
Unkechaug Dance Group
Paul Gibson's Baseball Clinic
Moriches Bay Civic Association
Moriches Chamber of Commerce's Town Fair Day
Center Moriches Drama Club
Center Moriches Music Award Associations' 'Amahl & the Night Visitors'
Saint John's Track and Field Program
Girl Scouts of Suffolk [C]ounty
Cub Scouts Pack 23
Boy Scout Troop # 414." 770 F. Supp. 91, 93, n. 4 (E.D.N.Y. 1991).

The Church claimed that the first three uses listed above demonstrated that Rule 10 actually permitted the District property to be used for religious purposes as well as a great assortment of other uses. The first item listed is particularly interesting and relevant to the issue before us. The District Court referred to this item as "a lecture series by the Mind Center, purportedly a New Age religious group." *Id.,* at 93. The Court of Appeals described it as follows: "The lecture series, 'Psychology and The Unknown,' by Jerry Huck, was sponsored by the Center Moriches Free Public Library. The library's newsletter characterized Mr. Huck as a psychotherapist who would discuss such topics as parapsychology, transpersonal psychology, physics and metaphysics in his 4-night series of lectures. Mr. Huck testified that he lectured principally on parapsychology, which he defined by 'reference to the human unconscious, the mind, the unconscious emotional system or the body system.' When asked whether his lecture involved matters of both a spiritual and a scientific nature, Mr. Huck responded: 'It was all science. Anything I speak on based on parapsychology, analytic, quantum physicists [sic].' Although some incidental reference to religious matters apparently was made in the lectures, Mr. Huck himself characterized such matters as 'a fascinating sideline' and 'not the purpose of the [lecture].'" 959 F.2d, at 388.

this case was that Rule 7 met this test. We cannot agree with this holding, for Rule 7 was unconstitutionally applied in this case.[201]

The Court of Appeals thought that the application of Rule 7 in this case was viewpoint neutral because it had been, and would be, applied in the same way to all uses of school property for religious purposes. That all religions and all uses for religious purposes are treated alike under Rule 7, however, does not answer the critical question whether it discriminates on the basis of viewpoint to permit school property to be used for the presentation of all views about family issues and child rearing except those dealing with the subject matter from a religious standpoint.

There is no suggestion from the courts below or from the District or the State that a lecture or film about child rearing and family values would not be a use for social or civic purposes otherwise permitted by Rule 10. That subject matter is not one that the District has placed off limits to any and all speakers. Nor is there any indication in the record before us that the application to exhibit the particular film series involved here was, or would have been, denied for any reason other than the fact that the presentation would have been from a religious perspective. In our view, denial on that basis was plainly invalid under our holding in *Cornelius, supra,* 473 U.S., at 806, 105 S. Ct., at 3451, that

> "[a]lthough a speaker may be excluded from a non-public forum if he wishes to address a topic not encompassed within the purpose of the forum . . . or if he is not a member of the class of speakers for whose especial benefit the forum was created . . . , the government violates the First Amendment when it denies access to a speaker solely to suppress the point of view he espouses on an otherwise includible subject."

The film series involved here no doubt dealt with a subject otherwise permissible under Rule 10, and its exhibition was denied solely because the series dealt with the subject from a religious standpoint. The principle that has emerged from our cases "is that the First Amendment forbids the government to regulate speech in ways that favor some viewpoints or ideas at the expense of others." *City Council of Los Angeles v. Taxpayers for Vincent,* 466 U.S. 789, 804, 104 S. Ct. 2118, 2128, 80 L. Ed. 2d 772 (1984). That principle applies in the circumstances of this case; as Judge Posner said for the Court of Appeals for the Seventh Circuit, to discriminate "against a particular point of view . . . would . . . flunk the test . . . [of] *Cornelius,* provided that the defendants have no defense based on the establishment clause." *May v. Evansville-Vanderburgh School Corp.,* 787 F.2d 1105, 1114 (1986).

The District, as a respondent, would save its judgment below on the ground that to permit its property to be used for religious purposes would be an establishment

---

201. Although the Court of Appeals apparently held that Rule 7 was reasonable as well as viewpoint neutral, the court uttered not a word in support of its reasonableness holding. If Rule 7 were to be held unreasonable, it could be held facially invalid, that is, it might be held that the rule could in no circumstances be applied to religious speech or religious communicative conduct. In view of our disposition of this case, we need not pursue this issue.

of religion forbidden by the First Amendment. This Court suggested in *Widmar v. Vincent,* 454 U.S. 263, 271, 102 S. Ct. 269, 275, 70 L. Ed. 2d 440 (1981), that the interest of the State in avoiding an Establishment Clause violation "may be [a] compelling" one justifying an abridgment of free speech otherwise protected by the First Amendment; but the Court went on to hold that permitting use of university property for religious purposes under the open access policy involved there would not be incompatible with the Court's Establishment Clause cases.

We have no more trouble than did the *Widmar* Court in disposing of the claimed defense on the ground that the posited fears of an Establishment Clause violation are unfounded. The showing of this film series would not have been during school hours, would not have been sponsored by the school, and would have been open to the public, not just to church members. The District property had repeatedly been used by a wide variety of private organizations. Under these circumstances, as in *Widmar,* there would have been no realistic danger that the community would think that the District was endorsing religion or any particular creed, and any benefit to religion or to the Church would have been no more than incidental. As in *Widmar, supra,* 454 U.S., at 271–272, 102 S. Ct., at 275–276, permitting District property to be used to exhibit the film series involved in this case would not have been an establishment of religion under the three-part test articulated in *Lemon v. Kurtzman,* 403 U.S. 602, 91 S. Ct. 2105, 29 L. Ed. 2d 745 (1971): The challenged governmental action has a secular purpose, does not have the principal or primary effect of advancing or inhibiting religion, and does not foster an excessive entanglement with religion.[202]

The District also submits that it justifiably denied use of its property to a "radical" church for the purpose of proselytizing, since to do so would lead to threats of public unrest and even violence. Brief for Respondent Center Moriches Union Free School District et al. 4–5, 11–12, 24. There is nothing in the record to support such a justification, which in any event would be difficult to defend as a reason to deny the presentation of a religious point of view about a subject the District otherwise opens to discussion on District property.

We note that the New York State Attorney General, a respondent here, does not rely on either the Establishment Clause or possible danger to the public peace in supporting the judgment below. Rather, he submits that the exclusion is justified because the purpose of the access rules is to promote the interests of the public in general rather than sectarian or other private interests. In light of the variety of the uses of District property that have been permitted under Rule 10, this approach has its difficulties. This is particularly so since Rule 10 states that District property

202. While we are somewhat diverted by Justice SCALIA's evening at the cinema, *post,* at 2149–2150, we return to the reality that there is a proper way to inter an established decision and *Lemon,* however frightening it might be to some, has not been overruled. This case, like *Corporation of Presiding Bishop of Church of Jesus Christ of Latter-day Saints v. Amos,* 483 U.S. 327, 107 S. Ct. 2862, 97 L. Ed. 2d 273 (1987), presents no occasion to do so. Justice SCALIA apparently was less haunted by the ghosts of the living when he joined the opinion of the Court in that case.

may be used for social, civic, or recreational use "only if it can be non-exclusive and open to all residents of the school district that form a homogeneous group deemed relevant to the event." App. to Pet. for Cert. 57a. At least arguably, the Rule does not require that permitted uses need be open to the public at large. However that may be, this was not the basis of the judgment that we are reviewing. The Court of Appeals, as we understand it, ruled that because the District had the power to permit or exclude certain subject matters, it was entitled to deny use for any religious purpose, including the purpose in this case. The Attorney General also defends this as a permissible subject-matter exclusion rather than a denial based on viewpoint, a submission that we have already rejected.

The Attorney General also argues that there is no express finding below that the Church's application would have been granted absent the religious connection. This fact is beside the point for the purposes of this opinion, which is concerned with the validity of the stated reason for denying the Church's application, namely, that the film series sought to be shown "appeared to be church related."

For the reasons stated in this opinion, the judgment of the Court of Appeals is

Reversed.

[Case No. 6-7]

Exclusion from a scholarship program based on the choice to pursue religious education is odious to our Constitution.

Espinoza v. Montana Department of Revenue

Supreme Court of the United States
591 U.S. __, 140 S. Ct. 2246 (2020)

Chief Justice ROBERTS delivered the opinion of the Court.

[1] The Montana Legislature established a program to provide tuition assistance to parents who send their children to private schools. The program grants a tax credit to anyone who donates to certain organizations that in turn award scholarships to selected students attending such schools. When petitioners sought to use the scholarships at a religious school, the Montana Supreme Court struck down the program. The Court relied on the "no-aid" provision of the State Constitution, which prohibits any aid to a school controlled by a "church, sect, or denomination." The question presented is whether the Free Exercise Clause of the United States Constitution barred that application of the no-aid provision.

I

A

In 2015, the Montana Legislature sought "to provide parental and student choice in education" by enacting a scholarship program for students attending private schools. 2015 Mont. Laws p. 2168, § 7. [2] The program grants a tax credit of up to $150 to any taxpayer who donates to a participating "student scholarship organization."

Mont. Code Ann. §§ 15-30-3103(1), -3111(1) (2019). The scholarship organizations then use the donations to award scholarships to children for tuition at a private school. §§ 15-30-3102(7)(a), -3103(1)(c).[203]

So far only one scholarship organization, Big Sky Scholarships, has participated in the program. Big Sky focuses on providing scholarships to families who face financial hardship or have children with disabilities. Scholarship organizations like Big Sky must, among other requirements, maintain an application process for awarding the scholarships; use at least 90% of all donations on scholarship awards; and comply with state reporting and monitoring requirements. §§ 15-30-3103(1), -3105(1), -3113(1).

[3] A family whose child is awarded a scholarship under the program may use it at any "qualified education provider"—that is, any private school that meets certain accreditation, testing, and safety requirements. See § 15-30-3102(7). Virtually every private school in Montana qualifies. [4] Upon receiving a scholarship, the family designates its school of choice, and the scholarship organization sends the scholarship funds directly to the school. § 15-30-3104(1). Neither the scholarship organization nor its donors can restrict awards to particular types of schools. See §§ 15-30-3103(1)(b), -3111(1).

The Montana Legislature allotted $3 million annually to fund the tax credits, beginning in 2016. § 15-30-3111(5)(a). If the annual allotment is exhausted, it increases by 10% the following year. *Ibid.* The program is slated to expire in 2023. 2015 Mont. Laws p. 2186, § 33.

[5] The Montana Legislature also directed that the program be administered in accordance with Article X, section 6, of the Montana Constitution, which contains a "no-aid" provision barring government aid to sectarian schools. See Mont. Code Ann. § 15-30-3101. In full, that provision states:

> "**Aid prohibited to sectarian schools.** . . . The legislature, counties, cities, towns, school districts, and public corporations shall not make any direct or indirect appropriation or payment from any public fund or monies, or any grant of lands or other property for any sectarian purpose or to aid any church, school, academy, seminary, college, university, or other literary or scientific institution, controlled in whole or in part by any church, sect, or denomination." Mont. Const., Art. X, § 6(1).

Shortly after the scholarship program was created, [6] the Montana Department of Revenue promulgated "Rule 1," over the objection of the Montana Attorney General. That administrative rule prohibited families from using scholarships at religious schools. Mont. Admin. Rule § 42.4.802(1)(a) (2015). It did so by changing the definition of "qualified education provider" to exclude any school "owned or

203. The Legislature provided the same tax credit to taxpayers who donate to public schools for the purpose of supporting innovative educational programs or curing technology deficiencies at such schools. See Mont. Code Ann. § 15-30-3110 (2019).

controlled in whole or in part by any church, religious sect, or denomination." *Ibid.* The Department explained that the Rule was needed to reconcile the scholarship program with the no-aid provision of the Montana Constitution.

The Montana Attorney General disagreed. In a letter to the Department, he advised that the Montana Constitution did not require excluding religious schools from the program, and if it did, it would "very likely" violate the United States Constitution by discriminating against the schools and their students. See Complaint in No. DV-15-1152A (Dist. Ct. Flathead Cty.), Exh. 3, pp. 2, 5–6. The Attorney General is not representing the Department in this case.

B

This suit was brought by three mothers whose children attend Stillwater Christian School in northwestern Montana. Stillwater is a private Christian school that meets the statutory criteria for "qualified education providers." It serves students in prekindergarten through 12th grade, and petitioners chose the school in large part because it "teaches the same Christian values that [they] teach at home." App. to Pet. for Cert. 152; see *id.*, at 138, 167. The child of one petitioner has already received scholarships from Big Sky, and the other petitioners' children are eligible for scholarships and planned to apply. While in effect, however, Rule 1 blocked petitioners from using scholarship funds for tuition at Stillwater. To overcome that obstacle, petitioners sued the Department of Revenue in Montana state court. Petitioners claimed that Rule 1 conflicted with the statute that created the scholarship program and could not be justified on the ground that it was compelled by the Montana Constitution's no-aid provision. Petitioners further alleged that the Rule discriminated on the basis of their religious views and the religious nature of the school they had chosen for their children.

The trial court enjoined Rule 1, holding that it was based on a mistake of law. The court explained that the Rule was not required by the no-aid provision, because that provision prohibits only "appropriations" that aid religious schools, "not tax credits." *Id.*, at 94.

The injunctive relief freed Big Sky to award scholarships to students regardless of whether they attended a religious or secular school. For the school year beginning in fall 2017, Big Sky received 59 applications and ultimately awarded 44 scholarships of $500 each. The next year, Big Sky received 90 applications and awarded 54 scholarships of $500 each. Several families, most with incomes of $30,000 or less, used the scholarships to send their children to Stillwater Christian.

In December 2018, the Montana Supreme Court reversed the trial court. 2018 MT 306, 393 Mont. 446, 435 P. 3d 603. The Court first addressed the scholarship program unmodified by Rule 1, holding that the program aided religious schools in violation of the no-aid provision of the Montana Constitution. In the Court's view, the no-aid provision "broadly and strictly prohibits aid to sectarian schools." *Id.*, at 459, 2018 MT 306, 435 P. 3d, at 609. The scholarship program provided such aid by using tax credits to "subsidize tuition payments" at private schools that are "religiously affiliated" or "controlled in whole or in part by churches." *Id.*, at 464–467, 2018 MT 306, 435 P. 3d, at 612–613. In that way, the scholarship program flouted the State Constitution's "guarantee to all Montanans that their government will not use state funds to aid religious schools." *Id.*, at 467, 2018 MT 306, 435 P. 3d, at 614.

The Montana Supreme Court went on to hold that the violation of the no-aid provision required invalidating the entire scholarship program. The Court explained that the program provided "no mechanism" for preventing aid from flowing to religious schools, and therefore the scholarship program could not "under *any* circumstance" be construed as consistent with the no-aid provision. *Id.*, at 466–468, 2018 MT 306, 435 P. 3d, at 613–614. As a result, the tax credit is no longer available to support scholarships at either religious or secular private schools.

The Montana Supreme Court acknowledged that "an overly-broad" application of the no-aid provision "could implicate free exercise concerns" and that "there may be a case" where "prohibiting the aid would violate the Free Exercise Clause." *Id.*, at 468, 435 P. 3d at 614. But, the Court concluded, "this is not one of those cases." *Ibid.*

Finally, the Court agreed with petitioners that the Department had exceeded its authority in promulgating Rule 1. The Court explained that the statute creating the scholarship program had broadly defined qualifying schools to include all private schools, including religious ones, and the Department lacked authority to "transform" that definition with an administrative rule. *Id.*, at 468–469, 2018 MT 306, 435 P. 3d, at 614–615.

Several Justices wrote separately. All agreed that Rule 1 was invalid, but they expressed differing views on whether the scholarship program was consistent with the Montana and United States Constitutions. Justice Gustafson's concurrence argued that the program violated not only Montana's no-aid provision but also the Federal Establishment and Free Exercise Clauses. *Id.*, at 475–479, 2018 MT 306, 435 P. 3d, at 619–621. Justice Sandefur echoed the majority's conclusion that applying the no-aid provision was consistent with the Free Exercise Clause, and he dismissed the "modern jurisprudence" of that Clause as "unnecessarily complicate[d]" due to "increasingly value-driven hairsplitting and overstretching." *Id.*, at 482–484, 2018 MT 306, 435 P. 3d, at 623–624.

Two Justices dissented. Justice Rice would have held that the scholarship program was permissible under the no-aid provision. He criticized the majority for invalidating the program "*sua sponte*," contending that no party had challenged it under the State Constitution. *Id.*, at 495, 2018 MT 306, 435 P. 3d, at 631. Justice Baker also would have upheld the program. In her view, the no-aid provision did not bar the use of scholarships at religious schools, and free exercise concerns could arise under the Federal Constitution if it did. *Id.*, at 493–494, 2018 MT 306, 435 P. 3d, at 630.

We granted certiorari. 588 U. S. ___, 139 S. Ct. 2777, 204 L. Ed. 2d 1157 (2019).

II

A

[7] The Religion Clauses of the First Amendment provide that "Congress shall make no law respecting an establishment of religion, or prohibiting the free exercise thereof." We have recognized a "'play in the joints' between what the Establishment Clause permits and the Free Exercise Clause compels." *Trinity Lutheran Church of Columbia, Inc.* v. *Comer*, 582 U. S. ___, ___, 137 S. Ct. 2012, 198 L. Ed. 2d 551, 559 (2017)) (quoting *Locke* v. *Davey*, 540 U. S. 712, 718, 124 S. Ct. 1307, 158 L. Ed. 2d 1 (2004)). Here, the parties do not dispute that the scholarship program is permissible under the Establishment Clause. Nor could they. [8] We have repeatedly held that the Establishment Clause is not offended when religious observers and organizations benefit from neutral government programs. See, *e.g.*, *Locke*, 540 U. S., at 719; *Rosenberger* v. *Rector and Visitors of Univ. of Va.*, 515 U. S. 819, 839, 115 S. Ct. 2510, 132 L. Ed. 2d 700 (1995). See also *Trinity Lutheran*, 582 U. S., at ___, 137 S. Ct. 2012, 198 L. Ed. 2d 551, 559) (noting the parties' agreement that the Establishment Clause was not violated by including churches in a playground resurfacing program). Any Establishment Clause objection to the scholarship program here is particularly unavailing because the government support makes its way to religious schools only as a result of Montanans independently choosing to spend their scholarships at such schools. See *Locke*, 540 U. S., at 719, 124 S. Ct. 1307, 158 L. Ed. 2d 1; *Zelman* v. *Simmons-Harris*, 536 U. S. 639, 649–653, 122 S. Ct. 2460, 153 L. Ed. 2d 604 (2002). The Montana Supreme Court, however, held as a matter of state law that even such indirect government support qualified as "aid" prohibited under the Montana Constitution.

The question for this Court is whether the Free Exercise Clause precluded the Montana Supreme Court from applying Montana's no-aid provision to bar religious schools from the scholarship program. For purposes of answering that question, we accept the Montana Supreme Court's interpretation of state law—including its determination that the scholarship program provided impermissible "aid" within the meaning of the Montana Constitution—and we assess whether excluding religious schools and affected families from that program was consistent with the Federal Constitution.[204]

[9] The Free Exercise Clause, which applies to the States under the Fourteenth Amendment, "protects religious observers against unequal treatment" and against "laws that impose special disabilities on the basis of religious status." *Trinity Lutheran*, 582 U. S., at ___, ___, 137 S. Ct. 2012, 198 L. Ed. 2d 551 (internal quotation

---

204. JUSTICE SOTOMAYOR. argues that the Montana Supreme Court "expressly declined to reach any federal issue." *Post*, at ___, 207 L. Ed. 2d, at 734 (dissenting opinion). Not so. As noted, *supra*, at ___, 207 L. Ed. 2d, at 696, the Montana Supreme Court recognized that certain applications of the no-aid provision could "violate the Free Exercise Clause." 2018 MT 306, 393 Mont. 446, 468, 435 P. 3d 603, 614 (2018). But the Court expressly concluded that "this is not one of those cases." *Ibid.*

marks and alterations omitted); see *Cantwell* v. *Connecticut*, 310 U. S. 296, 303, 60 S. Ct. 900, 84 L. Ed. 1213 (1940). Those "basic principle[s]" have long guided this Court. *Trinity Lutheran*, 582 U. S., at ___-___, 137 S. Ct. 2012, 198 L. Ed. 2d 551. See, *e.g.*, *Everson* v. *Board of Ed. of Ewing*, 330 U. S. 1, 16, 67 S. Ct. 504, 91 L. Ed. 711 (1947) (a State "cannot exclude individual Catholics, Lutherans, Mohammedans, Baptists, Jews, Methodists, Non-believers, Presbyterians, or the members of any other faith, *because of their faith, or lack of it*, from receiving the benefits of public welfare legislation"); *Lyng* v. *Northwest Indian Cemetery Protective Assn.*, 485 U.S. 439, 449, 108 S. Ct. 1319, 99 L. Ed. 2d 534 (1988) (the Free Exercise Clause protects against laws that "penalize religious activity by denying any person an equal share of the rights, benefits, and privileges enjoyed by other citizens").

Most recently, *Trinity Lutheran* distilled these and other decisions to the same effect into the "unremarkable" conclusion that disqualifying otherwise eligible recipients from a public benefit "solely because of their religious character" imposes "a penalty on the free exercise of religion that triggers the most exacting scrutiny." 582 U. S., at ___-___, 137 S. Ct. 2012, 198 L. Ed. 2d 551, 561). In *Trinity Lutheran*, Missouri provided grants to help nonprofit organizations pay for playground resurfacing, but a state policy disqualified any organization "owned or controlled by a church, sect, or other religious entity." *Id.*, at ___, 137 S. Ct. 2012, 198 L. Ed. 2d 551, 553). Because of that policy, an otherwise eligible church-owned preschool was denied a grant to resurface its playground. Missouri's policy discriminated against the Church "simply because of what it is—a church," and so the policy was subject to the "strictest scrutiny," which it failed. *Id.*, at ___-___, 137 S. Ct. 2012, 198 L. Ed. 2d 551, 555). We acknowledged that the State had not "criminalized" the way in which the Church worshipped or "told the Church that it cannot subscribe to a certain view of the Gospel." *Id.*, at ___, 137 S. Ct. 2012, 198 L. Ed. 2d 551, 562). But the State's discriminatory policy was "odious to our Constitution all the same." *Id.*, at ___, 137 S. Ct. 2012, 198 L. Ed. 2d 551, 565).

Here too Montana's no-aid provision bars religious schools from public benefits solely because of the religious character of the schools. The provision also bars parents who wish to send their children to a religious school from those same benefits, again solely because of the religious character of the school. This is apparent from the plain text. The provision bars aid to any school "controlled in whole or in part by any church, sect, or denomination." Mont. Const., Art. X, § 6(1). The provision's title—"Aid prohibited to sectarian schools"—confirms that the provision singles out schools based on their religious character. *Ibid.* And the Montana Supreme Court explained that the provision forbids aid to any school that is "sectarian," "religiously affiliated," or "controlled in whole or in part by churches." 393 Mont., at 464–467, 2018 MT 306, 435 P. 3d, at 612–613. The provision plainly excludes schools from government aid solely because of religious status. See *Trinity Lutheran*, 582 U. S., at ___-___, 137 S. Ct. 2012, 198 L. Ed. 2d 551.

The Department counters that *Trinity Lutheran* does not govern here because the no-aid provision applies not because of the religious character of the recipients, but because of how the funds would be used—for "religious education." Brief for Respondents 38. In *Trinity Lutheran*, a majority of the Court concluded that the Missouri policy violated the Free Exercise Clause because it discriminated on the basis of religious status. A plurality declined to address discrimination with respect to "religious uses of funding or other forms of discrimination." 582 U. S., at ___, n. 3, 137 S. Ct. 2012, 198 L. Ed. 2d 551, 564). The plurality saw no need to consider such concerns because Missouri had expressly discriminated "based on religious identity," *ibid.*, which was enough [***17] to invalidate the state policy without addressing how government funds were used.

This case also turns expressly on religious status and not religious use. The Montana Supreme Court applied the no-aid provision solely by reference to religious status. The Court repeatedly explained that the no-aid provision bars aid to "schools controlled in whole or in part by churches," "sectarian schools," and "religiously-affiliated schools." 393 Mont., at 463–467, 2018 MT 306, 435 P. 3d, at 611–613. Applying this provision to the scholarship program, the Montana Supreme Court noted that most of the private schools that would benefit from the program were "religiously affiliated" and "controlled by churches," and the Court ultimately concluded that the scholarship program ran afoul of the Montana Constitution by aiding "schools controlled by churches." *Id.*, at 466–467, 2018 MT 306, 435 P. 3d, at 613–614. The Montana Constitution discriminates based on religious status just like the Missouri policy in *Trinity Lutheran*, which excluded organizations "owned or controlled by a church, sect, or other religious entity." 582 U. S., at ___, 137 S. Ct. 2012, 198 L. Ed. 2d 551, 553).

The Department points to some language in the decision below indicating that the no-aid provision has the goal or effect of ensuring that government aid does not end up being used for "sectarian education" or "religious education." 393 Mont., at 460, 466–467, 2018 MT 306, 435 P. 3d, at 609, 613–614. The Department also contrasts what it characterizes as the "completely non-religious" benefit of playground resurfacing in *Trinity Lutheran* with the unrestricted tuition aid at issue here. Tr. of Oral Arg. 31. General school aid, the Department stresses, could be used for religious ends by some recipients, particularly schools that believe faith should "*permeate*[ ]" everything they do. Brief for Respondents 39 (quoting *State ex rel. Chambers* v. *School Dist. No. 10*, 155 Mont. 422, 438, 472 P. 2d 1013, 1021 (1970)). See also *post*, at ___, ___, 207 L. Ed. 2d, at 723, 726 (Breyer, J., dissenting).

Regardless, those considerations were not the Montana Supreme Court's basis for applying the no-aid provision to exclude religious schools; that hinged solely on religious status. [10] Status-based discrimination remains status based even if one of its goals or effects is preventing religious organizations from putting aid to religious uses.

Undeterred by *Trinity Lutheran*, the Montana Supreme Court applied the no-aid provision to hold that religious schools could not benefit from the scholarship program. 393 Mont., at 464–468, 2018 MT 306, 435 P. 3d, at 612–614. [11] So applied, the provision "impose[s] special disabilities on the basis of religious status" and "condition[s] the availability of benefits upon a recipient's willingness to surrender [its] religiously impelled status." *Trinity Lutheran*, 582 U. S., at ___-___, 137 S. Ct. 2012, 198 L. Ed. 2d 551 (quoting *Church of Lukumi Babalu Aye, Inc.* v. *Hialeah*, 508 U. S. 520, 533, 113 S. Ct. 2217, 124 L. Ed. 2d 472 (1993), and *McDaniel* v. *Paty*, 435 U. S. 618, 626, 98 S. Ct. 1322, 55 L. Ed. 2d 593 (1978) (plurality opinion) (alterations omitted)). To be eligible for government aid under the Montana Constitution, a school must divorce itself from any religious control or affiliation. Placing such a condition on benefits or privileges "inevitably deters or discourages the exercise of First Amendment rights." *Trinity Lutheran*, 582 U. S., at ___, 137 S. Ct. 2012, 198 L. Ed. 2d 551 (quoting *Sherbert* v. *Verner*, 374 U. S. 398, 405, 83 S. Ct. 1790, 10 L. Ed. 2d 965 (1963) (alterations omitted)). The Free Exercise Clause protects against even "indirect coercion," and a State "punishe[s] the free exercise of religion" by disqualifying the religious from government aid as Montana did here. *Trinity Lutheran*, 582 U. S., at ___-___, 137 S. Ct. 2012, [*2257] 198 L. Ed. 2d 551 (internal quotation marks omitted). Such status-based discrimination is subject to "the strictest scrutiny." *Id.*, at ___, 137 S. Ct. 2012, 198 L. Ed. 2d 551.

None of this is meant to suggest that we agree with the Department, Brief for Respondents 36–40, that some lesser degree of scrutiny applies to discrimination against religious uses of government aid. See *Lukumi*, 508 U. S., at 546, 533, 113 S. Ct. 2217, 124 L. Ed. 2d 472 (striking down law designed to ban religious practice involving alleged animal cruelty, explaining that a law "target[ing] religious conduct for distinctive treatment or advanc[ing] legitimate governmental interests only against conduct with a religious motivation will survive strict scrutiny only in rare cases"). Some Members of the Court, moreover, have questioned whether there is a meaningful distinction between discrimination based on use or conduct and that based on status. See *Trinity Lutheran*, 582 U. S., at ___-___, 137 S. Ct. 2012, 198 L. Ed. 2d 551 (GORSUCH, J., joined by THOMAS, J., concurring in part) (citing, *e.g.*, *Lukumi*, 508 U. S. 520, 113 S. Ct. 2217, 124 L. Ed. 2d 472, and *Thomas* v. *Review Bd. of Ind. Employment Security Div.*, 450 U. S. 707, 101 S. Ct. 1425, 67 L. Ed. 2d 624 (1981)). We acknowledge the point but need not examine it here. It is enough in this case to conclude that strict scrutiny applies under *Trinity Lutheran* because Montana's no-aid provision discriminates based on religious status.

B

Seeking to avoid *Trinity Lutheran*, the Department contends that this case is instead governed by *Locke* v. *Davey*, 540 U. S. 712, 124 S. Ct. 1307, 158 L. Ed. 2d 1 (2004). See also *post*, at ___, 207 L. Ed. 2d, at 726 (BREYER, J., dissenting); *post*, at ___, 207 L. Ed. 2d, at 736 (SOTOMAYOR, J., dissenting). *Locke* also involved a scholarship program. The State of Washington provided scholarships paid out of the State's general fund to help students pursuing postsecondary education. The scholarships could be used at accredited religious and nonreligious schools alike, but Washington prohibited students from using the scholarships to pursue devotional theology degrees, which prepared students for a calling as clergy. This prohibition prevented Davey from using his scholarship to obtain a degree that would have enabled him to become a pastor. We held that Washington had not violated the Free Exercise Clause.

Locke differs from this case in two critical ways. First, *Locke* explained that Washington had "merely chosen not to fund a distinct category of instruction": the "essentially religious endeavor" of training a minister "to lead a congregation." *Id.*, at 721, 124 S. Ct. 1307, 158 L. Ed. 2d 1. Thus, Davey "was denied a scholarship because of what he proposed *to do*—use the funds to prepare for the ministry." *Trinity Lutheran*, 582 U. S., at ___, 137 S. Ct. 2012, 198 L. Ed. 2d 551. Apart from that narrow restriction, Washington's program allowed scholarships to be used at "pervasively religious schools" that incorporated religious instruction throughout their classes. *Locke*, 540 U. S., at 724–725. By contrast, Montana's Constitution does not zero in on any particular "essentially religious" course of instruction at a religious school. Rather, as we have explained, the no-aid provision bars all aid to a religious school "simply because of what it is," putting the school to a choice between being religious or receiving government benefits. *Trinity Lutheran*, 582 U. S., at ___, 137 S. Ct. 2012, 198 L. Ed. 2d 551. At the same time, the provision puts families to a choice between sending their children to a religious school or receiving such benefits.

Second, *Locke* invoked a "historic and substantial" state interest in not funding the training of clergy, 540 U. S., at 725, 124 S. Ct. 1307, 158 L. Ed. 2d 1, explaining that "opposition to . . . funding 'to support church leaders' lay at the historic core of the Religion Clauses," *Trinity Lutheran*, 582 U. S., at ___, 137 S. Ct. 2012, 198 L. Ed. 2d 551 (quoting *Locke*, 540 U. S., at 722, 124 S. Ct. 1307, 158 L. Ed. 2d 1). As evidence of that tradition, the Court in *Locke* emphasized that the propriety of state-supported clergy was a central subject of founding-era debates, and that most state constitutions from that era prohibited the expenditure of tax dollars to support the clergy. See *id.*, at 722–723, 124 S. Ct. 1307, 158 L. Ed. 2d 1.

But no comparable "historic and substantial" tradition supports Montana's decision to disqualify religious schools from government aid. In the founding era and the early 19th century, governments provided financial support to private schools, including denominational ones. "Far from prohibiting such support, the early state constitutions and statutes actively encouraged this policy." L. Jorgenson, The State and the Non-Public School, 1825–1925, p. 4 (1987); *e.g.*, R. Gabel, Public Funds for Church and Private Schools 210, 217–218, 221, 241–243 (1937); C. Kaestle, Pillars of the Republic: Common Schools and American Society, 1760–1860, pp. 166–167 (1983). Local governments provided grants to private schools, including religious ones, for the education of the poor. M. McConnell, et al., Religion and the Constitution 318–319 (4th ed. 2016). Even States with bans on government-supported clergy, such as New Jersey, Pennsylvania, and Georgia, provided various forms of aid to religious schools. See Kaestle, *supra*, at 166–167; Gabel, *supra*, at 215–218, 241–245, 372–374; cf. *Locke*, 540 U. S., at 723, 124 S. Ct. 1307, 158 L. Ed. 2d 1. Early federal aid (often land grants) went to religious schools. McConnell, *supra*, at 319. Congress provided support to denominational schools in the District of Columbia until 1848, *ibid.*, and Congress paid churches to run schools for American Indians through the end of the 19th century, see *Quick Bear* v. *Leupp*, 210 U. S. 50, 78, 28 S. Ct. 690, 52 L. Ed. 954 (1908); Gabel, *supra*, at 521–523. After the Civil War, Congress spent large sums on education for emancipated freedmen, often by supporting denominational schools in the South through the Freedmen's Bureau. McConnell, *supra*, at 323.[205]

The Department argues that a tradition *against* state support for religious schools arose in the second half of the 19th century, as more than 30 States — including Montana — adopted no-aid provisions. See Brief for Respondents 40–42 and App. D. Such a development, of course, cannot by itself establish an early American tradition. Justice Sotomayor questions our reliance on aid provided during the same era by the Freedmen's Bureau, *post*, at ___, 207 L. Ed. 2d, at 737 (dissenting opinion), but we see no inconsistency in recognizing that such evidence may reinforce an early practice but cannot create one. In addition, many of the no-aid provisions belong to a more checkered tradition shared with the Blaine Amendment of the 1870s. That proposal — which Congress nearly passed — would have added to the Federal Constitution a provision similar to the state no-aid provisions, prohibiting States from aiding "sectarian" schools. See *Mitchell* v. *Helms*, 530 U. S. 793, 828, 120 S. Ct. 2530, 147 L. Ed. 2d 660 (2000) (plurality opinion). "[I]t was an open secret that 'sectarian' was code for 'Catholic.'" *Ibid.*; see Jorgenson, *supra*, at 70. The Blaine Amendment was "born of bigotry" and "arose at a time of pervasive hostility to the Catholic Church and to Catholics in general"; many of its state counterparts have a similarly "shameful pedigree." *Mitchell*, 530 U. S., at 828–829 (plurality opinion); see Jorgenson, *supra*, at 69–70, 216; Jeffries & Ryan, A Political History of the Establishment Clause, 100 Mich. L. Rev. 279, 301–305 (2001). The no-aid provisions of the 19th century hardly evince a tradition that should inform our understanding of the Free Exercise Clause.

The Department argues that several States have rejected referendums to overturn or limit their no-aid provisions, and that Montana even re-adopted its own in the 1970s, for reasons unrelated to anti-Catholic bigotry. See Brief for Respondents 20,

---

205. Justice Breyer. sees "no meaningful difference" between concerns animating bans on support for clergy and bans on support for religious schools. *Post*, at ___—___, 207 L. Ed. 2d, at 723–724. But evidently early American governments did. See *supra*, at ___, 207 L. Ed. 2d, at 693. Justice Breyer contests particular examples but acknowledges that some bans on clergy support did not bar certain "sponsorship" of religious schools. *Post*, at ___, 207 L. Ed. 2d, at 725. And, central to the issue here, he certainly does not identify a consistent early tradition, of the sort invoked in *Locke*, *against* support for religious schools. Virginia's opposition to establishing university theology professorships and chartering theological seminaries, see *ibid.*, do not fit the bill. Buckley, After Disestablishment: Thomas Jefferson's Wall of Separation in Antebellum Virginia, 61 J. So. Hist. 445, 452–453 (1995). Justice Breyer also invokes Madison's objections to the Virginia Assessment Bill, *post*, at ___—___, 207 L. Ed. 2d, at 724–725, but Madison objected in part because the Bill provided special support to certain churches and clergy, thereby "violat[ing] equality by subjecting some to peculiar burdens." Memorial and Remonstrance Against Religious Assessments, Art. 4, reprinted in *Everson*, 330 U. S., at 66, 16, 67 S. Ct. 504, 91 L. Ed. 711 (appendix to dissenting opinion of Rutledge, J.); see V. Muñoz, God and the Founders: Madison, Washington, and Jefferson 21–22, 27 (2009). It is far from clear that the same objections extend to programs that provide equal support to all private primary and secondary schools. If anything, excluding religious schools from such programs would appear to impose the "peculiar burdens" feared by Madison.

42. But, on the other side of the ledger, many States today—including those with no-aid provisions—provide support to religious schools through vouchers, scholarships, tax credits, and other measures. See Brief for Oklahoma et al. as *Amici Curiae* 29–31, 33–35; Brief for Petitioners 5. According to petitioners, 20 of 37 States with no-aid provisions allow religious options in publicly funded scholarship programs, and almost all allow religious options in tax credit programs. Reply Brief 22, n. 9.

All to say, we agree with the Department that the historical record is "complex." Brief for Respondents 41. And it is true that governments over time have taken a variety of approaches to religious schools. But it is clear that there is no "historic and substantial" tradition against aiding such schools comparable to the tradition against state-supported clergy invoked by *Locke*.

C

Two dissenters would chart new courses. JUSTICE SOTOMAYOR would grant the government "some room" to "single . . . out" religious entities "for exclusion," based on what she views as "the interests embodied in the Religion Clauses." *Post*, at ___, ___, 207 L. Ed. 2d, at 736, 736 (quoting *Trinity Lutheran*, 582 U. S., at ___, ___, 137 S. Ct. 2012, 198 L. Ed. 2d 551 (SOTOMAYOR, J., dissenting)). JUSTICE BREYER, building on his solo opinion in *Trinity Lutheran*, would adopt a "flexible, context-specific approach" that "may well vary" from case to case. *Post*, at ___, ___, 207 L. Ed. 2d, at 727, 729; see *Trinity Lutheran*, 582 U. S., at ___, 137 S. Ct. 2012, 198 L. Ed. 2d 551 (BREYER, J., concurring in judgment). As best we can tell, courts applying this approach would contemplate the particular benefit and restriction at issue and discern their relationship to religion and society, taking into account "context and consequences measured in light of [the] purposes" of the Religion Clauses. *Post*, at ___—___, ___, 207 L. Ed. 2d, at 728–730, 731 (quoting *Van Orden* v. *Perry*, 545 U. S. 677, 700, 125 S. Ct. 2854, 162 L. Ed. 2d 607 (2005) (BREYER, J., concurring in judgment)). What is clear is that JUSTICE BREYER would afford much freer rein to judges than our current regime, arguing that "there is 'no test-related substitute for the exercise of legal judgment.'" *Post*, at ___, 207 L. Ed. 2d, at 731 (quoting *Van Orden*, 545 U. S., at 700 (opinion of BREYER, J.)).

The simplest response is that these dissents follow from prior separate writings, not from the Court's decision in *Trinity Lutheran* or the decades of precedent on which it relied. [12] These precedents have "repeatedly confirmed" the straightforward rule that we apply today: When otherwise eligible recipients are disqualified from a public benefit "solely because of their religious character," we must apply strict scrutiny. *Trinity Lutheran*, 582 U. S., at ___-___, 137 S. Ct. 2012, 198 L. Ed. 2d 551. This rule against express religious discrimination is no "doctrinal innovation." *Post*, at ___, 207 L. Ed. 2d, at 727 (opinion of BREYER, J.). Far from it. As *Trinity Lutheran* explained, the rule is "unremarkable in light of our prior decisions." 582 U. S., at ___, 137 S. Ct. 2012, 198 L. Ed. 2d 551.

For innovation, one must look to the dissents. Their "room[y]" or "flexible" approaches to discrimination against religious organizations and observers would mark a significant departure from our free exercise precedents. [13] The protections of the Free Exercise Clause do not depend on a "judgment-by-judgment analysis" regarding whether discrimination against religious adherents would somehow serve ill-defined interests. Cf. *Medellín* v. *Texas*, 552 U. S. 491, 514, 128 S. Ct. 1346, 170 L. Ed. 2d 190 (2008).

D

[14] Because the Montana Supreme Court applied the no-aid provision to discriminate against schools and parents based on the religious character of the school, the "strictest scrutiny" is required. *Supra*, at ___, ___, 207 L. Ed. 2d, at 690, 692 (quoting *Trinity Lutheran*, 582 U. S., at ___, 137 S. Ct. 2012, 198 L. Ed. 2d 551). That "stringent standard," *id.*, at ___, 137 S. Ct. 2012, 198 L. Ed. 2d 551, is not "watered down but really means what it says," *Lukumi*, 508 U. S., at 546, 113 S. Ct. 2217, 124 L. Ed. 2d 472 (internal quotation marks and alterations omitted). To satisfy it, government action "must advance 'interests of the highest order' and must be narrowly tailored in pursuit of those interests." *Ibid.* (quoting *McDaniel*, 435 U. S., at 628, 98 S. Ct. 1322, 55 L. Ed. 2d 593).

The Montana Supreme Court asserted that the no-aid provision serves Montana's interest in separating church and State "more fiercely" than the Federal Constitution. 393 Mont., at 467, 2018 MT 306, 435 P. 3d, at 614. But "that interest cannot qualify as compelling" in the face of the infringement of free exercise here. *Trinity Lutheran*, 582 U. S., at ___, 137 S. Ct. 2012, 198 L. Ed. 2d 551. [15] A State's interest "in achieving greater separation of church and State than is already ensured under the Establishment Clause . . . is limited by the Free Exercise Clause." *Ibid.* (quoting *Widmar* v. *Vincent*, 454 U. S. 263, 276, 102 S. Ct. 269, 70 L. Ed. 2d 440 (1981)).

The Department, for its part, asserts that the no-aid provision actually *promotes* religious freedom. In the Department's view, the no-aid provision protects the religious liberty of taxpayers by ensuring that their taxes are not directed to religious organizations, and it safeguards the freedom of religious organizations by keeping the government out of their operations. See Brief for Respondents 17–23. [16] An infringement of First Amendment rights, however, cannot be justified by a State's alternative view that the infringement advances religious liberty. Our federal system prizes state experimentation, but not "state experimentation in the suppression of free speech," and the same goes for the free exercise of religion. *Boy Scouts of America* v. *Dale*, 530 U. S. 640, 660, 120 S. Ct. 2446, 147 L. Ed. 2d 554 (2000).

Furthermore, we do not see how the no-aid provision promotes religious freedom. [17] As noted, this Court has repeatedly upheld government programs that spend taxpayer funds on equal aid to religious observers and organizations, particularly when the link between government and religion is attenuated by private choices. A school, concerned about government involvement with its religious activities, might reasonably decide for itself not to participate in a government program. But we doubt that the school's liberty is enhanced by eliminating any option to participate in the first place.

The Department's argument is especially unconvincing because the infringement of religious liberty here broadly affects both religious schools and adherents. Montana's no-aid provision imposes a categorical ban—"broadly and strictly" prohibiting "*any* type of aid" to religious schools. 393 Mont., at 462–463, 2018 MT 306, 435 P. 3d, at 611. This prohibition is far more sweeping than the policy in *Trinity Lutheran*, which barred churches from one narrow program for playground resurfacing—causing "in all likelihood" only "a few extra scraped knees." 582 U. S., at ___, 137 S. Ct. 2012, 198 L. Ed. 2d 551.

And the prohibition before us today burdens not only religious schools but also the families whose children attend or hope to attend them. [18] Drawing on "enduring American tradition," we have long recognized the rights of parents to direct "the religious upbringing" of their children. *Wisconsin* v. *Yoder*, 406 U. S. 205, 213–214, 232, 92 S. Ct. 1526, 32 L. Ed. 2d 15 (1972). Many parents exercise that right by sending their children to religious schools, a choice protected by the Constitution. See *Pierce* v. *Society of Sisters*, 268 U. S. 510, 534–535, 45 S. Ct. 571, 69 L. Ed. 1070 (1925). But the no-aid provision penalizes that decision by cutting families off from otherwise available benefits if they choose a religious private school rather than a secular one, and for no other reason.

The Department also suggests that the no-aid provision advances Montana's interests in public education. According to the Department, the no-aid provision safeguards the public school system by ensuring that government support is not diverted to private schools. See Brief for Respondents 19, 25. But, under that framing, the no-aid provision is fatally underinclusive because its "proffered objectives are not pursued with respect to analogous nonreligious conduct." *Lukumi*, 508 U. S., at 546, 113 S. Ct. 2217, 124 L. Ed. 2d 472. On the Department's view, an interest in public education is undermined by diverting government support to *any* private school, yet the no-aid provision bars aid only to *religious* ones. A law does not advance "an interest of the highest order when it leaves appreciable damage to that supposedly vital interest unprohibited." *Id.*, at 547, 113 S. Ct. 2217, 124 L. Ed. 2d 472 (internal quotation marks and alterations omitted). Montana's interest in public education cannot justify a no-aid provision that requires only religious private schools to "bear [its] weight." *Ibid.*

[19] A State need not subsidize private education. But once a State decides to do so, it cannot disqualify some private schools solely because they are religious.

III

The Department argues that, at the end of the day, there is no free exercise violation here because the Montana Supreme Court ultimately eliminated the scholarship program altogether. According to the Department, now that there is no program, religious schools and adherents cannot complain that they are excluded from any generally available benefit.

Two dissenters agree. Justice Ginsburg reports that the State of Montana simply chose to "put all private school parents in the same boat" by invalidating the scholarship program, *post*, at ___—___, 207 L. Ed. 2d, at 719, and JUSTICE SOTOMAYOR describes the decision below as resting on state law grounds having nothing to do with the federal Free Exercise Clause, see *post*, at ___—___, 207 L. Ed. 2d, at 731, 734.

The descriptions are not accurate. The Montana Legislature created the scholarship program; the Legislature never chose to end it, for policy or other reasons. The program was eliminated by a court, and not based on some innocuous principle of state law. Rather, the Montana Supreme Court invalidated the program pursuant to a state law provision that expressly discriminates on the basis of religious status. The Court applied that provision to hold that religious schools were barred from participating in the program. Then, seeing no other "mechanism" to make absolutely sure that religious schools received no aid, the court chose to invalidate the entire program. 393 Mont., at 466–468, 2018 MT 306, 435 P. 3d, at 613–614.

The final step in this line of reasoning eliminated the program, to the detriment of religious and non-religious schools alike. But the Court's error of federal law occurred at the beginning. When the Court was called upon to apply a state law no-aid provision to exclude religious schools from the program, it was obligated by the Federal Constitution to reject the invitation. Had the Court recognized that this was, indeed, "one of those cases" in which application of the no-aid provision "would violate the Free Exercise Clause," *id.*, at 468, 2018 MT 306, 435 P. 3d, at 614, the Court would not have proceeded to find a violation of that provision. And, in the absence of such a state law violation, the Court would have had no basis for terminating the program. Because the elimination of the program flowed directly from the Montana Supreme Court's failure to follow the dictates of federal law, it cannot be defended as a neutral policy decision, or as resting on adequate and independent state law grounds.[206]

[20] The Supremacy Clause provides that "the Judges in every State shall be bound" by the Federal Constitution, "any Thing in the Constitution or Laws of any State to the Contrary notwithstanding." Art. VI, cl. 2. "[T]his Clause creates a rule of decision" directing state courts that they "must not give effect to state laws that conflict with federal law[ ]." *Armstrong* v. *Exceptional Child Center, Inc.*, 575 U. S. 320, 324, 135 S. Ct. 1378, 191 L. Ed. 2d 471 (2015). Given the conflict between the Free Exercise Clause and the application of the no-aid provision here, the Montana Supreme Court should have "disregard[ed]" the no-aid provision and decided this case "conformably to the [C]onstitution" of the United States. *Marbury* v. *Madison*, 5 U.S. 137, 1 Cranch 137, 178, 2 L. Ed. 60 (1803). [21] That "*supreme* law of the

206. JUSTICE SOTOMAYOR. worries that, in light of our decision, the Montana Supreme Court must "order the State to recreate" a scholarship program that "no longer exists." *Post*, at ___, 207 L. Ed. 2d, at 734 (dissenting opinion). But it was the Montana Supreme Court that eliminated the program, in the decision below, which remains under review. Our reversal of that decision simply restores the status quo established by the Montana Legislature before the Court's error of federal law. We do not consider any alterations the Legislature may choose to make in the future.

land" condemns discrimination against religious schools and the families whose children attend them. *Id.*, at 180. They are "member[s] of the community too," and their exclusion from the scholarship program here is "odious to our Constitution" and "cannot stand." *Trinity Lutheran*, 582 U. S., at ___, ___, 137 S. Ct. 2012, 198 L. Ed. 2d 551.[207]

* * *

The judgment of the Montana Supreme Court is reversed, and the case is remanded for further proceedings not inconsistent with this opinion.

It is so ordered.

207. In light of this holding, we do not address petitioners' claims that the no-aid provision, as applied, violates the Equal Protection Clause or the Establishment Clause.

Glossary of Terms

A fortiori: With stronger reason; much more.

A.B.A.: American Bar Association.

A.B.A.J.: American Bar Association Journal.

Ab initio: From the beginning; from the first fact; from the inception.

Abet: To encourage, incite, or set another to commit a crime.

Abstract: A lesser quantity containing the virtue and force of a greater quantity; an abridgement.

Academic freedom: The right to teach as one sees fit, but not necessarily the right to teach evil.

Actionable: That for which an action will lie; furnishing a legal ground for an action.

Ad valorem: According to the value; e.g., a duty or tax. A tax imposed on the value of property.

Administrative appeal: Quasi-judicial proceeding before an independent hearing officer or administrative law judge.

Administrative law judge: An individual presiding at an administrative due process hearing who has the power to administer oaths, hear testimony, rule out questions of evidence, and make determinations of fact. The role of an administrative law judge in IDEA proceedings is identical to that of an independent hearing officer.

Adversary process: The method courts use to resolve disputes in which each side presents its case, subject to rules of evidence; an independent fact finder (jury or judge) determines which side's evidence is more persuasive.

Adverse possession: A method of acquisition of title by possession for a statutory period under certain conditions.

Affiant: The person who makes and subscribes to an affidavit.

Affidavit: A written or printed declaration or statement of facts, made voluntarily, and confirmed by the oath or affirmation of the party making it, taken before a person having authority to administer such an oath.

AIDS: Acquired Immune Deficiency Syndrome. A virus that attacks a person's immune system and damages their ability to fight diseases.

Allegation: The assertion, claim, declaration, or statement of a party to an action, made in a pleading, setting out what he expects to prove.

Alternative Dispute Resolution: Procedures for settling disputes by means other than litigation; e.g., by arbitration or mediation. Such procedures are usually less costly and faster.

Amicus curiae: Friend of the court. Refers to one not a party to litigation who submits a brief to direct the court's attention to particular arguments.

Animo et facto: The required intent to change domicile; an intention to make the new place one's abode coupled with an actual transfer of bodily presence from one place to another.

Annotation: A remark, note, case summary, or commentary on some passage of a book, statutory provision, court decision, or the like, intended to illustrate or explain its meaning.

Annum: Year.

Appeal: An application by an appellant to a higher court to reconsider the order of the court below.

Appellant: One who appeals from a judicial decision.

Appellate court: A higher court that hears a case from a lower court on appeal.

Appellee: The person against whom an appeal is taken; the respondent to an appeal.

Arbitrary: In an unreasonable manner, fixed or done capriciously or at pleasure. Not founded in the nature of things.

Arbitration: A dispute resolution process in which a neutral third party renders a decision after a hearing at which both parties have an opportunity to be heard. The arbitrator has the power to render a binding decision.

Argument: An effort to establish belief by a course of reasoning.

Assault: The threat or use of force on another that causes that person to have a reasonable apprehension of imminent harmful or offensive contact.

Assumpsit: Suit on a contract.

Assumption of risk: Also known as volenti non fit injuria; denies legal recovery to a plaintiff for injuries to which they assent by voluntarily exposing themselves to a known and appreciated danger.

Banc: Bench; the place where a court permanently or regularly sits.

Battery: Intentional and wrongful physical contact with a person without his or her consent that entails some injury or offensive touching.

BFOQ: Bona Fide Occupational Qualification. An employment qualification that discriminates against a protected class (such as sex, religion, or national origin) but that also relates to an essential job duty and is reasonably necessary to the operations of the particular business; such a qualification is not illegal under federal employment discrimination laws.

Bill: A formal declaration, complaint, or statement of particular things in writing.

Bona fide: In good faith. Refers to action taken innocently and without notice of legal deficiencies or advises third party rights.

Bond: A written promise containing guarantees or security for performance.

Breve: A writ. A judicial order to perform a specified act, or giving authority to have it done.

Brief: Written argument presented by lawyers to a court.

C.F.R. (abbreviation for Code of Federal Regulations): The repository regulations promulgated by various federal agencies to implement laws passed by Congress.

Caveat: A warning to take care.

Certiorari: (To be more fully informed). An original writ or action whereby a cause is removed from an inferior to a superior court for consideration. The record of proceedings is then transmitted to the superior court. The term is most commonly used when requesting the U.S. Supreme Court hear a case from a lower court.

Class action: A suit brought on behalf of a large class of individuals by one or more representatives of that class.

Color of law: Under the appearance of legal authority.

Common law: Legal principles derived from usage and custom, or from court decision affirming such usages and customs.

Comparative negligence: Provides for a reduction in a plaintiff's recovery in an amount proportional to the plaintiff's fault in the damage.

Concurring opinion: A separate opinion delivered by one or more judges that agrees with the decision of the majority of the court but offers different reasons for that decision.

Conflict of interest: Term used in connection with public officials and fiduciaries and their relationship to matters of private interest or gain to them. A real or seeming incompatibility between one's private interests and one's public or fiduciary duties.

Contributory negligence: Negligence of the plaintiff which, combined with the negligence of the defendant, was the proximate cause of the injury in a complaint. Under the traditional concept of contributory negligence, a plaintiff's claim was completely barred if the damage suffered was partly the plaintiff's fault. See also Comparative Negligence.

Covenant: An agreement of promise.

Damages: A pecuniary compensation or indemnity, which may be recovered in the courts by any person who has suffered loss, detriment, or injury, whether to his person, property, or rights through the unlawful act or omission or negligence of another.

De facto:(in fact) Most commonly used in school law with desegregation. Segregation that is inadvertent and without assistance of school authorities and not caused by any state action, but rather by social, economic, and other determinants is de facto segregation.

De jure: Derived in law; i.e., founded in official governmental authority or action.

De minimis: A matter of minimal importance; insufficient to command judicial relief.

De novo: A legal proceeding, independent of prior finding. Arises frequently when an appellate court reviews a lower court's application of the law; the appellate court should consider the law anew, regardless of the lower court's holding.

Decency: Propriety of action, speech, dress, etc.

Declaratory relief: The opinion of a court on a question of law that, without ordering anything to be done, simply declares the rights of the parties.

Defamation: An intentional false communication, either published or publicly spoken, that injures another's reputation or good name.

Defendant: One required to make answer in a lawsuit; the one against whom the law is brought.

Defense: That which is offered and alleged by the party proceeded against in an action or lawsuit, as a reason in law or fact why the plaintiff should not recover or establish what they seek.

Demurrer: A plea by one of the parties to an action, who, while admitting for the sake of the argument all the material facts properly pleaded by the opposing party, contends the existence of the facts does not constitute grounds for action.

Deposition: Record of written testimony under oath, not taken at trial.

Dicta: Opinions of a judge that do not embody the resolution or determination of the specific case before the court.

Discretion: An exercise of judgment or choice.

Discrimination: In constitutional law, the effect of a statute or established practice that confers particular privileges on a class or that denies privileges to another class; differential treatment.

Disparate treatment: Differential treatment of employees or applicants on the basis of race, color, religion, sex, national origin, handicap, or veteran status.

Dissenting opinion: A minority opinion that disagrees with the outcome of the majority's decision, handed down by one or more members of the court.

Due process: Law in the regular course of administration, according to those rules and forms that have been established for the protection of private rights.

Duress: Unlawful coercion.

Ejusdem generis: Of the same kind, class, or nature.

Emancipation: Legal release from another's control. Surrender the right of care, custody and earnings of a child by his or her parents; the child assumes adult legal status.

Eminent domain: The power to take private property for public use by the state, municipalities, and private persons or corporations authorized to exercise functions of public character.

En banc: By the full bench.

Enjoin: To require; command; positively direct. To require a person, by writ of injunction to perform, or to abstain or desist, from some act.

Estop: To stop, bar, or impeded; to prevent; to preclude.

Et seq.: And the following, usually refers to pages following a referenced page.

Ex officio: By virtue of the office.

Ex parte: From or involving only one party to an action.

Ex post facto: (after the fact) Act passed after another act that retroactively changes the legal consequences of that act.

Ex rel.: Out of relations. Refers to proceedings instigated by the individual that is brought in the name of the state.

Expunge: To delete, erase, or destroy; e.g., from a court record.

F. Supp.: Federal Supplement. A unit of the National Reporter System covering cases decided in the U.S. district courts and the U.S. Court of International Trade.

Fatal errors: As grounds for a new trial, many harmful errors; reversible errors.

Federal question jurisdiction: Cases arising under the constitution of the United States, acts of Congress, or treaties, and involving their interpretations and applications.

Felony: A crime of a graver or more serious nature than those designated as misdemeanors.

Gender dysphoria: A clinical condition arising from debilitating anxiety and distress associated with reconciling the differences between the gender they identify with and the one they were assigned-at-birth.

Government tort: A wrong perpetrated by the government through an employee or agent or instrumentality under its control that may or may not be actionable, depending on whether there is governmental tort immunity.

Governmental act: An act in exercise of police power or in exercise of constitutional, legislative, administrative, or judicial powers conferred on federal, state, or local government for the benefit of the public.

Governmental function: A function conducted by a private actor that is designated as a state action for constitutional purposes.

Gravamen: The material part of a grievance, complaint, indictment, charge, cause of action, etc.

Grievance: In labor law, a complaint filed by an employee, or by his or her union representative, regarding working conditions and by which there is a procedural structure for resolution provided in the union contract.

Habeas corpus:(Latin; you have the body) The name given to a variety of writs, having as their objective to bring a party before a court or judge; usually arises when there is an issue as to the legality of a party's imprisonment.

Hearing de novo: Generally, a new hearing or a hearing for the second time. The reviewing court gives no deference to the lower court's findings. See also de novo.

Hearing on merits: A trial on the substance of a case, as opposed to consideration of procedure only.

Hearing: An oral proceeding before a court or quasi-judicial tribunal.

Hearsay evidence: Testimony given by witnesses who relate what others have told them or what they have heard said by others, rather than what they know personally.

Hold harmless agreement: A contractual arrangement whereby one party assumes the liability inherent in a situation, thereby relieving the other party of responsibility.

Holding: The legal principle to be drawn from the opinion (or decision) of the court.

Ib.: (Ibidem or Ibid.) In the same place.

Idem: (Id.) The same; used to indicate a reference previously made.

Illicit: Not permitted or allowed; prohibited; unlawful; as an illicit trade; illicit intercourse.

Immaterial: Not material; essential, or necessary; not important or pertinent; not decisive; of no substantial consequence.

Immunity: Exemption, as serving in an office, or performing duties that the law generally requires other citizens to perform; exemption from paying taxes. Freedom or exemption from penalty, burden, or duty.

Implied: Not expressed but inferred.

In camera: Latin for "in chambers"; in a judge's private chambers.

In loco parentis: In the place of the parent; instead of a parent; charged with a parent's rights, duties, and responsibilities.

In re: In the affair; in the matter of; concerning; regarding. Also, indicating that there are no adversarial parties in a judicial proceeding; refers to the fact that a court is only considering a res ("thing"), not a person.

Incite: To arouse, urge, provoke, encourage, or set in motion.

Indecent: Offensive to common propriety; offending against modesty or delicacy; grossly vulgar.

Independent hearing officer: An impartial third-party decision-maker who conducts an administrative hearing and renders a decision on the merits of the dispute.

Indictment: An accusation in writing found and presented by a grand jury, legally convoked and sworn to the court in which it is impaneled, charging that the person named has done some act, or been guilty of some omission, which by law is a public offense punishable on indictment.

Injunction: A court order prohibiting someone from doing some specified act or commanding someone to undo some wrong or injury.

Insubordination: Disobedience to constituted authority. Refusal to obey some order that a superior entity is entitled to give and have obeyed.

Inter alia: Latin for "among other things."

Invalid: Not legally binding.

Ipso facto: Latin for "by the fact itself"; as the necessary consequence of the act.

Ipso jure: Latin for "by the mere operation of the law."

Judgment: A decision by the court.

Judicial notice: The recognition by the judge that certain commonly known indisputable facts are true.

Judicial question: One proper for the determination of a court of justice, as distinguished from moot questions or from such questions as belong to the decision of a legislative or executive department of government.

Judicial review: Power of courts to review the decision of another department or level of government.

Judiciary: That branch of government invested with the judicial power; the system of courts in a country; the body of judges; the bench.

Jurisdiction: The right of a court to hear a case.

Jurisprudence: The study of law.

Justiciable: A term referring to a controversy or real dispute that a court may handle.

Juvenile: A young person who has not yet attained the age at which he or she should be treated as an adult for purposes of criminal law.

Laches: Negligence or unreasonable delay in pursuing a legal remedy, whereby a person forfeits their rights.

Law of the land: Due process of law. Body of law consisting of court decisions, statutes, and treaties.

Law: That which is laid down, ordained, or established. Generally contemplates both statutory and case law.

Lawsuit: A vernacular term for a suit, action, or cause instituted or depending between two private parties in the courts of law.

Legal liability: A liability which courts recognize and enforce against the party legally obligated or responsible.

Legislative history: The background and events, including committee reports, hearings, and floor debates, leading up to the enactment of a law.

Letter of the law: Expression used to denote the exact strict interpretation of a statute, ordinance, regulation, or law.

Lewd: Lustful; indecent; lascivious; lecherous; vulgar.

Liability: The quality or state of being legally obligated or responsible.

Liable: Bound or obliged in law or equity; responsible; chargeable.

Libel: A method of defamation expressed in print, writing, picture, or sign.

Liberty interest: An interest recognized as protected by the due process clauses of state and/or federal constitutions. Generally included are liberties guaranteed by the first eight amendments of the United States constitution, as well as interests created when the state either legislatively or administratively imposes limitations on their discretion and require that a specific standard prevail in decision-making.

Liberty: Freedom from all restraints except such as are justly imposed by law.

Liquidity: The status or condition of a person or a business in terms of their ability to convert assets into cash.

Litigant: A party to a lawsuit.

Litigate: To dispute or contend in form of law; to carry on a lawsuit.

Loyalty oath: An oath whereby an individual declares his allegiance to his government and its institutions and disclaims any support of foreign ideologies or associations.

Magistrate: A public civil officer, possessing such power—legislative, executive, or judicial—the government appointing them may ordain.

Majority opinion: The opinion of an appellate court in which the majority of its members join.

Malfeasance: The commission of an unlawful act.

Malice: Hatred; ill will; a formed design of doing an unlawful act.

Malpractice: Professional misconduct or unreasonable lack of skill.

Mandamus: Latin for "we command." This is the name of a writ to compel a public body or its officers to perform a duty.

Mandate: A legal command.

Mandatory statutes: Generic term describing statutes that require, not merely permit, a course of action.

Material witness: A person who can give testimony relating to a particular matter that no one else, or at least very few people, can give.

Mediation: Private, informal dispute resolution process in which a neutral third person, the mediator, helps disputing parties to reach an agreement. The mediator has no power to impose a binding decision on the parties.

Memorandum decision: A court's decision that gives the ruling (what it decides and orders done), but not opinion (reasoning for the decision).

Ministerial act: That which is done under authority or law, as opposed to discretion, judgment, or skill.

Minority: Not of legal age.

Misconduct of office: Any unlawful or unethical behavior by a public office in relation to the duties of their office, willful in character.

Misdemeanor: Offenses lower than felonies and generally those punishable by fine, penalty, forfeiture, or a small term of imprisonment.

Misfeasance: The wrongful performance of some act which a person may lawfully do.

Modus operandi: M.O.; method of operating or doing things.

Moot case: A case is "moot" when a determination is sought on a matter which, when rendered, cannot have any practical effect on the existing controversy.

Moral turpitude: An act of baseness or vileness; depravity in private and social duties that man owes to fellow man, or to society in general; contrary to accepted and customary rules of right and duty between man and man.

Motion: A request for a court ruling.

Municipal corporation: A body politic created by the incorporation of the inhabitants of an area to regulate and administer local affairs.

N.O.V.: (non obstante verdict) Notwithstanding the verdict. A judgment N.O.V. reverses the jury verdict as unsupported by law.

Negligence: The act or omission of doing something that a reasonable man, guided by those ordinary considerations that regulate human affairs, would not do; doing something that a reasonably prudent person would not do.

Nolens volens: Whether willing or unwilling; consenting or not.

Nolo contendere: Latin phrase meaning "I will not contest it." A plea in a criminal case that has a similar legal effect as pleading guilty.

Non sequitur: It does not follow.

Nonsuit: A term broadly applied to a variety of terminations of an action that do not adjudicate issues on the merits.

Nuisance: Nuisance is activity that arises from unreasonable, unwarranted, or unlawful use by a person of their own property; working obstruction or injury to the rights of another or to the public, producing material annoyance that the law will presume results in damage.

Oath: Any form of attestation by which a person signifies that they are bound in conscience to perform an act faithfully and truthfully.

Obscene: Objectionable or offensive to accepted standards of decency. Basic guidelines for a trier of fact in determining whether a work that depicts or describes sexual conduct is obscene are whether the average person, applying contemporary community standards, would find that the work, taken as a whole, appeals to the prurient interest, whether the work depicts or describes in a patently offensive way sexual conduct specifically defined by applicable state law, and whether the work, taken as a whole, lacks serious literary, artistic, political, or scientific value.

Opinion: A court's essay explaining the decision.

Ordinance: A rule established by authority; a permanent rule of action; a law or statute.

Original jurisdiction: Jurisdiction to consider a case at its inception in the first instance, as contrasted to appellate jurisdiction.

P.L.: An abbreviation for Public Law; a public law is a statute passed by Congress. The IDEA was initially referred to as P.L, 94–142, the 142nd piece of legislation introduced during the 94th Congress.

Parens patriae: Literally "parent of the country," refers traditionally to the role of the state as sovereign and guardian of a person under legal disability, such as juveniles or the insane.

Parish: A circuit of ground, committed to the care of one person or vicar, or other minister having cure of souls therein. In Louisiana, territorial governmental division elsewhere called a "county."

Parochial: Relating or belonging to a parish.

Parol: A word; speech; hence, oral or verbal.

Per curiam: By the court — usually signifying an unsigned judicial opinion.

Per se: By itself; in itself; taken alone; by means of itself; in its own nature without reference to its relation.

Persona non grata: Person not welcome; an undesirable person.

Petition: Written application or prayer to the court for the redress of a wrong or the grant of a privilege or license.

Plagiarism: The act of appropriating the literary composition of another, or parts or passages of their writings, or the ideas or language of the same, and passing them off as the product or one's own mind.

Plaintiff: A person who brings and action; the party who complains or sues in a civil action and is so named on the record.

Plenary: Full; conclusive.

Police power: Legislative power to enact laws for the health, comfort, and prosperity of the state.

Political question: Questions that high courts will refuse to take cognizance or to decide on account of their purely political character, or because their determination would involve an encroachment upon the executive or legislative powers.

Power of attorney: An instrument in writing whereby one person appoints another as his agent and confers authority to perform certain specified acts on behalf of the principal.

Power: The right, ability, authority, or faculty of doing something.

Prayer: The request contained in a bill in equity that the court will grant the process, aid, or relief that the complainant desires.

Precedent: An adjudged case or decision of a court, considered as furnishing an example or authority for an identical or similar case afterwards arising on a similar question of law.

Prejudice: A forejudgment; bias; partiality; preconceived opinion.

Prima facie: At first sight; on the first appearance; a fact presumed to be true unless disproved by some evidence to the contrary.

Principal: The source of authority or right. A superintendent, as of a school.

Prior restraint: A system of prior restraint is any scheme that gives public officials the power to deny use of a forum in advance of its actual expression.

Privacy, right of: The right to be let alone; right to live without unwarranted interference by the public in matters with which the public is not necessarily concerned.

Privilege: A particular and peculiar benefit or advantage enjoyed by a person, company, or class, beyond the common advantage of other citizens.

Pro se: Refers to a person who represents himself or herself in a court of law.

Probable cause: Reasonable cause; having more evidence for than against. A reasonable ground for belief in certain alleged facts.

Procedural due process: The guarantee of procedural fairness that flows from both the Fifth and Fourteenth Amendments' due process clauses contained in the constitution. It is necessary to show that significant deprivation of life, liberty, or property interest has occurred to invoke the due process clause.

Proprietary functions: Functions that a city or town, in its discretion, may perform when considered to be in the best interests of its citizens.

Protected class: Under Title VII of the Civil Rights Act of 1964, one of the groups the law seeks to protect, including groups based on race, sex, national origin, and religion.

Proximate cause: That which, in a natural and continuous sequence, unbroken by any efficient intervening cause, produces injury, and without which the result would not have occurred.

Prurient interest: A shameful or morbid interest in nudity, sex, or excretion. An obsessive interest in immoral and lascivious matters.

Publish: To make public; to circulate; to make known to people in general.

Punitive damages: Money awarded to a person that is over and above the damages actually sustained; usually incurred when the defendant acted recklessly, with malice, or with deceit. These damages are intended to punish and consequently deter blameworthy conduct.

Quantum meruit: The amount that is deserved. Recovery value to avoid unjust enrichment.

Quasi: As if; almost as it were; analogous to. A quasi-judicial act of a school board is holding a hearing before the dismissal of a teacher.

Quid pro quo: Latin for "something for something"; consideration.

Quo warranto:(By what authority); a method of trying title to a public office.

Quorum: The number of members required for lawful action by an official assembly.

Ratification: In a broad sense, the confirmation of a previous act done either by the party themselves or by another; a confirmation of a voidable act.

Rational basis test: Under this test, an appellate court will not second guess the legislature's wisdom or rationale in enacting a particular statute if there is a rational basis for its enactment, and if the challenged law bears a reasonable relationship to the attainment of some legitimate government objective.

Reasonable care: The degree of care that a person of ordinary prudence would exercise in the same or similar circumstances.

Reasonable doubt: The standard used to determine the guilt or innocence of a person criminally charged.

Reasonable man doctrine or standard: The standard that one must observe to avoid liability for negligence is the standard of the reasonable man under all the circumstances, including the foreseeability of harm to one such as the plaintiff.

Reasonable suspicion: A particularized and objective basis, supported by specific and articulable facts, for suspecting a person of criminal activity; this standard must be met for law enforcement to stop a person in a public place.

Redress: Satisfaction for an injury or damages sustained.

Reevaluation: Complete and thorough reassessment of a student. Generally, all the original assessments will be repeated, but additional assessments must be completed if necessary; the IDEA 2004 requires educators to reevaluate each child with a disability at least every three years.

Regulation: Rules for management or government.

Remand: To send back. The act of an appellate court when it sends a case back to the trial court and orders the trial court to conduct limited new hearings or an entirely new trial, or to take some further action.

Remedy: The means by which a right is enforced or the violation of a right is prevented, redressed, or compensated.

Res ipsa loquitur: The thing speaks for itself.

Res judicata: A matter adjudged; a thing judicially acted upon or decided; a thing or matter settled by judgment.

Respondeat superior: "Let the master answer." The responsibility and/or liability of a master for the acts of his servant.

Respondent: In equity practice, the party who makes an answer to a bill or other proceeding in equity.

Restitution: A remedy under which a person is restored to their original position prior to loss or injury.

Restraining order: An order in the nature of an injunction that forbids the defendant from doing the threatened act until a hearing on the application can be done.

Retroactive: A law that creates a new obligation on consideration already past, or destroys or impairs former privileges; extends scope or effect to matters that have occurred in the past.

Reverse: To overturn a decision; e.g., an appellate court can reverse the decision of a lower court.

Ripeness doctrine: The principle that the federal courts require an actual, present controversy, and therefore will not act when the issue is only hypothetical or the existence of a controversy is merely speculative.

Scheme: A design or plan formed to accomplish some purpose; a system.

Scienter: Knowingly; the knowing performance of an act.

Search: An examination of a person's house or other personal items with a view to the discovery of contraband or illicit or stolen property, or some evidence of guilt to be used in the prosecution of a criminal action for some crime or offense with which they are charged.

Sectarian: Denominational; devoted to, peculiar to, pertaining to, or promotive of, the interest of a sect or sects; religious.

Secular: Not spiritual; not ecclesiastical; relating to affairs of the present world; non-religious.

Seditious libel: A communication written with the intent to incite the people to change the government by other than lawful means, or to advocate the overthrow of the government.

Segregation: The act or process of separation. The unconstitutional policy and practice of separating people on the basis of color, nationality, religion, etc. in housing and schooling.

Seizure: The act of taking possession of property, for a violation of law or by virtue of an execution of a judgment.

Session: The sitting of a court, legislature, council, commission, etc., for the transaction of its proper business.

Sic: Latin, thus; so; in such a manner.

Sine qua non: Without which not. An indispensable requisite or condition.

Slander: The speaking of base and defamatory words tending to prejudice another in their reputation, community standing, office, trade, business, or means of livelihood.

Sovereign immunity: A judicial doctrine that precludes bringing suit against the government without its consent.

Standard of care: In the law of negligence, that degree of care that a reasonably prudent person should exercise in the same or similar circumstances.

Standing: A person's right to bring a lawsuit because he or she is directly affected by the issues raised.

Stare decisis: To abide by, or adhere to, previously decided cases.

State action: Anything done, performed, or enacted by the government, often a term used in connection with claims under the due process clause and the Civil Rights Act when a private citizen is seeking damages or redress because of improper governmental intrusion into their lives.

Statute: A formal written enactment of a legislative body.

Subpoena: A subpoena is a command to appear at a certain time and place to give testimony upon a certain matter.

Substantive due process: Doctrine that due process clauses of the Fifth and Fourteenth Amendments of the United States constitution require legislation to be fair and reasonable in content as well as application.

Substantive law: That part of law that creates, defines, and regulates rights and duties of parties, as opposed to procedural law, which prescribes methods of enforcing the rights or obtaining redress for their invasion.

Syllabus: An abstract; a headnote; a note prefixed to the report or opinion of an adjudged case, containing an epitome or brief statement of the rulings of the court upon the point or points decided in the case.

Temporary injunction: An injunction granted at the beginning of an action or lawsuit to restrain the defendant from performing some act, the right to which is in dispute and should be decided permanently at the conclusion of the action or lawsuit.

Tenure: Generally, tenure is a right, term, or mode of holding or occupying, and "tenure of an office" means the manner in which it is held, especially with regard to time.

Termination: End in time or existence; close; cessation; conclusion.

Theory of case: Facts on which the right of action is claimed to exist.

Theory of law: The legal premise or set of principles upon which a case rests.

Tort: A private or civil wrong or injury, including actions for bad faith breach of contract, for which the court will provide remedy in the form of an action for damages.

Tort-feasor: A wrong-doer; an individual or business that commits or is liable for a tort.

Transgender person: A person who identifies with a sex other than the one assigned at birth.

Trespass: An unlawful interference with one's person, property, or rights.

Trial: A judicial examination and determination of issues between parties to an action, whether they be issues of law, fact, or both, before a court that has jurisdiction.

Trier of fact: One or more persons — such as the jury in a jury trial or a judge in certain circumstances — who hear testimony and review evidence to make the ultimate ruling about a factual issue, such as whether certain events took place.

Turpitude: A term of frequent occurrence in statutes, especially those providing that a witness' conviction of a crime involving moral turpitude may be shown as tending to impeach their credibility. Anything done contrary to justice, honesty, modesty, or good morals.

U.S.C. **(abbreviation for United States Code):** The official compilation of statutes enacted by Congress.

Ultra vires: An act performed without any authority to act on the subject; outside the permissible scope.

Unfair labor practice: An act by an employer that in any way coerces or intimidates employees who wish to organize for collective bargaining.

Unilateral: One-sided.

Union shop: A place of work in which employees must join a union within a designated time or face dismissal.

Vacate: To annul; to set aside; to cancel or rescind.

Valid: Having legal strength or force, executed with proper formalities, incapable of being rightfully overthrown or set aside.

Vel non: Or not.

Venue: In common law pleading and practice, a neighborhood; the neighborhood, place, or county in which an injury is declared to have been done, or fact declared to have happened.

Verdict: The decision of the jury.

Vested interest: A present right or title to a thing, which carries with it an existing right of alienation, even though the right to possession or enjoyment may be postponed to some undetermined time in the future.

Void for vagueness doctrine: A law that is so obscure in its promulgation that a reasonable person could not determine from a reading what the law purports to do.

Void: Null; ineffectual; having no legal force or binding effect.

Volenti non fit injuria: A volunteer may not claim injury arising from his or her volunteered conduct, if that person knew of the risks when he or she consented to the conduct.

Waiver: The intentional or voluntary relinquishment of a known right.

Wanton: Reckless, heedless, malicious; characterized by extreme recklessness or foolhardiness; recklessly disregardful of the rights or safety of others or of consequences.

Whereas: A word that introduces a recital of fact.

Willful neglect: The intentional disregard of a plain or manifest duty, in the performance of which the public or the person injured has an interest.

Willful: Proceeding from a conscious motion of the will; voluntary; knowingly; deliberate.

Witness: In general, one who, being present, personally sees or perceives an event or thing; eyewitness. One who is called to testify in court.

Writ: A written judicial order to perform a specified act, or giving authority to have it done, as in a writ of mandamus or certiorari.

Index